CLASSICAL
ROMAN LAW

CLASSICAL
ROMAN LAW

BY

FRITZ SCHULZ

OXFORD
AT THE CLARENDON PRESS

Oxford University Press, Amen House, London E.C.4

GLASGOW NEW YORK TORONTO MELBOURNE WELLINGTON
BOMBAY CALCUTTA MADRAS KARACHI LAHORE DACCA
CAPE TOWN SALISBURY NAIROBI IBADAN ACCRA
KUALA LUMPUR HONG KONG

FIRST EDITION 1951
SET IN GREAT BRITAIN AT THE UNIVERSITY PRESS, OXFORD
AND REPRINTED LITHOGRAPHICALLY FROM SHEETS OF THE
FIRST EDITION 1954
REPRINTED LITHOGRAPHICALLY BY LATIMER, TREND & CO., LTD.
1961

PREFACE

THIS book was written in Oxford during the years 1945–9. The manuscript was finished and delivered to the Clarendon Press on the first of August 1949. Literature which came to my knowledge after that date could only be mentioned in the Addenda and references to this in the text are marked by asterisks.

I would like to thank all those who have helped me in my work, in particular the Clarendon Press and Mr. Kenneth Sisam, the then Secretary to the Delegates of the Press, who suggested the book and greatly contributed to making it a reality. I am, further, greatly indebted to Miss Margaret Alford, M.A. (Cantab.), Hon. M.A. (Oxon.), who assisted me with her great knowledge throughout several years.

OXFORD, 1950   F. S.

CONTENTS

CONTENTS

PART III

LAW OF SUCCESSION UPON DEATH

PART IV

LAW OF PROPERTY

CONTENTS

Part V
LAW OF OBLIGATIONS

LIST OF ABBREVIATIONS

ACI	= *Atti del Congresso Internazionale di Diritto Romano*, 1934–5.
Acta CII or *ACII*	= *Acta Congressus Iuridici Internationalis*, 1935.
AG	= *Archivio Giuridico.*
AJPH	= *American Journal of Philology.*
Ann. Catania	= *Annali del Seminario Giuridico dell' Università di Catania.*
Ann. Palermo	= *Annali del Seminario Giuridico dell' Università di Palermo.*
AP	= *Archiv für Papyrusforschung.*
Atti Napoli	= *Atti della Accademia di Scienze Morali e Politiche di Napoli.*
Atti Torino	= *Atti della Accademia delle Scienze di Torino.*
Beseler, *Beitr.*	= G. Beseler, *Beiträge zur Kritik der römischen Rechtsquellen.*
BGU	= *Aegyptische Urkunden aus den Kgl. Museen zu Berlin. Griechische Urkunden.*
Biondi, *Successione*	= Trattato di Diritto Romano ed. Albertario, vol. x (1943). Biondo Biondi, *Successione Testamentaria.* Donazioni.
Bremer	= *Iurisprudentiae antehadrianae quae supersunt*, ed. Bremer (Teubner).
Bruns or Bruns, *Fontes*	= *Fontes iuris Romani antiqui*, pars prior, ed. G. Bruns; 7th ed. by O. Gradenwitz, 1909.
Bull.	= *Bullettino dell' Istituto di Diritto Romano.*
C.	= *Codex Iustinianus.*
CAH	= *Cambridge Ancient History.*
C.Iust.	= *Codex Iustinianus.*
C.Th.	= *Codex Theodosianus.*
CIL	= *Corpus Inscriptionum Latinarum.*
Coll.	= *Mosaicarum et Romanarum Legum Collatio.*
Consult.	= *Veteris cuiusdam iurisconsulti consultatio.*
D.	= *Digesta Iustiniani.*
DP	= *Deutsches Privatrecht.*
Epit. Ulp.	= *Epitome Ulpiani.*
Ergänzungsindex	= *Ergänzungsindex zu Ius und Leges*, ed. E. Levy.
FIRA	= *Fontes Iuris Romani Anteiustiniani.*
Fr. Vat.	= *Fragmenta Vaticana.*

Gai.	= Gaius, *Institutiones*.
ILS	= *Inscriptiones Latinae Selectae*, ed. H. Dessau.
Inst. Iust.	= *Institutiones Iustiniani*.
Jolowicz, Introd.	= Jolowicz, *Historical Introduction to the Study of Roman Law*.
JRS	= *Journal of Roman Studies*.
Kaser, AR	= Max Kaser, *Altrömisches Ius*.
Kunkel	= Jörs–Kunkel–Wenger, *Römisches Recht*, 3rd ed. 1949.
l.c.	= loco citato.
Lenel, Edict.	= Lenel, *Das Edictum perpetuum*, 3rd ed. 1927.
LQR	= *Law Quarterly Review*.
Levy, Konkurrenz	= E. Levy, *Die Konkurrenz der Aktionen und Personen im klassischen römischen Recht*.
Mél.	= Mélanges.
Mitteis, Grundzüge	= Mitteis–Wilcken, *Grundzüge und Chrestomathie der Papyruskunde*.
Mitteis, RP	= Mitteis, *Römisches Privatrecht bis auf die Zeit Diokletians*, I (1908).
Mommsen, Schr.	= Th. Mommsen, *Gesammelte Schriften*.
Mommsen, StR.	= Th. Mommsen, *Römisches Staatsrecht*.
NRH	= *Nouvelle Revue Historique de Droit Français et Étranger*.
Pand.	= *Pandekten*.
Paul. Sent.	= *Pauli Sententiae*.
PW	= Pauly–Wissowa, *Realenzyklopaedie der klassischen Altertumswissenschaft*.
RE	= Pauly–Wissowa, *Realenzyklopaedie*.
Rend. Lomb.	= *Istituto Lombardo di Scienze e Lettere, Rendiconti*.
RH	= *Revue Historique de Droit Français et Étranger*.
Rhein. Mus.	= *Rheinisches Museum*.
RIDA	= *Revue Internationale des Droits de l'Antiquité*.
Riv. It.	= *Rivista Italiana per le Scienze Giuridiche*.
s.	= section.
Savigny, System	= Savigny, *System des heutigen Römischen Rechts*.
SB	= *Sitzungsberichte*.
Schulz, Einführung	= F. Schulz, *Einführung in das Studium der Digesten*.
Schulz, History	= F. Schulz, *History of Roman Legal Science*.
Schulz, Principles	= F. Schulz, *Principles of Roman Law*.
SD	= *Studia et Documenta Historiae et Iuris*.
Seckel, Handlex.	= Heumann–Seckel, *Handlexikon zu den Quellen des Römischen Rechts*.

Seckel–Kübler   = *Iurisprudentiae Anteiustinianae Reliquiae* (Teubner).

SHA   = *Scriptores Historiae Augustae.*

Solazzi, *Glosse a Gaio* I = *St. Riccobono*, I. 73 ff.

         II = *Per il XIV centenario delle Pandette e del Codice di Giustiniano* (Pavia, 1933).

St.   = *Studi.*

Stolz–Schmalz, *Lat. Grammatik*   = Stolz–Schmalz, *Lateinische Grammatik,* 5th ed. by Leumann and Hofmann, 1928.

T   = *Tijdschrift voor Rechtsgeschiedenis. Revue d'Histoire du Droit.*

Thes.   = *Thesaurus.*

Voc. or *Voc. Iur. Rom.* or *VIR*   = *Vocabularium Iurisprudentiae Romanae.*

Wenger, *CP*   = Wenger, *Institutes of the Roman Law of Civil Procedure,* translated by H. O. Fisk (1940).

Z   = *Zeitschrift der Savigny-Stiftung für Rechtsgeschichte, Romanistische Abteilung.*

Z (germ. Abt.)   = *Zeitschrift der Savigny-Stiftung für Rechtsgeschichte, Germanistische Abteilung.*

Z. f. RG   = *Zeitschrift für Rechtsgeschichte.*

INTRODUCTION

Sequemur hoc quidem tempore et hac in quaestione non interpretes,
sed, ut solemus, e fontibus eorum iudicio arbitrioque nostro quantum
quoquo modo videbitur hauriemus.

CICERO, *De Officiis*, i. 2. 6.

THE subject of this book is Roman Private Law. Con- 1. Subject:
stitutional Law and Administrative Law, Criminal Roman
Law, and Law of Procedure are excluded. Nor can the Law Private
history of Roman Legal Science and of the Sources of
Roman Law be discussed here, since neither is concerned
with private law alone. All those provinces of Roman Law,
important as they are for private law, cannot be adequately
treated within a system of private law and accounts of them
must therefore be sought in other books. This isolation of
private law inevitably entails certain disadvantages and
dangers, but in this we are only following the track of
Roman jurisprudence, and the outstanding importance of
Roman private law for legal science in general would in
itself be a sufficient reason for treating it separately.

Roman private law has a very long history extending
from the Twelve Tables of the fifth or fourth centuries B.C.
throughout the whole space of antiquity down to Justinian's
times (sixth century A.D.), and, further, throughout the
Middle Ages in both eastern and western Europe down to
our times; for this law is still alive and its history not yet
closed.

This long history cannot possibly be written within the 2. Classical
limits of a text-book, nor would the present state of know- Private
ledge permit it, since long periods are still insufficiently Law
explored. We must make a choice. We have chosen the
period of the Principate from Augustus to Diocletian.
Earlier and later law will be touched occasionally, but on
the whole we wish to confine this book to the law of that
period which we call the 'classical period' of Roman private
law. As the available sources of republican private law are
very scanty, classical law is for us the outstanding representative of true Roman private law—indeed, the centre of

B

any science of Roman law from which all inquiries inevitably must start and to which they must return. Classical private law is one of those vantage points on which the true historian loves to take his stand since it affords a free and comprehensive view of all sides of the development of Roman law.

> Mommsen (1854), *Schr. v.* 384: 'Die rechte Geschichtsforschung sucht nicht in möglichster Vollständigkeit das Tagebuch der Welt wiederherzustellen; sie sucht die Höhen und die Überblicke und von glücklichen Punkten in glücklichen Stunden gelingt es ihr herniederzusehen auf die unwandelbaren Gesetze des Notwendigen. . . .'

3. Static character   This choice is of course open to many criticisms. One may object that in this way we resign almost entirely a description of the development of Roman law. A system of classical private law is indeed of a mainly static character. But although the ambiguous term 'development' is a favourite with legal historians, they rarely give us more than accounts of ready-made legal rules chronologically arranged. 'Et puis . . . et puis . . . il y a beaucoup de "puis" dans cette histoire.' After all, no text-book of Roman private law has hitherto seriously attempted to give a description of its development. This book is still to be written.

4. Reasons for excluding Justinian's law   A more serious objection might be raised to our excluding Justinian's law. It is not classical law but rather Justinian's *Corpus Iuris* which has held its sway over the European continent for many centuries and has left conspicuous traces in the private law of today. Thus by excluding Justinian's law we are omitting the link which connects the law of antiquity with that of the Middle Ages and of later times. This is undoubtedly true. There are, however, two arguments in favour of isolating classical law, one of a scientific, the other of a pedagogic character.

The historical analysis of post-classical law in general and of Justinian's law in particular has barely begun. It must not be forgotten that the main part of Justinian's legislation—the *Institutes*, the *Digest*, and the *Codex Iustinianus* —are collections of pre-Justinianic texts. The compilers have adapted them to the usage of their day by numerous interpolations; but their classicism and the short time in which they had to accomplish their work prevented them from drastically transforming the texts. Thus the *Digest* still speaks of praetor and *aediles*, of edicts and their interpretation, still discusses whether an *actio directa* or *utilis* lies, still distinguishes between *actio* and *interdictum*, between *ius civile* and *ius honorarium*—all matters which had become irrelevant in the living post-classical law. It follows from this that the law which the compilers meant to become Justinian's own law is not to be discovered by straightforward reading of those compilations; one has to interpret them and to understand them in their Byzantine context. Moreover, there are numerous conflicting passages. What is Justinian's law in such cases? This question has only one meaning for us who no longer deal with the *Corpus Iuris* as a living code, namely: what is in such cases the law which the compilers meant to establish? The answer must be sought by historical research, not by 'dogmatic exegesis'. Suppose that there are two conflicting passages on a certain problem in two different places of the *Digest*, one attributed to Ulpian and the other to Paul. Close examination shows that the first text has suffered interpolation at the hands of the compilers, whereas the second remained unaltered by inadvertence. Obviously it is the interpolated text which gives Justinian's law. Whenever we fail to find an historical solution we have, as true historians to shrug our shoulders and practise the noble *ars nesciendi*. The further question as to the law actually applied by Byzantine practice on the basis of the *Corpus Iuris* is entirely distinct from the first. To answer it we must consult the writings of Byzantine lawyers and the Byzantine papyri. Thus to discern 'Justinian's law' is obviously no easy task, and it is small wonder that as yet there exists no book giving a true historical exposition of that law. Certainly the immense literature on the *Corpus Iuris*, from the times of the Bolognese Glossators (twelfth and thirteenth centuries) down to the German 'Pandecten-Wissenschaft' of the nineteenth century renders valuable service, but on the whole those books are not concerned with exploring Justinian's law by historical methods. Their aim is to build up a practical law on the basis of the *Corpus Iuris* and they contain to a considerable extent medieval and modern law sailing under Justinian's flag.

There is also a pedagogic reason for confining ourselves to classical law. Classical private law is a homogeneous, original and, in truth, quite unique system which is basically different from any other system of antiquity or of later times. It is this which makes its study both attractive and difficult. First and foremost students must attempt to make themselves familiar with classical law, and for that purpose it seems best to concentrate upon it.

The study of classical private law began with humanism. The so-called Glossators and Post-glossators (1100–1500) had confined themselves to the *Corpus Iuris* and to what they called 'Justinian's Law'. The humanistic lawyers were the first to investigate pre-Justinianic, in particular classical law. Supported by newly discovered pre-Justinianic sources they began to apply critical methods and to search after interpolations. The outstanding representatives of this new school were Jacobus Cuiacius (Jacques Cujas, 1520 or 1522–90) and Antonius Faber (Antoine Favre, 1557–1624), both men of genius, the latter in particular endowed with a rare and unswerving instinct for classical law, far in advance of his times.

The summer of this humanistic school was glorious but brief. To the traditionalists these newfangled inquiries seemed to be a strange and dangerous game threatening the authority of the *Corpus Iuris* and the *ius commune*. Faber's penetrating intuition was incomprehensible to unsympathetic minds and seemed to them either uncanny or foolish. It must indeed be admitted that the humanists did not sufficiently distinguish between historical research and interpretation of the *Corpus Iuris* as a living Code. A passage in the *Digest* sometimes requires a *duplex interpretatio*, since the meaning which it had in the classical original sometimes differs widely from that which is to be attributed to it within the framework of Justinian's legislation. Thus the anti-humanistic reaction became victorious. The searching

5. Study of Classical Private Law. The Humanists

6. Anti-humanistic reaction

inquiries of Cuiacius and Faber found no adequate continuation, the great Faber became a bogey for all 'sober-
minded' lawyers, and research into classical private law
made little, if any, progress throughout the seventeenth
and eighteenth centuries.

> Heineccius, 'De secta Tribonianomastigum', *Opera* (Genevae, 1748),
> tom. iii, Opusculorum variorum sylloge, iii, no. xi, p. 180: 'Ecquidem
> quantum detrimenti inde capiat iurisprudentiae studium, si in contemp-
> tum adducantur libri iuris nihilque in iis rectum, nihil sanum atque
> integrum esse quotidie inculcetur adulescentibus, neminem esse arbitra-
> mur quin intelligat. P. 179: . . . quo nemo ab insano illo antinomias et
> Tribonianismos venandi studio (!) magis abhorruit.'

A new approach to classical private law was made in the
first half of the nineteenth century under the leadership of
Friedrich Carl von Savigny. Humanistic investigation was
resumed and continued. Important pre-Justinianic sources
were discovered, particularly the Institutes of Gaius and
the so-called *Fragmenta Vaticana*. The lost manuscript of
the *Epitome Ulpiani* was rediscovered. Nevertheless, the
traditional reluctance to search after interpolations remained dominant. An almost incredible blindness towards
interpolations is a remarkable feature of Savigny and his
school and hampered considerably their investigations; the
most sophisticated solution seemed preferable to assuming
an interpolation. *(7. Savigny and his school)*

At last came Theodor Mommsen. He and his colla-
borators provided us with reliable editions of the sources,
particularly of the *Digest*. Mommsen's edition of Justinian's *Digesta* (the large edition in two volumes, 1870,
with which every serious student should become familiar)
will for ever remain *regina editionum*. On this solid basis,
schooled by Mommsen's numerous books and papers,
Italian and German scholars (I. Alibrandi, C. Ferrini, A.
Pernice, O. Lenel, O. Gradenwitz, and F. Eisele) made a
fresh start in the study of classical private law by applying
philological and historical methods. The work of Antonius
Faber after a long pause was resumed; his inquiries were at
last properly appreciated and vigorously continued. The
outstanding pioneers of the twentieth century were Emilio *(8. Mommsen and the modern school)*

Albertario and Gerhard von Beseler. We are still in this period. Innumerable more or less important problems are still *sub iudice* and many will probably remain so unless fresh sources turn up. However, an essential part of classical private law has been recovered *multaque pars vitavit vitabitque Libitinam*.

9. Scope of this book   In this book we do not aim at anything like completeness. We confine ourselves to classical legal institutions and principles, sociological and political aspects being predominant. For the fine network of juristic subtleties we refer the reader to other text-books and to the monographic literature. This book should be used both as an introduction and as a supplement to more comprehensive books. Having excluded Justinian's law (above, s. 4) we have also abstained from consistently comparing classical law with the law of other peoples. The unique character of classical law renders such comparison unprofitable and even confusing for the study of Roman law. Only occasionally have we made exceptions.

10. Our system   We have arranged our exposition following on the whole the so-called *Pandecten-System*, i.e. *not* the system of Justinian's *Pandectae sive Digesta*, but rather the system adopted by the German 'Pandecten-Lehrbücher' of the nineteenth century. This system contained five parts: I. General Part; II. Law of Things; III. Law of Obligation; IV. Family Law; V. Law of Succession upon Death. The 'General part' contained (1) a general theory of the rules of private law (of their interpretation and limits, including international private law) and of the individual rights originating from those rules. (2) The law of persons (natural and legal). (3) The general theory of the *negotium iuridicum*. (4) The legal protection of private law, in particular the law of actions. This 'General Part' was of a very doubtful value even in those text-books of modern 'Roman Law', but is definitely unsuitable for an historical exposition of classical private law. It contained a vast mass of generalities and abstractions, elaborated by post-classical, medieval, and modern jurisprudence, but more or less foreign to classical legal thinking. Aversion to far-reaching

abstractions is a characteristic feature of classical law which the historian has to preserve carefully. Those generalizations, conceptions, and abstract rules have their own history which requires and deserves a special treatment, but the historian must not import them into classical law which knew nothing of them. The historian must attempt to present the law of the past as far as possible in its historical form; he must not separate content and form (though this was of course permissible to lawyers who treated the *Corpus Iuris* as a living code):

> Natur hat weder Kern noch Schale,
> Alles ist sie mit einem Male. (Goethe)

Thus we have omitted the general theory of legal rules which obviously has its proper place within a history of legal sources. We have further omitted the general theory of *negotium iuridicum* which is an entirely modern creation. The law of persons we have combined with Family Law. What remains from that 'General Part' is the Law of Actions and that must indeed be preserved since to a considerable extent classical private law is still 'actional law' and so cannot be understood without a clear insight into the mechanism of the forms of action. Maitland has characterized the attitude of medieval English jurisprudence as follows:

> 'Legal remedies, legal procedure, these are the all-important topics for the student. These being mastered, a knowledge of substantive law will come of itself. Not the nature of rights but the nature of writs must be his theme . . . so thought our forefathers.' See Maitland, 'The History of the Register of Original Writs' (1889), *Select Essays in Anglo-American Legal History*, ii (1908), 549; *Collected Papers*, ii (1911), 110.

Maitland's dictum might with some restrictions be applied to classical jurisprudence, and the Law of Actions is therefore the proper and indispensable introduction to any system of classical private law. Like many introductions it should be read twice: at the beginning to obtain a preliminary survey and after having finished the study of substantive law. In truth the technicalities of the 'Law of Actions' have no particular difficulties even for a beginner.

11. We have abstained from providing our exposition with
Citations from the sources a running commentary of citations from the sources. Such citations are rarely looked up by students nor are students as a rule able to make a proper use of them without the help of a teacher. We have therefore confined ourselves to citing a few selected texts the reading of which we recommend.

In these citations spurious words are included in square brackets. In angular brackets we have included those words which were probably written by the classical writer but which are not transmitted in our texts.

12. *Biblio-graphy* For the full evidence we must refer to the literature.

With regard to the literature, we have given a list of modern text-books at the end of this introduction. We have further given bibliographic remarks in the course of our exposition. In the latter, text-books have as a rule been left unmentioned, since the reader can find the relevant pages in them by the help of indexes. We have mentioned standard works and of the monographic literature those books and papers which seemed to us of particular importance. As far as possible we have also cited the latest publications, but this book is no reference-book and is like other text-books here and there inevitably a little behind the latest discoveries. After all, the exploration of classical law is still in full swing.

BIBLIOGRAPHY

s. 1. For matters excluded from this book see Jolowicz, *Introd.* In particular for criminal law Brasiello, *La repressione penale in diritto romano* (1937); for civil procedure Wenger, *CP*; for history of legal science and sources Schulz, *History.* On legal isolation see Schulz, *Principles,* 19.

s. 2. On the classical period see Schulz, *History,* 99.

s. 3. On historical development see E. Landsberg, *Geschichte der deutschen Rechtswissenschaft,* iii. 2 (1910), 208; Ernst Troeltsch, *Ges. Schr.* iii (1922), 221 ff.

s. 4. On Justinian's classicism see Schulz, *History,* 278–85. The standard work for 'Pandectenwissenschaft' is Windscheid, *Lehrbuch des Pandektenrechts,* 9th ed. by Th. Kipp (1906). On the historical study of Justinian's law see Collinet, *Études historiques sur le droit de Justinien,* i (1912); ii. (1925); iv (1932); v (1947).

s. 5. There is no comprehensive work on the humanistic school. See Stintzing, *Geschichte der deutschen Rechtswissenschaft* i (1880); Coing, Z lix (1939), 697; Albertario, *Introd.* 142 with references; Koschaker,

Europa und das römische Recht (1947), 105 ff. On Cuiacius see Albertario, Z xxxi (1910), 158; on Faber De Medio, *Bull.* xiii (1901), 208; xiv (1902), 276; Albertario, *Contributi alla storia della ricerca delle interpolazioni* (1913).

s. 6. On the reaction see E. Spangenberg, *Einleitung in das Römisch-Justinianeische Rechtsbuch* (1817), 239. A good representative is the reactionary Albericus Gentilis who came to Oxford in 1580 and was a member of St. John's College. See Gentilis, *Dialogi de iuris interpretibus* (London, 1582), new edition by G. Astuti, 1937. On Gentilis see Holland, *An Inaugural Lecture on Albericus Gentilis* (1874); Speranza, *Alberico Gentili*, i (1876), ii (1910); G. Astuti, *Mos Italicus e Mos Gallicus nei dialoghi 'De iuris interpretibus' di Alberico Gentili* (1937); Th. F. Henderson in *Dictionary of National Biography*, vii. 1003–6.

s. 7. Koschaker, l.c. 270 ff.

s. 8. On the modern school see Schulz, *Einführung in das Studium der Digesten* (1916), 62. Reference books for the literature of that school: *Index interpolationum quae in Iustiniani Digestis inesse dicuntur* (ed. E. Levy and E. Rabel), i (1929), ii (1931), iii (1935); Supplementum I (1929). Guarneri Citati, *Indice delle parole, frasi e costrutti ritenuti indizio di interpolazione nei testi giuridici romani* (2nd ed. 1927); Supplementum I in *St. Riccobono*, i (1934), 701; Supplem. II in *Festschrift Paul Koschaker*, i (1939), 117. Ed. Volterra, 'Indice delle glosse, delle interpolazioni e delle principali ricostruzioni . . . nelle fonti pregiustinianee occidentali' in *Rivista di storia del diritto italiano*, viii (1935), ix (1936). P. de Francisci, *Il diritto romano* (guida bibliografica, 1923); Biondi, *Guide Bibliografiche;* iii. 1. *Diritto Romano* (1944); Monier, *Bibliographie des travaux récents de droit romain*, i (1944), ii (1949).

s. 9. Pringsheim, 'The Unique Character of Classical Roman Law, *JRS* xxxiv (1944), 60.

s. 10. See A. B. Schwarz, 'Zur Entstehung des modernen Pandekten-Systems', Z xlii (1921), 578.

s. 12. Modern text-books of Roman private law: DUTCH: J. C. van Oven, *Leerboek van Romeinsch Privatrecht* (1945). ENGLISH: H. J. Roby, *Roman Private Law in the Times of Cicero and the Antonines* (1902); W. W. Buckland, *A Textbook of Roman Law from Augustus to Justinian* (2nd ed. 1932); *A Manual of Roman Private Law* (2nd ed. 1939); Buckland and McNair, *Roman Law and Common Law* (1936); H. F. Jolowicz, *Historical Introduction to the Study of Roman Law* (1932); F. Schulz, *Principles of Roman Law* (1936); M. Radin, *Handbook of Roman Law* (1927). FRENCH: E. Cuq, *Manuel des Institutions Juridiques des Romains* (1917); R. Monier, *Manuel élémentaire de Droit Romain*, i (6th ed. 1947), ii (4th ed. 1948). GERMAN: L. Mitteis, *Römisches Privatrecht bis auf die Zeit Diokletians*, i (1908); E. Rabel, 'Grundzüge des römischen Privatrechts', in Holtzen-dorff–Kohler, *Enzyklopaedie der Rechtswissenschaft*, i (1915); Joers–Kunkel–Wenger, *Römisches Recht* (3rd ed. 1949); H. Siber, *Römisches Recht*, II. *Röm. Privatrecht* (1928); E. Weiss, *Institutionen des römischen Privatrechts* (2nd ed. 1949); E. Seidl, *Römisches Privatrecht* (1949),

112 pages. GREEK: G. A. Petropoulos, Ἱστορία καὶ εἰσηγήσεις τοῦ ῥωμαϊκοῦ δικαίου (1944). ITALIAN: S. Perozzi, *Istituzioni di diritto romano* (2nd 1928); E. Costa, *Storia del diritto romano privato* (2nd ed. 1925); *Cicerone giureconsulto* (2nd ed. 1927); P. Bonfante, *Istituzioni di diritto romano* (10th ed. by Albertario 1946); Arangio-Ruiz, *Istituzioni di diritto romano* (9th ed. 1947); B. Biondi, *Istituzioni di diritto romano* (1946); Di Marzo, *Istituzioni di diritto romano* (5th ed. 1946).

PART I

LAW OF ACTIONS

INTRODUCTION

TO a considerable extent classical private law might be 13. Law of actions called 'actional law' or 'law of actions', since it appears in the shape of statements about judicial remedies. Classical lawyers were not so much concerned with laying down rules on rights and duties as with discussing the conditions under which a certain action lies and the redress which might be obtained by it. The scope of this first part is much narrower. We only wish to give a clear idea of the various kinds of actions, the actions being taken in a wide sense to cover all judicial remedies. In other words we shall confine ourselves to the 'general law of actions'.

The classical law of actions was not fully discernible be- 14. Our main source fore the discovery of Gaius' *Institutes* in 1816. The classical system of actions did not survive the end of the classical period (above, s. 2); hence post-classical law-books, and particularly Justinian's compilations, afford only a defective and fallacious picture of that part of classical law. Thus the discovery of Gaius' *Institutes* was a veritable revelation since the whole of the fourth book deals with *ius quod ad actiones pertinet*. Although this part of the *Institutes* was completely obsolete by the fourth and fifth centuries, the classicism of the post-classical law-school has reverently preserved it without much tampering with the text. On the whole Gaius' exposition is a reliable source of classical law, but it would be silly to treat it as sacrosanct since it is (like the whole work) of an elementary character and therefore sometimes defective and inaccurate. On the other hand, post-classical interpolations are not entirely absent so that criticism is indispensable here as elsewhere.

SOURCES

s. 13. Read as examples for the actional style of the classics *D.* (4. 3) 35; (16. 3) 1. 38; (9. 2) 41 pr.: [*deleverit vel*]; [*in factum et*].

LAW OF ACTIONS

BIBLIOGRAPHY

s. 13. Standard works: O. Lenel, *Das Edictum Perpetuum* (3rd ed. 1927); L. Wenger, *Institutes of the Roman Law of Civil Procedure*, translated by H. O. Fisk (1940); Collinet, *Études historiques sur le droit de Justinien*, v: *La nature des actions, des interdits et des exceptions dans l'œuvre de Justinien* (1947); James Goldschmidt, *Der Prozess als Rechtslage* (1925), 6–67, 81, should not be ignored.

s. 14. The best edition of Gaius' *Institutes* for English-speaking students is F. De Zulueta, *The Institutes of Gaius*, Part I, text with critical notes and translation. On Gaius' *Institutes* see F. Schulz, *History* (1946), 159 ff., 281.

CHAPTER I

FUNDAMENTAL NOTIONS

1. *Iurisdictio and Iudicatio*

FUNDAMENTAL for the classical law of actions is the distinction between *iurisdictio* and *iudicatio*.

15. Iurisdictio and Iudicatio

Iurisdictio (ius dicere) means within the sphere of the ordinary civil procedure the authority to decide whether a plaintiff in an individual case should be permitted to pursue his claim before a judge. *Iudicatio (iudicare)* means the authority to pronounce judgment.

As a rule *iurisdictio* and *iudicatio* are not combined in one hand, *iurisdictio* being entrusted to a magistrate (particularly the praetor) and *iudicatio* to a private person (or several private persons). Both magistrate and *iudex* are regarded as representatives of common sense; they need not necessarily have a full knowledge of the law but are expected to act in close contact with professional lawyers. The terminology *iurisdictio—iudicatio* is somewhat artificial, since the natural sense of *ius dicere* comprehends any statement on law, including judgment. In ancient times, however, the praetor was called *iudex* and acted as a judge; *iurisdictio* was then the proper term to designate his functions and the customary term was preserved in later times in spite of the division of powers between magistrate and judge. Substantially the division is far from being artificial and has parallels in the law of other peoples. English law-students need only remember the medieval English procedure with writs.

16. Magistrate and Judge

Thus classical civil procedure begins with proceedings before a magistrate (proceedings *in iure*). If the magistrate declines to establish a *iudicium (denegare iudicium)*, the plaintiff's case is dismissed. The plaintiff may apply to the Emperor, who will perhaps instruct the magistrate to grant a *iudicium*; or he may wait for the end of the praetor's year of office and apply to the next praetor. If, on the other hand, the praetor grants a *iudicium (dare iudicium)*, the procedure

17. Proceeding in iure and apud iudicem

in iure is closed. This stage is marked by the calling up of witnesses (*litis contestatio*). The term *litis contestatio* is also used to designate the end of the proceeding *in iure* and even this proceeding as a whole. At the close of the proceedings *in iure* the second phase of the civil procedure begins, namely the *iudicium* or proceedings *apud iudicem*. At this point the plaintiff's claim is substantially examined and eventually judgment pronounced, viz. either the plaintiff is dismissed or the defendant condemned. In civil unlike criminal procedure it is not permissible to pronounce *non liquet*. Appeal from judgment is not permitted.

18. Juris-dictional magistrates   The jurisdictional magistrate within the limits of the City of Rome is the *praetor urbanus* if both parties are Roman citizens; if one or both are non-Romans the *praetor inter peregrinos* or *cives et peregrinos* (abbreviated to *praetor peregrinus*). For certain actions the *aediles curules* are competent (below, s. 926). In the *municipia*, municipal magistrates have a limited jurisdiction. In the provinces the governors are the jurisdictional magistrates, while in the senatorial provinces the jurisdiction of the *aediles* is exercised by *quaestores*.

19. The judges   As a rule *iudicatio* is entrusted to a single private person chosen by both parties and authorized by the magistrate. This judge is called *iudex*. Sometimes he is called *arbiter*. Originally the latter name was used when the judge had to give judgment at his discretion (within certain limits), but in classical times it is hardly more than a terminological variant. For certain claims (e.g. the *actio iniuriarum*, below, s. 1015) several judges (three or five) can be chosen and they are called *recuperatores*. For some claims parties may entrust *iudicatio* to the *centumviri* (e.g. for the *hereditatis petitio*).

20. Extra-ordinaria cognitio   The procedure which we have so far described we call the ordinary procedure (*Inst. Iust.* 3. 12 pr,). By the side of it there existed a different form of procedure which is termed in our sources (but never in Gaius *Institutes*, cf. 2. 278) *cognitio extra ordinem* or *extraordinaria cognitio*. Here the magistrate is entitled to exercise both *iurisdictio* and *iudicatio*, though he is free to charge a private person (*iudex*

pedaneus) with *iudicatio* and as a rule seems to have availed himself of that help. In classical times this is the only procedure available for a certain group of claims (e.g. for the action *ex fideicommisso*) which were excluded from the ordinary procedure. Moreover, it applies to all claims in those provinces of the Empire in which the ordinary procedure did not exist (e.g. in Egypt).

Obviously there are important differences between those two forms of procedure, but one must not exaggerate them, since in the *extraordinaria cognitio* the magistrate as a rule entrusted *iudicatio* to a private person. *Extraordinaria cognitio* was the later form, originating from public law and therefore more modern, flexible, and free from the harsh formalism of the older procedure. Thus the following two main differences are sufficiently explained: 21. Differences between the two forms of procedure

1. In the ordinary procedure the appointment of a *iudex* is compulsory, in the *extraordinaria cognitio* optional.
2. In the ordinary procedure no *iudicium* can take place without the parties having agreed upon the person of the judge and the programme of the *iudicium* (*formula* see below, s. 27). If the defendant refuses to co-operate, there is no such thing as judgment by default. In the *extraordinaria cognitio* an agreement of the parties is not compulsory and a judgment by default may be pronounced.

According to a modern theory propounded by Wlassak in numerous books and papers and accepted by many other scholars, the ordinary procedure is to be regarded as a sort of arbitration. Parties agreed before the magistrate not only on the person of the judge but also on the gist of the legal issue, viz. on the programme of the *iudicium*, and the judge is therefore to be regarded as a sort of arbitrator. The exposition of this theory has been marred by many unsound arguments, uncritical interpretations, and faulty deductions. It is true that the idea of arbitration was absent from Gaius' mind and probably also from the minds of the classical lawyers altogether. Of the legal thinking of the republican lawyers we know nothing. Of course they could not 22. Wlassak's theory speak of a *contractus*, this term having too narrow a sense; perhaps they did not even dare to call the agreement a *pactum*. Nevertheless, the historian is permitted to investigate the ideas working behind the scenes even if the actors themselves were not conscious of them. For the modern lawyer this agreement of the parties is indeed an instance of agreement to submit to arbitration. The absence of a judgment by default might well be explained without the help of this idea, but its driving force is palpable in the development of the actions, particularly of the *actiones bonae fidei* (below, s. 63). Thus the *iudex* may safely be styled an arbitrator, but a special sort of arbitrator, viz. an arbitrator authorized by the magistrate and therefore also a deputy of the magistrate, just like the *iudex pedaneus* in the *extraordinaria cognitio*. However, the importance of the whole issue has been considerably over-estimated; it is after all only a question of legal ideology or construction, not of law.

23.
Imperium

Besides *iurisdictio*, the jurisdictional magistrate had also *imperium* on the strength of which he was entitled to give orders at his discretion within the very wide limits allowed by the *leges*. In the ordinary procedure in particular the magistrate badly needs that power. As aforesaid there is no *iudicium* if the defendant refuses co-operation *in iure*. Here the magistrate's *imperium* comes in; he may, for example, order *missio actoris in bona rei*. The municipal magistrates had no *imperium*, but in such cases the Roman praetor, if necessary, came to the rescue, since the plaintiff might apply to him.

SOURCES
s. 18. Read Gai. 1. 6.

BIBLIOGRAPHY
s. 15. Wlassak, Z xxv (1904), 81; Bekker, Z xxvii (1906), 1–12; Steinwenter, *PW* x. 1155; Kaser, *AR* (1949), 358 f.

s. 16. Jolowicz, *ACI*, Bologna, ii (1934), 59; Hoetink, *Seminar*, v (1947), 16 ff.*

s. 17. Düll, *Denegationsrecht und praetorische Jurisdiction* (1915); Lévy-Bruhl, *La denegatio actionis sous la procédure formulaire* (1942);

Vojtěch Poláček, *Denegatio* (1947), Czech with an English summary; Z lxiii (1943), 406. On *litis contestatio* Beseler, Z xlvi (1926), 134, 138; lii (1932), 292. On *non liquet* Mommsen, *Römisches Strafrecht* (1899), 422.

s. 19. On *Iudex* see J. Mazeaud, *La Nomination du judex unus sous la procédure formulaire à Rome* (1933). On *arbiter* E. Levy, Z xxxvi (1915), 16. On *recuperatores* and *centumviri* Wenger, *CP*, p. 61.

s. 20. Mitteis, *Grundz.* 23; Arangio-Ruiz, *FIRA* iii, no. 170 with references; Balogh, *ACI*, Roma, ii (1935), 267 ff.; Santi di Paola, 'La litis contestatio nella cognitio extra ordinem, *Ann. Catania*, 1948.

s. 21. On judgment by default see A. Steinwenter, *Studien zum römischen Versäumnisverfahren* (1914); L. Arù, *Il processo civile contumaciale* (1934).

s. 22. Against Wlassak's theory see Beseler, Z xlvi (1926), 131 with references; *LI* (1931), 401; Mazeaud, l.c. 172 ff.; Gioffredi, *SD* xii (1946), 144, 146.

2. *Iurisdictio and Lex*

The jurisdictional magistrate is bound by *leges* (in classical times also by *senatusconsulta* and imperial constitutions), but only as far as they expressly order him to grant or to refuse *iudicium*. Such orders, however, are rare, since statutes generally confine themselves to laying down rules as to rights and duties of private persons. In such cases the magistrate is not bound by statute but is entitled to grant or to refuse *iudicium* at his discretion. This simple principle, which of course implies a very strict interpretation of statutes, must be firmly kept in mind by anybody who wishes to understand the discussions of republican and classical lawyers. It is a true Roman principle revealing the whole attitude of Roman jurists towards law-creating acts of State, viz. their unconcealed distaste for legislation.

24. The freedom of the magistrates

> One example will suffice. The Twelve Tables laid down rules on *iniuria* without speaking of actions. Tab. VIII. 2. 4: 'Si membrum rupsit, ni cum eo pacit, talio esto. Si iniuriam faxit, XXV poenae sunto.' The praetor did not feel bound by these rules and granted very different actions. (Lenel, *Edictum*, tit. xxxv, p. 397; Riccobono, *FIRA* 1. 369; See further the *actio furti manifesti* (below, s. 997).

This great freedom of the magistrates was considerably restricted not by statute but by the magistrates themselves,

25. Restrictions; ius honorarium

viz. by the development of the Edicts. Before entering office the jurisdictional magistrates were wont to publish a programme (*edictum*) in which they declared that under certain well-defined circumstances they would be prepared to grant or to refuse *iudicia* (*iudicium dabo; iudicium non dabo*). Each magistrate usually adopted the edict of his predecessor with certain modifications and additions so that a comprehensive system of rules was gradually developed (*ius honorarium* in contrast to *ius civile*) which the magistrates traditionally propounded again and again in their edicts. Eventually the whole body of *ius honorarium* was codified by Hadrian. This is not the place to describe the details of this development.

26. Gaius (4. 103–9) distinguishes between *iudicium legiti-*
Iudicium *mum* and *iudicium quod imperio continetur*. This distinction
legitimum
and has nothing to do with the difference between *ius civile* and
iudicium *ius honorarium*. *Iudicium legitimum* is a *iudicium* in the City
quod
imperio of Rome before a single judge, both parties as well as the
continetur judge being Roman citizens. Whenever any one of these requirements is absent there is a *iudicium quod imperio continetur*. Certainly there existed a *lex* which ordered magistrates to establish *iudicia* whenever the three conditions just mentioned were fulfilled and left the establishment of other *iudicia* to the discretion of the magistrates, but whether that *lex* was the *lex Iulia* of Augustus or the *lex Aebutia* which introduced the formulary procedure or even the *lex XII tabularum* cannot be determined.

SOURCES

s. 24. Read *D.* (14. 6) 1 pr.; (16. 1) 2. 1; Gai. 3. 223, 224 (to *fuerit*).
s. 26. Read Gai. 4. 103–5, 109.

BIBLIOGRAPHY

s. 24. F. Schulz, *Principles*, 6 ff.; *History*, 24, 60, 127 f.
s. 25. Schulz, *History*, 61, 127; Kaser, *Altröm. Ius* (1949), 96.
s. 26. Beseler, Z xlvi (1926), 131; Lenel, Z xlvii (1927), 29. Kaser, l.c. 73, 93. On the *lex Aebutia* (149–126 B.C.) see Berger, *PW*, Suppl. vii. 379.*

3. *Formula*

As we have stated above (s. 21), in the ordinary proce- 27. Conception of formula dure *iudicium* could only take place if the parties·had agreed upon the person of the judge as well as on the legal issue to be submitted to him, and then only if that agreement had been approved by the magistrate. When that was achieved, an official document was drawn up which was called the *formula*. This document has given its name to the whole procedure, the classical lawyers speaking of *agere per formulas* and modern students of 'formulary procedure'.

In an individual case the *formula* is substantially the work 28. Legal character of formula of the parties as well as of the magistrate. It was the business of the plaintiff to present a draft *formula*, but the defendant might propose modifications and the magistrate too might make his authorization to the proposed *formula* conditional on the plaintiff accepting certain changes in it. Thus agreement is achieved by the co-operation of all three, the plaintiff, the defendant, and the magistrate. The *formula*, however, is not cast in the style of a contractual document. In contractual documents all over the world the consent of parties is expressed in one way or the other, whereas in the *formula* it is never mentioned. The *formula* is rather a statement of the magistrate's decree in which he authorizes the agreement (*dare iudicium*) and orders the judge to pronounce judgment (*iubere iudicare*).

Cf. *Lex Rubria*, cap. xx, l. 21: 'dum in ea verba . . . iudicium det (scil. magistratus) itaque iudicare iubeat: Iudex esto', etc.; follows formula.

The *formula* is not a letter to the judge or even addressed to him but rather addressed 'to all', viz. *ad eos ad quos ea res pertinet*.

Similar is a *decretum pontificum ILS* 8381, Bruns no. 76, *FIRA* i, no. 63.

In the course of time numerous *formulae* became stereo- 29. Our sources typed and were incorporated in the Edict, but this official list of available *formulae* was never regarded as a closed list, not even after Hadrian's codification (above, s. 25).

Thus the classical lawyers were in possession of a large

stock of stereotyped *formulae* and many classical discussions are intelligible only to readers who have a full knowledge of the shape of the *formula* which the jurists had before them. Ulpian in his commentary on the Edict constantly transcribed the *formulae* propounded in the Edict and carefully explained them, but in our texts they have been omitted, not being any longer of practical use. Gaius in the fourth book of his *Institutes* attempted to expound a general doctrine of the various kinds of *formulae*, a 'Formenlehre', and this exposition has been preserved thanks to the classicism of the post-classical law-school (above, s. 14).

30. Formula certae creditae pecuniae as example   In these preliminary remarks we only wish to give one example. We have chosen the simplest of all *formulae*, namely the *formula* for a creditor who wished to recover the money which he has lent to a borrower (*formula certae creditae pecuniae*, below, s. 879).

Octavius iudex esto.

Si paret Numerium Negidium Aulo Agerio sestertium
    X milia dare oportere,
iudex Numerium Negidium Aulo Agerio sestertium
    X milia condemnato, si non paret, absolvito.

The model *formulae* propounded in the Edict used fictitious names for the parties, *Agerius* for the plaintiff (*actor*) and *Negidius* (*negans*) for the defendant. In republican times this usage was not yet fixed, as is shown by the *lex Rubria* which uses *L. Seius* for the plaintiff and *Q. Licinius* for the defendant. Of course these fictitious names had to be replaced by the real names of the parties and the judge when the *formula* was used in an actual case.

Our texts have sometimes *condemna* and *absolve* instead of *condemnato* and *absolvito*, probably blunders of the copyists who wrongly expanded the abbreviations *c* and *a*. Since the beginning of the document is styled in the third person the rest of it should be framed in the same way. However, formulas of that kind are always exposed to the danger of corruption since everybody knows their meaning and is inclined to overlook such formal trifles. The matter is without any importance.

The clause *si paret . . . oportere* is called *intentio*. Gaius 4. 41 defines *intentio* as follows: 'Intentio est ea pars formulae qua actor desiderium suum concludit.' This should be translated as follows: An *intentio* is that part of a *formula* by which the plaintiff defines (or circumscribes) his claim.

Professor De Zulueta's translation is not quite accurate. He translates: 'An *intentio* is the part of a *formula* in which the plaintiff expresses what he claims.' This translation would suit the *formula certae creditae pecuniae*, but not e.g. the *rei vindicatio*. Here the *intentio* runs as follows: 'Si paret mensam qua de agitur Auli Agerii esse ex iure Quiritium.' The plaintiff's claim is certainly *not* directly expressed in this clause.

The clause *Numerium Negidium . . . absolvito* is called *condemnatio*. This term must not be translated by 'condemnation', but by 'authorization to condemn or to absolve'. Gaius 4. 43 clearly says: 'Condemnatio est ea pars formulae qua iudici condemnandi absolvendive potestas permittitur.'

Now suppose the defendant declared *in iure* that the creditor had given him (by *pactum*) a year within which to repay the money and that this year had not yet elapsed. Then an *exceptio pacti* is inserted in the *formula*. And if the plaintiff objected that the defendant had induced him to grant that time by fraud a *replicatio doli* is inserted. The whole *formula* would now run as follows:

Octavius iudex esto.

Intentio	Si paret Numerium Negidium Aulo Agerio sestertium X milia dare oportere,
Exceptio pacti	si inter Aulum Agerium et Numerium Negidium non convenit, ne ea pecunia intra annum peteretur,
Replicatio doli	aut si quid dolo malo Numerii Negidii factum est iudex Numerium Negidium Aulo Agerio sestertium X milia condemnato, si non paret absolvito.
Condemnatio	

These preliminary remarks on the structure of *formulae* must suffice here; we shall return to the subject in the second chapter of this part (ss. 45 ff.).

In the *extraordinaria cognitio* the magistrate was entitled to entrust *iudicatio* to a judge (above, s. 20). In such cases he usually issued a written instruction which looked somewhat similar to a *formula*. However, these instructions remained flexible and a stock of stereotyped *formulae* was never developed. The days of formalism were coming to their end.

31. Formulae in extraordinaria cognitio

BIBLIOGRAPHY

s. 28. On Wlassak's idea of the formula see Wlassak, *Die klassische Prozessformel*, *SB Wien*, ccii. 3 (1924), and Wenger, *CP*; against Wlassak (rightly) Beseler, *Z* xlvi (1926), 131 ff.; Mazeaud, *La Nomination du judex unus* (1933), 154, 187 ff.

s. 29. On Ulpian's commentary see Schulz, *History*, 197.

s. 30. Lenel, *Edictum*, p. 237, 501; Gai. 4. 41, 43, 119, 126. On *condemna, absolve* instead of *condemnato, absolvito* see Lenel, Z xliii (1922), 574; *Edict*, p. 114; Beseler, Z xlvi (1926), 136. On *intentio* Lenel, *Beiträge zur Kunde des praetorischen Edicts* (1878), 107; J. Juncker, 'Die Gaianische Definition der Intentio', *St. Riccobono*, ii. 327 ff.

s. 31. J. Partsch, *Die Schriftformel im römischen Provinzialprozesse*, 69 ff. (Diss. Breslau, 1905); Boulard, *Les Instructions écrites du magistrat au juge-commissaire dans l'Égypte* (1906); Wlassak, *Zum römischen Provinzialprozess*, 11 ff. (*SB Wien*, cxc. 4, 1919); Arangio–Ruiz, *FIRA* iii, no. 170. On Byzantine law see Collinet, *Études*, 5 (1947), 182 ff.

4. Iudicium

32. Conception of iudicium   *Iudicium* in genuine classical texts always means precisely 'procedure *apud iudicem*' and never *formula*. If the praetor declared in the Edict: *Quae dolo malo facta esse dicentur ... iudicium dabo* that means: 'I shall be prepared to establish a proceeding before a judge *de dolo malo*.' This implies *formulam de dolo malo dabo*, since without a *formula* a proceeding before a judge cannot be established. *Iudicio de dolo potest consequi* means 'he can obtain redress before a judge'; one might also say *formula de dolo potest consequi*. Nevertheless, *iudicium* and *formula* are not synonyms. Whenever the clauses of the *formula* are discussed *formula* cannot be replaced by *iudicium*: one may say *formula in factum concepta* but never *iudicium in factum conceptum*.

33. Informal procedure   The procedure before the judge is entirely informal. Parties and their advocates plead their cases and produce evidence as far as required; ultimately the judge pronounces judgment.

34. Judge bound by formula   Whenever the judge has to perform his functions under instructions from the magistrate—always in the ordinary procedure, usually in the *extraordinaria cognitio*—he is bound by those instructions. He is not entitled to inquire into their legality, being sufficiently protected by the magistrate's authority. These instructions need legal interpretation particularly in the ordinary procedure, since the *formula* is both short and complex. Of course he is expected to follow well-established legal doctrines. As a rule he performed his office with the support of a *consilium*, which he assembled at his discretion. He might consult a lawyer and even ask him to be a member of his *consilium*. The dominant classical interpretation as expounded in the writings of the classical lawyers is not of a uniform character, some clauses of the *formula* being interpreted liberally and others very strictly.

Examples of liberal interpretation will be given later. An outstanding example of strict interpretation is the following. We have considered above (s. 30) the *formula certae creditae pecuniae*. The judge is instructed to find out whether the defendant owes *decem milia sestertium* or not. Now suppose the judge comes to the conclusion that the defendant owes only nine. According to classical strict interpretation the judge has to dismiss the action; he is not allowed to condemn the defendant to pay nine. He who owes nine does not owe ten, consequently the judge has to absolve the defendant, for the *formula* says *si non paret absolvito*. Cf. Blackstone, *Commentaries*, Book III, ch. 9, no. 1: 'In an action of debt the plaintiff must recover the whole debt he claims or nothing at all. For the debt is one single cause of action, fixed and determined; and which, therefore, if the proof varies from the claim, cannot be looked upon as the same contract whereof the performance is sued for. If therefore I bring an action of debt for 30l., I am not at liberty to prove a debt of 20l. and recover a verdict thereon, any more than if I bring an action of detinue for a horse, I can thereby recover an ox.' (N.B.)

Concerning evidence, complete freedom prevails. The classical lawyers, following the republican tradition, show only a mild interest in the law of evidence and even the question of the burden of proof was not discussed by them in detail. Parties may produce evidence at their discretion; only torture is excluded altogether, in remarkable contrast to Greek law. Rules of evidence do not exist. The judge decides at his discretion whether the assertions of the parties are true or not. *35. Evidence*

Finally the judge has to pronounce judgment. As aforesaid (s. 17), he has either to condemn or to absolve. If he establishes that the plaintiff is right he has—in the ordinary procedure—to condemn the defendant to pay a certain sum of money. In the *extraordinaria cognitio* he is entitled to order specific performance. *36. Judgment*

BIBLIOGRAPHY

s. 32. The right doctrine has been defended by Beseler, Z xlvi (1926), 131; li (1931), 401; lii (1932), 292; *Beitr.* v. 51; *Bull.* xxxix (1931), 320.

s. 34. Beseler, Z lxvi (1948), 299. For *consilium iudicis* see Schulz, *History*, 52, 117.

s. 35. Schulz, *Principles*, 32; *History*, 84. For testimonies of witnesses recently found in Herculaneum see Arangio-Ruiz, *La parola del passato* (1948), 146 ff., 171 ff. J. Ph. Levy, 'La Formation de la théorie romaine des preuves', *St. Solazzi* (1948), 418 ff.

s. 36. On judgment in *extraordinaria cognitio* see Mitteis, *Grundzüge*, 44; Wenger, *CP* 303; Biondi, *St. Bonfante*, iv. 61; Taubenschlag, *Law of Greco-Roman Egypt* (1944), § 56. On *condemnatio pecuniaria* see Gioffredi, *SD* xii (1946), 136 ff.

5. Actio

37.
Conception
of actio   Although the term *actio* occurs on almost every page of our law-books, modern lawyers have found difficulty in giving it an adequate definition. Both republican and classical jurists have obviously abstained from defining it, the only definition in our sources being certainly of post-classical origin. Nevertheless, the classical conception of *actio* is simple and clear.

The verb *agere* simply means 'to act' and *actio* means *actus*, comprehending every process of doing, indeed acts of every kind. In the legal language of classical lawyers both terms have a narrower technical sense, referring solely to civil procedure. *Agere* means to act in a lawsuit, *in iure* as well as *apud iudicem*; the plaintiff's acting in particular is called *agere*. *Actio* comprehends accordingly all acts of parties *in iure* as well as *apud iudicem*, and primarily the plaintiff's acts. In some typical legal phrases *actio* means only the proceeding *apud iudicem*: *actio a praetore danda est* means 'a procedure *apud iudicem* should be established by the praetor', *actio proposita est in edicto praetoris* means 'a procedure *apud iudicem* is promised in the Edict'. In these phrases *actio* is identical with *iudicium* (above, s. 32): *actio danda est* and *iudicium dandum est* mean the same. On the other hand, *mandare actionem* means 'to give somebody a mandate to act as an agent in a lawsuit, *in iure* as well as *apud iudicem*'.

38. Actio
and
formula   *Actio* never means *formula*. To be sure one might say *formulam praetor proposuit* as well as *actionem proposuit*, since the praetor could not promise an *actio* (= *iudicium*) without

promising a *formula* and by proposing a *formula* he proposed an *actio*. Even in cases in which the Edict contained solely a *formula*, a lawyer might safely say *praetor actionem proposuit* (Gaius 2. 253). Nevertheless, *actio* and *formula* are not identical. Whenever the structure of the *formula* is concerned, *actio* must not be substituted for *formula*: one may say *formula in factum concepta* (see below, s. 47), but not *actio in factum concepta* (cf. above, s. 32).

In classical legal language *actio* never means 'claim', either in the sense of a claim on a private person or a claim on the magistrate. *Actio mihi competit qua possum consequi* means 'I can sue somebody and by doing so obtain something'. This implies: 'I have a right to demand something', but that is only implied and not expressly said. Theoretical meditation on the relation between *actio* and 'right' the classics have purposely eschewed as belonging in their eyes to legal philosophy and not to jurisprudence.

Thus *actio* always means 'legal procedure'. To render *actio* in English by 'action' is therefore quite correct, provided one keeps in mind that 'action' means 'a process of acting'.

The classical lawyers have confined the term *actio* to the ordinary procedure, though it would have been suitable also to *extraordinaria cognitio*. All texts in which *actio* occurs referring to *extraordinaria cognitio* are spurious. Since for *fideicommissa* only *extraordinaria cognitio* is open (above, s. 20), there is for the classical lawyers no such thing as *actio ex fideicommisso* or *actio fideicommissi*, the classical term being *petitio* or *persecutio fideicommissi*. Of course the term *actio extraordinaria* is also unknown to them. *Interdictum* and *in integrum restitutio* are never called by them *actio* (see below, s. 111 and s. 119).

The classical terminology in our sources has been obscured by innumerable interpolations of the compilers as well as of pre-Justinianic authors. Thus *formula* has been extirpated from all texts of the *Digest* with only one exception (*D.* 47. 2. 42 pr.). *Fideicommissi actio* occurs as early as the post-classical *Sententiae Pauli* (4. 1. 6).

39. Actio and claim

40. Actio to be rendered by 'action'

41. Cognitio extraordinaria

42. Interpolations

SOURCES

s. 37. Read *D.* (44. 7) 51 = *Inst. Iust.* 4. 6 pr. (spurious: Schulz, *Principles*, 45). Apparently the compilers found no other passage containing a definition.

s. 38. Read Gai. 3. 224 and note *taxamus* '*formulam*' not *actionem*, since the *taxatio* had to be inserted in the *formula* (Lenel, *Edict.*, p. 399).

s. 41. Read Gai. 2. 278, 282 and note *agitur . . . persecutio* est.

BIBLIOGRAPHY

s. 37. Wlassak, *PW* i. 303; 'Der Judikationsbefehl im röm. Prozesse', *SB Wien*, cxcvii. 4 (1921), *passim* (see Index); 'Die klassische Prozessformel', *SB Wien*, ccii. 3 (1924), *passim* (see Index); J. Goldschmidt, *Prozess als Rechtslage* (1925), 42 ff. For materials see *Thes.* i. 438, 441, 48 ff. *Voc.* i. 103. On *actus* see *Thes.* i. 449 ff., 454, 53; Beseler, *Z* lvii (1937), 1.

s. 39. G. Pugliese, *Actio e diritto subiettivo* (1939), with references.

s. 41. On *petitio* see Schnorr v. Carolsfeld, *PW* xix, 1153. On *petere* = *agere* Beseler, *SD* iii (1937), 18. On *actio extraordinaria* Wlassak, *PW* i. 312 (uncritical). According to *Voc.* ii. 732 the term occurs solely in *D.* (19. 1) 52. 2 (certainly spurious).

6. *Executio*

43. Ordinary procedure The execution of a judgment pronounced in the ordinary procedure is conducted as follows. After the lapse of thirty days the defendant is summoned by the plaintiff to appear once more before the magistrate. The defendant might make reasonable objections to the execution, e.g. by alleging that he had already satisfied the plaintiff within the thirty days. Then a new *iudicium* might be established in order to examine the plaintiff's action (*actio iudicati*). As a rule, however, the defendant acknowledged the plaintiff's claim. There were two modes of execution.

1. Execution on the person of the defendant. The plaintiff was permitted to take the defendant home and to keep him there until the judgment was fulfilled. (For *beneficium competentiae* see below, ss. 793, 794.) This execution on the person existed throughout the whole classical period, though it is but rarely mentioned in our sources. Some rules of classical law remain unintelligible if one does not remember this form of execution. Thus in classical law the only penalty for theft is a fine (apart from *infamia*). Since as a

rule thieves have no property, that rule would be absurd if execution on the person did not exist.

2. Execution against the defendant's property. Only an execution against his property as a whole was permitted, all other creditors of the defendant being called up as in a case of bankruptcy. Execution against a single piece of his property was not possible.

In the *extraordinaria cognitio* execution was quite informal. Here too execution on the person existed, but execution against the defendant's property might be directed against single things.

44. Extraordinaria cognitio

BIBLIOGRAPHY

s. 43, 44. Woess, Z xliii (1922), 485 ff.; H. Lewald, *Die Personalexekution im Recht der Papyri* (1910); Mitteis, *Grundzüge*, 44; Wenger, *CP* 222 ff.; Taubenschlag, *Law of Greco-Roman Egypt* (1944), § 57.

CHAPTER II

CLASSIFICATION OF ACTIONS

1. *Actiones civiles and actiones honorariae*

45.
Definitions
AN action by which the plaintiff pursues a claim founded in civil law (*ius civile*) is called *actio civilis*; it may be specifically called *actio legitima* if the claim is recognized by *lex*. An action by which the plaintiff pursues a claim *ex iure honorario* (above, ss. 24, 25) is called *actio honoraria* (*praetoria* or *aedilicia*). Let us give a few preliminary examples. The Twelve Tables imposed a fine of double for non-manifest theft. The praetor proposed accordingly an *actio furti nec manifesti in duplum*: this is an *actio civilis*. On the other hand, the Twelve Tables imposed capital punishment for *furtum manifestum*. The praetor, however, replaced capital punishment by an *actio furti manifesti* for fourfold damages: this is an *actio honoraria* (*praetoria*). The *actio de dolo* was created by the praetor quite independently of *ius civile* and is therefore an *actio honoraria*.

46.
Actiones honorariae by statute
Students should be warned not to regard every action created by statute (*lex, senatusconsultum, constitutiones principum*) as an *actio civilis*. A statute might abstain from creating *ius civile* and simply order the magistrates to propose actions. These, then, are *actiones honorariae*.

SOURCES

s. 45. Read Gai. 3. 189, 190; 4. 76, 110, 111.
s. 46. Read Gai. 2. 253.

BIBLIOGRAPHY

s. 45. Wlassak, 'Die klassische Prozessformel', *SB Wien*, ccii. 3 (1924), 7. 22. Materials for *actio civilis Voc.* i. 749 ff.; for *actio honoraria Voc.* iii. 269. 4 ff.; Kaser, *Altröm. Jus* (1949), 94; for *aedilicia actio Voc.* i. 290. 39; for *praetoria actio* Seckel, *Handlex.* v. 'praetorius'; Kaser, l.c.; for *legitima actio Voc.* iii. 269. 11.
s. 46. Beseler, Z xlvii (1947), 356; Lenel, *Edictum*, § 68.

2. *Formulae in ius and in factum conceptae*

A formula is framed *in ius* (scil. *in ius civile*) if the con- 47.
demnation of the defendant is made conditional upon the $\quad$ Definitions
plaintiff having a right or claim *ex iure civili*. If that is not
the case and the condemnation is dependent only on the
existence of certain facts, the *formula* is called *in factum concepta*. An example of the former is the *formula certae creditae
pecuniae*, which we have discussed above (s. 30). An
example of the latter is the *formula* of the patron's action
against his freedman who has summoned him to court without the praetor's permission. This action is not founded in
ius civile and its *formula* runs as follows:

> 'Recuperatores sunto.
> 'Si paret illum patronum ab illo liberto contra edictum illius praetoris
> in ius vocatum esse, recuperatores illum libertum illi patrono sestertium
> X milia condemnanto, si non paret absolvunto.'

This distinction is quite clear, but Gaius (4. 45) fails to 48. Gaius'
give an accurate definition of the *formula in ius concepta*: 'eas $\quad$ Intentio
quidem formulas, in quibus de iure quaeritur, in ius con-
ceptas vocamus.' This is certainly faulty since also in a
formula in factum concepta 'de iure quaeritur' (e.g. in the
formula patroni, as to whether the defendant is the plaintiff's
freedman; whether the defendant summoned the plaintiff
to court; whether he summoned him without the praetor's
permission). Gaius' definition of the *formula in factum concepta* is correct: 'initio formulae nominato eo quod factum
est, adiciuntur ea verba, per quae iudici damnandi absolvendive potestas datur.' It follows from this that no *formula
in factum concepta* can ever have an *intentio* (above, s. 30),
since the condemnation is not made conditional on a right
or claim of the plaintiff. Gaius 4. 46. 60, where the contrary
is asserted, are passages which obviously have suffered
interpolation.

Artificial but ingenious specimens of *formulae in factum* 49.
conceptae are the *formulae ficticiae*. One example must suffice $\quad$ ficticiae
here. The heir *ex iure praetorio* (called *bonorum possessor*) was
entitled to assert the rights of the *de cuius*. Suppose the *de
cuius* had given a loan which the *bonorum possessor* wished to

recover. He could not make use of the *formula certae creditae pecuniae* (above, s. 30) since he was not the heir *ex iure civili* (*heres*) and consequently not the creditor. The praetor, however, permitted him to sue the borrower *ficto se herede* with the following formula:

'Si Aulus Agerius (scil. the bonorum possessor) L. Titio heres esset, tum si pareret Numerium Negidium Aulo Agerio sestertium X milia dare oportere, iudex Numerium Negidio Aulo Agerio sestertium X milia condemnato, si non pareret absolvito.'

This is not a *formula in ius concepta*, since the condemnation is made conditional on a hypothetical right or claim of the plaintiff. But a hypothetical right not being an actual right, the *formula* is substantially *in factum concepta*. This simple truth could hardly escape the notice of the acute classical lawyers.

We cannot discuss here the difficult question of *consumption*. Gai. 4. 106, 107 are in any case inaccurate.

50. The different construction of the *formula* (*in ius—in* **Corollaries** *factum*) renders apparent the difference between *actiones civiles* and *actiones honorariae* (above, s. 45):

All *actiones civiles* have *formulae in ius conceptae* and conversely all *formulae in ius conceptae* belong to *actiones civiles*.

On the other hand, all *actiones honorariae* have *formulae in factum conceptae* and conversely all *formulae in factum conceptae* belong to *actiones honorariae*.

These propositions are logical necessities, being only corollaries of the definitions given above (s. 47).

51. Agere We frequently meet in our sources the terms *agere in* **in factum.** *factum* and *actio in factum*. The former is possibly classical **Actio in** **factum** (Gaius 4. 107 is spurious) and its meaning is to act *in iure* (above, s. 17) by pleading certain facts and not a right or claim *ex iure civili*. The terms *actio in factum* or *iudicium in factum* are very often, perhaps always, interpolated, though in themselves they are not objectionable. So far, however, this is only a question of terminology. What is substantially important is the following: *agere in factum* inevitably leads to a *formula in factum concepta* and every *actio in factum* (if that was a classical term) requires a *formula in factum con-cepta*. *Actio in factum civilis* is for the classics an absurdity and the term occurs only in spurious texts.

SOURCES

ss. 47, 48. Read Gai. 4. 45. 46.
s. 49. Read Gai. 4. 34.

BIBLIOGRAPHY

ss. 47–51. Pokrowsky, 'Die actiones in factum des klass. Rechts', Z xvi (1895), 7 ff.; Erman, Z xix (1898), 261 ff.; xxiii (1902), 445; Audibert, 'L'Expression *civilis in factum*; son caractère byzantin', *Mél. Fitting*, i (1907); 'Formules sans intentio', *Mél. Girard*, i (1912), 35 ff.; De Visscher, 'Les Formules in factum', *RH* iv (1925), 193 ff. = *Études de droit Romain* (1931), 361 ff.; Perozzi, 'Intorno a Gaio, 4. 60', *Mél. Cornil*, ii (1926), 199; Beseler, Z xlvi (1926), 268; Lenel, *Edictum* (1927), pp. 129, 203; Z xlviii (1928), 1 ff.; Riccobono, 'Formulae ficticiae', *T* ix (1929), 1 ff.; Beseler, *T* x (1930), 169 ff.; 'Meletemata', *Mnemosyna Pappoulia* (1934), 61; Solazzi, 'Appunti Gaiani', *Rend. Lomb.* lxxiv (1940–1), 587. On the Byzantine *actio in factum* see Collinet, *Études*, v (1947), 337 ff.*

3. *Actiones utiles*

Actio utilis is an action arising from the imitation of another action promised in the Edict. The word *utilis* means 'accommodated', i.e. adapted to a case not covered by the original action.

52. Definition

Cf. Cicero, *De lege agraria*, 2. 6. 14; '... hoc animo me ad legendam legem cognoscendamque venisse ut, si eam vobis accommodatam atque utilem esse intellegerem, auctor eius atque adiutor essem.'

For the original action a fixed designation apparently did not exist in classical times. In our sources sometimes occur the names *actio directa* or *actio vulgaris*, but the texts are partly interpolated, partly at least suspect.

53. Actio directa?

The original action may be an *actio civilis* or an *actio honoraria* (above, s. 45), but the *actio utilis* is of course always an *actio honoraria* and therefore has always a *formula in factum concepta* (above, s. 50). The *formulae ficticiae* are *formulae in factum conceptae* (above, s. 49).

54. Actio utilis sub-stituted by actio in factum

For that reason the classical lawyers sometimes substi-tuted *in factum agere* for *actio utilis* (above, s. 51). They might say: 'Actio legis Aquiliae non competit sed utili actione agendum est.' But they might equally well say: 'Actio legis Aquiliae non competit sed in factum agendum est.' In choosing the latter phrase they did not emphasize the dependence of the action upon an original action. However, if the original action was an *actio honoraria* the *actio utilis* could not properly be specified by *in factum agere* since the original action too had a *formula in factum concepta*. In our sources *actio utilis* has often been changed into *actio in factum* by post-classical hands.

55. Action on the case The English lawyers of the thirteenth century, who knew of the Roman terminology, have very properly rendered *actio utilis* or *actio in factum* by *breve in consimili casu* (action on the case).

SOURCES

s. 52. Read Gai. 3. 219.
s. 53. Read Gai. 4. 34 ['*non habet . . . et*']; 4. 38 ['*nec directo . . . oportere*']; Paul. *Sent.* 2. 12. 8 (post-classical).
s. 54. Read Gai. 3. 202 = *Inst. Iust.* 4. 1. 11 (Gaius *actio utilis*, Iust. *in factum actio*).

BIBLIOGRAPHY

ss. 52–4. Alibrandi, 'Delle azioni dirette ed utili', *Opere*, i (1896), pp. 149 ff.; Collinet, *Études*, v (1947), 403 ff. Materials for *agere in factum, actio in factum*, and *iudicium in factum, Voc.* ii. 786. 40 ff.; for *actio in factum civilis, Voc.* i. 749. 26 ff. On the English *breve in consimili casu* see Statute of Westminster, 13 Edw. 7, cap. 24 (1285), *Statutes of the Realm*, i. 83; Holdsworth, *History*, i (1927), 398; ii (1936), 300.

4. *Actiones in rem and in personam*

56. Definitions The peculiarity of the classical *actio in rem* lies in the proceeding *in iure* (above, s. 17). We have stated above (ss. 21–3) that in the ordinary procedure no *iudicium* could be instituted without the defendant's consent, but that the praetor's *imperium* came in if the defendant refused his consent. This rule is usually rendered as follows: the defendant has to defend his case *in iure*, i.e. he has to accept a *formula* approved by the praetor and consequently a proceeding before a judge (*iudicium*). There is, however, a small number of actions which entail no such duty, the defendant being free to abandon his case. These actions are called *actiones in rem*, the Roman idea being that here the plaintiff's action *in iure* is not directed against the defendant's person but against a thing (*in rem*) which the defendant is at liberty either to protect or to abandon. In contrast to them, all actions which entail a duty to make defence in court are called *actiones in personam*. An example of an *actio in personam* is the *actio certae creditae pecuniae*, which we have mentioned above (s. 30). The outstanding example of an *actio in rem* is the *rei vindicatio*, i.e. the action of the owner of a thing to recover it from the defendant who is in possession of it. Here the defendant is free to abandon the thing. If the thing was a movable, the praetor ordered the plaintiff to take it home (*duci vel ferri iubere*). If the thing was an immovable, the praetor ordered the defendant to restore it by issuing the *interdictum* '*quem fundum*' (below, ss. 647 ff.).

In classical times the distinction between *actiones in rem* and *actiones in personam* is crossed by the distinction between *actiones civiles* and *actiones honorariae* (above, s. 45). Both *actiones civiles* and *honorariae* may be either *in rem* or *in personam*.

57. Actiones honorariae in rem

The Roman makers of the *formulae* attempted to render the distinction (*actio in rem* and *in personam*) clear by a different construction of the *formulae*. *Actiones civiles in rem* have as a rule (below, s. 651) an *intentio* framed *in rem*, i.e. not mentioning the defendant's name, whereas in the *intentio* of an *actio civilis in personam* the defendant's name is mentioned. See for *actiones civiles in personam* the *formula certae creditae pecuniae*, which we have given above (s. 30). The *formula* of the *rei vindicatio* runs as follows:

58. Formulae in rem

'Si paret fundum Cornelianum, quo de agitur, ex iure Quiritium Auli
    Agerii esse,
neque is fundus Aulo Agerio restituetur,
quanti is fundus erit, tantam pecuniam iudex Numerium Negidium Aulo
    Agerio condemnato, si non paret absolvito.'

The defendant's name appears only in the *condemnatio*, whereas the *intentio* (*si paret . . . esse*) is framed *in rem*. In the *formula* of an *actio honoraria in rem* which has no *intentio* (above, ss. 48, 50) the name of the defendant is similarly omitted as far as possible in wording the facts on which the condemnation is made conditional (above, s. 47).

59. Unclassical ideas   This is the classical meaning of the distinction between *actiones in rem* and *actiones in personam*. Students should be warned not to confuse it by introducing other ideas. It would be wrong to say that *actiones in rem* are those actions by which *iura in re* (or *in rem*) are protected. It would also be wrong to define *actiones in rem* as those actions which lie against anybody who violates a *ius in re* (or *in rem*). Both *actio legis Aquiliae* and *condictio furtiva* are actions by which a *ius in re* (*dominium*) is protected and which lie against anybody who violates the *ius in re* (*dominium*): nevertheless, they are *actiones in personam* and not *in rem*. For the classics the decisive question is solely whether the defendant has to make defence *in iure* or whether he is free to abandon the case. *Actiones mixtae tam in rem quam in personam* are unknown in classical law. The queer idea of an *actio in personam in rem scripta* is also entirely unclassical. The English distinctions between real actions, personal actions, and mixed actions, though obviously inspired by the Roman sources, in no way correspond to the classical distinctions.

SOURCES

Read Gai. 4. 2 and 3; [*Actio ex . . . negativa*]. *D.* (50. 17) 156 pr. Gai. 4. 87 from the words *sed cum*.

BIBLIOGRAPHY

s. 56. Wlassak, *Z* xxv (1904), 141 ff., 153 ff.; *PW* i. 313; Pissard, 'Duci vel ferri iubere', *Études Girard*, i (1912), 241 ff.; Lenel, *Edict.* § 248; J. Goldschmidt, *Prozess als Rechtslage* (1925), 82.*

s. 57. Albertario, 'In tema di classificazione delle azioni', *Riv. di diritto processuale civile*, v (1928), 185 ff. = *Studi*, iv (1946), 219 ff. Against him (rightly) G. Segrè, 'Sulla distinzione delle actiones in rem e in personam per raporti estranei al ius civile nel diritto rom. classico', *Bull.* xli (1933), 81 ff.

s. 58. On the last words of Gai. 4. 3 see Beseler, *Z* xlvi (1926), 268; for the *formula* of the *actio negatoria* see Lenel, *Edict.* §§ 72, 73.

s. 59. On *actiones mixtae tam in rem quam in personam*: *Inst. Iust.* 4. 6. 20 and Paul. *Sent.* 1. 7. 4 (post-classical: Schulz, *Z* xliii, 1922, 229). On *actio in rem scripta* (which occurs only *D.* 4. 2, 9. 8) see Lenel, *Edict.* p. 113. On the English classification see Blackstone, *Commentaries*, Book

III, ch. 8 init. and modern text-books. *Actio realis* (real action) does not occur in our sources; *actio personalis* (personal action) occurs but is always unclassical (Schulz, *Einführung*, 91).

5. *Bonae fidei iudicia*

Classical legal language knows only of *bonae fidei iudicium*, not of *bonae fidei actio*. The terms *bona fide iudicium*, *bonae fidei contractus*, *bonae fidei negotium* are likewise unclassical. 60. Terminology

A *bonae fidei iudicium* is a procedure before a judge under a *formula* in which by a special clause the judge is ordered to pronounce judgment according to good faith. Let us take as an example the action of a seller of goods claiming the price (*actio venditi*). The *formula* is framed as follows: 61. Definition and example

'Quod Aulus Agerius (the seller) Numerio Negidio (the buyer) fundum Cornelianum, quo de agitur, vendidit,
quidquid paret ob eam rem Numerium Negidium dare facere oportere ex fide bona,
eius iudex Numerium Negidium Aulo Agerio condemnato, si non paret absolvito.'

It is the clause *ex fide bona* which renders the *iudicium venditi* a *bonae fidei iudicium*. The *formula* as a whole needs some explanatory remarks.

The words *quidquid* . . . *ex fide bona* contain the *intentio* (above, s. 30). It is an *intentio incerta*, the judge being authorized to fix the sum due to the plaintiff according to good faith. This sum may be more or less than the stipulated price: more, if, for example, the defendant is *in mora* and owes interest; less, if, for example, parties had agreed that the price should be paid by instalments and only the first instalment is due. The clause *quod* . . . *vendidit* is called *demonstratio* and is indispensable whenever there is an *incerta intentio*. The word *quod* should be rendered by 'if' or 'whereas'; *eius* is a 'genitive of respect' or 'relation' (genitive with judicial words, Stolz–Schmalz, *Lat. Grammatik*, p. 402); this usage is in conformity with republican official style. The meaning of *eius* is here as always in these *formulae*: 'on the strength of what has been said in the preceding part of the *formula* the judge shall make a valuation in money and condemn the defendant to pay a fixed sum'.

As a rule the clause is framed as in the *formula venditi*, viz. by adding *ex fide bona* to the *intentio*. Exceptionally it is framed differently (*actio fiduciae*, *actio rei uxoriae*), but the meaning is the same. After all, these *formulae* have been 62. Form of the clause composed by various hands at various times and we must not expect uniformity.

63. Legal meaning The original meaning of a *bonae fidei iudicium* was as follows: the judge shall decide what as a matter of good faith (not *ex iure Quiritium*) was due from the defendant to the plaintiff. In the time at which, for example, the *formula venditi* was created a formless contract of sale was not yet recognized by *ius civile*. Thus an *actio venditi* could not be founded on *ius civile* but only on good faith. Here it is particularly evident that the agreement of the parties *in iure* which we have discussed above (ss. 21, 22) was indeed an agreement to submit to arbitration. In classical times, however, the meaning of the clause *ex fide bona* is different. A formless contract of sale being now recognized by *ius civile*, that clause was no longer the basis of the action but was only meant to determine the measure of such performance as might be due.

64. Classical law of bona fides The judge was free to interpret these clauses at his discretion. But here as elsewhere he was expected to follow well-established legal doctrines (above, ss. 11 and 34). Thus the classical lawyers have developed an important group of rules by interpreting these clauses. These rules cannot be given here but will be discussed later in due course.

65. List of bonae fidei iudicia Nor can a list of the *bonae fidei iudicia* be given at this point. The praetorian Edict had a special section *de bonae fidei iudiciis*, but it did not contain all of them. Gaius 4. 62 gives a list which apparently was meant to be complete, but it is doubtful whether it really is. Anyhow, the list shows the well-known feeling for law of the Roman jurists, though it is not quite free from historical arbitrariness and chance. As aforesaid, these *formulae* were gradually developed and were not framed by one man according to a comprehensive plan.

66. Iudicia stricti iuris? The *iudicia* which were not *bonae fidei iudicia* had no common designation in classical times; in particular they were not called *iudicia stricta* or *iudicia stricti iuris*. Such a name would indeed have been very improper, since in many of them *bona fides* prevailed as well as in the *bonae fidei iudicia*.

SOURCES

Read Gai. 4. 40, 41, 48, 62. Cicero, *De officiis*, 3. 16. 66.

BIBLIOGRAPHY

s. 60. Gradenwitz, *Interpolationen in den Pandekten* (1887), 105 ff. (out of date). Materials: *bonae fidei iudicium, Voc.* i. 598.43; *bonae fidei actio* within the materials of the *Voc.* only once, *D.* (16. 3) 1. 23 (spurious), within the *Cod. Iust.* only once, *C.* (4. 65) 17 (Diocletian); *bona fide iudicium* only once *D.* (27. 7) 8. 1 (spurious: Beseler, 'Meletemata', *Mnemosyna Pappoulia*, 1934, p. 53); on *bonae fidei contractus* and *negotium* see Schulz, Z xliii (1922), 189 with references. *Bonae fidei iudex* only *D.* (12. 3) 4. 2 (spurious). On the Byzantine *actiones bonae fidei*, see Collinet, *Études*, v (1947), 225 ff.

s. 61. Lenel, *Edict.* § 110. On *quod* and *eius* within the *formulae* Schulz, *History*, 259, 258.

s. 63. Schulz, *History*, 83, with references; Kaser, *Altröm. Jus* (1949), 289 ff.

s. 64. B. Biondi, *Iudicia bonae fidei*, i (1920), 3 ff.; G. Grosso, 'L'efficacia dei patti nei bonae fidei iudicia', *Studi Urbinati*, i and ii (1927–8); 'Efficacia dei patti nei bonae fidei iudicia', *Memorie dell' istituto giuridico Torino*, Ser. II, Memoria iii (1928); Koschembahr–Lyskowski, 'Quid veniat in bonae fidei iudicium en droit classique romain', *St. Riccobono*, ii (1936), 149.

s. 65. Had *actio commodati* and *actio pigneraticia* 'bonae fidei iudicia'? Lenel, *Edict.* §§ 98, 99; G. Segrè, 'Sull' età dei giudizi di buona fede di commodato e di pegno', *St. Fadda*, vi (1905), 339 ff.; Biondi, l.c. 176 ff.; G. Grosso, 'Ricerche intorno all' elenco classico dei bonae fidei iudicia', *Riv. It.* N.S. iii (1928), fasc. 1.*

s. 66. Materials: *Voc.* v. 696. 27 ff. Naber, De 'strictis iudiciis', Mnemosyne, xxiv (1896), 55 ff.; Biondi, 'Actiones stricti iuris', *Bull.* xxxii (1922), 61 ff.; Pringsheim, Z xlii (1921), 653.

6. *So-called actiones arbitrariae*

In one group of actions the *formulae* have a clause *nisi* 67. *restituetur* or *neque restituetur* inserted immediately before the *condemnatio*. Take as an example the *formula* of the *rei vindicatio* which we have given above (s. 58). Such actions were called *actiones arbitrariae* by earlier Romanists, since it was believed that this clause ran *nisi* (or *neque*) *arbitrio iudicis restituetur*. Today we know (or should know) that the clause did not mention an *arbitrium iudicis*, and further

Definition

that those actions were never called *actiones arbitrariae* by the classical lawyers. Gaius was content to mention twice (4. 141, 163) a *formula arbitraria*, making it quite clear that this was a *formula* in which an *arbiter* instead of a *iudex* was appointed (above, s. 19).

68. Legal meaning   This clause means that if the judge comes to the conclusion that the plaintiff is right, he shall not immediately condemn the defendant to pay an amount of money but rather issue a *pronuntiatio* ordering specific restitution. It is only if that order is not obeyed that he shall condemn the defendant to pay money. Thus the harshness of the *condemnatio pecuniaria* is considerably mitigated by that clause. Moreover, the classical lawyers interpreted the clause very liberally so that the judge is not only authorized to order the restitution of the *res* but also to award fruits of the *res* and damages. The word *restituere* is taken as *in integrum restituere* (*D.* 21. 1. 23. 7: 'quodammodo in integrum restituere'; 43. 8. 2. 43: 'restituere videtur qui in pristinum statum reducit').

69. Formulae with restituere and similar formulae   A list of the *formulae* with *nisi* (or *neque*) *restituetur* cannot be given here; it need only be noted that all *actiones in rem* (but not they alone) were provided with that clause. Upon examining those *formulae* which we know to have contained it we realize again that much arbitrariness and individual idiosyncrasy were at work in building up the *formulae*. Take, for example, the *formula* of the *actio commodati* by which the lender of a thing claims to have it returned to him. It might well have been provided with a clause *nisi restituetur*; actually, however, the *formula commodati* (*in factum concepta*) ran as follows:

> 'Si paret Aulum Agerium (the lender) Numerio Negidio (the borrower) rem qua de agitur commodasse eamque Aulo Agerio redditam non esse, quanti ea res erit, tantam pecuniam iudex Numerium Negidium Aulo Agerio condemnato si non paret absolvito.'

The *reddere* clause is similar to the *restituere* clause but not identical with it. However, on the strength of the *reddere* clause the judge was equally entitled to issue a *pronuntiatio* ordering specific restoring of the thing. Moreover, the legal meaning of *reddere* was apparently assimilated to that of *restituere* by the classical lawyers. Finally, in the *bonae fidei iudicia* (above, s. 61) the judge was equally allowed to order specific performance before condemning the defendant to pay money. Thus the result is that in classical law the judge is as a rule entitled to order specific restitution or performance (this is not the case in the actions *ex stipulatu*, *ex testamento*, and the *condictiones*). Nevertheless, the classical lawyers carefully kept apart the various kinds of actions and in spite of all assimilations full uniformity was neither achieved nor apparently sought. Differences in detail remained, but they can hardly be discerned in full from available sources. The process of assimilation was continued in post-classical times with the usual effect that the texts were interpolated and the classical differences obliterated. In this book, however, we are not concerned with these vexed questions.

SOURCES

s. 67. Read Gai. 4. 163 to *condemnatur*; *Inst. Iust.* (4. 6) 31; *D.* (4. 2) 14. 11: 'et hoc fit his verbis ⟨formulae⟩ [edicti]: neque ea res [arbitrio iudicis] restituetur': the compilers after having substituted *edicti* for *formulae* (right Lenel, *Edict.* p. 113, see above, s. 42; wrong Levy 21 ff., Schönbauer, 375) were led to add *arbitrio iudicis* in order to make the text quite clear which had become ambiguous by their first alteration.

s. 68. Read (for the classical interpretation of *restituere* in the *formula* of the *rei vindicatio*) *D.* (6. 1) 17. 1 to *esse*; (6. 1) 33 and 79.

BIBLIOGRAPHY

ss. 67, 68. Windscheid, *Pand.* i (1906), § 46; Biondi, *Sulla dottrina Romana dell' Actio arbitraria* (1911, Estratto d. *Annali Palermo*, i); May, 'Observations sur les actiones arbitrariae', *Mél. Girard*, ii (1912), 151; Segrè, 'La denominazione di actio confessoria', *Mél. Girard*, ii (1912), 511 ff.; Biondi, *Studi sulle actiones arbitrariae e l'arbitrium iudicis*, fasc. 1 (1913); 'Di nuovo sulla dottrina Romana dell' actio arbitraria', *Bull.* xxvi (1913), 1 ff., 153; O Lenel, 'Zur Lehre von den actiones arbitrariae', *Festgabe f. R. Sohm* (1914), 201 ff.; Levy, *Zur Lehre von den sog. actiones arbitrariae* (1915) = Z xxxvi (1915), 1 ff.; Herdliczka, *Zur Lehre vom Zwischenurteil (pronuntiatio) bei den actiones arbitrariae* (1930); M. Kaser, *Restituere als Prozessgegenstand* (1932); v. Lübtow, *der Ediktstitel quod metus causa gestum erit* (1932), 136 ff.; Herdliczka, *Skizzen zum röm. Zivilprozess: formula arbitraria, iudicium arbitrarium und actiones arbitrariae* (1934); Scheltema, *Proeve eener theorie der actiones arbitrariae* (1934); Schönbauer, 'Vom Wesen der iudicia arbitraria', *St. Riccobono*, ii (1936), 371; Albertario, 'Due osservazioni sul fragmentum de formula Fabiana', *Studi*, v (1937), 603 ff.; Collinet, *Études*, v (1947), 229.

s. 69. For a list see particularly Biondi, *Studi sulle actiones arbitrariae* (1913), 38 ff. For *reddere* see Levy, l.c. 72.

7. *So-called actiones directae and actiones contrariae*

70. Classical terminology   On the strength of a contract of sale the seller has an *actio venditi* and the buyer an *actio empti*. Similarly from a contract of hire arise an *actio locati* for the *locator* and an *actio conducti* for the *conductor*. In other contracts, however (*mandatum, societas, commodatum, depositi, pignus, fiducia*), though both parties have actions these are not differentiated terminologically. In a contract of mandate, for example, the *mandator* might sue the agent for damages if he did not properly perform his job, and the agent might sue the *mandator* in order to recover the expenses which he had incurred in carrying out the *mandator's* orders. Both actions were simply called *actio mandati* by the classical lawyers, and this could safely be done since the connexion in which the term is used makes it sufficiently clear whether the action of the *mandator* is meant or that of the agent. The *formulae* for the two actions of course differed slightly.

Action of the *mandator*:

'Quod Aulus Agerius (the mandator) Numerio Negidio (the agent)
     mandavit ut . . ., qua de re agitur,
quidquid paret ob eam rem Numerium Negidium Aulo Agerio dare
     facere oportere ex fide bona,
eius iudex Numerium Negidium Aulo Agerio condemnato', etc.

Action of the agent:

'Quod Numerius Negidius (the mandator) Aulo Agerio (the agent)
     mandavit, ut . . . qua de re agitur,
quidquid paret', etc.

Why were the two actions on the contracts of sale and hire designated by specific names and not similarly the actions on other contracts? The simple answer is that the Latin language did not possess different terms for designating the two sides of a contract of *mandatum, commodatum, depositum*, etc. Mysterious legal thought certainly does not lie behind this phenomenon.

To be sure in our sources the action of the agent, de- 71.
pository, etc., is often called *actio contraria* or *iudicium con-* Justinian's
trarium; the term *actio directa* for the action of the mandator, logy
depositor, etc., occurs but rarely (as far as I can see only
once in the *Digest D.* (3. 5) 19). This terminology, however, is definitely Justinianic and not classical. It is of course
impossible to prove interpolation in every text by special
arguments since the simple adding of *contraria* or *contrarium*
as a rule does not leave further traces of interpolation. But
three facts cannot be denied: (1) the terms *actio contraria*,
iudicium contrarium and in contrast to them *actio directa* do
not occur in any text outside the *Corpus iuris*. (2) Gaius uses
the term *actio contraria* in a different sense (Gaius 4. 177–
81). (3) In some cases interpolation is evident. These facts
point to the conclusion that the classical lawyers knew
nothing of this terminology.

SOURCES

s. 70. Read Gai. 3. 127, 161; Paul. *Sent.* 2. 13. 7; 2. 15. 2.
s. 71. Read Inst. Iust. (4. 16) 2 to *notatur* and Gai. 4. 182 to *depositi*.
D. (17. 1) 12. 9: 'mandati actionem [N.B. not *contrariam*] . . . erit [con-
traria] mandati actio'.

BIBLIOGRAPHY

Materials for *actio contraria*, *Voc.* i. 1005, 26 ff.; for *iudicium contrarium*, *Voc.* i. 1005. 44 ff. Gradenwitz, *Interpolationen in den Pandekten*
(1887), 111 ff.; Partsch, 'Studien zur negotiorum gestio', i, *SB Heidelberg*
(1913), 54; Kübler, Z xxxviii (1917), 73 ff.; Beseler, *Beitr.* iv (1920),
255; Biondi, *Iudicia bonae fidei*, i (1920), 59 ff. (Estr. d. *Annali Palermo*,
vii); Lenel, *Edict.* (1927), 254; Kreller, *Arch. f. ziv. Praxis*, cxxxiii,
Beiheft (1931), 131 ff; Arangio-Ruiz, *Il mandato* (1949), 97 ff.; Provera,
SD viii (1942), 113 ff.; *St. Solazzi* (1948), 345 ff. On *D.* (3. 2) 1 and
(3. 2) 6. 7 see Schulz, *Festschrift für Zitelmann* (1913), 19 ff.; on *D.*
(47. 2) 62. 1 see Beseler, Z liii (1933), 61. Manigk *PW* ix. 2481, is not
helpful.*

8. *Actiones poenales and actiones rem persequentes*

In classical law an *actio poenalis* is an action which results 72.
from an offence and by means of which a fine may be im- Definitions
posed upon the delinquent; the fine is as a rule payable to

the plaintiff. All other actions are called *actiones rem perse-quentes*. Penal actions (as well as *actiones rem persequentes*) are either *actiones civiles* or *actiones honorariae* (above, s. 45). The fine sometimes amounts to a multiple of damages (*duplum, triplum, quadruplum*), sometimes only to the *simplum* (*actio de dolo*), but even in the latter case the action must not be regarded as an action for damages.

73. Four rules   The classical lawyers have carried through this distinction with their usual clearness and precision. All classical penal actions without any exception are subject to the following four rules.

1. Co-delinquents are liable cumulatively. Suppose that three thieves co-operated in a *furtum nec manifestum*. The owner may sue each of them for double value so that the whole sum due to him is the sixfold value of the stolen thing. This rule clearly reveals the penal character of an action, even when the amount of the fine does not exceed the *simplum*. Damages can only be claimed once, and if one of the delinquents pays the whole, the others become free from any liability. A fine, however, is very reasonably held to be due from each of them.

2. No penal action is transmissible to the heir of the delinquent. The great Roman principle, never to punish the heirs of delinquents, is firmly maintained although of course if the offender dies after the *litis contestatio* (above, s. 17), his heir becomes responsible, since the plaintiff is entitled to obtain what was due to him at the time of the *litis contestatio*.

3. Whenever the delinquent was *filius in potestate patris* or a slave, he himself was not liable for the fine. The penal action lay against the father or the master, but they were entitled to escape liability by surrendering the offender to the plaintiff by *manicipatio* (*noxae datio, actio noxalis*). Out-side the group of penal actions *noxae datio* is not admissible in classical law.

4. Each penal action can be brought in addition to any *actio rem persequens*. Thus the owner can sue the thief (*fur nec manifestus*) by the *actio furti* for double value and in addition by the *rei vindicatio* (above, s. 58) for the stolen thing. If in a contract of hire the slave of the lessee has damaged

the hired thing, the lessor can sue the lessee by the *actio legis Aquiliae noxalis*. If an *actio locati* also lay against the lessee, both actions could be brought together, the classical *actio legis Aquiliae* being a pure penal action (below, s. 1009).

No classical action is partly penal and partly *rem persequens*. There is only one exception to this rule. In a small group of actions *lis infitiando crescit in duplum*, the outstanding example being the action resulting from *legatum per damnationem*. As regards the *actio ex testamento* resulting from such a legacy, Gaius' statement (4. 9) is true: *rem et poenam persequimur*. Other *actiones mixtae* do not exist in classical law. **74. Actiones mixtae**

These classical principles were variously altered in post-classical times. The far-going classical cumulation of actions seemed too harsh and was therefore restricted; *noxae datio* was no longer confined to penal actions and some penal actions (*actio vi bonorum raptorum, actio legis Aquiliae*) were rendered *actiones mixtae* (*et rem et poenam persequentes*). These innovations were carried through by innumerable interpolations and our sources are, therefore, in a horrid state. It would be an interesting task to write the history of that post-classical development in full detail; this, however, lies outside the scope of this book (above, s. 2.). **75. Post-classical law**

Sometimes a penal action can be brought by any Roman citizen or by any citizen of a *municipium*. These *actiones populares* were introduced partly by *leges*, partly by the praetor's Edict in cases in which public interest prevailed. The outstanding example is the *actio honoraria de sepulcro violato*. The fine obtained from the delinquent accrued either to the plaintiff or to the State or *municipium*. It remains, however, doubtful how far these actions could be pursued in the ordinary civil procedure. The Roman *actiones populares* certainly were the model of the numerous 'popular actions' which have been introduced by English statutes since the Middle Ages. In continental law they disappeared at an early date, for they presuppose a vigorous and active public spirit which on the Continent did not exist. **76. Actiones populares**

77. Some penal actions are extinguished by the death of the
Actiones
vindictam injured party. Modern students used to designate them as
spirantes *actiones vindictam spirantes* (cf. *D*. 37. 6. 2. 4). The outstanding example is the *actio iniuriarum*.

78. The classical penal actions afford a powerful protection
Evaluation of material and immaterial interests against aggression,
of classical
penal since it is always easier for a plaintiff to claim a fine than to
actions claim and prove damages. The *actio iniuriarum*, for example, is a sharp-edged remedy against any violation of
honour. Of course it has to be borne in mind that execution
on the person still existed in classical law (above, s. 43),
otherwise this system of fines cannot be properly understood.

SOURCES

s. 72. Read Gai. 4. 6–9; [*et iniuriarum . . . raptorum*]; [*quod . . . sunt*];
cf. Gai. 4. 112.

s. 73. 1. Read *D*. (9. 2) 11. 2; (47. 4) 1. 19; (47. 2) 21. 9 (Jolowicz,
Digest, xlvii. 2, *De furtis*, 1940, p. 34).

s. 73. 2. Read Gai. 4. 112.

s. 73. 3. Read Gai. 4. 75, 76.

s. 73. 4. Read Gai. 4. 4; Coll. 12. 7. 9 ([*ita ut . . . agendum*].

s. 74. Read Gai. 4. 9. 171.

s. 75. Read *D*. (2. 10) 1. 4 (spurious); *Coll.* 12. 7. 9 [*ita ut . . . agendum*];
Paul. *Sent.* (2. 31) 13; *D*. (17. 1) 26. 7 (spurious: note *actio mandati
noxalis!*); *Inst. Iust.* (4. 6) 19.

s. 76. Read *D*. (47. 12) 3 pr. Cf. Lenel, *Edict.* § 93.

s. 77. Read Gai. 4. 112 in fine.

BIBLIOGRAPHY

s. 72. E. Levy. *Privatstrafe und Schadensersatz im klassischen römischen
Recht* (1915); against him (rightly) Beseler, *Beitr.* iv (1920), 258 ff.;
Juristische Miniaturen (1929), 129; P. Voci, *Risarcimento e pena privata
nel dir. Rom. class.* (1939) i; on Gai. 4. 9 Beseler Z xlvii (1927), 65;
Scritti Ferrini, iii (1948) 283; Voci, l.c. 94. Wlassak, *PW* i. 316 ff.

s. 73. 1. Bonfante, *Scritti*, iii (1926), 209 ff.

s. 73. 2. Schulz, *Principles*, 203 f.; Riccobono, Z xlvii (1927), 75 ff.;
Lenel, Z xlviii (1928), 563; Voci, l.c. 107 ff.

s. 73. 3. Girard, 'Les Actions noxales', *NRH* xi (1887), 409 ff.; xii
(1888), 31 ff. = *Mélanges*, ii (1923), 309 ff.; Biondi, *Actiones noxales*
(1925, Estr. d. *Annali Palermo*, x); Beseler, Z xlvi (1926), 104 ff.; Lenel,
Z xlvii (1927), 1 ff.; Biondi, *Bull.* xxxvi (1928), 99 ff.; F. de Visscher,
'La Nature juridique de l'abandon noxal', *RH* ix (1930), 411; *Le Régime
romain de la noxalité* (1947), now the standard work on the subject;

Beseler, Z l (1930), 29; 'Lucubrationes Balticae', *SD* iii (1937), 380 ff.; Lisowski, *PW*, Suppl. vii. 604–63; Kaser, *Altröm. Jus* (1949), 225 ff.*

s. 73. 4. Beseler, *Beitr.* iv (1920), 258 ff. against Levy, l.c.; on *Coll.* 12. 7. 9 see Beseler, Z l (1930), 74; Niedermeyer, *ACI* 1933, Roma, i. 379.

s. 74. Voci, l.c., 5. 91 ff., 182.

s. 75. See Bonfante, Beseler ll. cc.; on Paul. *Sent.* 2. 31. 13 see M. Conrat, *Paulus*, 184; De Visscher, *Le Régime etc.* 470 ff.; Voci, l.c. 91 ff.

s. 76. Bruns, 'Die römischen Popularklagen', *Z f. RG* iii (1864), 341 ff. = *Kleinere Schriften*, i (1882), 313 ff.; Mommsen, *Schr.* iii. 374 ff.; *StR* ii. 70; Strachan-Davidson, *Problems of the Roman Criminal Law* i (1912), 180; Wlassak, *PW* i. 318; *Der Judikationsbefehl (SB Wien*, cxcvii. 4. 1921), p. 271; E. Weiss. Z xlv (1925), 494. On English popular actions see Holdsworth, *History*, iv (1937), 356; ix (1926), 240.

s. 77. On Gai. 3. 112 see Albertario, 'Elementi postgaiani', *Studi*, v. 448; Beseler, Z liii (1933), 20; cf. Levy, Z xlvi (1926), 416.

9. *So-called actiones famosae*

In some actions enumerated in the praetor's Edict the condemnation involved *infamia*. The praetor stated that persons condemned in these actions were not allowed to appoint an agent (*cognitor* or *procurator*) for a civil procedure and he limited their right to appear in court on another's behalf (*postulare pro aliis*). He did not expressly say that he regarded them as *infames* or *ignominiosi*, but that was certainly implied by his rules. Some of these actions were penal (*actio furti, vi bonorum raptorum, de dolo*), some non-penal actions (*actio mandati, depositi, fiduciae, pro socio*). 79. Definition

The classical list of actions has been gradually developed, as is shown by the so-called *lex Iulia municipalis*, and even in its ultimate form it was not quite free from arbitrariness, since the exclusion of the *actio commodati* cannot be reasonably explained. The list as transmitted to us by Justinian's *Digest* is not quite complete, since the compilers have eliminated some actions, for example, the *actio fiduciae* and the so-called *actiones contrariae* (above, s. 70). The list given by Gaius 4. 182 is also incomplete (e.g. the *actio de dolo* is omitted). 80. The classical list of actions

In our sources these actions are called *actiones famosae* or *iudicia famosa*, but these terms are hardly classical. 81. Post-classical terminology

SOURCES

s. 79. Read Gai. 4. 182.

s. 80. Read *Lex Iulia municipalis*, l. 111 (Bruns, *Fontes*, no. 18; *FIRA* i, no. 13; E. G. Hardy, *Roman Laws and Charters*, i, 1911, p. 136); *D.* (3. 2) 1 to *damnatus erit*; *Inst. Iust.* 4. 16. 2, cf. Gai. 4. 182; *D.* (3. 2) 6. 7 (entirely spurious).

BIBLIOGRAPHY

s. 79. Lenel, *Edict.* pp. 77, 90.

s. 80. Lenel, *Edict.* pp. 79 f.; Schulz, *Festschrift f. Zitelmann* (1913), pp. 17 ff.; Beseler, *Beitr.* iv (1920), 255.

s. 81. See materials in *Voc.* ii. 813. 33 ff.

10. *Actiones perpetuae and actiones temporales*

82.
Praetorian
prescrip-
tion

A general limitation of actions did not exist in classical law, but the praetor sometimes declared in his Edict that he would grant a certain action (e.g. the *actio de dolo*) only within a space of one year to be counted from the day *cum primum experiundi potestas fuerit*. This praetorian praescription of actions was stated in the Edict rather arbitrarily and without a fixed principle.

83.
Cassius'
rules

The jurist Cassius, however (consul A.D. 30), surveying the whole mass of actions, framed the following three rules:

1. All *actiones civiles* (above, s. 45) are *actiones perpetuae*.
2. All *actiones honorariae rem persequentes* (above, ss. 45, 72) are also *actiones perpetuae*.
3. All honorary penal actions (s. 72) are available only for one year.

84.
Julian's
Edict

According to these rules even those penal actions for which the praetor had not expressly fixed the limitation of time were now regarded by the lawyers as being available only for a year. Cassius' idea was that an injured man should obtain satisfaction only as long as the injury was still fresh in his mind, though he could not apply this principle to the civil penal actions.

In the time of Gaius Cassius' rules were no longer quite true. There were now honorary penal actions which were *actiones perpetuae* like the *actio furti manifesti* (above, s. 45) and the *actio vi bonorum raptorum in simplum*, and there were other exceptions to these rules. Apparently the Edict had been altered in the period after Cassius, probably by Julian when he revised the Edict for Hadrian (above, s. 25). Some of these exceptions, however, are of post-classical origin.

The classical term for an action available only for a year is *actio annua*, not *actio annalis*. Both *actio temporaria* and *actio temporalis* seem to be classical terms. **85. Classical terminology**

SOURCES

s. 83. Read *D.* (44. 7) 35 to *dandae sunt*; Gai. 4. 110, 111.

s. 84. Read Gai. 4. 112; 3. 209. *D.* (39. 4) 13. 4 (spurious; the style is that of a legislator, not of a lawyer); *D.* (11. 3) 13 pr. (spurious).

BIBLIOGRAPHY

s. 82. Lenel, *Edict.* p. 64, n. 2; Wlassak, *PW* i. 320; P. Voci, *Risarcimento e pena privata* (1939), 104 f.

ss. 83. 84. Beseler, *Beitr.* iv (1920), 258 ff.

s. 85. Beseler, *Beitr.* v (1931), 53. Materials for *actio annalis* in *Voc.* i. 448. 44; for *actio annua* in *Voc.* i. 458. 30; for *actio temporaria* and *actio temporalis* in *Voc.* v. 969.

11. *So-called iudicia divisoria*

The following three actions form a special group in the praetor's Edict: *actio familiae erciscundae*, *actio communi dividundo*, *actio finium regundorum*. They are usually called *iudicia divisoria* by modern students, a misleading term which never occurs in our sources and should be avoided altogether. **86. The three actions**

1. Co-heirs are co-owners of the inherited property. Each of them can demand division, and if that could not be achieved by agreement, he may sue his co-heirs by an action which bears the old-Latin name *actio familiae erciscundae* (or *herciscundae*). *Familia* means in classical times the estate, *erciscere* (or *herciscere*) means *dividere*. The judge has a far-reaching discretionary power in this proceeding. Suppose three co-heirs are co-owners of a piece of land. The judge may make three lots and assign one to each of them. Or he may assign the whole land to one of them and oblige him to

indemnify the other two by paying a sum of money. By this assignment, which is called *adiudicatio*, the recipient becomes owner *ex iure Quiritium*.

2. The *actio communi dividundo* is a very similar action applicable to any other kind of joint ownership.

3. The *actio finium regundorum* is an action for regulating boundary disputes. Obviously this is not a *iudicium divisorium* like the other two, since the parties are not joint owners of the disputed land. But here too the boundary is fixed by *adiudicatio*.

87.   The shape of the *formulae* for these three actions is much
Formula
and legal disputed. It contained a special clause, called *adiudicatio*,
charter by which the judge was authorized to assign the disputed thing. The clause *ex fide bona* was certainly absent and these *iudicia* were therefore not regarded as *bonae fidei iudicia* by the classical lawyers (above, s. 60). Justinian's compilers, however, styled them *bonae fidei iudicia* and they have carried through this idea by means of interpolations. The actions were *actiones in personam*, not *in rem*, since the defendant was bound to defend himself (above, s. 56). Each party had in these proceedings the legal position of both a plaintiff and a defendant, but the term *iudicia duplicia* seems of post-classical origin.

SOURCES

s. 86. Read Gai. 4. 42 and *Epit. Ulp.* 19. 16; *Lex Rubria,* cap. xxiii, l. 54; Gai. 3. 154*a*.

s. 87. Read Gai. 4. 42. 62; *Inst. Iust.* (4. 6) 20. 28; *C. Iust.* (3. 38) 3, spurious as shown by Consult. 2. 6; *D.* (10. 1) 1 [*licet . . . est*], *licet* with indicative!; *D.* (10. 2) 2. 3; (10. 1) 10; *D.* (10. 3) 2. 1 interpolated as shown by *D.* (5. 1) 13.

BIBLIOGRAPHY

ss. 86, 87. A. Berger, *Zur Entwicklungsgeschichte der Teilungsklagen* (1912); Arangio-Ruiz, 'Appunti sui giudizi divisori', *Riv. It.* lii (1913); Biondi, *Bonae fidei iudicia,* i (1920) (Estr. d. *Annali Palermo,* vii), pp. 218 ff.; Arangio-Ruiz, 'Studi formulari II. In tema di adiudicatio', *Bull.* xxxii (1922), 1 ff.; Lenel, *Edict.* (1927), §§ 79–81 with references; Frezza, 'Actio communi dividundo', *Riv. It.* N.S. vii (1932, not available); Albertario, *Studi,* iv (1946), 165 ff.; Sciascia, 'In tema di actio familiae erciscundae', *AG* cxxxii (1945); Beseler, *Scritti Ferrini,* iii (1948), 281.*

12. *Praeiudicia*

A *praeiudicium* is an *actio* in which the plaintiff demands 88.
the ascertainment of a fact or a legal relation. Such an Definition
action is sometimes preparatory to another lawsuit and is
therefore called 'preceding proceeding' (*prae-iudicium*).
The plaintiff may, for example, assert that the defendant is
his freedman whereas the defendant denies this relation. If
the judge pronounces judgment for the plaintiff, the latter
may sue the defendant by another action resting on the
relation between patron and freedman (for an example see
above, s. 47). We know of one *praeiudicium* ordered by a
lex; others were mentioned in the praetor's Edict.

The *formula* of these actions is not known to us. Gaius 89.
4. 44 states that it contained only an *intentio*, but the text is Formula
hardly reliable. Perhaps the *formula* ran as follows: and legal
character

'Octavius iudex esto pronuntiatoque an Numerius Negidius libertus
Auli Agerii sit.'

Certainly these actions were not *actiones in rem* since the 90. Extra-
defendant was bound to defend himself (above, s. 56). ordinaria
cognitio
In the *extraordinaria cognitio praeiudicia* apparently
played an important part.

SOURCES

s. 88. Read Gai. 4. 44; 3. 123.

s. 89. Read *Inst. Iust.* 4. 6. 13 (not classical).

s. 90. Read the two following opinions: *P. Michigan* iii, no. 159 = Z
xlvi (1926), 276 and *P. Oxy.* i, no. 37 = Mitteis, *Chrest.* no. 79, *FIRA*
iii, no. 170.

BIBLIOGRAPHY

Pissard, *Les Questions préjudicielles en droit Romain* (1907); Lenel,
Edict. (1927), Index, s.v. 'praeiudicia'; Beseler, *T* x (1930), 170; H.
Krüger, *St. Riccobono*, ii (1936), 229 ff.*

CHAPTER III

EXCEPTIONES

1. *Conception of the classical exceptio*

91.
Definition
IN republican and early classical times an *exceptio* was a defence incorporated in the *formula* in the interest of the defendant as an exception to the *condemnatio* (above, s. 30). Suppose the defendant objected to an *actio certae creditae pecuniae* that the creditor had given him a year's time for repaying the money and that this year had not yet elapsed. Then an *exceptio pacti* had to be inserted at the defendant's request and the whole *formula* now ran as follows:

> 'Si paret Numerium Negidium Aulo Agerio sestertium X milia dare oportere
>
> extra quam si inter Aulum Agerium et Numerium Negidium convenit, ne ea pecunia intra annum peteretur,
>
> eius iudex Numerium Negidium Aulo Agerio condemnato', etc.
>
> *Extra quam si* = 'except that' is republican official usage: *Senatus consultum de Bacchanalibus*, l. 29 (186 B.C., Bruns, no. 36; *FIRA* i, no. 30).

The clause *extra . . . peteretur* was in truth an exception to the order to condemn (*condemnatio*) and was therefore very properly called *exceptio*. In Hadrian's Edict, however (above, s. 25), perhaps already in earlier praetorian edicts, these exceptions have a different form. The *condemnatio* is now made conditional on the non-existence of the facts alleged by the defendant. The *exceptio pacti*, for example, now ran as follows:

> 'si inter Aulum Agerium et Numerium Negidium non convenit ne ea pecunia intra annum peteretur.'

Obviously this is no longer an exception to, but rather a negative condition of the *condemnatio*. The term *exceptio* is now no longer a proper designation for that clause, and, what is worse, the exceptions now come near to other clauses containing negative conditions of the condemnation (e.g. *nisi restituetur*, above, s. 67) which were never called *exceptiones* by the classical lawyers. The inevitable consequence of this transformation is therefore that it is no longer possible to give a logical definition of *exceptio*. The formal peculiarity of the clause (*extra quam si*) was the *differentia specifica*; this having disappeared, only an 'historical' definition is possible. The classical *exceptiones*, at least after Hadrian, are particular defences of the defendant covered by a special clause of the *formula*, objections which in earlier times were inserted by *extra quam si* or would have been inserted in that way if the individual *exceptio* had already been known to these times. The most essential point, however, is: the classical (like the pre-classical) *exceptio* is always a special clause of the *formula*. Students should hold fast to this statement; all texts conflicting with it should be relentlessly condemned as post-classical.

Since the classical *exceptio* is a clause of the *formula*, the defendant has to require its insertion during the proceeding *in iure* (above, s. 17). If he forgets to do so it cannot be added later and he can obtain relief only by *in integrum restitutio* (Gai. 4. 125). Like the whole *formula*, the *exceptio* needs the praetor's approval; he may or may not approve it (*dare exceptionem . . . denegare exceptionem*) at his discretion. If the plaintiff refuses to accept the *formula* with *exceptio*, the praetor may threaten him with *denegatio actionis* (above, ss. 17, 24). 92. To be added in iure

An *exceptio* has to be inserted in the *formula* if the objections of the defendant cannot be taken into consideration by the judge without such a clause. 93. When is an exceptio required?

> Suppose that the plaintiff asserts that he has lent a sum of money to the defendant which he now wishes to recover. The defendant objects that he has never received the money or that he has already paid it back. To insert an *exceptio* would be both superfluous and illogical. If the judge comes to the conclusion that the defendant's assertions are true, he has to acquit him *officio iudicis*, since the *formula* says:
>
> 'Si paret Numerium Negidium Aulo Agerio centum dare oportere, eius iudex Numerium Negidium Aulo Agerio condemnato, si non paret absolvito.'
>
> If the defendant did not receive the money or has already paid it back, there is no *dare oportere*. If, however, the defendant pleads a *pactum ne ea pecunia intra annum peteretur*, the judge must not consider this defence without special authorization, for in spite of such a *pactum* (even if the year has not yet elapsed) it remains true that the defendant *centum dare*

oportet iure civili. On the strength of such a *pactum* the judge cannot acquit the defendant *officio iudicis* but only *per exceptionem* or *exceptione opposita* (scil. in *formula*). Modern students usually say that in such cases the defendant can obtain relief only *ope exceptionis*, but this phrase was coined in Bologna and not in Rome and, though harmless, should be avoided.

If you finally raise the question as to which sorts of defences require *exceptiones* and which may be considered by the judge *officio iudicis*, there is one simple answer. In this matter the construction of the *formula* and its interpretation by the judge and the lawyers (above, s. 64) are decisive and nothing else. The judge is bound to the *formula* (above, s. 34) and it depends on its wording (as understood by the lawyers) whether or not he needs an *exceptio* in order to consider an individual defence. Students should be content with this 'formal' answer and not seek for 'substantial' reasons; such attempts have been made and proved entirely futile.

94.
Exceptio
and
denegatio
actionis

As we have stated above (s. 17), the praetor was entitled *denegare actionem* at his discretion. If the defendant pleaded a certain defence which the praetor regarded as well founded and not requiring further evidence, he might dismiss the plaintiff's action by refusing to grant a *iudicium*. But this way of dispatching the matter entailed a serious drawback for the defendant; although it spared him the trouble of a proceeding *apud iudicem*, the praetor's decree had not the force of *res iudicata* and the plaintiff might therefore try his luck with another praetor. For that reason the praetor (at least according to Hadrian's Edict, above, s. 25) abstained in such cases from *denegatio actionis*, confining himself as a rule to granting an *exceptio*.

Take the following example. A *Senatusconsultum Macedonianum* (under Vespasian, below, s. 880) prohibited the giving of a loan to a son *in potestate patris*. The text of the decree expressly ordered *denegatio actionis* in case of contravention. Nevertheless the praetor (according to Hadrian's Edict) was as a rule content with inserting an *exceptio* (of course, he did so *officio praetoris* and not only at the defendant's request). The *formula* ran in such a case as follows:

'Si paret Numerium Negidium (scil. filium) Aulo Agerio sestertium
    decem milia dare oportere,
si in ea re nihil contra senatus consultum Macedonianum factum est,
iudex Numerium Negidium Aulo Agerio decem milia condemnato', etc.

The classical *exceptio* being a clause of the *formula* was confined to the ordinary procedure. In the *extraordinaria cognitio* there is no *formula* and therefore no *exceptio*. To be sure the instructions given to a *iudex pedaneus* (above, ss. 20, 31) imitated in a way the *formula* and might have imitated exceptions too. But the predilection of classical lawyers for terminological neatness would not allow them to call defences based on such instructions *exceptiones*; instead of that term they used *praescriptio* (objection). 95. No *exceptio* in *extraordinaria cognitio*; *praescriptio*

The classical *exceptio* could not survive the death of the formulary procedure. Nevertheless, the term *exceptio* was retained in post-classical times, but it was now used as being synonymous with *praescriptio* and so comprehended all sorts of objections to the plaintiff's claim. While Gaius' section on the classical *exceptio* (4. 115 ff.) was on the whole faithfully preserved by the classicism of the post-classical law-school (above, s. 14), numerous other texts were ruthlessly adapted to the usage of the day by interpolation. 96. Exceptio in post-class. times; interpolations

1. Gaius abstained from giving a definition of *exceptio*; the definitions which we meet in our sources were obviously framed in post-classical times.

2. Wherever we meet in apparently classical texts the term *exceptio* with reference to the *extraordinaria cognitio* and conversely the term *praescriptio* with reference to the formulary procedure we are certain of interpolation.

3. In a *bonae fidei iudicium* the judge was entitled to regard informal *pacta* as well as any *dolus* of the plaintiff, simply on the strength of the clause *ex fide bona* or a similar clause (above, s. 61). An *exceptio pacti* or *doli* was not required and therefore not admitted. No classical lawyer can ever have expressed that rule by such sentences as the following: 'exceptio pacti [or doli] bonae fidei iudiciis inest'; or 'exceptio pacti [or doli] in bonae fidei iudiciis officio iudicis continetur'. Such phrases, though intelligible from the post-classical point of view, would have been sheer nonsense to classical lawyers, an *exceptio* not incorporated in the *formula* being for them a contradiction in terms. All such phrases should be regarded as post-classical.

4. A very important corollary of the post-classical

conception of *exceptio* is the following. In classical times the judge had to find for the defendant, if he discovered the *exceptio* to be well founded. This follows inevitably from the construction of the *formula*.

Suppose the plaintiff claims a sum of 100 which he has lent to the defendant. The latter replies: this may be true, but the plaintiff owes me a sum of 60 on the strength of another contract; thus I have only to pay the difference on the ground *dolo facit qui petit quod redditurus est.* The plaintiff denies the defendant's objection. The *formula certae creditae pecuniae* is now framed containing an *exceptio doli* as follows:

'Si paret Numerium Negidium Aulo Agerio centum dare oportere, si in ea re nihil dolo malo Auli Agerii factum sit neque fiat, centum iudex Numerium Negidium Aulo Agerio condemnato', etc.

The judge comes to the conclusion: (1) that the defendant owes the plaintiff 100; (2) that the plaintiff owes the defendant 60. Judgment? The *exceptio doli* is well founded, for 60 of the sum claimed by the plaintiff must be returned; hence his action must be dismissed. The judge cannot condemn the defendant to pay the difference (40) since the *formula* does not allow that. The classical *exceptio* never has a so-called 'diminishing effect'. In the *extraordinaria cognitio* this formal harshness did not exist; here the judge was entitled to condemn the plaintiff to pay the difference. But wherever we meet the 'diminishing effect' of *exceptio* in connexion with the formulary procedure, we have to regard the passage in question as interpolated.

5. Sometimes the *exceptio* mentioned in classical texts was eliminated, and with good reason from the post-classical point of view.

97. **History of the post-classical development** Thus there is considerable confusion in available sources dealing with *exceptio* and it is small wonder that uncritical inquiries during the nineteenth century and the beginning of the present century have not achieved satisfying results. The interesting history of the post-classical *exceptio* and the hardly less interesting history of its development from the days of the Glossators down to modern times are still unwritten.

SOURCES

s. 91. Read *D.* (43. 12) 1. 16, *Labeo* (times of Augustus), the only passage with *extra quam si* in our law-books; cf. Cicero, *De invent.* 1. 33. 56. Gai. 4. 119.

s. 94. Read *D.* (14. 6) 1 pr.; (14. 6) 7. 4, 6, 7 to *dederit.*

s. 96. *Exceptio vel praescriptio*: see C. Iust. 8. 35 rubr.

s. 96. 1. Read *D.* (44. 1) 2 pr. and 22 pr. (both spurious).

s. 96. 2. Read *D.* (31) 34. 2: [*ipso iure*]; [*sed nec . . . fecisse*]. *Fideicommissum,* therefore *extraord. cognitio* (above, s. 20) therefore no *exceptio.*
s. 96. 4. Read *D.* (44. 1) 22 pr. [*modo*]; [*modo minuit damnationem*].

BIBLIOGRAPHY

s. 91. For the literature till 1906 see Windscheid–Kipp, *Lehrbuch des Pandektenrechts,* i (1906), § 47; particularly important P. Krüger, *Prozessualische Konsumption und Rechtskraft des Erkenntnisses* (1864), § 5, and *Z f. RG* vii (1868), 219 ff. and Kipp's remarks in Windscheid–Kipp, l.c., pp. 205 ff. For Wlassak's numerous writings see Wenger, *CP* 155 with references; *PW* vi. 1553 ff. See further Seckel's important art. 'exceptio' in Heumann–Seckel, *Handlexikon* and *Generalregister* for Z i–l (1930), v. 'exceptio'.

s. 92. Guarneri-Citati, 'Exceptio omissa initio—in integrum restitutio —appellatio', *St. Perozzi* (1925), 245 ff.

s. 93. P. Krüger and Kipp, loc. cit.

s. 94. R. Schott, *Das Gewähren des Rechtsschutzes im röm. Civilprozess* (1903); R. Mewald, *Denegare actionem in röm. Formularprozess* (Diss. Erlangen, 1912); Wlassak, Z xxxiii (1912), 136 ff., 147 ff.; Lévy–Bruhl, *La denegatio actionis sous la procédure formulaire* (1924) and *T* v (1924), 383 ff.; Wlassak, *Die klassische Prozessformel,* i (*SB Wien,* ccii. 3, 1924), 138 N. 28; Lenel, *Edict.* §§ 278, 279.

s. 95. For materials see Schlossmann, *Praescriptiones und praescripta verba* (1907), 32; J. Partsch, *Longi temporis praescriptio* (1906), 70 ff. and Z xxviii (1907), 444. The materials need a critical examination.

s. 96. 2. For materials see Partsch and Schlossmann, loc. cit.

s. 96. 3. Biondi, *Iudicia bonae fidei,* i (1920, Estratto d. *Annali Palermo,* vii), 3 ff.; Beseler, Z xlv (1925), 191.

s. 96. 4. Pernice, *Labeo,* ii. 1 (1895), 261 ff.; Arangio-Ruiz, *L'exceptio in diminuzione della condanna* (1930); Solazzi, 'Sull' exceptio in diminuzione della condanna', *Bull.* N.S. i (1934), 268 ff.; Biondi, *La compensazione nel diritto romano* (1927, Estratto d. *Annali Palermo,* xii), 43 f., 141 f. with references.

s. 97. Ernst Heymann, *Das Vorschützen der Verjährung. Zugleich ein Beitrag zur Lehre von Exceptio und Einrede* (1895).*

2. *Classification of exceptions*

After having dealt in the preceding chapter (ss. 45 ff.) with various groups of actions we now wish to point out the extent to which there were analogous groups of exceptions. *Exceptiones civiles* and *honorariae* (cf. above, s. 45). This distinction is never mentioned in our sources. As a rule exceptions are *exceptiones honorariae*; the only *exceptio civilis* known to us is apparently the *exceptio dominii* in the

98. Exc. civiles and honorariae

formula Publiciana (below, s. 653). The exceptio mentioned by Labeo *D.* (43. 12) 1. 16 is also an *exceptio civilis*, but it is an exception directed against an *interdictum* (see below, ss. 106 ff.), not against an action. To be sure some exceptions were propounded in the Edict by order of a *lex* or *senatusconsultum* [*exceptio legis Cinciae* (below, s. 973), *legis Laetoriae* (below, s. 328), *senatusconsulti Macedoniani* (s. 94), *Vellaeani* (below, s. 975)], but these statutes did not create *ius civile* and the exceptions ordered by them should therefore be regarded as *exceptiones honorariae* (above, s. 46).

99. Exc. in ius and in factum conceptae   *Exceptiones in ius* and *in factum conceptae* (cf. above, s. 47). According to what has just been said exceptions are as a rule *in factum conceptae*; the *exceptio dominii* in the *formula Publiciana* is, of course, in *ius* (scil. *civile*) *concepta*.

100. Exc. utiles   *Exceptiones utiles* (cf. above, s. 52). An *exceptio utilis* is an exception framed upon the model of an existing exception. The latter had no fixed name: *exceptio directa* never occurs in our sources, *exceptio vulgaris* only once *D.* (47. 23) 3. In some passages *exceptio in factum* is used as a substitute for *exceptio utilis*, but they all seem to be spurious.

101. Exc. in rem and in personam   *Exceptiones in rem* and *in personam* (cf. above, s. 56). This distinction was entirely unknown to classical lawyers. It occurs only in two passages, both taken from the 76th book of Ulpian's *Ad edictum*. The *exceptio metus* is here called *exceptio in rem* since the name of the plaintiff is not mentioned in it: 'si in ea re nihil metus causa factum sit', whereas the *exceptio doli* is called *exceptio in personam*, since it contains the plaintiff's name: 'si in ea re nihil dolo malo Auli Agerii factum sit neque fiat.' Both passages are obviously spurious. A post-classical revisor of Ulpian's work has attempted to introduce this terminology, but without success.

102. Exc. rei and personae cohaerentes   *Exceptiones rei* and *personae cohaerentes*. This distinction, too, is post-classical, the two passages in which it occurs being certainly spurious. By *exceptio personae cohaerens* is here understood an exception which is available only to an individual person, not, for example, to his surety. The *exceptio competentiae* is an example (below, ss. 793, 794).

Exceptiones perpetuae and *temporariae* (cf. above, s. 82). 103. Exc.
There is no limitation of exceptions. Nevertheless an *excep-* perpetuae
tio is sometimes available only for a time. Suppose the credi- porariae
tor has promised by an informal *pactum* not to demand the
repayment of a loan for one year. If he demands the money
earlier, the borrower has an *exceptio pacti* which after the
lapse of the year is no longer available. This *exceptio pacti*
is an *exceptio temporaria* (or *temporalis*). If, however, the
creditor has promised by *pactum* never to demand the
money, the *exceptio pacti* is an *exceptio perpetua*. It should,
however, be observed that it does not make any difference
for the judge whether an *exceptio* inserted in the *formula* is
temporaria or *perpetua*. If he comes to the conclusion that
the *exceptio* is well founded, he has in both cases to dismiss
the plaintiff's action; he cannot condemn the defendant to
pay the money after the lapse of the year, since the classical
exceptio has no diminishing effect (above, s. 96. 4). Gaius—
and apparently he alone among the classical lawyers, for
D. (44. 1) 2. 4 Ulpian is spurious—calls the *exceptio tem-*
poraria an *exceptio dilatoria* and the *exceptio perpetua* an
exceptio peremptoria—infelicitous terms, since the *exceptio*
perpetua destroys (*perimit*) neither obligation nor action.
This terminology was retained in post-classical times and
led to the idea that there is no obligation if the debtor has an
exceptio perpetua. This is, of course, a heresy in the eyes of
classical lawyers and is always post-classical wherever we
meet it in the sources.

An *exceptio popularis* analogous to *actio popularis* (above, 104. Exc.
s. 76) is an absurdity. Nevertheless, we meet it once in our popularis
sources (*Fr. Vat.* 266), certainly an addition made by an
unusually silly interpolator.

Finally, the *replicatio* may be mentioned here as an *exceptio* 105.
of a special kind, viz. an exception to an exception. It con- Replicatio
tains the plaintiff's objection to the *exceptio* as set forth by
the defendant and has to be added to the *exceptio* with the
words *aut si*. We have already given an example above
(s. 30). A further discussion of the *replicatio* is not required.
For this present purpose the defendant who makes use
of an *exceptio* may be regarded as a plaintiff: *reus* (the

defendant) *in excipiendo actor est*; thus the rules which we have stated above for the *exceptio* have to be applied to the *replicatio*.

SOURCES

s. 98. Read Gai. 4. 118.

s. 100. Read *D.* (14. 6) 7. 1; *D.* (7. 9) 4 [*aut . . . in factum*] ⟨*de dolo*⟩; cf. *D.* (44. 4) 4. 15.

s. 101. Read *D.* (44. 4) 2. 1, 2; (44. 4) 4. 33 to *qui agit* (both spurious).

s. 102. *D.* (44. 1) 7. 1; (44. 4) 4. 27.

s. 103. Read Gai. 4. 120–2 to *locum exceptio*; 123. *Fr. Vat.* 266 to *exceptionem*; *D.* (50. 16) 10; (44. 7) 42. 1; (50. 17) 112.

s. 105. Read Gai. 4. 126 with De Zulueta's footnote in his edition of Gaius. *D.* (44. 1) 1; (22. 3) 19 pr.

BIBLIOGRAPHY

s. 98 ff. Wenger, *PW* vi. 1560 ff.; *CP* 156 ff.

s. 98. P. Krüger, *Prozessualische Konsumption* (1864), §.5 and *Z f. RG* vii (1868), 220; Windscheid–Kipp, *Lehrb. d. Pandektenrechts* i (1906), § 47, p. 205; Beseler, Z xliv (1924), 362.

s. 100. For materials see *Voc.* ii. 661. 8 ff.; ii. 787. 4 ff., 15 ff.

s. 101. Schulz, Z xliii (1922), 427; Beseler, *Beitr.* iii (1913), 58; iv (1920), 86; Z lvii (1937), 34 and 37.

s. 102. G. Rotondi, *Scritti*, ii. 341 f.; Beseler, Z xlv (1925), 456; *St. Bonfante*, ii (1930), 60 f.

s. 103. Th. Kipp, 'Über dilatorische und peremptorische Exzeptionen', Z xlii (1921), 328 ff.; Riccobono, Z xliii (1922), 293; Beseler, *Juristische Miniaturen* (1929), 124; *St. Bonfante*, ii (1930), 59; *Beitr.* v (1931), 52; Z liii (1933)), 20; lvii (1937), 46.*

s. 104. Beseler, Z lvii (1937), 46.

CHAPTER IV
INTERDICTA

1. *Interdicto experiri*

BESIDES the procedure *per formulam* and the *extraor-dinaria cognitio* there is, for one group of claims, a third procedure in classical law, the procedure *per interdictum*. Though stamped with archaic features it played an important part throughout the whole classical period. Its long history is only partly discernible from available sources and even the classical law, to which we here confine ourselves, is not known to us in all details since our main source, Gaius' description in 4. 139 ff., is silent upon important points and moreover not fully preserved to us. Leaving aside all intricate details we may describe the classical procedure as follows.

After having summoned the defendant before the magistrate (the praetor or the provincial governor) the plaintiff pleaded his case, eventually asking the magistrate to issue an individual *interdictum*. Then the defendant pleaded his case making objections and possibly asking the magistrate to insert an *exceptio* in the *formula interdicti*. After a more or less summary examination of the case (*causae cognitio*) the magistrate either refused to issue the interdict (*denegare interdictum*) or agreed to grant it (*reddere interdictum*). In the latter case he pronounced the *formula interdicti*, just as he pronounced a *formula actionis*. Of course, the *formula interdicti* was taken down on record like the *formula actionis*. The *formula interdicti*, however, did not contain the appointment of a judge like the *formula actionis* but only a command substantially addressed to both parties, although in form it was sometimes addressed to the plaintiff alone, sometimes to the defendant alone, sometimes to both, sometimes 'to all', i.e. *ad quos ea res pertinet*. These forms have been gradually developed by a long series of anonymous praetors and lawyers and for that reason we cannot expect uniformity. In any case such stylistic variants are of small importance. Let us consider a few examples.

1. *Interdictum de glande legenda* (Lenel, *Edict.* § 260). The plaintiff has a piece of land adjoining the defendant's land. On the plaintiff's land near the boundary there is an oak. According to the Twelve Tables (vii. 10) the plaintiff is entitled to enter the defendant's land in order to collect the acorns fallen from his tree. If the defendant prohibits the plaintiff from doing so the latter may demand this interdict, which runs as follows:

'Glandem, quae ex illius agro in tuum cadat, quo minus illi tertio quoque die legere auferre liceat, vim fieri veto.'

'I forbid force to be used by you to prevent the plaintiff from collecting and carrying away acorns *tertio quoque die*' (e.g. Monday, Wednesday, Friday, and so on). This interdict is addressed only to the defendant. In an actual case the words *illius* and *illi* have, of course, to be replaced by the plaintiff's name.

2. *Interdictum de fonte* (Lenel, *Edict.* § 253). This interdict is addressed only to the plaintiff.

3. *Interdictum de loco sacro religioso sancto* (Lenel, *Edict.* § 235). 'In loco sacro religioso sancto facere inve eum immittere quid veto.' This interdict is addressed 'to all'.

4. *Interdictum uti possidetis* (Lenel, *Edict.* § 247).

'Uti nunc eas aedes, quibus de agitur, nec vi nec clam nec precario alter ab altero possidetis, quo minus ita possideatis, vim fieri veto.'

'I forbid force to be used to prevent him of you two who is at present in faultless possession (*nec vi nec clam nec precario*) of the disputed building from possessing it as he at present does.' This interdict is addressed to both parties.

5. *Interdictum de vi armata* (Lenel, *Edict.* § 245. 2.). 'Unde tu illum vi hominibus coactis armatisve deiecisti, aut familia tua deiecit, eo illum quaeque ille tunc ibi habuit restituas.'

'Bring the plaintiff back to the place from which (*unde = a quo*, see Stolz–Schmalz, *Syntax*, § 87, p. 491) you have expelled him by force and restore also the things which the plaintiff had in that place.' This is in the form of an absolute order addressed to the defendant; actually, however, it is only meant to be a hypothetical command since the magistrate has not yet stated that the defendant has indeed expelled the plaintiff.

108. Legal meaning of interdict These examples make it quite clear that the interdict is not a decision of an individual case, nor is it meant to coerce the defendant into satisfying the plaintiff. In classical times it is nothing but a formal preliminary act.

Sometimes (if the plaintiff demands *restituere* or *exhibere*) 109.
the defendant may ask for an arbiter. Then a *formula* is Formula
drafted in which an arbiter is appointed (therefore called arbitraria
formula arbitraria; above, s. 67) who is ordered to condemn
the defendant to pay *quanti ea res est* if he has contravened
the interdict.

If the defendant cannot or will not make use of that 110.
opportunity the first act of the procedure is closed. The Wager of
wrongdoer is now regarded as having committed contempt law
of court. In classical times this is merely a fiction, as Lenel
has rightly pointed out, for the trespasser has to obey at
once before the magistrate (*antequam ex iure exeat*); this,
however, is actually impossible in many cases, for example,
if the restitution of land is required or in the *interdictum de
glande legenda*. Parties now leave the tribunal of the magistrate, but this, too, is in classical times merely a fiction. In
truth they withdraw only to return after a short interval and
to begin the second act of this archaic drama. The plaintiff
now challenges the defendant to a wager of law and each
party has to promise the other to pay a sum of money in case
he should be found out to be wrong. Now two *formulae* are
drafted concerning these promises (*formulae ex stipulatu*),
and the trial is transmitted to the judge appointed in those
formulae. If the plaintiff claims *restituere* or *exhibere* another
iudicium (*iudicium secutorium in quanti ea res est*) is added in
his *formula* so that, should he be victorious, he obtains the
thing or its value and moreover the amount of the wager.
A similar *iudicium secutorium* was added to the plaintiff's
formula in case of an *interdictum prohibitorium* (below,
s. 113 d).

This archaic procedure is neither the ordinary procedure 111.
per formulas nor the simple *extraordinaria cognitio* but a mix- Classical
ture of both. At the outset it is an *extraordinaria cognitio*, but logy
it leads to a procedure *per formulas* since the judge is not a
iudex pedaneus (above, s. 20). The issue of the interdict
belongs to the first part; hence the classical lawyers never
call the interdict *actio* since this term is confined by them
to the ordinary procedure *per formulas* (above, s. 27). To
apply for an interdict is accordingly never called *agere* by

them; *agere interdicto* is the shortened form of *agere inter-dicto reddito*, meaning the *actio arbitraria* and the *actiones ex sponsionibus*. Nor have the classical lawyers ever used *inter-dicere* with reference to the plaintiff, though non-lawyers had no scruple about doing so. The classical jurists know only the terms *interdicto uti* and *experiri*. Finally, the parties to whom an interdict is addressed are never called *actor* and *reus*. It should be observed that in the edictal forms of inter-dicts the fictitious names *Aulus Agerius* and *Numerius Negi-dius* are invariably avoided.

112. Post-classical interdicts In post-classical times the classical procedure *per inter-dictum* was abrogated. Already in classical times it was a strange survival from much earlier days, an archaic and artificial theatre-piece difficult to perform and dangerous for both parties. As Frontinus (under Domitian) puts it (ed. Lachmann, p. 44; ed. Thulin, p. 34): 'Magna enim alea est litem ad interdictum deducere, cuius est executio perplexissima.' It had been retained too long, thanks to the extreme conservatism and passive attitude of the classical lawyers, and its abrogation was indeed overdue. Eventually it was replaced by the *extraordinaria cognitio*, which in post-classical times became the ordinary procedure. The inter-dicts became now simple actions by which the plaintiff might obtain restitution, discovery (*exhibere*), or damages. The name *interdictum* and the special names of the various interdicts were retained. The classicism of the post-classical law-school and—under its influence—of the compilers of the *Digest* went so far as to preserve the forms of the *inter-dicta* as propounded in the Edict.

113. Inter-polations This transformation inevitably led to numerous altera-tions of classical texts. Thus we meet in pseudo-classical texts interdicts called *actiones*, the plaintiff called *actor*, *interdicere* used for *agere interdicto*, to say nothing of more substantial alterations. This practice had already begun in early post-classical times; it should be particularly noted that even our text of Gaius' *Institutes* is not quite free from interpolations of this kind.

SOURCES

s. 109. Read Gai. 4. 162–4.

s. 110. Read Gai. 4. 165.

s. 111. Read Agennius Urbicus, *De controversiis agrorum*, B. 41 (ed. Lachmann, p. 63; ed. Thulin, p. 24): 'Videbimus tamen an interdicere quis possit hoc est ad interdictum provocare de eiusmodi possessione.' Quint. *Declam.* 3. 6. 71. Paul. *Sent.* 4. 7. 6.

s. 112. Read *D.* (43. 1) rubr.; *Inst. Iust.* (4. 15) pr. and 8; *D.* (6. 1) 68 (spurious).

s. 113. Read *D.* (43. 16) 1 pr. with Lenel, *Edict.* 462 ff.; Gai. 4. 155: [*nam . . . possessionem*]; Gai. 4. 157–60 are also heavily interpolated. *D.* (44. 7) 37 pr. (spurious); Paul. *Sent.* (4. 8) 5: the *interdictum Quorum bonorum* is called *praetoria actio*.

BIBLIOGRAPHY

ss. 106 ff. A. Berger, *PW* ix. 1609 ff. with references; A. Biscardi, *La protezione interdittale nel processo romano* (1938); E. Gintowt, 'Über den Charakter der Interdikte und der iudicia ex interdicto', *St. Albertoni*, ii (1937), 233 ff.

s. 107. Berger, l.c. 1687; Biscardi, l.c. 25 ff.

s. 108. Lenel, *Edict.* 448; against him (wrongly) Gintowt, l.c. 254 ff.

s. 109. Berger, l.c. 1698.

s. 110. Berger, l.c. 1693; Lenel, *Edict.* 447 f.; Gintowt, l.c. 254 ff. is wrong.

s. 111. Wlassak, Z xxv (1904), 138 ff.; Berger, l.c. 1611; Biscardi, l.c. 14; Regensburg, *Die in ius vocatio als Einleitung des Interdikten Verfahrens* (Diss. Münster, 1924), 5 ff. Materials for *experiri interdicto, Voc.* ii. 709. 43; for *uti interdicto, Voc.* iii. 853. 11; for *postulare interdictum, D.* (3. 3) 35. 2; Berger, l.c. 1688.

s. 112. Schulz, *History*, 128, 278 ff., 284; Berger, l.c. 1703 ff.*

s. 113. Albertario, *Actio e interdictum* (1911); *Contributi allo studio della procedura civile giustinianea*, I. *Actiones e interdicta* (1912, estratto d. *Riv. It.* lii) = *Studi*, iv (1946), 117 ff.; 'Elementi postgaiani nelle Istituzioni di Gaio', *Studi*, v (1937), 450; Beseler, *Beitr.* iv (1920), 208; Z xlvii (1927), 359; lii (1932), 293; lvii (1937), 25; Riccobono, 'Interdictum-Actio', *Festschrift Paul Koschaker*, ii (1939), 368. Materials for *interdicere = uti interdicto*: Heumann–Seckel, *Handlexikon*, p. 280; *Voc.* iii. 840. 44; cf. Beseler, *Subsiciva* (1929), 8. Materials for *interdicto agere, Voc.* iii. 851. 51; cf. Beseler, *Beitr.* iv (1920), 298.

2. *Classification of interdicts*

We will now describe the classical varieties of interdicts, just as we have discussed above (ss. 45 ff., 91 ff.) the various kinds of actions and exceptions. It should be noted that we are dealing here solely with *interdicta*, i.e. the *formulae*

pronounced by the magistrate, and not with the actions
which were granted in the course of this procedure (*actio
arbitraria*, *actiones ex sponsionibus*; see above, ss. 109,
110); those actions require no further discussion.

113*a*.
Interdicta
honoraria
All *interdicta* are *honoraria*; *interdicta civilia* do not exist.
Even the *interdictum de glande legenda* (above, s. 107)
though founded in the Twelve Tables is not to be regarded
as *interdictum civile*. A statute might order the granting of
an *interdictum*, but that did not render it an *interdictum
civile* (see above, ss. 46, 98). Accordingly all *interdicta* are
in *factum concepta* (above, s. 50).

113*b*. No
interdicta
in rem
The distinction between *actiones in rem* and *in personam*
(above, s. 56) is not transferable to *interdicta*. In one text we
meet the mysterious dictum: 'Interdicta omnia, licet in rem
videantur concepta, vi tamen ipsa personalia sunt' (*D*. 43.
1. 1. 3). This probably means that although in some interdicts the defendant's name is not mentioned, they are nevertheless *in personam*. This text is, of course, spurious.

113*c*.
Interdic-
tum utile
Interdictum utile is the classical term for an interdict
framed after the model of another, the original, interdict
(above, ss. 52, 100). For the latter there is no special name,
the terms *interdictum directum*, *interdictum vulgare* not occurring in classical writings. *Interdictum in factum* is not used
as a substitute for *interdictum utile*.

113*d*. The
classical
trichotomy
Classical is the dichotomy: 'praetor aut iubet aliquid
fieri aut fieri prohibet'; the magistrate either orders or for-
bids something to be done. In the former case he orders
something to be restored or to be produced so that one
might also form a trichotomy: 'aut prohibitoria sunt interdicta aut restitutoria aut exhibitoria'; all interdicts are either
prohibitory or restitutory or exhibitory. The *interdictum
de glande legenda*, for instance, is prohibitory; the *interdictum de vi armata* restitutory (above, s. 107). This distinction is of importance, since it is only after the issue of a
restitutory or exhibitory interdict that the defendant is permitted to demand an arbiter in order to avoid the wager of
law (above, s. 109). Each classical interdict falls into one of
these three classes, but only one, since *interdicta mixta* are
unknown in classical law.

Penal interdicts do not exist since the order of the magis- 113*e*. No trate does not impose a penalty; hence there is no place for interdicta poenalia *noxae datio* (above, s. 73. 3). On the strength of an interdict issued against somebody his heir cannot be challenged to the wager. But the question would very seldom arise since the wager follows almost immediately after the issue of the interdict (above, s. 110). Incidentally it may be observed that the actions granted in the course of this procedure (above, ss. 109, 110) likewise do not bear a penal character; neither the *actio arbitraria* nor the actions *ex sponsionibus* are *actiones poenales*.

Some interdicts are available to *quivis ex populo* (see 113*f*. above, s. 76). Whenever in the *formula* of an interdict popularia nothing is said about the person of the plaintiff the interdict was apparently regarded as *populare*. An example is the *interdictum ne quid in loco sacro fiat* (above, s. 107. 3).

Some interdicts are available only for a year (*interdicta* 113*g*. *temporaria*). The *formula* of the *interdictum de vi non armata*, perpetua— for instance, begins with the clause: 'unde in hoc anno tu temporaria illum vi deiecisti.' As a rule the interdicts are *perpetua*. A principle lying behind this distinction is not discernible; Cassius' rules (above, s. 83) were not transferable to inter- dicts since there were no *interdicta poenalia*.

All classical interdicts are either *simplicia* or *duplicia*. As 113*h*. a rule they are *simplicia*; an example of *interdictum duplex* is simplicia— the *interdictum uti possidetis* which we have given above duplicia (s. 107. 4). We shall discuss the significance of this distinc- tion below (ss. 781, 782).

SOURCES

s. 113*d*. Read Gai. 4. 140, 141.
s. 113*h*. Read Gai. 4. 156–60.

BIBLIOGRAPHY

Berger, *PW* ix. 1613 ff.; Z xxxvi (1915), 176 ff.
s. 113*b*.. Berger, *PW* ix. 1625.
s. 113*c*. Berger, *PW* ix. 1623.
s. 113*d*. Berger, *PW* ix. 1613; Z l.c. 198; Lenel, *Edict.* pp. 455, 480.
s. 113*e*. Biondi, *Studi sulle actiones arbitrariae*, i (1913), 179 ff.; *Actiones noxales* (Estr. d. *Annali Palermo*, x, 1925), 78 ff.; Gintowt, *St.*

Albertoni, ii (1937), 238 ff.; Berger, *PW* ix. 1618 ff.; Z xxxvi (1915), 183 ff.

    s. 113*f*. Berger, *PW* ix. 1621.

    s. 113*g*. Berger, *PW* ix. 1689.

    s. 113*h*. Berger, *PW* ix. 1616; Z xxxvi (1915), 222. On Gai. 4. 157–60 see E. Weiss, Z l (1930), 266; Ed. Fraenkel, Z liv (1934), 313; Beseler, Z lvii (1937), 25.

CHAPTER V

STIPULATIONES HONORARIAE AND IN INTEGRUM RESTITUTIO

1. *Stipulationes honorariae*

STIPULATIONES praetoriae are stipulations which a jurisdictional magistrate (consul, praetor, *aedilis*, provincial governor) is prepared to enforce. Let us take as an example the *cautio* (= *stipulatio*) *usufructuaria*.

114. Definition

> A testator has in his will appointed H to be his heir and given a usufruct by legacy to L. A usufruct is a *ius in re aliena* which entails no obligations between the owner of the thing and the *usufructuarius*. But the praetor may—at the request of the heir—order L to make a promise to H in the following form:
>
> > 'Cuius rei usus fructus testamento Lucii Titii tibi legatus est, ea re boni viri arbitratu usurum fruiturum te et, cum usus fructus ad te pertinere desinet, id quod inde extabit restitutum iri dolumque malum abesse afuturumque esse spondesne?—Spondeo.'
>
> If L refused to make such a promise the praetor threatened him with *denegatio actionis*.

For a considerable number of cases this remedy was expressly provided by the Edicts of the praetors, provincial governors, and *aediles curules*. In some cases the promise had to be made by order of a statute; as a rule it had to be made with sureties (*satisdatio*). All these stipulations fall into one of two groups:

115. Stipulations propounded in the Edicts

1. Some of them are meant to be substitutes for missing actions; an example is the *cautio usufructuaria*.
2. Others only serve to enhance the creditor's security by furnishing him with sureties.

The stipulations of the first group bear archaic features and apparently go back to the times before the *Lex Aebutia*. In later republican times the praetor might have created the missing action and we cannot discern the reason why this was not done. But even throughout the classical period these old-fashioned remedies were preserved thanks to the conservatism of the classical lawyers.

116. Post-   In post-classical times the *stipulationes honorariae* were
classical   subsumed under *actio*. But even the compilers did not dare
termino-
logy to take the last step and to replace them by actions. The
interesting history of the post-classical development is still
unwritten.

SOURCES

s. 114. Read Gai. 4. 88.

s. 116. Read *D*. (44. 7) 37 pr. [*stipulationes . . . continentur*]; *D*. (46. 5)
1 pr.—5; [*Praetoriarum . . . stipulatione*]; [*istarum*].

BIBLIOGRAPHY

ss. 114 ff. E. I. Bekker, *Die Aktionen des römischen Privatrechts*, ii
(1873), 35; Wlassak, *PW* iv. 309; E. Weiss, *PW* iiiA. 2547; H. Krüger,
Z xlv (1925), 46 ff.; v. Woess, Z liii (1933), 372 ff.; Guarino, *SD* viii
(1942), 316 ff.

s. 114. Lenel, *Edict.* § 286.

s. 115. Lenel, *Edict.* pp. 514 ff., 567.

s. 116. Beseler, *Beitr.* iii (1913), 130; on *D*. (46. 8) 20 Beseler, Z lvii
(1937), 28; on *D*. (45. 1) 52 pr. Beseler, Z lvii. 37; on *D*. (7. 1) 13 pr.—2
Beseler, Z lvii. 28 and *Index Interp.*, Lenel, *Edict.* § 171.

2. *In integrum restitutio*

117.   The classical *in integrum restitutio* is the restitution of a
Definition legal *status quo ante* by decree of a magistrate. The magistrate does not order something to be restored but he himself restores the earlier status by his decree. Hence only the
restitution of a legal status can come in question since facts
cannot be undone by decree.

> Let us give an example. A owes B 100 by stipulation. Now A is
> adopted (*adrogatio*, see below, s. 242) by C. According to *ius civile*
> A's obligation is destroyed by *capitis deminutio* (below, s. 123); the
> praetor, however, restores the obligation *iure praetorio* by his decree and
> grants B an *actio utilis* the *formula* of which runs as follows:
>
> 'Si Numerius Negidius capite deminutus non esset, tum si
> Numerium Negidium Aulo Agerio centum dare oporteret, iudex
> Numerium Negidium Aulo Agerio centum condemnato', etc.
>
> This is a *formula ficticia* (above, s. 49).

118.   The praetor had enumerated in a special section of his
Edictal   Edict—Lenel, *Edict.* §§ 39 ff.—certain cases in which he
cases
would be prepared to grant *in integrum restitutio* after a

causae cognitio. In other cases he might grant it at his discretion. The request of a party for *in integrum restitutio* (*postulare in integrum restitutionem*) was of course never called *actio* by classical lawyers, though in post-classical times we sometimes meet this designation. The compilers have sometimes replaced *in integrum restitutio* by *actio.* These and other interpolations cannot be discussed here.

119. Interpolations

SOURCES

s. 117. Read Gai. 4. 38.
s. 118. Read Paul. *Sent.* 1. 7. 1 (post-classical).

BIBLIOGRAPHY

Windscheid–Kipp, *Lehrbuch des Pandektenrechts,* i (1906), § 114, with references; Ed. Carrelli, *Decretum e sententia nella restitutio in integrum* (1938), not available, but see *SD* iii (1937); iv (1938), 5 ff.
s. 117. Lenel, *Edict.* § 42; Beseler, *T* viii (1928), 315 ff.
s. 119. Lenel, *Edict.* § 225; Schulz, Z xliii (1922), 228 ff.

EPILOGUE

120. Epilogue to the first part Looking back at the whole complicated apparatus of legal remedies we can scarcely hesitate to admire it as a great juristic achievement; and to contemplate the classical lawyers working with it will always afford instructive pleasure both to lawyers and historians. It should, however, not be overlooked that this cleverly devised but highly artificial system was already out of date in the second century A.D. The classical lawyers failed to realize that it could not possibly endure and that the *extraordinaria cognitio* was the procedure of the future. When at last, at the beginning of the post-classical period, the formulary procedure was replaced by the *extraordinaria cognitio*, the fine classical books could no longer be used in their original sense. The law-school tried to adapt them to the usage of the day by shortening and interpolating them, but only made things worse by that method, a terrible muddle being the inevitable consequence. The post-classical lawyers unfortunately did not possess the strength of mind to free themselves from the classical system of actions, and to give a clear and complete exposition of the living law. 'The forms of action they had buried but they still ruled them from their graves.'[1]

---

[1] Maitland, *Equity, also the forms of action at common law* (1909), p. 296.

PART II

LAW OF PERSONS AND FAMILY LAW

CHAPTER I

SINGLE PERSONS

1. *Persona, Status, Caput*

THE term *persona* is used by classical lawyers as an 121. equivalent to *homo* and in no other sense.

1. All human beings, including slaves, are styled *personae*. Gaius makes that quite clear by dealing with the law of slavery in his exposition of *ius quod ad personas pertinet* and speaking without scruple of a *persona servilis* (1. 121) and a *persona servi* (2. 187; 3. 189). It is not in conflict with this usage that he denotes slaves as *res corporales*; a slave is both *persona* and *res*. The Roman lawyers never regarded a slave as an animal, nor could they legally do so since they could not deny his capacity for doing legal acts. Ulpian's dictum (*D.* 50. 17. 32): 'Quod attinet ad ius civile servi pro nullis habentur', has been torn from its context by the compilers and was not meant to be a legal maxim (Lenel, *Pal.* ii. 1173).

2. On the other hand, human beings alone are styled *personae*, both the conception and the term 'legal persons' being entirely absent. It suffices to refer to Gaius. In his 'law of persons' he is dealing with 'natural persons' only and you will seek in vain for the law of legal persons. The classical lawyers rightly regarded corporations as 'joint tenants' (*Gesamthand*) and not as persons distinct from their human members (below, s. 145). It is true that already in the classical period geodesists (*agrimensores*) occasionally spoke of a *persona coloniae*, but this usage remained outside legal language.

3. In post-classical times slaves were excluded from the class of *personae* and on the other hand corporations were called *personae vice*. But this new conception of *persona*

remained in the background in antiquity and it was not before the scholasticism of the Middle Ages that the idea of legal persons became current in legal science.

122. Status *Status* is not a technical term of classical legal language. The word is sometimes used by the lawyers, but without a precise meaning. Continental jurisprudence of the sixteenth, seventeenth, and eighteenth centuries has elaborated a comprehensive system of various status, but this system was eventually rightly rejected by Hugo and Savigny. Modern students of Roman law are inclined to retain at least three status: *status libertatis, status civitatis, status familiae,* but this arbitrary trichotomy is entirely unknown to classical lawyers.

123. Caput and capitis deminutio *Caput,* metaphorically used, is a technical term of classical legal literature, but it is simply synonymous with *persona.* This is particularly true in the case of the doctrine of *capitis deminutio.* This term originally meant the diminution of a group of persons by the loss of a member. Where a Roman citizen lost citizenship the Roman people was diminished to that extent, *populus Romanus capite deminutus est.* And where a son *in potestate patris* was adopted *familia capite deminuta est.* Quintus Mucius was probably the first to form the trichotomy.

   capitis deminutio maxima: by the loss of liberty;
   capitis deminutio media: by the loss of citizenship;
   capitis deminutio minima: by changing the family.
This trichotomy was retained in later times, but the term *capitis deminutio* gradually obtained a different meaning. It now referred to the eliminated member and signified 'deterioration of status'. This member was now called *capite deminutus,* i.e. deteriorated with respect to his person (*capite deminutus = persona deminutus, Ablativus respectus* or *limitationis* like *lumine uno luscus* = 'blind of one eye'). One may safely talk of deterioration in the case of *capitis deminutio maxima* and *media,* since here the new status is indeed inferior to the old status. But in cases of *capitis deminutio minima* this is not always true. Suppose that an adopted son is adopted by another. This is regarded as *capitis deminutio,* though obviously the new status does not

differ from the old status. If a father emancipates his son the latter obtains the superior status of a *homo sui iuris*, yet this was regarded as a case of *capitis deminutio minima*. This sounds indeed odd, but the matter becomes at once intelligible if you remember the original meaning of *capitis deminutio*. A father emancipated his son: this is *capitis deminutio*, since *familia capite deminuta est*. A son *in potestate* becomes *sui iuris* by his father's death: this is not *capitis deminutio*, since the family, being dissolved by the father's death, does not lose a member. An adopted son is adopted by another: this is *capitis deminutio*, since the family of the first adoptive father loses a member. The cases of *capitis deminutio* as developed under the earlier usage were left unaltered, though the new terminology was not suitable for all of them.

The legal consequences of *capitis deminutio* will be referred to from time to time in due course.

SOURCES

s. 121. Read Gai. 1. 121; *D*. (46. 1) 22 (interpolated).

s. 123. Read *D*. (26. 1) 1 pr.; Gai. 1. 159–62; *Epit. Ulp*. xi. 10–13; *D*. (4. 5) 11.

BIBLIOGRAPHY

s. 121. Schlossmann, *Persona und πρόσωπον im Recht und im christlichen Dogma* (Universitäts-Programm Kiel, 1906) and Z xxvii (1906), 358; Trendelenburg, *Kantstudien*, xiii (1908), 8 f.; Hirzel, *Die Person, Begriff und Namen derselben im Altertum* (SB. der Bayr. Akad. der Wiss. 1914, Abhandl. 10); Rheinfelder, 'Das Wort Persona', *Beihefte zur Z für roman. Philologie*, Heft lxxvii (1928); Schnorr v. Carolsfeld, *Geschichte der juristischen Person*, i (1933), 52 ff.; Düll, *PW* xix. 1036; Beseler, Z xlv (1925), 188; xlvi (1926), 83; Duff, *Personality in Roman Private Law* (1928), 1 ff.

s. 122. Pernice, *Labeo*, i (1873), 96; Savigny, *System*, ii (1840), 443 ff.; Svennung, *Orosiana* (1922), 127 ff.; Köstermann, *Rhein. Mus.* lxxxvi (1937), 225.

s. 123. Pernice, *Labeo*, i. 97, 172; H. Krüger, *Geschichte der capitis deminutio*, i (1887); Desserteaux, *Études sur la formation historique de la capitis deminutio*, i (1909); ii (1919–26); iii (1928); on this work see H. Krüger, Z xlix (1929), 541; U. Coli, *Saggi critici sulle fonti del diritto romano I. Capitis deminutio* (1922, not available, but see Steinwenter, Z xlix (1929), 661); M. Radin, 'Caput et σῶμα', *Mél. Paul Fournier* (1929), 651; Beseler, *Beitr.* iv (1920), 92; E. Levy, *Die röm.*

Kapitalstrafe (*SB Heidelberg*, 1930–1, 5. Abhandl.), p. 8 with references; Duff, *Personality in Roman Private Law* (1938), 25; Ambrosino, 'Il simbolismo nella capitis deminutio', *SD* vi (1940), 369 ff. (hardly acceptable); Gioffredi, 'Caput', *SD* xi (1945), 301 ff.

2. *Birth and Death*

124. A person in the sense defined above (s. 121) comes to existence at the birth of a living child. The child *en ventre sa mère* (*qui in utero est*, not '*nasciturus*', see *Vov*. iv. 11 ff.) is not yet a person, nor is the existence of a born child antedated to the beginning of the pregnancy. The misleading maxim *nasciturus pro iam nato habetur* is of modern origin. The classical lawyers used similar phrases for scholastic purposes, but never without emphasizing their true meaning. They might safely say that, with respect to certain legal rules, a child *in utero* is regarded as if already born, for such a statement did not imply that a child existed as *persona* before its birth. A father, for example, might appoint a *tutor* by will to a child not yet born, the child being treated in this particular respect as if already born (Gai. 1. 147). Further, the classical lawyers of the first two centuries have framed the following rule: The status of a legitimate child (procreated in a *matrimonium iustum*, see below, ss. 186 ff.) is determined as if it were born at the beginning of the pregnancy: 'statum sumit ex eo tempore, quo mater eius concepit'. Thus, if the mother has lost citizenship during her pregnancy the child's status is not impaired by that. In connexion with status one might say: 'qui in utero est pro iam nato habetur, si ex iusto matrimonio procreatus fuit'. In post-classical times this rule was extended to illegitimate children. Whereas *Epitome Gai.* (1. 4. 9) still gives the classical law, the *Sententiae Pauli* (2. 24. 1–3) have already the post-classical rule which was also incorporated in the *Digest* by interpolating classical texts.

Nasciturus pro iam nato habetur

125. The first cry   It is sometimes not easy to state whether a new-born child was alive for a short time or was still-born. Early Roman law decided the issue rather roughly by requiring as evidence of life that somebody should have heard the child cry. It is remarkable that this archaic rule, which we

frequently meet in Germanic sources, was still defended by the Proculians; the Sabinians disputed it, but the controversy continued till Justinian decided in favour of the Sabinians.

Augustus was the first to introduce a registration of births. By two statutes—*Lex Aelia Sentia* (A.D. 4) and *Lex Papia Poppaea* (A.D. 9)—it was enacted that a legitimate child enjoying Roman citizenship had to be registered within a period of thirty days after its birth. The purpose of the registration was to facilitate proof of the date of birth and of the child's status, although the register only raised a presumption or furnished prima-facie evidence. Parents and child were entitled to obtain a birth certificate which contained the name of the child, the names of the parents, the date of the birth, and a statement that the child was in possession of Roman citizenship. Such a certificate might well have served as a substitute for a passport. The Roman register of births was barred to illegitimate children until the Emperor Marcus opened it to them. In our law-books registration is but rarely mentioned, though it still existed in post-classical times. But since the beginning of this century a considerable number of certificates have been discovered from time to time in Egypt and these have furnished us with a clear picture of this institution. Registration of deaths was unknown to Roman legislation. Local regulations concerning the registration of both births and deaths existed but do not concern us here. *126. Registration of births*

Since the Middle Ages continental law has developed a variety of rather complicated rules governing presumptions in cases where it is doubtful whether an absent person is dead or still alive. Such rules are entirely unknown to classical law. Magistrates and judges were free to regard an absent person as dead or as still living at their discretion; a declaration of death by way of a *praeiudicium* (above, s. 88) was apparently unknown. On the whole Justinian has preserved the classical law. *127. No presumption in case of absence*

In Justinian's *Digest* the following presumption is laid down. Where parents have died together with their children in the same accident (e.g. in the same shipwreck) *filii* *128. Commorientes puberes* are presumed to have died after their parents, *filii impuberes* before them. But the relevant texts are heavily interpolated; apparently the classical lawyers knew of no presumptions concerning *commorientes*.

SOURCES

s. 124. Read Gai. 1. 89–91; *Epit. Gai.* 1. 4. 9; Paul. *Sent.* (2. 24) 1–3. *D.* (1. .5) 7; (50. 16) 231.

s. 125. Read *C. Iust.* (6. 29) 3.

s. 127. Read *D.* (23. 2) 10, spurious, see *Index Interp.*

s. 128. Read *D.* (34. 5) 22, obviously interpolated; *D.* (34. 5) 9. 4, entirely spurious; *D.* (23. 4) 26 pr. [*quia . . . perisse*]; Law of Property Act 1925, s. 184.

BIBLIOGRAPHY

s. 124. Pernice, *Labeo*, i (1873), 196; Albertario, 'Conceptus pro iam nato habetur', *Studi*, i (1933), 3 ff. with references; Archi, *L'epitome Gai* (1937), 133 ff.*

s. 125. Pernice, *Labeo*, i. 204; Grimm, *Deutsche Rechtsaltertümer*, 4th ed. i (1899), 106; Gierke, *Deutsches Privatrecht*, i (1895), 358. For English law see Pollock and Maitland, *History*, ii (1898), 418; Bateson, *Borough Customs*, ii (Seldon Society, xxi, 1906), p. 112 f.

s. 126. Schulz, 'Roman Registers of Births and Birth Certificates', *JRS* xxxii (1942), 79 ff.; xxxiii (1943), 55 ff.; *FIRA* iii (1943), nos. 1–5; Teresa Grassi, *Aegyptus*, iii (1922), 206 ff.; Orsolina Montevecchi, *Aegyptus*, xx (1940), 39; xxviii (1948), 129 ff.

s. 127. E. Levy, 'Verschollenheit und Ehe in antiken Rechten', *Gedächtnisschrift für Emil Seckel* (1927), 145 ff.

s. 128. Ferrini, 'Le presunzioni in diritto romano' (1892), *Opere*, iii (1929), 444 ff.; Beseler, Z xliv (1924), 372; G. Donatuti, *Le praesumptiones iuris in diritto romano* (1930), 20 ff.; 'Le praesumptiones iuris come mezzi di svoglimento del diritto sostanziale romano', *Riv. di dir. priv.* iii (1933), 198; Beseler, *Bull.* xii (1948), 98.

3. *Cives Romani, Latini, Peregrini*

129.
Principle of
personality

Within a system of Roman private law we have to deal with these classes only in so far as questions of private law are raised. It is the domain of classical private law which we have to define here, a law which had not a territorial character but on principle applied only to persons in possession of Roman citizenship. To understand the bearing of this so-called 'principle of personality' one has to remember the construction of the Roman Empire under the Principate.

The Roman Empire is a federal body consisting of the Roman State and its free allies.

The Roman State comprehends geographically the territory under the direct *imperium* of the Roman magistrates; personally it comprehends Roman citizens and those 'foreigners' (*peregrini*) who are subjects of the Roman State. The latter are called *peregrini dediticii* in the broader sense of that term (Gai. 1. 14). To a considerable extent the Roman State allowed them to live in communities which had their own territory, their own law, and their own administration, subject only to permanent control and power of intervention vested in the provincial governors. Peregrine subjects of the Roman State who were not citizens of such a community (*nullius certae civitatis cives*) were called *peregrini dediticii* in the narrower sense of the term (*Epit. Ulp.* 20. 14). The allies of Rome were such peregrine communities as had concluded a permanent alliance with the Roman State (*civitates liberae*). They were exempt from the rule of the provincial governors and had their own territory, their own law, and their own administration granted to them by treaty. Differences of opinion between a *civitas* and the Roman State were adjusted by means of negotiation in the Roman Senate. Though these *civitates* were without any political power, their freedom was as a rule scrupulously observed by the Roman government.

Finally there were peregrines living outside the Roman Empire but occasionally visiting Roman territory.

We may now define the scope of Roman private law in its application to these classes of persons and the significance of the principle of personality.

1. Roman private law applies to Roman citizens wherever they may live within the Roman Empire. They have to observe its rules and if they appear before a Roman court these rules are applied to them. Romans living in an Eastern province might of course draft contracts and wills according to Hellenistic usage, but such documents would be considered by a Roman court according to Roman law, and if parties had contravened cogent Roman rules the court would regard the document as void. If a Roman citizen

130. Construction of the Roman empire

131. Cives Romani

living, for example, in Egypt made a will in Greek any Roman court in Egypt as well as elsewhere would consider it to be void. It should, however, be borne in mind that 'Roman private law' was not quite uniform throughout the Empire but contained rules of a territorial character. The Edicts of the provincial governors in so far as they concerned Roman citizens did not exactly agree with the Edict of the *praetor urbanus*. In Egypt, for example, the formulary procedure did not exist; the close connexion of the formula with private law has been pointed out in the preceding part. Further, some *leges* did not apply to the provinces and there were other differences.

132.
Peregrini
2. In accordance with the principle of personality Roman private law as a rule did not apply to peregrines. If they were citizens of a community with self-government (*civitates liberae* or *quasi liberae*), they had of course their own law-courts, which decided according to peregrine private law. Even Roman citizens who had recently obtained citizenship were sometimes entitled to apply to such peregrine courts. Where peregrines appeared before a Roman magistrate the latter was free to decide the issue at his discretion. Apparently, the private law which he administered was a mixture of both Roman and peregrine law, for what we call to-day 'international private law' did not exist in antiquity. In Rome there was a special magistrate, the *praetor inter peregrinos*, called for short *praetor peregrinus*, who had to decide disputes if one or both of the parties were peregrines. He as well as the *praetor urbanus* issued an Edict containing rules which he would observe during his year of office. But whereas the Edict of the *praetor urbanus* is known to us fairly well, the Edict of the *praetor peregrinus* is entirely lost. We know that some Roman institutions (e.g. *stipulatio*, contract of sale, *actio furti*, and *legis Aquiliae*) were open to peregrines and others (e.g. *sponsio*, *testamentum*) barred to them. The provincial governors proceeded in much the same way as the *praetor peregrinus*, but they applied peregrine law much more liberally, simply because they had a better knowledge of it than the Roman praetor could have. If both parties were

peregrines they applied as a rule peregrine private law. The law to be applied if one party was a peregrine and the other a Roman citizen was apparently still to a considerable extent unsettled in classical times and there were many local differences.

3. Some peregrines enjoyed a privileged status, having the *ius commercii et conubii* or one of them. The *ius commercii* enabled them to use certain Roman contracts barred to other peregrines, particularly the *mancipatio*. On the strength of the *ius conubii* a peregrine might contract a *iustum matrimonium* with a Roman citizen.

133. Ius commercii et conubii

4. Midway between Roman citizens and *peregrini* stand the *Latini*. On the one hand they are not Roman citizens, on the other they are not styled *peregrini* in official usage. The old Italian *Latini* (*prisci Latini*) had long since ceased to exist since they all had become Roman citizens after the Social War. The *Latini* of the classical period fall into two groups.

134. Latini

a. Latini coloniarii. They are the citizens of *coloniae Latinae*, i.e. *coloniae* endowed with Latin law, which still existed outside of Italy. They had self-government and their own Latin law, which of course was very similar to Roman law. Considerable fragments of the statutes of Salpensa and Malacca—two Spanish *coloniae Latinae*—have been preserved to us. Before Roman magistrates these *Latini* had the status of privileged peregrines, being in possession of the *ius commercii* and some of them also of the *ius conubii*.

b. Latini Iuniani. This artificial group was created by the *lex Iunia* (A.D. 19). Slaves released by their masters without due observance of civil law rules became free but not Roman citizens. Their status was similar to that of the *Latini coloniarii*. They enjoyed the *ius commercii* and exceptionally *ius conubii*, but were of course not members of an autonomous community as were the *Latini coloniarii*.

On the whole, leading Roman lawyers showed only a mild interest in all these questions, confining themselves mainly to the study of pure Roman private law. Labeo, it is true, commented on the Edict of the *praetor peregrinus*,

135. Attitude of the Roman lawyers

but later commentaries *ad Edictum* are only concerned with the Edict of the *praetor urbanus*. Gaius—and apparently he alone—wrote a commentary on the *edictum provinciale*, but what this book really contained cannot be clearly discerned from available fragments. None of these lawyers seems to have given *responsa* on peregrine or Latin law. Obviously they were loath to recognize that Rome was no longer a City-State but an Empire, and, stout conservatives that they were, they still preserved the traditional attitude of lawyers of the City of Rome, just as Aristotle in his *Politics* was concerned only with the Greek polis and had no eyes for the empire which his pupil Alexander was building up.

136. Constitutio Antoniniana But the days of the Roman City-State were drawing to an end, and as the whole empire needed concentration and centralization of available forces, so the complicated particularism of private law was doomed. In A.D. 212 the Emperor Antoninus Magnus (Caracalla) bestowed Roman citizenship generally, though not without exceptions, on all non-Roman subjects of the Empire. We possess this important enactment, the so-called *Constitutio Antoniniana*, in a papyrus, but unfortunately the decisive clause of it remains obscure in spite of the searching scrutiny to which it has been subjected. In any case Roman private law now applied without discrimination to the great mass of the population of the Roman Empire. The manner of this drastic innovation and the extent to which it was carried through in practice are another matter. A considerable muddle may have been the immediate effect, since a great many of the former peregrines knew neither Roman private law nor even the language of its sources. Gregorius Thaumaturgus, a contemporary of Ulpian's pupil Modestinus (about the middle of the third century), and himself an advocate, makes the following touching statement: 'The marvellous law of Rome which now applies to all subjects of the empire (N.B.) is difficult to learn, because, for all its excellence, it is in Latin and very difficult to read'. But our treatise on classical private law is not the proper place for writing the history of the *Constitutio Antoniniana*. It is

enough to state that by that constitution Roman citizenship lost almost all its importance for Roman private law. The unification of private law was, at least legally, achieved.

SOURCES

s. 131. Read Gai. 3. 121–2 (local differences).
s. 132. Read Gai. 3. 92, 93; 4. 37.
ss. 133, 134. Read *Epit. Ulp.* 19. 4 and 5 (19. 5 spurious); Gai. 1. 56; *Epit. Ulp.* 5. 4.
s. 136. Read the *constitutio Antoniniana* in *FIRA* i, no. 88.

BIBLIOGRAPHY

Mitteis, *Grundzüge*, p. xvi f.; R. Taubenschlag, *The Law of Greco-Roman Egypt* (1944), ch. i, with references.

s. 130. Schulz, *Principles*, 144; Sherwin-White, *The Roman Citizenship* (1939), particularly 167 ff.; F. de Visscher, *Le Statut juridique des nouveaux citoyens Romains et l'inscription de Rhosos* (Extrait de l'*Antiquité Classique*, xiii (1945), 11 ff.; xiv (1945), 29 ff.), 1946.

s. 131. E. Weiss, *Studien zu den römischen Rechtsquellen* (1914), 66.

s. 132. Kübler, *PW* xix. 639; H. Lewald, 'Conflict de lois dans le monde Grec et Romain', Ἀρχεῖον ἰδιωτικοῦ δικαίου, xiii (1946); Beseler, *Bull.* xii–xiii (1948), 119.

s. 134. Steinwenter, *PW* x, 1260; xii. 910.

s. 136. For literature on the *constitutio Antoniniana* see *FIRA* i, no. 88 and Taubenschlag ,l.c. 5. 28.*

4. *Enslavement and release from slavery*

The law of slavery is so closely connected with a variety of subjects of Roman private law that in this place we can deal only with its two fundamental issues, the modes of enslavement and release from slavery.

Classical Roman law knows only of the following causes of slavery:

137. Classical cases of enslavement

1. Persons captured in war became slaves of the Roman State which might keep them for its own use or sell them.

2. A child borne by a female slave became a slave. To this rule there is only the one exception which we have already mentioned (s. 124): 'qui in utero est pro iam nato habetur, si in iusto matrimonio conceptus fuit': where

a wife became a slave during her pregnancy, the child born to her is free.

3. Condemnation in a criminal procedure sometimes entailed penal slavery (*servus poenae*).

4. According to a *Senatusconsultum Claudianum* (A.D. 52) a free woman who persisted in cohabitation with a slave in spite of a warning (*denuntiatio*) from the master became his slave. This harsh law remained in force even in post-classical times till it was eventually abrogated by Justinian.

138.
Unclassical
cases
Other modes of enslavement were unknown to classical law.

1. There was no rule according to which a patron might claim the re-enslavement of his freedman as a punishment for ingratitude. Quite exceptionally the Emperor might condemn a freedman to re-enslavement in an *extraordinaria cognitio*.

2. A free man who sold himself fraudulently as a slave did not thereby become a slave. He himself was not entitled to *proclamatio ad libertatem* unless he returned the money to the buyer, but this was a matter of procedure and did not imply legal enslavement.

3. Where parents sold their children into slavery they remained free. Children exposed by their parents and picked up by somebody who treated them as slaves did not become slaves; still less did persons stolen by man-hunters and sold as slaves. Roman law is in so far unimpeachable. Nevertheless, innumerable free men and women may actually have lived as slaves (cf. Sueton., *De gramm.* 21) because they could not prove their legal status and the lawyers could only afford them the meagre consolation, *non deficit ius sed probatio*.

139.
Release
without
manumis-
sion
A slave might be released from slavery by an act of State as a reward for his services to the State. Further, in a few cases a slave became automatically free on the strength of imperial constitutions. According to an Edict of Claudius, for instance, a slave became free who had been dismissed by his master on account of old age or illness. But the outstanding mode of release was that effected by an act of the owner of the slave (*manumissio*).

In the republican period there were already three forms
of *manumissio*: *testamento, vindicta, censu*. Manumission by
will is perfectly clear. Any owner of a slave might release
him in a valid *testamentum* using the traditional formulas:
'Stichus servus meus liber esto!' or 'Stichum servum meum
liberum esse iubeo' (Gai. 2. 267). The two other forms of
manumission are doubtful. *Manumissio vindicta* was apparently performed in the following way. The slave and his
master appeared before a Roman magistrate, in particular
the praetor. The magistrate vindicated the slave as being
a Roman citizen, pronouncing a certain form of words and
touching him with a staff, *vindicta* (as a rule by the hand of
his lictor). He did not release the slave from slavery by his
declaration, but asserted that he was already free, being a
Roman citizen. The master too spoke a formula probably
containing his consent or he remained silent. The widely
held opinion that *manumissio vindicta* was a case of *in iure
cessio* (below, s. 610) can no longer be maintained. *Manumissio censu* was a very similar act. Here it was the censor
who, drafting the list of Roman citizens, claimed the slave
to be a Roman citizen and declared that he would register
him in the list. He did not bestow citizenship on him, for
he had no competence to do so and the registration of the
slave in the roll of citizens had legally only a declaratory
effect (Cicero, *pro Archia* 5. 11). Just like the magistrate in
the *manumissio vindicta*, he declared that he regarded the
person who actually was a slave as a Roman citizen and the
master declared his consent. No form of words was pronounced in this act either by the censor or by the master.
Whereas *manumissio testamento* and *vindicta* were still practised throughout the classical period, the *manumissio censu*
became obsolete after Vespasian, since a census was no
longer held in Rome, and the provincial census could
hardly have been a substitute. Nevertheless, Caius treats
manumissio censu as a living institution.

Besides these three forms of manumission there existed
by the end of the republican period an informal quasi-manu-
mission protected by the praetor. By the *lex Iunia* (A.D. 19)
it was raised to a veritable manumission, which was called

140.
Manumis-
sio testa-
mento,
vindicta,
censu

141.
Manumis-
sio inter
amicos

manumissio inter amicos. This term does not mean that the manumission was performed in the presence of friends but rather that it was acted *inter dominum et servum ut inter amicos*, i.e. in an informal manner. The master might of course make his declaration before his friends as witnesses, but he might well choose another method, for example, he might write a letter to the slave.

142.   The legal effect of any manumission valid *iure civili* was
Manumis- in republican times inevitably that the former slave became
sion and
citizenship a Roman citizen. Any slave of a Roman master—regardless of the slave's race—acquired Roman citizenship automatically by manumission, no consent of the State being required. This outstanding example of Roman liberalism seemed remarkable to ancient observers. Philip V of Macedon, Hannibal's ally, in a letter extant in an inscription, refers to it and declares it to be an important source of Rome's strength. With her released slaves, he says, Rome not only increased the number of her citizens, but was even enabled to found numerous colonies. The beginning of the Principate shows in this respect a reaction. According to the *lex Aelia Sentia* (A.D. 4) certain classes of ill-famed slaves though becoming free by manumission did not acquire citizenship but were ranked among the *peregrini dediticii* (above, s. 130). The status of these *peregrini dediticii ex lege Aelia Sentia* was even worse than that of other *peregrini dediticii*, since they had no possibility of acquiring citizenship in any way. The *lex Iunia* (A.D. 19) bestowed on slaves released by *manumissio inter amicos* the status of *Latini*, thus creating the artificial group of *Latini Iuniani* which we have already mentioned above (s. 134). We cannot dwell here on other restrictions to manumission.

SOURCES

s. 137. 4. Read Gai. 1. 160; Paul. *Sent.* 2. 21*a.* 1; *C. Iust.* (7. 24) 1 pr.

s. 138. 1. Read *C. Iust.* (6. 3) 12; [*nisi . . . probentur*].

s. 138. 2. Read *D.* (40. 14) 2 pr.; (40. 13) 1 pr.

s. 138. 3. Read Pliny *ad Traian.* 65, 66.

s. 139. Read Cicero, *pro Balbo* 9. 24 in fine.

s. 140. Read Gai. 1. 17; 2. 267; *Epit. Ulp.* 1. 6–8; Cicero, *Top.* 2. 10; Boethius, ad Cic. *Top.* l.c. Bruns, *Fontes,* ii.

s. 141. Read Gai. 3. 56 to *non essent cives Romani*; *Epit. Ulp.* 1. 10;
Fr. Dosith. 7; *D.* (41. 2) 38 pr.; *C. Iust.* (7. 6) 1. 11.
   s. 142. Philip's letter see in Dittenberger, *Sylloge* (3rd ed.), ii, no. 543;
ILS no. 8763. Read Gai. 1. 13–15.

BIBLIOGRAPHY

W. Westermann, art. 'Sklaverei', *PW* Suppl. vi. 894 ff.; R. H. Barrow,
Slavery in the Roman Empire (1928); M. Bang, 'Die Herkunft der
römischen Sklaven', *Mitteilungen des deutschen archäolog. Instituts*, Röm.
Abteil. xxv (1910), 223 ff.; xxvi (1912), 189 ff.; Buckland, *The Roman
Law of Slavery* (1908), 397 ff.; Duff, *Freedmen in the Early Roman
Empire* (1928); Cosentini, *Studi sui liberti*, i (1948).
   s. 137. Buckland, l.c. 397 ff.; Bang, l.c. xxvi. 189 ff.; Mommsen,
Röm. Strafrecht (1899), 947; Castello, *St. Salazzi* (1948), 232 ff.
   s. 138. 1. De Francisci, 'La revocatio in servitutem del liberto ingrato',
Mélanges Cornil, ii (1926), 297 ff.; M. Kaser, Z lviii (1938), 129 ff.
   s. 138. 3. E. Weiss, *PW* xi. 463 ff.; R. Taubenschlag, Z l (1930), 146;
The Law of Greco-Roman Egypt in the Light of the Papyri (1944), 53 and
55; Bang, l.c. xxvi. 200; Nani, *Epigraphica*, v (1943–4), 45 ff., 67 ff.
   s. 139. Buckland, *Slavery*, 598 ff.
   s. 140. Duff, *Freedmen*, 23 ff.; H. Lévy-Bruhl, 'L'Affranchissement
par la vindicte', *St. Riccobono*, iii (1936), 1 ff. = *Quelques problèmes du
très ancien droit Romain* (1934), 56 ff.; L. Aru, 'Breve nota sulla manumissio vindicta', *Studi Solmi*, ii (1941), 303 ff.; Kaser, Z lxi (1941),
172 ff.; Cosentini, l.c. 9 ff.; Kaser, *Altröm. Jus* (1949), 104; on *manumissio censu* D. Daube, *JRS* xxxvi (1946), 57 ff.; Lemosse, *RH* xxvii
(1949), 161 ff.
   s. 141. Wlassak, Z xxvi (1905), 367 ff.; A. Biscardi, *Manumissio per
mensam e affrancazioni pretorie* (1939). On the date of the *Lex Iunia* see
Kübler, *Geschichte des röm. Rechts* (1925), 243; Balog, *Études Girard*, ii
(1913), 473 ff.; H. Last, *CAH* x. 888; Duff, *Freedmen*, Append. I,
pp. 210 ff.
   s. 142. Schulz, *Principles*, 120 ff.; Duff, l.c. 30 ff., 72 ff., De Visscher,
SD xii (1946), 69 ff.; Cosentini, 'A proposito di un recente ipotese sull'
origine delle forme civili di manomissione', *Ann. Catania*, 1948.

CHAPTER II

CORPORATIONS

1. *Introduction*

143. Scarcity of sources 'IN the whole sphere of Roman law there is hardly a problem so obscure and vexing as that concerning so-called legal persons.' It was with these words that Mommsen, at the beginning of this century, commenced his last paper on Roman corporations, and his verdict is on the whole still valid today. It cannot be otherwise. The materials furnished by our law-books are unusually scanty. The rich stock of inscriptions, important and interesting from the sociological point of view, rarely gives information upon legal questions. The *Lex Iulia de collegiis*, the basis of the classical law of private corporations, has not been preserved to us; we do not even possess a reliable account of its contents. The numerous *senatusconsulta* and imperial constitutions issued to carry through or modify this statute are also lost. In these circumstances important details are inevitably still matters of conjecture and will remain so unless fresh materials are discovered.

144. No independent foundation Classical law knows only one type of so-called legal persons, namely the corporation. The independent foundation well known in continental law is absent in classical law as well as in modern English law. Foundations were created in classical times by instituting a person (as a rule a corporation) a trustee with a quantity of property. Thus we have to deal at this point only with corporations.

145. Classical terminology Classical legal language has no term for what we call today a corporation. The term *corporatio* was entirely unknown, nor was *universitas* a technical term to designate a corporation. The words *collegium* and *corpus* were used to specify certain kinds of corporations. Above all, both the conception and the term 'legal persons' were completely unknown to the classical lawyers. This does them credit, for the idea of a legal person is not only superfluous and useless but leads to many self-induced difficulties and has called into being a confused mass of absurd literature on the supposedly mysterious 'essence' of legal persons.

For the classical lawyers the corporation is simply an organized body of human persons. Classical law knows only two kinds of such bodies.

146. Societas and corporation

1. *Societas* (partnership). This is an organized body of persons with a fixed number of members, each partner having a disposable share of the common property. The number of partners is invariable. Where a partner dies or withdraws the *societas* is inevitably dissolved. The remaining partners might of course continue the society, but then a new contract was required. If a new partner wished to join the society a new contract had also to be made between him and each of the existing members. However, each partner had a disposable share of the common property. He might sell his share, and if he did so the buyer became the owner of the share though not a partner of the *societas*.

2. *Corporation*. In contrast to *societas* this is an organized body of persons with a variable number of members, no member having a fixed and disposable share of the common property. Thus, where a member dies or withdraws the corporation is not dissolved. On the other hand no member has a disposable share of the common property, which nevertheless belongs to the members. It is the members and not a fictitious 'legal person' who are the owners of the property, though not as single persons but rather as 'joint tenants' (*zur gesamten Hand*, with joint hands), and they can make use and dispose of that property only within the framework of the corporation. An organized body of this kind we will call a 'corporation', though this term as aforesaid was unknown to the classical lawyers.

Suppose that two men are carrying a beam of timber which one of them alone would not be able to carry. Both are carrying the whole beam and the share of the burden borne by each of them cannot be fixed. Nevertheless, it is true that the two men 'with joint hands' (*zu gesamter Hand*) are carrying the beam and not a mysterious third person.

Besides *societas* and corporation as described above two further types are conceivable: (1) an organization with variable members each of them having a disposable share of the common property; (2) an organization with invariable members none of them having a disposable share. However, classical law did not make use of these possibilities.

147. The classical lawyers showed only a mild interest in the law of corporations and dealt with it very superficially. This attitude, which seems so strange to modern observers, must not be explained by assuming that corporate life was not sufficiently developed to attract the attention of the lawyers; in fact corporations existed in great number, as inscriptions and papyri show. The true reason for the classical reluctance to deal with the law of corporations is the following. In conformity with republican tradition the classical lawyers confined themselves on principle to the study of private law, and the law of corporations was to a considerable extent a question of public law. As a matter of fact the corporations existing within the sphere of Roman law were of a public character since even those which we call 'private corporations' were created and worked in the public interest. Sports clubs and commercial or industrial corporations hardly existed. They could only be created by permission of the government, which as a rule was refused for political reasons. Even if the government exceptionally gave consent, the number of such corporations was certainly negligible. This was the reason why the classical lawyers discussed the law of corporations only occasionally and in connexion with other subjects. The Edict of the *praetor urbanus* dealt in three places with the actions brought by and against a corporation (Lenel, *Edict.* §§ 31, 33, 34). Ulpian in his big commentary *ad edictum* discussed these rubrics in his ninth and tenth books, but both were concerned with so many other subjects that only a very modest space can have remained for the law of corporations. In the systems of Q. Mucius and Sabinus there was no place for it. It is remarkable that no classical lawyer has ever commented on the *lex Iulia de collegiis*. We know of no monographic work on this important statute. The classical so-called *Digesta*-systems dealt with a traditional series of leges, but the *lex Iulia* was not among them. All this shows clearly that the law of corporations lay at the periphery of the classical sphere of interest; it was the

classical isolation of private law which prevented the lawyers from developing a full theory of the law of corporations. It is for this reason that the law of corporations as given in Justinian's Digest is so exceedingly poor (*D.* 3. 4 and 47. 22).

BIBLIOGRAPHY

s. 143. Savigny, *System des heutigen römischen Rechts*, ii (1840), §§ 85 ff.; Pernice, *Labeo*, i (1873), 254 ff.; Mommsen, *Z.* xxv (1904), 33 ff. = *Schr.* iii. 53 ff.; Mitteis, *RP* i (1908), § 18; Schnorr v. Carolsfeld, *Geschichte der juristischen Person*, i (1933); P. W. Duff, *Personality in Roman Private Law* (1938).

s. 144. Pernice, *Labeo*, i (1873), 254 ff.; iii. 1 (1892), 57 ff., 150 ff.; Mommsen, *Schr.* iii. 63; Mitteis, *RP* i. 414 ff.; Laum, *Stiftungen in der griech. und röm. Antike*, 2 vols. (1914); Beseler, *Z* xlvi (1926), 87 f.; Schnorr, l.c. 14 ff.; Le Bras, 'Les Fondations privées du Haut Empire', *St. Riccobono*, iii (1936), 23 ff.; Bruck, 'The Growth of Foundations in Roman Law and Civilization', *Seminar*, vi (1948), 1 ff. For the literature on the so-called alimentary foundations see *FIRA* iii, no. 116, with references.

s. 145. On *corporatio* see *Novella Severi* ii and *Thes.* iv. 995; on *universitas, corpus, collegium* see Schnorr, l.c. 59 ff.; Albertario, *Studi*, i (1933), 99 ff.*

s. 146. Beseler, *Juristische Miniaturen* (1929), 132–51; *Z* xlv (1925), 188 ff.; xlvi (1926), 83 ff.; Schnorr, l.c. 403; Albertario, l.c.*

s. 147. Schulz, *Principles*, 27 ff.; *History*, 84; on Q. Mucius and Sabinus see Schulz, *History*, 95, 157; on the *Digesta*-system ibid. 226.

2. *Populus Romanus as a corporation*

The Roman people is a corporation. Its variable members are the body of Roman citizens (*cives Romani*) who are the joint owners of the common property (*res publicae*). The term *res publicae* means 'things belonging to the people' (*publicus = poplicus = populicus*), i.e. the *res communes populi Romani*, or *civium Romanorum*, for *communis* is sometimes used as an equivalent to *publicus*. The treasury of this corporation is called *aerarium populi Romani*; for short, *aerarium*.

_{148. Populus Romanus as gesamte Hand}

The Roman people is capable of acquiring land and chattels, of making contracts, of being creditor as well as debtor, of being appointed heir by will and even of being a tutor, but Roman private law does not apply to this sphere of law. The people is the owner of the *ager publicus*

_{149. Public law of property}

but not *dominus ex iure Quiritium*; contracts made by the people are not subject to Roman private law. The people cannot be summoned before the praetor, nor does the people sue its debtors before the praetor. It is the representative of the people who has to decide disputes of this kind, acting as both party and judge.

150.
Attitude of
the classi-
cal lawyers
The classical lawyers did not discuss the law of this corporation, even in so far as it was law of property, since it did not belong to what they called private law (above, s. 147). This isolation of private law had the strange effect that legal institutions well established in the sphere of public law were dogmatically excluded as heresies from private law. Modern critics of classical private law should not forget that the sometimes stubborn and prejudiced orthodoxy of Roman jurisprudence was confined to private law.

BIBLIOGRAPHY

s. 148. Beseler, *Juristische Miniaturen* (1929), 132 ff.; Z xlv (1925), 188. On *publicus* see Alois Walde, *Lat. Etym. Wörterbuch* (1949), v. 'poplicus'; Stolz–Schmalz, *Lat. Grammatik* (5th ed. 1928), 194; Mommsen, *Schr.* iii. 56; Kornemann, *PW* iv. 778 (art. 'communis'); *Thes.* iii. 1977. 51 ff.

s. 149. Pernice, *Labeo*, i (1873), 263 ff.; Mommsen, *Röm. Staatsrecht* i (1887), 169 ff.; ii (1887), 461 ff., 556; *Schr.* iii. 132 ff.; Mitteis, *RP* i (1908), 347 ff.; Duff, *Personality in Roman Private Law* (1938), 51 ff.; Sibylle Bolla, *Die Entwicklung des Fiskus zum Privatrechtssubjekt mit Beiträgen zur Lehre vom Aerarium* (1938, not available but see Schnorr, Z lx, 1940, 260); Ed. Volterra, 'Sulla capacità del "populus romanus" di essere istituto erede', *St. Sassaresi*, xvi (1938); Biondi, *Successione testamentaria* (1943), 122; Sutherland, 'Aerarium and Fiscus during the Early Empire', *AJPh* lxvi (1945), 151 ff.; Luzzatto, *Epigrafia giuridica Greca e Romana* (1942), 45 ff.: Il problema della capacità a succedere del popolo Romano.'

s. 150. Schulz, *Principles*, 27 ff.

3. *Princeps*

151.
Princeps as
a corpora-
tion sole
As a rule there is but one *princeps* at a time. He is the sole owner of certain funds destined for public purposes which after his death do not fall to his heir *iure civili* but to his successor in office. Adopting the English conception of 'corporation sole', we may simply say that the *princeps* is a

corporation sole. It is true that from the time of Marcus there are sometimes two or three *principes* at a time; in such cases the corporation consists of several joint *principes*.

The property of this corporation is called *fiscus Caesaris*, *fiscus Augusti*, or for short *fiscus*. The word *fiscus* originally means 'basket', particularly 'money-basket'; but in republican times it is already used for 'public chest', 'public treasury'. In classical times the technical meaning of *fiscus* is 'chest (treasury) of the emperor', in contrast to *aerarium*, the chest or treasury of the people. As the people is the owner of the *aerarium*, so the *princeps* is the owner of the fiscal property, but he is so as a representative of the corporation and not as individual private person. Augustus, for example, instituted in his will two heirs, Tiberius (two-thirds) and Livia (one-third). Livia cannot possibly have inherited one-third of the fiscal property, which certainly as a whole fell to Tiberius as successor in office. Fiscal property was originally subject to private law; from the time of Claudius, however, it was more and more exempted from it and assimilated to the *aerarium*. Also claims on behalf of and against the *fiscus* became now a matter of special administrative procedure.

152. Fiscus

Besides the *fiscus* the *princeps* had his private property (*patrimonium, res privata*) to which private law applied and which fell to his heir and not to his successor in office. Gradually a third fund was developed which was regarded as the property of the corporation sole but was—in contrast to the *fiscus*—destined to the personal use of the Emperor. It was subject to private law, but fell to his successor in office and not to his heir.

153. Patrimonium principis

The classical lawyers of the first two centuries discussed fiscal law only in close connexion with issues of private law. Monographic works on this subject did not appear before the third century and were of comparatively small volume.

154. Classical literature on fiscal law

In post-classical times the *aerarium populi Romani* was absorbed by the *fiscus*. Accordingly the classical texts have sometimes been altered by interpolating *fiscus* for *aerarium* or *populus*; the text of the *Institutes* of Gaius, however, remained free from interpolations of this kind.

155. Interpolations

SOURCES

s. 152. Read *D*. (43. 8) 2. 4.

s. 153. Read *D*. (31) 56.

s. 155. Read *D*. (40. 4) 50, pr. where *fisco* is interpolated for *populo*, as Papinian's *responsa (Collectio libror.* 3. 293) show.

BIBLIOGRAPHY

s. 151. Beseler, Z xlvi (1926), 84; *Jurist. Miniaturen* (1929), 141 ff. On the English corporation sole see Blackstone, *Commentaries*, Book I, ch. 18; Maitland, 'The Corporation Sole', *LQR* 1900 = *Collected Papers*, iii (1911), 240 ff.; *Selected Essays* (1936), 73 ff.; J. Salmond, *Jurisprudence* (10th ed. 1947), 117, 122; Halsbury's *Laws of England*, viii (1933), 8.

s. 152. Mommsen, *Röm. Staatsrecht*, ii (1887), 998 ff.; Mitteis, *RP* i (1908), 349 ff.; Rostowzew, *PW* vi. 2385 ff.; F. E. Vassalli, 'Concetto e natura del fisco', *Studi Senesi*, xxv (1908) = *Scritti*, ii (1939), 5 ff.; Duff, *Personality in Roman Private Law* (1938), 51 ff.; Sibylle Bolla, *Die Entwicklung des Fiskus zum Privatrechtssubjekt* (1938); H. Last, 'The Fiscus', *JRS* xxxiv (1944), 51 ff., with references; R. Taubenschlag, *The Law of Greco-Roman Egypt* (1944), 43 ff.; Sutherland, 'Aerarium and Fiscus during the Early Empire', *AJPh* lxvi (1945), 151 ff.*

s. 153. Mitteis, *RP* i. 354 ff.; O. Hirschfeld, *Die kaiserlichen Verwaltungsbeamten* (1905), 8 ff.; Beseler, Z xlvii (1927), 372; J. H. Oliver, *AJPh* lxvii (1946), 312.

s. 154. Schulz, *History*, 257.

4. *Municipia civium Romanorum*

156. Sources The Edict of the *praetor urbanus* contained two rubrics concerning these corporations: *quibus municipum nomine agere liceat* (Lenel, § 31) and *quod adversus municipes agatur* (Lenel, § 33). The classical lawyers commenting on the Edict could not, therefore, avoid a discussion of these corporations but did not of course give a full exposition of the law concerning them. They confined themselves to private law and particularly to the law of actions. The texts which have been preserved to us are poor and have suffered various interpolations, so that important legal points remain unsettled.

157. Legal nature Like the *populus Romanus* a *municipium* is an organized body of persons with variable members none of them having a disposable share of the common property (*res communes*, *res publicae*). The property belongs to the *municipes* and not to a legal person distinct from the *municipes*, but these own the property as persons joined together and united by the organization (*zu gesamter Hand*) and not as single and private persons. The terminology of the sources is perfectly clear in this respect. The Edict speaks of actions *municipum* (not *municipii*) *nomine* and *adversus municipes* (not *municipium*), and the lawyers speak, for example, of a *servus municipum*. In a statement like the following: 'Si quid universitati debetur singulis non debetur, nec quod debet universitas singuli debent', '*universitas*' means '*universitas civium*', and '*singuli*' means the '*municipes* as single and private persons'. The idea of a legal person is entirely absent, and if sometimes the *municipium* is called the owner of the *res communes*, this is only a stylistic variant.

The law which applies to the *municipia* is partly public, partly private law. The whole organization, *comitia*, *curia*, and magistrates, is ruled by public law. Since the competence of the magistrates is regulated by public law, they are capable of acquiring property for the *municipes* and the rigid principle of private law: 'per liberam personam adquiri nobis non potest' does not apply to them. In this respect the municipal magistrates have the same legal position as the *magistratus populi Romani*. Our sources are silent upon this rule; nevertheless, it must have existed. It has been suggested that all acquisitive acts had to be performed by the slaves of the *municipium*, but this is hardly plausible and confronts us with the question as to how a *municipium* acquired its first slave (see also below, s. 163). _{158. Mixture of public and private}

A *municipium* could not be instituted as *heres*. According to classical private law an *incerta persona* could not be instituted (below, ss. 450 ff.) and an institution like the following: 'Quicumque ad funus meum venerint heredes mihi sunto', would be void. Since the classical lawyers did not regard the *municipium* as a legal person, the institution of a *municipium* as heir meant the institution of a variable number of *municipes* and therefore of *incertae personae*. The *populus Romanus* could be instituted (above, s. 149), but the Roman people was not subject to private law. To the _{159. Heredis institutio}

municipia, however, private law was applied in this connexion, apparently for political reasons. There were exceptions even in classical times. By a *senatusconsultum* of unknown date freedmen of a *municipium* were allowed to institute that *municipium* and particular *municipia* may have obtained a privilege; but before the post-classical period *municipia* were not generally regarded as capable of being instituted heir.

160.
Legata
Legacies too could not be given to a *municipium* since legacies could not be given to an *incerta persona* just as an *incerta persona* could not be instituted heir. From the time of Nerva, however, *municipia* could be appointed as legatees.

161. Fidei-commissa
Fideicommissa could from the beginning be left to an *incerta persona* and therefore also to a *municipium*. A *senatusconsultum* under Hadrian prohibited *fideicommissa* in favour of a *persona incerta*, but a *fideicommissum* of *singulae res* given to a *municipium* must nevertheless have been valid, as from Nerva's time a *legatum* was valid. A *fideicommissum hereditatis* in favour of a *municipium* was expressly allowed by a *senatusconsultum Apronianum* (A.D. 117 or 123).

162.
Usufruct
A *usufruct* could not be created in favour of a *municipium*. According to classical law a usufruct inevitably ends at the death of the *usufructuarius* if it does not end earlier. A usufruct belonging to a *municipium* might therefore continue as long as the *municipium* exists and render ownership a *nudum ius Quiritium*. It was for this reason that classical law prohibited a *usufruct* of a *municipium* altogether. Justinian permitted such a usufruct, but limited it to a period of a hundred years.

163. Debts
The *municipes* were capable of being debtors, as is shown by the edictal rubric *quod adversus municipes agatur*. The municipal magistrates must therefore have been competent to bind the *municipium* by their contracts (above, s. 158). The action lay in such cases against the *duoviri*. All further details, notably the execution, remain uncertain. The magistrates did not by their delicts render the *municipes* liable.

SOURCES

s. 157. Read *D*. (3. 4) 7 pr. § 1; *D*. (3. 4) 9; (1. 8) 6. 1; (48. 18) 1. 7.

s. 159. Read *Epit. Ulp*. 22. 4, 5 [*et . . . fiant*].

s. 160. Read *Epit. Ulp*. 24. 18. 28.

s. 161. Read Gai. 2. 287; *D*. (36. 1) 27 to *iubet*; *Epit. Ulp*. 22. 5.

s. 162. Read *D*. (7. 1) 56; (33. 2) 8. Both texts are interpolated; see *Index Interp*. and Beseler, *Beitr*. v. 22; Solazzi, *Bull*. xix–l (1948), 393 ff.

s. 163. Read *D*. (44. 7) 35. 1; (4. 3) 15. 1 (interpolated).

BIBLIOGRAPHY

Pernice, *Labeo*, i (1873), 277 ff.; Mommsen, *Schr*. iii. 53 ff.; Mitteis, *RP* i (1908), 376 ff.; Duff, *Personality in Roman Private Law* (1938), 62 ff.

s. 157. Albertario, *Studi*, i. 99 ff.; Beseler, Z xlv (1925), 188; *Jur. Miniaturen* (1929), 132 ff.

s. 158. Mitteis, l.c. 380 ff. (unsatisfactory).

s. 159. Biondi, *Successione testamentaria* (1943), 124.

s. 162. See below, s. 664.

s. 163. Mitteis, l.c. 380, 383; Lenel, *Edict*. § 33 (both unsatisfactory).

5. *Collegia*

Numerous corporations of the kind which the classical lawyers called *collegia* are known to us, and, taking into account that our knowledge mainly depends on inscriptions and papyri and thus on casual information, we may safely assume that their number was immense. But with the great number of individual *collegia* may be contrasted their lack of variety, for all *collegia* known to us may be assigned to one of the following three classes:

1. Professional corporations, guilds of mechanics, artisans, merchants, ship-owners, etc.
2. Burial corporations which provided their members with a decent funeral.
3. Sacred corporations devoted to special religious worship.

There occur mixtures of these three types, but *collegia* for other purposes, commercial and industrial corporations, social, political, and sports clubs are apparently absent, and if exceptionally *collegia* of this kind existed their number was certainly very small.

Hence we can well understand why in the eyes of the classical lawyers the law concerning *collegia* lay at the periphery of the sphere of private law. The *collegia* known to

164. Classification

165. The public character of the classical collegia

them had a public character, since they were created and worked in the public interest, a sort of appendix to the administration of the State and the *municipia*, and as the lawyers on principle confined themselves to private law they treated the *collegia* in a rather casual way (above, s. 147). To be sure the Edict of the *praetor urbanus* had a rubric concerning actions on behalf of and against *collegia* and the lawyers did of course discuss it, but here too (above, 2. 156) they were content with discussing the law of actions and left aside the organization of the *collegia*. Very little of these discussions has survived, for some passages in the *Digest* in which *collegia* are mentioned originally dealt only with *municipia* and were extended to *collegia* by interpolations of the compilers.

166. Lex Iulia de collegiis and later regulations   The legal basis of the classical law concerning *collegia* was a *lex Iulia* either of Iulius Caesar or of Augustus, but probably of the latter. Unfortunately the important statute has not been preserved to us, we do not even possess a full and reliable account of its content, as it is only once mentioned in an inscription. Regulations implementing the *lex Iulia* (*leges*, *senatusconsulta* and imperial constitutions) did exist, but none of them has survived. Taking, however, into account all available materials, the outlines at least of these statutes may be described as follows:

They were not concerned with corporations but with assemblies and meetings and required a permission by the Senate for all organizations whose statutes provided for assemblies of their members. In some inscriptions in which it is emphasized that the individual *collegium* had obtained the approval of the Senate, this is expressed by stating that the Senate had permitted the *collegium* to hold meetings of the members, for example, 'quibus senatus coire convenire convocari permisit'. This formula, familiar in connexion with the convoking of the *populus* and the *senatus*, means that the *collegium* is permitted to assemble its members. Another inscription gives a *caput ex senatusconsulto* with the heading 'quibus coire convenire collegiumque habere liceat'. Here *collegium habere* is similar to *senatum habere* (to hold a meeting of the Senate) and means to hold a meeting of the members. That *convenire* in this formula means 'to come together', 'to assemble' is made perfectly clear by the following words *nisi semel in mense coeant* which can only mean that an assembly is allowed only once a month. Other inscriptions are content with shorter formulas, for example, 'quibus ex senatus consulto coire permissum est', but the meaning is certainly the same. Thus if the statutes were expressly concerned with assemblies, they might have been applied not alone to corporations but also to *societates* (above, s. 146) with numerous members, which would have been in conformity with the clear purpose of the *lex Iulia*, namely to control the political clubs which in the last century of the republic had played a fateful part. In fact in some passages of our sources the *societas* is mentioned together with the *collegium*. But be that as it may, corporations whose statutes provided for assemblies of their members could not be legally created without the permission of the Senate. Regulations following the *lex Iulia* somewhat relaxed its rigidity; the Senate gave general permission to create *collegia* composed of persons of low estate (*collegia tenuiorum*), particularly burial corporations; moreover, the Senate seems to have delegated its power to the *princeps*.

But apart from this, the rules of the *lex Iulia* were strictly observed throughout the classical period. The exaggerated timidity of the Roman government towards political corporations remained unaltered; the official licence was only reluctantly given and indeed was refused as a matter of course where a *collegium* did not belong to one of the traditional groups (above, s. 166). The policy of the government is clearly revealed by a letter of Pliny to Trajan and by Trajan's answer. The emperor refused to grant a concession to a voluntary fire-brigade in Nicomedia although a serious fire had lately demonstrated the need for such an institution, and although the governor Pliny, a friend of the Emperor, lent his support to the application. The emperor expressly says that the reason for his negative answer is the fear lest the fire-brigade might develop into a sort of political club. If even in such a case the concession was refused because the government suspected political

167. Roman policy concerning collegia

tendencies you may imagine how rarely the concession was granted to *collegia* not belonging to the traditional groups; Gaius was therefore quite right in stating that '*paucis admodum in causis* concessa sunt huiusmodi corpora'. Under such a policy a full development of private corporations was of course impossible, in particular capitalistic corporations of the modern type could not come into existence: their absence is a remarkable feature of Roman economic life.

168. The concession given by the Senate or the *princeps* did
Collegia not imply a grant of legal personality (above, ss. 145, 146),
illicita but a non-licensed *collegium* was a *collegium illicitum* and therefore legally void. There was, however, still another kind of *collegium illicitum*, namely such *collegia* as had obtained the concession but were actually pursuing illicit objects; it was the duty of the Roman magistrates to dissolve such *collegia* and to punish their members.

169. In this connexion a few remarks are required on the legal
Christian character of Christian congregations in the days before
congre-
gations Constantine. The subject has been frequently discussed, but the results of the numerous inquiries are unsatisfactory since the available sources, both Christian and pagan, are entirely silent on the legal basis of the persecutions of the Christians. We know that Ulpian in his *libri de officio proconsulis* had made a careful collection of the *senatusconsulta* and imperial constitutions which concerned the Christians, but neither Justinian's *Digest* nor other sources have preserved this important chapter. It should, however, no longer be doubted that certainly from the time of Domitian and probably from the first persecution under Nero (A.D. 64) Christian congregations had no means of obtaining a legal status. Even where they attempted to organize themselves as *collegia funeraticia*, which required no special licence (above, s. 166), such corporations would have been *collegia illicita* since the Christian cult was prohibited, probably by a *senatus consultum*. Nevertheless, the congregations may actually have lived as legally void *collegia funeraticia*. It was the duty of the Roman magistrates to prohibit them and to punish their members, but there were periods

in which the magistrates overlooked their existence and only where informers were busy or in times of a general persecution was the law rigidly applied. On the whole the number of Christian martyrs down to the middle of the third century was not considerable; Origen states that 'those who died for their faith are few and easy to count'.

Turning now to some details, we have to begin by stating that the law which applies to the *collegia* is only in part private law. In fact the life of the *collegia* remains incomprehensible if we do not realize that to some extent they were ruled by public law (above, s. 158). 170. Public and private law

A *collegium* is founded by an agreement of the first members (*constitutores collegii*) for which formalities are not required (*pactio, lex et conventio*). A statute (*lex collegii*), to be framed by the first members, was of course indispensable where a special concession was required; in other cases it was optional, but *collegia* without a statute can hardly have existed since neither public nor private law contained rules concerning the organization of *collegia*. The statutes preserved to us in inscriptions are not numerous, obviously because the publication on stone was too expensive. Moreover, they are substantially incomplete; either the inscriptions give us only extracts from the full statutes or the statutes confined themselves to the most important points. 171. Foundation

The promoters of the *collegium* were its first members. New members could join the *collegium* according to the rules laid down in the statute; they were admitted by decree of the assembly or by special agents (*curatores, adlectores*). Women were eligible as members of some *collegia*; there even existed special *collegia* for women. Frequently we meet slaves among the members, which in itself shows that we are here outside the sphere of pure private law. Sometimes the number of members was limited by the statute. According to Marcian no one was allowed to be a member of several *collegia* at a time, but the inscriptions show that this rule was not always observed. Membership was sometimes transferable by sale, gift, or legacy. The rights and duties of the members were of course regulated by the statute. Each member had the right to attend the meetings of the 172. Members *collegium*. In a burial corporation the heir of a member was entitled to a sum of money for the funeral expenses. The members were bound to pay a fixed contribution to the *arca communis*. However, all these rights and obligations between a *collegium* and its members were outside the sphere of private law and no action lay to enforce them. Some statutes provided for private law-courts, but we hear nothing of the mode of execution. It is therefore conceivable that the classical lawyers excluded this internal law of the *collegia* entirely from their discussions; it was no part of what they regarded as private law.

173.
'Joint tenants'   The *collegium* was capable of having rights and duties towards non-members. The property of the *collegium* is the common property of the members (*res communes, arca communis*) as of 'joint tenants' united by the statute. Accordingly the debts of the *collegium* are the debts of the members. These rights and duties are created by the legal acts of the director of the *collegium* or any other agent appointed by the statute. The maxim of Roman private law, 'per liberam personam adquiri nobis non potest', does not apply to these acts, 'ad exemplum rei publicae', i.e. according to the model of the *municipia* (above, s. 158). This rule is expressly stated by Gaius, and his statement must be substantially correct since without this rule rights and duties of the *collegium* could not have come into existence. These rights and duties are with some exceptions subject to private law.

174. Manu-mission   Manumission of a slave belonging to a *collegium* was prohibited, certainly for political reasons, since *liberti* of a *collegium* seemed to be too dangerous. This prohibition, apparently introduced by an unknown statute, was abrogated by the Emperor Marcus.

175.
Usufruct   A usufruct could not be created in favour of a *collegium* (above, s. 162), though our sources are silent on this point.

176. Heres   A *collegium* could not be instituted as heir, since it was a *persona incerta* (above, s. 159); where we meet such an institution in inscriptions it was either legally void or valid only on the strength of a privilege.

177.
Legata   *Legata* could be given to a *collegium* according to a *senatusconsultum* passed under Marcus. In earlier times such

legacies were void, since the *collegium* was a *persona incerta* (above, s. 160).

Fideicommissa left to a *collegium* were originally valid, then prohibited by Hadrian (above, s. 161), and finally permitted by the *senatusconsultum* which we have just mentioned. **178. Fidei-commissa**

A *collegium* ceases to exist if the number of its members decreases to less than three, since at that point a decree by a majority is no longer possible; the one-man corporation was unknown to classical law. The *collegium* can be dissolved by decree of the assembly and, where the *collegium* is *illicitum*, by an act of State. **179. Termination**

SOURCES

s. 165. For the edictal rubric see Lenel, *Edict*. § 34. Examples of interpolations: *D*. (2. 4) 10. 4; see Albertario, *Studi*, i. 105, *Index Interp.*, *D.* (48. 18) 1. 7; see Albertario, l.c. i. 102; *Index Interp.*

s. 166. Read Bruns, *Fontes*, 174 = *ILS* 4996 with Berger, *Epigraphica*, ix (1947), 44 ff.; *D*. (3. 4) 1 pr.; Bruns, *Fontes*, 175 (Kaput ex senatus-consulto populi Romani) = *ILS* 7212; *FIRA* iii, 35; *D.* (47. 22) 1 pr.

s. 167. Read Pliny, *ad Trajanum* 33 and 34; 92 and 93; *D*. (3. 4) 1 pr.

s. 169. Read Lactant. *Div. inst.* 5. 11; Pliny, *ad Trajan.* 96 and 97; Origenes, *Contra Cels.* 3. 8.

s. 171. For *leges collegiorum* see Bruns, *Fontes*, 175 ff.; *ILS* 7212 ff.; *FIRA* iii. 32 ff.

s. 173. Read *D*. (3. 4) 1. 1; 7 pr.; 9; Bruns, *Fontes*, 138 (= *ILS* 7313; *FIRA* 93).

s. 177. Read *D*. (34. 5) 20.

s. 179. Read *D*. (50. 16) 85; (3. 4) 7. 2 (itp. see Albertario, *Studi*, i, 109); Bruns, *Fontes*, 177 (= *ILS* 7215*a*, *FIRA* iii. 41).

BIBLIOGRAPHY

s. 164 ff. Mommsen, *De collegiis et sodaliciis Romanorum* (1843); Pernice, *Labeo*, i (1873), 254 ff.; Max Conrat (Cohn), *Zum römischen Vereinsrecht. Abhandlungen aus der Rechtsgeschichte* (1873); O. Gierke, *Das deutsche Genossenschaftsrecht*, iii (1881), 77 ff.; Liebenam, *Zur Geschichte und Organisation des römischen Vereinswesens* (1890); Waltzing, *Étude historique sur les corporations professionnelles chez les Romains*, i (1895), ii (1896), iii (1899), iv. (1900); Kornemann, art. 'collegium', *PW* iv (1900), 779 ff.; Mommsen, 'Zur Lehre von den römischen Korporationen', *Z* xxv (1904), 33 ff. = *Schr*. iii. 53 ff.; Mitteis, *RP* 1 (1908), § 18; San Nicoló, *Aegyptisches Vereinswesen zur Zeit der Ptolemaeer und*

Römer, i (1913), ii (1915); Albertario, 'Corpus e Universitas nella designazione della persona giuridica', *Studi*, i (1933), 97 ff.; Schnorr v. Carolsfeld, *Geschichte der juristischen Person*, i (1933); F. M. de Robertis, *Contributi alla storia delle corporazioni a Roma*, i (1933), ii (1934); G. M. Monti, *Le corporazioni nell' evo antico e nell' alto medio evo. Lineamenti e ricerche* (1934); Gerda Krüger, *Die Rechtsstellung der vorkonstantinischen Kirche* (1935), 1–68; Bandini, *Appunti sulle corporazioni Romane* (1937); F. M. de Robertis, *Il diritto associativo Romano* (1938); P. W. Duff, *Personality in Roman Private Law* (1938), 95 ff.; Taubenschlag, *The Law of Greco-Roman Egypt* (1944), 43.

s. 164. See Waltzing, l.c.; Rostovtzeff, *The Social and Economic History of the Roman Empire* (1926), Index, under vv. 'associations', 'corporations', 'professional corporations'.

s. 165. Mommsen, *De collegiis*, 117: 'Collegium instituitur ad exemplum municipii, qua in re tota eorum natura conclusa est'; Rostovtzeff, l.c. 532, n. 22.

s. 166. Mommsen, *Schr.* iii. 113 ff.; Rotondi, *Leges publicae* (1912), 442; *Acta divi Augusti*, i (1945), 160; De Robertis, *Contributi*, i. 43 ff., ii. 89 ff.; Berger, *Epigraphica*, ix (1947), 44 ff., with references.

s. 167. Rostovtzeff, l.c. 159 f.

s. 168. Schnorr, l.c. 236 ff. (unacceptable); De Robertis, *Contributi*, ii. 122 ff.

s. 169. Waltzing, art. 'collegia', in Cabrol–Leclercq, *Dictionnaire d'archéologie chrét.* iii (1914); Saleilles, 'L'Organisation juridique des premières communautés chrétiennes', *Mélanges Girard*, ii (1912), 469 ff.; M. Roberti, 'Le associazioni funerarie cristiane', *Studi Zanzucchi* (1927), 89 ff.; F. M. de Robertis, *Contributi*, ii. 183 ff.; Gerda Krüger, *Die Rechtsstellung der vorkonstantinischen Kirche* (Kirchenrechtliche Abhandlungen, cxv–cxvi, 1935); G.M. Monti, 'i collegia tenuiorum e la condizione giuridica della proprietà ecclesiastica nei primi tre secoli del cristianesimo', *St. Riccobono*, iii (1936), 71 ff.*

s. 176. Biondi, *Successione testamentaria* (1943), 126.

CHAPTER III

HUSBAND AND WIFE

1. *Introduction*

THE classical law of marriage is an imposing, perhaps the most imposing, achievement of the Roman legal genius. For the first time in the history of civilization there appeared a purely humanistic law of marriage, viz. a law founded on a purely humanistic idea of marriage as being a free and freely dissoluble union of two equal partners for life. Historians, including legal historians, biased by religious and patriarchal ideas, have hitherto failed to realize the true origin and character of the classical law of marriage and still regard it as a sign of decadence and demoralization. 'In the last century of the Roman Republic', declared Jhering in 1880, 'the traditional Roman matrimony in which the wife was *in manu mariti*, grew out of fashion and even where it continued to exist *manus mariti* was dwindling to a mere fiction. Better natures, however, far from seeing progress in this evolution rightly regarded it as a sign of ever-spreading demoralization.' As a representative of those 'better natures' he cited old Cato Censorius, with whom a patriarchal husband like Jhering naturally sympathized. Jhering's evaluation is dominant still today. Actually the classical law was not created by libertines or licentious persons but rather by the best stock which Rome ever possessed, and it was accordingly not a sign of pervasive decadence but of the strength of the Roman humanistic movement. The Greeks discovered the idea of *humanitas*, but they failed to carry it through in law, and particularly in the law of marriage; it was, however, adopted by the Romans and in their hands soon took practical effect. At first confined to a small group of noble and highly educated men surrounding the younger Scipio, the humanistic movement spread ever more widely and soon led to legal reforms. Not in all parts of Roman law was the movement equally successful, but the law of marriage was

180. Humanistic character of the classical law of marriage

indeed radically humanized in a surprisingly short time. Already the Twelve Tables knew a so-called 'free marriage' as well as the patriarchal marriage in which the wife stood *in manu mariti*. To be sure the former was designed by the authors of the Code as an anomalous and provisional institution and in fact played only a modest part down to the middle of the second century B.C.; then the humanistic movement thrust it into the foreground. Leading Roman society refused to conclude marriages with *manus*; it preferred the free marriage, and together with open-minded and creative lawyers, praetors, and judges developed a new and humanistic law of marriage without any aid from the legislature. The old patriarchal marriage continued to exist and was, therefore, still discussed by the classical lawyers, but it no longer played a significant part in social life.

181. Fate of the classical law of marriage   This fine achievement of republican jurisprudence was preserved throughout antiquity, though not without certain modifications which will be mentioned in due course. With Augustus there began a reaction, but its pace was comparatively slow and even in Justinian's *Corpus Iuris* the principles of the humanistic law of marriage were maintained. The patriarchal law did not revive, and the attempt of the Church to introduce a specifically Christian law remained unsuccessful. However, in the course of the Middle Ages the Roman law of marriage was almost completely abandoned in western Europe. On the basis of well-known passages of the New Testament the Church developed an anti-humanistic law of divorce which entailed artificial rules on impediments to marriage. On the other hand, the patriarchal marriage to which the Teutonic peoples in western Europe were accustomed was not to be easily relinquished. Thus the revival of the *Corpus Iuris* down from the twelfth century could not possibly entail a revival of the Roman law of marriage. The Roman law of divorce, in fact the keystone of the Roman legal building, was abrogated by canon law and (after the Reformation) by protestant municipal law. The Roman law of matrimonial property became subsidiary law in many parts of the Con-

tinent, but the patriarchal law was tenaciously maintained by municipal law so that the Roman law more or less remained a law of text-books. The humanistic movement of the eighteenth century sometimes stimulated continental legislators to follow the Roman model. The *Code Civil*, art. 233, permitted a divorce by consent; the Prussian *Allgemeine Landrecht*, ii. 1. 716–18, recognized a divorce by consent and even divorce on account of unilateral disinclination. Unfortunately this movement lasted only a short time and was too soon followed by the vigorous reaction of romanticism and nationalism. The humanization of the law of marriage was not continued and some of the results achieved were abandoned: art. 233 of the *Code Civil* was abrogated in 1884 and the progressive Prussian law replaced by the reactionary German *Bürgerliche Gesetzbuch* of 1896. Since the last decades of the nineteenth century a new movement tending to humanize the law of marriage is perceptible and has already achieved remarkable results in Scandinavia.

As this rapid survey shows, the Roman law of marriage as a whole has never been in force in western Europe since the Middle Ages. It is, nevertheless, of great importance for the history of civilization as well as for critical jurisprudence. It reminds us that a humanistic law of marriage did exist in antiquity for five hundred years and stimulates us to throw off the fetters both of canon law and of patriarchal philistinism. The classical law of marriage bides its time; it is still a living force.

As far as we can see, the humanistic law of marriage as created in republican times has not led to evil consequences. It must, however, be admitted that the humanistic movement (not the law itself) did sometimes influence actual matrimonial life in an anti-social way. It could not be otherwise. The Roman *humanitas* emphasizing the value and dignity of human personality was inevitably individualistic and thus sometimes came into conflict with the interests of the community.

182. Humanistic movement and Roman population

1. A widespread aversion to matrimony did not exist, either in the last century of the Republic or during the

Principate; occasional morose remarks on matrimonial life do not prove much, since similar remarks might be collected from other peoples and other times. It is, however, true that *humanitas* sometimes hindered the conclusion of a second and further marriage. Emperor Marcus, for example, did not marry again after Faustina's death because he did not wish to give a stepmother to his many children. The republican code of honour prevented a widow from marrying again.

2. It was still more dangerous that the humanistic movement led to birth-control in the form of the 'one or two child families'. Even today any population is endangered by this system; in antiquity—owing to the undeveloped state of medicine and hygiene—its effects were catastrophic. The old noble families died out in the course of the last century B.C. and the new aristocracy soon suffered the same fate. At least one important cause of this collapse, which happened just in the period at which the humanistic movement reached its high tide, was *humanitas*: to use Malthus' terminology, the check was virtue and not vice; the polarity between 'nature' and 'humanitas' became once again manifest.

Read the admirable *Report of the Royal Commission on Population* (1949), in particular the following paragraphs:

'617. Numbers of births have fallen at a much faster rate than deaths. ... This is not due to any change in the proportion of people marrying ... but to a decline in the number of children born per married couple. ... Couples married in the mid-Victorian era produced on the average $5\frac{1}{2}$ to 6 live-born children. ... Among the couples married in 1925–29 the figure may be estimated as 2·2. This reduction of 60 per cent. has been achieved by the substitution of one or two child families for families of five, six, or seven children as the most common sizes of family and by the virtual disappearance of families of more than six children which formerly were very numerous.'

'619. Although it is theoretically possible that there has been some decline in the reproductive capacity of the population of Great Britain since the mid-19th century, there is no positive evidence to this effect. ... Certainly the main cause, and very probably the only cause, of this fall was the spread of deliberate family limitation.'

'96. The explanation lies we think in the profound changes that were taking place in the outlook and ways of living of the people during the 19th century. The main features of these changes are well-known. They include . . . the growth of humanitarianism and the emancipation of women.'

'103. Unrestricted childbearing, which involved hardship and danger to women, became increasingly incompatible with the rising status of women and the development of a more considerate attitude of husbands to wives.'

'100. The number of children tended to be limited also, not merely because the expenditure upon them might handicap parents in maintaining their own standards or achieving their ambitions, but because the fewer the children in the family the more could be spent on each child, and the better start it might have in life.'

'411. Even without statistical evidence of this sort, it would be justifiable from our knowledge of the spread of the small family system to infer that . . . the more educated persons in all classes would have smaller families than the less educated. . . .'

'156. Since there are two parents to every child, since a small fraction of the children born must always be expected to die before they reach marriageable age, and some further fraction must be expected to remain unmarried, there is obviously a strong presumption that an average family of no more than 2·2 children per married couple must be below replacement level.'

'626. The number of 2·2 children per married couple is insufficient for the replacement of the population.'

Everybody who wishes to understand the decline of the Roman population during the last century of the Republic and during the classical period should study the report. It is much more illuminating than anything that has been written by historians of antiquity. The true cause of the decline was not debauchery, not a general aversion to marriage, not a mysterious decline in the reproductive capacity of the Roman population, not race-mixture, and least of all the liberal Roman law of marriage. The main cause was Roman *humanitas*. It led to drastic birthcontrol, i.e. to one- or two-child families which, owing to the state of medicine and hygiene, was glaringly insufficient for the replacement of the population.

Augustus realized the danger and attempted to stop this pernicious development. In two statutes—a *lex Iulia de maritandis ordinibus*, a plebiscite of 18 B.C., and a consular *lex Papia Poppaea* of A.D. 9—he built up a comprehensive system of social rules by which he hoped to prevent a further shrinking of the Roman population. Unfortunately only a few fragments of these statutes have been preserved and even their content is not fully known to us. The Emperor and his lawyers obviously bestowed great pains on this work; nevertheless, it turned out to be entirely ineffectual. By granting petty honours, theatre-tickets, and privileges in the field of the law of guardianship and succession, the Roman population could not possibly be saved. Substantial financial support granted by the State to parents blessed with large families (cf. the above-cited *Report*, paragraphs 419 ff.) might have been effective, but the financial policy of Augustus did not venture on so bold a step. Though the failure of this legislation was evident at the latest by the times of Trajan, it remained in force throughout the whole classical period; in the Christian period it was abrogated under the influence of ascetic tendencies.

SOURCES

s. 180. An important document is the *Laudatio Turiae* (time of Augustus); best edition *FIRA* iii, no. 69, with references. Read *D.* (23. 2) 1 with Schulz, *Principles*, 46 n. 5; Ehrhardt, Z lvii (1937), 357.*

s. 182. Read *SHA*, Marcus, 29. 10. Juvenal, 6. 594. Tacitus, *Ann.* 3. 25, 28 i.f.

BIBLIOGRAPHY

s. 180 ff. On the whole classical law of marriage see Bonfante, *Corso*, i (1925); Corbett, *The Roman Law of Marriage* (1930); Orestano, 'La struttura giuridica del matrimonio Romano dal dir. class. al diritto giustinianeo', *Bull.* xlvii (1940), 154 and xlviii (1941), 88 (excellent work but unfinished).

s. 180. Schulz, *Principles*, 189 ff., 192 ff. For materials see L. Friedländer, *Darstellungen aus der Sittengeschichte Roms*, 9th ed. by Wissowa, i (1919), 265 ff.; W. Kroll, *Die Kultur der Ciceronischen Zeit*, ii (1933), 26 ff. On free marriage Schulz, *Principles*, 192 n. 1; Lévy-Bruhl, *T* xiv (1936), 462.

s. 181. A history of the Roman law of marriage since the beginning of the Middle Ages does not yet exist. See P. Vaccari, *Matrimonio franco e matrimonio romano* (1913); *Nota per la storia del matrimonio romano dall' ultima legislazione imperiale alle compilazioni romano-barbariche* (1936); E. Glasson, *Le Mariage civil et le divorce dans l'antiquité et dans les principales législations modernes*, 3rd ed. 1880. On canon law see A. Esmein, *Le Mariage en droit canonique*, 2nd ed. par Genestal 1929–35; Orestano, ll. cc. *passim*; Willystine Goodsell. *Problems of the Family* (1930).

s. 182. On the *leges Iulia et Papia Poppaea* see *Acta divi Augusti*, i (1945), 166 ff. with references.

2. *Betrothal*

The classical betrothal (*sponsalia*) consists of two pro- 183. Act
mises of marriage, the parties being the intending husband of betrothal
or his *pater familias* on the one side and the intending bride
or (more usually) her *pater familias* on the other. In republican times these promises had to be made by two *sponsiones*,
hence the term *sponsalia*. In classical law, however, *sponsiones* are no longer required, an informal agreement being
sufficient; the term *sponsalia* was nevertheless retained.
Where the future husband and wife were not the parties,
their informal consent had to be added. As a rule witnesses
were called up to attest the engagement and a deed was
drafted, but the law did not require such formalities.

In classical law no action lay for the breach of the betro- 184.
thal. In earlier republican law an action for damages (not for Libera
matrimonia
specific performance) existed, for we know that according esse debent
to the law of the Latin communities (before their incorpora-
tion with the Roman State) there was such an action. Any
constraint, however, seemed to be incompatible with the
humanistic idea of marriage (*libera esse debent matrimonia*),
and this action therefore ceased to exist as early as the time
of Cicero. Accordingly it was not permitted to stipulate
a penalty in the event of marriage not taking place and an
arrha sponsalicia was equally void. Finally, an engagement
could be dissolved by a declaration on either side.

Thus the classical betrothal is mainly of a social and non- 185.
legal character, but legal effects are not entirely absent. Legal
effects
Where a *dos* was given to the intending husband he was
entitled to keep it as long as the betrothal held good.
Neither of the parties might legally conclude a further
engagement before having dissolved the first, contravention of this rule rendering the offender infamous. Where
a son-in-law was exempted by statute from the obligation
to give evidence, a *sponsus* was also exempted.

In post-classical times further legal effects were attached
to betrothal, apparently under the influence of Eastern and
Christian ideas. Penal stipulations, to be sure, were bravely
rejected by post-classical and even by Justinian's law, but

eventually they were admitted by the Emperor Leo in his *Novella* 18. *Arrha sponsalicia* intruded into Roman law in pre-Justinianic times, a result of the influence of oriental customs. Infidelity of the *sponsa* was now regarded as *adulterium*; *Iniuria* committed against a *sponsa* entitled her *sponsus* to an *actio iniuriarum*; the action for recovery of a *dos* given to the *sponsus* was assimilated to the *actio de dote*. Thus *sponsalia* were in later law assimilated to marriage, whereas classical law had kept both strictly apart.

SOURCES

s. 183. Read *D.* (23. 1) 1–3, 4 (with Beseler, Z liv. 33), 7, 9 (cf. *D.* 24. 1. 32. 27), 11, 12 ([*tunc* . . . *eligat*]); 18.

s. 184. Read Gellius, 4. 4 (= Seckel–Kübler, *Iurisprud. anteiust.* 1. 33); *C.* (5. 1) 1; (8. 38) 2; *D.* (45. 1) 134 pr.

s. 185. Read the passage of the Edict, Lenel, *Edict.* § 16, p. 78; *D.* (22. 5) 5; *Schol. Sinait.* § 4; *D.* (42. 5) 17. 1 [*tametsi*]; [*tamen* . . . *contractum est*] with *Index Interp.*

BIBLIOGRAPHY

s. 183 ff. Marquardt–Mau, *Privatleben der Römer* (1886), 39 ff., 261; Friedländer–Wissowa, *Röm. Sittengeschichte*, i (1919), 273 ff., iv (1921), 133; W. Kroll, *Die Kultur der Ciceronischen Zeit*, ii (1933), 30 f., 70.

Bonfante, *Corso*, i (1925), 225; Corbett, *The Roman Law of Marriage* (1930), 1 ff.; ed. Volterra, 'Studio sull' arrha sponsalicia', I (*Riv. It.* N.S. ii, 1927, pp. 581 ff.); II (*Riv. It.* iv, 1929, pp. 3 ff.); III (*Riv. It.* v, 1930, pp. 155 ff.); 'Ricerche intorno agli sponsali', *Bull.* xl (1932), 260 ff.; *Sul consenso della filia familias agli sponsali* (1929); *Diritto romano e diritti orientali* (1937), 123 ff.; P. Aemilius Hermann, 'Die Schliessung der Verlöbnisse im Recht Justinians und der späteren byzantinischen Gesetzgebung', *Analecta Gregoriana*, viii (1935), 79 ff.; Schulz, *Principles* (1936), 200; Massei, *Bull.* xlvii (1940), 148; Gaudemet, 'La Conclusion des fiançailles à Rome à l'époque préclassique', *RIDA* i (1948), 79 ff.

3. *Conclusion of marriage*

186.
Consensus
facit
nuptias

Nuptias non concubitus sed consensus facit. Justinian's compilers read this rule in the post-classical edition of Ulpian's *Ad Sabinum*, and although it can scarcely have been written by Ulpian, it reveals in the form of a maxim (and therefore not with detailed accuracy) the humanistic principle which governs the whole classical law of marriage. In classical law marriage is concluded by an informal agreement. No oral formula or symbolic acts are legally required, no collaboration of a priest or a magistrate, not even an official registration, although Augustus had introduced registration of births (above, s. 126). Formalities of any kind did not seem compatible with the particular dignity of this unique act. Roman *humanitas* wished to emphasize that it is the free will of man and woman which is the constitutive element of this act and did not even shrink from recognizing clandestine marriage. The primitive rule which required sexual intercourse for the consummation of marriage was of course rejected.

The classical law was maintained throughout the post-classical period and even in Justinian's law. Even the Church was content with an informal agreement and did not (down to the *concilium Tridentinum*, 1545–63) require the collaboration of a priest. Very early, however, the Church regarded *copula carnalis* as essential for the consummation of marriage, but this was apparently meant as a mitigation of the harsh Christian law of divorce; in any case it worked in this way.

However, though it is true that *consensus facit nuptias* marriage is not (like *societas*) a consensual contract, since it does not create obligations but a status. Just as ownership cannot be transferred *nudo consensu* but only (leaving here apart *mancipatio* and *in iure cessio*) by *traditio*, even so a 'real act' is required for the consummation of marriage. A *traditio puellae* seemed incompatible with *humanitas*, but the customary *deductio uxoris in domum mariti* was maintained as a requirement of marriage. In the true manner of late-republican and classical jurisprudence this *deductio* was stripped of its festive and symbolic character and an informal *deductio* was regarded as legally sufficient. There was no notion of affording publicity to the marriage. Where, for example, the house of the bride's family was the first marital domicile, a real *deductio* was impossible. Further, if immediately after the wedding the young couple started for a wedding tour, marriage was concluded at once and its

187.
Deductio
in domum
mariti

consummation not delayed until the return to the husband's house. On the other hand, *deductio* was valid if the husband was absent from his house. If you keep in mind the character of *deductio*, you cannot put it on a par with *consensus*, the former obviously not being an indispensable requirement.

Concerning the further conditions of a *matrimonium iustum* we will confine ourselves to the following notes.

188.
Consent of parents

1. The consent of the intending husband and bride is not sufficient where either of them is *in patria potestate*; here the consent of the *pater familias* is required. However, if the *pater familias* of the bride refused to consent without sufficient reason, he might be compelled to consent in a procedure *extra ordinem* on the strength of a clause of the *lex Iulia de maritandis ordinibus* (above, s. 182). No such redress existed where the *pater familias* of the intending husband refused his consent. Here classical law firmly maintained the principle *nemini invito suus heres adgnascitur*, the legitimate children of a son *in potestate* being *sui heredes* of their grandfather. With regard to the law governing the position of children, the humanistic movement, as we shall point out later, had only a modest success, for *patria potestas* appeared to the classical lawyers as a veritable sanctuary of Romanism which they did not dare to violate. It was Justinian who in this case put the son on a par with the daughter.

189.
Monogamy

2. The principle of monogamy was strictly maintained by Roman law of all times. The rumour that Julius Caesar intended to allow polygamy (on account of the declining Roman population) was probably mere slander. The principle was so deep rooted that a severe punishment of a bigamist seemed superfluous; he became infamous according to the praetor's Edict which in classical times was regarded as a sufficient punishment. However, polygamy was forbidden only to Roman citizens and not also to peregrines. Thus polygamy was permitted to Jews according to their law (provided they were not Roman citizens); eventually it was expressly forbidden them by Theodosius I.

190.
Exogamy

3. The rules as to consanguinity and affinity by marriage

as impediments to marriage admit of many variations and Roman law, like other systems, changed repeatedly in this respect. The classical law was on the whole sound, particularly when compared with the exaggerated rules of canon law; for the not very interesting details we may refer to other books.

4. Differences of race and status (by birth or profession) of Roman citizens were in principle no impediment to marriage. Marriages between patricians and plebeians were already permitted by a *lex Canuleia* (445 B.C.). Marriages between free-born and freed persons were apparently not allowed in earlier republican law, but at the end of the Republic this prohibition had disappeared, undoubtedly under the influence of *humanitas*. Even coloured slaves when set free by their Roman master became Roman citizens (above, s. 142) and might conclude a *matrimonium iustum* with any Roman citizen. Augustus here as elsewhere initiates a reaction. It is true his idea to keep Roman population free from peregrine and slavish blood had only small influence on the law of marriage; he prohibited marriage between members of the senatorial class and freed persons, further between free-born citizens and members of disreputable professions. The legal effect of these prohibitions was apparently at first only that marriages concluded in contravention of them were not *matrimonia secundum legem Iuliam et Papiam*, viz. they did not exempt spouses from the disadvantages which celibacy and childlessness entailed but were nevertheless legally valid. It was, however, a terrible blunder of Augustus to prohibit soldiers of the rank and file from marrying. This interdict was not only inhuman but also had a serious effect on the Roman population; as the length of service was very long a particularly vigorous part of the Roman population was debarred from marrying for the best part of its life. Thus the soldiers were inevitably doomed to concubinage. Citizenship was granted to their children as a matter of course after *honesta missio*, but the concubines were as a rule peregrine or freed women; the Emperor seems to have entirely forgotten his racial ideas. The interdict glaringly

191. Different status

reveals Augustus' dilettantism in this field of policy, although, of course, it must not be forgotten that it was quite new to statesmen and legislators of his time. Eventually the interdict was abrogated by Septimius Severus, two hundred years too late.

SOURCES

s. 186. Read *D.* (35. 1) 15 = (50. 17) 30; Conc. Trid. *Decretum de reformatione matrimonii*, c. i.

s. 187. Read *D.* (23. 2) 5 [*non in uxoris*]; (23. 2) 6 ⟨*absens*⟩ [*absentem*].

s. 188. Read *Epit. Ulp.* 5. 2; *D.* (23. 2) 19 (interpolated, see *Index Interp.*).

s. 189. Read Laberius, fr. 63, *Necyomantia*, p. 351 ed. Ribbeck (with Schanz–Hosius, *Gesch. d. röm. Lit.* i, 1928, p. 259); Sueton. *Caes.* 52; Lenel, *Edict.* 78; *C.* (9. 9) 18 pr.; (1. 9) 7. *C.* (5. 5) 2 must be interpolated or shortened.

s. 191. Read Sueton. *Aug.* 40. 3 with Schulz, *Principles*, 120.

BIBLIOGRAPHY

s. 186. E. Levy, *Der Hergang der römischen Ehescheidung* (1925), 70; Orestano, *Bull.* xlvii (1940), 154 ff.; Volterra, *La Conception du mariage d'après les juristes romains* (1940). On Rasi, *Consensus facit nuptias* (1946) see Volterra, *Riv. It.* i (1947), 399 ff.; *RIDA* i (1948), 213 ff.; Taubenschlag, *Law of Greco-Roman Egypt* (1944), 88.*

s. 187. Levy, l.c. 68 ff.; Corbett, *The Roman Law of Marriage* (1930), 93; Ehrhardt, *Symbolae Friburgenses* (1933), 102; *PW* xvii. 1479; Orestano, l.c. in particular 306 ff.: 'La pretesa essenzialità della deductio in domum'; Volterra, 'Quelques observations sur le mariage des filiifamilias', *RIDA* i (1948), 213 ff. On the customary formes of *deductio* see Kunkel, § 175, n. 8, with references.

s. 188. On the *lex Iulia* and *D.* (23. 2) 19 see literature in the *Index Interp.* and Biondi in *Acta divi Augusti*, i (1945), 188; Volterra, *Revue intern.* l.c.

s. 189. Mommsen, *Röm. Strafrecht* (1899), 701; Ed. Volterra, 'Per la storia del reato di bigamia in diritto romano', *Studi Ratti* (1933), 389 ff., 419; Taubenschlag, l.c. 77. On Sueton, *Caes.* 52 see L. Rubinson, *Freedom of Speech in the Rom. Republic* (1940), 14 ff.*

s. 190. Kunkel, *PW* xiv. 2266; Taubenschlag, l.c. 83.

s. 191. Kunkel, *PW* xiv. 2262; Nardi, *SD* vii (1941), 112 ff.; *La reciproca posizione successoria dei coniugi privi di conubium* (1938), 14 ff.; Solazzi, 'Prostitute e donne di teatro nelle legge augustee', *Bull.* xlvi (1939), 49. On the marriage of soldiers see Schulz, *JRS* xxxiii (1943), 61, n. 63, with references; Taubenschlag, l.c. 82.*

4. *Personal effects of marriage*

The immediate effects of classical marriage are very few 192. and the rules concerning the personal relations between *Immediate effects* husband and wife are mainly negative. The husband has no legal power whatever over his wife, he is *not* 'the 'wife's head' (St. Paul, i Cor. xi. 3; Eph. v. 22), and both are regarded as equal partners. The wife retains her family name; the name of Cicero's wife was Terentia, that of his brother's wife Pomponia (she was a sister of Pomponius Atticus). As a rule the wife does not acquire the rank of her husband, an exception being made only for the wife of a senator. The wife shares her husband's domicile. Legal duties as to sexual intercourse do not exist between husband and wife, nor are they bound to respect and maintain each other. Such duties are sometimes mentioned in modern law as their infringement may justify divorce; the liberal classical law of divorce renders them superfluous. The wife is liable for sexual infidelity, but not equally the husband; it was the Church which required fidelity from the husband too. *Iniuria* committed against the wife entitled the husband to an *actio iniuriarum*, apparently whether or not the wife was *in manu*. Thus the classical law concerning personal relations between husband and wife is rather scanty, but it is just this legal reserve which is required by *humanitas*. Legal regulation of these most intimate and delicate relations seems, and indeed is, 'inhuman'.

The indirect effect of marriage is that it provides the 193. basis for establishing *manus mariti*. As already said above *Manus* (s. 180), patriarchal marriages still existed in classical law, *mariti* though actually they occurred but rarely. *Manus*, however, never came into existence automatically by the conclusion of marriage but required a special legal act. Classical law knew only two forms of this act, *confarreatio* and *coemptio*, which in classical times—as must be emphasized in contrast to the predominant doctrine—were two modes of creating *manus mariti* and not two modes of concluding marriage.

1. *Confarreatio* was a sacred act the details of which are 194. Con-*farreatio*

unknown to us. It took its name from the sacred bread or cake (*panis farreus*) which was required for the ceremony. Priests (a *pontifex* and a *flamen*) had to collaborate, oral formulas had to be pronounced, and witnesses had to be called. This ceremony was practised throughout the whole classical period and even in post-classical times as long as pagan Roman priests existed, but only in highly conservative and orthodox circles. For admission to some branches of the priesthood birth from a marriage with *confarreatio* was essential, but even by the end of the Republic there were sometimes not sufficient eligible candidates. The post of the *flamen Dialis* remained vacant for want of candidates from 87 to 12 B.C. and a *senatusconsultum* (in 12 B.C.) was required to declare that a *confarreatio* might be performed *ad sacra tantum*, viz. with the effect that the wife was *in manu* only with regard to sacred but not to civil law. This rule had to be reinforced by a *lex* under Tiberius (A.D. 23), so strong was the aversion of noble ladies to submit themselves to *manus mariti*.

195.
Coemptio
2. *Coemptio* was a *mancipatio* by which a wife was sold (or sold herself) to her husband *nummo uno*. By a special clause of the *nuncupatio* it was expressly said that the wife was sold *matrimonii causa* and not as a slave, and the effect was accordingly that the wife was now *in manu* and not *in mancipio* (below, s. 257). However, *coemptio* too was dying out in the last century of the Republic, the reason being that women, inspired by the humanistic movement, rejected it. In Cicero's *De or.* 1. 56. 237 the orator Antonius declares that judicial orators were as a rule ignorant of the details of the ceremony. In classical times a genuine *coemptio* occurred but only very rarely, and as a living institution there only survived *coemptio fiduciae causa facta* which was not effected *matrimonii causa* (s. 319). It is significant that in the post-classical *Epitome Ulpiani coemptio* to a husband is no longer mentioned.

196. Usus
3. The republican law knew a third mode. Where the marriage had been concluded without *confarreatio* or *coemptio* the rules of *usucapio* were applied and *manus* was acquired by the husband *usu*, viz. by having the wife in his

possession for one year. The wife might interrupt *usucapio* by staying away from her husband's home for three nights (*trinoctium*). This archaic mode was still living law in the time of Cicero, but it was too much in conflict with *humanitas* to survive the end of the Republic. It was apparently Augustus who abolished it; anyhow, it no longer existed in the classical period.

To define the legal position of the wife *in manu* the classical lawyers used the paradoxical and over-subtle formula *loco filiae mariti est*. Neither her social nor her legal position is adequately characterized by this formula. The legal power which the husband has over his wife *in manu* differs widely from that over his children and it is with good reason that the term *potestas* is avoided and his power called *manus*. In historical times the husband never possessed *ius vitae necisque* over his wife or the right to sell her. It is, however, true that where the bride was also *in patria potestate* or *in tutela mulierum* both are absorbed by *manus*. With regard to her capacity to hold property, she is in the position of a child *in potestate* and she is *heres legitima* of her husband like one of his children. 197.
Filiae loco

Where the wife is not *in manu* (and that, as aforesaid, was the rule in classical times) the husband has no legal power whatever over her. The consequence is that if she was *in potestate patris* at the time of marriage, this continues unaltered. If she is not *in potestate patris*, a *tutor* has to be appointed for her; her husband is not her *tutor* by law nor is he as a rule appointed as her *tutor*. 198. Free
wife

SOURCES

s. 192. Read *D.* (50. 1) 32; 38. 3 (domicile); Plautus, *Mercator*, 817 ff.; Gellius, 10. 23. 5; Hieronym., *Epist.* 77. 3; *CSEL* 55. 39 (infidelity); *D.* (47. 10) 1. 3 (*iniuria*); Gai. 3. 221 (*iniuria*).

s. 193. Read Gai. 1. 108–10.

s. 194. Read Gai. 1. 112; *Epit. Ulp.* 9. 1; Gai. 1. 136; Tacitus, *Ann.* 4. 16.

· 195. Read Gai. 1. 113, 114, 123, last sentence.

s. 196. Read Gai. 1. 111.

s. 197. Read Gai. 1. 114. 136.

s. 198. Read Gai. 1. 144.

BIBLIOGRAPHY

s. 192. Kunkel, *PW* xiv. 2283; Schulz, *Principles*, 22. 195; Beseler, *Beitr.* v (1931), 43 on *D.* (47. 10) 1. 3; Esmein, *Le mariage en droit canonique*, ii (1935), 1 ff.

s. 193. Ed. Volterra, *La Conception du mariage d'après les juristes rom.* (1940); 'Ancora sulla manus e sul matrimonio', *St. Solazzi* (1948), 675 ff.; Köstler, Z lv (1947), 65.*

s. 194. Wissowa, *Religion* (1912), 118; Kunkel, *PW* xiv. 2270; Brassloff, *St. Bonfante*, ii (1930), 365; Corbett, *Roman Law of Marriage* (1930), 71; Schulz, *Principles*, 193; Köster, 44.

s. 195. Kunkel, *PW* l.c.; Corbett, l.c. 78; Carrelli, *Coemptio matrimonii causa* (1933), not available; Köstler, 42. On *coemptio fiduciae causa* see W. Erbe, *Die Fiducia* (1940), 165 ff.

s. 196. Corbett, l.c. 85; Schulz, *Principles*, 192; H. J. Wolff, 'Trino-ctium', *T* xvi (1939), 145.

s. 197. Schulz, *Principles*, 193 f.

5. *Law of matrimonial property. Principles*

199. Wife in manu   When the wife was *in manu mariti* she was incapable of having any property of her own (above, s. 197). All property which she possessed before marriage and that which she acquired later was automatically acquired by her husband, who alone was the owner of such property and was entitled to dispose of it at his discretion *inter vivos* as well as *mortis causa*. On the other hand, the wife was *heres legitima* of her husband like any child *in potestate*.

200. Separation of goods   However, in the classical period when *manus* was dying out and free marriage becoming predominant the humanistic aim of putting husband and wife on a par was radically carried through. Free marriage had no immediate effects on property. Wife and husband alike remained the owners of their respective property which they possessed when marrying; property gained by one of them during matrimony was his or her property. Each spouse may freely dispose of his property *inter vivos* and *mortis causa*. The wife in particular needs no marital consent to her legal acts; the husband, on the other hand, is not liable for her debts. In short, it is the system of separation of goods (which is now, since 1882, also the English system) and it is resolutely carried through in Roman free marriage. This system is

somewhat unfavourable to the wife, since she has no share of the property acquired by her husband during matrimony, though this property is very frequently acquired by her help in the form of her domestic work. It is for this reason that modern defenders of women's rights sometimes prefer the system of community of acquests (of income and profit). However, the Roman ideal wife for whom well-born lawyers framed the law had no wish to acquire property in matrimony. Turia's husband declared in his *laudatio*, l. 37:

'Omne tuom patrimonium acceptum a parentibus communi diligentia conservavimus: neque enim erat adquirendi tibi cura.'

Moreover, the keen individualism of the Roman lawyers had no sympathy with matrimonial community of any kind.

The two following rules are corollaries to the classical system.

1. The husband was not legally bound to maintain his wife.
2. The wife was not (like the *uxor in manu*) *heres legitima* of her husband nor was the husband *heres legitimus* of his wife. The praetor granted *bonorum possessio sine tabulis* to each of the spouses, but only in default of *cognati* (below, s. 417).

This was the classical law. We must, however, keep in mind that there was a fixed matrimonial custom in Rome. The lawyers with their strictly legal outlook mentioned it only occasionally, but they presupposed it and wished to give it ample working space, since in this way a regulation might be reached which best suited individual cases. The main principles of this custom are the following: **201. Law and custom**

1. It is Roman custom that both husband and wife like any Roman citizen make a will (each of course separately) and appoint the other spouse as heir (at least *pro parte*) or legatee. The want of a sufficient law of intestacy was thus hardly felt. **202. Succession by will**

2. It is customary for spouses in a *bene concordans matrimonium* to treat their respective property as though it were property common to both, the wife entrusting her husband **203. Community of goods**

with the management of her property and confining herself to domestic work. Turia's husband declared in his *laudatio*, l. 37:

> 'Omne tuom patrimonium acceptum a parentibus communi diligentia conservavimus: neque enim erat acquirendi tibi cura, quod totum mihi tradidisti. Officia ita partiti sumus ut ego tutelam tuae fortunae gererem, tu meae custodiam sustineres.'

There were, of course, exceptional cases in which the wife took the administration of her property into her own hands. A well-known example is Cicero's wife Terentia, whose independent management sometimes irritated Cicero (who was often in pecuniary embarrassment) and finally led him to divorce her.

204. Maintenance of the wife. Dos
3. Actually (not legally, see above, s. 200) the husband has to maintain his wife as well as his children and to defray the expenses of the household. It is customary for the wife or her parents to make a contribution towards these expenses by giving the husband a sum of money or certain things. This gift is called *dos*. The husband acquires ownership of this property, but the idea is that he should spend only the income gained from it and preserve the capital as a provision for his wife in case the marriage is dissolved by the husband's death or by divorce. Thus *dos* has a twofold character: on the one hand it is a contribution to the costs of matrimonial life; on the other it is a fund to secure the maintenance of the wife in the period after the end of the marriage.

205. Donatio ante nuptias
4. Even in the classical period this mode of securing the maintenance of the widowed or divorced wife seemed insufficient, hence a *donatio ante nuptias* became more or less usual. The intending husband made a gift to the bride which the latter gave back to him as a part of the *dos*. The post-classical development of this type of *donatio* lies outside the scope of this book.

206. Donationes inter virum et uxorem
Within the framework of this homogeneous and carefully considered law the rule prohibiting donations between spouses seems an uncouth intruder. According to our sources the prohibition was introduced in republican times by custom *ne mutuo amore invicem spoliarentur donationibus*;

ne venalia essent matrimonia; *ne concordia pretio conciliari videretur*. But these reports are hardly credible. The romantic morality and doctrinaire illiberality of the prohibition renders it ill suited to a system in which the regulation of mutual relations is entrusted to the spouses to such a great extent; on the other hand, it suits excellently the Augustan legislation. The predominant opinion which attributes the interdict to Augustus is therefore probably right. The classical lawyers restricted it as far as they could, excepting in particular from its operation a *donatio mortis causa*. According to a *senatusconsultum* under Severus which was enlarged later by a *senatusconsultum* under Caracalla, A.D. 206, donations between spouses became valid (*convalescunt*) when the donator died without having revoked his gift. With this modification the prohibition became Justinian's law and later European common law, but in some territorial laws the pre-Severan law sometimes revived (e.g. in England).

SOURCES

s. 199. Read Gai. 2. 90.

s. 200. Best editions of the 'laudatio Turiae': *ILS* 8393 (with Addenda in vol. iii. 2, p. cxc); *FIRA* iii, no. 69.*

s. 202. Read Pliny, *Epist.* viii. 18. 7, 8.

s. 203. Read Columella, *De re rust.*, praef. lib. xii.

s. 205. Read *C.* (5. 3) 1.

s. 206. Read *Epit. Ulp.* 7. 1; *D.* (24. 1) 1–3 pr.; 32 pr., 2. *Fr. Vat.* 276. Bracton's interesting chapter fol. 29 needs a commentary.

BIBLIOGRAPHY

s. 200. On Roman individualism Schulz, *Principles*, 146 ff. On maintenance of the wife see Koschaker, 'Unterhalt der Ehefrau und Früchte der dos', *St. Bonfante*, iv (1930), 1 ff.

s. 202. F. v. Woess, *Das römische Erbrecht und die Erbanwärter* (1911), 36 ff., 45 ff.; Brandileone, *Scritti* i (1931), 128; Esmein, 'Le testament du mari', *Mél. d'hist. du droit et de critique* (1886), 37 ff.

s. 203. On the passage in the *laudatio Turiae* see Arangio-Ruiz, *FIRA* iii. 213, n. 1, with references; Schulz, *Principles*, 148.*

s. 205. Brandileone, *Scritti*, i (1931), 117 ff., 215 ff., 229 ff.; Scherillo, *Riv. di Storia del diritto ital.* iii (1930), 69 ff.; Corbett, *Roman Law of Marriage* (1930), 205 ff.

s. 206. F. Dumont, *Les Donations entre époux en droit romain* (1928, see Kaden, Z 1, 1930, 611); J. B. Thayer, *On Gifts between Husband and Wife*

(1929); Lauria, 'Il devieto delle donazioni fra coniugi', *Studi Albertoni*, ii (1937), 513 ff.; G. Scherillo, 'Il devieto delle donazioni tra coniugi', *St. Solmi*, i (1941), 171 ff.; Biondi, *Acta divi Augusti*, i. 1 (1945), 182; Siber, 'Confirmatio donationis', Z liii (1933), 99 ff., 103 ff.; De Robertis, 'La convalescenza delle donazioni fra coniugi nelle orationes di Severo e Caracalla', *St. Barillari* (1936); R. Besnier, 'Les Donations entre époux ou futurs époux en Normandie', *RH* xv (1936), 701 ff.

6. *Law of matrimonial property. Dos*

The classical *dos* (above, s. 204) needs further discussion.

i. *Assignment of dos*

207. Dos and manus   A *dos* could be assigned to the husband irrespective of whether he was in possession of *manus* or not. Available texts apparently presuppose a free marriage, and this is quite understandable as *manus* was already dying out in the classical period.

208. Dos assigned before wedding   A *dos* might be given before or after the marriage itself, but in the former case the assignment of *dos* is *in pendenti*; though the husband becomes at once the owner of the property given, this is as yet not *dos* and becomes such only by the conclusion of marriage; where marriage definitely did not take place, the restitution of the property might be claimed by *condictio causa non secuta*.

209. Acts of assignment   The assignment of *dos* requires a legal act sufficing to confer a right on the husband. As a rule this right is ownership, but it might also be a right of any other kind, usufruct, *servitus*, or a mere claim. Hence, where ownership is the right, *mancipatio*, *in iure cessio*, *traditio*, or *legatum per vindicationem* is required; if a claim has to be assigned, *cessio actionis* or *promissio dotis* by stipulation has to take place. All these legal acts are obviously not confined to the assignment of a *dos*; there existed, however, one act which was so confined, the *dotis dictio*. This was a declaration addressed to the husband that a certain property should be *dos*, for example, *dotis filiae meae erunt centum*; from this act sprang an obligation which had to be fulfilled after the marriage had taken place. The details of this act are still doubtful for want of sources. Since *dotis dictio* disappeared in post-classi-

cal times, the Byzantine compilers eliminated it entirely from classical texts and replaced it by *promissio dotis*. Further investigations may perhaps succeed in finding out the classical content of these interpolated texts.

A *dos tacita* is unknown to classical law. Where a divorced wife returned to her former husband and concluded a new marriage with him, the renewal of the *dos* was not implied by that act even if the husband still had the property in his hands; in such a case, however, an informal declaration sufficed to render it a *dos* again. The compilers have smuggled *dos tacita* into the classical texts, and modern lawyers, stimulated by these interpolations, sometimes went still farther in assuming that the whole property of the bride is (in default of express protest) to be regarded as *dos tacita*. This of course meant turning the classical system upside down. For the classical law wishes the wife to have property of her own and for that reason requires an express legal act for the assignment of *dos*. _{placeholder}

A *dos* might be given by the bride or wife, by her father or grandfather, or by any other person. The *dos* assigned by her father or grandfather was termed *dos profecticia* (*quia proficiscitur a patre*); for other sorts of *dos* there were no special names in classical law. In post-classical times the ill-starred term *dos adventicia* arose to designate any *dos* which was not *dos profecticia*; to call the *dos* assigned by the wife *dos adventicia* is certainly both improper and confusing.

ii. *Dos during marriage*

The legal position of *dos* during marriage is in classical law very simple and clear: the husband has the right which has been conferred to him by the assignment of *dos*. As aforesaid (s. 209), this right might be a mere usufruct, and if usufruct had become the regular subject of *dotis datio*, the Roman *dos* would have become something similar to the Greek προίξ or φέρνη. However, the republican cautelary jurisprudence apparently pressed parties to prefer a conveyance of ownership and succeeded in its object, for in classical times the husband is as a rule the owner of the *dos*;

210. Dos tacita

211. Dos profecticia and adventicia

212. Roman dos and Greek dowry

anyhow, we shall confine ourselves in the following discussion to this case.

213. The classical principle

The husband and he alone is the owner of the property assigned to him as *dos*. He has the right to use, manage, and even dispose of it at his discretion, though he may be made responsible later if he has to restore the *dos*. During matrimony the wife has no right to interfere and is in no way protected against her husband's possible squandering of the *dos*. However, the liberal Roman law of divorce has to be kept in mind; the wife might check her husband at once by divorcing him and claiming the restitution of the *dos*.

The husband has full, unrestricted ownership of the *dos*. The idea of a mere fiduciary ownership or trusteeship is entirely foreign to classical law. It is true that the praetor's Edict had a rubric *de re uxoria* (Lenel, *Edict.* tit. xx) and the praetorian action for recovery of the *dos* was called *actio rei uxoriae*, but it is not proved by this usage that the *dos* during marriage was officially called *res uxoria*. This term referred only to the *dos* after the dissolution of marriage by divorce or by the husband's death. After such a dissolution the property assigned as *dos* was strictly speaking no longer *dos* and the term *res uxoria* was a very proper one with which to describe the property which had to be restored to the wife.

214. Lex Iulia de fundo dotali

There was only one exception to this classical principle: the husband was not allowed to alienate Italian estates, given as *dos*, without the consent of his wife; he could not mortgage them even with his wife's consent. These prohibitions were introduced by Augustus' *lex Iulia de adulteriis*, the relevant chapter being cited as *lex Iulia de fundo dotali*. It was the conception of the *dos* as a provision for the divorced or widowed wife (above, s. 204) which was at work here.

215. Fruits of dos

The husband has the right to use the property given as *dos* and to gather the fruits of it; these he may keep even when he is bound to restore the *dos*. The underlying idea was certainly this: *dos* is meant to be a contribution towards the expenses of matrimonial life (*onera matrimonii*), but this idea was apparently never expressly mentioned by the classical lawyers, all classical texts in which it occurs being interpolated. These interpolations are not all of Byzantine origin, for we meet them in pre-Justinianic texts; it was probably in the late classical or post-classical law-school that these interpolations originated. At all events, the idea itself is substantially classical and, therefore, the assignment of *dos* never a donation.

In post-classical jurisprudence we meet the tendency to regard *dos* as a trust, the husband as a trustee and the wife as *cestui que* trust. A fixed terminology was not reached, but the idea is visible in various formulas. Boethius (who died in A.D. 525) declared in his commentary on Cicero's *Topica* (6. 17. 65):

> 'Dos enim licet matrimonio constante in bonis viri sit, est tamen in uxoris iure.'

We do not know Boethius' source, which certainly was a post classical law-book; anyhow we meet a similar formula in a post-classical text attributed to Tryphoninus:

> *D.* (23. 3) 75. 'Quamvis in bonis mariti dos sit, mulieris tamen est.'

In another post-classical text (*D.* 11. 7. 16) *dos* is called *quasi patrimonium uxoris*. Justinian declared that both husband and wife are owners of the things given as *dos*, the wife *iure naturali*, the husband *legum subtilitate*, thus coming very near to the English formula which calls the *cestui que* trust 'equitable owner' and the trustee 'legal' or 'nominal owner'; it is even possible that the English formula rests on Justinian. In pre-Justinianic times this new idea led but rarely to substantial alterations of the classical law; as a rule it was only used to supply reasons for classical decisions. Where, however, the husband gave the fruits of the *dos* to his wife during matrimony and their value exceeded the costs of her maintenance, this was according to classical law a forbidden donation, whereas the post-classical lawyers denied its being a donation at all, apparently because they regarded *dos* as a trust. More important were the following rules created by Justinian. Since he regarded the wife as a *cestui que* trust, he granted her after the end of matrimony a *rei vindicatio*. Moreover, the wife might recover the *dos* even during matrimony, where it was endangered by the husband's mismanagement. Such protection of the wife would have seemed superfluous to classical lawyers on account of the liberal law of divorce, but this freedom no longer existed in Justinian's law; moreover, Justinian did not wish to encourage the wife to divorce her husband. Finally, Justinian prohibited any alienation of things forming part of the *dos* even with the wife's consent and allowed the *dos* to be restored to the wife during matrimony. Thus it is clear that the idea of trust had made considerable progress. Unfortunately these innovations were carried through within the compilation so imperfectly and the classical texts remained unaltered to such an extent that the exact legal nature of the Roman *dos* has been a vexed problem in the doctrine since the Glossators; an all-satisfying formula was not found to describe it, since the conception of the trust was foreign to continental common law.

iii. *Dos after the end of matrimony*

217.
Cautio and
actio rei
uxoriae

At or before the assignment of *dos* the giver might stipulate for its restitution after the end of matrimony (*cautio rei uxoriae*). In default of such a stipulation there lay a praetorian action for recovery of the *dos* called *actio rei uxoriae* (above, s. 213). This action was created by the praetor in republican times (it was known to Cicero), but to a certain extent reformed by Augustan legislation. However, the early history of the action remains obscure and it is only the classical action which is known to us fairly well. Its *formula* is doubtful, but it is certainly an *actio in personam* (above, s. 56) and an *actio bonae fidei* (above, s. 60), though apparently not on the strength of the usual clause *ex fide bona*.

218.
Conditions
of actio
rei uxoriae

The conditions of the *actio rei uxoriae* were the following:

1. Where the wife died in matrimony, the so-called *dos adventicia* (above, s. 211) remained permanently with the husband and the wife's heir was excluded. *Dos profecticia* (above, s. 211) had to be restored (minus ⅕th for each child) to the father if he were still alive; if he had already died, it remained with the husband.

2. Where the marriage was dissolved by the husband's death or by divorce, *dos* both *profecticia* and *adventicia* had

to be restored. If the wife were still *in potestate patris*, the action had to be brought by the father *adiuncta filiae persona*, the wife's name being apparently mentioned in the *formula*. If the wife were *sui iuris*, the action appertained to herself. In any case the action was not transmissible to the heir of the father or the wife except when the husband was *in mora debitoris*.

This regulation needs an explanation. It seems strange that the *dos* remained with the husband to such a great extent without regard to whether or not there were children. It is further strange that the action was not transmissible to the heir of the person entitled to it. The whole position was probably established by Augustan legislation and the underlying idea was perhaps the following:

1. Where the wife died during matrimony, *dos* remained on principle with the husband on account of the children, and where there were no children it remained with him, in order to facilitate a new marriage of the widower. Due regard, however, was paid to *patria potestas* (above, s. 188); hence *dos profecticia* had always to be restored to the wife's *pater familias* if he was still alive.

2. Where the wife was alive, *dos* had to be restored in every case, for it was meant to provide for her maintenance and to help her to conclude another marriage.

3. If parties wished the rule to be different they might so order it by stipulation.

Concerning the restitution of the *dos* the following notes must suffice here:

219.
Restitution
of dos

1. The husband had to restore what had been conferred on him as *dos* including anything that had accrued to him as a result of the *dos*. He was only entitled to keep the fruits of the *dos* (above, s. 215).

2. In the case of things alienated by the husband he was bound to restore their value, and of things which had deteriorated or perished by his fault he had to pay damages.

3. Fungible things had to be restored by three yearly instalments (*annua bima trima die*), other things at once. This rule certainly goes back to the Augustan legislation

which, however, may have only adopted republican cautelary practice.

4. The *quinque retentiones* in their classical form also derived from an Augustan statute. For any one of five reasons the husband was entitled to retain a part of the *dos*:

(a) *propter liberos*; one-sixth of the *dos* for each child but in any case not more than three-sixths (one-half).*

(b) *propter mores uxoris*, for moral offences of the wife; one-eighth of the *dos* in minor cases, one-sixth in more serious cases.

(c) *propter impensas*, for expenditure on the *dos*.

(d) *propter res donatas*. As aforesaid (s. 206), donations between husband and wife were void, hence the husband might claim the restitution of his gifts. In so far as he had not yet recovered them, he might retain an equivalent part of the *dos*.

(e) *propter res amotas*. Where a wife appropriated things belonging to her husband after divorce in order to recover her *dos* by a sort of self-help, this was not regarded as *furtum*. The things taken by the wife were therefore not *res furtivae* but were called *res amotae*. The praetor granted the *actio rerum amotarum* to the husband which did not entail infamy; moreover, the husband might retain an adequate part of the *dos propter res amotas*.

220.
Justinian's
law   Justinian drastically reformed the classical action for recovery of the *dos*. Now *dos* never remained with the husband; it had always to be returned and the action was always transmissible to the heir of the person entitled to it. Land had to be returned at once, all other things after the lapse of one year. The *scrupulositas retentionum* (above, s. 219) was entirely wiped out. Not even the classical name of the action was retained. Justinian declared that this action should be regarded on the one hand as resulting from a *stipulatio tacita* and so like an *actio ex stipulatu* but nevertheless as an *actio bonae fidei* like the *actio rei uxoriae*. The compilers accordingly eliminated the term *actio rei uxoriae* from the classical texts and replaced it by *actio de dote*; their

reverentia antiquitatis and their literary taste prevented them from inserting in classical texts the monstrous *actio bonae fidei ex stipulatione tacita*. The Justinianic action is an *actio in personam* like the classical action, but it is secured by a *hypotheca generalis* on the whole property of the husband; moreover, a *rei vindicatio* is granted to the wife, as we have already mentioned (s. 216). The *actio rerum amotarum* (above, s. 219) was already altered in pre-Justinianic law; it was now granted also to the wife against her husband. Finally, all *actiones famosae* (above, s. 79) between husband and wife were barred.

SOURCES

s. 208. Read *D.* (23. 1) 10 [*nisi . . . fin.*]; *D.* (23. 3) 47; Paul. *Sent.* (2. 21*b*) 1.

s. 209. Read Gai. 2. 63; *Epit. Ulp.* 6. 1 and 2; *CTh.* 3. 13. 4.

s. 210. Read *D.* (23. 3) 30 [*dum . . . convenisse*]; (23. 3) 31; (23. 3) 64 (spurious). The classical tendency is revealed by the question in *Fr. Vat.* 115.

s. 211. Read *Epit. Ulp.* 6. 3; *D.* (23. 3) 5 pr.

s. 214. Read Paul. *Sent.* (2. 21*b*) 2; Gai. 2. 63; *C.* (5. 13) 1. 15; *Inst. Iust.* (2. 8) pr.

s. 215. Read *D.* (23. 3) 7 pr. (entirely spurious, but substantially classical) and § 1 [*nisi . . . redduntur*]; Fragm. Oxon. (Seckel–Kübler, *Jurisprud. anteiust.* ii. 1, p. 163 [*quia . . . sustinet*].

s. 216. Read *C.* (5. 12) 30 pr. 1; *C.Th.* (3. 13) 3. 1; cf. *C. Just.* (5. 19) 1 with Koschaker, l.c. 19.

s. 217. Read Gellius, 4. 3. 2 (= Seckel–Kübler, *Jurisprud. anteiust.* 1. 33); *Epit. Ulp.* 6. 4; Gai. 4. 62; Lenel's problematical reconstruction of the *formula*: Lenel, *Edict.* p. 305.

s. 218. Read *Epit. Ulp.* 6. 4–7; *Laudatio Murdiae* (*FIRA* iii, no. 70), l. 6.

s. 219. 1. Read *D.* (23. 3) 4; 10. 1. 2, 32, 65.

s. 219. 2. Read *D.* (24. 3) 66 pr. (23. 3) 17 pr. [*sed . . . exhibet*].

s. 219. 3. Read *Epit. Ulp.* 6. 8.

s. 219. 4. Read *Epit. Ulp.* vi. 9, 10, 12, 14–17; *D.* (25. 2) 1.

s. 220. See *C.* (5. 13) 1; on the post-class. *actio rerum amotarum* read *C.* (5. 21) 2, interp., and *Epit. Ulp.* 7. 2.

BIBLIOGRAPHY

ss. 207 ff. For the literature of the 19th century see Windscheid, *Pand.* iii, §§ 492 ff. Modern literature: Bonfante, *Corso*, i (1925), 283 ff.; Corbett, *Roman Law of marriage* (1930), 147 ff.; M. Lauria, 'La dote romana'

(1938), estratto dagli *Atti dell' Accademia di scienze morali e politiche della Società reale di Napoli*, vol. lviii.*

s. 208. Albertario, 'Sulla dotis datio ante nuptias', *Studi*, i (1933), 317 ff.

s. 209. Berger, 'Dotis dictio in röm. Recht', *Bulletin de l'Académie des Sciences de Cracovie* (1909), 75 ff.; Lauria, l.c. 7 ff.; Daube, *Juridical Review*, li (1939), 11 ff.; Berger, *Journal of Juristic Papyrology*, i (1945), 13 ff.; Riccobono, *Bull*. viii–ix (1947), 39.

s. 210. E. Levy, *Der Hergang der röm. Ehescheidung* (1925), 12; Windscheid, *Pand*. iii, § 494, notes 12 and 13.*

s. 211. Albertario, 'Dos profecticia e dos adventicia', *Studi*, i (1933), 281.

s. 212. Beauchet, *Histoire du droit privé de la république Athénienne*, i (1897), 303; R. Taubenschlag, *The Law of Greco-Roman Egypt* (1944), 95.

s. 213. Albertario, 'Subtilitas legum e moderamen naturalis iuris nel diritto dotale romano-giustinianeo', *Studi*, i (1933), 369 ff.; H. J. Wolff, Z liii (1933), 297 ff. with references.

s. 214. Windscheid, *Pand*. iii, § 497, with references; Biondi in *Acta divi Augusti*, i (1945), 127.

s. 215. Koschaker, 'Unterhalt der Ehefrau und Früchte der dos', *St. Bonfante*, iv (1930), 3 ff.; Albertario, 'La connessione della dote con gli oneri del matrimonio', *Studi*, i (1933), 293 ff.; H. J. Wolff, Z liii (1933), 360 ff.; Beseler, Z lxvi (1948), 337, 291 f.; *Dos* a donation? Wrongly Albertario, *Studi*, i (1933), 373; Lauria, l.c. 19; cf. Windscheid, *Pand*. iii, § 492.

s. 216. Concerning fruits see Koschaker, l.c. 5 and 12; on Justinian's law see Partsch, *Aus nachgelassenen und kleineren verstreuten Schriften* (1931), 345; Taubenschlag, *The Law of Greco-Roman Egypt* (1944), 96; on continental common law Haenel, *Dissensiones dominorum* (1834), § 266; Windscheid, *Pand*. iii, § 496.*

s. 217. Solazzi, *La restituzione della dote nel diritto romano* (1899); E. Levy, *Privatstrafe und Schadensersatz* (1915), 35, with references; Biondi, *Iudicia bonae fidei*, i (1920), 178 ff.; Lenel, *Edict*. (1927), § 113; Capocci, *Bull*. xxxvi (1928), 139; H. J. Wolff, Z liii (1933), 300 ff.*

s. 218. On 'actio adiuncta filiae persona' see Wolff, l.c. 301 ff.*

s. 219. 2. Arangio-Ruiz, *Responsabilità contrattuale in diritto romano* (1933), 201 ff.; Pflüger, Z lxv (1947), 147 ff.

s. 219. 4*c*. Schulz, Z xxxiv (1913), 57 ff.; Riccobono, *Annali Palermo* iii/iv (1915), 409 ff.; J. Ph. Levy, *Les Impenses dotales en droit classique* (1937).

s. 219. 4*e*. Zanzucchi, *Riv. It.*, xlii (1906), 1 ff.; E. Levy, *Privatstrafe und Schadensersatz* (1915), 114 ff.; Schulz, *Epit. Ulp.* (1926), 32; Lenel, *Edict*. (1927), § 115.

s. 220. Tripiccione, *L'actio rei uxoriae e l'actio ex stipulatu nella restituzione della dote secondo il diritto giustinianeo* (1920).*

7. *Law of matrimonial property. Parapherna*

The wife in a free marriage is capable of having property of her own (above, s. 200). Where she had such property her ownership was unrestricted and she might manage and dispose of it without her husband's consent. She might of course allow her husband to manage it; then the general rules of *mandatum* or *locatio conductio operarum* applied. Once in our classical texts this kind of property is called *parapherna*, viz. *res quae extra dotem sunt*, but the text is spurious. Nevertheless, the word has become a modern term of art, since lawyers like to show that they know some Greek. 221. Res uxoris extra dotem

There existed in classical law the presumption that all property which the wife had acquired during matrimony had been acquired from her husband, counter-evidence being admissible. This presumption is first mentioned in our sources by Q. Mucius, and though he was only concerned to report the practice of the courts, it was called *praesumptio Muciana*. This did not mean that all acquests of the wife during matrimony were supposed to have been acquired through a donation of her husband, but it was understood in this way by the doctrine of European common law, and as donations between spouses were void the result was that all acquests of the wife during matrimony are supposed to belong to the husband. It was the patriarchal attitude of the lawyers which led to this interpretation, but it had already been suggested by the compilers who inserted the text in the *Digest* under the title *de donationibus inter virum et uxorem*. 222. Praesumptio Muciana

SOURCES

s. 221. Read *D*. (35. 2) 95 pr.; (23. 3) 9. 3, first sentence.
s. 222. Read *D*. (24. 1) 51 [*et verius . . . habeat*]; [*evitandi . . . probasse*].

BIBLIOGRAPHY

s. 221. Windscheid, *Pand.* iii, § 507; Castelli, *Scritti giuridici*, i (1923), 1 ff.
s. 222. Lenel, *Pal.* 2. 64; *Index Interp.* ad *D*. (24. 1) 51; Schulz, *History*, 205, n. 1; Scherillo, *Studi Solmi*, i (1941), 174; Windscheid, *Pand.* iii, § 509. 5.

8. *End of matrimony*

Matrimony is terminated by divorce (*divortium*, *re-pudium*), by certain alterations of status, and by death.

i. *Divorce* (*divortium*, *repudium*)

223.
Freedom of
divorce

In classical law any marriage, without regard to whether the husband has *manus* or not, can be dissolved by agreement of the spouses or by notice given by one of them. Agreements which attempt to exclude or to limit divorce are void, nor is it possible to stipulate for a penalty to be paid in case of divorce. It is this unlimited and illimitable freedom of divorce which seemed so highly objectionable to modern moralists and lawyers and so obviously a sign of Roman decadence. In truth, as we have already emphasized above (s. 180 f.), this freedom is the inevitable and indispensable keystone of the classical humanistic law of marriage; this is clearly stated in our sources.

The Emperor Alexander declared in a rescript of A.D. 223:

C. (8. 38) 2: 'Libera matrimonia esse antiquitus placuit. Ideoque pacta, ne liceret divertere, non valere et stipulationes quibus poenae inrogarentur ei qui divortium fecisset, ratas non haberi constat.'

We meet the same decision in a *responsum* by Paulus:

D. (45. 1) 134. 1: '. . . quia inhonestum visum est vinculo poenae matrimonia obstringi sive futura sive iam contracta.'

This sentence is probably spurious, but nevertheless substantially classical. Even the author of the so-called *scholia Sinaitica* declares:

§ 6. ἄτοπον γὰρ τὸν γάμον διηνεκοῦς τῆς ὁμονοίας δεόμενον διὰ τῆς poenas καὶ μὴ διαθέσει συνίστασθαι.

(Translation: 'absurdum enim, matrimonium perpetuae concordiae indigens poena et non consensu consistere.')

This text is particularly valuable since at the time of the author the principle was no longer valid without qualification. This shows how firmly and deeply rooted it was in both Roman morality and Roman legal doctrine.

Societas could be renounced at any time, and any limitation by agreement was void; full freedom of divorce was therefore inevitable, since the personal freedom is so much more strongly affected by marriage than by *societas*. Conscious of the true limits of law as were the Roman lawyers, in contrast to Greek and oriental lawyers, they realized that it is beyond the strength of law to preserve matrimony against the will of the spouses, since law can never compel them to live peacefully together. Law can maintain matrimony in the legal sense, but neither morality nor the community is in the least interested in the existence of a mere legal marriage. In the great majority of cases forcible maintenance of marriage has only the effect of dooming spouses to concubinage or other illegitimate intercourse, not to speak of the devices applied by parties and their advocates in order to elude the legal rules.

Reliable facts and reports are not available concerning the social effects of the Roman classical freedom of divorce. It is certainly true that in the last century of the Republic the number of divorces was greater than in earlier times, but that does not necessarily mean a decay of morals. The development of the individual personality of both men and women inevitably enhanced the difficulties of a permanent matrimonial life. A good example is Cicero's matrimony with Terentia, who in many respects was his superior. Moreover, the unrest of revolutionary times had an adverse effect on matrimony in that stratum of society which furnished the political figures. Turia's husband declared (l. 27):

224. Stability of marriage

> 'Rara sunt tam diuturna matrimonia, finita morte, non divertio interrupta: nam contigit nobis ut ad annum XXXXI sine offensa perduceretur.'

However, marriages lasting for forty-one years are always rare. In the period of the Principate stability of marriages was apparently normal. In the inscriptions we meet many marriages of long duration. Trimalchio posing as a true Roman declares (Petron. *Cena*, 74. 16): 'It was suggested to me to divorce my wife because we have no children, but I declined to do so, since I am a jolly good fellow and do not wish to appear frivolous' (*dum bonatus ago et nolo videri levis*). Roman *gravitas* required by customary sanction was more effective than legal prohibitions and impediments.

Penalties for frivolous divorcing were unknown to republican law, but the husband's duty to restore *dos* actually

225. Penalties for divorcing

worked as a sort of penalty. Cicero came into financial difficulties when he had to return Terentia's *dos* and so did his
son-in-law Dolabella when his marriage with Tullia came
to and end. The *retentio propter liberos* (above, s. 219) had a
similar effect. Only in one case was divorce forbidden by
Augustus. A freedwoman who had married her patron was
not allowed to divorce her husband without his consent. In
the event of contravention of this rule marriage was dissolved but the wife lost *conubium* if she wished to conclude
a new marriage. Christian legislation allowed divorce only
for certain reasons and instituted penalties in case of contravention. We will not follow this development here. The
important thing to note is that in Justinian's law the classical principle was maintained to the extent that even the forbidden divorce was valid, though penalized, and the former
spouses might therefore conclude a new marriage. It was
canon law which abandoned this principle.

226.   Each of the spouses was entitled to divorce. Where they
Divorce were *in patria potestate* their fathers had the right to dissolve
effected by
parents the marriage—even a *bene concordans matrimonium*—and
the consent of their children was not required. This
patriarchal rule was of course in open conflict with *humanitas*, but—as already said above (s. 188)—classical lawyers
were shy of interfering with *patria potestas*. Eventually this
archaic rule was abrogated by Pius or Marcus.

227. Act   Divorce was effected in classical times by informal agree-
of divorce ment or by a declaration of one of the spouses; in both cases
actual dissolution of the common life was also required.
An exception to this rule was made by the *lex Iulia de adulteriis*. A husband was thereby bound to divorce his adulter-
ous wife, otherwise he made himself guilty of *lenocinium*,
and for the divorce a declaration before seven witnesses was
compulsory. However, even in this case an informal declaration sufficed to dissolve marriage though not to avoid
punishment.

In post-classical times a deed of divorce became more
and more usual and was finally required by law. This
requirement was maintained by Justinian, but the compilers of the *Digest* also permitted a declaration before seven

witnesses, generalizing the rule of the *lex Iulia* which we have just mentioned. Probably they wished to make compulsory a written declaration signed by seven witnesses.

ii. *Alteration of status*

Marriage is further dissolved by certain alterations of status, above all by *capitis deminutio maxima* and *media* (above, s. 123). Marriage is further dissolved where the husband of a freedwoman enters the senatorial class (see above, s. 191) and where the husband joins the army (down to Severus; see above, s. 191.)

228. Alterations of status

iii. *Death*

Finally, matrimony ends by death. Where one of the spouses was absent for such a long time that it was doubtful whether he or she was still alive, the other spouse probably might dissolve marriage by a declaration 'to whom it may concern'; the concluding of a new marriage was certainly a sufficient manifestation of the intention to dissolve marriage.

229. Death and absence

iv. *Legal effects of the end of matrimony*

The restitution of the *dos* has been sufficiently discussed above (ss. 217 ff.). We have also already stated (s. 200) that the wife had no legal claim to be maintained by her husband during matrimony. Nor had she such a claim after the termination of matrimony, even if marriage had been dissolved *culpa mariti*. This negative rule is by no means an inevitable corollary of the freedom of divorce, but Roman lawyers apparently regarded it as such. They held that the maintenance of the divorced or widowed wife was sufficiently secured by *dos* and *donatio ante nuptias* (above, s. 204). Where these funds were insufficient they argued that the wife or her parents should have stipulated for a more ample provision before the wedding. This rather casual *laisser-faire* attitude reveals again the fact that Roman lawyers provided mainly for the *beati possidentes*.

230. Maintenance of the wife

Where marriage was dissolved by divorce, *manus mariti* (in so far as it still existed) did not cease automatically.

231. End of manus

If a *coemptio* had taken place (above, s. 195) a *remancipatio* was required and in cases of *confarreatio* (above, s. 194) a *diffarreatio*. The husband might be forced to effect these acts.

232.
Waiting-
time

After the termination of the marriage each spouse was entitled to conclude a new marriage. Where, however, marriage was dissolved by the husband's death the wife had, according to the praetor's Edict, to wait for the specified time of mourning (ten months) to elapse before marrying again. The idea was not to prevent *turbatio sanguinis*, for if that had been the purpose of the waiting period it would also have been required where the marriage was dissolved by divorce. Hence the wife had to observe the full time even if a child had been born to her shortly after her husband's death. In the post-classical period the mourning-time was fixed at one year. The duties to be observed by the wife in mourning were mitigated by a *senatusconsultum* at some date before 240; the compilers, however, took this statute as having entirely abrogated compulsory mourning. Henceforth the waiting period could only have had the purpose of preventing *turbatio sanguinis*; therefore they transformed the classical texts so as to conform to that purpose and extended the rule as to the waiting period to divorced women. To conclude, it may be added that the idea of preventing *turbatio sanguinis* by a second marriage (after the dissolution of the first by divorce as well as by the husband's death) was well known in republican and classical times, but it was the pontifical law and not the praetor's Edict which was concerned with it.

SOURCES

s. 224. See the following inscriptions (the number of the years of matrimony are given in round brackets): *ILS* 1397 (31); 1259 (40); 1526 (44); 1612 (24); 1756 (38); 7789 (51); 1763 (45); 8140 (30); 8393 (41); 8401 (60); 8430*a* (15 and 28).

s. 226. Read Paul, *Sent.* (5. 6) 15; C. (5. 17) 5 pr. [*nisi* . . . *fecerit*].

s. 227. Read *D.* (24. 2) 2 pr. § 1; *C.* (5. 17) 6; *Nov. Theod.* xii pr. = *C.* (5. 17) 8 pr.; *D.* (24. 2) 9.

s. 231. Read Gai. 1. 137*a*.

s. 232. Read *D.* (3. 2) 11. 1–3 (heavily interpolated).

BIBLIOGRAPHY

s. 224. Friedländer–Wissowa, *Sittengeschichte*, i. 283 ff.; W. Kroll, *Die Kultur der Ciceronischen Zeit*, ii (1933), 38, 47 ff., 52 f.

s. 225. On the *liberta* see E. Levy, *Der Hergang der röm. Ehescheidung* (1925), 137 ff.; Solazzi, *Bull.* xxxiv (1925), 295 ff.; Corbett, *Roman Law of Marriage* (1930), 243; Volterra, 'Sul divorzio della liberta', *St. Riccobono*, iii (1936), 203 ff.*

s. 226. Solazzi, *Bull.* xxxiv (1925), 1 ff.; Levy, l.c. 145; G. Longo, *Bull.* xl (1932); Kaser, *Z* lviii (1928), 83; Taubenschlag, *Law of Greco-Roman Egypt* (1944), 106.

s. 227. Levy, l.c.; Solazzi, l.c. 312 ff.; Corbett, l.c. 218 ff.

s. 228. Kunkel, *PW* xiv. 2273; Corbett, *Roman Law of Marriage* (1930), 211.

s. 229. E. Levy, 'Verschollenheit und Ehe in antiken Rechten', in *Gedächtnisschrift für Emil Seckel* (1927), 145 ff.; Kunkel, l.c. 2272.

s. 231. Kaser, l.c. with references.*

s. 232. Karlowa, *ZfRG.* ix (1870), 229 ff.; Windscheid, *Pand.* iii, § 512; Corbett, l.c. 249; Volterra, 'Un' osservazione in tema di impedimenti matrimoniali', *Studi Albertoni*, i (1933), 401 ff.; 'Osservazioni sull' obbligo del lutto nell' editto pretorie', *Riv. It.* viii (N.S., 1933), 1 ff.; Rasi, *Scritti Ferrini*, i (1947), 393 ff. with references; Kübler, *PW* xiii. 1607.

Appendix. Concubinatus

Classical *concubinatus* is an allowed but illegitimate permanent union of man and woman, the latter being defined as 'femina quae cum uxor non esset, cum aliquo tamen vivebat, femina pro uxore', an unmarried wife, a woman living with somebody as his wife. The woman's so to speak official designation is *concubina*; thus an inscription on a tombstone mentions a freedwoman Lysistrate, *concubina divi Pii*. In unofficial usage other designations occur, *amica, hospita, focaria*. 233. Terminology

A Roman *concubina* is basically different from a *meretrix* and the difference is sometimes emphasized in our sources. To have a concubine is not against Roman morality (even good emperors like Pius and Marcus had concubines) and it was no stigma on a woman to be a concubine. Concubinage with free and slave women occurred as early as the republican period, but it became apparently more frequent during the Principate, an undesired effect of the Augustan 234. Social character legislation since parties chose concubinage in cases in which their marriage was prohibited by law. In particular soldiers of the rank and file barred from marrying commonly resorted to concubinage (above, s. 191).

235.
Legal
character

However, *concubinatus* had purely social recognition in the classical period. The Augustan legislation neither permitted nor regulated, nor even mentioned it; it did not develop into a sort of marriage but remained an illegitimate relation like any other. The children of a *concubina* were simply illegitimate children (*spurii*); a *concubina* could not commit *adulterium*. Donations between the quasi-spouses were valid; it was only the 'soldiers' emperor' Caracalla who prohibited donations given by a soldier to his concubine (not vice versa). Thus there remained only one question for the classical lawyers: under what conditions is *concubinatus* permitted? The simple answer was that *concubinatus* is permitted (leaving aside a special imperial licence) with those women only with whom any other illegitimate intercourse is permitted. The Augustan legislation prohibited illegitimate intercourse with freeborn and respectable women under penalty of *stuprum*. Illegitimate intercourse was permitted with freedwomen and with women of bad repute; it is with this group of women that Ovid dealt in his *Ars amatoria*:

> 1. 33. Nos Venerem tutam concessaque furta canemus
> Inque meo nullum carmine crimen erit.

and it is also with this group that *concubinatus* was allowed.

236. Con-
cubinatus
and mono-
gamy

Keeping these facts in mind, one cannot be surprised that a man might have two concubines at the same time; Roman *concubinatus* was not a monogamous union. Even a husband was allowed to have a concubine, since any illegitimate intercourse was allowed to him and was never regarded as *adulterium*. (Of course his intercourse with a married woman would be *adulterium* and his intercourse with a freeborn respectable unmarried woman *stuprum*.) As aforesaid (s. 189) the Romans never wavered in maintaining the principle of monogamy, but that meant for them only that a man cannot have two legitimate wives. Where a legitimate wife did not like her husband's having a concubine she might divorce him; she might further stipulate for a penalty before or at the wedding in the event of his taking a concubine.

In a sepulchre at Concordia (Gallia Cisalpina) a husband was buried together with his wife and his concubine. The tombstone shows the husband's head and to the right and left of it the heads of the two women. The inscription runs as follows: *P. Cervonius P. F. Marinus testamento fieri iussit sibi et Cinciai Sex. F. Secundai uxori Chiai concubinai.* When Cervonius made his will his wife was obviously still alive.

Even a polyandrous concubinage was not prohibited, but the much discussed sepulchre of Allia Potestas furnishes no evidence for its existence. Allia was a freedwoman who lived in concubinage with her patron, the designation *uxor* being carefully avoided. The *duo iuvenes amantes* mentioned in the inscription as living in the same house were certainly not Allia's sons (sons would have been mentioned among her *laudes*); nor were they the legitimate sons of the patron; if they were so, the patron could not say (as he does in the inscription) that he knew no one who would carry through his will. Thus they are simply two young men living in the house but not lovers of Allia.

237. Polyandrous concubinage?

From the legal point of view *concubinatus* differed widely from *matrimonium*, but in actual fact they might easily have been mistaken the one for the other. For where both marriage and concubinage were permitted (above, s. 235) it was only the intention of parties which could be decisive in distinguishing the two. This want of a clear demarcation between matrimony and concubinage seems hardly tolerable to us, but the inertia of the Roman Government and of the law in the sphere of status is a well-known and remarkable fact. Registration of births was only introduced by Augustus (above, s. 126), and neither he nor any of his successors supplemented it with a registration of marriages.

238. Concubinatus and matrimonium

In post-classical times Roman *concubinatus* was considerably transformed. The Church regarded any illegitimate intercourse as sinful and legislation took a hostile attitude towards concubinage. We will not describe this development but confine ourselves to a sketch of Justinian's law as it was at the time when the *Digest* was made (A.D. 533), since this law was declared by interpolating classical texts.

239. Post-classical law

1. *Concubinatus* was now permitted even with freeborn respectable women (cf. above, s. 235).

2. Constantine had already forbidden a husband to have

a concubine and this was adopted by Justinian. An unmarried man, however, might still have several concubines at the same time and it was only by Justinian's *Novellae* that polygamous concubinage was abrogated.

3. The conditions of concubinage were assimilated to those of marriage. The woman must be at least twelve years old and the former concubine of a man must not become the concubine of his son or grandson.

4. Infidelity of a concubine is now regarded as *adulterium*.

5. A freedwoman who is her patron's *concubina* must not leave him without his consent (cf. above, s. 225); contravention renders her incapable of concluding a marriage and perhaps also of entering into a new concubinage.

6. The children of a *concubina* are privileged, as we shall point out later (below, ss. 253, 278).

7. Intestate succession was granted to the concubine only by Justinian's *Novellae*.

SOURCES

s. 233. Read *D.* (50. 16) 144; *CIL* vi. 8972 = *ILS* 1836; *CIL* v. 4923; cf. *Statute Rules and Orders*, 1939, no. 1221, ss. 14 and 43; 1940, no. 1469.

s. 234. Read Sueton., Vespasian 21; *SHA* Pius 8. 9; Marcus, 29. 10.

s. 235. Read *C.* (5. 16) 2; *D.* (25. 7) 1. 1.

s. 236. Read *D.* (45. 1) 121. 1; *C.* (5. 26) 1; *CIL* v. 1918.

s. 237. Read *CIL* vi. 37965 = Bücheler–Lommatzch, *Carm. Lat. epigr. supplem.* (1926), 1988.

s. 239. Read *D.* (48. 5) 35 pr. [*Excepta . . . concubina*]; (25. 7) 3 [*et m. . . . fecit*]; [*sine . . . committere*] ⟨*stuprum committit*⟩; *D.* (25. 7) 1. 4 [*nisi . . . sit*]; (25. 7) 1. 3 [*quia . . . est*]; (25. 7) 1 pr. The compilers forgot to insert *an* before *ab invito*; cancel the interrogation mark and [*ego . . . habere*] and you have the classical text.

BIBLIOGRAPHY

ss. 233 ff. P. M. Meyer, *Der römische Konkubinat nach den Rechtsquellen und den Inschriften* (1895); Kübler, Z xvii (1896), 357 ff.; Costa, *Bull.* xi (1898), 233; Mitteis, Z xxiii (1902), 304 ff.; Castelli, 'Il concubinato e la legislazione Augustea', *Bull.* xxvii (1914), 55 ff. = *Scritti giuridici* (1923), 143 ff.; J. Plassard, *Le Concubinat Romain sous le Haut Empire* (1921); Volterra, *St. Riccobono*, iii (1936), 212; *ACI Bologna*, i (1934), 134; Sargenti, *Il diritto privato nella legislazione di Costantino*

(1938), 133; Esmein, *Le Mariage en droit canonique*, ii (1935), 125 ff.; Friedländer–Wissowa, *Sittengeshichte*, i (1919), 64 ff.; 218; 278; 304; Solazzi, 'Il concubinato con l'oscuro loco nata', *SD* xiii–xiv (1947–8), 269 ff.

s. 237. Bücheler–Lommatzch, *Carm. Lat. epigr. suppl.* (1926), with references; Castelli, *Scritti giur.* (1923), 101 ff.; Brugi, *Atti Veneto* lxxiii (1914), ii. 415; Zocco-Rosa, *La laudatio Alliae* (1914).

s. 239. Bonfante, 'Nota sulla riforma giustinianea e la legislazione del concubinato', *St. Perozzi* (1925), 285; Castelli, 'Concubinato', l.c.

CHAPTER IV

PARENTS AND CHILDREN

1. *Introduction*

240.
General
character

THE classical law of marriage is an impressive creation of Roman *humanitas* and it is for this reason that it appeals to us as so amazingly modern. The classical law concerning parents and children is the very reverse: the old, harsh patriarchal law was in principle maintained; the influence of the humanistic movement, though appreciable in this field also, did not touch the roots of the old law. *Patria potestas* remained the central institution of the law concerning parents and children. The idea of a *materna potestas* was never taken into consideration by the orthodox Roman lawyers, though it was suggested to them by provincial law and custom. Legal relations between parents and children, apart from *patria potestas*, were insufficiently developed. It is true that the harshness of the old *patria potestas* was somewhat mitigated, but this was done reluctantly and by artificial devices, the lawyers being obviously averse to drastic reforms. *Patria potestas* was regarded as a palladium of Romanism (above, s. 188), and it was with obstinate pride that the unique character of Roman *patria potestas* was still emphasized by the classical lawyers (below, s. 254). Thus—in contrast to the Roman law of marriage—the law concerning parents and children impresses us as old-fashioned; in fact it was already out of date in the classical period. It was only in Christian times that the law was further humanized and long overdue reforms were carried through.

BIBLIOGRAPHY

Taubenschlag, *The Law of Greco-Roman Egypt* (1944), §§ 4, 5.

2. *Beginning of patria potestas*

241. Patria
potestas
created by
birth

A legitimate child is at birth subjected to the *potestas* of his father. A child is legitimate if it was begotten in a *matri-*

monium iustum; where it was begotten before the marriage it was illegitimate even if it was born in lawful wedlock.

With regard to proof of legitimacy there were no presumptions in classical law. The maxim *pater is est quem nuptiae demonstrant* occurs only once in our sources. If Paul really wrote this sentence he did so commenting on the praetor's Edict, 'parentem . . . in ius sine permissu meo ne quis vocet', and his meaning was that the praetor does not investigate whether the plaintiff was in truth the legitimate child of the defendant, but is content with the fact that he was born in lawful wedlock. This did not imply a general presumption that a child born in lawful wedlock is the legitimate child of the husband (counter-evidence reserved). However, the whole text seems to be spurious, since the classical lawyers do not pronounce sibylline maxims. As regards the time of conception classical law knew no presumption; the rule of continental common law that conception has to be assumed between the 182nd and the 300th day before birth is not classical.

Apart from the artificial cases mentioned by Gaius (1. 65 ff.) classical law knew only one legal act which brought *patria potestas* into existence, namely *adoptio* (*optio* = choice, option), which is either *adoptio* of a *homo sui iuris* (*adrogatio*) or *adoptio* of a *homo alieni iuris* (*adoptio* in the narrower sense). A legitimation of illegitimate children by their fathers (distinct from *adoptio*) did not exist in classical law. Where the parents married, the child did not become automatically a legitimate child, *legitimatio per subsequens matrimonium* being unknown to classical law (it was introduced into English law only by the Legitimacy Act, 1926). Legitimation *per rescriptum principis* was also unknown. As aforesaid (s. 191) soldiers of the rank and file were debarred from marrying down to the time of Septimius Severus and only concubinage was open to them. Children born to a soldier's concubine were illegitimate children (above, s. 235). At the *missio honesta* of a soldier, Roman citizenship was conferred upon his children as a matter of course, but they were not necessarily subjected thereby to the *patria potestas* of their father (cf. Gai. 2, 135a).

242. Patria potestas created by legal acts

243.   The only purpose of *adoptio* is to bring *patria potestas* into
Purpose of existence and it cannot be applied to other purposes. A mere
adoptio
relationship of parent and child without *patria potestas*
cannot be created by *adoptio*. It is for this reason that women
were inevitably debarred from adopting, since a woman
cannot have *patria potestas* and *materna potestas* did not
exist (above, s. 240). An *adoptio in fratrem* known to peregrine law was expressly rejected by Roman law.

244.   *Adrogatio* was effected by a decree of the *comitia curiata*.
Adrogatio This was originally a genuine legislative act, but it early
as a legisla-
tive act degenerated into a mere formality, the ten *curiae* being
represented by ten lictors; however, this formality was
observed throughout the whole classical period. The
comitia were convoked originally by the *pontifex maximus*, in
classical times (since the Emperor was *pontifex maximus*) by
his deputy. The *formula* of his motion ran as follows:

> Gellius 5. 19. 9: 'Velitis iubeatis, uti L. Valerius L. Titio tam iure
> legeque filius siet, quam si ex eo patre matreque familias eius natus esset,
> utique ei vitae necisque in eum potestas siet, uti patri endo filio est. Haec
> ita, uti dixi, ita vos Quirites rogo.'

This motion (like any other motion in legislative *comitia*)
was called *rogatio* and has given the name *adrogatio* to the
whole ceremony. Gaius' explanation (1. 99: 'dicitur "adrogatio", quia et is qui adoptat, rogatur . . . et is qui adopta-
tur . . .') is certainly erroneous. To be sure the *pontifex* did
not bring in his motion without the consent of the *adoptans*
and the *adoptandus*; it is also possible that both appeared in
the *comitia* and declared their consent; but neither their
presence nor their consent was legally required. Though
the decree of the *comitia* was now a mere formality, the
forms of a legislative act were still observed and for such an
act the motion of the presiding magistrate and the vote of
the assembly were the only requirements. The rule that
women could not be adrogated must, therefore, not be
explained by their incapacity to appear in the *comitia*, for
the presence of the *adroganda* would not have been essential. The republican pontiffs apparently did not wish to have
families maintained by the adoption of women and therefore traditionally declined to bring in a motion for the adro-

gation of a woman; indeed this is implied by Gaius in 1. 101 (*nam id magis placuit*).

Since the presence of the *adoptans* was not required, a posthumous *adrogatio* (viz. after the death of the *adoptans*) was possible. Where a testator instituted somebody as his heir under the condition that he took the testator's *nomen gentile*, the instituted person might fulfil the condition, accept the inheritance, and apply to the pontiffs for *adrogatio*. The deputy of the *pontifex maximus* might now bring in a motion adapting the usual formula to the special case: _{245. Adrogatio per testamentum}

> 'Velitis iubeatis, uti L. Valerius L. Titio tam iure legeque filius siet, quam si ex eo patre matreque familias eius natus esset ante testamentum a L. Titio factum' (above, s. 244).

This is certainly an artificial act, but not more artificial than other creations of the pontifical jurisprudence. Actually Octavius (later the Emperor Augustus) was adrogated by Julius Caesar after the latter's death, and anyone who knows Augustus' methods will be satisfied that here as always he scrupulously observed legal rules. This form of *adrogatio* may have occurred only rarely, since the pontiffs were loath to bring in a motion in such a case. Our lawbooks are silent upon it, but that Gaius in his elementary treatise does not mention it is small wonder, nor can it come as a surprise that the *Digest* is silent on it, for even if the compilers had found it mentioned in classical texts they had to omit those texts.

Since *adrogatio* was a legislative act, it was irrelevant whether the pontiff brought in his motion with or without the consent of the *collegium pontificum*, just as it was legally irrelevant whether a consul bringing in a motion before the *comitia centuriata* acted with or without the consent of the Senate. As a rule the pontiff brought in the motion *de decreto collegii*, but, according to Cicero, no such decree had been carried in the adrogation of Clodius. It was for that reason (among others; see below, s. 250. 4) that Cicero disputed the validity of the *adrogatio* (*De domo*, 14. 38), but this was merely irresponsible rhetoric. _{246. De decreto collegii}

As a rule *adrogatio* was preceded by a *detestatio sacrorum*, viz. a declaration of the *adoptandus* before witnesses in _{247. Detestatio sacrorum}

which he renounced his *sacra familiari*. This act too was irrelevant to the validity of *adrogatio* and for that reason is not mentioned by Gaius.

248. Finally it should be noted that *adrogatio* could be effected *Adrogatio confined to Rome* only in the City of Rome, since *comitia* could not be held elsewhere. However, where parties were living in a province, they might apply to the pontiffs by letter or by a deputy and the pontiffs might effect *adrogatio* since, as aforesaid (above, s. 244), the presence of the parties was not required.

249. Act *of adoptio* *Adoptio* in the narrower sense (above, s. 242), viz. *adoptio* of a *homo alieni iuris*, was a no less artificial act, obviously created by the cautelary jurisprudence of the early Republic. First the *patria potestas* had to be abolished and this was done by selling a son three times by *mancipatio* (one sale of a daughter or a grandchild was sufficient) according to the rule of the Twelve Tables (iv. 2): 'Si pater filium ter venum duuit, filius a patre liber esto.' Then followed an *in iure cessio* by which the *adoptans* claimed the *adoptandus* as his son. Later republican jurisprudence would have been content with *in iure cessio*, but the pedantic jurisprudence of earlier times did not dare to eliminate the 'sacred' *patria potestas* without an authorization by the Twelve Tables.

With regard to the conditions of *adoptio* we have again to distinguish between *adrogatio* and *adoptio* in the narrower sense (above, s. 242).

250. Con-*ditions of adrogatio* In the case of *adrogatio*, legal rules did not exist as it was a legislative act (above, s. 244) and the *comitia* were sovereign. Since the decree of the *comitia curiata* had become a mere formality (above, s. 244), it was actually the *pontifex* who decided at his discretion whether he would bring in the motion. Of course some traditional rules were developed from which the pontiffs departed only in case of emergency.

1. The *adoptandus* had to be *sui iuris*. It may be that originally a *homo alieni iuris* could also be adrogated, but since a special form of adoption for a *homo alieni iuris* had been developed, *adrogatio* was confined to *homines sui iuris*.

2. Women could not be adrogated, as we have already

stated above (s. 244); this rule was observed throughout the whole classical period. The important consequence was that a person could not adopt his illegitimate daughter: he could not adrogate her and *adoptio* in the narrower sense did not apply, since an illegitimate child was *sui iuris*.

3. *Impuberes* were not adrogated in republican and early classical times. The pontiffs with a view to guarding *impuberes* from possible disadvantages actually declined to bring in a motion. This, however, was only a pontifical practice so that Antoninus Pius as *pontifex maximus* could make an order by a letter addressed to the pontiffs that an *adrogatio* of an *impubes* might be effected if certain precautions were taken.

4. The *adrogans* had to be *pubes*, but there were no rules as to the difference of age between *adoptans* and *adoptandus* and the former might even be younger than the latter; Cicero's maxim (*De domo sua* 14. 36): 'ut adoptio fili quam maxime veritatem illam suscipiendorum liberorum imitata esse videatur' was certainly not an inviolable principle for the pontiffs. Clodius was older than his *pater adoptans*; indeed he might have been his father, as Cicero (*De domo* 13. 35 *in fine*) observed. This was one of the grounds on which Cicero disputed the validity of the *adrogatio*, but this is as weak as his other arguments (above, s. 246). Such an *adrogatio* was certainly unusual (it is significant that in Clodius' case Julius Caesar was *pontifex maximus*), but it was nevertheless valid.

5. A person who had legitimate children was not debarred from adrogating, though the pontiffs were of course reluctant to bring in a motion in such cases out of regard for the legitimate children. Where the *adoptans* was still of an age to expect legitimate children the pontiffs as a rule declined adrogation, but the fixed age limit of 60 years did not exist in classical times.

6. The *adoptans*, if the pontiffs required it, had to swear on oath that he had good ground for the adrogation (*iusiurandum calumniae*). The formula of the oath was framed by Quintus Mucius Scaevola, but is not preserved to us.

251. Conditions of adoptio (in the narrower sense)   As regards the adoption of a *homo alieni iuris*, the magistrate who had to pronounce his *addictio* in effecting *in iure cessio* might have played a part similar to that of the *pontifex* in the *adrogatio*. However, the magistrates regarded *addictio* in this case as a mere matter of form, leaving the whole business substantially to the discretion of the parties; the reason was certainly that they did not wish to interfere with the *patria potestas* of the father of the *adoptandus*. Thus women as well as men could be adopted, *impuberes* as well as *puberes*. Even slaves could be adopted in republican times, whereas under the Principate the magistrates apparently refused *addictio* in such cases. Finally it was not required that the *adoptans* should be older than the *adoptandus*; the idea of an artificial *imitatio naturae* remained foreign to this kind of adoption.

252. Effect of adrogatio and adoptio   In conclusion it must once more (above, s. 243) be emphasized that the effect of classical *adoptio* was always the creation of *patria potestas* of the *adoptans* over the *adoptandus*. Where the latter was *homo sui iuris* his children in power were now subjected to the *potestas* of the *adoptans*, and where he had a wife *in manu* this *manus* was now transferred to the *pater adoptivus*; his property fell to the *adoptans*.

253. Postclassical law   This archaic and petrified law was drastically reformed in the post-classical period. *Adrogatio* was now effected by *rescriptum principis*; *adoptio* of *homo alieni iuris* by an agreement (of *adoptans*, *adoptandus*, and the father of the latter) in court. *Adrogatio* of women was now at last permitted. The *adoptans* had to be eighteen years older than the *adoptandus*; *adoptio naturam imitatur*, as the compilers declared, remembering Cicero's formula (above, s. 250). *Adrogatio* by imperial rescript was as a rule refused where the *adoptans* was not yet 60 years old. In Justinian's law *adoptio* did not necessarily lead to *patria potestas*; hence women too were now entitled to adopt. By the side of adoption there now existed a special legitimation of illegitimate children by their father. A father might legitimize his children born to his concubine either *per subsequens matrimonium* or *per rescriptum principis*. On the other hand, adoption of an illegitimate child by his father was now prohibited.

SOURCES

s. 241. Read Gai. 1. 55, first sentence; *D.* (2. 4) 5; (1. 6) 6; (1. 5) 12 [*et ideo . . . esse*]; (38. 16) 3. 11–12.

s. 243. Read Gai. 1. 104.

s. 244. Read Cicero, *De lege agrar.* 2. 31; Gai. 1. 97–9, 104; Gellius, 5. 19. 1–10.

s. 248. Read Gai. 1. 100; *Epit. Ulp.* 8. 4.

s. 249. Read Gai. 1. 97–9, 132.

s. 250. 1. Read Gai. 1. 99.

s. 250. 3. Read Gai. 1. 102, first sentence; Gellius, 5. 19. 10.

s. 250. 4. Read Gai. 1. 106 (spurious).

s. 250. 5. Read *D.* (1. 7) 17. 3; Gellius, 5. 19. 5, 6 (cf. Cicero, *De domo* 13. 34 in fine; 14. 36); *D.* (1. 7) 15. 2.

s. 250. 6. Gellius, 5. 19. 6.

s. 251. Read Gai. 1. 100–2; Gellius, 5. 19. 11–14; *Inst. Iust.* (1. 11) 12.

s. 252. Read Gai. 1. 107; Gellius, 18. 6. 9.; Gai. 2. 159 is inaccurate.

BIBLIOGRAPHY

s. 241. Windscheid, *Pand.* i (1906), § 56*b*; Stobbe–Lehmann, *Deutsch. Privatrecht*, iv (1900), 373 ff.; Pollock and Maitland, *History*, ii (1911), 398.

ss. 242 ff. Mommsen, *Staatsrecht*, ii (1887), 37; iii (1887), 36 ff.; Gunnar Bergman, *Beiträge zum röm. Adoptionsrecht* (1912). On *adrogatio libertorum* see Lavaggi, *SD* xii (1946), 115. Cosentini, *Annali Catania*, ii (1948).

s. 243. On *adoptio in fratrem*, see Schulz, *Gedächtnisschrift f. Seckel* (1927), 105; Marongiou, 'L'affratellamento', *St. Solmi*, ii (1941), 261 ff.; see further Cassin, *L'Adoption à Nuzi* (1938), 38, 311.*

s. 244. Mommsen, *Staatsrecht*, ii. 38; iii. 303 f.; Solazzi, *Rend. Lomb.* lxxiv (1940–1), 575 on Gai. 1. 101.*

s. 245. Mommsen, *Staatsrecht*, iii. 39; Lefas, 'L'Adoption testamentaire à Rome', *NRH* xxi (1897), 721 ff.*

s. 246. Mommsen, *Staatsrecht*, ii. 37, n. 3; Rostowzeff, *Tesserarum Urbis Romae et Suburbi Plumbearum Sylloge* (1903), no. 98; *Tesserae plumbeae urbis Romae et suburbi* ed. Rostowzeff (1903), Tab. ii. 17 (picture of a *collegium pontif.* performing an *adrogatio*).

s. 247. Mommsen, *Staatsrecht*, iii. 38; Wissowa, *Religion und Kultus der Römer* (1912), 512.

s. 249. Mommsen, *Staatsrecht*, iii. 36; W. Erbe, *Die Fiducia* (1940), 170 ff.*

s. 250. 3. G. Beseler, 'Die adrogatio impuberis in klassischer Zeit', *Subsiciva* (1929), 1 ff.

s. 253. Windscheid, *Pand.* iii (1906), §§ 522–4; Bergman, l.c. 1 ff.; Castelli, *Scritti giur.* (1923), 165 ff. (*adrogatio feminarum*), 179 ff., 189 ff.

(*adrogatio per rescriptum*); Monier, *St. Albertoni*, i (1935), 235 ff. (*adoptio plena*); Albertario, 'La donna addottante', *Mnemosyna Pappoulia* (1934), 17 ff. = *AG* cxii (1934); Bellelli, *SD* iii (1937), 140; H. Janeau, *Recherches sur la légitimation en droit romain*; *de l'adrogation des liberi naturales à la légitimation par rescrit du prince* (1947); Lavaggi, 'Una riforma ignorata di Giustiniano. Adrogatio plena e minus plena', *SD* xii (1946), 45 ff.

3. Rights of the paterfamilias over the child's person

254.
Archaic character

The archaic character of the classical *patria potestas* is glaringly revealed by the immense power which the father has over the person of his child *in potestate*. Cicero says (*Pro Plancio* 12.29) that a father has to be revered by his children almost like a god ('quem veretur ut deum, neque enim multo secus est parens liberis'). As Shakespeare, following Cicero, put it (*Midsummer Night's Dream*, 1. i. 46 ff.):

> *Theseus.* What say you, Hermia? be advis'd, fair maid,
> To you, your father should be as a god;
> One that compos'd your beauties, yea, and one
> To whom you are but as a form of wax
> By him imprinted, and within his power
> To leave the figure or disfigure it.

The status of a child in power was actually similar to that of a slave. *Patria potestas* was in no sense a sort of guardianship; it did not cease to exist when the child grew up but remained so long as the father lived, unless he released the child by a special legal act (*emancipatio*). However, this comprehensive and almost unlimited power was not a peculiarity of Roman law. To be sure, Gaius declares (1. 55):

> 'Quod ius proprium civium Romanorum est (fere enim nulli alii sunt homines, qui talem in filios suos habent potestatem, qualem nos habemus) idque divi Hadriani edicto, quod proposuit de his, qui sibi liberisque suis ab eo civitatem Romanam petebant, significatur. [nec me praeterit Galatarum gentem credere in potestate parentum liberos esse.]'

This is true with regard to Hellenistic law, but Gaius had, of course, no knowledge of primitive law. Even a post-classical annotator could add that the law of the *Galatae* knew a similar *potestas*. Actually he had in mind the law of the *Galli* (not of the *Galatae* in Asia Minor to whom St. Paul wrote one of his epistles), remembering Caesar's remark (*Bell. Gall.* 6. 19. 3):

'Viri in uxores sicut in liberos vitae necisque habent potestatem.'

Moreover, Germanic *patria potestas* was no less harsh and rigid than the Roman *potestas*. Thus it is not the unqualified rigour of Roman *patria potestas* which comes as a surprise but rather that it was preserved (with slight mitigations) in classical times in spite of the humanistic movement. This, indeed, needs an explanation, and a reference to the well-known conservatism of Romans does not suffice. It was the true Roman feeling for authority and discipline which inspired the lawyers; the Roman home seemed to them to be the high school of Roman *disciplina* and the unlimited *patria potestas* an indispensable requirement. Moreover, the Roman respect for individual freedom rendered them loath to interfere with the internal management of the Roman home. At all events Roman private law ended at the threshold of the Roman house: 'My home is my castle', or, as Cicero puts it (*In Vatinium* 9. 22), *domus exsilium est.*

Let us now turn to the details.

Domestic discipline lies in the hands of the father and this implies even the right to kill the child in the course of managing domestic affairs. This *potestas vitae necisque* expressly mentioned in the Twelve Tables (iv. 2) seemed to the lawyers the core of Roman *patria potestas*, as the old formula of *adrogatio* (above, s. 244) clearly shows. It was maintained throughout the classical period and even Constantine mentions it as being still in force; eventually it was abrogated by Valentinian and Valens. Occasionally the classical emperors interfered with its exercise. Trajan compelled a father who had chastised his son *contra pietatem* to emancipate him. Hadrian punished a father who had killed his son in hunting (not in the course of a domestic procedure) by *relegatio*. **255. Potestas vitae necisque**

The father had the right to expose or to kill his new-born child and only Valentinian abolished this. **256. New-born children**

Originally the father had the right to sell his child. Where he sold it abroad (*trans Tiberim*, as the old formula put it) it became a slave, but such sales early went out of use, **257. Sale of children** so that Constantine could (erroneously) declare 'that our forefathers never allowed a father to deprive his child of his freedom'. Where a father sold his child within the frontiers of the Roman State the child acquired a special status (*in mancipio est* or *in causa mancipii est*). The child was a free person *quoad ius publicum*, remaining in particular a Roman citizen, but *quoad ius privatum* his status was similar to that of a slave. In the classical period such a sale occurred only in case of *noxae datio* (above, s. 73. 3); apart from this it was only practised *dicis causa*, for example, in effecting adoption of a *homo alieni iuris* (above, s. 249). Thus far *humanitas* was victorious; but in post-classical times the sale of new-born children revived.

258.
Right to betroth children and to give them in marriage
Originally the father had the right to betroth his children and give them in marriage even without their consent. As aforesaid (ss. 183, 186), *humanitas* abolished this right in classical law, the consent of the children being now required. The post-classical period shows again a reaction; the father might betroth his daughter and give her in marriage provided that the husband was not an unworthy person.

259.
Right of dissolving marriage
The father had the right to dissolve the marriage of his children, a right which was abolished only by Pius or Marcus (above, s. 226).

260. Datio tutoris and substitutio pupillaris
The father had the right to appoint a *tutor* or an heir to his children. This will be discussed later (below, ss. 286, 458).

261. The father no tutor legitimus
In conclusion it must be emphasized once more (above, s. 254) that *patria potestas* was not a type of guardianship and that the father must not be regarded as *tutor legitimus* of his child. Hence a *filius impubes* in power was not capable of binding himself by a legal act, even with the father's consent; for there was no such thing as *interpositio auctoritatis patris* (below, s. 302). Still less was the father entitled to act as his child's legal representative.

SOURCES

s. 255. Read *C.Th.* (4. 8) 6, pr. cf. *C. Iust.* (8. 46) 10; *D.* (37. 12) 5, first sentence; (48. 9) 5.

s. 256. Read *C.Th.* (9. 14) 1.

s. 257. Read Gai. 1. 116, 117, 138, 141; even if 1. 141 were spurious (Solazzi, 'Glosse a Gaio I', *St. Riccobono*, i. 164; Beseler, *St. Albertoni*, i. 435), the words *sed ... mancipantur* are substantially classical. *C.* (7. 16) 1; *C. Th.* (4. 8) 6 pr.

s. 261. Read *D.* (45. 1) 141, 2; *Inst. Iust.* (3. 19) 10, last sentence; *D.* (50. 12) 2. 1 [*sine ... auctoritate*]; (37. 1) 7. 2 [*et ...filio*]; [*aut pater*].

BIBLIOGRAPHY

ss. 254 ff. Cornil, 'Contribution à l'étude de la *patria potestas*', *NRH* xxi (1897), 416 ff.; Wenger, 'Hausgewalt und Staatsgewalt im röm. Altertum', *Miscellanea F. Ehrle*, i (1924), 33 ff.; Schulz, *Principles*, 198; Kaser, Z lviii (1938), 62 ff.; Roberti, *St. Albertoni*, i (1935), 259.

s. 254. On Germanic law see A. Heusler, *Institutionen des deutschen Privatrechts*, ii (1886), 431; see further Westrup, *Introduction to Early Roman Law*, iii. 1 (1939), 143 ff., 162 ff.

s. 255. Albanese, 'Note sull' evoluzione del ius vitae ac necis', *Scritti Ferrini*, iii (1948), 343 ff. (not convincing); Volterra, 'Il pretese tribunale domestico in diritto romano', *Riv. It.* 1948, pp. 103 ff.; Düll, Z lxiii (1943), 52 ff.

s. 257. Mommsen, *Schr.* iii. 5 ff.; Pampaloni, *Bull.* xvii (1905), 123 ff.; Steinwenter, *RE* xiv. 1010; Schulz, *Principles*, 199.

s. 261. On the father as the 'natural guardian' of the child see Windscheid–Kipp, *Pand.* iii (1906), p. 62; Lee, *Introduction to Roman-Dutch Law* (1946), 37.

4. *Proprietary incapacity of a child in power*

A child in power, like a slave, could own no property and whatever it acquired fell automatically to the father. It is of course possible that in prehistoric times there was in Rome as elsewhere a house-community, father and children being regarded as co-owners of the property of the house. However, if such a community ever existed, it disappeared early and the classical lawyers have no reminiscence of it. *262. No house-community*

The child in power is incapable of owning property. This dogma completely dominated the minds of the lawyers in the late Republic as well as under the Principate, though it was already out of date at the end of the Republic in that it was in open conflict with the realities of life. The child's proprietary incapacity had become no less than an article of faith for the lawyers and they could at the most reconcile themselves only to half-measures and compromises, which inevitably rendered the law highly complicated; but they *263. Classical dogma and peculium and profecticium*

preferred to accept artificialities rather than abandon the sacred dogma and left the long overdue reform to the post-classical age. Where an adult son no longer lived in the household of his father, the latter could not help granting his son separate property, particularly any property which the son acquired by his own work. The son might manage this separate property (*peculium*, literally 'property in cattle') like an owner and even dispose of it or charge it with his debts, but the father was sole legal owner, and he could deprive the son of his *peculium* at his discretion even if it had been acquired by the son's work (*adimere peculium*). When the father died the *peculium* simply became part of his estate; when the son died he could have no heirs either by will or by intestacy. This artificial and, in its details, intricate institution already existed in republican times.

264. Under the Principate, with its big standing army, the
Peculium system was supplemented by recognizing a special *peculium*
castrense *castrense*. (In contrast to it the *peculium* which we have just mentioned is usually called *peculium profecticium*, but this term is post-Justinianic.) A son in power who joined the army and had to live during his long period of service far from Rome and Italy could not possibly be content with a *peculium profecticium*; hence imperial constitutions began a reform which was carried through by the lawyers. The property which the soldier acquired on service (and, after Severus, donations given to him on account of the service) formed a special property over which the son's control was considerably more complete than over the *peculium profecticium*. The owner of the *peculium castrense* was again the father; so far the orthodox dogma was maintained. The son, however, might manage the property and freely dispose of it not only *inter vivos* but also (in contrast to *peculium profecticium*) by will, and the father was not entitled to deprive him of it (again in contrast to *peculium profecticium*). Thus the ownership of the father was as a rule merely a *nudum ius*, but it became of practical significance (1) When the son ceased to be a soldier, for then *peculium castrense* ceased to exist; it was only Hadrian who extended *peculium castrense* to discharged soldiers (*veterani*); (2) When the

soldier died intestate the property fell to the father *iure peculii* and not to the intestate heirs of the soldier.

This artificial compromise was the most to which the classical lawyers could reconcile themselves. It would have been easy to assign ownership of the *peculium castrense* to the soldier and the lawyers were, from the time of Hadrian, strong enough to force through that reform by imperial constitutions, but their doctrinarian attitude did not allow them so to act.

In the post-classical period the classical law was gradu- **265. Post-classical law** ally reformed and eventually the archaic principle was thrown overboard: in Justinian's law the proprietary capacity of the child in power was at last recognized. The child now became the owner of his acquest, though the father as a rule had the right to manage it and to have a usufruct in it. Property which the child acquired from the father became *peculium profecticium* as in classical law. *Peculium castrense* too still existed and was even supplemented by a *peculium quasi castrense*. To describe this evolution in detail lies outside the scope of this book.

SOURCES

s. 263. Read Gai. 2. 86–7.

s. 264. Read *Epit. Ulp.* 20. 10; *D.* (49. 17) 2; *Inst. Iust.* (2. 12) pr. to *numerantur*.

BIBLIOGRAPHY

ss. 263 ff. G. Mandry, *Das gemeine Familiengüterrecht*, i (1871); ii (1876), out of date but still very valuable; Windscheid, *Pand.* iii (1906), §§ 515 ff.; *Micolier, Pécule et capacité patrimoniale*, ii (1922); Kaser, Z lviii (1938), 85 ff.

s. 263. Albertario, 'Libera administratio peculii', *Studi*, i (1933), 139 ff.; G. Longo, 'Libera administratio peculii', *Bull.* xxxviii (1930), 29 ff.

s. 264. H. Fitting, *Das castrense peculium* (1871); Appleton, *NRH* xxxv (1911), 593 ff.; Albertario, *Studi*, i (1933), 159 ff.; Guarino, 'L'oggetto del castrense peculium', *Bull.* xlviii (1941), 41 ff.

s. 265. Archi, 'In tema di peculio quasi castrense', *St. Besta*, i (1939), 117 ff.

5. *Obligations of a child in power*

266.
Principle
The child's incapacity to own property does not necessarily imply its incapacity to be legally bound. This is easy
to understand, for the child's proprietary incapacity has the
consequence that all acquests of the child automatically fall
to the father, whereas its incapacity to be a debtor could not
have the consequence that the father was bound by the
child's acts. Nevertheless, it seems natural to exempt a
child from obligations if it cannot be the owner of property.
This was indeed the principle of republican and classical
law, but with one important exception.

267.
Liability
for
contracts
1. Originally a child in power could not bind himself by
contracts. In classical law this rule was still in force with
respect to a *filiafamilias*, whereas a son in power was now
capable of binding himself by contract. A son might even
be sued and condemned in a civil procedure, but an execution (including execution on his person; above, s. 43) was
impossible unless he had a *peculium castrense*.

268.
Liability
for delicts
2. Children in power, like slaves, were, *manente potestate*,
not liable for their delicts.

In both cases actions lay against the father.

269.
Actiones
adiecticiae
1. On account of the contractual obligations of a *filiusfamilias* the praetor granted (under certain conditions) the
creditor an action against the father. Let us take the *actio
de peculio* as an example.

> Where a father granted a *peculium profecticium* to his son the former,
> as aforesaid (s. 263), remained the owner of the property. Now suppose
> the son promised somebody by *stipulatio* to pay a sum of 100. The
> creditor might sue the son, but, *durante potestate*, there was no execution.
> Hence the praetor added to this action an action against the father
> (*adiecit actionem*), by which the latter might be condemned up to the
> extent of the *peculium* (*de peculio*). The formula probably ran as follows:
>
> 'Si paret L. Titium, qui in potestate Numerii Negidii est, Aulo
> Agerio centum dare oportere, iudex Numerium Negidium Aulo
> Agerio centum dumtaxat de peculio condemnato', etc.

The praetor's Edict granted several such actions by which,
when the son had bound himself by contract, the creditor
could sue the father. From the time of the Glossators these
actions have been called *actiones adiecticiae qualitatis* or

actiones adiecticiae (*quia adiciuntur actionibus in filium*); on the basis of them the classical lawyers developed a fine but intricate network of rules which we will not describe here.

2. The father was liable for the delicts of his children in power, but this was only a noxal liability which we have already described above (s. 73); the *noxae datus* was now *in causa mancipii* (above, s. 257). *Noxae datio* of a daughter was apparently no longer practised in classical times for reasons of *humanitas*; certainly Gaius mentions only *noxae datio* of a son. 270. Actio noxalis

Actionable obligations between father and child on principle did not exist, but since the second century A.D. a mutual liability for maintenance was recognized by imperial constitutions, *extraordinaria cognitio* being available to enforce these obligations. However, in classical law the father was not yet bound to assign a *dos* to the husband of his daughter. 271. Obligations between father and child

SOURCES

s. 267. Gai. 3. 104; *Fr. Vat.* 99; *D.* (44. 7) 39; (45. 1) 1, 141, 2 [*impubere*].

s. 268. Gai. 4. 77, first sentence. *D.* (44. 7) 14 and (5. 1) 57 are interpolated.

s. 271. Read Gai. 4. 78 to *nasci potest*.

BIBLIOGRAPHY

s. 267. Perozzi, *Ist.* i (1928), 428 f.; Siber, *Röm. Privatrecht* (1928), 310.

s. 268. Siber, *Naturalis obligatio* (1925).

s. 269. Kunkel, §§ 165 ff.; Lenel, *Édict.* (1927), §§ 101 ff.

s. 271. Mandry, l.c. i. 279 ff.; Albertario, *Studi*, i (1933), 251 ff.; Kunkel, § 184. 6; Castelli, *Scritti giur.* (1923), 129 ff.

6. *End of patria potestas*

Patria potestas ended: 272. Termination

1. By the death or *capitis deminutio* (above, s. 123) of either the father or the child; mere absence, however, did not terminate *potestas*.

2. *Potestas* over a daughter ended by her becoming a Vestal virgin and that over a son by his becoming *flamen Dialis*.

3. *Potestas* over a daughter ended by her becoming

subjected to *manus mariti*. Coexistence of *manus* and *potestas* is in itself conceivable but was rejected by the lawyers. The consequence is that when the husband of an *uxor in manu* died, the wife became *sui iuris* and did not return into her father's *potestas*.

4. *Potestas* over a daughter ended by selling her into *causam mancipii*; *potestas* over a son by selling him three times (above, s. 249). Hence after the first and second sale the son was *in causa mancipii* as well as *in potestate patris*. This co-existence of two powers, however, was so little in harmony with classical tendencies that in the only case in which *in causa mancipii esse* meant a real power and not only a formality, viz. in case of *noxae datio* (above, s. 257), the Sabinians asserted that *patria potestas* over a son ended at the first sale (Gai. 4. 79).

5. Finally *patria potestas* ended by *adoptio* and *emancipatio* since both were effected by selling the child *in causam mancipii* (a son three times). As regards emancipation, the son was as a rule remancipated to the father by the 'purchaser' after the third *mancipatio*. The father then set his son free by *manumissio*, whereby the father became the patron of his emancipated son (*parens manumissor*).

273. Legal effects   As regards the legal effects of the termination of *patria potestas* there were three possibilities:

1. Either the child became subjected to a new *potestas* or to *manus*. In case of adoption the child was now *in potestate patris adoptivi*. Where the child was *in potestate* of his grandfather and the latter died, he became subjected to the *potestas* of his father if the latter was still alive and not emancipated by the grandfather.

2. Or the child was now free from *potestas* and acquired, as the Romans put it, *potestas* over himself, *in suam tutelam et potestatem pervenit*; it is now *sui iuris* (= *suae potestatis*).

3. Or none of these cases happened, viz. if the son died or suffered *capitis deminutio maxima* or *media* (above, s. 123).

274. Liability for contracts and delicts   In conclusion we will add a few remarks on the liability for contracts effected and delicts committed during the former *potestas*.

1. As aforesaid (above, s. 267) a *filiusfamilias* (but not a *filiafamilias*) was liable for contractual obligations. Where the son became *sui iuris*, he could be sued for them (if the obligations were extinguished by *capitis deminutio* they might be restored by *in integrum restitutio*) and even an execution was now possible; but execution on the person was sometimes barred (so-called *beneficium competentiae*; below, s. 793).

2. Where a child in power (son or daughter) committed a delict it was, as aforesaid (above, s. 268), not liable *durante potestate*, but it became liable when it became *sui iuris* on the strength of the rule *noxa caput sequitur*.

3. The *actiones adiecticiae* (above, s. 269) against the former *paterfamilias* were not affected by the end of *potestas* but in case of the *actio de peculio* there was a time limit (*actio de peculio annalis*; see above, ss. 82 ff.).

4. The *actio noxalis* was extinguished with the end of *potestas*; when the child entered a new *potestas* the action was now available against the new *paterfamilias*: *noxa caput sequitur*.

SOURCES

s. 272. Read Gai. 1. 127, first sentence; 1. 128; *D.* (23. 2) 10, entirely spurious; Gai. 1. 130; 1. 136; 1. 132; 4. 79 (Gai. 1. 138 is inaccurate); 1. 134.

s. 273. Read Gai. 1. 127.

s. 274. Read *D.* (14. 5) 5 pr.; Gai. 4. 77.

BIBLIOGRAPHY

s. 272. W. Erbe, *Die Fiducia* (1940), 170 ff.; Lévy–Bruhl, *Nouvelles Études* (1947), 80 ff.; Goethe, *Faust* I: 'Du must es dreimal sagen'; Grimm, *Deutsche Rechtsaltertümer*, i (1899), 286.*

s. 274. Mandry, l.c. i. 414 ff. On *beneficium competentiae* see Lenel, *Edict.* (1927), 278; A. Levet, *Le Bénéfice de compétence* (1927), 61 ff.

7. *Relations between parents and children apart from patria potestas*

i. *Legitimate children*

The child is bound to show *obsequium* and *pietas* towards his parents. This leads to the following legal rules:

275.
Obsequium
and pietas

1. The child must not summon his parents (mother as well as father) to court without the permission of the praetor.

2. The child must not bring *actiones famosae* against his parents (above, s. 79).

3. The child must not effect execution on the person of either parent (so-called *beneficium competentiae*, below, s. 793).

276. Education The father's right to educate the child (in so far as it was *not* in his power) is apparently not mentioned in our sources. As regards the right of the mother, Emperor Pius stated that she might keep the child herself if it was not well looked after at the father's house. In actual fact education lay to a wide extent in the hands of the mother, particularly after the father's death, but legally she needed the permission of him who had the right to educate the child, in particular the permission of the guardian.

277. Mainten- ance Claims for maintenance between parents and children were recognized from the second century A.D.

ii. *Illegitimate children*

278. Ille- gitimate children The relationship between illegitimate children (*spurii, vulgo quaesiti*) and their mother was apparently the same as that between legitimate children and their mother. A legal relationship between the child and its father was in principle not recognized; in particular the father was not bound to maintain his child. Justinian finally made the father liable to maintain his child born to his concubine. Hadrian granted *bonorum possessio ab intestato* to the illegitimate children of soldiers (below, s. 415). Evidently the illegitimate child was not as yet a social problem. It is significant that Augustus barred illegitimate children from his register of births; it was only opened to them by Marcus (above, s. 126), and even the so-called 'alimentary foundations' paid but little regard to them. In the foundation mentioned in the beginning of the tablet of Velleia support was given to 245 legitimate boys, 34 legitimate girls, 1 illegitimate boy, and 1 illegitimate girl. The classical lawyers

hardly ever considered the problem seriously which evidently lay entirely beyond their horizon. Justinian's statement (*Novella* 89 praef.) is perfectly true: 'Naturalium liberorum nomini in legislatione Romana olim opera data non erat neque ulla ei humanitas favebat, sed tamquam peregrinum et plane alienum a re publica existimabatur.'

SOURCES

s. 276. Read *D.* (43. 30) 1. 3 and 3. 5.

s. 277. Read *C.* (5. 25) 1–4.

s. 278. Hadrian's *epistula*: *FIRA* i, no. 78 with Berger, *Journal of Juristic Papyrology*, i (1945), 28; Foundation of Velleia: Bruns, *Fontes*, no. 145a; *FIRA* iii, no. 116.

BIBLIOGRAPHY

s. 275. Bonfante, *Corso*, i (1925), 278.

s. 276. Taubenschlag, *Law of Greco-Roman Egypt* (1944), 113 ff.; Jolowicz, *JRS* xxxvii (1947), 87.

s. 277. Albertario, *Studi*, i (1933), 251 ff.; Taubenschlag, *St. Riccobono*, i (1936), 507 ff.; *Law of Greco-Roman Egypt*, 107, 114.

s. 278. E. Weiss, Z xlix (1929), 260 ff.; *PW* iiiA, 1889; H. J. Wolff, 'The background of the post-classical legislation on illegitimacy', *Seminar*, iii (1945), 21.

CHAPTER V
GUARDIANSHIP

1. *Introduction*

279.
Evaluation

THE classical law of guardianship does not deserve the adverse criticism pronounced by scholars without a full knowledge of what was really classical law. Taken as a whole it is far from being a contemptible achievement; it is carefully and cleverly elaborated; it pays regard to various interests; it is humane, liberal, and non-bureaucratic: These are the prominent features of the law. It is governed by three leading principles.

280.
Principles

1. The classical conception of guardianship is that of disinterested care for a person needing protection. Originally in Roman law the guardian exercised an authority which was granted to him in his own interest and in that of the family, but this principle had already lost the day in the late Republic, and in classical law only a few survivals remind us of the primitive *munt* (to use the term of Teutonic law) which once the Roman guardian also possessed. At quite an early period Servius Sulpicius (consul 51 B.C.) defined *tutela* as 'vis ac potestas in capite libero ad tuendum eum qui propter aetatem sexumve sua sponte se defendere nequit'. The important part of this definition is that which contains the *differentia specifica* (*ad tuendum* rel.); *patria potestas* is also *vis ac potestas in capite libero*, but it is a power wielded in self-interest, whereas classical *tutela* is of a disinterested character.

2. The classical guardian is a private person and not a public servant; he discharges his functions in principle without interference from governmental authority. This non-bureaucratic system is in conformity with that liberalism which dominates Roman private law. As a rule the guardian is a near relative or a friend of the family; the idea of a professional guardian was not contemplated by the lawyers since the illegitimate child was not yet a social problem (above, s. 278).

3. There is a court for the protection of wards which has as its primary duty to provide a guardian wherever one is required by law.

It is true that the classical law of guardianship shows several vital defects. Some parts have archaic features, especially the *tutela mulierum*, which the classical lawyers unfortunately failed to abolish. Another serious fault is the exclusion of women from guardianship, though they are obviously the born guardians of *impuberes*. Thus a widow could not be the guardian of her children, and as there was no *materna potestas* (above, s. 240), another person had to be guardian. Finally classical law, as regards legal technique, was too complicated. The different strata—law of the Twelve Tables and of later statutes, praetorian and consular law, law of *senatusconsulta* and imperial constitutions —needed to be welded together. These defects, however, were to a considerable extent remedied in the postclassical period. On the whole the law of the *Corpus iuris* was greatly superior to medieval Germanic law and it is small wonder that in European legal development since the thirteenth century Roman influence is discernible everywhere.

Classical legal language has no general term for 'guardian'; it distinguishes between *tutor* (protector) and *tutela* on the one hand and *curator* (caretaker) and *cura* on the other. In the following exposition these two institutions have to be carefully distinguished.

It is not an easy task to ascertain the classical law of guardianship from available sources, although the lengthy description given in Gaius' *Institutes* is preserved to us almost complete. The different sources of classical law— *leges, senatusconsulta, constitutiones principum*—are not in our hands; quotations often lack accuracy and important details may have been lost by post-classical abbreviation of classical texts. Moreover, the post-classical period reformed the classical law to a considerable extent and this inevitably led to a mutilation of classical texts by interpolations. Thus it is only by careful critical examination of the texts that the classical law can be restored. In the course of

281. Terminology

282. State of sources and modern research

the last fifty years a considerable part of this work has been performed, especially by Siro Solazzi in numerous books and papers. In the following account we confine ourselves to the main features of the classical law of guardianship.

SOURCES

s. 280. 1. Read *D.* (26. 1) 1 pr. The text is corrupt (the compilers have eliminated *tutela mulierum*) and the original cannot be restored with certainty. The words *ad tuendum . . . nequit* must not be cancelled since that would render the definition trivial, *patria potestas* being also a *potestas in capite libero.* See Kübler, *St. Besta,* i (1939), 75; Z lix (1939), 562; H. J. Wolff, *St. Riccobono,* iii (1936), 461, n. 124; Beseler, *Scritti Ferrini,* iii (1948), 284.

BIBLIOGRAPHY

ss. 279 ff. Rudorff, *Das Recht. der Vormundschaft,* i (1832); ii (1833); iii (1834); Windscheid, *Pand.* iii (1906), 113 ff. Modern literature: Bonfante, *Corso,* i (1925), 403 ff.; E. Sachers, *PW* viiA, 1497 ff. (a very useful survey with full references); R. Taubenschlag, *The Law of Greco-Roman Egypt* (1944), 119 ff.

s. 280. 1. Solazzi, *Istituti tutelari* (1929), 1 ff.; A. Heusler, *Institutionen des deutschen Privatrechts,* ii (1886), 480 ff.; Pollock and Maitland, *History,* i (1911), 323; ii (1911), 444; H. Mitteis, Z (germ. Abt.), lxiii (1943), 179 ff.; Molitor, Z (germ. Abt.), lxiv (1944), 112 ff.

s. 281. On the Roman goddess *Tutela* see *PW* viiA. 1599 ff.

2. *Impuberes*

283.
Pupilli

Impuberes who are not under one of the three classical kinds of power (*potestas, manus, mancipium*) need and receive a guardian, who is called a *tutor.* The term *pupillus* ('little doll' from Lat. *pupus*) is used sometimes synonymously with *impubes,* sometimes to designate an *impubes* who has, or should have, a *tutor.*

284.
Puberty

Impuberes are in classical law young persons who have not yet reached the age of puberty. Girls become legally *puberes* at the end of their 12th year. In the case of boys puberty was according to Roman custom a matter of recognition by the family and was celebrated by a family feast at which the boy donned the *toga virilis*; sometimes he was enrolled in a public register. At the end of the Republic there arose a tendency to fix puberty of boys at the end of their 14th year and this was adopted by the school of the Proculians, whereas the Sabinians defended the old custom. From the second century A.D. there existed a third doctrine to the effect that a boy was legally *pubes* when he was both 14 years old and actually *pubes*. Apparently these conflicting opinions had supporters in the law-schools down to Justinian, but the practice was evidently to follow the third doctrine (even the Sabinian Gaius was sometimes content with 14 years); eventually the Proculian doctrine was confirmed by Justinian.

SOURCES

s. 283. Read Gai. 1. 142, 189.

s. 284. Read Gai. 1. 196; 1. 40; 2. 112, 113; *Epit. Ulp.* 11. 28; cf. *lex Urson.* cap. 98; *lex Pap. Pop., Epit. Ulp.* 16. 1*a*; *C. Th.* (2. 17) 1. 1 (N.B. *viros non sera pubertate*); *C. Iust.* (5. 60) 3; *Inst. Iust.* (1. 22) pr.; *Michigan Papyri*, vii (1947), no. 433: registration of boys who had assumed the *toga virilis*.

BIBLIOGRAPHY

ss. 283, 284. Pernice, *Labeo*, i (1873), 206 ff.; Rotondi, *Scritti giur.*, iii (1922), 488.

3. *The three kinds of tutela impuberum*

The classical law distinguishes between three kinds of *tutela impuberum* according to the mode in which it originates: {285. Three kinds of tutela impuberum terminology}

i. *Tutela testamentaria*; here the guardian is appointed by the will of the child's father.

ii. *Tutela legitima*; here the guardian is appointed directly by the Twelve Tables.

iii. *Tutela decretalis*; here the guardian is appointed by the decree of a magistrate.

Tutela testamentaria (*tutor testamentarius*) and *tutela decretalis* (*tutor decretalis*) are not classical terms but they are indispensable for the following discussion. Justinian termed '*tutor dativus*' a *tutor* appointed by a magistrate (*C. Iust.* 1. 3. 51 pr.; never in *Inst. Iust.*) an infelicitous terminology which should be avoided altogether. Gaius (1. 154) styles a *tutor mulieris* appointed by name in her husband's will '*tutor dativus*' (in contrast to '*tutor optivus*', see below, s. 314). The post-classical author of the *Epit. Ulp.* misunderstanding Gaius called any *tutor* appointed by will '*tutor dativus*' (*Epit. Ulp.* 11. 14).

The mode of origin determined fundamentally the character of the resulting *tutela*, which therefore has to be described in close connexion with the different modes of origin.

i. *Tutela impuberum testamentaria*

286.   The right of the father to appoint a *tutor* by will for his children in power is founded by the lawyers on the Twelve Tables; the mother has no such right, since there is no *materna potestas* (above, s. 240). The father must not interfere with another person's *potestas*. Suppose A has in his power both his son B and his grandson C (son of B). A must not appoint a *tutor* for C since at A's death C falls into the power of B (above, s. 273). The father has to apply a certain formula, taking as a model either the formula of the *legatum per vindicationem* (below, s. 555) or that of the *heredis institutio* (below, s. 443). The appointed person becomes *tutor* automatically at the moment at which the will comes into force, neither confirmation by an authority nor acceptance by the appointed person being required. The latter, however, is entitled to reject the guardianship (*se abdicare tutela*); so far this kind of *tutela* has preserved the character of an archaic *munt* (above, s. 280), as it entailed a right, but not a corresponding duty, to act as a *tutor*. From the time of Claudius the *tutor testamentarius* was bound to discharge his functions and the former *ius se abdicandi* was replaced by a mere *ius se excusandi* (below, s. 292).

Tutela impuberum testamentaria

ii. *Tutela impuberum legitima*

287.   In default of a *tutor testamentarius* the Twelve Tables entrusted *tutela* to the person who would be the nearest male heir of the ward according to that code (*heres legitimus*; see below, ss. 389 ff.).

Tutela impuberum legitima

> English and French jurisprudence has strongly censured this rule on the ground that to appoint the nearest heir of the ward as *tutor* means *quasi agnum committere lupo ad devorandum*. However, the fear that the presumptive heir of the ward might misuse his position as a guardian to murder the ward in order to become his heir is actually unfounded and apparently was called forth only by Persius, 2. 12. We meet the Roman rule in continental common law as well as in other laws and the English misgivings have (as far as we know) proved unwarranted.

The *tutor legitimus* became automatically a *tutor* at the moment at which the need for guardianship arose. In contrast to the *tutor testamentarius* he never had a right to abdicate, though he might transfer *tutela* to another person by *in iure cessio*. This rule certainly originated when *tutela decretalis* was not yet known, or at least not yet practised as a matter of course. As the law of that period aimed at providing a *tutor* in every case, it could not allow the *tutor legitimus* to abdicate but only to convey *tutela* to another person. If he could find no such person he had to remain *tutor*, which implied no hardship since he was not bound to act as a *tutor*, *tutela legitima* being—as originally the *tutela testamentaria* also—as yet a mere *munt* (above, s. 286). This archaic *tutela legitima* was, unlike *tutela testamentaria*, preserved throughout the classical period; apparently the *tutor legitimus* had still no *ius se abdicandi*. It would have been in harmony with the tendencies of the age to grant him this right in order to make room for the more modern *tutela decretalis*, but apparently this did not happen. Nor had the *tutor legitimus* a *ius se excusandi*, since he was not bound to discharge his functions.

The *tutela legitima adgnatorum* over female wards was abolished by Claudius, so that only the *tutela legitima* of the patron over his *liberta* remained (below, s. 395). Further, the *tutor legitimus* over male wards lost (we do not know when) the right to convey *tutela* to another person by *in iure cessio*.

iii. *Tutela impuberum decretalis*

In default of a *tutor testamentarius* or *legitimus* the *impubes* was by the law of the Twelve Tables left without a *tutor*. We do not know whether in such cases the consuls and later the *praetor urbanus* interfered and appointed a *tutor*, but it seems hardly credible. It has been asserted that such appointments must have been made since the *pupillus* could not have been left unprotected. However, in medieval Germany down to the thirteenth century numerous minors were actually without guardians and it is not at all improbable that the same thing occurred in Rome in early republican times.

288.
Tutela
decretalis
before the
lex Atilia

289. Lex
Atilia

Whatever the earlier position may have been a *lex Atilia* ordered the *praetor urbanus* to appoint a *tutor* when an *impubes* had neither a *tutor testamentarius* nor a *tutor legitimus*. A guardian appointed in this way was called *tutor Atilianus*.

The *lex Atilia* was probably a plebiscite and Atilius a *tribunus plebis*. The date of the statute is unknown, but since Livy in his account of the *senatusconsultum de Baccanalibus* (186 b.c.) mentions a *tutor Atilianus* (39. 9. 7) the *lex Atilia* must be earlier than 186; it is well known that Livy's report is based on very good sources.

290. Lex
Iulia et
Titia

A *lex Iulia et Titia* (31 b.c.) extended the *lex Atilia* to the provinces, authorizing the provincial governors to appoint a *tutor*.

To-day, in view of the papyri, there can be no doubt that the formula '*lex Iulia et Titia*' means a single, consular *lex* moved by the consuls Iulius and Titius, and not two statutes (a *lex Iulia* and a *lex Titia*). In 31 b.c. Octavianus (since his adoption by C. Iulius Caesar his proper name was C. Iulius Caesar) was consul for the third time; in the same year M. Titius L. F. was *consul suffectus* from May to October. Thus 31 b.c. has to be taken as the date of the statute. That the *lex* is sometimes cited shortly as *lex Titia* or *lex Iulia* is not surprising. Theoph. *Paraphras.* 1, 20 pr. is sheer fantasy.

291. Lex
Salpensana
and lex
Ursonensis

Neither the *lex Atilia* nor the *lex Iulia Titia* is in our hands, though a summary of their contents is given by Gaius (1. 185). Fortunately, however, we possess ch. 29 of the *lex Salpensana*—the statute of the Latin *municipium Salpensa* in Spain granted under Domitianus—which deals with *tutoris datio*. Moreover, the corresponding ch. 109 of the *lex coloniae Genetivae Iuliae sive Ursonensis* published after Caesar's death by Antonius has been recently found. Both statutes apparently took the *Lex Atilia* as a model. With the help of these materials we are able to ascertain the rules given by the *lex Atilia* and the *lex Iulia Titia*.

292. The
law of the
leges Atilia
and Iulia
Titia

(*a*) A *tutor* has to be appointed *cui tutor non erit incertusve erit*, i.e. where a *pupillus* either has no *tutor* or it is legally uncertain whether he has one or not (cf. Gai. 1. 187).

(*b*) A *tutor* is only appointed if somebody (*quivis ex populo*) makes an application (*postulare*), proposing a certain person (*nominare*).

(*c*) According to the *lex Atilia* the *tutor* has to be appointed by the *praetor urbanus de maioris partis tribunorum plebis sententia*; according to the *lex Iulia Titia* by the provincial governor. The magistrate has to pronounce his decree *causa cognita*, probably—as it is so stated in the *lex Salpensana*—within a space of ten days.

(*d*) The form of the decree is shown by Egyptian documents. The magistrate declared *illum tutorem do*, adding *quo ne ab iusto tutore tutela abeat*. The meaning of the last clause, which follows exactly the wording of the *leges* (as both *lex Salpensana* and *lex Ursonensis* show), was that if a tutor *testamentarius* or *legitimus* already existed he was not deprived of the *tutela* by this appointment. In such cases the decree was valid, since otherwise no one would have done any business with a *tutor decretalis*, but the appointed *tutor* (a *tutor adiunctus*) was dismissed as soon as the magistrate realized that a *tutor testamentarius* or *legitimus* existed.

(*e*) *Tutor decretalis* 'tam iustus tutor esto quam si is adgnatus proximus tutor esset', i.e. as if he were a *tutor legitimus*. In an Egyptian document the magistrate declared accordingly, *M. Longum legitimum tutorem do*. Why did the statute not simply declare *iustus tutor esto*? Because at that time the *tutor testamentarius* still had the *ius se abdicandi* (above, s. 286) and the legislator did not wish to grant this right to the *tutor decretalis*. It is true that the position of a *tutor decretalis* was in spite of the words of the statute not quite identical with that of a *tutor legitimus*. The latter had no *ius abdicandi*, but on the other hand he was not bound to discharge his functions (above, s. 287). The *tutor decretalis*, however, was from the very beginning bound to act as a *tutor*, for the purpose of the appointment was of course not to bestow a mere title. It was for this reason that a person whom the magistrate intended to appoint might excuse himself (*se excusare*) by bringing forward certain grounds (*causae excusationis*) which were examined by the magistrate and either accepted or rejected by him. Even an appointed *tutor* might plead such an excuse, and if the magistrate approved it he was dismissed.

Both the *lex Atilia* and *lex Iulia Titia* remained in force throughout the classical period; the report given in

293.
Classical
magistrates

Justinian's *Institutes* (1. 20. 3) is wrong, as Egyptian documents show. However, in addition to the *praetor urbanus* the consuls were (from the time of Claudius) competent to appoint a *tutor*. Moreover, there was (from the time of Marcus) a special *praetor tutelarius* (*tutelaris* is a post-classical term); the *Italici iuridici* too were made competent by Marcus. In the Latin *municipia* (above, s. 134) the *duoviri* were entitled to appoint a *tutor*, whereas in the Roman *municipia* the municipal magistrates were as a rule restricted to making proposals; but in Urso (a *colonia civium Romanorum*) the *duoviri* were competent to appoint a *tutor*, as the newly found fragments plainly show. In the provinces the governors might delegate the power of appointment to other authorities. The details belong rather to the history of administrative law than to the law of guardianship.

294.
Procedure before the magistrates
In the course of the classical period rules governing the procedure before the magistrates were gradually developed, especially concerning the *ius se excusandi*. Although the fine network of these rules is interesting in many respects, we must leave it aside here.

295.
Tutela decretalis outside the scope of the leges Atilia and Iulia Titia
The *lex Atilia* as well as the *lex Iulia Titia* ordered the magistrates to appoint a *tutor* only in default of a testamentary or a statutory guardian, but *tutela decretalis* was not confined to such cases; the maxim *tutorem habenti tutor non datur* is not classical. In republican times the *praetor urbanus* regarded himself as competent to appoint a *tutor* although a *tutor legitimus* or *testamentarius* already existed, but we know of only one situation in which he used this power, viz. where the *tutor* wished to sue the ward or vice versa. Such a *tutor* was called *tutor praetorius*, since he was appointed by the *praetor* without any statutory authorization. In classical times the magistrates were not competent to appoint a *tutor* without being authorized by *lex*, *senatusconsultum*, or *constitutio principis*. Thus, according to a *senatusconsultum*, the *praetor urbanus* might appoint a *tutor* when the *tutor testamentarius* had been removed from office or excused. The *tutor legitimus* was not allowed to come in since the testator by his appointment had plainly shown that he did not wish him to become *tutor*; besides we have

already observed the tendency to push the old-fashioned *tutela legitima* into the background (above, s. 287). This same tendency led to the confirmation of an invalid appointment by will. Where a father had made a valid will containing an invalid *datio tutoris* (because the father had failed to observe the required form) the appointment might be confirmed by the magistrates on the strength of imperial constitutions. This *tutor* was in truth a *tutor decretalis* and not a *tutor testamentarius*, but he eliminated the *tutor legitimus* like a *tutor testamentarius*. Though the *tutor legitimus* was not deprived of his *tutela*, he was not allowed to exercise the power of administration; this was permitted only to the *tutor confirmatus*. The cases in which confirmation was permissible were not determined by any abstract rule. The emperors allowed confirmation in individual cases, and magistrates together with the lawyers generalized and supplemented the imperial decisions by interpretation.

SOURCES

s. 285. *Tutela legitima* and *tutor legitimus* are classical terms: Gai. 1. 155, 165. The terms *tutela testamentaria* and *tutor testamentarius* never occur in Gai. *Inst.* (cf. Gai. 1. 155 *tutor testamento datus*); the passages in the *Digest* which contain them (*Voc. Iur. Rom.* v. 1021. 14 ff.) are spurious. *Tutor dativus* occurs in the *Digest* only once (*Voc. Iur. Rom.* ii. 18. 24): *D.* (46. 6) 7, interpolated.

s. 286. Read *Epit. Ulp.* 11. 14; Gai. 1. 144, 146, 189. Form of *datio tutoris*: Gai. 1. 149; 2. 289; cf. Gai. 2. 117, 193. *Abdicatio* and *excusatio*: BGU 1113, l. 8 (Mitteis, *Chrest.* no. 169; *FIRA* iii, no. 31 with a Latin translation); Gai. 1. 182 (N.B. referring to *tutela testamentaria* only); *Fr. Vat.* 223 i.f., cf. *FIRA* iii, no. 30 (*excusatio tutoris testamentarii*).

s. 287. Read Gai. 1. 155, 164, 165. *In iure cessio*: Gai. 1. 168, 169; *Epit. Ulp.* 11. 17 (referring to *tutela mulierum* only). *Lex Claudia*: Gai. 1. 157, 171.

ss. 289, 290. Read Gai. 1. 185.

s. 291. Ch. 29 of the *lex Salp.* (Bruns, *Fontes*, no. 30; *FIRA* i, no. 23) is difficult to understand since its author clumsily re-elaborated a model (*lex Atilia* or *lex Urson.*); see O. Gradenwitz, 'Die Stadtrechte von Urso, Salpensa, Malaca' (*Heidelberg. SB*, Phil. hist. Kl. 1920. 17. Abhandl.); F. Schulz, *St. Solazzi* (1948), 451 ff. Engl. translation: Hardy, *Three Spanish Charters* (1912), 83 ff. For the new fragments of the *lex Ursonensis* see d'Ors, 'Los bronces de El Rubrio', *Emerita, Boletin de linguistica y filologia class.* ix (1941), 138 ff.; J. Mallon, 'Les Fragments de El Rubrio et leur appartenance à la lex Coloniae Genetivae Iuliae', *Emerita*, xii

(1944), 1 ff.; the texts were reprinted in *Rev. Archaeol.* xxvi (1946), nos. 120–2 and *Année épigr.* See Schulz, l.c.

s. 292. Read *P. Oxy.* iv 720 (= *FIRA* iii, no. 24); further, the document published by Sanders, *Z. f. d. neutestamentliche Wissenschaft* xxxvii (1938, published 1939), pp. 191 ff. (Sanders's remarks on *legitimus* are wrong) = *L'Année épigr.* 1947, no. 12; cf. *FIRA* iii, no. 25. These documents deal with *tutor mulierum*, but the form of a *datio tutoris impuberum* was the same.

s. 294. Read *Fr. Vat.* 149, 150 (cf. *D.* 27. 1, 6. 2 and 12 with Schulz, *History*, 273, n. 12); *Fr. Vat.* 186, [*vel . . . curator*], 189.

s. 295. *D.* (26. 1) 6. 2; Gai. 1. 184; 1. 182 (referring only to *tutela testamentaria*); *D.* (26. 3) 1 pr. § 1.

BIBLIOGRAPHY

s. 285. Solazzi, *Studi sulla tutela*, i (1925), 1 ff.

s. 286. Solazzi, *Istituti tutelari* (1929), 12 ff., 155 ff.; Bonfante, *Corso*, I (1925), 427; Beseler, Z l (1930), 443 (not acceptable); Sachers, *PW* viiA. 1508, 1532; Lévy–Bruhl, *St. Solazzi* (1948), 318 ff.; Guarino, ibid. 31. On *BGU* 1113 see Solazzi, 'L'abdicatio tutelae e BGU 1113', *Rend. Lomb.* xlviii (1915), 985 ff.*

s. 287. Sachers, l.c. 1505, 1533, 1534; Solazzi, *La legge delle XII Tavole sulla tutela* (1928). On the English criticism see *Leges Henrici*, 70, 19; Liebermann, *Gesetze der Angelsachsen* i (1903), 589 with ref.; Fortescue, *De laudibus legum Angliae* (ed. Chrimes, *Cambridge Studies in English Legal History*, 1942), c. 44; Coke, *Inst.* i. 88*b* (ed. 1794, i, s. 123); Blackstone, *Commentaries*, bk. i, ch. 17, no. 1; Jolowicz, *JRS* xxxvii (1947), 88.

s. 288. Mitteis, *RP* i (1908), 41 n. 4 (wrong); A. Heusler, *Institutionen des deutschen Privatrechts*, ii (1886), 484.

s. 289. Kübler, 'Privatrechtliche Competenzen der Volkstribunen in der Kaiserzeit', *Festschrift zu O. Hirschfelds 60. Geburtstag* (1903), 51; Solazzi, 'La lex Atilia nel Digesto', *Studi sulla tutela*, i (1925), 29 ff.; Sachers, l.c. 1512.

s. 290. On the modes of citing Roman *leges* see Mommsen, *Röm. Staatsrecht*, iii (1887), 315; on Octavianus' third consulate see Fitzler–Seeck, *PW* x. 327; on Titius' consulate see Hanslik, *PW* viA, 1561; *ILS* 891, 6123. On the whole question whether *lex Iulia et Titia* means a single *lex* or two *leges* see Taubenschlag, *PW* xii. 2392; *Law of Greco-Roman Egypt* (1944), 131; Biondi in *Acta divi Augusti*, i (1945), 199, with full references.

s. 291. On cap. 29 of the 1. *Salp.* see Mommsen, *Schr.* i (1905), 330; on the *lex Ursonensis* Schulz, *History*, 88.

s. 292a. Mommsen, l.c. 233.

s. 292d. Mommsen, l.c. 233 (wrong).

s. 293. P. Joers, *Untersuchungen zur Gerichtsverfassung der röm. Kaiserzeit* (1892), 4 ff., 31 ff., 66 ff.; Solazzi, 'Console e pretore urbano nella datio tutoris', *AG* lxxxv (1921), 279 ff.; *Istituti tutelari* (1929), 54 ff.; Sachers, *PW* viiA, 1513 ff.; D'Ors, *Emerita*, ix (1941), 145, with references; K. Schneider, *PW* vii 1608; on the term *praetor tutelarius* see Schulz, *History*, 247.

s. 294. Sachers, l.c. 1534 ff.

s. 295. Beseler, Z l (1930), 443; Solazzi, 'Sulla regola *tutorem habenti tutor dari non potest*', *Rend. Lomb.* 1919, pp. 227 ff.; 'La conferma del tutore', *Rend. Lomb.* 1920, pp. 359 ff.; *Istituti tutelari* (1929), 54 ff.; Sachers, l.c. 1511 f., 1520 f., 1524.

4. *Functions of the tutor impuberis*

The *tutor testamentarius* as well as the *tutor legitimus* originally discharged his duties at his discretion without being controlled or directed by a magistrate. Under the *lex Atilia*, however, the praetor certainly began to control the *tutor decretalis* whenever he received complaints about the latter and eventually he no doubt acted similarly towards the testamentary and statutory guardian. In the classical period rules were developed concerning *tutela* which the *tutor* had to observe, but their number apparently remained small and the control of the magistrates slight, in harmony with the classical liberalistic tendency to give the *tutor* a free hand. It was the bureaucratic tendency of the post-classical age which gradually restricted the freedom of the *tutor*.

296. Freedom of the guardian

The *tutor* has a legal power over the ward's person, but it differs widely from *patria potestas*. According to classical usage, a ward *in tutela* is not *in potestate* but rather *sui iuris* (= *suae potestatis*; see above, s. 273), whereas the republican lawyers had no scruple about calling *tutela* a *potestas* (above, s. 280). The *tutor* has no *potestas vitae necisque* and no *ius vendendi* (cf. above, ss. 255 f.); he cannot give the ward *in adoptionem* nor can he even consent to an *adrogatio* of the ward. Thus the power over the ward's person implies only the right to determine the ward's dwelling place, his education and maintenance. Complaints about this part of the *tutor's* administration might be brought before the magistrate, but it is significant that the title of the *Digest* dealing with this subject (27. 2) contains to a considerable extent post-classical material (Fr. 1 was originally not concerned with *tutela* at all) and that the corresponding titles

297. Guardian's power over the ward's person

of the *Codex Iustinianus* (5. 49 and 5. 50) contain only a few rescripts, all belonging to the third century. Further, the *tutor* has to administer the ward's property according to the following rules.

298.   1. The *tutor legitimus* was, as aforesaid (above, s. 286), not bound to take the administration upon himself. If he wished to take it into his hands, the consuls (above, s. 293) required, before admitting him to the administration, that he should guarantee the safety of the property by a *cautio rem pupilli salvam fore*. The praetor's Edict did not demand this *cautio* of the tutor *legitimus*, which implies that it was the consuls and not the *praetor urbanus* who first imposed the *cautio* on the *tutor legitimus*; but the other magistrates who were entrusted with the control of *tutela* (above, s. 293) seem to have followed the example of the consuls. No such *cautio* was required of the *tutor testamentarius*, since he was the trusted nominee of the father ('fides eius et diligentia ab ipso testatore probata est'). However, the praetor declared in his Edict that when the father had appointed several tutors the administration would be granted to him who was prepared to provide the *cautio*. The tutor *decretalis* was as a rule also exempt from the *cautio*, since the magistrate had ample opportunity to examine the trustworthiness of the tutor before appointing him. The *lex Atilia* (as the *lex Salpensana* shows) was therefore silent upon the *cautio*.

299.   2. The *tutor* is entitled to administer and dispose of the ward's property at his discretion, *domini loco* (provided that he was admitted to the administration by the magistrate). he might alienate property of the ward by *mancipatio* as well as by *traditio*: Mitteis's opinion that he was excluded from *mancipatio* is certainly erroneous. He might also collect any money which was owed to the ward and sue the ward's debtors. Fixed rules of general application to be observed by the *tutor* apparently did not yet exist; the lawyers discuss only individual cases. Of course he had to invest money as profitably as possible, but he was not yet bound to invest it in land. The *tutor*'s duty to make an inventory of the goods of the ward at the beginning of his administration seems to be classical.

Cautio rem pupilli salvam fore

Freedom of the tutor

A new trend began with a *senatusconsultum* of A.D. 195
under Septimius Severus, whose *oratio* is preserved to us.
The tutor is prohibited from alienating and mortgaging
praedia rustica vel suburbana belonging to the ward, except
when the father had permitted alienation in his will. Where
alienation and mortgaging was necessary in order to pay
the debts of the ward the *tutor* had to apply to the *praetor
urbanus* for special permission. The *tutor* might alienate
praedia urbana since they were not regarded as a thoroughly
safe investment on account of the danger of fire. We will
not describe the further development in detail. An enactment of Constantine in A.D. 326 marks the final victory of
bureaucracy. Now the *tutor* is entirely incapable of alienating the ward's property (except valueless and superfluous
things) without the consent of an authority; according to
Justinian's statute he cannot call in assets of the ward
without an official decree.

3. As regards the technical side of the administration of
the ward's property it has to be borne in mind that direct
agency was unknown to classical law; accordingly legal
acts of the *tutor* effect immediately only the legal position of
the *tutor*. When, for instance, the *tutor* sold a thing belonging to the ward it was the *tutor* and not the ward who was
bound and acquired rights by the contract; and when the
tutor bought a thing for the ward it was equally the *tutor*
and not the ward who became the owner of the thing. At
the end of *tutela* these rights and duties had to be transferred to the ward by special acts. This is the classical
principle of indirect agency to which no exceptions
were made in classical times; where we meet such exceptions in our sources, they should be condemned as post-
classical.

4. There were, however, three modes of causing rights
and duties to arise directly in the *pupillus*:

(*a*) The tutor orders a slave of the ward to effect a certain
legal act. Whatever the slave acquired fell automatically to
the *pupillus* (above, s. 262); as for obligations originating
from a slave's contract, there were the *actiones adiecticiae*
(above, s. 269).

302. Acts of the ward tutore auctore

(b) The *pupillus* himself might effect the legal act with the consent of the *tutor* (*tutore auctore, interpositio tutoris auctoritatis*). An informal consent was sufficient but it had to be declared at the moment at which the legal act was performed. Where, for example, a contract of sale was made by a *pupillus tutore auctore*, the actions resulting from this contract (*actio empti, actio venditi*) lay on behalf of and against the ward. This mode, however, was only available if the *pupillus* was no longer an *infans* (*infantia maior*). In classical law *infantes* are children who are not yet able to speak, *qui fari non possunt*; it was Justinian who designated children as *infantes* until the end of their 7th year, certainly a paradoxical terminology. Distinctions drawn between *impuberes infantia maiores* (*infantiae proximi—pubertati proximi*) are not classical.

303. Acts of the ward without auctoritas

(c) The *pupillus* might effect a legal act even without the *auctoritas* of the guardian if, and in so far as, the act entailed a legal profit for him. But here too it was required that the *pupillus* should be *infantia maior* (though one cannot understand why it was not legally permitted to convey the ownership, for example, of an apple to a child which could not yet speak). Where the act entailed both advantages and disadvantages to the *pupillus*, the classical law was as follows:

i. A debtor of a *pupillus* pays to him what he owes without the guardian's consent. The ward became the owner of the money, but the obligation of the debtor nevertheless remained. If the guardian now sued the debtor, the latter might refuse to make a second payment only in so far as the *pupillus* was still enriched by the first payment.

ii. Somebody gave a loan (*mutuum*) to a *pupillus* without the *auctoritas* of the *tutor*. The ward acquired ownership of the money, but the contract was void and no contractual action lay against him.

iii. When a *pupillus* bought goods without the *auctoritas* of the *tutor*, he acquired the *actio empti* but was not liable for the price, the seller not having an *actio venditi* (so-called *negotium claudicans*). If the *tutor* sued the seller for delivery of the goods sold, the latter might refuse delivery if the purchase price was not offered to him. When the seller had already delivered the goods without having received the price, he was without a contractual remedy.

The question to what extent in such cases there lay actions against the ward for the restoration of his enrichment is still *sub iudice*, since available sources are heavily interpolated. This much is certain, that the classical lawyers were loath to grant such actions and with good reason: people should abstain from doing business with *impuberes* without the guardian's consent.

SOURCES

s. 298. Read Gai. 1. 199, 200 (hardly genuine, but substantially on the whole classical).

s. 300. Read *D*. (27. 9) 1 pr.–2.

s. 301. Read Gai. 2. 95; *C. Iust.* (5. 37) 26. 3; *D*. (41. 1) 13. 1 [*Et tutor . . . ignorantibus*].

s. 302. Read Gai. 3. 107, 109 [*et qui . . . est*]; [*sed in his . . . facta est*]; *D*. (26. 8) 3; (26. 8) 9. 5–6.

s. 303. Read Gai. 2. 83, 84; 3. 91; *Inst. Iust.* (1. 21) pr.

BIBLIOGRAPHY

s. 297. Kübler, 'Die vormundschaftliche Gewalt im röm. Recht', *St. Besta*, i (1939), 75 ff.; Sachers, *PW* viiA. 1543; Beseler, *Scritti Ferrini*, iii (1948), 284.

s. 298. Lenel, *Edict.* (1927), §§ 121, 288; Solazzi, *Istituti tutelari* (1929), 88 ff.; Sachers, l.c. 1569.

s. 299. Pernice, Z xix (1898), 123; Kübler, l.c. 77 ff., 81 ff. (against Mitteis, *RP* i. 208); Sachers, l.c. 1544 ff.

s. 300. Bachofen, 'Das Veräusserungsverbot der oratio Severi', *Ausgewählte Lehren des röm. Civilrechts* (1848), 119 ff.; Sachers, l.c. 1550; Brasiello, *St. Solazzi* (1948), 689; reconstruction of the *oratio* p. 723 (hardly acceptable).

s. 301. Kübler, l.c. 84 ff. with references; Kunkel, § 58; Sachers, l.c. 1549.

s. 302. On *infantes* see Windscheid, *Pand.* i (1906), § 54 note 4. 5 with references; Tumedei, *Distinzioni postclassiche riguardo all' età. Infantiae proximus e pubertati proximus* (1922); Albertario, *Bull.* xxxiii (1933), 81 ff., (1923), 71 f.; 'Infanti proximus e pubertati proximus', *Studi*, i (1933), 81 ff.*

s. 303. On *negotia claudicantia* see Windscheid, *Pand.* ii (1906), § 321, n. 23. Actions against the ward on account of his enrichment: H. Siber, *Röm. Privatrecht* (1928), 45, 222, 316 (probably right); 'Das angebliche rescriptum divi Pii über Bereicherungsklagen gegen Mündel', Z liii (1933), 471; G. H. Maier, *Praetorische Bereiche ungsklagen* (1932),

3 ff., 5 (not helpful); Albertario, *Studi*, iv (1946), 339. See further van Oven, 'Handelingen door den pupil zonder bijstand van den voogd verricht', *Tydskrif vir hedendaagse Romeins-Hollandse Reg*, 1939, pp. 87–129.

5. *Liability of the tutor impuberis*

The classical law knew five different remedies against the *tutor impuberis*.

i. *Accusatio suspecti tutoris*

304.
Accusatio
suspecti
tutoris
This was an *actio popularis* (above, s. 76) which lay only against the *tutor testamentarius*; if the suspicion proved true the *tutor* was dismissed. The testamentary *tutor* could abdicate (above, s. 286); accordingly he could also be dismissed. The action was founded by the classical lawyers on the Twelve Tables.

ii. *Actio rationibus distrahendis*

305.
Actio
rationibus
distra-
hendis
This was a penal action *in duplum* which lay only against a *tutor legitimus*. The term *rationes distrahere* occurs only in legal literature and its meaning is probably simply 'to control accounts'. The statutory *tutor* had no *ius abdicandi* (above, s. 287) and accordingly could not be dismissed; but the ward might with this action demand of him a rendering of accounts, and if it was thereby established that the *tutor* had converted his ward's property to his own use, he was condemned to pay double damages. This action too goes back to the Twelve Tables.

iii. *Actio tutelae*

306. Actio
tutelae
Originally there was no special action against the *tutor decretalis*. The *lex Atilia* was silent on the matter (as the *lex Salpensana* shows); apparently it was held that the *causae cognitio* which preceded the appointment would protect the ward against an unfaithful *tutor*. However, from the beginning of the last century B.C. we know of a new action called *arbitrium* (or *actio*) *tutelae*. This action cannot be older than the *lex Aebutia* which introduced the formulary procedure (above, s. 26); nor can it be older than the *lex*

Atilia (above, s. 289), for originally it lay solely against the *tutor decretalis*; in classical law it lay also against the *tutor testamentarius*. Whether it lay against the *tutor legitimus* is, in view of the sources, problematical. The action was conditioned by *gestio tutoris* and for that reason came near to the *actio negotiorum gestorum* (see below, s. 1064); it did not lie when the *tutor* had caused damage to the ward by mere non-feasance in the form of complete failure to attend to the administration. The *formula* of the action contained the clause *ex fide bona* (above, ss. 60 ff.), which inevitably involved responsibility of the *tutor* for *dolus*, *culpa* (*culpa in faciendo* and lack of *diligentia*), however the classical lawyers may have expressed it.

iv. *Actio tutelae utilis*

The *actio tutelae* presupposed *gestio* and did not lie when the *tutor* failed entirely to act. From the time of Marcus, however, there was an *actio tutelae utilis* against the *tutor cessans*, but only where he was *tutor testamentarius* or *decretalis*, since the *tutor legitimus* was not bound to attend to the administration (above, s. 287). 307. Actio tutelae utilis

v. *Dismissal of the tutor*

A *tutor decretalis* could be dismissed at any time by the magistrate who had appointed him. A *tutor testamentarius* might be removed as a result of the *accusatio suspecti tutoris* (above, s. 304), but possibly also by a simple act of the magistrate (simple *remotio*). A *tutor legitimus* could not be removed, but he might be rendered innocuous by the appointment of a *curator impuberis* or a *tutor adiunctus* to whom would be granted the power of administration; the *tutela* of the *tutor legitimus* became thus a *nudum ius*. To be sure there was no such thing as *interpositio auctoritatis curatoris*, nor did the *actio tutelae* lie against such a *curator*, but the *actio negotiorum gestorum* was a sufficient substitute. A *tutor adiunctus* could be appointed together with a *tutor legitimus* only in so far as this was authorized by *lex*, *senatusconsultum*, or *constitutio principis* (above, s. 295). 308. Dismissal Curator impuberis

s. 304. Read Gai. 1. 182, referring only to the *tutor testamentarius*.

s. 305. Read Paul. *Sent.* (2. 30) 1; *D.* (27. 3) 2 [*per quam ... poena est*], see above, s. 73, 4.

s. 306. Read Gai. 1. 191; 4. 62.

BIBLIOGRAPHY

s. 304. R. Taubenschlag, *Vormundschaftsrechtliche Studien* (1913), 27 ff.; Berger, Z xxxv (1914), 39 ff.; Solazzi, *Istituti tutelari* (1929), 207 ff.; Sachers, *PW* viiA, 1556 ff.

s. 305. Sachers, l.c. 1563.

s. 306. Lenel, *Edict.* (1927), § 124; Lauria, 'Periculum tutoris', *St. Riccobono*, iii (1936), 285 ff.; Solazzi, *SD* iv (1938), 135 ff.; Sachers, l.c. 1565 ff.; Pflüger, Z lxv (1947), 162 ff.*

s. 307. Lenel, *Edict.* p. 318 n. 10; Sachers, l.c. 1568.

s. 308. On simple *remotio* see Sachers, l.c. 1561; on *tutor adiunctus* and *curator impuberis* see Sachers, l.c. 1524 and 1526; Solazzi, *Curator impuberis* (1917).

6. *Irrationality of the classical tutela mulierum*

309.
Conception of tutela mulierum and sources
The *tutela* over *feminae puberes* (which we call shortly 'tutelage of women', *tutela mulierum*) who did not stand either *in patria potestate* or *in manu* or *in mancipio* existed throughout the whole classical period, as the available documents plainly show. It was still in force under Diocletian, but was abrogated in the fourth or fifth century and so is absent from the *Codex Theodosianus* as well as from Justinian's *Corpus iuris*; Justinian's compilers have either cancelled *tutela mulierum* where they met it in classical texts or replaced it by *tutela impuberum*. Thus available materials are comparatively scarce, but they suffice for discerning the classical law in all essential details.

310.
Tutela mulierum and ius liberorum
The classical *tutela mulierum* is of particular interest to the legal historian. It is true that tutelage of women occurs in many other laws, for example, in Greek and Germanic law; but a comparison between the Greek 'lord' (κύριος) and the German *Vogt* or *Muntwalt* on the one hand and the Roman 'protector' (*tutor*) on the other shows at once the genuinely Roman character of *tutela mulierum*. The high social position of Roman women (as compared with that of

Greek and German women) influenced the institution even in early republican times and the humanistic movement (above, s. 180) played its part in liberalizing it further. One may justly raise the question as to how this *tutela* could be preserved throughout the classical period although its abolition was already due at the end of the Republic, but the answer is very simple. During the troublous times of the late Republic the Romans did not find time to abolish it, and the reactionary legislation of Augustus could certainly not be expected to do so. On the contrary, *tutela mulierum* was by now 'anchored' in the *leges Iulia et Papia Poppaea*: A woman was set free from *tutela* when she had borne three children (or four if she was *liberta* and in *tutela legitima*), and it was this close connexion with the rules inspired by population policy which kept alive this antiquated institution during the classical period, although the effect of those rules remained small (above, s. 182) and the emperors frequently gave dispensation from them by granting the *ius liberorum* as a privilege. In Christian times the Augustan population policy was abandoned under the influence of the Christian ascetic conception of marriage and at this point the *tutela mulierum* lost its last ideological support.

As regards the rational force behind the *tutela mulierum* we meet in Cicero's speech *pro Murena* (12. 27) the following phrase: 'Mulieres omnes propter infirmitatem consilii maiores in tutorum potestate esse voluerunt.' This formula apparently has its origin in Greek philosophy, for it sounds like a translation of a well-known dictum of Aristotle: 311. Infirmitas sexus

> *Politica* 1260a (I, cap. v): ὁ μὲν γὰρ δοῦλος ὅλως οὐκ ἔχει τὸ βου-λευτικόν, τὸ δὲ θῆλυ ἔχει μέν, ἀλλ' ἄκυρον, ὁ δὲ παῖς ἔχει μέν, ἀλλ' ἀτελές.

> Let us translate it into Latin (available English translations are hardly intelligible): 'servus nullum omnino consilium habet; femina habet quidem sed infirmum; puer habet quidem sed immaturum.' Obviously Cicero's *infirmitas consilii* is a translation of βουλευτικὸν ἄκυρον.

This dictum was wrong with respect to Roman women in Cicero's own time, as Cicero himself knew very well; his own wife administered her property quite independently.

Nevertheless, it was repeated by rhetorical writers (Val. Max. 9. 1. 3: *imbecillitas mentis*; Seneca, *Controv.* 1. 6. 5: *imbecillitas*; Seneca *ad Marciam* in princ.: *infirmitas muliebris animi*) and Gaius too reproduced it (1. 144 *propter animi levitatem*). However, after the *leges Iulia et Papia Poppaea* this reasoning was really absurd. If the *infirmitas sexus* were a fact the *ius liberorum* would have been a punishment and not a reward, since the granting of the *ius liberorum* could not possibly remove this infirmity. Thus it cannot come as a surprise that in another passage of Gaius' *Institutes* (1. 190) the traditional reasoning is expressly rejected and though Gaius' authorship is doubtful the text speaks the truth and is the more remarkable because in post-classical times the old phrase was repeated again and again, now, of course, under the influence of the Christian-oriental evaluation of women.

312. A woman's place is at home   Thus the tutelage of women cannot be motivated by arguments as to *infirmitas sexus* so far as the last century of the Republic and the classical period are concerned; nor was that the decisive motive with the legislators of the Twelve Tables; such persons are not likely to have speculated as to whether a woman is 'by nature' capable or incapable of administering her property. On the other hand, regard for family interests was not the prevailing motive, as the *tutela testamentaria* plainly shows (below, s. 314). A woman seemed to need protection like a *pupillus* and for that reason received a protector (*tutor*), who originally had the same power as the *tutor impuberis*. A woman did indeed need protection, but not by nature (φύσει); rather the need was a consequence of the social order (θέσει). It was an immutable dogma of the old Roman moral code that a woman's place is at home and that she should not take part in public life. For that reason she is excluded from the *comitia*, from the Senate, and from magistracy. Even at the time of the Twelve Tables a Roman woman was not (like a decent Greek woman) actually excluded from domestic social life; she was legally excluded neither from business life nor from appearing and acting in court. Convential decorum, however, required that women should not engage in public life,

and as this rule of etiquette was in fact observed women certainly lacked experience of business life and were in particular ignorant of the law, not because by nature (φύσει) mastery of the law was beyond their intelligence but because it seemed not to be fitting that they should learn and know it. As the prophet of old Roman custom, Cato Censorius, put it: 'If women kept within their proper sphere, they would not care for legislation at all.'

Livy, 34. 2. 8 f.: 'Equidem non sine rubore quodam paulo ante per medium agmen mulierum in forum perveni. Quod nisi me verecundia singularum magis maiestatis et pudoris quam universarum tenuisset, ne compellatae a consule viderentur, dixissem: Qui hic mos est in publicum procurrendi et obsidendi vias et viros alienos appellandi? istud ipsum suos quaeque domi rogare non potuistis? . . . quamquam ne domi quidem vos si sui iuris finibus matronas contineret pudor, quae leges hic rogarentur abrogarenturve, curare decuit.' (N.B.)

This is the basis of the Roman tutelage of women; not *infirmitas sexus* or even the belief that such *infirmitas* existed, but rather this tenet of old Roman custom: public life is exclusively the business of the man; it forms part of his *officium*. It is significant that the *senatusconsultum Vellaeanum* (under Nero), which prohibited women from becoming sureties, gave this justification: *cum eas virilibus officiis fungi non sit aequum*; it was only a post-classical glossator who referred to *imbecillitas sexus*.

However, the emancipation of women during the last century B.C. resulted in the overthrow of this old Roman custom. Roman women were no longer content to sit at the distaff or the weaving-loom and to do domestic work (οὐ ταλασίαν οὐδὲ οἰκουρίαν φρονοῦσαι, Plutarch, *Antonius*, 10. 5); they took part in public life, though they remained excluded from the *comitia*, the Senate, and the magistracies. One need only refer to Terentia's activity in the suppression of the Catilinarian conspiracy; even in the conspiracy against Caesar a woman (Porcia) was let into the secret. Caecina Severus made (A.D. 20) a vehement speech against the political activities of the wives of provincial governors (Tacitus, *Ann.* 3. 33). Further, women began to act as advocates, which they were permitted to do until the middle of the last century B.C. There was even a comedy by Titinius

313. Emancipation of women

(probably earlier than Terence) with the title 'the lady-lawyer' (*iuris perita*), of which, unfortunately, only a few insignificant fragments are preserved to us. However, the bad behaviour of the lady-advocate C. Afrania (who died 48 B.C.) led the *praetor urbanus* to exclude women altogether from *postulare pro aliis* (Lenel, *Edict.* § 15). Above all, women now began to enter business life. Again Cicero's wife Terentia is a good example; she administered her property quite independently with the help of her freedmen. She was not *in manu*, but her *tutor* is never mentioned. Thus the old basis of *tutela mulierum* disappeared and to justify it by referring to *infirmitas sexus* was ridiculous in view of actual life in Rome at the end of the Republic. Cicero wrote to Terentia at the beginning of the civil war with Caesar (*Ad fam.* 14. 7. 2): 'I should exhort you to be courageous if I did not know that you are more courageous than any man.' And Turia's husband declared (2. 15):

'Repentinis nuntiis ad praesentia et imminentia pericula evoctatus tuis consiliis conservatus sum.'

Such were the realities of Roman life in contrast to the professorial wisdom of Hellenistic philosophers and rhetors. The tutelage of women was by the end of the Republic an irrational institution; the classical lawyers realized this (Gai. 1. 190) and treated it accordingly, in spite of reactionary philistines and Hellenistic professors.

SOURCES

s. 309. Read *Fr. Vat.* 325, first sentence (Diocletian); *D.* (18. 1) 27 which originally dealt with *tutela mulieris* as *Fr. Vat.* 1 shows; *D.* (26. 2) 1 pr., *tutor mulieris* has been cancelled as Gai. 1. 144, *Fr. Vat.* 229, first sentence, show.

s. 310. Read Gai. 1. 145, 194.

s. 311. Read Gai. 1. 144, 190; *Epit. Ulp.* 11. 1.

s. 312. Read Corn. Nepos praef. 6–7; *ILS* 8403; Laudatio Murdiae, ll. 20 ff., *CIL* vi, 10230; *ILS* 8394; *D.* (16. 1) 2. 1 and 2; § 2 is spurious.

s. 313. On C. Afrania: Val. Max. 8. 3. 2; *D.* (3. 1) 1. 5.*

BIBLIOGRAPHY

ss. 309 ff. On *tutela mulierum* see Bonfante, *Corso,* i (1925), 407 ff. Taubenschlag, *Vormundschaftsrechtliche Studien* (1913), 69 ff.; *Archives d'histoire du droit oriental*, ii (1938), 293 ff. (materials); *Law of Greco-Roman Egypt* (1944), 128 ff.; Sachers, *PW* viiA. 1588 ff.

s. 309. Savigny, *Vermischte Schriften*, i (1850), 262 ff.; Mitteis, *Grund-züge* (1912), 252; Taubenschlag, *Vormundschaftsr. Studien*, 85; Solazzi, *Rend. Lomb.* li (1918), 586 ff.; 'Sulle tracce del tutor mulieris', *Studi sulla tutela* (1925), 16 ff.; Sachers, l.c. 1598.

s. 310. Kübler, Z xxx (1909), 154 ff.; xxxi (1910), 176 ff.; Stein-wenter, *PW* x. 1281; Sachers, l.c. 1598; Biondi in *Acta divi Augusti* i (1945), 179.

s. 311. Solazzi, 'Infirmitas aetatis e infirmitas sexus', *AG* civ (1930), 1 ff. On Gai. 1. 190, Solazzi, 29; Beseler, *Beiträge*, v (1931), 2 f. On *fragilitas sexus* see materials in *Thes. L. L.* vi. 1230. 65; on *imbecillitas sexus* ibid. vii. 415. 43. On *fragilitas sexus* in the papyri see Taubenschlag, *Vormundschaftsrechtl. Studien*, 85.

s. 312. Gide, *Étude sur la condition privée de la femme* (1885); Warde Fowler, *Social Life at Rome in the Age of Cicero* (1908); Schroff, *PW* xiv 2300 ff.; W. Kroll, *Die Kultur der Ciceronischen Zeit*, ii (1930), 26 ff. On the *senatusconsultum Vellaeanum* see Albertario, 'Providentia', *Athe-naeum*, vi (1928), 171; Beseler, *Beiträge*, ii (1911), 106; Solazzi, 'Infir-mitas aetatis', l.c. 19.

s. 313. W. Kroll, l.c. 26 ff., 32 ff.; on C. Afrania see Münzer, *PW* iii. 1589; on Titinius' comedy see Schanz–Hosius, *Geschichte der röm. Literatur*, i (1927), 142 ff.; Weinstock, *PW* viA. 1540 ff.; on Terentia Weinstock, *PW* vA. 710 ff.

7. *The three kinds of tutela mulierum*

Tutelage of women, like *tutela impuberum*, originated in one of three ways: it was created by will or was based directly on the Twelve Tables or arose by official appointment.

i. *Tutela mulierum testamentaria*

The father might appoint a *tutor* by will on the strength of his *patria potestas* and a husband might also appoint for his wife *in manu*. The latter alone might appoint an unspecified *tutor*: *Titiae uxori meae tutoris optionem do* (*tutor optivus*). On the strength of such an appointment the wife was entitled to choose a *tutor* either generally for every business for which she needed *auctoritas*, or for specified types of business, or even for one single business only. We do not know when and in what way this *tutela optiva* was introduced, but it certainly existed in A.D. 186. Obviously a woman chose

314. Tutela mulierum testamentaria

only a person whom she could rely on to raise no difficulties about giving his *auctoritas*; in particular, when she chose a *tutor in unam rem* she selected a person who had promised in advance to give his consent. The testamentary *tutor* had a *ius abdicandi* and retained it in contrast to the testamentary *tutor impuberum* (above, s. 286), throughout the classical period; for that reason he did not need a *ius se excusandi*.

ii. *Tutela mulierum legitima*

315.
Tutela
mulierum
legitima
In default of a testamentary *tutor* the next heir of the woman (*proximus adgnatus* or her patron) is *tutor legitimus*. Since the *uxor in manu* was *filiae loco* (above, s. 197), her son might be *proximus adgnatus* and accordingly (as in Greek and Germanic law) her *tutor*. The *tutor legitimus* had no *ius abdicandi*, but he might transfer *tutela* to another person by *in iure cessio* and he retained this right, again in contrast to the *tutor legitimus impuberum* (above, s. 287), in classical times. Claudius abolished the *tutela adgnatorum* but not the *tutela patroni* (above, s. 287).

iii. *Tutela mulierum decretalis*

316. Tutor
mulierum e
lege Iulia
et Titia
In default of a testamentary or statutory *tutor*, one had to be appointed by a magistrate on the strength of the *lex Atilia* and the *lex Iulia Titia* (see above, s. 289 f.).

The *lex Atilia* expressly mentioned the *tutor mulierum*, as the newly found fragments of the *lex Ursonensis* show. Ch. 29 of the *lex Salpensana* also comprehended *tutela mulierum*, though its author has framed the text so clumsily that modern readers have been sometimes misled into believing that tutelage of women was on purpose omitted.

In our Egyptian documents the *tutor mulieris* is always appointed *ex lege Iulia et Titia et ex senatus consulto*, the reference being perhaps to the *senatusconsultum* mentioned by Gaius (1. 173–82). A *tutor mulieris* too was appointed only if an application was made to the magistrate, but only the woman herself was entitled to make it, not *quivis ex populo* (above, s. 292).

317. Tutor
adiunctus
Again a *tutor mulieris* (like a *tutor impuberis*; above, s. 295) was not only appointed in default of a testamentary or statutory *tutor* but (apart from the *tutor praetorius*; above,

s. 295), solely on the strength of a special authorization by
lex, senatusconsultum, or *constitutio principis.* Thus a *tutor
dotis constituendae causa* might be appointed by the *praetor
urbanus* when the *tutor legitimus* was *impubes,* dumb, or a
madman, in accordance with the *lex Iulia de maritandis
ordinibus* and a *senatusconsultum.* We meet here the archaic
figure of a *tutor* who is incapable of acting as a *tutor,* an
interesting survival of the primitive *munt* (above, s. 280)
which in the sphere of *tutela impuberum* had long disappeared (Gai. 1. 157, verb. *puberem*). It was of a particular
importance that the Senate permitted a woman to apply for
a *tutor* when her *tutor* was absent. This meant a further
toning down of tutelage, since the lawyers interpreted this
rule liberally by holding even a short absence to be sufficient. Thus a woman might appear in court, declare that her
tutor was absent, and ask the magistrate to appoint a *tutor,*
proposing a man who had promised her in advance that he
would give his consent. Such an interpretation is of course
only intelligible if we assume that the classical lawyers
realized the irrationality of the tutelage of women (above,
ss. 309 ff.) and did what they could to render it a mere formality. In all these cases the old *tutor* was not deprived of
his *tutela* by the appointment and the newly appointed *tutor*
was a *tutor adiunctus* (above, s. 308).

SOURCES

s. 314. Read Gai. 1. 144, 145, 148–54; *Epit. Ulp.* 11. 1 (post-classical
text, but substantially classical); *Epit. Ulp.* 11. 17 (referring to *tutela
mulierum* only).

s. 315. Read Gai. 1. 155, 157, 165, 168, 171; *Epit. Ulp.* 11. 17.

s. 316. Read Gai. 1. 185; *Epit. Ulp.* 1. 18. On *lex Salp.* and the new
fragments of the *lex Ursonensis* see above, s. 291. Read *FIRA* iii, nos. 24,
25 and the document published by Sanders, *Z. f. d. neutestamentliche
Wissenschaft,* xxxvii (1938, published 1939), 191 ff. = *L'Année épigr.*
1947, no. 12.

s. 317. Read Gai. 1. 173 [*quo . . . desinit*]; 174, 176–81; *D.* (26. 1)
6. 2.

BIBLIOGRAPHY

ss. 314 ff. Sachers, *PW* viiA. 1590 ff. with references.

s. 314. Solazzi, *Aegyptus,* ii (1921), 174.

s. 316. On *lex Salp.* c. 29 see Mommsen, *Schr.* i. 330 ff.; erroneously

D'Ors, *Emerita*, ix (1941), 145. For documents see Taubenschlag, *Studi Bonfante*, i (1930), 390; *Law of Greco-Roman Egypt* (1944), 131; Solazzi, 'Il consenso del tutor mulieris alla sua nomina nei papiri e nei testi romani', *Aegyptus*, ii (1921), 155 ff.

s. 317. On Gai. 1. 173 see Solazzi, *Istituti pupillari* (1929), 15; 'Glosse a Gaio', *St. Riccobono*, i (1936), 184; Beseler, Z l (1930), 443. On *tutor impubes* see Solazzi, 'L'età del tutore', *Riv. It*. lxiv (1920); Bonfante, *Corso*, i (1925), 408, 429. Solazzi, *Aegyptus*, l.c.

8. Functions of the tutor mulieris

318. Auctori-tatis inter-positio   Originally the functions of a *tutor mulieris* did not differ from those of a *tutor impuberis*, but in classical times the differences between the two kinds of *tutela* were very considerable. The *tutor mulieris* had no power over the person of the woman or over her property, but she needed his *auctoritas* for certain legal acts; this *auctoritatis interpositio* was now his only function. But even with respect to *auctoritas* the woman's position was privileged as compared with that of a *pupillus*. She no longer needed *auctoritas* for an alienation of *res nec mancipi* (below, s. 605), where the mode of conveyance was informal. Thus she might give a loan (*mutuum*) without the *tutor's* consent because that contract was performed by *traditio* of a *res nec mancipi*; and when her debtor paid her what he owed, the woman not only acquired ownership but the debtor became free from the debt, since the woman's claim was a *res nec mancipi*. A woman was further capable of making a will *tutore auctore*, whereas a *pupillus* could not make a will even with his *tutor's* consent.

319. Tutor fiduciarius   These limited functions of a *tutor mulieris* were further restricted by permitting the woman to apply to the magistrate when the *tutor* refused to give his consent. The magistrate might then compel the *tutor* to give his *auctoritas*, even a *tutor legitimus* if there was a weighty reason. Such official pressure was certainly exerted even in early republican times when a woman wished to effect *confarreatio* or *coemptio* (see above, ss. 194 f.). Cautelary jurisprudence by making use of this created a remedy by which a woman could easily get rid of a troublesome *tutor*.

A woman might effect a *coemptio* with a man *dicis causa*;

if her *tutor* refused *auctoritas* she applied to the magistrate, who had power to enforce it. By this *coemptio* the woman fell into the man's *manus*, whereby *tutela* came to an end (above, s. 309). Now the man mancipated the woman to B (whom of course the woman had selected in advance), so that she was now *in causa mancipii* (above, s. 257); B manumitted her and thus became her patron and thereby *tutor legitimus* (above, ss. 287, 315). This procedure smacks of old-republican jurisprudence and certainly originated at a time at which the magistrate did not yet enforce *auctoritatis interpositio* as a matter of course.

Taking all this into account, it becomes evident that in classical times *auctoritatis interpositio* had become a mere formality. The *tutor* gave his consent blindly as he knew that if he refused it, the magistrate had power to enforce it; the *auctoritas* of the *tutor legitimus* alone was still of some importance, since the magistrate exercised compulsion only *ex magna causa*. It was for this reason that the *senatusconsultum Vellaeanum* (under Nero; below, s. 975) which prohibited women from becoming sureties did not distinguish between women *in tutela* and women set free from it (on the strength of the *ius liberorum*; above, s. 310). *Tutela mulierum* no longer meant protection for women, since the *tutor* gave his consent as a matter of course.

320.
Auctoritatis interpositio a formality

SOURCES

s. 318. Read Gai. 2. 80–5; 1. 192; 2. 113, 118; *Fr. Vat.* 45; *Epit. Ulp.* 11. 27.

s. 319. Read Gai. 1. 190 *in fine*, 192; 1. 114–15.

BIBLIOGRAPHY

s. 318. Solazzi, 'Glosse a Gaio, Seconda Puntata', Studi Pavia, *Per il XIV centenario delle Pandette e del Codice di Giustiniano* (1933), 319 ff.; Sachers, *PW* viiA. 1596 f.; Volterra, 'Sulla capacità delle donne a far testamento', *Bull.* xlviii (1941), 74 ff.

9. *Liability of the tutor mulieris*

Both *accusatio suspecti tutoris* and *actio rationibus distrahendis* (above, ss. 304 f.) were excluded, since the administration of the woman's property was not in the hands of the

321. No liability

tutor. The *actio tutelae* (above, s. 306) might have been given against him to make him responsible for having been negligent in giving his consent, but actually this did not happen. The lawyers wished to make it easy for the *tutor* to give his consent and for that reason set him free from any liability; thus he might safely give his consent because he could not be made responsible for having given it. The tendency of the lawyers to minimize the importance of the antiquated institution of *tutela mulierum* is again manifest. Of course general actions, for example *actio de dolo* or *actio legis Aquiliae*, lay against the *tutor* as well as against anybody else.

SOURCES

s. 321. Read Gai. 1. 191.

BIBLIOGRAPHY

s. 321. Taubenschlag, *Law of Greco-Roman Egypt* (1944), 133.

10. *Cura minorum*

322. Need for protection of a minor   *Tutela* over male persons ended when they attained puberty (above, s. 284); in classical law this was as a rule at the end of their 14th year. Thus a young man who was not in *potestate patris* became legally independent very early, too early according to modern opinion. But this rule goes back to very early times and in a primitive age a young man of 14 might quite reasonably be regarded as an adult. In medieval Teutonic law a boy came of age even earlier, namely at twelve years, for example, in later Anglo-Saxon law; in earlier Anglo-Saxon law even at ten years. In a more advanced civilization with its complicated business life the term of fourteen years was certainly no longer suitable; but though the Romans realized that comparatively early, their liberalism prevented them from raising the age-limit; the protection of the minor was achieved by other remedies.

323. Lex Laetoria (not Plaetoria)   A *lex Laetoria* in the first decade of the second century B.C. granted special legal protection to persons who had not yet completed their 25th year (*minores viginti quinque*

annis); in the following discussion we shall call them briefly
minores or *minors*.

The true name of the statute is *lex Laetoria*, not *Plaetoria*, as modern
students commonly designate it. We know of a *lex Plaetoria de iuris-
dictione* (Bruns, *Fontes*, p. 45; *FIRA* i, p. 80; G. Rotondi, *Leges publicae*,
p. 245) and a *lex Plaetoria de dedicatione* (*CIL* vi. 3732; Rotondi, l.c.
p. 478), but the statute concerning *minores* is called *lex Plaetoria* only
once, namely in the so-called *lex Iulia municipalis* (Bruns, l.c. no. 18,
l. 112; *FIRA* i, p. 149). All other passages in which the name of the
statute is mentioned—among them *Cod. Theod.* 8. 12. 2 and official
documents (see R. Taubenschlag, *Law of Greco-Roman Egypt*, p. 135)—
have *Laetoria*; where you meet in Cicero, *De nat. deor.* 3. 30. 74 and
De off. 3. 15. 61 '*Plaetoria*', the editor has carelessly replaced the
'*Laetoria*' of his manuscripts by '*Plaetoria*'. In these circumstances
sound criticism inevitably leads one to abandon the name *Plaetoria*. The
lex Iulia municipalis—a draft published by Antonius from Caesar's
papers which shows many blunders and inaccuracies—has no authority
in such a matter; it would be preposterous to 'correct' the name in all
other passages solely on the strength of this inscription.

The *lex Laetoria* protected all those who had not yet completed their 25th year; thus it included those who had
begun their 25th year. This was formerly disputed, but is
now definitely established by an *oratio Claudii* (*FIRA* i,
p. 286).

324. Meaning of minor xxv annis

Persons who had reached the age of puberty but had not yet finished
their 25th year were usually called by the lawyers *minores viginti
quinque annis* (*Ablativus comparationis*), or *minores viginti quinque
annorum* (*Genetiv. comp.*). The rubric of the Edict had *De minoribus
xxv annis*, but the Edict itself began with the words: 'Quod cum
minore quam viginti quinque annis natu gestum esse dicetur.' Accordingly, the lawyers sometimes say *minores quam xxv annis*. *Iuvenis,
adulescens, adultus* instead of *minor xxv annis* are post-classical usage.
The age of xxv years is called in our sources *aetas legitima*. The term
was already used in classical times (*Fr. Vat.* 69 by a testator) but the
classical lawyers used it, if at all, but rarely.

325. Terminology

The *lex Laetoria* granted protection to all minors
whether male or female, *sui iuris* or *in potestate*, and, in the
case of female minors, without regard to whether they were
in tutela or not. The remedy which the statute accorded to
minors was a special action which lay against anybody who
had fraudulently taken advantage of the inexperience of the
minor (*circumscribere*). This action, which still existed in

326. Actio legis Laetoriae

classical times, was a popular penal action (above, ss. 72 ff.) and therefore an *actio noxalis* (above, s. 73); condemnation involved infamy. This is all we know about the action. Of course the praetor must have propounded a *formula* in his Edict and the lawyers must have discussed it in their commentaries on the Edict, but the compilers have carefully eliminated these discussions so that we do not know even the place in the Edict in which the *formula* was propounded.

327. Two actiones leg. Laetoriae?

The so-called *lex Iulia municipalis* appears to mention two actions: l. 112 ... 'queive lege Plaetoria ob eamve rem, quod adversus eam legem fecit fecerit, condemnatus est erit'. However, two substantially different actions are scarcely conceivable. Most probably only one action is meant and the wording is tautological. As aforesaid, this *lex* is a hastily published draft.

The *actio legis Laetoriae* was the only remedy granted by the statute. The praetor added two further remedies:

328. Exceptio legis Laetoriae

1. An exception against the action of a person who had fraudulently taken advantage of the minor. This exception was not expressly specified in the Edict, but was contained in the general exception 'si in ea re nihil contra legem senatusve consultum factum est' (Lenel, *Edict.* § 279). The lawyers certainly discussed this *exceptio legis Laetoriae*, but nothing of their discussions has remained.

329. In integrum restitutio

2. The praetor promised an *in integrum restitutio* (above, s. 117), at his discretion and not only in cases of fraud. The Edict ran as follows: 'Quod cum minore viginti quinque annis natu gestum esse dicetur, uti quaeque res erit, animadvertam.'

330. Disadvantages of the remedies

These three remedies (*actio, exceptio,* and *in integrum restitutio*) involved a serious disadvantage to the minor; they destroyed or at least impaired his credit, since many people might hesitate to do any business with a minor at all. Thus in Plautus' *Pseudolus* v. 303 (first performance 191 B.C.) a minor complains:

> Perii, annorum lex me perdit quinavicinaria,
> Metuunt credere omnes.

331. Introduction of cura minorum

Nevertheless, these remedies remained in force and it was only by the Emperor Marcus that a better remedy was afforded to the minor. Henceforth he might apply to the praetor (in the provinces to the governor) for a *curator* (*cura minorum*). It is of course possible that the praetor occasionally granted such a *curator* before the time of Marcus, but it was only by a constitution of Marcus that *cura minorum* became a legal institution.

Our only information about the introduction of the *cura minorum* is given by the so-called *Scriptores Historiae Augustae* (Capitolinus, Marcus Antoninus Philosophus 10. 12). The author—a post-classical non-legal writer—is unreliable in details, especially whenever law is concerned; but as a rule there is a kernel of truth in his information. The text runs as follows:

'. . . de curatoribus vero, cum ante non nisi ex lege Laetoria, vel propter lasciviam vel propter dementiam darentur, ita statuit, ut omnes adulti curatores acciperent non redditis causis.'

For every unbiased reader the meaning is:

Whereas before Marcus a *curator* was given to a minor only on the strength of the *lex Laetoria*, namely, where he was either a lunatic or a spendthrift, according to Marcus' constitution a *curator* had to be given to the minor in any case, if requested, *non redditis causis*, viz. even if the applicant did not allege lunacy or prodigality.

The author is in error in so far as he believes that a *curator furiosi* and *prodigi* were given *e lege Laetoria*; but apart from that his account is right: before Marcus a *curator* was only given to a minor if he was either a lunatic or a spendthrift, whereas Marcus ordered a *curator* to be given in other cases as well. Any other interpretation of the text is evidently in conflict with the wording.

The classical *cura minorum* was fundamentally different from *tutela*.

1. First and foremost *cura* was always optional and never, like *tutela*, compulsory. A *curator* was only appointed if the minor applied for one: *inviti adulescentes curatores non accipiunt*. Apparently there was no exception to this rule in classical times. Even where somebody wished to sue a minor, a *curator* was not appointed against the minor's will. The plaintiff or the magistrate might urge him to apply for a *curator*, but if he remained obstinate there was no redress and the plaintiff had to sue the minor even though he had no *curator*.

2. Women might apply for a *curator* even if they were *in tutela*. Tutelage of women had become a mere formality

Marginal notes: 332. The vexed text in the Vita Marci — 333. Cura minorum optional — 334. Curator of a woman in tutela

(above, ss. 319, 320), and yet a woman sometimes needed substantial help in her business affairs.

335.
Consensus
curatoris

3. There was no such thing as *auctoritatis interpositio curatoris* (cf. above, s. 302). A male minor enjoyed full legal capacity even if he had a *curator*; for a female minor *in tutela* there were restrictions which we have mentioned above (s. 318). But the minor might consult the *curator* when he wished to carry out some individual transaction and ask him for his consent (*consensus*). Although all passages in which this *consensus* is mentioned seem to be spurious, such a consent cannot have been lacking, since otherwise *cura minorum* would have been without any content. The lawyers mention it but rarely since it had no legal effect. Even if the *curator* gave his consent, the magistrate was nevertheless free to grant *actio* and *exceptio legis Laetoriae* and also *in integrum restitutio*. Actually, however, he refused these remedies as a general rule when the *curator* had given his consent. It was by such a practice that the credit of the minor was restored.

336.
Curator
as adminis-
trator of
property

4. The *curator* had no right to administer the minor's property, otherwise *cura minorum* would have been a *quasi-tutela*. It is common opinion that a *curator mulieris* at any rate had the right of administration, but even this seems most unlikely. The lawyers had minimized the effects of *tutela mulierum* and in classical times a *tutor mulieris* was debarred from administering her property. No reaction can be detected during the classical period, and for that reason a *curator mulieris* cannot have become automatically the administrator of her property. But, of course, a minor might entrust the *curator* with the administration of all his property or of part of it, and the magistrate too might, on application of the minor, order him to take the administration into his hands. In particular provincial women who were too ignorant to administer their property alone may frequently have entrusted the *curator* with administration, and it is for this reason that the administration of a *curator mulieris* is repeatedly mentioned in our sources. Texts speaking of the administration by a *curator* of a male minor are in part clearly spurious, in part at least suspect. Never-

theless, even a male minor must have had the right to entrust his *curator* with administration (possibly with the help of the magistrate) and must have made use of that right; otherwise the post-classical development (of which we shall presently speak) would remain unintelligible. It has been objected that a *curator minoris* cannot have lacked the right of administration, since without it *cura minoris* would have been a poor thing; but such an argument springs from a bureaucratic attitude. Bureaucracy, of course, is eager to intervene, to be busy, and to publicize the importance of a job. The classical period, however, was not yet the age of bureaucracy and the classical *curator* was not a bureaucrat; he was rather, so to speak, an officially appointed 'good uncle' or *prochein amy* (Pollock and Maitland, ii. 441) who was quite satisfied with being occasionally consulted by his ward or administering the property at his request.

5. As regards the liability of the *curator*, the actions which lay against the *tutor impuberum* (above, ss. 304 ff.) did not lie against the *curator*. When he acted as an administrator he might be rendered liable on an *actio negotiorum gestorum* or *mandati*.

337. Liability of the curator

Such was the classical and truly Roman *cura minorum*. To set a young person free from *tutela* at an early date (though the end of the 14th year was certainly too early in the classical period) and to give him at his option a 'caretaker' or *prochein amy* who might advise him and, if requested, administer his property: that was indeed an ingenious idea which reveals again the irrepressibly individualistic spirit of Roman law. It was, however, just for this reason that the post-classical bureaucratic age failed to appreciate the classical institution. *Cura minorum* was increasingly assimilated to *tutela impuberum*, although a *quasi-tutela* lasting till the end of the 25th year was absurd. *Cura minorum* was now no longer optional; the *Epitome Gai*, 1.8 clearly reveals the law of the fifth century. Justinian's compilers too wished to render *cura minorum* compulsory, as their interpolation in *D.* (4. 4) 1. 3 irrefutably proves, and it was only by inadvertence that conflicting classical texts were left unaltered. Notably the compilers of

338. Character of the classical cura and postclassical development

the *Institutes* (1, 23, 2) retained the fundamental classical principle *inviti adulescentes curatores non accipiunt*. A complete amalgamation of *tutela impuberum* and *cura minorum* was not achieved, nor apparently attempted, but the classical texts were heavily interpolated. To a considerable extent these interpolations must not be attributed to Justinian's compilers but to the post-classical law-school (end of the third and beginning of the fourth century). The state of our sources is, therefore, really appalling and it is only by methodical criticism that the classical law can be re-established; unfortunately the page in Gaius' *Institutes* which contained his exposition of *cura* has not been preserved to us. The pioneers in this field were E. Albertario and S. Solazzi. A detailed description of the post-classical development lies outside the scope of this book.

SOURCES

s. 329. Read *D.* (4. 4) 27. 2.

s. 333. Read *C.* (5. 31) 1 and 6.

s. 336. Read *C.* (5. 37) 12 [*vel . . . curatoribus*]; *Fr. Vat.* 110.

s. 338. Read *Epit. Gaii* 1. 8; *D.* (4.4) 1 [*Hoc edictum . . . opitulationem*]; [*Apparet . . . gerentibus*]; *C.* (2. 21) 3 [*hunc contractum . . . fecisti*].

BIBLIOGRAPHY

ss. 322 ff. Modern standard work: S. Solazzi, *La minore età* (1912); Berger, *PW* xv. 1860 ff. with references.

s. 322. Gierke, *Deutsches Privatrecht*, i (1895), 382; Heusler, *Institutionen des deutsch. Privatrechts*, i (1885), 55; F. Liebermann, *Gesetze der Angelsachsen*, ii. 1 (1906), 589.

s. 323. Weiss, *PW*, Suppl. v. 578 ff.; Berger, l.c. 1867.

s. 324. Berger, l.c. 1865.

s. 325. Berger, l.c. 1860 f.; Weiss, l.c. 579; Solazzi, l.c. 285 (*adultus*); Albertario, *Studi*, i (1933), 513 ff.

ss. 326, 327. Savigny, *Vermischte Schriften*, ii (1850), 336; Duquesne, *Mélanges Cornil*, i (1926), 217 ff.; Debray, *Mélanges Girard*, i (1912), 265 ff., 305; Lenel, *Edict.* (1927), 80.

s. 328. Debray, l.c. 282 ff.; Lenel, *Edict.* 513.

s. 329. Lenel, *Edict.* 116.

s. 330. Costa, *Bull.* ii (1889), 72 ff.

ss. 331, 332. Berger, l.c. 1869 with references.

s. 335. Berger, l.c. 1875 ff., 1880.

s. 336. Berger, l.c. 1873 ff. with references.

s. 337. Lenel, *Edict.* 319.

s. 338. Solazzi, *Minore età* (the whole book, especially 239 ff.); Albertario, *Studi*, i (1933), 407 ff., 427 ff., 475 ff., 499 ff., 511 ff.; Archi, *L'Epitome Gai* (1937), 221 ff.; Berger, l.c. 1871 ff., 1876, 1881 ff., 1884.

11. *Cura furiosi*

The classical law concerning lunatics was still remarkably primitive. Unfortunately it is not completely known to us since the relevant page in Gaius' *Institutes* has not been preserved, but the primitive character of this part of Roman law is nevertheless quite apparent.

339. Character and sources

According to the Twelve Tables both the person and property of a *furiosus* were *in potestate* of the *proximus adgnatus* or the *gens*. The classical lawyers avoided the term *potestas* here as well as in *tutela* (above, s. 297) and specified the *proximus adgnatus* as '*curator furiosi*' (the *cura* of the *gens* had disappeared). A procedure in which a person might be officially declared insane did not exist; a *furiosus* fell automatically into the *potestas* of the *adgnatus* and became free from it when he recovered. Persons mentally affected who were *in potestate patris* or *in tutela* did not fall under the *cura furiosi*.

340. Cura legitima

Where there was no *curator legitimus* (a *cura furiosi testamentaria* did not exist) the praetor (in the provinces the governor) might appoint a *curator*. Though available sources are in an unsatisfactory condition, such a *cura furiosi decretalis* (see above, s. 285) certainly existed, although there was no statute like the *lex Atilia* (above, s. 289) which provided for the appointment of such a *curator*. The magistrates acted at their discretion and very often a *furiosus* may have been without a *curator*: primitive times show but little sympathy with lunatics, who are merely regarded as a burden; they are left to the care of their relatives or friends and if they are dangerous they are thrown into prison, for asylums do not exist in primitive society.

341. Cura decretalis

A *curator furiosi* had to care for the lunatic's person as well as for his property. Like the *tutor impuberum* (above, s. 299), the *curator legitimus* was *vice domini* and, therefore, entitled *iure civili* to dispose of the lunatic's property. Nevertheless, it was the *furiosus* and not the *curator* who was

342. Administration by curator legitimus

regarded as the owner of the property; the idea of the *curator* being a trustee remained foreign to Roman thinking (above, s. 213). Cicero' sstatement (Tusc. 3. 5. 11): 'furiosum dominum esse rerum suarum vetant duodecim tabulae' is, as usual, rhetorical and legally inaccurate.

343.
Administration by curator decretalis
A *curator furiosi decretalis* could dispose of the lunatic's property.only *iure praetorio*.

344.
Incapacity of furiosus
A *furiosus* entirely lacked legal capacity, whether he had or had not a *curator*. Any *negotium* effected by him was void *iure civili* even if the other party was ignorant of his state. Delicts committed by him did not render him liable to a fine or damages, though this rule was only reluctantly acknowledged in the classical period.

345. Quid est furor?
Thus the protection afforded both to the mentally afflicted person and to the person who came in legal contact or conflict with him was insufficient. Above all, the lawyers had apparently no clear conceptions of mental diseases. Although Greek doctors of classical times already possessed a considerable stock of knowledge and their writings were known in Rome, the lawyers clearly did not pay any attention to them. The fundamental question, when is a person to be regarded as *furiosus*? was never discussed by them and simply left to the magistrates and the judges. In the eyes of the classical lawyers this was a *quaestio facti* and they remained true to the principle of the republican *iurisconsulti*, which is thus expressed by Aquilius Gallus:

' "Nihil hoc ad ius; ad Ciceronem," inquiebat Gallus noster, si quis ad eum quid tale rettulerat, ut de facto quaereretur.' (Cicero, *Topica*, 12. 51.)

Thus this important question was indeed discussed by 'Cicero', i.e. by the judicial orators and *quid sit dementia*? was a stock question for discussion in the rhetorical schools. Nothing good could come of such discussions, though the rhetors knew of the medical literature and made use of it. The classical lawyers as usual took no notice of them, but some post-classical interpolations are obviously influenced by them.

346. Lucid intervals
The doctors knew well that in some sorts of mental disease there occur lucid intervals.

Caelius Aurelianus, *De morbis chronicis*, 1. 5. 151 (a Latin translation of a Greek work of Soranus written in the first half of the second century A.D.): 'Est autem insania sive furor nunc iugis nunc temporis interiecti requie levigatus.'

Aretaeus 1. 7 (p. 79 ed. Kühn): μανίη δὲ καὶ διαλείπει.

Accordingly the rhetors taught their pupils to plead 'id genus furoris fuisse ut intermissionem haberet'. Wherever we meet this idea in our legal sources the texts are either of post-classical origin or interpolated. This statement does not mean that lucid intervals were disregarded by the practice of classical times, but only that classical lawyers did not discuss the subject in their writings.

Further, we meet in the rhetorical writings the terms *dementia* and *demens* used together with, or instead, of *furor* and *furiosus*. This usage intruded into the classical legal writings and gave rise to the false belief that the classical lawyers knew two sorts of insanity. In truth they only used the terms *furor* and *furiosus*. In law-books outside the *Corpus iuris* the terms *dementia* and *demens* occur only in *C. Th.* (9. 43) 1 (only metaphorically they are used in a few other texts); in the *C. Iust.* they occur only in Justinian's enactments. This is in itself a powerful argument against the classicality of the few passages in the *Digest* in which these terms occur. In some of them the interpolation can be proved: I think that is as much proof as can reasonably be required. The term *mente captus* was also avoided by the classical lawyers.

347. Dementia and furor

In early post-classical times *cura legitima* disappeared since the *adgnatus* now needed official confirmation.

348. Disappearance of cura legitima

SOURCES

s. 340. Read XII Tab. v. 7*a* and 7*b*.

s. 341. Read *D.* (27. 10) 13; (1. 18) 13. 1.

s. 342. Read Gai. 2. 64; *D.* (47. 2) 57. 4, interpolated [*sed et . . . possunt*] but substantially classical; (40. 1) 13 [*tradendum*] ⟨*mancipandum*⟩, [*traditus*] ⟨*mancipatus*⟩.

s. 344. Read Gai. 3. 106; *D.* (44. 7) 1. 12; (44. 4) 16 [*quem . . . existimabat*] [*in id . . . processit*]. Delicts: *D.* (9. 2) 5. 2 to *verissimum*; (1. 18) 14 to *pertinebit*.

s. 346. Read Paul. *Sent.* (3. 4*a*) 5; *Epit. Gai.* (2. 2) 3; *D.* (5. 1) 12. 2 [*perpetuo*]; *C.* (5. 70) 6 (*antiquitas* means post-classical jurisprudence).

s. 347. Read *D.* (4. 8) 27. 5 [*vel demente*], cf. *D.* (4. 8) 47. 1–49 pr.; (5. 2) 2 [*vel demens*], cf. *Inst.* (2. 18) pr.

s. 348. Read *Epit. Ulp.* 12. 1 (N.B. *dantur*).

BIBLIOGRAPHY

ss. 339 ff. Audibert, *Études sur l'histoire du droit Romain*, I. *La Folie et la prodigalité* (1892); H. Krüger, Z xiv (1893), 260; Bonfante, *Corso*, i (1925), 473 ff.*

s. 340. De Visscher, 'Potestas et Cura', *St. Perozzi* (1925), 399 ff. = *Études de droit Rom.* (1931); Guarino, *SD* x (1944), 374 ff., 406 ff.

s. 344. Beseler, *Z* lvii (1937), 12 ff.; Pernice, *Labeo*, i (1873), 238 f.

s. 345. I. L. Heiberg, *Geisteskrankheiten im klass. Altertum* (1927).

s. 346. Solazzi, 'I lucidi "intervalla" del furioso', *AG* lxxxix (1923); Lenel, 'Intervalla insaniae', *Bull.* i (1924), 227 ff.; Lanfranchi, *Il diritto nei retori Romani* (1938), 197 ff.; De Francisci, *Bull.* xxx (1921), 154 ff.

s. 347. Solazzi, 'Furor vel dementia', *Rivista di antichità Μουσεῖον*, ii (1924); Lenel, *Z* xlv (1925), 514 ff.; Lanfranchi, l.c.*

s. 348. Audibert, 'Comment la curatelle légitime se transforma en curatelle dative', *NRH* xv (1891), 310 ff.; Solazzi, 'Interpolazioni in Ulp. XII', *Rend. Lomb.* lv (1922); Bonfante, *Corso*, i. 479.

12. *Cura prodigi*

349. Sources

The classical law concerning the spendthrift cannot be ascertained from available sources with full certainty. Gaius' exposition in his *Institutes* has not been preserved to us; the text in the post-classical *Epitome Ulpiani* (12. 1–3) is far from being classical; the passage in the post-classical *Sententiae Pauli* (3. 4a. 7) is short and insufficient; the relevant passages in the *Corpus iuris* are heavily interpolated. Without fresh sources full certainty cannot possibly be achieved, but the classical law was in all probability as follows.

350. The Twelve Tables

1. The Twelve Tables stated (the wording is not preserved) that a person who wasted the property which he had inherited by succession on intestacy from his father or grandfather should be in the *potestas* of the *proximus adgnatus* or the *gens* after having been certified as a *prodigus* by a magistrate (originally the consuls, later the *praetor urbanus* and the provincial governors). The magistrate effected this by issuing an *interdictio bonorum*: 'tibi ea re commercioque (a so-called hendiadys) *interdico*'. In classical law the *proximus adgnatus* was called *curator prodigi* (above, s. 340); he was a *curator legitimus*.

351. Praetorian law

2. Later (we do not know since when) the praetor issued an *interdictio bonorum* in the following two cases as well: (*a*) when a freedman wasted his property (the law was clearly concerned with the patron's right of succession);

(*b*) when an *ingenuus* wasted the property which he had inherited by will of his father or grandfather. In these two cases the praetor appointed a *curator* at his discretion; he was a *curator honorarius*.

3. Ultimately Antoninus Pius ordered that a *curator* should also be given in other cases of prodigality. Accordingly the praetor issued an *interdictio bonorum* and appointed a *curator*. This *cura* was also a *cura honoraria*.

352. Antoninus Pius

The *curator legitimus* was—like the *curator furiosi legitimus*—*iure civili vice domini* and, therefore, entitled to administer and to dispose of the property. The *prodigus* himself was incapable of alienating this property. He was also debarred from making a will and any contract which involved being bound himself. Nor could he do so even with the curator's consent, since there was no such thing as *interpositio auctoritatis curatoris* (above, ss. 302, 335). Most probably he was also debarred from accepting a *hereditas* since that implied the possible assumption of legal duties. Further details remain obscure. For example, when a *prodigus* made a contract of sale, was that a *negotium claudicans*? (above, s. 303). Was a *prodigus* capable of making a so-called praetorian will (below, s. 436)?

353. Effects of cura legitima

The *curator honorarius* was also entitled to administer and to dispose of the property, but only *iure praetorio*. Legal acts of the spendthrift himself were valid *iure civili*, but alienations and contracts resulting in his being legally bound were void *iure praetorio*.

354. Effects of cura honoraria

In all cases *cura prodigi* did not end automatically when the spendthrift ceased to be a *prodigus*, but only when the magistrate cancelled the *interdictio bonorum*.

355. End of cura prodigi

The fundamental and difficult question as to the circumstances in which a person might be regarded as a *prodigus* was apparently never discussed by the classical lawyers; in their eyes it was a *quaestio facti* which lay outside the scope of their activities (above, s. 345).

356. Who is a spendthrift

The post-classical age attempted a fusion of *ius civile* and *ius honorarium*, with the usual result of a confusion of classical texts. *Cura legitima*—like *cura furiosi legitima* (above, s. 348)—disappeared in early post-classical times since the

357. Post-classical development

proximus adgnatus now needed the confirmation of the magistrate.

SOURCES

Read Gai. 1. 53; Paul. *Sent.* (3. 4*a*) 7; *Epit. Ulp.* 12. 1–3; 20. 13; D. (45. 1) 6 [*tradere*] ⟨*mancipare*⟩; ⟨*lege*⟩ *bonis*; (29. 2) 5. 1 (spurious); (27. 10) 1 pr. [*quod . . . curatorum*]; (26. 5) 12. 2.

BIBLIOGRAPHY

Audibert, *Études sur l'histoire du droit Romain*, I. *La folie et la prodigalité* (1892); 'Comment la curatelle légitime se transforma en curatelle dative', *NRH* xv (1891), 310 ff.; H. Krüger, Z xiv (1893), 260 ff.; Ivo Pfaff, *Zur Geschichte der Prodigalitätserklärung* (1911); Mitteis, 'Zu der Stelle des Ulpian, 27. 10. 1 pr.', *Berichte der Verhandlungen der Kgl. Sächs. Gesellschaft der Wiss. Phil.-Hist. Klasse*, lxii (1910), 265; Beseler, *Beitr.* ii. 99 f.; E. Weiss, Z xxxiii (1912), 488; De Visscher, 'Potestas et Cura', *Studi Perozzi* (1925), 399 ff. = *Études de droit Romain* (1931), 5 ff.; 'La Curatelle et l'interdiction des prodigues', *Mélanges Cornil*, ii (1926), 539 ff.; *Études*, 21 ff.; Collinet, 'L'Origine du decret de l'interdiction des prodigues', *Mélanges Cornil*, i (1926), 147 ff.; Solazzi, 'Interpolazioni in Ulp. XII', *Rend. Lomb.* lv (1922); 'Interdizione e cura del prodigo nella legge delle XII tavole', *St. Bonfante*, i (1930), 45 ff.; Beseler, *Byzantinisch-Neugriechische Jahrbücher*, vi (1928), 554 f.; Berger, *St. Riccobono*, i (1936), 597.*

PART III

LAW OF SUCCESSION UPON DEATH

INTRODUCTION

RIGHTS and duties of a person are as a rule not extinguished with that person's death. There are exceptions to this rule: *patria potestas* and *manus mariti* are extinguished with the death of the father and husband; usufruct is extinguished by the death of the usufructuary; penal actions (above, s. 73) are extinguished by the debtor's death; accessory obligations resulting from *sponsio* and *fidepromissio* are extinguished with the surety's death (Gai. 3. 120). However, the number of these exceptions is small if compared with the bulk of rights and duties which survive the death of the person who was their bearer. The rules which regulate the legal fate of rights and duties after the death of their former bearers we call 'the law of succession upon death', or shortly 'the law of succession'. 358. Conception of the law of succession

> The idea of a law of succession as a systematic unity meets us for the first time in Gaius' *Institutes* (2. 97–3. 87). Though this exposition shows considerable systematic defects, it is remarkable as a first attempt. Justinian's *Institutes* (2. 6–3. 12) follow the system devised by Gaius and further development was not achieved until the jurisprudence of natural law (seventeenth and eighteenth centuries) which eventually set forth the law of succession on death in close connexion with family law.

Classical jurisprudence discussed the law of succession on death with obvious predilection and at the same time admirable delicacy, but it is with mixed feelings that a modern observer contemplates this enormous display of legal ingenuity. This part of classical law was highly complicated and to a large extent perplexedly entangled, but the classical lawyers did little to simplify it. Their professional relish for details and for vexed questions was too strong for them, and, absorbed in the spinning of this fine network, they forgot the maxim *simplicitas legum amica*. Unification and simplification of the law was overdue, but 359. Technical character. Sources the task was shirked and was left to be carried out by a later age which had neither the leisure nor the capacity it demanded. Justinian's compilers—the authors of the *Codex Iustinianus*, the *Digest*, and the *Institutes*—did not and could not attempt a thorough reform. After these compilations had been accomplished, Justinian issued some important reformatory enactments, but it was left to the law-school and to practice to carry them through, sometimes in harmony with and sometimes in contrast to the law as given in the three compilations. Taking also into account the fact that numerous classical texts collected in these compilations had been rendered obscure and even contradictory by shortening and interpolation, the ultimate verdict must inevitably be that the unification and simplification of the Roman law of succession, objects so dear to Justinian, were not achieved, and that since the beginning of the twelfth century, when Justinian's law was regarded and cultivated as a living law, the law of succession has always presented enormous difficulties to lawyers.

However, it is just this characteristic of the Roman law of succession which renders it a particularly interesting field for legal historians. The labyrinthine law cries out for historical analysis; available materials are unusually rich; all factors in Roman legal evolution are clearly visible, in particular the strength of Roman jurisprudence as well as its limits and shortcomings. Bonfante's dictum is no exaggeration:

'Nessun istituto del diritto romano rispecchia più luminosamente il carattere organico del diritto. L'eredità è il vero campo di battaglia e di studio dei principi generali e eccezionali.'

The Roman law of succession is indeed the focus of the Roman 'will to law'.

360. Liberal character of the Roman law of succession   So far we have described the character of the classical law of succession from the technical point of view; we will now characterize its fundamental ideology. It bears an outspokenly liberal character and operated, for that reason, as a stimulating model in the continental liberal movement of the nineteenth century. Liberalism as applied to the law of succession produced the following principles.

The will (*testamentum*) appears in Roman legal history at a very early date since it was already known to the Twelve Tables. The Roman code was certainly inspired by the law of Athens, for Attic law, at least from the time of the laws of Solon (594 B.C.), knew of disposition by will. But though the idea was of Greek origin, it was carried through in true Roman style. Solon's law permitted a will only in default of legitimate children. This restriction was not adopted by the Roman legislators, but the freedom of a testator was confined within flexible limits. The original Roman will was the *testamentum calatis comitiis*; such a will could only be effected where the *pontifex maximus* brought a motion before the *comitia* and whenever the *pontifex* disapproved of the will, he might refuse to bring in the motion (above, s. 244). But these restrictions disappeared comparatively early, and from the third century B.C. a Roman citizen enjoyed almost unlimited freedom in disposing of his property by will. Roman custom impressed upon a good *pater familias* the need to make use of this liberty and not to live a single day after reaching the age of puberty without a will; the lawyers did their best to maintain a will even by strained constructions (*favor testamenti*). The idea was to replace intestate succession as far as possible by succession on will, since the former was inevitably schematic while the latter might pay regard to the individual case. If you compare the slow development of wills and testamentary freedom in Teutonic law, this Roman attitude, far from being inevitable, reveals clearly the strong Roman individualistic liberalism. The *lex Voconia* (169 B.C.) by which citizens belonging to the first census class were forbidden to institute women as heirs marks an anti-liberal reaction (it was advocated by Cato Censorius). It was still in force in classical times, but its effect was deliberately minimized by the lawyers who permitted a *fideicommissum hereditatis* in favour of women which differed only technically from *institutio heredis*. The freedom of leaving legacies was restricted by various statutes, ultimately by the ill-starred *lex Falcidia* (40 B.C.) which permitted legacies only up to three-quarters of the property. In the last decades of the Republic the freedom of a testator was restricted by according to certain near relations a reasonable share of which the testator could not deprive them by will (*portio debita*); in classical law this was one-quarter of their intestate portion. The *lex Papia Poppaea* (above, s. 182) introduced further restrictions, but on the whole the freedom in classical law was very extensive. In Justinian's law the *pars debita* was somewhat higher; on the other hand, the restrictions of the *lex Papia Poppaea* no longer existed, so that in the law of the *Corpus iuris* the freedom of the testator still remained as one of the most conspicuous features of the Roman law of succession.

362. Pacts on succession Pacts on succession have no binding force under classical law; freedom to regulate succession upon death must not be impaired in any way. This liberal principle is carried through without any exception.

(*a*) A pact between A and B by which A appoints B or C as heir or legatee (or by which both A and B mutually appoint each other as heirs or legatees) is invalid. This rule is all the more remarkable as under Greek law such pacts were recognized, particularly in matrimonial and adoptive pacts. It is no less significant that the mancipatory will (below, s. 432), though a true inheritance pact, never implied a binding of the testator, who might revoke at any time without the consent of the other party (the *familiae emptor*).

(*b*) A contract in which a person promised to make or not to make, to revoke or not to revoke, a will was void.

(*c*) Joint wills were prohibited. Provisions contained in such wills are sometimes meant to be interdependent, so that if one of the testators died the other could no longer revoke his own dispositions. It was for this reason that joint wills were not allowed under classical law.

363. Freedom of heir and legatee Liberal individualism endeavours to grant full freedom to both heir and legatee.

(*a*) Where there are co-heirs, each of them may claim partition of the common property at any time. The testator cannot either exclude or restrict this right.

(*b*) Both heir and legatee are perfectly free to dispose of the inherited property; prohibitive clauses in the testator's will are void. In particular the testator cannot prohibit the alienation of anything inherited.

(*c*) Substitutions were kept within very narrow limits. A testator cannot institute Titius and substitute Seius in the following way: 'Titius heres meus esto; post mortem Titii (or *post decem annos*) Seius mihi heres esto'. Under classical law the testator might bind Titius to restore the inherited property to Seius by a *fideicommissum hereditatis*, but he could not create a *fideicommissum familiae*. A disposition of the following kind: 'A shall be my heir; after his death the property shall pass to his eldest son, after the latter's death to his eldest son and so on' would be void under classical law, since the *fideicommissarius* must be a *persona certa* (below, s. 561) and alive at the testator's death. Of course, such things as entails and trusts were entirely unknown. Thus classical law meets fully the demands of the radical French liberals of the Revolution who passionately fought against substitutions and eventually abolished them (*Code civ.* 896).

> See Portalis, *Discours* (Locré, *La Législation civile, commerciale et criminelle de la France*, i (1827), 314): 'Sans doute on a bien fait, pour la liberté de la circulation et pour le bien de l'agriculture, de proscrire ces substitutions absurdes qui subordonnent les intérêts du peuple vivant aux caprices du peuple mort, et dans lesquelles, par la volonté de la génération qui n'est plus, la génération qui est se trouve constamment sacrifiée à celle qui n'est point encore. Il est prudent de soumettre à des règles la faculté de tester et de lui donner des bornes. . . . See further Exposé des motifs' (Locré, l.c. xi. 1827, 358 ff.).

364. Principle of equality

The liberal principle of equality (*la loi inviolable de l'égalité*, as Mirabeau put it) rejects in intestate succession any priority of males over females and excludes primogeniture and similar institutions (e.g. secundogeniture). It demands further that a reasonable portion of the inheritance should be left to certain near relations and so to this extent is in conflict with the freedom of disposition by will. The rules concerning intestate succession as laid down by the Twelve Tables did not discriminate between males and females; sons and daughters got equal shares of their father's property. This order is amazingly progressive if compared with continental non-Roman laws of the Middle Ages. Primogeniture and similar institutions always remained foreign to Roman law. A republican statute, possibly the *lex Voconia*, diminished the rights of females, but only within the second class of intestate heirs (below, s. 392). In the conflict between the principle of equality and that of testamentary freedom, the latter was victorious and it was only at the end of the Republic that a *pars debita* was granted to certain near relations (below, s. 480).

365. **Estate duty**   Finally, the Roman disinclination to establish an estate duty is in conformity with liberalism. Such a duty was introduced by Augustus, but he had to bear down strong opposition. The duty came to 5 per cent., but near relations and small inheritances remained free.

366. **Economic effects of the Roman law of succession**   The liberal law of succession which after the French Revolution more and more influenced continental legislation has sometimes led to evil results: estates had to be parcelled out or encumbered with mortgages, both eventually leading to the disappearance of small farmers and the creation of large estates.

> Suppose a farmer has four sons. Under Roman law he might appoint one of them as his heir, but he was bound to leave to his other sons the *debita portio* (under Justinian's law one-third of the intestate portion). Thus, if the value of the inheritance was 120, the heir had to pay to each of his brothers 10. If he had no money to pay them off, he had either to sell a part of the estate or to encumber it with a mortgage. If he chose neither of these modes, he had to sell the whole estate and thereupon as a rule ceased to be an independent farmer. If the father did not make a will, his four sons became co-owners of the estate (each of them at one-quarter). As aforesaid (s. 363), each of them might claim partition at any time. If a partition of the land was unworkable because the resulting allotments would be too small, one of the sons might take over the estate, but he had to pay off his brothers, altogether the huge amount of 90, i.e. three-quarters of the value of the whole estate. The inevitable result is that estates are split up or encumbered with mortgages or fall into the hands of big capitalists.

We do not know whether the Roman law of succession worked similarly in antiquity. As long as a *debita portio* was not yet recognized, a farmer might institute one of his children as heir, disinherit the others, and grant them only small legacies. But it is doubtful whether an average farmer really acted as a *homo oeconomicus* and not rather as a father who did not wish to prefer any one of his children. After the *debita portio* had been recognized, the danger became more serious and the liberal Roman law was perhaps—at least in Italy—one of the factors which led to the disappearance of small farmers and to the increase of *latifundia*. As yet we know nothing about the economic effects of the Roman law of succession. Empty declamations on the increase of *latifundia* tell us nothing; Roman lawyers as usual had no eyes for such problems, but the Roman government too apparently did not realize the economic dangers inherent in the law of succession. The literature on the economic history of the Roman Empire has hardly touched the problem.

SOURCES

s. 361. Read Twelve Tables, v. 3; on *lex Voconia* Gai. 2. 274. Gellius 20. 1. 23. Read further Plutarch, *Cato maior*, ix. 6.

s. 362. Read *D.* (17. 2) 52. 9; (38. 16) 16; (45. 1) 61; *C.* (2. 3) 15; (2. 4) 34 i.f.; (5. 14) 5; (6. 20) 3; (8. 38) 4. Joint will permitted to soldiers by Diocletian *C.* (2. 3) 19.

s. 363. Read Gai. 2. 238, 287.

BIBLIOGRAPHY

ss. 358 ff. A modern comprehensive exposition of the whole law of succession does not yet exist. Indispensable are still Vangerow, *Lehrbuch der Pandekten*, ii (1876); Windscheid, *Lehrbuch des Pandektenrechts*, iii (1906), 184 ff. Manigk, *PW* viii. 622 ff. is insufficient.*

s. 358. On the systematic question see Schwarz, *Z* xlii (1921), 604, 606.

s. 359. Bonfante, *Corso*, vi (1930), 78.

s. 360. Schulz, *Principles*, 156; Hedemann, *Die Fortschritte des Zivilrechts im XIX. Jahrh.* ii. 1 (1930), 47 ff.

s. 361. On Solon's law see Beauchet, *Histoire du droit privé de la république Athénienne*, iii (1897), 426; Kübler, *PW* VA. 968. On the *lex Voconia* see Steinwenter, *PW* xii. 2418. On the predominance of will Schulz, l.c.*

s. 362. Windscheid, *Pand.* iii, §§ 529 n. 2; 564 n. 3; 568; Vismara, *Storia dei patti successori*, 2 volumes (1941); Re, 'Del patto successorio. Studio di legislazione comparato', *Studi e documenti di storia e diritto*, vii, viii. On Greek law see Mitteis, *Grundzüge* (1911), 241 ff.; Kreller, *Erbrechtliche Untersuchungen* (1920), 223 ff.; Taubenschlag, *Law of Greco-Roman Egypt* (1944), 156.

s. 363*a*. Schulz, *Principles*, 150 f.; Hedemann, l.c. 62.

s. 363*b*. Windscheid, *Pand.* iii, § 678. 3.

s. 363*c*. Windscheid, *Pand.* iii, §§ 554. 4, 637; Hedemann, l.c. 53 ff.

s. 364. Hedemann, l.c. 66 ff.; v. Woess, *Das röm. Erbrecht und die Erbanwärter* (1911), 65 ff.; Kübler, Z xli (1920), 15 ff.

s. 365. On Augustus' *lex de vicesima hereditatum* see Biondi in *Acta divi Augusti*, i (1945), 219, with references; De Laet, *L'Antiquité classique*, xvi (1947), 29.

s. 366. Hedemann, l.c. 79 ff.; Max Weber, *Dir röm. Agrargeschichte* (1891), 67 f.

CHAPTER I

FUNDAMENTAL NOTIONS

1. *Successor, Successio, Succedere*

*S*UCCEDERE in classical legal usage, like the English verb 'to succeed', means 'to take the place previously filled by another person or thing' and in particular 'the succeeding of an heir *in locum* or *in ius defuncti*'. If used in the latter, narrower sense the meaning is that the heir takes the legal position of the *defunctus*; with regard to private law (with which alone we are concerned in this book) it means that the *successor* succeeds to the rights and duties of the *de cuius*[1] *en bloc*, in so far as such rights and duties survive the death of the *de cuius* (above, s. 358).

Gaius, dealing in his *Institutes* (2. 18 ff.) with the acquisition of things, distinguishes between the acquisition of single things (2. 97: *quemadmodum singulae res adquirantur*) and the acquisition of a plurality of things *en bloc* (2. 97, 191: *quibus modis per universitatem res nobis adquirantur*); the latter mode he describes as *successio* (2. 157; 3. 77; 3. 82). Within this conception of *successio* he makes the following subdivisions: (1) the succession of the heir (*iure civili* as well as *iure praetorio*); (2) other cases of *adquirere per universitatem*, e.g. where the *pater adrogans* acquired by *adrogatio* the property of the adopted son (Gai. 3. 82 and above, s. 252). Modern students designate these two kinds of succession by the phrases '*successio mortis causa*' and '*successio inter vivos*', but Gaius does not use these terms. Obviously *successio* as used here by Gaius means a mode of acquiring things (namely *adquirere per universitatem*, i.e. *en bloc*) and does not imply an assumption of duties, for the *pater adrogans* does not 'succeed to' the duties of the adopted son. It is, however, doubtful whether this conception of *successio* was current among classical lawyers or was peculiar to Gaius himself; in any case it is hardly felicitous. Suppose somebody sells all the goods stored in a warehouse and transfers ownership by giving the key to the buyer. The latter acquires the goods *uno actu, en bloc* (*per universitatem*), but Gaius would hardly be prepared to describe this mode as a *successio*.

Another thing is quite certain. Wherever a person acquired ownership of a single thing or of several things by

---

[1] *De cuius* (in English, French, Italian, and Spanish legal language the current term to designate the *defunctus*) is an abbreviation of *is de cuius hereditate quaeritur* (or *agitur*); see *Inst. Iust.* (3. 2) 6; D. (38. 8) 1. 11; (38. 6) 5 pr.

sale (*mancipatio* or *traditio*), by donation, by legacy, or by *usucapio*, the classical lawyers never described this acquisition as *successio*; they never said that in such cases the new owner 'succeeded' to the former owner.

370. Post-classical conception of successio However, the post-classical lawyers, apparently influenced by Gaius, applied the term *successio* also to *adquirere singulas res*. They felt no scruple about regarding the buyer, the legatee, etc., as 'successors' and called this succession *successio in unam rem*; what Gaius had simply called *successio*, they termed *successio in universum ius*, *in universitatem* or some similar expression. Modern lawyers accordingly distinguish between 'universal' and 'singular' succession. These conceptions and terms are entirely unknown to classical lawyers; they never occur in Gaius' *Institutes* and wherever we meet them in our sources the texts are either of post-classical origin or interpolated. As usual the new terminology was not established with any thoroughness, and in many passages of the *Corpus iuris*, even in interpolated passages, *successor* means nothing else but 'heir'. In conclusion we may emphasize that the post-classical conception of *successio* and the distinction between universal and singular succession are obscure as well as unnecessary.

SOURCES

s. 367. Read Gai. 4. 34 to *directas actiones* (Ambrosino's suggestion, l.c. p. 96, is unacceptable); *D.* (50. 17) 42.

s. 368. Read *D.* (41. 1) 62 [*ad heredem*]; (23. 5) 1. 1 [*secundum . . . est*].

s. 370. Compare Gai. 3. 82 with *Inst. Iust.* (3. 10) pr.; Gai. 3. 77 with *Inst. Iust.* (3. 12) pr. Read further *D.* (43. 3) 1. 13 [*in locum . . . successum*]; (39. 2) 24. 1*a* [*successores . . . continentur*].

BIBLIOGRAPHY

C. Longo, 'L'origine della successione particolare nelle fonti di diritto romano', *Bull.* xiv (1902), 127 ff., 224 ff.; xv (1903), 283 ff.; Bonfante, *Scritti giuridici*, i (1916), nos. v–ix, xv; *Corso*, vi (1930), 1 ff.; Rightly, against Bonfante, Ambrosino, 'Successio in ius, successio in locum', *successio*, *SD* xi (1945), 64–192; Catalano, 'Successio in universum ius', *Ann. Catania*, i (1946–7), 314 ff., rightly against Ambrosino's exaggerations. For materials see *VIR* v. 732, 734 ff.; *Ergänzungsindex*, 188 f. On succession in general see Windscheid, *Pand.* i (1906), § 64.2.*

2. *Heres, Hereditas*

In classical law *heres* is a *successor mortis causa ex iure civili*. He succeeds *uno actu in locum defuncti* which, as regards private law, means that he succeeds to all those rights and duties of the *de cuius* which survive the latter's death. There may be several heirs, but only as to specified fractions of the inheritance (e.g. A to one-third; B to two-thirds); to confine an *heres* to certain things belonging to the inheritance would have been incompatible with the Roman conception of an *heres*. A testator cannot, for instance, appoint A as heir of his landed property and B as heir of his money. The *heres* inevitably assumes the debts of the *de cuius*; where there are several heirs each of them owes a fraction of that debt. If, for example, A is *heres* to one-third, B *heres* to two-thirds, and the *de cuius* owed 90, then A owes 30 and B 60. Other limitations to the heir's liability are inconsistent with the classical conception of an *heres*. The testator cannot institute A as his *heres* liable only for debts of a certain kind. Above all, the liability of an *heres* cannot be limited to the amount of the inherited property. If, for example, A is the sole heir and the *de cuius* owed 100, then A too owes 100, even if the value of the inherited estate is only 60; under classical law A has no means of restricting his liability to the amount of the inheritance.

371. Conception of heres

This harsh and inescapable rule as to the unlimited liability of the classical *heres* is apparently quite unique. In other laws we meet, more or less strongly marked, the idea that the debts of the *de cuius* are an encumbrance lying upon the inherited estate; accordingly the heir has never to pay more than the value of the estate. Thus the classical rule seems to require special explanation. It has been attempted by Bonfante and his followers to understand it as a survival of prehistoric Roman law. In prehistoric times, it is said, the Roman *heres* succeeded to the head of a *gens* (or house) who possessed a kind of public sovereignty over the *gens* (or house). The *heres* succeeded to that sovereignty and for that reason also to the obligations of the previous sovereign. 'Sed hoc divinare est et relinquatur pertinacibus.' This theory, passionately defended by Bonfante, is, to say the least, unproved and indeed unprovable with the aid of available materials, since all legal rules taken as survivals can be explained differently and much more simply. Even if this theory were right, it would not explain how unlimited liability could survive the disappearance of the prehistoric order for such a long time; reference to

372. Unlimited liability for debts

the *vis inertiae* and to Roman conservatism does not suffice here. The liability has to be explained within the framework of classical law.

In fact the remarkable liability of the *heres* can be explained without the help of speculative reasoning. What puzzles modern observers is the following consideration.

If the *de cuius* were still alive, his creditors might claim satisfaction out of his property, and if that turned out to be insufficient they had to face a loss. Why should the debtor's death yield a gain to the creditors? The unlimited liability of the *heres* implies such an unjustified advantage, since now the creditors might obtain satisfaction not only out of the inheritance but also out of the heir's property. Hence we have to seek an explanation of this strange liability.

This mode of arguing is perfectly right from the standpoint of modern law, but it is wrong from that of republican and classical Roman law, since the possibility of execution on the person of the debtor (above, s. 43) is ignored. A debtor was subjected to execution on his person for the amount of his debt, e.g. if he owed 100, for the amount of 100, and he could not object that the value of his property was only 60. Now suppose the debtor dies and an *heres* succeeds *in locum defuncti*. It is only logical to say that the *heres* is subjected to an execution on his person to the same extent as the *de cuius* was, i.e. for the full amount of the debt; this implies unlimited liability. If execution on the heir's person were permitted only for the amount of the debt as far as it is covered by the inherited assets (*dumtaxat de hereditate*), his liability would be less than that of the previous debtor and the position of the creditor would deteriorate as a result of the death of the original debtor. The fact that the liability of the *heres* is not limited to the value of the inherited assets is thus fully explained: it is the logical and inevitable consequence of the conception of *heres* as a *successor in locum defuncti* as long as execution on the person is the primary mode of execution, as in fact it was in republican times and in the classical period within the ordinary procedure (above, s. 43). To be sure the classical lawyers might have pushed the execution on the person into the background. Under Augustus' *lex Iulia de cessione bonorum* a debtor was (within certain limits) entitled to evade execution on his person by abandoning his property to his creditors. One might have allowed the *heres* to avert execution on his person on account of a debt of the *de cuius* by abandoning the inheritance. But this could not be achieved by a liberal interpretation of the *lex Iulia*; it would have required a statute (*lex, senatusconsultum, constitutio principis*) which was actually never issued. The *cessio bonorum* of the *lex Iulia* was regarded as an exceptional privilege and not as the starting-point of a new development in the law of execution. Execution on the person still seemed too important to allow it to be restricted any further. It was only Justinian who by granting the *beneficium inventarii* opened a way to restricting the liability to the amount of the inherited estate. But under Justinian's law *cessio bonorum* was facilitated to such an extent that execution on the person was pushed into the background; it is hardly ever mentioned in the *Corpus iuris*.

After what has been stated so far it is evident that the appointment of an *heres* by testament does not necessarily imply the assignment of a benefit. Suppose that the testator had no property at all but only debts. Even in such a case an *institutio heredis* is perfectly valid: the appointed person succeeds *in locum defuncti* and all other provisions made in the will—*tutoris datio, manumissio testamento*—come into force. Occasionally it is said in our sources that an *heres* who obtains no advantage by the inheritance has only *inane nomen heredis* (Gai. 2. 224, *C. Iust.* 3. 29. 3), but this is a misleading expression. If a testator wishes to assign a pure advantage to somebody he must not appoint him as *heres*, since an *heres* is always at least potentially liable for the debts of the *de cuius*. He must choose another mode of disposition: *legatum, fideicommissum, donatio mortis causa, modus, manumissio testamento*. In these cases, with which we shall deal later, the recipient is (leaving apart the irregular *fideicommissum hereditatis*) not liable for the debts of the *defunctus*.

373.
Institutio
heredis and
assignment
of
advantages

In primitive law the idea is widespread that the father survives in his sons and, as these are his heirs, survives in his heirs. The heir, so to speak, reproduces the father, embodies in himself and perpetuates the father's personality. In the development of the Roman law of succession this idea plays no part. The heir appointed by testament is, as aforesaid (s. 361), predominant and to regard such an heir as the perpetuator of the testator's personality would be absurd. In our sources the idea occurs only once, in one of Justinian's *Novellae* (Nov. 48 praef.), where it is only an empty rhetorical phrase. In the nineteenth century Hegelianism attempted to resuscitate the old idea, which even today occasionally finds advocates. A similar idea is the regarding of the heir as a representative of the *de cuius*, but this too is entirely foreign to the classical lawyers.

374.
Heres
neither
perpetuator
nor repre-
sentative of
the
defunctus

The term *hereditas* is used in a double sense by the classical lawyers. It means (1) *successio mortis causa ex iure civili*, i.e. the succeeding itself and the right to succeed (*ius*

375.
Hereditas

successionis); (2) the estate of the deceased person (*bona defuncti*). For both meanings we possess reliable texts, but the classical lawyers never use the term *hereditas* in the sense of a unit comprehending both the assets and the debts of the *de cuius*.

Hereditas (= *successio*) is either *hereditas ex testamento* or *ab intestato* or *contra testamentum*; we shall expound these kinds of succession below (ss. 381, 426, 459).

376.
Deferre hereditatem adire hereditatem
An *heres* sometimes succeeds automatically upon the death of the *de cuius* or at the opening of his will; sometimes a special act of acceptance is required. In the latter case the classical lawyers distinguish between *deferre hereditatem* (to offer the inheritance) and *adire hereditatem* (to enter on the inheritance).

Our text-books distinguish between *delatio* and *adquisitio hereditatis*, an entirely non-classical terminology. The terms *delatio* and *adquisitio hereditatis* do not occur in classical sources. *Deferre hereditatem* is classical. *Adquirere hereditatem* is also classical, but does not mean acquisition in contrast to *delatio*. *Accipere hereditatem* does not mean 'to accept an offered inheritance' but 'to receive (to obtain, to get) an inheritance'.

SOURCES

s. 375. For *hereditas* = *successio*, see Gai. 2. 14; *D.* (50. 17) 62 [*universum*]; (50. 16) 24 [*universum*]; for *hereditas* = *bona defuncti* see Cicero, *Topica*, 6. 29; *D.* (36. 3) 5. 3; (26. 7) 39. 3.

s. 376. *Adquisitio hereditatis* occurs *D.* (36. 1) 67 pr., but the text is spurious: Beseler, *Beitr.* iv (1920), 187; Z xlvi (1926), 141; lii (1932), 42; liii (1933), 38. For the classical usage see *D.* (50. 16) 151; (41. 1) 10. 1; (28. 7) 13.

BIBLIOGRAPHY

s. 372. Bonfante's writings, see above, ss. 367–70, Bibliography. Further Rabel, Z l (1930), 295 ff.; Korosec, *Die Erbenhaftung nach röm. Recht*, i (1927); Siber, 'Geschichtliches und Rechtsvergleichendes über die Haftung für Nachlaßschulden', *Acta Academiae Universalis Jurisprudentiae Comparativae*, i (1928), 986 ff. Rightly against Bonfante Ambrosino, *SD* xi (1945), 184; Volterra, *Bull.* xlviii (1941), 76. For the execution on the person see v. Woess, Z xliii (1922), 485 ff. On Justinian's *beneficium inventarii* see Windscheid, *Pand.* iii (1906), § 606. On Greek law see Pringsheim, Z xli (1920), 349 ff.; Taubenschlag, *Law of Greco-Roman Egypt* (1944), 163, with references; on Germanic law Gierke, 'Grundzüge des deutschen Privatrechts', § 117 (Holtzendorff–Kohler, *Enzyklopädie der Rechtswissenschaft*, i, 1915, 291).*

s. 374. Windscheid, *Pand.* iii (1906), § 528; Mitteis, *RP* i (1908), 93 ff.; Bonfante, *Scritti*, i (1916), 158 ff.; Solazzi, 'Contro la rappresentanza del defunto', *Riv. It.* 1916; Saleilles, 'Le Principe de la continuation de la personne du defunt par l'héritier en droit romain', *Festschrift für Otto Gierke* (1911), 1015 ff.; Planiol, *Traité élémentaire de droit civil*, iii (1946), s. 2213 with references; Solazzi, *Diritto ereditario romano*, i (1932), 199 ff.

3. *Bonorum possessor, bonorum possessio*

Under classical law the *bonorum possessor* is the *successor mortis causa ex iure praetorio (honorario)*. The term is somewhat confusing since this *possessor* is not a *possessor rerum* (below, s. 751); he is a person to whom the praetor grants *successio iuris praetorii*. The *bonorum possessor* might obtain *possessio rei* by bringing the inheritance under his actual power, but he acquired *bonorum possessio* immediately by the praetor's decree. Like the *heres*, the *bonorum possessor* is a *successor mortis causa* and succeeds *uno actu in locum defuncti*; but the *bonorum possessor* is only a *successor iure praetorio*, which implies numerous technical peculiarities.

377. Conception of bonorum possessio

> Suppose that Sempronius has given a loan of 100 to Titius; then Sempronius dies. If Seius is Sempronius' *heres*, he may sue Titius with the usual *formula certae creditae pecuniae* (above, s. 30): 'Si paret Titium Seio centum dare oportere', etc. If Seius was not *heres* but only *bonorum possessor*, he cannot sue Titius in this way, since Seius is not *creditor iure civili*. Hence he has to use a *formula ficticia* (above, s. 49): 'Si Seius Sempronio heres esset, tum si pareret Titium Seio centum dare oportere', etc.

The praetor might grant *bonorum possessio* to an *heres*, who then enjoyed the praetorian remedies as well as those accorded to him by *ius civile*; here the praetor bestowed *bonorum possessio* in support of *ius civile (adiuvandi iuris civilis gratia)*. The praetor might also grant *bonorum possessio* to a *non-heres*, who then had only the praetorian remedies. If in the latter case an *heres* did not exist, the praetor merely filled in the gap left by *ius civile (supplendi iuris civilis gratia)*, but where an *heres* existed (A is *heres* and B *bonorum possessor*) there are two conflicting rights, and in such a case it is sometimes the *bonorum possessor* who is

378. Kinds of bonorum possessio

legally superior to the *heres* (the *bonorum possessio* is then called *bonorum possessio cum re* and the praetor acts in such cases *corrigendi iuris civilis gratia*); sometimes the *heres* is superior to the *bonorum possessor* (the *bonorum possessio* is then called *bonorum possessio sine re*). We shall point out later those cases in which the *bonorum possessio* was *cum re* and those in which it was *sine re*, but it should be noted from the beginning that *sine re* does not mean *sine effectu*, as the post-classical author of the *Epitome Ulpiani* (23. 6) believed. *Bonorum possessio sine re* also bestows upon the *possessor* the praetorian remedies.

Bonorum possessio is granted (1) *secundum tabulas testamenti*, i.e. to the person appointed heir in a testament; (2) *ab intestato, si tabulae testamenti non extabunt*; (3) *contra tabulas testamenti*. The details will be given later (ss. 436, 404, 468). *Bonorum possessio* never falls automatically to a person as *hereditas* sometimes does (above, s. 376); *bonorum possessio* can only be acquired by a decree of the praetor granting *bonorum possessio* to the applicant. For this reason the distinction between *bonorum possessio decretalis* and *edictalis* cannot possibly be classical; actually the term *bonorum possessio decretalis* occurs only once and then in an interpolated text.

379.
Classical
termino-
logy

Petere or *adgnoscere bonorum possessionem* means 'to apply to the magistrate for *bonorum possessio*'. The noun *adgnitio bonorum possessionis* occurs in classical writings only once, *D.* (38. 15) 5 pr. (spurious). *Deferre bonorum possessionem* corresponds to *deferre hereditatem* (above, s. 376). *Dare bonorum possessionem* means 'to grant *bonorum possessio* by decree'. *Bonorum possessio decretalis* occurs only in a single passage, *D.* (38. 9) 1. 7, which is evidently interpolated [*Decretalis*]; [*nondum . . . quia*]. The term is absent from Inst. Iust., C. Iust., C. Theod., Nov. Posttheodosianae, and from the materials of the Ergänzungs-Index. *Bonorum possessio edictalis* occurs only twice: *D.* (29. 2) 30. 1 and (38. 6) 1. 4; both texts are spurious.

380.
Republican
and post-
classical
law

In the following we confine ourselves to the *bonorum possessio* under the praetorian Edict as codified by Julian and Hadrian (above, s. 25). Our knowledge of the earlier law and of its historical evolution is rather slight; the post-classical development urgently needs a critical analysis.

SOURCES

s. 377. Read Gai. 3. 32; 4. 34; *D.* (50. 17) 117; (37. 1) 2; (50. 16) 119; (37. 1) 3. 1 [*Hereditatis . . . bonorumve*] ⟨*Bonorum*⟩.

s. 378. Read *D.* (1. 1) 7. 1; Gai. 3. 33*b*, 34 (*remota bonorum possessione = bonorum possessio* set aside); 3. 35, 36; *Epit. Ulp.* 28. 1.

s. 379. Read *D.* (37. 1) 3. 3.

BIBLIOGRAPHY

A modern (critical) work on the whole law of *bonorum possessio* does not yet exist. K. F. Fabricius, *Histor. Forschungen I. Ursprung und Entwicklung der bonorum possessio bis zum Aufhören des ordo iudiciorum privatorum* (1837); B. W. Leist, *Die bonorum possessio*, 2 vols. (1844, 1848); Glück–Leist, *Erläuterung der Pand.*, Serie der Bücher, 37–8, i–v (1870–9); Alibrandi, *Opere*, i. 65 ff.; C. Arnò, 'La bonorum possessio sine re', *Memorie della R. Accademia di scienze, lettere ed arti in Modena*, Serie III, vol. xii (Sezione scienze), 1914; Bonfante, *Corso*, vi (1930), 416 ff.; Lenel, *Edict.* (1927), 342 ff. For documents containing an *adgnitio bonorum possessionis* see Taubenschlag, *Law of Greco-Roman Egypt* (1944), 162. On *bonorum possessio decretalis* see Solazzi, *AG* c (1928), 17 ff.

CHAPTER II
INTESTATE SUCCESSION

1. *Introduction*

381. The relevant moment INTESTATE succession takes place when it is legally certain that a valid and effective testament does not exist; at that moment (which we will shortly call 'the relevant moment') the inheritance (*hereditas* and *bonorum possessio*) is offered to a certain person or to certain persons.

> Suppose the *de cuius* left a valid testament in which he instituted A and B as his heirs. After the death of the *de cuius* A refused the inheritance and some days later B did so as well. At the moment at which B refuses it is certain that an effective will does not exist and the inheritance is offered to the intestate successors.

If a person at the relevant moment no longer exists, he or she cannot be intestate heir.

> Suppose the testator has a son A and a brother B; he institutes his friend F as *heres*. Four weeks after the testator's death F refuses the inheritance. A was alive at his father's death, but died three weeks later without leaving children. The only intestate heir is B; the heir of A cannot claim the inheritance.

It is true that *bonorum possessio ab intestato* might be claimed and obtained even if a valid testament existed, but this is only *bonorum possessio sine re* (Gai. 3. 35, 36; above, s. 378).

382. Sources The classical law springs from several very different sources, namely the Twelve Tables, the *lex Voconia of* 169 B.C., the praetorian Edict, two *senatusconsulta*, and the *lex Iulia de maritandis ordinibus*. We are not concerned here with the original meaning of the rules laid down by the Twelve Tables, which probably differed from that attributed to them by later jurisprudence; we take them as they were understood by the classical lawyers. As regards the Edict we confine ourselves to the Edict as codified by Hadrian (above, s. 25), since of that alone have we a sufficient knowledge.

BIBLIOGRAPHY

La Pira, *La successione ereditaria intestata e contro il testamento in diritto romano* (1930).

2. *Intestate succession under the Twelve Tables and the lex Voconia*

Persons appointed intestate successors by the Twelve Tables are called *heredes legitimi*; they fall into three classes. 383. Heredes legitimi

i. *Sui*

Sui are persons who would be *in potestate* or *in manu* of the *de cuius*, if the latter were still alive. Blood-relationship with the *de cuius* is neither required nor in itself sufficient: *uxor in manu* and *filius adoptivus* belong to the *sui* but are not consanguineous; on the other hand, an *emancipated* son of the *de cuius* is consanguineous but not a *suus*. As already stated above (s. 364), the Twelve Tables did not differentiate between males and females and no later statute, not even the *lex Voconia*, dared to depart from this liberal law. 384. Sui heredes

Where there is a plurality of *sui*, the so-called 'principle of representation' applies which means that descendants of a son are excluded by their father but represent him when he is either not a *suus* or no longer alive at the relevant moment. 385. Principle of repre- sentation

Take the following case:

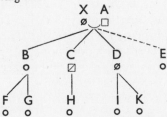

At the death of the *de cuius* X, the following were alive: his wife *in manu* A; his son B and the latter's sons F and G; the son H of his deceased daughter C; the sons I and K of his deceased son D; his emancipated son E. Now A is *filiae loco* (above, s. 197) and therefore *sua*; F and G are excluded by their father B; H is not a *suus* of the *de cuius* but of C's husband; E is emancipated and therefore not a *suus*. Thus ABIK are *heredes legitimi*, A and B to one-third each, I and K to one-sixth each.

We do not know whether this 'principle of representation' was already applied in the times of the Twelve Tables, since that code does not expressly mention it. In any case it is very old and was firmly maintained in later times.

386. Suus conceptus pro iam nato habetur
A *suus* can only be *heres legitimus* if he was already in existence at the death of the *de cuius*, but it suffices if at that time he was *en ventre sa mère* and was born alive later: 'postumus suus conceptus pro iam nato habetur' (above, s. 124).

387. No aditio, no repudiatio
The *sui* became *heredes* automatically, no acceptance of the inheritance (*aditio hereditatis*; above, s. 376) being required; nor were they entitled to refuse the inheritance. We shall deal with this rule later (below, s. 488).

388. A woman has no sui heredes
Where the *de cuius* is a woman, this first class of heirs does not exist since a woman can have no *sui*, not being capable of exercising *potestas* (above, s. 240).

ii. *Adgnatus proximus and patronus*

389. Proximus adgnatus
Where the *de cuius* is free-born and *sui* do not exist, the *proximus adgnatus* is *heres legitimus*.

390. Conception of adgnati
Adgnati in the Roman sense are persons who, together with the *de cuius*, descend from the same male ancestor and would at the relevant moment stand in the same *patria potestas*, if the common ancestor were still alive. Adopted persons are regarded as being *adgnatorum loco*, an *uxor in manu* as *filiae loco* (above, s. 197). This conception comprehends the *sui*,.but the rule of the Twelve Tables is only con-

391. Succession per capita
cerned with the *adgnati* who are not *sui*. In this class the principle of representation does not apply; the agnate who, at the relevant moment, is nearest in degree excludes all other agnates. Several agnates of equal degree take *per capita* and not (as in the first class) *per stirpes*.

Take the following example:

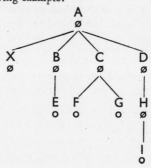

At the death of the *de cuius* X there were alive: E, son of a deceased brother B; F and G, sons of a deceased brother C; and I, grandson of a deceased brother D. They are all *adgnati*, for they would be under the *patria potestas* of their common ancestor, A, if the latter were still alive. EFG are *heredes legitimi* (of the third degree), I is excluded, since he is of the fourth degree. EFG are *heredes per capita*, each as to one-third.

Under the Twelve Tables males and females were in this second class also on a par; a later statute, however, admitted female agnates only if they were sisters of the *de cuius*. This statute was probably the *lex Voconia* of 169 B.C.

392. Female agnates

> The post-classical *Sententiae Pauli* (4. 8. 20) state:
>
> 'Feminae ad hereditates legitimas ultra consanguineas successiones non admittuntur: idque iure civili Voconiana ratione videtur effectum; ceterum lex XII tabularum sine ulla discretione sexus adgnatos admittit.'

The wording of this much disputed text should not be stressed too much; it should rather be borne in mind that the author was a post-classical lawyer. Either he knew nothing of the origin of this rule and his reference to the *lex Voconia* is merely a conjecture; or he knew that the *lex Voconia* was its source and *Voconiana ratione* is only a rhetorical variant of *lege Voconia*. We know the timid attitude of republican jurisprudence towards *leges*, and it is quite out of the question that the lawyers should have dared to introduce such an innovation in defiance of the Twelve Tables without the express order of a statute.

An agnate could only become *heres* if he was alive at the death of the *de cuius*; the rule *conceptus pro iam nato habetur* was not applied in this class as it was in the first.

393. Adgnatus conceptus pro iam nato non habetur

The *proximus adgnatus*—in contrast to the *suus* (above, s. 387)—did not become *heres* automatically, but only if he accepted the inheritance by *aditio hereditatis*. If he refused, the inheritance was not offered to the *adgnatus* of the next degree.

394. No successio graduum

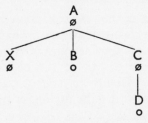

B is *proximus adgnatus*. If he refuses the inheritance it is not offered to D.

395. The patron as heres legitimus Where the *de cuius* was a freedman, he had no agnates. If he had *sui*, these were his *legitimi heredes*. Failing *sui* the inheritance fell under the Twelve Tables to his patron, and if the patron was not alive, to the patron's agnatic descendants. It should be borne in mind that where a father emancipated his child he became therewith as a rule his patron (*parens manumissor*; above, s. 272).

iii. *Gens*

396. Succession of the gens The Twelve Tables (v. 5) stated: 'Si adgnatus nec escit, gentiles familiam habento.' *Gentiles* means the organized members of a *gens*, the *gens* as a unit (*gesammte Hand*), just as *municipes* means *municipium* (above, s. 157). It is to this unit that the inheritance falls, *si adgnatus non est*. If you take these words literally they are absurd, for the *gens* was an agnatic union and where there was no agnate there was no *gens*. Thus the true meaning of this laconic sentence must needs be that if the *proximus adgnatus* refused the inheritance, it fell to the *gens*.

397. The rule in legitimis hereditatibus successio non est Most scholars reject this interpretation as being irreconcilable with the wording of the Twelve Tables and with the rule *in legitimis hereditatibus successio non est*. However, this rule occurs only in a post-classical text (*Epit. Ulp.* 26. 5) with reference to heirs of the second class. In post-classical times the rule was perfectly correct. The succession of the *gens* had disappeared and within the first class a succession such as that rule contemplated was out of the question, since a *suus* could not refuse the inheritance. Thus in post-classical times this apparently general rule could only refer to the second class. The prevailing opinion leads one to the absurd conclusion that if the *proximus adgnatus* refused the inheritance, it became *res nullius* and might be occupied by anybody; and this in an age in which the *gens* was at the height of its strength! This is incredible. Moreover, according to the popular interpretation, there would be no case at all in which the *gens* could succeed.

398. Disappearance of the succession of the gens The succession of the *gens* still existed at the end of the Republic and the classical lawyers probably discussed it in their writings as a living institution. Actually, however, it disappeared in the course of the classical period since organized *gentes* ceased to exist. Post-classical writers, for that reason, declared it to be no longer in use.

Gaius states in two passages of his *Institutes* that the succession of the *gens* was no longer actual law. Only one of these passages is preserved to us (3. 17), but its queer wording renders Gaius' authorship doubtful. The post-classical *liber singularis regularum*, attributed to Ulpian, likewise declared the succession of the *gens* to be outmoded (*Coll.* 16. 4. 2). In the post-classical *Epitome Ulpiani* the succession of the *gens* is deliberately omitted. The post-classical *Sententiae Pauli* (4. 8. 3) say:

> 'Intestatorum hereditas lege duodecim tabularum primum suis heredibus, deinde adgnatis et aliquando quoque gentilibus deferebatur.'

Aliquando here means 'finally', 'at last'.

iv. *General character of the hereditas legitima*

The preceding description makes it quite clear that this law of intestate succession is a pure agnatic law. Blood-relationship alone does not bestow a right of succession. An emancipated person cannot be *heres* in any of the three classes. A mother (if she is not *uxor in manu*) cannot be *heres* to her children and the children cannot be *heredes* to their mother. Further, succession between husband and wife does not exist. The *uxor in manu* is *filiae loco* and might, therefore, succeed to her husband as a *sua*. Any succession to the *uxor in manu* is out of the question, since she is incapable of having property (above, s. 199).

399.
Agnatic
character
of hereditas
legitima

SOURCES

s. 383. Read *D.* (38. 16) 11.
s. 384. Read XII Tab. v. 4; Gai. 3. 1–3.
s. 385. Read Gai. 3. 7–8.
s. 386. Read Gai. 3. 4; *D.* (38. 16) 6 [*neque*]; [*neque . . . cognatus*]; ⟨*non*⟩ *potest*; (38. 16) 3. 9, first sentence; (38. 16) 4; *Epit. Ulp.* 26. 3.
s. 389. Read XII Tab. v. 4; Gai. 3. 9.
s. 390. Read Gai. 1. 156; 3. 10.
s. 391. Read Gai. 3. 11; 3. 15–16.
s. 392. Read Gai. 3. 14.
s. 394. Read Gai. 3. 12.
s. 395. Read XII Tab. v. 8; Gai. 3. 40.
s. 396. Read XII Tab. v. 5.

BIBLIOGRAPHY

ss. 383 ff. *Michon*, 'La Succession ab intestat dans le plus ancien droit romain', *NRH* xlv (1921), 119 ff.; La Pira, *La successione ereditaria intestata e contro il testamento* (1930), 163 ff.
s. 383. Mommsen, *Schr.* iii (1907), 361; Lenel, *Z* xlvi (1926), 31; Beseler, *Bemerkungen zu Z* 1927 (1927), 4.*

s. 384. Kirk, 'Suus heres', Z lviii (1938), 161; Lepri, *St. Solazzi* (1948), 299, with references; v. Woess, *Das röm. Erbrecht und die Erbanwärter* (1911), 65 ff.; Kübler, 'Das Intestaterbrecht der Frauen im alten Rom', Z xli (1920), 15 ff.; Brassloff, *Studien zur röm. Rechtsgeschichte*, i (1925), 35 ff.

s. 386. Albertario, 'Conceptus pro iam nato habetur', *Bull.* xxxiii (1923), 12 ff. = *Scritti*, i (1933), 16 ff.*

s. 389. Lenel, 'Die Rechtsstellung des proximus adgnatus und der gentiles im altröm. Erbrecht', Z xxxvii (1916), 129 ff.; Carcaterra, *La successione intestata dell' adgnatus proximus nella legge delle XII Tavole* (1939, inaccessible).

s. 390. Guarino, 'Questioni intorno a Gai. 3. 10', *SD* x (1944), 290 f.

s. 392. Kübler, l.c. 24.*

s. 396. Lenel, l.c.; Kübler, *PW* vii. 1176 ff.

s. 398. Beseler, *Scritti Ferrini*, iii (1948), 269; Z lxvi (1948), 381.

3. *Senatusconsultum Tertullianum and Orfitianum*

400.
S. C. Tertullianum
Under a *senatusconsultum Tertullianum* (issued in the time of Hadrian) the non-agnatic mother of the *de cuius* (i.e. the mother who was not *in manu* of the father of the *de cuius*) was placed in the second class of intestate heirs (above, s. 389) if she was in possession of the *ius liberorum* (above, s. 310). The details are very complicated and cannot be described here. The whole matter is in need of fresh examination.

As aforesaid (s. 388), a woman cannot have *sui* (above, ss. 384 ff.).

401.
S. C. Orfitianum
A *senatusconsultum Orfitianum* (A.D. 178) permitted children to succeed to their mother in the first class of heirs (above, s. 384); the privilege was not extended to grandchildren.

402.
Classical and post-classical terminology
The law established by these statutes was *vice iuris civilis* (Gai. 1. 4), but the classical lawyers never described these kinds of succession as *hereditas legitima* (*heredes legitimi*). This term was limited to the intestate succession of the Twelve Tables (above, s. 384), and it was only the post-classical lawyers who, in numerous interpolations, designated succession under these *senatusconsulta* as *hereditas legitima*.

403.
Classical conservatism
What puzzles us concerning these two enactments is not that succession is granted to blood-relations, but that this

was done so reluctantly and incompletely. If a child under the *senatusconsultum Orfitianum* could succeed *iure civili* to his mother, why could not also an emancipated child to his father? The classical lawyers would perhaps have answered that the emancipated child might apply for *bonorum possessio* (below, s. 405); but that is hardly a satisfactory answer.

SOURCES

s. 400. Read *Epit. Ulp.* 26. 8.

s. 401. Read *Epit. Ulp.* 26. 7. In 178 consuls were Ser. Scipio Orfitus (with *f* and not with *ph*) and D. Velius Rufus; see *CIL* xvi (*Diplomata Milit.* ed. Nesselhauf), no. 128, p. 114; *CIL* xiii. 6629, 6630.

s. 402. The interpolation of *legitimam* is clear in *D.* (38. 17) 1. 8; likewise the interpolation of *legitima* in *D.* (38. 17) 1. 9, first sentence; but the non-classical usage occurs already in the post-classical *Epit. Ulp.* 26. 7 and 8 and in the post-classical *Sententiae Pauli*, iv. 9 and 10.

BIBLIOGRAPHY

Vangerow, *Pand.* ii (1876), § 408; La Pira, *La successione etc.* (1930), 277 ff.; Beseler, *Bemerkungen zu Z 1927* (1927), 4; Lavaggi, 'La successione della libertà e il SC. Orfitiano', *SD* xii (1946), 174 ff.*

4. *Bonorum possessio ab intestato*

At the side of intestate succession *iure civili* there stands in classical times intestate succession *iure honorario, bonorum possessio ab intestato*. We know little of the development of this institution and must confine ourselves to the rules of the Edict codified by Julian and Hadrian (above, s. 25). Under the rubric *si tabulae testamenti nullae extabunt* (Lenel, *Edict.* p. 355) the *praetor urbanus* (in the provinces the governor) promised to grant *bonorum possessio*, distinguishing the following classes of heirs.

404. Scope of the following exposition

Class I

In the first place *bonorum possessio* was granted to the *liberi* of the *de cuius*. The wording of the Edict has not been preserved, but it can hardly have used the term *liberi*. The classical lawyers discussing this clause of the Edict used the word *liberi* in a technical and rather artificial sense. *Liberi* in this sense are the *sui* of the *de cuius* (above, s. 384)

405. Conception of liberi

and those persons who would be *sui* if *capitis deminutio* (above, s. 123) had not prevented them (provided they are not in another person's *potestas*). The lawyers designated this type of *bonorum possessio* as *bonorum possessio unde liberi*, an abbreviation of 'bonorum possessio ex illa parte edicti unde liberi ad bonorum possessionem vocantur' (*unde* is particularly frequent in official language).

Take the following example:

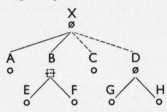

At the death of the *de cuius* there existed the following persons: A, a son of the *de cuius* X and in his *potestas*; E and F, sons of a deceased daughter B; C, an emancipated son; and G and H, sons of an emancipated and deceased son D. Now A is *suus* and consequently belongs to the *liberi*; E and F are neither *sui* nor *liberi*, C is not *suus*, but would be *suus* if he had not suffered *capitis deminutio* by emancipation; he belongs, therefore, to the *liberi*; G and H were never X's *sui*, but they would be his *sui* if their father D had not suffered *capitis deminutio* by emancipation; they belong, therefore, to the *liberi*.

406. A woman cannot have liberi   When the *de cuius* is a woman, there is no *bonorum possessio unde liberi*, since a woman can have no *sui* and consequently (and paradoxically) no *liberi*. Even under the *senatusconsultum Orfitianum* (above, s. 401) the children cannot claim *bonorum possessio unde liberi*, but only *unde legitimi* (below, s. 414).

407. Mode of succession   The *liberi* succeeded according to the same rules as the *sui* in the *legitima hereditas* (above, ss. 384 ff.); males and females are, therefore, on a par and the principle of representation applies. However, the *liberi* never acquire *bonorum possessio ipso iure* (above, s. 378), whereas the *sui* acquire the *hereditas ipso iure*. An exception to the principle of representation is laid down by a clause of the Edict which was called 'nova clausula Iuliani de coniungendis cum emancipato liberis eius' (Lenel, *Edict.* § 146).

Suppose that X has emancipated his son A but has retained his grandsons B and C in his *potestas*. B and C are X's *sui*, A, B, and C are his *liberi*. According to the principle of representation A alone would be entitled to *bonorum possessio* to the exclusion of his sons B and C. According to the *nova clausula* all three obtain *bonorum possessio*, A as to one-half, B and C as to one-quarter each. The *ratio* of this exception is nowhere given in our sources, but it was probably the following. *Bonorum possessio unde liberi* was originally *sine re* (above, s. 378). Already at the end of the Republic or in the early days of the Principate it became *cum re*; only in Julian's case the *bonorum possessio* granted to the emancipated A remained *sine re*, otherwise his *bonorum possessio* would have entirely deprived the *heredes iuris civilis* B and C, of their rights. Julian granted to the emancipated A a *bonorum possessio cum re*, but only as to one-half, reserving the other half to the *sui* B and C. Thus he avoided the complete exclusion of the *heredes iuris civilis*. The inverse case shows that this was the *ratio*. Suppose X has emancipated his grandsons B and C and retained A *in potestate*. Here *bonorum possessio* is granted to A alone following the principle of representation, since this *bonorum possessio* does not exclude *heredes iuris civilis*; B and C are excluded, but they are not *sui*.

After the *bonorum possessio* granted to the *liberi non sui* had become *cum re*—but probably not much later—the institution of *collatio bonorum* was developed. Whenever *sui* together with *liberi non sui* claimed *bonorum possessio unde liberi*, the unconditional granting of *bonorum possessio* to the *non sui* would sometimes result in a gross injustice towards the *sui*. Suppose the *de cuius* had two sons, A and B; he had emancipated B but retained A in his *potestas*. A is a *suus*, B a *non suus*, but both being *liberi* they might claim *bonorum possessio* as to one-half each. Now A had no proprietary capacity as long as his father lived, since he was in his *potestas* (above, s. 263); whatever he acquired fell automatically to his father and, if it still existed at his father's death, became part of the inheritance (let us leave aside *peculium castrense*; above, s. 264). Thus the emancipated B would take a share in the property acquired by A, but A would have no share in the property acquired by B after his emancipation. This would indeed be unjust, and for that reason the praetor declared in his Edict under the rubric *de collatione bonorum* (Lenel, *Edict.* § 144) that he would not grant *bonorum possessio* to B, unless he promised A to give him a reasonable share of his own property which he (B) possessed at his father's death; he had to promise in the form of a *stipulatio*: 'quidquid moriente patre in bonis habui id boni viri arbitratu me collaturum'. For this promise (*cautio de conferendis bonis*) the Edict contained a precedent among the *stipulationes praetoriae* (Lenel, *Edict.* § 283 and above, s. 114). The details of this *collatio* were not expounded in the Edict, but the lawyers construed the Edict in the following way: B, who impairs A's civil right by *bonorum possessio*, is bound to promise him a portion of his own·property; this portion corresponds to A's share of the *bonorum possessio*. In the present case A claims *bonorum possessio* as to one-half; accordingly B has to promise him one-half of the property which he (B) happens to possess at his father's death. When there are several *emancipati* (e.g. A is *suus*, B and C *emancipati*) each of them has to give such a promise to A; in fixing the portion to be contributed by them the other emancipated son is regarded as not existing, so that in this second case also B and C have to promise A one-half of their respective property. This is the classical notion of *collatio*. Students should be expressly warned against believing that the *emancipati*, before sharing the inheritance with *sui*, had to pool their property with the inherited property.

Let us consider another case in which there are two *sui* and two *emancipati*. The *de cuius* had four sons; two of them, A and B, remained *in patria potestate*, whereas C and D were emancipated. At the death of the father C had a property of 90, D a property of 60. The value of the father's estate was 400. A, B, C, and D are *liberi* and each of them may claim *bonorum possessio* as to one-quarter, but C and D cannot obtain *bonorum possessio* unless they promise A as well as B one-third of their respective property. Thus we arrive finally at the following result:

A obtains one-quarter of the inheritance (= 100); further, from C he obtains one-third of his property (= 30) and from D one-third of his property (= 20); consequently he obtains altogether 150.

B also obtains one-quarter of the inheritance (= 100); further, he obtains from C one-third of his property (= 30) and from D one-third of his property (= 20), thus he obtains in all 150.

C obtains one-quarter of the inheritance (= 100); he retains of his own property 90–60 (= 30); thus he has now altogether 130 and so has gained 40 by the *bonorum possessio.*

D obtains one-quarter of the inheritance (= 100); he retains of his own property 60–40 (= 20); thus he has now in all 120, having gained 60 by the *bonorum possessio.*

By this mode of *collatio* it may happen that the *emancipatus* suffers a loss by *bonorum possessio*; but in such a case he should abstain from *bonorum possessio* altogether and if he applied for it by inadvertence, 'de se quaeri debet: iura vigilantibus scripta sunt'.

Suppose a father had three sons; A was *in potestate*, B and C were emancipated. At the father's death B had a property of 80, C had no property at all; the value of the father's estate was 90. A, B, and C are *liberi* and may claim *bonorum possessio* as to one-third each, but B has to promise A to contribute one-half of his property. We have the following result:

A obtains one-third of the inheritance (= 30); further he acquired from B one-half of his property (= 40); thus he gets in all 70.

B obtains one-third of the inheritance (= 30) and retains of his own property 80 − 40 (= 40); thus he has now 70, i.e. he has lost 10.

C obtains one-third of the inheritance (= 30).

Thus the *ratio* of the classical *collatio bonorum* is quite clear: when the civil right of a *suus* is impaired by the *bonorum possessio* of an *emancipatus*, the latter is bound to recompense the *suus* for that loss by promising him a part of his own property. The same idea underlies the classical *collatio dotis* which was regulated under a special rubric of the Edict (*de collatione dotis*; Lenel, *Edict.* §§ 145, 283). Available sources are unfortunately unsatisfactory. 410. Collatio dotis

Most probably the classical rule was the following. Suppose the *de cuius* had a son A *in potestate* and a daughter B whom he had emancipated. B married (free marriage; above, s. 180) when her father was still alive and a *dos* (above, s. 204) was given to her husband either by her father or by herself or by somebody else. At her father's death the marriage still existed. B might claim *bonorum possessio unde liberi* as to one-half; if she had property of her own she had to promise a contribution from this property according to the rules which we have just described. But the *dos* does not belong to her property: the sole owner of the *dos* is her husband (above, s. 213), nor is the *dos in bonis uxoris*. Thus under the edict *de collatione bonorum* B would not be bound *conferre dotem*. On the other hand, B had at her father's death an expectancy concerning the *dos*, for if later the matrimony was dissolved by divorce or by the husband's death, she might recover the *dos* (above, s. 218). For these reasons the praetor declared under the rubric *de collatione dotis* that the emancipated daughter was bound to give the *suus* a *cautio de conferenda dote*; she had to promise *me dotem meam boni viri arbitratu collaturam*, which means that if she actually recovered the *dos* later, she had to surrender a part of her *dos* (in the present case, one-half) to the *suus*. If the daughter was still *in potestate patris* the Edict did not apply. Take the following case. The *de cuius* had a son A and a daughter B; both were in his *potestas*. B married (free marriage) during her father's life and her husband received a *dos*. A and B are *sui* and *liberi* and each of them may claim *bonorum possessio unde liberi* as to one-half. B is not bound *conferre dotem* and with good reason, for in this case B's *bonorum possessio* does not impair the right which A has *iure civili*. However, on the strength of a rescript of Antoninus Pius, B is bound *iure civili conferre dotem*: the judge who has to divide the inheritance (*iudicium familiae erciscundae*; above, s. 86) imposes on B the obligation to give A a *cautio de conferenda dote*. The *ratio* of this imperial *collatio* was different· from that of the praetorian *collatio*. To be sure, in this case also B acquired an expectancy *vivente patre* just as in the first case, but the purpose of the imperial *collatio* was not to indemnify the *suus* for the loss which he suffered by B's *bonorum possessio*. The Edict was not added to after Pius' rescript, nor was that required. When in the present case B claimed *bonorum possessio*, the praetor granted it without requiring a *cautio*. But if now B claimed partition as *bonorum possessor*, i.e. by the *actio familiae erciscundae ficticia*, the judge imposed on her the duty to give a *cautio de conferenda dote*.

411. Contribution of gifts The idea that a child has to contribute what he or she had received from the father *inter vivos* remained entirely foreign to classical law. If a father of two sons (A and B) had emancipated B and conveyed to him a certain property, B claiming *bonorum possessio unde liberi* together with A had to contribute from this property as far as it existed at the father's death, just as from other property which he acquired after the emancipation; but if both A and B were emancipated the latter was not bound *conferre donationem*. This is perfectly right. If the father regarded the donation as an advance payment on B's future share of the inheritance, he should make an adequate disposition by testament. Accordingly a daughter is under classical law never

bound to contribute from her *dos profecticia* (above, s. 211) to her *emancipated* brother.

In post-classical times the classical *collatio* lost its rational basis, since the proprietary incapacity of a child in power disappeared; but we cannot describe the history of the post-classical *collatio* here. 412. Post-classical collatio

So much about the *bonorum possessio unde liberi*. When the *de cuius* was a *libertus* the patron might sometimes claim *bonorum possessio* together with the *liberi*, viz. in so far as the *liberi* were *liberi non naturales* (*filius adoptivus* and *uxor in manu*). In such cases the patron might claim *bonorum possessio* of half of the portion which fell to the *liberi non naturales*. 413. The patron in the first class

> Suppose that a *libertus* had a son A and an adopted son B. The patron might claim *bonorum possessio* as to one-quarter, A to one-half, B to one-quarter.

Class II

If there were no *liberi*, or if these did not claim *bonorum possessio*, the praetor granted *bonorum possessio* to the *heredes legitimi*, i.e. to those persons who were *heredes* according to the rules of the Twelve Tables (*bonorum possessio unde legitimi*; see above, ss. 384 ff.). Those persons who were *heredes* under the *senatusconsultum Tertullianum* and *Orfitianum* (above, ss. 400, 401) were not *heredes legitimi* (above, s. 402), but the praetor granted to them *bonorum possessio unde legitimi*, i.e. 'ex ea parte edicti unde legitimi ad bonorum possessionem vocantur'. 414. Unde legitimi

Class III

The third class comprehends the *cognati* of the *de cuius*, i.e. his blood-relations; his agnates, in so far as they are not blood-relations (above, s. 390), are *cognatorum loco*. *Bonorum possessio unde cognati* is granted to the *proximus cognatus* down to the sixth degree; to a *cognatus* of the seventh degree only if the parent of the cognate and the *de cuius* were grandchildren of brothers or sisters or of brother and sister. 415. Unde cognati

> If G is the *de cuius*, H might claim *bonorum possessio unde cognati*. H is of the seventh degree, but his parent F and the *de cuius* G are

grandchildren of brothers (B and C). If the *de cuius* was E, H's son could not claim *bonorum possessio*, though he is also of the seventh degree.

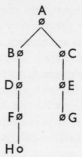

It was certainly reasonable to limit the granting of *bonorum possessio*, but the praetor was too liberal (he took the limit from the *lex Cincia* and the *lex Furia testamentaria*); he ought to have stopped at the fourth degree. However, Roman liberalism was loath to let the inheritance fall to the State. On the strength of an *epistula Hadriani*, *bonorum possessio unde cognati* was granted to the illegitimate children of a soldier (above, s. 278).

Classes IV and V

416. Unde familia patroni, Unde patronus patroni   In the fourth class stood the patron and his family when they had suffered *capitis deminutio* (above, s. 123) and therefore did not belong to the *legitimi*. In the fifth class stood the *patronus patroni*.

Class VI

417. Unde vir et uxor   In this class *bonorum possessio* was granted to the husband or wife of the *de cuius* (*bonorum possessio unde vir et uxor*).

Class VII

418. Unde cognati manumissoris   In the last class were the *cognati* of the patron.

General rules

419. Conceptus pro iam nato habetur   As regards the praetorian heirs of class I the praetor applied the principle *conceptus pro iam nato habetur* (above, ss. 124, 386). It sufficed, therefore, that these persons were *iam concepti* at the death of the *de cuius*. Under post-classical law the principle also applied to other classes.

Persons to whom *bonorum possessio ab intestato* is offered
have to apply for it within a certain time, as a rule within
100 days *intra dies centum quibus scierit potueritque*; parents
and children of the *de cuius* were allowed a year. This time-
limit was expressly stated in the Edict (Lenel, *Edict.* § 165).

420.
Time-
limit

Where the members of a certain class did not make use
of the *bonorum possessio* offered to them, it was offered to the
members of the next class in so far as they did *not* belong to
one of the preceding classes (so-called *successio ordinum*).
The clause of the Edict which stated this rule was called
edictum successorium (Lenel, *Edict.* § 165).

421.
Successio
ordinum

> Suppose the *de cuius* had only one child, A, who was in his *potestas*.
> *Bonorum possessio unde liberi* is offered to A, but he does not claim it
> *intra annum*. Now *bonorum possessio* is offered to the *heredes legitimi*.
> A as a *suus* is *heres legitimus*: is *bonorum possessio* offered to him a second
> time? If again A does not claim *bonorum possessio*, it is offered to the
> *cognati*; A is *proximus cognatus*: is *bonorum possessio* offered to him a third
> time? Prevailing opinion answers these questions in the affirmative; but
> they have to be answered in the negative. Such a repeated offering is
> unjustified and in open conflict with the wording of the Edict. The
> praetor expressly declared in the *edictum successorium*:
>
> > 'Quibus ex edicto bonorum possessio dari potest, si quis eorum aut
> > dari sibi noluerit aut intra dies centum quibus scierit potueritque non
> > admiserit, tunc *ceteris* (N.B.) bonorum possessionem perinde dabo *ac
> > si prior ex eo numero non fuerit.*' (N.B.).
>
> The popular but incorrect view is due to *D.* (38. 9) 1. 11, which is
> obviously spurious.

In the third class there was also a *successio graduum*; when
the *proximus cognatus* did not claim *bonorum possessio*, it was
offered to the cognate of the next degree.

422.
Successio
graduum

To conclude, it must be particularly emphasized that the
bonorum possessio ab intestato granted according to the Edict
was as a rule a *possessio sine re* (above, s. 378), i.e. not protected against the *heredes*. It is only the *bonorum possessio
unde liberi* which is *cum re* as against the *heredes legitimi*
(above, s. 420).

423.
Bonorum
possessio
cum re,
sine re

> Suppose the *de cuius* had two sons A and B; the former was *suus*, the
> latter *emancipatus*. B might obtain *bonorum possessio* as to one-half which
> is *cum re* as regards A. Suppose that the *de cuius* had only one emanci-
> pated son who obtained *bonorum possessio unde liberi*; this *bonorum
> possessio* too is *cum re* as regards the *proximus adgnatus*. On the other

hand, suppose that there was only one single *suus* who did not apply for *bonorum possessio unde liberi*. After the lapse of a year (above, s. 420) the *proximus adgnatus* claimed and obtained *bonorum possessio unde legitimi*. This *bonorum possessio* is *sine re*, since the *suus* might claim the inheritance by *hereditatis petitio*.

Let us examine the following case: *Liberi* did not exist and the *proximus adgnatus* acquired the *hereditas iure civili* by *aditio* (above, s. 376), but did not apply for *bonorum possessio unde legitimi*. After the lapse of 100 days (above, s. 420) the *proximus cognatus* might claim and obtain *bonorum possessio unde cognati*, but it would be *sine re*, since the *proximus adgnatus* might claim the inheritance *iure civili* by *hereditatis petitio*.

SOURCES

ss. 405–7. Read Gai. 3. 26; *Epit. Ulp.* 28. 8; *D.* (38. 6) 5. 1.

s. 409. Read *Coll.* 16. 7. 2 (cf. Gai. 3. 20 and above, s. 242); *Paul. Sent.* (5. 9) 4; *D.* (37. 6) 1. 24; (37. 6) 2. 5; (37. 6) 3. 2 [1. 24 and 3. 2 are non-classical texts but substantially classical].

s. 410. Read *D.* (37. 7) 1 pr. (a post-classical paraphrase).

s. 411. Read *C.* (6. 20) 4 [*dotem in medium*]; *si* ⟨*bonorum possessionem*⟩; [*succedant*]; [*seu adventiciam*]; [*a patre . . . constitutam*]; [*his etenim . . . placuit*].

s. 413. Gai. 3. 40, 41.

s. 414. Read *Epit. Ulp.* 28. 7; *D.* (38. 7) 2. 4 [*legitimum*]; [*legitimam*]; read the *agnitio bonorum possessionis* in a papyrus of A.D. 249, Z xxxii (1911), 278; *FIRA* iii, no. 61.

s. 415. *Epit. Ulp.* 28. 7 and 9; *D.* (38. 8) 1. 3. For the *lex Cincia* see *Fr. Vat.* 298; for the *lex Furia Fr. Vat.* 301. *Epistula Hadriani*: Mitteis, *Chrest.* no. 373; *FIRA* i, no 78, with Berger, *Journal of Juristic Papyrology*, i (1945), 28.

ss. 416–18. Read *Epit. Ulp.* 28. 7.

ss. 420–1. Read *D.* (38. 9) 1. 10, 11 with Beseler, *Beiträge*, iv (1920), 158; v (1931), 66.

s. 422. See Gai. 3. 28: *successio graduum* in class II?

s. 423. Read Gai. 3. 37.

BIBLIOGRAPHY

ss. 404 ff. Lenel, *Edict.* (1927), 155 ff.; La Pira, *La successione ereditaria intestata* (1930), 227 ff.

s. 408. Cosentini 'Breve nota sull' origine dell' edictum de coniungendis cum emancipato liberis eius' (disputing Julian's authorship), *St. Solazzi* (1948), 219 ff. with references.

s. 409. Windscheid, *Pand.* iii (1906), § 609, with references; Guarino, *Collatio bonorum* (1937); 'Sul modo di attuazione della *collatio emancipati*', *SD* iv (1938), 521 ff.; 'Über den Begriff der Kollation', Z lix (1939), 509 ff.; Beseler, *Scritti Ferrini*, iii (1948), 303 f. is not acceptable.

s. 410. Lenel, *Edict.* § 145; Guarino, 'Collatio dotis', *Bull.* viii–ix (1947), 259, hardly acceptable.

s. 411. Pringsheim, 'Die *Collatio dotis* an die *emancipati*', *SD* iv (1938), 533; Guarino, Z lix (1939), 533.

s. 412. Windscheid, l.c. §§ 609 ff.; Guarino, ll. cc. *passim*.

s. 414. On the *heredes ex senatusconsulto Tertulliano and Orfitiano* see above, s. 402, and Beseler, *Bemerkungen zu Z 1927* (1927), 4 f. On the text of the Edict see Lenel, *Edict*. § 157; Solazzi, *Studi Besta*, i (1939), 210.

s. 419. Albertario, 'Conceptus pro iam nato habetur', *Bull*. xxxiii (1923), 14 f., modified in *Scritti*, i (1933), 18 f.

s. 420–1. Beseler, *Beiträge*, iv (1920), 158; v (1931), 66.

s. 423. C. Arnò, 'La bonorum possessio sine re', *Memoria della R. Accademia di scienze, lettere ed arti in Modena*, Serie III, vol. xii (sezione scienze), Estratto, pp. 18 ff.

5. *Bona vacantia*

Where an inheritance was not claimed either *iure civili* or *iure honorario*, the inheritance fell under Augustus' *lex Iulia de maritandis ordinibus* to the *aerarium populi Romani* (above, s. 148) as *bona vacantia*; later, apparently already under Tiberius (Tacitus, *Ann*. 2. 48), it fell to the *fiscus* (above, s. 152). Neither the *aerarium* nor the *fiscus* was regarded as *heres*, but their position was similar to that of an *heres*. By special privilege *bona vacantia* sometimes fell to a *municipium*.

424. Bona vacantia

SOURCES

Read Gai. 2. 150; *Epit. Ulp*. 28. 7 in fine; Pliny *Epist. ad Traianum*, 84; *Edictum Claudii de civitate Volubilitanorum*, Chatelain, *Inscr. Lat. de Maroc*, i (1942), no. 116 = *FIRA* i, p. 416.

BIBLIOGRAPHY

Vangerow, *Pand*. ii (1876), § 564; Biondi in *Acta divi Augusti*, i (1945), 195, with references; Fitzler–Seeck, *PW* x. 354 n. 2; Weiss, *PW* xii. 2363; Z liii (1933), 256; Beseler, Z xlv (1925), 548; O. Hirschfeld, *Die Kaiserlichen Verwaltungsbeamten* (1905), 116; *FIRA* i. 471 (concerning the *Forma Idiologi*, § 4).

6. *Post-classical intestate succession*

Classical intestate succession was considerably modified in the course of the post-classical period; in particular, *ius civile* and *ius praetorium* were more and more assimilated and amalgamated with each other; but in the Eastern

425. Post-classical intestate succession

Empire the two kinds of law continued, at least in principle, to exist. A survey of Justinian's law as it was in 533 is given in Justinian's *Institutes*, 3. 1–9. However, this law was drastically reformed in Justinian's *Novella* 118 (A.D. 543, some additions in *Novella* 127 of 548). This post-classical evolution requires a special description which lies outside the scope of this book.

BIBLIOGRAPHY

Windscheid, *Pand.* iii (1906), §§ 569 ff.; La Pira, *La successione ereditaria* (1930), 296 ff.; Archi, *L'Epitome Gai* (1937), 317 ff.; Bossowski, 'Die Novelle 118 Justinians und deren Vorgeschichte', *Festschrift P. Koschaker*, ii (1939), 277 ff.

CHAPTER III

SUCCESSION UPON TESTAMENT

1. *Introduction*

UNDER classical law a will (*testamentum*) is a legal act in which somebody is appointed heir (*heres*). A will might contain other provisions besides the institution of an heir (legacy, *exheredatio*, *datio tutoris*, *manumissio*), but such dispositions were only regarded as supplements and additions to the *institutio heredis* and the latter alone was essential for the existence of a valid will: 'caput et fundamentum intellegitur totius testamenti heredis institutio' (Gai. 2. 229). Without an *institutio heredis* there was no valid will, and when none of the appointed heirs accepted the inheritance the whole will (not only the institutions of heirs) broke down. On the other hand, where a legacy left in a will was void this did not affect the institution of the heir (or heirs). A will might contain nothing but an *institutio heredis*, but it could not contain only legacies. When a person wished to make a gift *mortis causa* to somebody without altering the intestate succession, he might do so by *donatio mortis causa* or in *codicilli* (below, ss. 543, 549, 574), but such acts do not amount to wills.

426. Classical conception of testamentum

This simple conception of a will already existed in early republican times; indeed, it is scarcely credible that under the Twelve Tables the will could contain nothing but legacies. In any case we have no reliable evidence for the existence of such a will and need not discuss the question here.

427. Republican conception

As usual, etymology tells us but little. *Testamentum* is derived from *testari* and *testis*, but it does not mean 'a legal act attested by witnesses'. As *ornamentum* means something which *ornat*, *documentum* something which *docet*, *monumentum* something which *monet*, thus *testamentum* means something (an oral declaration or a document) which attests, shows, proves, declares. *Testator* is a person who declares and not a witness.

428. Etymology of testamentum

The definitions of the testament which we meet in our sources are unsatisfactory; the strength of Roman lawyers did not lie in their definitions.

429. Roman definitions of testamentum

430. Scope
of ch. III

At this point we have only to deal with the will as a basis for succession, i.e. so far as *institutio heredis* is concerned. We shall therefore describe the different forms of a will, the revocation of a will, and the kinds of *heredis institutio*. Acquisition of the inheritance by the instituted heir must be discussed together with acquisition by an *heres ab intestato*. Other possible contents of a will, particularly legacies, need likewise a separate description (below, ss. 539 ff.).

SOURCES

s. 429. Read Gellius, 7. 12. 1 (Servius Sulpicius); *Epit. Ulp.* 20. 1; *D.* (28. 1) 1.

BIBLIOGRAPHY

ss. 426 ff. Windscheid, *Pand.* iii (1906), §§ 538 ff.; Kübler, *PW* vA. 985 ff.; Biondi, *Successione testamentaria* (*Trattato di diritto romano*, ed. E. Albertario, vol. x, 1943).*

s. 426. Biondi, l.c. 17 ff., 179 ff.; Sanfilippo, *Studi sulla hereditas*, i (1937), 142 ff. (Estratto dal vol. xvii degli *Annali Palermo*); Vismara, *St. Besta*, iii (1939), 303 ff.

s. 427. Lenel, 'Zur Geschichte der heredis institutio' in *Essays in Legal History*, ed. P. Vinogradoff (1913); Solazzi, *Diritto ereditario romano*, i (1932), 89 ff.; Bonfante, *Corso*, vi (1930), 64 ff.

s. 429. Biondi, l.c. 19 ff.; Vismara, *St. Besta*, iii (1939), 358 ff.

2. *Testamentum per aes et libram*

431.
Testamen-
tum calatis
comitiis
and in
procinctu

It has already been said (s. 361) that will was already known to the Twelve Tables. There were two forms, the *testamentum calatis comitiis* and the *testamentum in procinctu*. The former was made, like *adrogatio* (above, s. 244), by a decree of the *comitia curiata* on a motion of the *pontifex maximus*. Since it was left to the discretion of the *pontifex* to bring in the motion, he had an immense influence upon the framing of the will. The *pontifex* did not bring in a motion without the testator's consent; on the other hand, the testator needed the consent of the *pontifex*, since otherwise the *pontifex* would refuse to bring in the motion. Thus at least some of the rules to be observed in making an *institutio heredis* originated from the cautelary jurisprudence of the pontiffs. The *testamentum in procinctu* was a military will, for *in procinctu* means *in acie procincta*, in girded-up battle-array, ready for battle. It was made within the framework of a sacred ritual which preceded the beginning of the battle; an informal oral declaration addressed to those comrades who stood nearest to the *testator* was sufficient. Neither of these types of will was abrogated, but they were in practice replaced by the will by bronze and balance (*per aes et libram*). Even the military will passed out of use, since it was too closely connected with a form of archaic ritual which in the course of the second century B.C. became obsolete. In the last century B.C. soldiers made use of the ordinary *testamentum per aes et libram* (Caesar, *Bell. Gall.* 1. 39. 4, though the text is interpolated); the classical military will has no direct connexion with the *testamentum in procinctu*.

The will by bronze and balance was not known to the Twelve Tables. Gaius expressly states (2. 101) that 'in the beginning' (*initio*) there existed only the two wills which we have just described, and that the will by bronze and balance came later (*accessit deinde*). 'In the beginning' can only mean 'in the Twelve Tables', since Gaius could not possibly know anything about the law before that code. The will by bronze and balance is the artificial product of early Roman cautelary jurisprudence; it was made in the following way. The testator conveyed his whole estate, both present and future, by *mancipatio nummo uno* to another person (*familiae emptor*), who thereby became owner at the testator's death. In effecting this conveyance the testator gave instructions to the *familiae emptor* concerning the distribution of the estate after the testator's death, either orally in the *nuncupatio* or in the *tabulae testamenti* to which he referred in the *nuncupatio*.

432. Original character of the testamentum per aes et libram

> The formulas to be pronounced by parties in making this *mancipatio* are preserved to us in Gaius' *Institutes* (2. 104). *Familia pecuniaque* simply means 'estate'. *Familiae emptor* means *emptor familiae pecuniaeque*, i.e. buyer of the whole estate. See Beseler, Z liv (1934), 323.

Strictly speaking, this *mancipatio* is no testament at all, since it does not imply the appointment of an *heres*: the *familiae emptor* is not an *heres* (Gaius, 2. 103, expressly says: *heredis locum optinebat*); still less is an *heres* to be found in the person or persons to whom the *familiae emptor* had to furnish something according to the instructions given by the testator. On the other hand, the *mancipatio* was not meant to be an act *inter vivos* but rather *mortis causa*, since it was not to come into force before the testator's death. It can never have been otherwise. It is incredible that a testator should ever have conveyed his whole present and future estate to somebody with immediate effect: he would then have been entirely dependent upon the goodwill of the *familiae emptor*. In truth the *mancipatio* was made conditional upon the testator's death by the clause *quo tu iure testamentum facere possis*; by describing the act as a will it was sufficiently expressed that the *mancipatio* should come into force with the testator's death and not earlier. This clause further implied that the testator might revoke the *mancipatio* at his discretion. With the death of the testator the *familiae emptor* became owner of the estate, but only as a trustee. This was expressed by the words 'familiam pecuniamque tuam endo mandatela tua custodelaque mea esse aio'; the *familiae emptor* has to act according to the instructions given by the testator (*mandata*) and to protect the estate (*custodire*) which implies that he should *not* be entitled to use the estate for his own benefit.

433. Late republican testamentum per aes et libram This was the original character of the mancipatory will. It was in truth a conveyance *mortis causa* by which the *familiae emptor* was appointed as a trustee and had to carry out the instructions given by the testator. The legal position of the trustee was similar to that of an executor. If the republican lawyers had retained and further developed this idea, they might have arrived eventually at the present English law of succession. Actually, however, the reverse happened. The *mancipatio* was deprived of its original effects; it no longer conveyed the estate to the *familiae emptor*, who was in consequence no longer a trustee and executor but substantially only a witness. The *mancipatio* degenerated into a mere formality (*dicis causa*) and the idea of an executor disappeared so completely that it was entirely unknown to classical orthodoxy (below, s. 576). On the other hand, the testator's *nuncupatio* and *tabulae testamenti* were now assimilated to the *testamentum calatis*

comitiis. A mancipatory will now had to contain the appointment of an *heres*, whose position differed in no way from
that of an *heres* appointed in a *testamentum calatis comitiis.*
This development is described by Gaius (2. 103), unfortunately without details and accurate dates. It should,
however, be kept in mind that the original mancipatory testament was unknown to the Twelve Tables (above, s. 432)
and that its later form is probably to be attributed to the
second century B.C. and not to an earlier period, since otherwise Gaius would hardly have known anything about the
original form.

During the last century of the Republic the mancipatory 434.
will was the only Roman will, during the classical period Classical
the only *ordinary* will (on the extraordinary military will see testament
below, s. 435). In the eyes of a non-lawyer it was now
nothing but a declaration of the testator before seven witnesses (the five witnesses required in every *mancipatio*, the
libripens and the *familiae emptor*) that one or more wax
tablets contained his will, which he sometimes, but not
necessarily, read to them. Thus the act appeared already
to a non-lawyer like Cicero. The lawyers, however, while
realizing that the *mancipatio* was now a mere archaic drama
(Gaius, 2. 103: *dicis causa propter veteris iuris imitationem*)
nevertheless reverently preserved the traditional forms: the
man with the balance had to be present and the *familiae
emptor* had to pronounce the old formula as if he were still
the trustee of the testator as of yore. In short, the whole
ritual had to be scrupulously performed and if any important part of it were omitted, the testament was relentlessly
condemned as void *iure civili*, at least by the orthodox
lawyers in Rome. It may, however, be doubted whether—
in particular in the provinces and after the *constitutio Antoniniana* of A.D. 312 (above, s. 136)—this *mancipatio mortis
causa* was still actually performed. On this point our documents do not furnish reliable evidence: they may record an
act as having taken place which in truth did not take place
at all. Gordian's enactment of A.D. 242 (*C.* 6. 11. 2) seems
to imply that a will could be made *iure civili* by an oral
declaration before seven witnesses. We possess some

mancipatory wills partly in Latin, partly in Greek translation, above all the amazingly well-preserved five wax
tablets which contain the will of the cavalryman Antonius
Silvanus made 142 A.D.

SOURCES

s. 431. Read Gai. 2. 101; for the ritual to which *test. in procinctu*
belonged see *Schol. Veron. ad Vergil. Aen.* 10. 241 in *Servii grammatici
quae feruntur in Verg. carm. commentaria*, ed. Thilo–Hagen, iii. 2 (1902),
446; Bruns, *Fontes*, ii (1909), 77 f.; cf. Plutarch, *Coriol.* 9.

s. 432. Read Gai. 2. 102, 104.

s. 433. Read Gai. 2. 103.

s. 434. Read *C.* (6. 11) 2 [*bonorum possessionem*] ⟨*hereditatem*⟩ *deferri*.

BIBLIOGRAPHY

s. 431. Kübler, *PW* va. 985 f.; *FIRA* i. 37, with references; Biondi,
Successione testamentaria (1943), 35 ff.; Kaser, *Altröm. Jus* (1949), 148.

s. 432. Weiss, Z xlii (1921), 102 ff.; Beseler, Z xliii (1922), 535;
Solazzi, *Diritto ereditario*, i (1932), 89 ff.; *Glossae a Gaio*, ii (1933), 404;
Kübler, l.c. 987, 996 ff.; Biondi, l.c. 39 ff.; Kaser, 149.*

s. 434. E. Costa, *Cicerone giureconsulto*, i (1927), 218. For the testament
of Ant. Silvanus see Guéraud–Jouget, *Études de papyrologie*, vi (1940),
1 ff., the text also in *FIRA* iii, no. 47, commentary: Macqueron, 'Le
Testament d'Antonius Silvanus', *RH* xxiv (1943), 123 ff. For further
documents see *FIRA* iii, pp. 129 ff.; Taubenschlag, *Law of Greco-Roman
Egypt* (1944), 145, with references.

3. *The classical military testament*

435.
Military
testament

A soldier might of course make an ordinary will *per aes
et libram* and the will of Silvanus which we have just mentioned is such a will. But from the time of Julius Caesar
soldiers were frequently granted special privilege by the
emperors in making wills, as the old *testamentum in procinctu* had disappeared long before (above, s. 431). We only
possess the text of a constitution of Trajan (or part of it)
according to which no form whatever had to be observed
by a soldier in making his will, a dangerous liberty, since
it was now sometimes difficult to discern a true will from
casual remarks. Trajan realized this danger, but did not
come to a workable method of distinguishing. In any case
a military will was extinguished when a year had elapsed

after the *missio honesta*, and immediately after *missio inhonesta*.

SOURCES

Read *D*. (29. 1) 1 pr.; *P. Fay*. x, to be used not in the ed. princeps (1900) but in Ferrini, *Scritti*, i (1929), 454; Gai. 2. 109, 114 *in fine*; *D*. (29. 1) 24.

BIBLIOGRAPHY

Arangio-Ruiz, *Bull*. xviii (1906), 157 ff.; Calderini, *Atene e Roma* xviii (1915), 259 ff.; Kübler, *PW* va. 1000; Biondi, *Successione testamentaria* (1943), 73 ff. with references; Levy, Z lii (1932), 526; Guarino, 'Sull' origine del testamento dei militari', *Rend. Lomb.* lxxii (1938–9). On Gai. 2. 109 see Beseler, Z lvii (1937), 44; Solazzi, *Glosse a Gaio*, ii (1933), 413 ff. On Gnom. Idiol. see *FIRA* i. 475, with references.

4. *The so-called praetorian will*

The praetor promised in his Edict (Lenel, *Edict*. §§ 149, 155) to grant *bonorum possessio secundum testamentum* (above, s. 378), i.e. to the heirs appointed in a mancipatory or military will. As regards the latter the praetor simply referred to imperial constitutions (the text of the Edict is not preserved at this point). Concerning the mancipatory will the praetor declared that when 'tabulae testamenti non minus quam septem testium signis signatae' were brought before him he would grant *bonorum possessio* to the *heres* or *heredes* appointed in such tablets. The terminology of the Edict is significant, for the seven 'witnesses' required by the praetor were the five witnesses required in any *mancipatio*, the *libripens*, and the *familiae emptor*. By thus describing both *libripens* and *familiae emptor* as witnesses the praetor made it clear that he no longer paid regard to the old ritual and that he would grant *bonorum possessio* even if a *mancipatio* had not taken place at all. We may therefore speak of a 'praetorian will', requiring a document in which an *heres* was appointed and which was sealed by seven witnesses. This kind of testament already existed in the time of Cicero; but when *bonorum possessio* was granted although no valid *mancipatio* had been effected, it was a *bonorum possessio sine re* (above, s. 378) and so was not protected against the intestate heir who might claim the

436.
Praetorian testament

inheritance *iure civili* by *hereditatis petitio*. Eventually Antoninus Pius granted an *exceptio doli* to the *bonorum possessor*, thus changing his *bonorum possessio sine re* into *bonorum possessio cum re*. Throughout the classical period *bonorum possessio* was only granted *secundum tabulas testamenti*. If therefore a testament was made orally before seven witnesses, the heir could not apply for *bonorum possessio*; Gordian's enactment (*C.* 6. 11. 2) which states the contrary is evidently interpolated.

SOURCES

Read Gai. 2. 119, 120, 149*a*; *Epit. Ulp.* 28. 6; *C.* (6. 11) 2 [*bonorum possessionem*] ⟨*hereditatem*⟩ *deferri*.

BIBLIOGRAPHY

Lenel, *Edict.* (1927), § 149; Kübler, *PW* VA. 989; Biondi, *Successione testamentaria* (1943), 49 ff.*

5. *Absence of public wills. Post-classical forms*

436*a*. No public testaments

A so-called public will, i.e. a will made before an authority, was unknown to classical law. Although the law of wills was already so complicated that a non-lawyer could not be expected to be fully master of it, the lawyers insisted upon the liberal point of view: a non-lawyer should make a will only with the help of a lawyer, and if he neglected this help, he acted at his peril. It was indeed a well-established Roman custom to make a will with the assistance of a lawyer, and it is with ill-concealed delight that Cervidius Scaevola (*D.* 31. 88. 17) reports a case in which a testator emphatically claimed to have made his testament 'sine iuris consulto, rationem animi mei potius secutus quam nimiam et miseram diligentiam', and the will turned out to be invalid.

437. Post-classical forms

In post-classical times the mancipatory will was at last abandoned; *ius civile* and *ius praetorium* were amalgamated. Under Justinian's law the ordinary private will had to be made by an oral or written declaration before seven witnesses. *Bonorum possessio secundum tabulas* was nevertheless maintained, but it was now obtainable even if there were no *tabulae*, upon an oral declaration before seven witnesses. Besides the military will other kinds of extraordinary wills were developed. There were in addition public wills (*testamentum principi oblatum* and *apud acta conditum*). This post-classical development cannot be described here.

SOURCES

s. 437. Read *C.* (6. 11) 2 [*bonorum possessionem*] ⟨*hereditatem*⟩ *deferri*.

BIBLIOGRAPHY

s. 437. David, Z lii (1932), 314 ff.; Kübler, *PW* va. 990, 1002; Kunkel, § 202; Biondi, *Successione testamentaria* (1943), 52 ff.

6. *Revocation of the will*

As aforesaid (above, s. 362), the Roman will could be revoked by the testator at any time, but the twofold law of wills (*ius civile* and *ius praetorium*) rendered the matter somewhat complicated.

438. Revocation of a testament

1. A valid mancipatory will could only be revoked by another valid mancipatory will (see below, s. 446). Where the testator deliberately destroyed the *tabulae testamenti*, the will remained nevertheless valid *iure civili*. The *testamentum per aes et libram* was legally an oral testament; the tablets were purely evidential and only served to simplify the oral declaration (*nuncupatio*) by providing a means of reference. But in such a case *bonorum possessio ab intestato* (above, ss. 404 ff.) might be obtained by the intestate heir and this *bonorum possessio* after the rescript of Antoninus Pius (above, s. 436) was *cum re* and so protected against the *heres scriptus*.

2. Where a valid mancipatory will was revoked in a praetorian will, the former remained valid *iure civili*, but the heir appointed in the praetorian will might claim *bonorum possessio secundum tabulas supremas* (i.e. according to the praetorian will) and from the time of Pius this was *bonorum possessio cum re*, i.e. protected against the heir appointed in the first will.

3. A praetorian will might of course be revoked by the testator's deliberate destruction of the tablets, since it was

only *secundum tabulas* that *bonorum possessio* could be obtained by the *heres scriptus*. But the same result inevitably occurred when the tablets were destroyed by the testator inadvertently or by another person or were lost in an accident. Where there were no *tabulae testamenti*, *bonorum possessio secundum tabulas* was out of the question; this is simply required by logic and texts which state the contrary cannot possibly be classical.

On the post-classical doctrine concerning the revocation of wills we will not dwell.

SOURCES

s. 438. 1. Read Gai. 2. 151, 151*a*.

s. 438. 3. Read *D.* (37. 11) 1. 10 and 11. The texts are heavily interpolated and the original wording cannot be recovered; substantially, Ulpian declined *bonorum possessio*; cf. Beseler, Z xlv (1925), 477 (reconstruction hardly acceptable).

BIBLIOGRAPHY

Biondi, *Successione testamentaria* (1943), 591 ff.*

7. *General character of the rules concerning institutio heredis*

439.
Origin of
the rules
A testator in appointing an *heres* had to observe certain rules which are highly characteristic of Roman law in general and of the Roman law of succession in particular. They were not fixed by statute but were created by the republican cautelary jurisprudence, to a considerable extent by the *pontifices*. In making a *testamentum calatis comitiis* the *pontifex* had to bring in a draft of the will. This was of course substantially worked out by the testator, but the pontiff had to approve it, and for that reason could demand that certain rules were observed. These rules were applied to the mancipatory will and added to by the later cautelary jurisprudence. Thus a stock of rules was developed which the classical lawyers did not dare to abandon.

440.
Criticism
of the rules
These rules have been censured by modern students as harsh, archaic, unjust, and partly unintelligible, but this criticism is not justified. The true Roman tendency towards simplicity, clearness, and freedom is discernible in them.

The appointment of an heir which was vital to the whole will (above, s. 426) should be expressed as plainly and unmistakably as possible. To give a testator full freedom and to charge the judge with finding out the true intention of the testator often buried in obscure and ambiguous phrases, must lead to disputes and expensive litigation. The creators of these Roman rules wished to compel a testator by indirect means to make a will only with the assistance of a lawyer. The rules are harsh only to a testator who is ignorant of them and is therefore in danger of offending against them and as a result making an invalid will; to a testator well advised by a lawyer they are beneficial, for they compel him to use simple, typical, and unambiguous terms. Considering the rules from this point of view, one can only admire the wisdom and the political sense of those who fashioned them.

441. Military testament

A soldier making a military will was not bound to observe all of these rules since he could not be expected to consult a lawyer. To be sure Trajan's enactment (above, s. 435) wished first and foremost to set a soldier free from the mancipatory ritual, but the soldier was likewise freed from some other rules. How far the classical lawyers went in this respect is for the time being difficult to say since available sources are not quite reliable; in any case it is clear that there were rules which even a soldier had to observe in a military will. In the following discussion we shall only mark those rules with which a soldier could undoubtedly dispense in making a military will.

We will now consider these rules in detail.

BIBLIOGRAPHY

s. 439. Schulz, *History of Roman Legal Science* (1946), 19.

s. 441. Kübler, *PW* va. 1001; Levy, Z lii (1932), 526, with references; Biondi, l.c. 74 ff.

8. *Formula for the institutio heredis*

442. Republican law

The appointment of an *heres* must be effected in Latin and contain the word *heres*. Paraphrases of this word were not allowed, since they might lead to doubts as to whether the testator intended in truth to make an *institutio heredis*. Thus 'Titius shall have my whole estate' would be an inadequate formula, since the *heres* necessarily succeeds also to the obligations of the testator (above, s. 571). The idea of the lawyers was that a testator should follow the good example given by the lawyers themselves in their writings and observe the *proprietas verborum*, i.e. should designate a matter with its unambiguous, technical term.

443.
Classical
and post-
classical
law

Within these limits the classical lawyers disputed about permissible variants, but the traditional formula *Titius heres mihi esto* remained the stock phrase. After the *constitutio Antoniniana* (above, s. 136) this formal requirement could not be maintained any longer. Alexander Severus permitted an *institutio heredis* in Greek, either generally or only with respect to certain parts of the Empire. Constantine abolished formalism altogether and declared any expression to be sufficient.

SOURCES

s. 442. Read Gai. 2. 117, 281; *Epit. Ulp.* 21; 25. 9; Gnom. Idiol. § 8 (*FIRA* 1. 471); *D.* (28. 5) 1. 3; 1, 5–7, interpolated see *Index Interp.*

s. 443. For Alexander's constitution read the text given by Mitteis, *RP* i (1908), 282 n. 60, or *Studien zur Palaeographie u. Papyruskunde*, ed. C. Wessely, xx (1921), no. 35. Constantine's constitution: *C.* (6. 23) 15.

BIBLIOGRAPHY

ss. 442, 443. Kreller, *Erbrechtliche Untersuchungen* (1919), 331; Uxkull–Gyllenband, *BGU* v. 2, p. 29 f.; *FIRA* iii, no. 51, with references; Maschi, 'La solennità della heredis institutio', *Aegyptus*, xvii (1937), 197 ff., 226 ff.; Sanfilippo, *Studi sulla hereditas*, i (1937), 142 ff.; Biondi, *Successione testamentaria* (1943), 58, 215 ff. On Hadrian's privilege (*graece testari*) granted to the *schola Epicurea* at Athens see Schulz, *History* (1946), 121.

9. *Place of the institutio heredis within the text of the will*

444.
Institutio
heredis
caput
testamenti

The classical will had to begin with the *institutio heredis*. All other provisions to be made by will were regarded as merely supplementary and as modifications of the institution of a heir; their validity depended on the *institutio heredis*. The *institutio heredis* is, so to speak, the foundation-stone of the will and building up a will had accordingly to begin with the laying of that stone. This was the rather primitive reasoning of the republican draftsmen and their usage eventually became a legal rule which was still observed in classical times. What followed the institution in a will was visibly covered by it and so belonged to the will without question; what preceded was not visibly a part of the will and for that reason void. If the testator wished to institute his own slave he might of course begin with his manumission, 'Servus meus Stichus liber et heres mihi esto', but this is not an exception to the rule, since the manumission is an indispensable part of the institution. Other kinds of manumission by will (i.e. without instituting the slave heir) could not be made prior to the institution of an heir. Labeo and Proculus asserted that a *tutoris datio* (above, s. 285) might be written before the institution of an heir 'quod nihil ex hereditate erogatur tutoris datione' (Gai. 2. 231), but their opinion was apparently rejected by the majority of jurists. Trajan is said to have allowed a will to begin with an *exheredatio* (below, s. 464), but the only text which we possess is probably spurious.

Constantine, of course, abandoned the old rule (above, s. 443); the post-classical age had no taste for legal architecture.

SOURCES

Read Gai. 2. 229–31; *Inst. Iust.* (2. 20) 34; Gai. 2. 186; *D.* (28. 5) 9. 14; (28. 5) 1 pr. interpolated.

BIBLIOGRAPHY

Biondi, *Successione testamentaria* (1943), 188 ff.; Maschi, *Aegyptus*, xvii (1937), 223 ff.; G. Vismara, 'Appunti intorno alla heredis institutio', *St. Besta*, iii (1939), 301 ff.*

10. *Completeness of the will*

A will has to be complete as regards the institution of *heredes*. This principle leads to the following important rules.

i. *Codicilli are no substitute for a will*

The proper place for an *institutio heredis* is the will itself and not *codicilli* (see below, s. 543). *Codicilli* cannot contain

445:
Codicilli no place for institutio heredis

a valid institution even if the testator refers to them in his will. A queer testamentary institution such as *quem heredem codicillis fecero, heres esto* (so-called *testamentum mysticum*) was void under classical law.

ii. *No plurality of wills*

446. Nemo cum duobus testamentis decedere potest

1. A will which was valid *iure civili* was 'broken' (*rumpitur*) by a subsequent will also valid *iure civili*. This is a sound rule, for if both wills remained in force and the former were only abrogated so far as it was in conflict with the latter, the judge would have to decide to what extent the former is compatible with the latter. This is sometimes a difficult business (I know of a case in which a testator had made more than twenty additional testaments) which in any case might have been done much better and more quickly by the testator himself. Modern lawyers who regard this rule as archaic and plead for its abandonment have no sense of legal policy.

Suppose a testator declared in his first will:

'Titius heres et dare damnas esto centum Publio; Seius heres et dare damnas esto viginti Sempronio.'

In a subsequent will the testator declared:

'Cornelius heres et dare damnas esto triginta sorori meae Attiae.'
What is the meaning of the second will? Are Titius and Seius replaced by Cornelius? or is Cornelius meant to be a co-heir together with Titius and Seius? Under classical law these awkward questions could not arise; only the second will was valid and Cornelius became sole heir. If the testator wishes something else, he ought to have gone to the small trouble of rewriting the first testament. Such is the teaching of Roman *disciplina*.

2. Where a testament valid *iure civili* was followed by a praetorian will, the first was not 'broken'; the praetor merely granted *bonorum possessio secundum supremas tabulas* (as was expressly said in the Edict) and this *bonorum possessio* was *cum re* from the time of the rescript of Antoninus Pius (above, s. 436).

3. Where a praetorian will was followed by a valid mancipatory will, the former was not 'broken', but the praetor accorded *bonorum possessio* only to the heir appointed in the mancipatory will (*secundum supremas tabulas*).

4. Where a praetorian will was followed by another praetorian will, the former was not 'broken', but the praetor granted *bonorum possessio* only *secundum tabulas supremas*.

5. These rules applied even if the subsequent will though validly made did not come into force, in particular if the heirs appointed in the second will refused to accept the inheritance. In such cases the praetor did not grant *bonorum possessio* to the heirs appointed in the first will, since he did so only *secundum tabulas supremas*.

These rules did not apply to a military will.

It is of course impossible to make two wills at the same time. A testator might write his will on two or more tablets, but they would form only one will, being covered, in a mancipatory will, by the same *nuncupatio*.

iii. *The sum of the portions to which heirs are instituted must be the whole inheritance*

Where a testator instituted heirs to portions of the inheritance, these must exhaust the whole inheritance. If the sum of the portions was not the whole inheritance, they were rectified (either increased or diminished) by legal construction. In particular it must be noted that when the sum was less than the whole inheritance, the remainder did not fall to the intestate successors but to the instituted heirs. This last rule was cast into the form of a maxim in post-classical times: 'Nemo pro (or *ex*) parte testatus, pro (or *ex*) parte intestatus decedere potest'. The classical lawyers did not use this maxim; under classical law it was not quite accurate, since succession against the testament (below, s. 483) sometimes led to a combination of intestate succession with testamentary succession. Cicero, *De inventione* (2. 21. 63) might say:

> 'Supponatur enim ab heredibus haec ratio: Unius pecuniae plures dissimilibus de causis heredes esse non possunt, nec umquam factum est, ut eiusdem pecuniae alius testamento alius lege heres esset.'

This is evidently not a legal rule taken from a text-book but a fictitious proposition set forth by a party in a lawsuit.

In Justinian's collection of maxims *D*. (50. 17) 7 we read the following text:

[margin note:] 447. Rectification of portions. Nemo pro parte testatus pro parte intestatus decedere potest

'Ius nostrum non patitur eundem in paganis et testato et intestato decessisse, earumque 'rerum naturaliter inter se pugna est "testatus" et "intestatus".'

The baroque and rhetorical form of this text reveals its post-classical origin (*in paganis* = a non-soldier; *decessisse* instead of *decedere*; *naturaliter*, though the rule is far from being natural; *pugna*); see *Index Interp.*; David, *Studien zur heredis institutio ex re certa* (1930), 34. *Inst. Iust.* (2. 14) 5; probably derived from this text;

'. . . neque enim idem ex parte testatus et ex parte intestatus decedere potest.'

The rule 'miles pro parte testatus pro parte intestatus decedere potest' is likewise spurious: *D.* (29. 1), 6 cf. Beseler, *Studi Riccobono*, i. 297; *D.* (29. 1) 19 pr. [*hoc est . . . decedere*]; *D.* (49. 17) 19. 2, cf. Beseler, l.c. 299. *Miles pro parte testari potest D.* (29. 1) 37 or *miles ex parte heredem instituere potest*, *D.* (29. 1) 19 pr., is perfectly correct.

Classical law knew only one rule concerning *institutio heredis*: the appointment of an heir or of a plurality of heirs must regulate the succession exhaustively. If a person once sets up the apparatus of a *testamentum calatis comitiis* or *per aes et libram*, he should do the job thoroughly. He should not say: Titius shall be my heir to one-half, and be silent upon the other half with the intention of leaving it to the intestate heirs. To let intestate succession come in involves unnecessary trouble, since relationship has to be proved. If the testator actually wished the intestate successors to be his heirs to one-half, why did he not properly institute them? It was for these reasons that the lawyers excluded the intestate successors altogether by raising the portion of the instituted heir. Thus on the legal construction of the will Titius was regarded as universal heir (*heres ex asse*). Of course this result was *not* in conformity with the testator's intention, but the lawyers deliberately neglected it in order to compel him to avoid appointments of that kind. When the lawyers' rule was once established this extreme case would hardly ever happen, since any professional scribe of wills, let alone a lawyer, would know the rule and prevent a testator from making such a disposition. There remained only cases in which by inadvertence the portions did not exhaust the whole inheritance, but in such cases the construction of the lawyers was not in conflict with the testator's intention.

Let us consider the following cases.

1. A testator had three sons *in potestate*. Without any reference to them he instituted his four friends A to one-third, B to one-quarter, C to one-fifth, and D to one-fifth. By inadvertence he did not realize that the sum of the portions is 59/60ths and not the whole inheritance. Would it not be just to give the remaining 1/60th to the intestate successors? The answer is that under republican and classical law the testament would be void, since the testator (as we shall see later, s. 460) had expressly to disinherit his *sui*. Thus in this present case the whole inheritance fell to the intestate heirs, i.e. to the *sui*.

2. Suppose the testator had disinherited his *sui* and instituted A, B, C, and D as in the first case. What about the remaining 1/60th? Should it fall to the intestate successors? But that would mean it would fall to the *sui* whom the testator has expressly disinherited. The lawyers raised the quotas of the instituted heirs so that A obtains 20/59ths, B 15/59ths, C 12/59ths, and D 12/59ths. This construction is probably in harmony with the testator's intention.

3. Suppose the testator had no children and instituted his friends as above. Again the lawyers raised the portions and thus came much nearer to the testator's intention than if the remaining 1/60th fell to the *proximus adgnatus*, who perhaps was a distant relative.

Thus the famous rule 'nemo pro parte testatus pro parte intestatus decedere potest' is fully explained and—under republican and classical law—fully justified. The rule has been censured as manifestly unjust or enigmatical; much has been written on it; prehistoric law has been invoked to explain it, all this because the basic attitude of the republican lawyers was ignored. These lawyers were not yet mere dialectical interpreters of statutes but rather political men who felt themselves entrusted with the development of the law. They wished to teach testators to make clear and complete testaments in order to save trouble and expense. For that reason the lawyers did not shrink from the extreme case; if the testator instituted A to one-half, and said nothing about the other half, according to the lawyers' construction A became universal heir. This case would arise but rarely, and the lawyers had no intention of framing the law with regard to an extreme and exceptional case. Even if it happened, it would have had a deterrent effect which the lawyers would have welcomed.

A soldier making a military will was not required to observe this rule.

SOURCES

s. 445. Read Gai. 2. 273. Interpolated: *D.* (28. 5) 78; (28. 7) 10 pr.
s. 446. Read Gai. 2. 144; *Inst. Iust.* (2. 17) 2.
s. 447. Read *D.* (28. 5) 13. 1–4; (28. 5) 79. 1; *Inst. Iust.* (2. 14) 5
and 7.

BIBLIOGRAPHY

s. 445. Windscheid, *Pand.* iii (1906), § 546 n. 10; Beseler, Z xliii
(1922), 437; *Beiträge* v (1931), 47; Biondi, *Successione testamentaria*
(1943), 620; Vismara, *St. Besta,* iii (1939), 343 ff.
s. 446. Windscheid, l.c. § 565; Sanfilippo, *Studi sulla hereditas* i
(1937), 73 ff.; Biondi, l.c. 33.
s. 447. Windscheid, l.c. §§ 537, 552; Lenel, 'Zur Geschichte der heredis institutio' in *Essays in Legal History,* ed. P. Vinogradoff (1913), 127 f.;
Bonfante, *Scritti,* i (1916), 140; *Corso,* vi (1930), 81; Rabel, Z l (1930),
306, 308; Solazzi, *Diritto ereditario romano* i (1932), 212 ff.; Sanfilippo,
l.c. 187 ff.; Sciascia, 'Miles pro parte testatus pro parte intestatus decedere
potest', *Seminar,* v (1947), 31 ff.*

11. *Heredis institutio ex re certa*

448. Heres ex re certa   When a testator instituted a single heir as follows:
'Titius mihi heres esto ex fundo meo Corneliano', the institution, though in itself not absurd, regulated the succession
but incompletely, for the testator was silent with regard to
the rest of his property and to the question of assumption of
his obligations. When a testator appointed Titius and
Seius as follows: 'Titius shall be heir of my landed property
and Seius the heir of the rest of my property', this institution too regulated the succession but incompletely, since
nothing was said about the testator's obligations. In the
latter case the will might be supplemented by construction;
the value of the real estate on the one hand and the value of
the chattels on the other might be ascertained and according to the proportion of the first value to the second one
might regard Titius and Seius as liable for the testator's
obligations. But such a construction would involve technical difficulties; an inventory would have to be made and
the value of the two parts of the property ascertained. The
republican lawyers, here as elsewhere, were not prepared
to tackle unnecessary difficulties, which the testator by
exercising a little care might have spared them. The

testator—such was their idea—should take thought and institute the heirs to portions, thereby rendering the whole legal situation simple and clear. *Institutio heredis* and *legatum* are provisions fundamentally different—the former, unlike the latter, is not a gift (above, s. 373)—and they should not be confused. If in the second case the testator wished to leave his real estate to Titius, he should leave it to him by legacy (*praelegatum*; below, s. 555). It was for these reasons that it was not permitted under republican law to institute an heir *ex re certa*. If such a disposition was made by a testator, it was perhaps regarded as entirely invalid by the earlier republican jurists, but by Cicero's time the *institutio heredis* was preserved *favore testamenti* and only the limitation to *res certa* was regarded as void. This rule too was obviously of an educational character, for the lawyers were of course conscious that they were not implementing the testator's intention in their construction. The republican rule was maintained throughout the whole classical period; the classical lawyers were only concerned with carrying it through and improving it in detail.

Classical law may be illustrated by the following cases:

1. The testator instituted one single heir: 'Titius mihi heres esto ex fundo Corneliano.' The lawyers regard the words *ex fundo Corneliano* as if they had not been written; Titius becomes universal heir. Any other solution is impossible on account of the rule *nemo pro parte*, etc. (above, s. 447).

2. 'Titius ex fundo Corneliano mihi heres esto, Seius ex fundo Iuliano.' Titius and Seius are regarded as instituted heirs each to one-half of the whole inheritance.

3. 'Titius mihi heres esto ex parte tertia fundi Corneliani, Seius ex besse (= two-thirds) eiusdem fundi.' Titius is regarded as instituted to one-third of the whole inheritance, Seius to two-thirds.

4. 'Attius mihi heres esto fundi Corneliani, duo Titii fundi Iuliani heredes mihi sunto.' Attius is regarded as instituted to one-half of the whole inheritance, the two brothers to one-quarter each.

5. 'Titius heres mihi esto exceptio fundo Corneliano.' The exception is ignored and so Titius is regarded as instituted *ex asse*.

In a military testament the limitation to *certa res* was equally inoperative but if a plurality of *heredes* was instituted, it was maintained as a legacy. When a soldier made the following will: 'Titius shall be heir to my *bona castrensia*,

449. Miitary testament

Seius to my other property', Julian suggested a more complicated solution. Titius obtains the *bona castrensia* and Seius the other property; Titius is liable for the debts which pertain to the *bona castrensia* and Seius to the debts which pertain to the other property. This opinion apparently prevailed.

449a. **Post-classical law** In the post-classical period the classical doctrine was modified in details; in particular the limitations to *certae res* were in the case of a plurality of *heredes* constructed as regulations to be observed by the *iudex familiae erciscundae* (above, s. 86). All passages in classical writings which contain this construction are interpolated.

SOURCES

s. 448. Read *D.* (28. 5) 11 (genuine); (28. 5) 9. 13, evidently interpolated [*quasi sine partibus*], [*si modo . . . refragatur*]; (28. 5) 75 [*excepto usu fructu*]; [*ea re*] ⟨*exceptione*⟩; (28. 5) 1. 4 *Si* ⟨*quis*⟩; [*aliquis solus*]; *Cod. Greg.* (3. 8) 1. 1—preserved to us by the *lex Romana Visigothorum* of A.D. 506 (N.B.)—[*sane . . . potuisset*]; the *interpretatio* knows nothing of these words (N.B.); read text and *interpretatio* in Mommsen, Krüger, Studemund, *Collectio librorum iuris anteiustiniani*, iii (1890), 229 f.

BIBLIOGRAPHY

ss. 448, 449. M. David, *Studien zur heredis institutio ex re certa im klassischen römischen und justinianischen Recht* (1930); Kunkel, Z li (1931), 535 ff.; Beseler, *St. Riccobono*, i (1936), 294 ff.; Sanfilippo, *Studi sulla hereditas*, i (1937), 227 ff.

12. *Certa persona*

450. Certa persona Only a *certa persona* can be instituted *heres*, i.e. a person of whose individuality the testator in making his will had or might have a clear notion. Thus the following institution would be void: 'Qui primus ad funus meum venerit heres mihi esto.' On the other hand, the following institution would be valid: 'Ex cognatis meis qui nunc sunt, qui primus ad funus meum venerit heres mihi esto.' These are of course cases primarily of academic interest, but the eminently practical nature of the rule is revealed by its corollaries.

451. Legal persons 1. A so-called legal (or juristic) person could not be instituted *heres*. As we have stated above (s. 146), what is called today a legal person was regarded by the classical lawyers as a variable *Gesamthand*; the owners of the rights belonging to the legal person were the varying members. Now it is evident that a testator might perhaps know the present members of a legal person, though as a rule the members are so numerous that this is hardly possible, as, for example, in the case of a *municipium*. But even if the testator actually knew all persons who were members at the time when the will was made, that would not suffice, for the institution of a legal person does not mean the institution of the present members, but of the members at the time when the inheritance will be acquired. Thus the institution of a legal person is the institution of an *incerta persona* and for that reason void. Under classical law an exception was made when a *libertus* of a *municipium* instituted that *municipium*, a singular case introduced by a *senatusconsultum* (above, s. 159). An individual legal person might obtain as a special privilege the capacity to be instituted (above, s. 176). Further, the *populus Romanus* and *fiscus* might be instituted, but they stood outside the sphere of private law (above, s. 149).

2. No less important is another corollary. A person could only be instituted if he or she already existed at the time when the institution was made. *Postumi*—the term, which has a different meaning in intestate succession (see above, s. 386), means here persons who were born after the will was made—as a rule could not be instituted. Exceptions were made *iure civili* in favour of the testator's *postumi sui* (above, s. 384) and *iure praetorio* in favour of the testator's *liberi* (above, s. 405), provided they were *iam concepti* at the time when the will was made. These exceptions were necessary, as we shall point out later (below, s. 462). The details are too complicated to be described in this place; available texts are heavily interpolated.

452. Postumi

The requirement of a *persona certa* was introduced by the republican lawyers not for theoretical but for very practical reasons. The lawyers did not wish legal persons to become heirs, to accumulate wealth, and thereby to develop into

453. Practical purpose of the requirement

powerful and dangerous bodies within the State. The traditional Roman dread of legal persons (above, s. 167) was certainly exaggerated, but modern laws too sometimes grant to legal persons only a limited capacity of acquiring property by inheritance. Further, the lawyers wished to check substitutions; we shall presently return to this issue (below, s. 456).

454. Post-classical law Post-classical law entirely abandoned the classical rule. *Postumi* could now be instituted indiscriminately provided that they were *iam concepti* at the time of the institution. Private legal persons could only be instituted on the strength of a special privilege.

SOURCES

s. 450. Read Gai. 2. 238; *Epit. Ulp.* 22. 4.
s. 451. Read *Epit. Ulp.* 22. 5.
s. 452. Read Gai. 2. 242; 1. 147.
s. 454. Read *Inst. Iust.* (2. 20) 25–8; *C.* (6. 48) 1.

BIBLIOGRAPHY

ss. 450 ff. Windscheid, *Pand.* iii (1906), §§ 547 n. 2; 535. 2; Biondi, *Successione testamentaria* (1943), 113 ff.
s. 451. Biondi, l.c. 121 ff.
s. 452. Siber, *Röm. Privatrecht* (1928), 344; Albertario, 'Conceptus pro iam nato habetur', in *Scritti*, i (1933), 14 f., 18. 50 (in this revised edition of his paper, originally *Bull.* xxxiii, 1923, 1 ff., Albertario has accepted Siber's view); La Pira, *La successione ereditaria intestata e contro il testamento* (1930), 67 ff.; Robbe, *I postumi nella successione testamentaria romana* (1937); Biondi, l.c. 114 ff.*

13. *Substitutiones*

i. *Substitutio vulgaris*

455. Substitutio vulgaris A testator could institute a person subject to a suspensive condition, for example, *Titia heres esto si Sempronio nupserit*. A special kind of a conditional institution is the *substitutio vulgaris*. A testator instituted A *primo gradu* and B *secundo gradu* under the condition that A did not become heir either because he could not become heir (e.g. because he died before the testator), or did not wish to become heir and so refused the inheritance. The institution of B was called *substitutio vulgaris* because a substitution of that kind was admissible in all cases, in contrast to *substitutio pupillaris*, which we shall presently describe (below, s. 459). The usual classical formula of a *substitutio vulgaris* ran as follows:

'L. Titius heres esto cernitoque in diebus centum proximis quibus scierit potueritque. Quod ni ita creverit, exheres esto. Tum Maevius heres esto cernitoque in diebus centum quibus scierit potueritque.'

Cernere hereditatem means to accept the inheritance by a formal declaration (below, s. 497). When Titius did not effect the *cretio* in time, he was excluded by the clause *quod ni* (= *si non*; see Stolz–Schmalz, *Lat. Grammatik*, 1928, § 342) *ita creverit exheres esto* and the substitution of Maevius came into force.

Suppose the testator omitted the clause *quod ni . . . exheres esto*. Titius did not effect the *cretio* but accepted the inheritance by informal *aditio* (below, s. 496). A very narrow construction of the wording led the classical lawyers to the following result: (1) Titius has become heir. (2) The substitution has come into force as the condition (*si non creverit*) is fulfilled. (3) Thus both Titius and Maevius become heirs each to one-half (Gai. 2. 177). It was only the Emperor Marcus who granted the whole inheritance to Titius (*Epit. Ulp.* 22. 34).

Since the whole will broke down when none of the instituted heirs accepted the inheritance (above, s. 426), substitutions of this kind were frequently made in Roman wills. A substitute might also be appointed to a substitute, and so on. ('A shall be my heir; if A does not become heir, then B shall be my heir,' and so on.)

ii. *Semel heres, semper heres*

A testator cannot institute an *heres* under a resolutive condition or for a certain period of time; modern students have accordingly framed the maxim (foreign to our sources, but see *D.* 28. 5. 89) *semel heres, semper heres*. When a testator declared: 'Titius shall be my sole heir but only for ten years', that would be in conflict with the rule *nemo pro parte testatus*, etc. (above, s. 446). But the specific purpose of the rule *semel heres*, etc., was to prevent substitutions by which an heir is appointed to succeed after the *heres primi gradus* has been heir for a certain time.

456.
Semel heres, semper heres

Under classical law the following substitutions were not permitted:

1. 'My wife shall be my sole heir; after her death my children shall be my heirs.'

2. 'My wife shall be my sole heir. My children shall be my heirs when they reach the age of 25.'

It was substitutions of this kind that the French liberals had in mind when they fought so passionately against the 'nuisance of substitutions' (above, s. 363). The wisdom of republican lawyers guarded republican and classical law against that nuisance. Substitutions to take effect in the far distant future were already excluded by the requirement of a *persona certa*, but even if substitutes were *certae personae*, substitutions of this kind were not permitted: republican liberalism wished to preserve for the heir the full freedom of disposal, which would inevitably be compromised if such substitutions were recognized.

457.
Fideicommissary substitution
However, in this respect Roman liberalism was too radical. Substitutions of *personae certae* do not involve serious dangers and can hardly be spared entirely. The classical lawyers realized that and, too conservative to abandon the old rule altogether, they created the hybrid institution of a *fideicommissum hereditatis* (below, s. 561). Now a testator might institute A and impose upon him a *fideicommissum* to restore the inheritance to B after a certain or uncertain time, e.g. after ten years, after A's death, after B has become of age, and so on. B was strictly speaking not *heres* but only recipient of a *fideicommissum*, but his legal position was assimilated to that of an *heres* (below, s. 568). But even now the 'nuisance of substitutions' could not develop since the requirement of *persona certa* applied also to *fideicommissa* (Gai. 2. 287).

To a military testament the rule *semel heres, semper heres* did not apply.

iii. *Substitutio pupillaris*

458.
Substitutio pupillaris
A *pupillus* (above, s. 283) could not make a will even *tutore auctore*; hence intestate succession would have inevitably taken place if he had died *intra pubertatem*, had not the Roman aversion to intestate succession (above,

s. 361) led to the creation of an expedient: the *substitutio pupillaris*. It was already well known in Cicero's time. On the strength of *patria potestas* a father might appoint to his *filius impubes* an heir, the appointment being subject to the condition that the son died *intra pubertatem*.

Originally such a substitution was combined with an *institutio pupilli* and a *substitutio vulgaris* (above, s. 455). Thus the earliest formula drafted by republican cautelary jurisprudence (for this kind of substitution was not introduced by statute) ran as follows:

'Titius filius meus mihi heres esto. Si filius meus mihi heres non erit, sive heres mihi erit et is prius moriatur quam in suam tutelam venerit, tunc Seius heres esto.'

This formula comprehended three different provisions: (1) the *pupillus* was unconditionally instituted as *heres patris*. (2) Seius was instituted as *heres patris* subject to the condition that the son did not become heir because he died before the testator. (3) The same Seius was instituted as *heres pupilli* subject to the condition that the son became *heres patris* but died *intra pubertatem*.

In the course of its further development the *substitutio pupillaris* became independent. A testator might omit the *substitutio vulgaris* and eventually even the *institutio pupilli*, disinheriting him expressly. Now *substitutio pupillaris* appeared in its pure form as follows:

'Titius filius meus exheres esto. Si filius meus prius moriatur quam in suam tutelam venerit, tunc Seius heres esto.'

Pupillary substitution was now usually written on special tablets (*secundae tabulae*, which of course must not be rendered by 'second testament'; see above, s. 446); the testator declared in his *primae tabulae* that the *tabulae secundae* should not be opened as long as his son was alive and *intra pubertatem*. Testators were afraid lest the substitute might endanger the *pupillus'* life when he knew of the substitution.

The consistent classical doctrine concerning *substitutio pupillaris* is lucidly expounded in Gaius' *Institutes* (2. 179 ff.). The substitute is *heres pupilli* and nothing else; he is not the heir both of the son and the father. It is evident when the father disinherited the *pupillus*, that the substitute was only the heir of the *pupillus*. But when the father instituted his son and appointed a pupillary substitute, the latter was still exclusively the heir of the *pupillus* and not also of the father. To be sure, in the latter case the substitute acquired the father's property in so far as it still existed in the inheritance of the *pupillus*, but that did not make him *heres patris*. As *heres pupilli* the substitute naturally obtained all the property held by the *pupillus* at his death, including the property which he had acquired after his father's death. This was the classical doctrine and most probably also that of the republican lawyers. In truth, we have not a single reliable text which indicates a republican doctrine different from that which is given in Gaius' *Institutes*.

1. In republican and classical times a *substitutio pupillaris* was sometimes made with the following formula: 'Si filius meus intra pubertatem decesserit, tunc Seius mihi heres esto.' *Mihi* here does not indicate that originally the substitute was regarded as *heres patris*. The original form of a pupillary substitution combined *substitutio vulgaris* with *substitutio pupillaris* (above, s. 458) so that *mihi* was justified. In the pure form of a pupillary substitution *mihi* though harmless was certainly inaccurate, as the classical lawyers expressly said. Gaius for that reason rightly omitted *mihi*.

2. The substitute is called *heres secundus* like the *substitutus vulgaris*. This usage again does not indicate that the pupillary substitute was regarded as *heres patris*. *Heres secundus* means *heres secundo loco institutus*, since a will cannot begin with a substitution. For the same reason the pupillary substitute is called *substitutus*, i.e. *sub-institutus, secundo loco institutus*.

3. The father could impose *legata* upon the pupillary substitute, though the rule was that a testator could only charge his own *heres* with *legata*. Of course this is an exception to the rule, but the whole *substitutio pupillaris* is an exception to the rule that a testator could only appoint an *heres* to his own property. The exception regarding *legata* was suggested by the original combination of *substitutio pupillaris* with *substitutio vulgaris* (above, s. 458). It is significant that *legata* could not be imposed upon the pupillary substitute when the father had disinherited his son and thus a *substitutio vulgaris* was quite out of the question.

SOURCES

s. 455. Read Gai. 2. 174–7; *Epit. Ulp.* 22. 34.
s. 456. Read Gai. 2. 184; 2. 287; *D.* (28. 5) 34.
s. 458. Read Gai. 2. 179–82; *D.* (37. 11) 8. 1.

BIBLIOGRAPHY

s. 455. Windscheid, *Pand.* iii (1906), § 557; Biondi, *Successione testa-mentaria* (1943), 245.*

s. 456. Windscheid, l.c. §§ 554. 4; 561; Biondi, l.c. 48; Guarino, *St. Solazzi* (1948), 45.

s. 458. Windscheid, l.c. § 558; Costa, *Bull.* vi (1893), 245 ff.; La Pira, *St. Bonfante*, iii (1930), 273 ff.; H. J. Wolff, *St. Riccobono*, iii (1936), 437 ff.; Vážný, *Bull.* xlvi (1939), 67 ff.; xlvii (1940), 31 ff.; Biondi, l.c. 252.*

The post-classical lawyers confused the simple classical doctrine, particularly by introducing into it the idea that the substitute was also *heres patris* if the *impubes* became his father's heir. The heavily interpolated texts cannot be analysed here and Justinian's *substitutio quasi pupillaris* lies outside the scope of this book.

CHAPTER IV

SUCCESSION AGAINST THE WILL

1. *Introduction*

459.
Survey of
the classical
remedies

THE classical law of succession against the will is somewhat complicated, since three different institutions
must be distinguished:

1. The succession *iure civili* upon *praeteritio* of the
   testator's *sui*.
2. The *bonorum possessio contra tabulas testamenti* (above,
   s. 378).
3. The *querella inofficiosi testamenti*.

All three show a tendency to restrict the testator's freedom
of disposal: the goal was the same, the legal ways in which
it was attained were different. The lawyers of the second and
third centuries A.D. ought to have summed up the historical
development by amalgamating the three institutions into
one, but here as elsewhere they were reluctant to tackle the
unification and simplification of the law. Even in Justinian's compilations (*Codex Iustinianus*, *Digest*, and *Institutes*) a unification was not seriously attempted and it was
only Justinian's *Novella* 115 of A.D. 542 which at last
attained that aim.

BIBLIOGRAPHY

Windscheid, *Pand.* iii (1906), §§ 575 ff. with references; F. v. Woess,
Das römische Erbrecht und die Erbanwärter (1911), 131 ff.; La Pira,
La successione ereditaria intestata e contro il testamento (1930), 309 ff.,
67 ff., 95 ff.

2. *Succession iure civili upon praeteritio of sui*

460.
Praeteritio
of sui

When a testator failed to institute his *sui* (above, s. 384)
as heirs or to disinherit them, the will was either completely
invalid or modified in favour of the *sui* whom the testator
had passed over in silence (*praeterire*).

As regards further details, three classes of *sui* must be
distinguished.

1. Sons who were in the testator's power at the time when the testament was made had to be instituted as heirs or disinherited *nominatim*. *Nominatim* means 'calling the son by his proper name': *Titius filius meus exheres esto*. It was only when a testator had but one son that the formula *filius meus exheres esto* (without adding the son's name) was sufficient. If a son in power was neither instituted nor properly disinherited, the whole will was void *iure civili* and intestate succession ensued.

2. Daughters and grandchildren in the testator's power might be disinherited by a general clause without being mentioned by name: *ceteri omnes exheredes sunto*. If they were neither instituted nor disinherited the will was nevertheless valid but they obtained a share of the inheritance (*scriptis heredibus in partem adcrescunt*). Where the instituted heirs were *sui* this share was the intestate portion; where the instituted heirs were non-*sui* (*extranei*) the share was the half of the estate.

Gai. 2. 124 is very brief and not quite clear, but what is meant is probably the following:

461. In partem adcrescere in particular

(*a*) The testator had two sons A and B and a daughter C. He instituted A to two-thirds and B to one-third, passing over his daughter altogether. C receives her intestate portion (one-third; above, s. 384) from A and B, i.e. from A 2/9ths and from B 1/9th.

(*b*) The testator had only a daughter in power. He instituted his friend F as his universal heir, passing over his daughter. The daughter obtains one-half of the inheritance from F, i.e. less than her intestate portion which would be the whole inheritance.

(*c*) The testator had a son A and a daughter B, both in his power. He instituted A and his friend F each to one-half, passing over his daughter. B obtains her intestate portion (one-half from A, i.e. one-quarter, and from F half of his share, i.e. one-quarter, so that altogether she receives her full intestate portion (one-half).

(*d*) The testator had two sons A and B and a daughter C. He instituted A to one-quarter, B to one-quarter, and his friend F to one-half. C was passed over. C obtains from A and B her intestate portion (one-third), i.e. from A one-twelfth and from B one-twelfth. From F she receives half of his share, i.e. one-quarter. Thus C obtains on the whole five-twelfths of the inheritance which is more than her intestate portion ($\frac{1}{3} = \frac{4}{12}$).

(*e*) The testator has a son A and two grandsons C and D, sons of his son B who predeceased him. He instituted A and C each to one-half.

D was passed over. D obtains his intestate portion, one-quarter (half of C's share), from C.

In these cases of *in partem adcrescere* there is substantially a combination of testamentary succession with intestate succession and thus an exception to the maxim 'nemo pro parte testatus pro parte intestatus decedere potest' (above, s. 447). But the lawyers apparently regarded these *sui adcrescentes* as *quasi scripti heredes*; at any rate they were liable to pay the legacies (*C*. 6. 28. 4. 1).

462.
Postumi sui
3. The third group is formed by the testator's *postumi sui*, i.e. by the *sui* who were *iam concepti* at the time when the will was made and were born later (above, s. 452). If the testator failed to institute or to disinherit them, the will was void whatever the sex of the *postumi* (*adgnatione postumi rumpitur testamentum*). We need not discuss the complicated details.

463.
History of the rules
These strange and intricate rules want a short explanation. Unfortunately we know nothing of their genesis, for even Justinian's remark (*C*. (6. 28) 4. 2) hardly implies that originally an *exheredatio inter ceteros* was sufficient for the disinheritance of sons as of daughters and grandchildren. On the whole the rules look old, though they certainly do not go back to the Twelve Tables. We must first ask ourselves why so much stress was laid on the father's instituting or disinheriting his *sui*. Why could he not choose the milder way of passing them over in silence?

464.
Bartolus' theory
First and foremost the explanation which has been repeated again and again since Bartolus should be abandoned altogether. Originally, it is said, the *sui* were co-owners of the family property together with their father. For that reason the father was bound to expropriate them by a special act, viz. by disinheriting them expressly by. *exheredatio*, or implicitly by instituting them to a portion smaller than their intestate share. In truth the idea of a family property had long disappeared when these rules were made. If the *exheredatio* were meant to be an expropriation, its proper place would have been at the beginning of the will in order to make the way clear for institutions; actually, however, an *exheredatio* had to follow the institu-

tions. Moreover, the praetor, as we shall presently show (below, s. 468), also required the express institution or disinheritance of *liberi*, who certainly were never co-owners of the family property. Thus an appeal to prehistoric law turns out once again to be futile.

Another theory widely accepted should also be finally discarded. A father, it is said, was bound to institute or to disinherit his *sui* as a token of his respect to them (*honos institutionis vel exheredationis*); to pass them over in silence as if they did not exist at all would be an affront to them. This is a queer idea, for in truth the *sui* had not the least interest in such individual attention. On the contrary, any son would have preferred to be passed over in silence rather than to be stigmatized by an *exheredatio nominatim facta*. Thus this explanation should also be rejected.

465. Honos institutionis vel exheredationis

In truth the republican and classical lawyers never had the idea that the father was bound to institute or to disinherit his *sui*. The maxim *sui heredes instituendi sunt vel exheredandi* was framed by the post-classical author of the *Epitome Ulpiani* (22. 14) who had before him Gai. 2. 123, which runs differently. Accordingly succession against the will was not meant to punish the father for having failed to fulfil an obligation. The republican lawyers had the very natural desire to save the inheritance for the *sui*, but did not venture to impugn openly the father's will and for that reason did not interfere when he had instituted or disinherited them. But if the will was silent with regard to them, they then dared to help the *sui*. When a son was passed over (which seemed to the old lawyers to be the most important case) they annulled the will altogether; in all other cases they were content to make a compromise. Seen in this light, the rules concerning *praeteritio* are fully intelligible. They represent a stage in a development which eventually led to the *querella inofficiosi testamenti*. Both institutions show the same tendency to restrict the testator's liberty of disposal.

466. The true explanation

The popular explanations fail to recognize the ideological connexion between the *querella* and the law of *praeteritio*, but on the contrary throw the two institutions into sharp contrast.

Under the *querella*, it is said, the testator was bound to provide his

467. Formelles and Materielles Noterbrecht

nearest relatives with a substantial share of the inheritance (*Materielles Noterbrecht*); under the law of *praeteritio* the testator had to render them a purely formal tribute, viz. the *honos institutionis vel exheredationis* (*Formelles Noterbrecht*). Thus one arrived at an obligation of the testator which defies all explanation. The distinction between *Materielles* and *Formelles Noterbrecht* is misleading and should be abandoned.

SOURCES

ss. 460, 461. Read Gai. 2. 123, 124, 127, 128; *Epit. Ulp.* 22. 16, 17; Paul. *Sent.* 3. 4*b*. 8.

s. 462. Read Gai. 2. 130.

s. 464. Place of *exheredatio* within the will: Gai. 2. 128. *D.* (28. 5) 1 pr. is interpolated (above, s. 444).

BIBLIOGRAPHY

ss. 460 ff. Windscheid, l.c. § 576; Karlowa, *Röm. Rechtsgeschichte* ii (1901), 885 ff.; v. Woess, l.c. 131 ff.; Beseler, *Beiträge*, ii (1911), 33 f.; Kübler, Z xli (1920), 28 ff.; La Pira, l.c. 67 ff., 95 ff.; Solazzi, *Diritto ereditario rom.* i (1932), 220 ff., 227 ff.; Sanfilippo, *Studi sull' hereditas*, i (1937), 215 f.

s. 462. La Pira, l.c. 67 ff.; Robbe, *I postumi nella successione testamentaria romana* (1937), 21 ff., 211 ff., 263 ff.; Solazzi, *Athenaeum*, viii (1930), 45.

s. 463. v. Woess, l.c. 152 ff. (wrong). In truth the words *scimus etenim*, etc. in *C.* (6. 28) 4. 2 mean: 'males and females could be equally disinherited, whereas the *centumviri* granted a *querella* if the disinheritance was not justified' (below, s. 477).

s. 464. Bartolus ad *D.* (28. 2) 11; Karlowa, l.c. 886, with references; v. Woess, l.c. 138, with references; Westrup, *Introduction to Early Roman Law*, ii (1934), 85; iii. 1 (1939), 259.*

s. 465. v. Woess, l.c. 140 ff.; Karlowa, l.c. 888. Woess's own theory is mere fantasy; in historical times an *exheredatio inter ceteros* is no condition of a valid will.

s. 467. Windscheid, l.c. 370.

3. *Bonorum possessio contra tabulas testamenti*

i. *Bonorum possessio* granted to the *liberi*

468.
Principle

The praetor promised in his Edict (Lenel, *Edict.* § 142) to grant a *bonorum possessio contra tabulas* to the *liberi* (above, s. 405) whom the testator had passed over in silence, neither instituting them as heirs nor disinheriting them properly (according to the Edict male *liberi* including grandsons had to be disinherited *nominatim*). This kind of *bonorum possessio* only originated at the end of the Republic and in establishing it the praetor was certainly not inspired by any memory of the prehistoric house-community. Like the creators of the rules which we have just described (above, s. 466), the praetor wished to preserve the inheritance for the testator's children. His Edict marks the second stage in the process of evolution, for the praetor at the end of the Republic had considerably less scruple in pursuing his aim than his predecessors in earlier times. Let us consider his regulations in detail.

1. Whenever *praeteritio* of *liberi* rendered the testament void *iure civili* (i.e. when a son *in potestate* was passed over; above, s. 460), the praetor followed *ius civile* since that was thus far in harmony with his own policy. Accordingly he granted *bonorum possessio ab intestato* (*unde liberi*; above, s. 405) and not *bonorum possessio contra tabulas*. 469. The praetorian law in detail

2. *Where praeteritio* did not make the testament void *iure civili* (i.e. where a daughter in power or grandchildren in power had been passed over), he granted *bonorum possessio contra tabulas* according to the portions of *bonorum possessio unde liberi*, eliminating entirely instituted heirs (*heredes scripti*) who were not *liberi*. In the same way he protected *liberi* who were not the *sui* (above, s. 405). It should, however, be remembered (above, s. 406) that a woman could have no *liberi* in the sense in which that word was employed by the lawyers in this connexion; *bonorum possessio contra tabulas matris* was, therefore, out of the question.

3. When a testator had instituted his son, but had passed over his daughter, the son was not entitled to *bonorum possessio contra tabulas*. But if the daughter obtained that *bonorum possessio*, the son too might receive it to the extent of his intestate portion, *commisso per alium edicto*, i.e. the Edict having been made applicable to him by another (his sister).

4. The praetor when granting *bonorum possessio contra tabulas* preserved an *exheredatio*; a disinherited child was regarded as non-existent so far as *bonorum possessio* was concerned. Hence it is evident that although *bonorum possessio contra tabulas* was granted according to the portions of the *bonorum possessio ab intestato*, it sometimes led to a result

different from that reached by *bonorum possessio unde liberi*; the recipient of a *bonorum possessio contra tabulas* sometimes received more than he would have obtained by *bonorum possessio ab intestato*, since he participated in the portion of the disinherited child.

5. In a special clause of the Edict the praetor preserved the legacies left by the testator to his near relatives or his wife or daughter-in-law (*De legatis praestandis*; see Lenel, *Edict.* § 143).

6. The *bonorum possessio contra tabulas* was always *cum re* (above, s. 378).

470.
Testamentary succession and intestate succession combined

Thus it is by no means true to say that the praetor annulled the will altogether; the succession according to his rules is rather a combination of testamentary succession and intestate succession, a further exception to the rule 'nemo pro parte testatus pro parte intestatus decedere potest' (above, s. 447). At first sight this praetorian law looks perhaps very intricate. But consider the following cases and you will see at once that it is in truth simple and cleverly devised, provided you keep in mind what has been said above (s. 447) about *bonorum possessio unde liberi*.

When a testator had passed over his son in power in silence, the will was *iure civili* void and the praetor accordingly granted *bonorum possessio ab intestato* (*unde liberi*). This causes no difficulty whatever. Now consider the following cases of *bonorum possessio contra tabulas*.

(*a*) The testator had a son A and a daughter B, both in his power. Passing over his daughter he instituted A to one-quarter and his friend F to three-quarters. According to *ius civile* (above, s. 460) B would obtain one-half of her brother's portion, i.e. one-eighth of the inheritance, and from F one-half of his portion, i.e. three-eighths of the inheritance; thus altogether she would receive one-half of the inheritance, i.e. her full intestate share, while her brother A would receive only one-eighth of the inheritance. If, however, the daughter obtained *bonorum possessio contra tabulas*, F received nothing, the daughter B one-half of the inheritance and her brother A (*commisso per alium edicto*) the other half.

(*b*) The testator had a son A and two grandsons C and D, sons of his son B who had predeceased him. He instituted A and C as heirs, each to one-half, passing over D in silence. If D obtained *bonorum possessio contra tabulas* he received one-quarter of the inheritance, C also one-quarter and A one-half, for this is the distribution in *bonorum possessio unde liberi* (above, s. 407).

(*c*) The testator had one son A and two grandsons C and D, sons of a second son B who had predeceased him. He disinherited A and instituted his friend F as universal heir, passing over C and D in silence. C and D were entitled to *bonorum possessio contra tabulas* each to one-half of the inheritance, since A is to be regarded as non-existent.

To conclude two additional remarks must be made:

1. *Bonorum possessio contra tabulas* was, as aforesaid, granted according to the portions of *bonorum possessio unde liberi*. The rules concerning *collatio bonorum* and *collatio dotis* (which we have expounded above, ss. 409 ff., when dealing with *bonorum possessio unde liberi*) also applied to *bonorum possessio contra tabulas*.

471.
Collatio

> As a matter of fact the title *De bonorum possessionibus* in the Edict began with *bonorum possessio contra tabulas* and in this connexion dealt with *collatio bonorum et dotis* (Lenel, *Edict*. pp. 342 ff.). Later, under the rubric *unde liberi*, the Edict referred to the rules concerning *collatio* which had been given before. In this book we have observed the reverse order, dealing first with *bonorum possessio unde liberi* (above, s. 405), since one cannot properly understand *bonorum possessio contra tabulas* without first mastering *bonorum possessio unde liberi*.

2. Like any other *bonorum possessio* (see above, s. 378), a *bonorum possessio contra tabulas* was granted only if a person entitled to it applied for it. This application had to be made within a certain time, as we have already mentioned (s. 420).

472.
Application
required

ii. *Bonorum possessio contra tabulas granted to the testator's patron*

We have already mentioned (s. 413) the *bonorum possessio ab intestato* granted to the patron. When a freedman made a will and did not leave thereby half of the inheritance to his patron, the latter might claim *bonorum possessio contra tabulas* to one-half, but never in competition with the testator's natural *liberi* (as distinguished from *filii adoptivi* and from his *uxor in manu* who was *filiae loco*; above, s. 197).

473.
Dimidia
pars

> Suppose a freedman had one son only. He instituted his friend F as universal heir, disinherited his son, and left nothing to his patron. The patron might claim *bonorum possessio* to one-half of the inheritance, the other half remaining to F.

T

A freedman had two daughters, A and B. He instituted his friend F as universal heir, passing over his daughters and leaving nothing to the patron. A and B might claim *bonorum possessio contra tabulas*, each to one-half of the inheritance. If they did so, the patron was excluded; if they failed to do so in time, the patron might claim *bonorum possessio contra tabulas* to one-half, the other half remaining to F.

474.
Character
This kind of *bonorum possessio* originated in the last century of the Republic, possibly somewhat earlier than the *bonorum possessio* granted to the children. It is interesting as a further stage in the process of development. The praetor granted to the patron a fixed share of the freedman's inheritance (*dimidia pars*) which he might claim even if the freedman had expressly disinherited him or instituted him to less than one-half of the inheritance. This idea of a fixed portion to be left to a certain person was taken up by the *querella inofficiosi testamenti*, as we shall presently see (below, s. 480).

475. Lex
Papia. Pars
debita
The right of the patron was increased later by the *lex Papia* (Gai. 3. 42), but we may leave that aside. It should, however, be noted that Justinian's compilers have on principle interpolated *debita pars* to replace *dimidia pars* since in this respect Justinian's law differed from classical law (*Inst. Iust.* 3. 7. 3).

SOURCES

s. 468. Read Gai. 2. 135, 125; *Epit. Ulp.* 22. 23.

s. 469. 1. Read *D*. (28. 2) 32; (38. 6) 1. 9.

s. 469. 2. Read Gai. 2. 124, 125.

s. 469. 2, 3. Read *D*. (37. 4) 8. 14; (37. 4) 11. 1.

s. 469. 4. Read *D*. (37. 4) 8 pr. 10. 5.

s. 469. 5. Read *D*. (37. 5) 1 pr. (Post-classical text but substantially classical.)

s. 473. Read Gai. 3. 39–41; (38. 2) 1 [*certae*] ⟨*dimidiae*⟩.

s. 475. Gai. 3. 42. Read *D*. (38. 2) 20. 5 [*debitae*] ⟨*dimidiae*⟩. Justinian's law: *Inst. Iust.* (3. 7) 3.

BIBLIOGRAPHY

ss. 468 ff. Lenel, *Edict.* (1927), §§ 142 ff.; Windscheid, *Pand.* iii, § 577; La Pira, l.c. 311 ff.; Sanfilippo, l.c. 219 ff.

ss. 473 ff. Ad. Schmidt von Ilmenau, *Das Pflichtteilsrecht des Patronus und des Parens Manumissor* (1868); La Pira, l.c. 376 ff.

4. *Querella inofficiosi testamenti*

This remedy marks the last stage of development as far 476. as Roman law is concerned. Unfortunately our knowledge Sources of the classical *querella* is exceedingly slight. Gaius' *Institutes* are silent upon it; the short title of the post-classical *Sententiae Pauli* (4. 5) and what has been preserved to us of the title *De inofficioso testamento* in the *Codex Theodosianus* (2. 19) do not help us much. Thus we are almost exclusively dependent on the texts in Justinian's law-books which, however, are heavily interpolated. No wonder, therefore, that the repeated attempts to disentangle the ravelled skein have not fully succeeded. It should be realized that absolute certainty cannot possibly be attained with available sources and that important issues must needs remain in doubt for ever, unless fresh sources turn up to give us a further clue. In the following description we confine ourselves to the basic rules which we regard—more or less confidently—as classical, leaving entirely aside the post-classical development.

We know little about the history of the *querella*. It cer- 477. tainly did not originate earlier than the end of the Republic History and perhaps considerably later. At any rate it existed as an established institution in Trajan's age. Apparently it was developed in the practice of the court of the *Centumviri*.

The starting-point was the *testamentum inofficiosum*, i.e. 478. a will in which a testator offended against his *officium* Conception of testa- *pietatis* by not providing for his nearest relatives, particu- mentum larly for his children; in short a will which public opinion inofficio- stigmatized as unduteous. The law now punished this sum offence against morality by granting to the offended rela- tives a remedy (*querella*) against the instituted heirs (*scripti heredes*). The details of the development cannot be ascer- tained from available sources. We must content ourselves with an exposition of the rules as recognized in the age of the Severi (first half of the third century A.D.).

1. As regards the group of relatives who were entitled 479. Who to bring a *querella*, it is quite certain that the remedy was might bring in the available to the testator's descendants, not only to the *liberi* querella

in the sense employed by the lawyers with respect to the Edict (above, ss. 405, 406). This implies that as well as a father's a mother's will might be impugned by her descendants. It is less certain whether in classical times the ascendants of the testator and his brothers and sisters were already protected by that remedy. The post-classical *Sententiae Pauli* knew only a *querella* of the *liberi* and began the title *De inofficiosi querella* (4. 5) with the definition:

> 'Inofficiosum dicitur testamentum, quod frustra liberis exheredatis non ex officio pietatis videtur esse conscriptum.'

But this is hardly conclusive as we possess only the Visigothic *Epitome* of the *Sententiae*. Indeed, it seems probable that already in classical times ascendants as well as brother and sister of the testator might bring a *querella*.

480. Quarta pars 2. The *querella* was excluded when the testator had left to his relatives a quarter of their intestate portion. He was not bound to institute them as heirs to that quarter; he might leave to them its value by legacies or *donatio mortis causa*, just as a freedman might leave the *dimidia pars* to his patron (above, s. 473) by way of legacies or *donatio mortis causa*. The classical lawyers had no special term to designate this *quarta*; in particular, they never called it *portio legitima* for the simple reason that the amount was fixed by court-practice and not by a *lex*. The post-classical term *portio legitima* and the English term 'the legitim' should, therefore, be avoided as far as classical law is concerned.

481. Non-classical terminology   *Legitima portio* or *legitima pars* in classical writings means 'the intestate portion according to the Twelve Tables' and nothing else (above, s. 383). The classical lawyers could not call the 'reasonable share' *quarta legitimae partis* (thus Justinian's *Institutes*, 2. 18. 3) since emancipated children and heirs *ex senatusconsulto Orfitiano* and *Tertulliano* (above, s. 402) were not *heredes legitimi*. Nor could they call it *quarta debitae portionis* (thus *D*. 5. 2. 8. 8), since the intestate portion was not a *portio debita*. Finally, they hardly ever called it *pars debita*, a term which has produced the German *Pflichtteil*. *Pars debita* frequently occurs in the *Digest* in connexion with the *bonorum possessio contra tabulas* granted to the patron (above, s. 473), but as already said above (s. 475), it is here always interpolated to replace *dimidia pars*.

482. Grounds of disinheritance   3. The *querella* was also excluded when the testator had sufficient reasons for leaving nothing, or less than the *quarta*, to his relatives. It was for the court to decide whether such reasons existed or not; a fixed list of grounds for disinheritance was as yet unknown.

4. When the court pronounced a will to be unduteous, it was not thereby cancelled entirely. On the other hand, the plaintiff received now his full intestate portion, not only, as might be expected, the *quarta*. The will was only cancelled in so far as that was necessary to accord him his intestate share. In this respect the *querella* followed the example of the *bonorum possessio contra tabulas*. The plaintiff might claim his full intestate portion even when the testator had left to him some portion of the *quarta*; he was not confined to a *querella ad supplendam quartam*. 483. Testamentary succession and intestate succession combined

(*a*) The testator had three sons A, B, and C. He instituted A and B each to one-half and disinherited C without sufficient reason. C might sue both A and B with the *querella* and obtain his intestate portion (one-third), i.e. from A one-third of his share = one-sixth of the inheritance, and from B equally one-third of his share = one-sixth of the inheritance. If C did so, then each of the three brothers received his intestate portion (one-third). But suppose C was content with suing A; then he received from A one-sixth, A kept one-third, and B one-half of the inheritance. 484. Cases

(*b*) The testator had two sons A and B. He disinherited both *sine iusta causa* and instituted his friend F as universal heir. Both A and B might sue F with the *querella*. If they did so, each of them obtained his intestate portion, i.e. one-half of the inheritance; F received nothing. But suppose that only A sued F while B respected his father's will. Then A received his full intestate portion, i.e. one-half of the inheritance; the other half was retained by F.

5. The classical *querella* was, as said above (s. 477), developed in the practice of the Centumviral Court. In the first and second century A.D., as at the end of the Republic, this court was the arena for the virtuosi of rhetoric. These people on principle did not call things by their right names; they were trained to exaggerate, to distort, and to confuse. Thus when pleading for the plaintiff in a *querella inofficiosi testamenti* they liked to describe an unduteous will as a will made by a testator of unsettled mind (*a furioso factum*), here as elsewhere imitating Greek models. They called this *agere colore insaniae* or *non sanae mentis* (*color* in rhetorical slang means 'argument', 'pretext', 'device'; see *Thes. Linguae Lat.* iii. 1721, 47 ff.; 1722, 23 ff.). Such phrases 485. Color insaniae

might impress the non-legal members of the court, hence the orators used them without scruple.

'Rhetori concessum est sententiis uti falsis, audacibus, versutis, subdolis, captiosis, si veri modo similes sint et possint movendos hominum animos qualicumque astu (dexterity, cunning) inrepere.' (Gellius 1. 6.)

The lawyers, however, cannot have been influenced by such rhetorical stuff, for they knew too well that *testamentum inofficiosum* and *testamentum a furioso factum* were fundamentally different things. As usual they ignored this rhetorical wisdom, but in post-classical times the baneful weed of rhetoric crept into the classical writings; in a few passages of the *Digest* (never in the *Sententiae Pauli* or in the *Codex Theodosianus*) we meet the *color insaniae*, but they are all obviously interpolated. Most scholars have been misled by these texts and still believe in the far-reaching influence of the rhetoricians upon the Roman lawyers. In truth the lawyers, here as elsewhere, did not pay any regard to the pseudo-wisdom of the orators and the rhetorical schools: 'ineptias ac stultitias non ferebant iracundiusque respuebant ingenuo liberoque fastidio' (Cicero, *Brutus*, 67. 236).

The post-classical development was apparently influenced by rhetorical slang, but we will not discuss this question here.

486.   The *querella inofficiosae donationis*, though originating in
Querella late-classical times (Alexander Severus), was fully de-
inofficiosae
donationis veloped only in the post-classical period and may, therefore, be left aside here.

SOURCES

s. 479. Read *D.* (5. 2) 1, completely spurious.

s. 480. Read *D.* (5. 2) 8. 6, cf. *D.* (38. 2) 3. 15 and 17; doubtful texts see Beseler, *T* x (1930), 236 f., read further *D.* (5. 2) 8. 8 [*et si dicam . . . petere*].

s. 483. Read *C.* (3. 28) 22; Paul. *Sent.* 4. 5. 7 (spurious).

s. 484. Read *D.* (5. 2) 15. 2; *C.* (3..28) 13; *D.* (5. 2) 23. 2, corrupt text, probably ⟨non⟩ adcrescit.

s. 485. Read *D.* (5. 2) 2, completely spurious; *D.* (5. 2) 5 [*resque . . . ordinaret*].

BIBLIOGRAPHY

ss. 476 ff. Windscheid, *Pand.* iii (1906), §§ 575, 578 ff., with refer-

ences; Eisele, *Z* xv (1894), 256 ff.; Brugi, *Mélanges Fitting*, i (1907);
v. Woess, *Das röm. Erbrecht und die Erbanwärter* (1911), 178 ff.; Beseler,
Beiträge, ii (1911), 34; H. Siber, *Röm. Privatrecht* (1928), 374 ff.; La
Pira, *La successione ereditaria* (1930), 412 ff.; H. Krüger, *Z* lvii (1937),
94 ff.; *Festschrift P. Koschaker*, ii (1939), 256 ff.; *Bull.* xlvii (1940),
63 ff.; Timbal, *RH* xix/xx (1940/1), 386 ff.; Renier, *Étude sur l'histoire
de la querella inofficiosi testamenti en droit romain* (1942).

   s. 477. See H. Krüger, *Festschrift Koschaker*, 256 ff. For the court of
the *centumviri* see Wlassak, *PW* iii. 1935; Wenger, *CP* (1940).

   s. 481. On the term *portio legitima* see H. Krüger, *Bull.* xlvii. 72.

   s. 483. Windscheid, l.c. § 584; La Pira, l.c. 449 ff.; Solazzi, *Diritto
ereditario*, i (1932), 229 ff.; Sanfilippo, *Studi sull' hereditas*, i (1937),
194 ff. For the *actio ad supplendam quartam* see Windscheid, § 584 n. 1;
La Pira, l.c. 470; Seckel–Kübler in their edition of *Paul. Sent.* ad 4. 5. 7;
Beseler, *Beiträge*, ii (1911), 33; v. Woess, l.c. 253 (wrong).

   s. 484. Windscheid, l.c. § 584 nn. 20 ff.

   s. 485. v. Woess, l.c. 191 ff. (uncritical); Beseler, *St. Bonfante*, ii (1930),
82; Schulz, *Principles* (1936), 129 f.; La Pira, l.c. 531 ff. On the attitude
of the republican and classical lawyers towards rhetoric see Schulz, *History*,
54 f., 119, 125, 259. On post-classical law, La Pira, 456 ff.

   s. 486. Windscheid, l.c. § 586; Donatuti, 'L'origine della *querella
inofficiosae donationis*', *St. Riccobono*, iii (1936), 427 ff.; H. Krüger, *Z* lx
(1940), 83 ff.

CHAPTER V

ACQUISITION AND REFUSAL OF THE INHERITANCE

1. *Introduction*

487.
Survey

IN the preceding three chapters of this part we have expounded the conditions upon which any acquisition of an inheritance depended. The scope of the present chapter is to describe the acquisition itself and, in connexion with it, refusal of the inheritance.

First and foremost we must again distinguish between *hereditas* and *bonorum possessio* (above, ss. 377 f.). As regards the latter, only a few additional remarks are required, since we have already emphasized repeatedly that under classical law any *bonorum possessio* was acquired by a decree of the praetor or the provincial governor. For that reason there could, strictly speaking, be no refusal of *bonorum possessio* but only an abstention from it by not applying to the magistrate for it.

With regard to the acquisition and refusal of *hereditas* we must distinguish between *hereditas ab intestato* and *a testamento*. Although both have much in common, it is convenient to deal with them separately. Succession against the will (above, ss. 459 ff.) needs no further discussion. The victorious plaintiff in a *querella inofficiosi testamenti* acquired his intestate portion (above, s. 483) by the judgment of the court; succession upon *praeteritio* (above, s. 460) is covered by the rules of intestate and testamentary succession.

Thus we arrive at the following four sections:

1. Acquisition and refusal of *hereditas ab intestato*.
2. Acquisition and refusal of *hereditas a testamento*.
3. The inheritance during the interval between the death of the *de cuius* and the acquisition (*hereditas iacens*).
4. Acquisition of *bonorum possessio*.

2. *Acquisition and refusal of hereditas ab intestato*

i. *Sui heredes*

Sui heredes (above, s. 384) acquired the estate of their father or grandfather automatically when it was legally certain that a valid and effective will did not exist (above, s. 381). This might be at the time of the death of the *de cuius*, but possibly at a later time.

488. Principle

> Suppose a testator had made a will and instituted his friend F, disinheriting his only son A. After the testator's death F refused the inheritance, thereby rendering the will invalid. It was at this moment that the *suus* A acquired the inheritance *ab intestato*.
>
> The *suus* must be alive (at least *iam conceptus*) at the time when F refused the inheritance, as well as at the time when the testator died. If A was alive at his father's death but died before F refused the inheritance, the inheritance fell to that person who would be intestate heir if A had never existed. Suppose that B was a grandson of the testator (son of A) who did not yet exist at the testator's death. When F refused the inheritance, B existed, but his father A had died. B cannot inherit the estate of his grandfather.

Since *sui* acquired the inheritance automatically, even a *suus infans* (above, s. 302) or *furiosus* (above, s. 344) might acquire it. On the other hand, the acquisition was definitive; the *sui* were not entitled to refuse the inheritance: *semel heres, semper heres* (above, s. 456). For that reason the *sui* were called *sui et necessarii heredes*. If you keep in mind that the classical *heres* was liable for the debts of the *de cuius*, even *ultra vires hereditatis* (above, s. 371), and that there was an execution upon the person of the debtor (above, ss. 43, 372), the harshness of this rule is manifest. The aim of the old republican law was evidently to provide a father as far as possible with a *heres* without paying any regard to the interests of the *sui*; the harsh *patria potestas* was in this case effective even after the father's death.

489. Sui et necessarii heredes

However, the harsh rule of *ius civile* was considerably mitigated by the praetor. We do not know the time when he first interfered, but it can hardly have been earlier than the last century of the Republic. The praetor allowed a *suus* 'to abstain from the inheritance' and thereby to become free from his father's debts. Modern students are wont to

490. Beneficium abstinendi

call this right *beneficium abstinendi*, but the classical lawyers did not as yet have a fixed term.

> *Facultas abstinendi*: D. (29. 2) 57 pr. *Potestas abstinendi*: Gai. 2.
> 160, 163. *Ius abstinendi*: D. (28. 5) 87. 1. *Beneficium.abstinendi* only
> once in classical writings: D. (29. 2) 71. 4.

Where a *suus heres* availed himself of that *beneficium* (*tutor impuberis* and *curator furiosi* might claim that right for their wards) the praetor protected him against the creditors by *denegatio actionis* (above, s. 17); on the other hand, he denied to the *suus* the actions which would pass to him with the inheritance. The estate was delivered to the creditors, who might now proceed to *bonorum venditio* (above, s. 43). The creditors might demand a declaration from the *suus* whether or not he wished to make use of the *beneficium*; the *suus* could then ask for a *spatium deliberandi* to be fixed, if necessary, by the praetor. The *beneficium* could not be claimed if the *suus* meddled with the estate (*se immiscere bonis hereditariis*), i.e. if he did what might be termed as *pro herede gestio* (below, s. 496); and if it had already been obtained was lost when he did so. A single exception was made by the praetor in favour of a *suus pupillus* (Lenel, *Edict.* §§ 209, 210).

We may describe this *ius abstinendi* as a praetorian right to refuse the inheritance, provided we keep in mind that *ius civile* was not altered by that right. When a *suus* abstained from the estate, he nevertheless remained *heres iure civili*. The important consequence is that by the abstention the inheritance does not pass to the next intestate heir. Suppose that the *de cuius* had only one *suus* and that he made use of the *beneficium*. The inheritance was not offered to the *proximus adgnatus*, e.g. to the father's brother. In post-classical times the amalgamation of *ius civile* and *ius honorarium* led to the opposite result, as a (probably interpolated) rescript of Diocletian shows (*C.* 6. 58. 6). That the *suus abstentus* was still *heres* was now regarded as a mere matter of style (*nudum nomen heredis*).

491. The theory of the family property The *sui* alone acquired the inheritance automatically; all other intestate heirs acquired only by a special act of acceptance. How is this different treatment to be ex-

plained? Again the attempt has been made to find the explanation in prehistorical law. Originally, it is said, the *sui* were co-owners of the family property together with their father. Thus when the father died the *sui* did not acquire the estate but remained what they were before, co-owners, only now they were free from their father's *potestas*. This idea, it is said, was retained even when the idea of family property had long disappeared and led to the rule that *sui* acquire the inheritance automatically. This explanation should be rejected. In truth the republican and classical lawyers were guided by the desire to provide a father with an heir who could not decline the inheritance. Only the *sui* could be in question. Thus the lawyers regarded the *sui* as *heredes necessarii* and this implied that they acquired the inheritance *ipso iure*, as it would have been absurd to require an acceptance of the inheritance from a person who could not refuse it. That this was the leading idea is made abundantly clear by the fact that a *servus cum libertate heres institutus* was also a *heres necessarius* (below, s. 502) and consequently acquired the inheritance *ipso iure*: certainly such a freedman was never co-owner of the family property.

ii. *Heredes voluntarii*

All other intestate heirs (*iuris civilis*) except the *sui* acquired the inheritance by a special act which was called *aditio hereditatis* (*adire hereditatem* = to approach the inheritance). As these persons were free to accept or to decline the inheritance they were called (though perhaps not as early as classical times) *heredes voluntarii*.

492. Heredes voluntarii

> The term was apparently not known to Gaius who was led to the illogical distinction between *heredes necessarii* and *extranei* (Gai. 2. 152). Wherever the term occurs in classical writings the texts are suspect, including Papin. Fragmenta Paris. § 18, a note added by a post-classical editor of Papinian's *responsa* (Schulz, *History*, 219 ff., 237).

This group comprehends (leaving aside the *gens*; above, s. 396) the *proximus adgnatus* (above, s. 389), and the heirs *ex senatus consulto Tertulliano* (above, s. 400), and *Orfitiano* (above, s. 401). They all are non-*sui* and in this sense *extranei*.

493.
Hereditas
delata

A *suus* acquired the inheritance at the moment at which it was offered to him. As regards *heredes voluntarii* we must carefully distinguish between the moment at which the inheritance was offered to him and the moment at which he acquired it; modern students are wont to say 'between *delatio* and *adquisitio hereditatis*', but this terminology is non-classical (above, s. 376). The *heres* could neither accept nor refuse the inheritance before it has been offered to him.

The inheritance was offered to an *heres voluntarius ab intestato* when it was certain that a valid and effective will did not exist and, therefore, intestate succession took place (above, s. 381). As a rule this was at the death of the *de cuius*, but sometimes at a later time, viz. when an inheritance fell to an heir after it had been refused by another heir.

The *senatusconsultum Orfitianum* (above, s. 401) stated expressly that if the children refused their mother's inheritance the *ius antiquum* should take effect (Bruns, *Fontes*, no. 64), i.e. the inheritance fell to the *proximus adgnatus* of the mother. The *senatusconsultum Tertullianum* probably contained a similar clause. When a *proximus adgnatus* declined an inheritance, the inheritance was not offered to the next agnate (above, s. 394).

Like a *suus*, a *voluntarius heres* must be alive at the death of the *de cuius* and at the time when the inheritance was offered to him (above, s. 488); the rule *nasciturus pro iam nato habetur* did not apply here (above, s. 393).

494.
Transmissio
hereditatis
delatae

At the moment when the inheritance was offered to the *heres voluntarius* he acquired not the inheritance, but a right to acquire (or to refuse) it. He might transfer this right to another by *in iure cessio*, but when the heir died without having exercised his right to acquire the inheritance, his heir was not entitled to do so. It was only Justinian who permitted the heir's heir under certain conditions to acquire the inheritance.

495. Aditio
hereditatis

Under classical law there were two modes of accepting an inheritance (*adire hereditatem*): *pro herede gestio* and *cretio*.

496. Pro
herede
gestio

Originally there existed only one mode, the *pro herede gestio*. *Gerere pro herede* means 'to act as an heir'. Since acceptance was conditional on the heir's knowledge of the death of the *de cuius*, any act of the heir concerning the estate amounted as a rule to a *pro herede gestio*. If, for example, the heir applied to the praetor for *bonorum possessio ab intestato*, or if he sued the hereditary debtors or sold the inherited property, this would amount to *pro herede gestio*. The sources furnish on this subject a rich fund of legal subtleties.

Under classical law an inheritance *ab intestato* might also be accepted by *cretio* (Gai. 2. 167), i.e. by a formal declaration which contained the words *hereditatem adeo cernoque*.

> This use of *cernere* is peculiar to legal language. *Cernere*, says Varro, *De lingua Lat.* 7. 98, means *constituere*; 'itaque heres cum constituit se heredem esse dicitur "cernere".' The word *hereditas* means in this connexion 'succession' and not 'estate' (above, s. 375); *cernere hereditatem* means 'to settle the succession'.

This act did not require the presence of witnesses like the *mancipatio*, but a *testatio* (a declaration before witnesses) was nevertheless indispensable, since a declaration made to the walls of one's room would have been absurd.

The *cretio* evidently originated in testamentary succession, since the testator usually demanded a formal acceptance (below, s. 506). It is significant that Gaius deals with *cretio* in his section on testamentary succession and only incidentally does he mention that it was also available to intestate heirs. Whether *cretio* was compulsory when a *filius familias* wished to accept an inheritance *ab intestato* remains doubtful (the question could only arise when he was heir of his mother's estate *ex senatus consulto Orfitiano*).

In post-classical times the *cretio* was abolished. Justinian's compilers have accordingly eliminated the terms *cretio* and *cernere* from the classical texts and sometimes replaced them by *aditio* and *adire*.

Pro herede gestio and *cretio* were the only classical modes of *aditio hereditatis*. Gaius 2. 167 seems to mention a third mode when he states 'potest aut cernendo aut pro herede gerendo vel etiam nuda voluntate suscipiendae hereditatis heres fieri'. But the text is suspect. An informal declaration before witnesses might have been regarded as *pro herede gestio*.

497. Cretio

497a. A third mode of aditio?

498. Legal
capacity
Both *pro herede gestio* and *cretio* were legal acts and therefore required legal capacity. Hence a woman under a *tutor mulieris* and a *pupillus infantia maior* (above, s. 302) could only effect them *tutore auctore*. An *infans* or a *furiosus* was incapable of acquiring an inheritance and a *tutor impuberis* or *curator furiosi* could not act in the name of his ward, since direct agency was unknown to classical law. A spendthrift under *cura* was probably also incapable of acquiring an inheritance even with the curator's consent, and the curator could not act in his name.

499.
Repudiation
No formality was required for a *repudiatio hereditatis*; any manifestation of an intention not to become heir (*omittere, repudiare hereditatem*) was sufficient. The informal refusal corresponds with the informal *pro herede gestio* which originally was the only mode of accepting an inheritance. It was a legal act like *aditio* and required legal capacity.

500.
Spatium
deliberandi
A time-limit for accepting or refusing the inheritance did not exist *iure civili*. The creditors, however, might summon the heir before the praetor and demand a definite declaration as to whether or not he wished to accept the inheritance. The heir might then ask for a *spatium deliberandi*, and if he did not accept within this time he was excluded. If the heir refused to appear in court the praetor apparently fixed a *spatium deliberandi*. Gaius 2. 167 just mentions the point and his short discussion is not quite accurate.

SOURCES

s. 488. Read Gai. 2. 152, 156; *D.* (38. 16) 14; (38. 16) 6 [*neque*]; [*neque bonorum . . . cognatus*]; ⟨non⟩ potest; *Inst. Iust.* (3. 1) 7.

s. 489. Read *Inst. Iust.* (3. 1) 3; Paul. *Sent.* 4. 8. 5 [*quibus . . . necessaria*].

s. 490. Read Gai. 2. 158, 159, 163; *D.* (29. 2) 57 pr. ⟨*suis et*⟩ *necessariis*; *C.* (6. 58) 6 [*vel . . . hereditatem*]; *succedere* ⟨*non*⟩ *potest*.

s. 491. Read Gai. 2. 157; *D.* (28. 2) 11.

s. 493. Read *D.* (50. 16) 151; Gai. 3. 11–13.

s. 494. Read Gai. 2. 35 to *esset*; 3. 85 to *vocaretur*; *C.* (6. 30) 7 = Consult. 6. 19.

s. 496. Read *Epit. Ulp.* 22. 26.

s. 497. Compare *C.* (6. 30) 7 with Consult. 6. 19; the compilers have eliminated the *cretio*.

s. 497*a*. Read Gai. 2. 167 [*vel etiam . . . hereditatis*].

s. 498. Read Gai. 1. 176; *D.* (29. 2) 8 pr. [*pupilla*] ⟨*mulier*⟩.

s. 499. Read Gai. 2. 169; *Epit. Ulp.* 22. 29; Paul. *Sent.* 4. 4. 1.

s. 500. Read Gai. 2. 167.

BIBLIOGRAPHY

ss. 488 ff. Windscheid, *Pand.* iii (1906), §§ 595 ff.; Bonfante, *Corso*, vi (1930), 182 ff.; Solazzi, *Diritto ereditario romano,* ii (1933), 5 ff.

s. 490. Lenel, *Edict.* (1927), §§ 209, 210; Beseler, *St. Bonfante* ii (1930), 81 ff.; Solazzi, l.c. ii. 221 ff.

s. 491. Solazzi, l.c. i (1932), 160 ff.; Schulz, *JRS* xxxii (1942), 132, with references.*

s. 492. For texts with *heres voluntarius* see Solazzi, l.c. ii. 7.*

s. 494. Garaud, 'L'In iure cessio hereditatis', *RH* i (1922), 141 ff.; Ambrosino, *SD* x (1944), 3 ff.; De Martino, *St. Solazzi* (1948), 568 ff.; Guarino, ibid. 38.

s. 496. Solazzi, l.c. ii 62 ff.; Sanfilippo, 'La valutazione dell' animus nella pro herede gestio', *Ann. Catania,* 1948.

s. 497. Lévy–Bruhl, *NRH* xxxviii (1914), 153 ff.; Buckland, *T* iii (1922), 239 ff.; Solazzi, l.c. ii. 35 ff.; Biondi, 'Degenerazione della cretio', *St. Solazzi* (1948), 67 ff.

s. 497*a*. Solazzi, l.c. ii. 21 ff.; *SD* vi (1940), 323.*

s. 498. Solazzi, l.c. ii. 73 ff.; H. Krüger, Z lxiv (1944), 402 ff.

s. 499. Solazzi, l.c. ii. 181 ff.

s. 500. Lenel, *Edict.* § 208; Solazzi, *Spatium deliberandi* (1912), *Diritto ereditario,* ii. 160 ff.

3. *Acquisition and refusal of hereditas a testamento*

i. *Sui heredes*

When a testator instituted his *suus* as heir, the latter acquired the estate automatically as if he were *heres ab intestato* (above, s. 488). The time at which this acquisition took place was under republican law the time of the testator's death, or if the *suus* was instituted under a condition, the time of the fulfilment of that condition. The testator might even institute his *suus* under the condition *si volet*; in such a case the *suus* was of course not *heres necessarius*, since he acquired the inheritance only after having fulfilled that condition. In the classical period, under the Augustan *lex vicesimaria* (above, s. 365), the will had to be opened officially and under the *lex Papia* (above, s. 182) *delatio hereditatis* was postponed until the moment of the opening

501. Sui instituted as heirs

of the will. It is, however, doubtful whether this rule applied to the *suus*; our knowledge of the *lex Papia* is too inadequate to allow a definite statement. The *suus* who had acquired the inheritance might avail himself of the *beneficium abstinendi*, but in this respect we have nothing to add to our previous remarks (above, s. 490).

ii. *Necessarii heredes*

502.
Necessarii
heredes
A testator might set free his slave in his will (*manumissio testamento*; above, s. 140) and appoint him heir. When the will came into force, the slave became free and acquired the inheritance automatically. Under the *lex Papia* the time at which this occurred was apparently that of the opening of the will, but it might be a later moment if the testator had made the appointment conditional. The freedman acquired the inheritance like a *suus* in that he could not refuse it but, unlike a *suus*, he had no *beneficium abstinendi*. Gaius calls such heirs simply *heredes necessarii* in contrast to the *sui et necessarii heredes*.

iii. *Heredes voluntarii*

503.
Voluntarii
heredes
All persons instituted heirs who did not belong to the *heredes sui et necessarii* or to the *necessarii heredes* acquired the inheritance by accepting it after it had been offered to them.

504.
Hereditas
delata
Under republican law the inheritance was offered to them at the testator's death or if the institution was conditional, at the time of the fulfilment of the condition. Under the *lex Papia* the inheritance was apparently offered with the formal opening of the will; whether exceptionally the *ius antiquum* took place (*delatio* with the death of the testator) we cannot tell. At any rate, the heir must be alive at the testator's death, and at the time of the *delatio*.

505. Aditio
hereditatis
The acceptance of the inheritance (*aditio hereditatis*) had to be effected either by *pro herede gestio* or by *cretio*. Concerning *pro herede gestio* we may refer to what has been said above (s. 496), but *cretio* needs a special discussion with regard to testamentary succession.

506. Cretio
Cretio originated in succession upon the will and was

only transferred later to intestate succession (above, s. 497). It was republican cautelary jurisprudence which suggested to testators the imposition of a *cretio* upon the instituted heir. The idea of the lawyers was to press the instituted heir to come to a decision within a definite time as to whether or not he was prepared to accept the inheritance. The *spatium deliberandi* which in intestate succession could only be obtained with the help of the praetor (above, s. 500) could in testamentary succession be fixed by the testator; and as it is sometimes doubtful whether an act of the instituted heir is to be regarded as *pro herede gestio* (above, s. 496), the testator might demand an express and unmistakable declaration. Accordingly, the formula to be used by the testator might run as follows:

'Titius mihi heres esto cernitoque in centum diebus proximis'.

The declaration required from Titius ran as follows:

'Quod (= 'if' or 'whereas'; above, s. 61) me P. Maevius testamento suo heredem instituit, eam hereditatem adeo cernoque'.

Although this expedient is apparently not very old (it is never mentioned in Plautus' comedies), it goes back to the time in which formalistic interpretation of the will was still in full blossom. What happened if Titius did not obey the testator's order? A liberal construction of the testator's words might have taken the institution as conditional upon the effecting of the *cretio*, but the old lawyers felt themselves bound by the wording. Taken literally the institution was not subject to a condition and the inevitable consequence was that the testator's order concerning *cretio* was without any legal force. Titius might obey or neglect it; he might accept the inheritance by *cretio* or *pro herede gestio* within the hundred days or later. Even when the testator, had added, as was usually done, a *substitutio vulgaris*:

'Titius mihi heres esto cernitoque in diebus centum proximis; quodni ita creverit tum Sempronius mihi heres esto',

the conditional substitution did not induce the lawyers to regard the *institutio Titii* as also conditional.

We have already mentioned this narrow construction of the will (above, s. 455). Suppose that Titius accepted the inheritance by *pro herede*

U

gestio and that Sempronius too accepted. Then both became heirs, each to one-half. It was only the Emperor Marcus who rejected this conclusion, but he, too, did not regard the institution of Titius as conditional but attributed the whole inheritance to Titius (*Epit. Ulp.* 22. 34).

Thus for an order to perform a *cretio* to be effective the testator had to use the following formula:

'Titius mihi heres esto cernitoque in diebus centum proximis; quodni ita creverit, exheres esto.'

Now it was made quite clear that Titius could only accept the inheritance by performing *cretio* within the specified time; if he failed to do so, he was excluded by the clause *exheres esto*.

507.
Spatium deliberandi

The *spatium deliberandi* might be fixed by the testator in two ways: (1) 'cernitoque in diebus centum proximis', to be counted from the death of the testator (*cretio certarum dierum*); (2) 'cernitoque in diebus centum proximis quibus scierit poteritque' (*cretio vulgaris*). When the time fixed by the testator seemed too long, the creditors might apply to the praetor and obtain a restriction. When a testator had not ordered a *cretio*, the creditors might obtain the fixing of a *spatium deliberandi* in the procedure which we have described above (s. 500).

508.
Acquisition by a filius familias or by a slave

A testator might institute a *filius familias* not in his (the testator's) power or a slave not in his ownership. Only the son or the slave could acquire the inheritance, but the estate fell inevitably to the *pater familias* or to the owner of the slave and they were also responsible for the testator's debts. For that reason the son as well as the slave could only accept upon an order (*iussum*) of his *pater familias* or owner. If the inheritance was properly acquired by the son or the slave, the legal position of the *paterfamilias* or the owner of the slave was that of an *heres* and the lawyers had no scruple about designating them as heirs.

The corollaries of this principle are the following:

1. A son in power was properly instituted; later he was emancipated. He could acquire the inheritance for himself.

2. A slave was properly instituted but was later emancipated. He could acquire the inheritance for himself.

3. A slave belonging to A was instituted but later alienated to B. The slave might acquire the inheritance upon the *iussum* of B.

4. If the son in power or the slave died without having accepted the inheritance, the *pater familias* or the owner could not accept it. A very singular exception to this rule attributed to the Emperor Pius is suspect (*D.* 29. 2. 30 pr., 86 pr. with *Index Interp.*).

The ill-starred Augustan legislation on population (*lex Iulia et Papia Poppaea*; above, s. 182) restricted the capacity to accept an inheritance under a will. Unmarried persons (*caelibes*) and persons with no children or with only few children (*orbi*) could be validly instituted but were (with exceptions) incapable of acquiring the inheritance. These artificial and complicated regulations are only imperfectly known to us. Available sources need a fresh critical examination but here it is sufficient just to mention these rules.

509. Incapacitas ex l. Iulia et Papia

SOURCES

s. 501. Read *D.* (28. 7) 12.
s. 502. Read Gai. 2. 152–4.
s. 503. Read Gai. 2. 161–2.
s. 506. Read Gai. 2. 164–8; *Epit. Ulp.* 22. 33, 34.
s. 507. Read Gai. 2. 170–3.
s. 508. Read Gai. 2. 87. 189.

BIBLIOGRAPHY

ss. 501 ff. See references above, ss. 488 ff. Bibliography.

s. 501. Siber, *Röm. Privatrecht* (1928), 402 n. 3; Bachofen, *Ausgewählte Lehren des röm. Civilrechts* (1848), 366 ff.; Biondi in *Acta divi Augusti*, i (1945), 193. On *institutio 'si volet'* see Solazzi, l.c. ii. 15.

s. 506. See references above, s. 497, Bibliography. In particular on *cretio* ordered by will see Beseler, *Z* xliii (1922), 536; xlvii (1927), 62; *St. Riccobono*, i (1936), 301 ff.; Solazzi, *Diritto ereditario*, ii. 135 ff. Lenel, 'Zur Geschichte der heredis institutio', *Essays in Legal History*, ed. P. Vinogradoff (1913), 123 f. For documents concerning *cretio* see *FIRA* iii, nos. 60, 61, with references; Taubenschlag, *Law of Greco-Roman Egypt* (1944), 160 f.*

s. 508. Solazzi, l.c. ii. 84 ff.

s. 509. Bonfante, *Corso*, vi (1930), 281 ff.; Biondi, l.c. 181 ff.; *Successione testamentaria* (1943) = *Trattato di dir. Rom.* ed. Albertario, vol. x, pp. 133 ff.

4. Hereditas iacens

According to the preceding statements the heir appointed by law (intestate succession) or by will (testamentary succession) does not always succeed immediately

510. Conception and terminology

upon the death of the *de cuius*. In the interval between the death of the *de cuius* and the acquisition of the inheritance the estate is, as modern students say, *hereditas iacens*. The term does not appear in classical writings, but *hereditas iacet* and *bona iacent* are perhaps classical expressions.

The legal position of the *hereditas iacens* was much discussed by the classical lawyers, but a comprehensive theory was not reached, the lawyers as usual confining themselves to individual cases. Available texts (we depend entirely on texts in Justinian's law-books) are insufficient and heavily interpolated; only the broad outlines of the classical doctrine are discernible.

511.
Republican law
To a modern continental lawyer the issue implies no difficulties. An *hereditas iacens* is an estate not vested in an owner. A *servus hereditarius* is a slave *in potestate* but for the time being without a master. A thing belonging to the inheritance is *in dominio* but without a *dominus*. Debts of the *de cuius* still exist but, for the time being, there is no debtor. The conceptions 'ownership without owner', '*potestas* without a *dominus*', 'debts without a debtor' are not at all in conflict with logic; rather they are indispensable for a clear and realistic analysis of the *hereditas iacens*, but they were much too artificial for republican jurisprudence. The republican lawyers regarded *hereditas iacens* as a *res nullius*, like a wild animal that had not been captured. Of course the inheritance could not, like wild animals, be appropriated by anybody who chose, but *res hereditariae*, like such animals, were regarded, *hereditate iacente*, as *res extra dominium*, not merely as things *in dominio* without an owner. When the heir acquired the inheritance, he acquired ownership, but this acquisition was not dated back to the time of death of the *de cuius*. The inevitable consequence was that when a thing belonging to the estate was stolen *hereditate iacente*, an *actio furti* did not lie.

512.
Classical law
The classical lawyers attempted to remedy this rather primitive law. Cassius suggested that the acquisition of the inheritance should be dated back to the death of the *de cuius*, but he did not succeed. The dominant classical doc-

trine substantially acknowledged rights not vested in any individual and debts without a debtor; it was the classical aversion to generalizations which prevented the lawyers from expressing these conceptions. When a delict was committed against a hereditary thing *hereditate iacente*, they granted an action to the heir after his acquisition of the inheritance. The technicalities are not fully discernible but they are of minor importance. When a slave belonging to the estate was killed or hurt by somebody *hereditate iacente*, Celsus granted an *actio legis Aquiliae* to the heir (apparently only an *actio utilis*). He could only have reached this decision by assuming that the slave was, *hereditate iacente*, *in dominio*, though without a master. Likewise other actions *ex delicto* were given to the heir. But with regard to the *actio furti* the classical lawyers had to retain the republican rule, since on the absence of the *actio furti* depended the institution of *usucapio pro herede* with which we shall deal later (below, s. 628). The lawyers might somewhat restrict the old rule; they might create a new delict (*crimen expilatae hereditatis*), but they could not grant an *actio furti* without destroying *usucapio pro herede* altogether. A slave belonging to the estate might acquire by *stipulatio*, *mancipatio*, or *traditio*, *hereditate iacente*; the acquest fell to the estate (*hereditati adquiritur*), i.e. it was in the same legal position as the property left by the *de cuius*. This implied that the slave, *hereditate iacente*, was *in potestate* and that the *potestas* belonged to the inheritance, being like the whole estate *sine domino*. A *servus hereditarius* might be instituted by a testator other than his former master if the latter might have been instituted. In this case the sources use the argument *hereditas defuncti locum optinet* or *hereditas personae defuncti vice fungitur*. The meaning of these obscure formulas is probably: 'the *successio* (*hereditas = successio*, see above, s. 375) functions instead of the deceased'; in other words, the estate is subject to the right of succession and this right preserves the power over the slave, though it is a power not vested in a *dominus*. Be that as it may, the classical decision obviously depends on the slave being *in potestate* during the critical interval.

513. Post-classical law   In post-classical times *hereditas iacens* was regarded as a legal person. The preposterous idea crept into the classical texts which are quite clearly interpolated; this is not disputed today.

SOURCES

ss. 510 ff. Read *D.* (47. 2) 69 (with Jolowicz, *Digest* 47, 2 *de furtis*, p. 108); (9. 2) 13. 2 [*dominus . . . habebitur*]; ⟨*utili actione*⟩ *experiri*; (43. 24) 13. 5 [*accedit . . . admissum*]; *Inst. Iust.* (3. 17) pr.; (41. 1) 33. 2 [*per traditionem*] ⟨*mancipio*⟩, [*cuius . . . opinantis*]; (45. 3) 28. 4 (with Beseler, *Beiträge*, v. 80); (28. 5) 31. 1 [*dominam esse*]; (28. 5) 53 and 65; (30) 116. 3.

BIBLIOGRAPHY

s. 510. On terminology see *Voc. Jur. Rom.* iii. 283. 11–13.

ss. 511 ff. Windscheid, *Pand.* iii (1906), § 531, with references; Scaduto, 'Contributo esegetico alla dottrina romana dell' eredità giacente', *Annali Palermo*, viii (1921), i ff. See further on the relevant texts, discussed by Scaduto, *Index Interp.* with references.

5. Acquisition of bonorum possessio

514. Classical bonorum possessio always decretalis   Whoever wished to acquire *bonorum possessio* had to apply for it to the praetor or the provincial governor and it was acquired upon grant to him by a decree of the magistrate. Any classical *bonorum possessio* was a *bonorum possessio decretalis* (above, s. 378).

515. Details   Before pronouncing this decree the magistrate might, at his discretion, have a *causae cognitio*, but in the second century A.D. the granting of those kinds of *bonorum possessio* which we have described before (leaving aside special other kinds) had apparently become a matter of routine which was discharged without any, or without any serious, *causae cognitio*. Thus a plurality of *bonorum possessiones* might arise upon the same estate. Suppose that A appeared before the praetor and claimed and obtained *bonorum possessio ab intestato* (above, ss. 404 ff.). Some days later B appeared and producing a will obtained *bonorum possessio secundum tabulas* (above, s. 436). At last C appeared and claimed and received *bonorum possessio contra tabulas* (above, s. 468). The order of precedence of these three *bonorum possessiones* is quite clear, being implied by the order of the Edict: (1) *bonorum possessio contra tabulas*; (2) *bonorum possessio* *secundum tabulas*; (3) *bonorum possessio ab intestato*. Nevertheless, the legal situation is far from plain. Further, *bonorum possessio* might be claimed and received in advance and then the *bonorum possessio* obtained might at a later date turn out to be ineffective or to bear a different character. Suppose the *de cuius* had two emancipated sons, A and B. He instituted A to one-quarter and his friend F to three-quarters, passing over B in silence. B might claim *bonorum possessio contra tabulas* to one-half, and if he did so, then A likewise would receive *bonorum possessio contra tabulas* to one-half, *commisso per alium edicto* (above, s. 469). Now, suppose that A claimed *bonorum possessio contra tabulas* to one-half in advance, hoping that B would do the same. B, however, failed to claim *bonorum possessio contra tabulas* in time. The *bonorum possessio contra tabulas* obtained by A now changed into a *bonorum possessio secundum tabulas* to one-quarter. This, at least, must be concluded from our sources. However, we will not dwell upon these and other rather intricate details, particularly as the heavily interpolated texts are not yet fully disentangled.

In post-classical times those kinds of *bonorum possessio* 516. Postclassical law which alone we have discussed above were acquired by a declaration before an authority and a decree was only required in special cases. Accordingly, one distinguished now between *bonorum possessio edictalis* and *decretalis*. We have already pointed out above that this distinction was entirely foreign to the classical lawyers (above, s. 378).

The whole issue urgently needs a critical revision.

SOURCES

Read *D.* (37. 4) 10. 6; (37. 5) 14 pr.; (37. 5) 15. 1.

BIBLIOGRAPHY

Solazzi, *AG* c (1928), 17 ff.; La Pira, *La successione ereditaria intestata e contro il testamento* (1930), *passim*; H. Krüger, 'Erwerb und Ausschlagung der bonorum possessio durch das Hauskind, den pupillus und den furiosus', Z lxiv (1944), 394 ff. For the rest see Bibliography to ss. 377 ff.

CHAPTER VI

THE HEIR
AFTER THE ACQUISITION
OF THE INHERITANCE

1. *Introduction*

517.
Survey THE object of the present chapter is to expound the legal position of an heir or a plurality of heirs after the acquisition of the inheritance has taken place as described in the preceding chapter. There are three main issues which we have to consider:

1. The heir and the inherited property, i.e. the rights to which he has succeeded.
2. The heir and the debts to which he has succeeded.
3. The legal protection of the heir, i.e. the actions which are available to him.

We shall premise some remarks on the doctrine of accrual (*ius adcrescendi*), since a more convenient place within the system cannot be found (Windscheid, *Pand.* iii, § 603 n. 6). *Heres* and *bonorum possessor* will be treated together.

2. *Ius adcrescendi*

518. Here-
ditas ab
intestato Let us start with the following simple case. The *de cuius* died without making a will and intestate succession took place. As he had no *sui* the inheritance was offered to the *proximus adgnatus* (above, s. 389); there were, however, two agnates of the same degree, A and B, each of them entitled to one-half of the inheritance. Now suppose that A accepted the share offered to him, and after a while B refused his share. With B's refusal his share 'accrued' to A's share, so that A is now universal heir. The acquisition of B's share took place automatically; although the *proximus adgnatus* acquired the inheritance only by *cretio* or *pro herede gestio* (above, s. 492), no further *aditio* is required for the accruing portion. The Roman idea was that the whole

inheritance is offered *in solidum* to both A and B, and A's acceptance comprehends the whole estate, *partes concursu fiunt*. Thus, if B refuses his share, there is no longer a *concursus*; the *delatio* of the inheritance to A and his *aditio* now display their full force; no fresh *delatio* and *aditio* of the accruing portion is required. Even if A had already died at the time when B refused, the accrual took place; B's share fell to A's heir. When B did not refuse his share but died without having accepted it, the effect would be the same (above, s. 494): his share inevitably and automatically accrued to A's share.

Suppose that neither of the agnates had acquired the inheritance, when B refused his share or died. In this case also B's share accrued to A's portion, who now could only accept the whole or nothing.

The same principle applied when *bonorum possessio ab intestato* took place.

519.
Bonorum
possessio
ab
intestato

Suppose the *de cuius* had an emancipated son A and two emancipated grandsons C and D, sons of a son B who had predeceased the *de cuius*. A and C applied for *bonorum possessio unde liberi*, while D failed to do so in due time. D's share accrued to C and not also to A according to the principle of distribution within the class *unde liberi* (above, s. 407).

Finally the principle of accrual also applied to succession under a will. But here, too—as in the case of *bonorum possessio unde liberi* which we have just mentioned—the accrual sometimes took place within a smaller group of heirs. For instance: The testator instituted A to one-half and B and C together to the other half. If B refused his share (one-quarter), or if he died without having accepted it, his share accrued to C and not also to A. This was, of course, a question of the construction of the will, but the classical lawyers stuck to the wording of the will and if the testator had instituted a plurality of heirs to the same share (as in the example which we have just given), the accrual was always confined to the 'united heirs' (*re coniuncti*), whereas in all other cases general accrual among all co-heirs took place. The classical decisions provide significant information as to the classical methods of constructing a will and should, therefore, be read with particular attention as the available texts are in a rather good state.

520.
Succession
under a will

521. Lex Papia   Under the *lex Papia* the right of accrual was considerably restricted, as far as the succession upon the will was concerned. As a rule the quota (*pars caduca*) now fell to privileged persons mentioned in the will and in default of them to the *aerarium populi Romani*, later to the *fiscus*. The *ius antiquum* was maintained only in favour of descendants and ascendants of the testator down to the third degree.

SOURCES

s. 518. Read *Epit. Ulp.* 26. 5; *D.* (38. 16) 9.

s. 519. Read *D.* (37. 4) 12 pr.

s. 520. Read *D.* (50. 16) 142; (32) 80; (28. 5) 67; (28. 5) 17. 1; (28. 5) 15 pr.; (28. 5) 60. 3; (28. 5) 64 [*hoc*] ⟨*nihil*⟩; [*non ad ... separatis*].

BIBLIOGRAPHY

ss. 518–20. Windscheid, *Pand.* iii (1906), §§ 603, 604; Bonfante, *Corso*, vi (1930), 253 ff.; Vaccaro–Delogu, *L'Accrescimento nel diritto ereditario romano* (1941, not available); see Guarino, *SD* ix (1943), 301 ff.

s. 521. Windscheid, § 604 n. 1, with references.

3. *The heir and the inherited property*

522. Universal heres   If in an individual case only one *heres* had acquired the whole estate, the legal situation was simple. *Heres succedit in locum defuncti* (above, s. 367), i.e. the rights of the *de cuius* are now vested in the *heres* in so far as they were not extinguished by the death of the *de cuius* (above, s. 358). If the *de cuius* was owner *ex iure Quiritium*, the ownership is now vested in the *heres*; and if the *defunctus* was a creditor, the obligatory right is now vested in the person of the *heres*. Where a thing belonging to the estate was in the hands of another person the heir might sue the latter using the usual formula 'Si paret rem Auli Agerii (the name of the heir had to be inserted) esse etc'. (above, s. 58). He might equally sue a debtor of the *de cuius*, e.g. with the *actio certae creditae pecuniae* 'Si paret Numerium Negidium Aulo Agerio centum dare oportere etc.' (above, s. 30).

523. Universal bonorum possessor   The *bonorum possessor* was not a *successor iuris civilis*. Take the following simple case: A *de cuius* who died intestate had only one emancipated son who received *bonorum possessio unde liberi*. The son was not owner of the estate *ex*

iure Quiritium; even if he took the estate into his possession, *iure civili* the estate was *hereditas iacens* (above, s. 510). Thus if, for example, a piece of land belonging to the estate was in the possession of another person, the *bonorum possessor* could not sue the latter with the *rei vindicatio*, but the praetor granted him a *rei vindicatio utilis* with a *formula ficticia* (*ficto eo herede*) which we have already described (s. 49). The *bonorum possessor* might later acquire *dominium ex iure Quiritium* by *usucapio*, but for the time being he was entirely dependent on the protection of the praetor. Accordingly, the *bonorum possessor* could not alienate the land by *mancipatio*; all he could do was to transfer 'praetorian ownership', i.e. a possession protected by the praetor. Likewise the *bonorum possessor* could not sue a hereditary debtor with the usual formulas; he needed *actiones ficticiae*. Thus, seen from the technical point of view, *heres* and *bonorum possessor* differed widely and to call the *bonorum possessor* a *successor* at all might seem objectionable; but in practice these differences were hardly felt by parties. These technicalities were the concern of the lawyers and scribes, who dealt with them as a matter of course. Moreover, in the *extraordinaria cognitio* (in the provinces where the formulary procedure did not exist; above, s. 20) the contrast was not as manifest as in the ordinary procedure.

Sometimes the right of the *heres* is in conflict with that of the *bonorum possessor*; then we have to consider whether the *bonorum possessio* is *cum re* or *sine re*. The *bonorum possessor cum re* is protected by the praetor against the *heres*, the *bonorum possessor sine re* is not (above, s. 378). 524. Heres in conflict with bonorum possessor

> Consider the following case of a *bonorum possessio cum re*. The *de cuius* died intestate leaving only one emancipated son A and an agnatic brother (of the *de cuius*) B. A received *bonorum possessio unde liberi*, B who was sole heir *iure civili* accepted the inheritance by *cretio*. Now B alone is owner of the estate *iure civili*, but A's *bonorum possessio* is *cum re*. A might therefore claim the estate from B, but B could not claim it from A and the hereditary actions were denied to B by the praetor.

When a plurality of *heredes* had acquired the estate, e.g. A to one-third and B to two-thirds, every right belonging to it was now vested in their persons according to their 525. Coheredes shares. If a piece of land belonged to the estate, A and B were now co-owners; the ownership, not the land, was divided so that A had one-third of the *dominium* and B two-thirds. A *servus hereditarius* had now two masters, A having one-third of the *potestas* and B two-thirds. In conformity with Roman liberalism (above, s. 363) each co-heir was entitled to dispose of his share of the single things without the consent of the other; of the whole thing they could of course dispose only together. Further, each co-heir might demand partition at any time. The partition might be effected by agreement between the co-heirs or, if that could not be reached, by the judge in the *iudicium familiae erciscundae* to which we shall return later (below, s. 538). There was only one exception to these rules. According to the old republican maxim *nomina ipso iure divisa sunt* (*nomen* = 'entry in the creditor's ledger', 'debt', 'obligation'), divisible claims were automatically apportioned. Suppose the *de cuius* had made a loan of 90 to somebody; then the recipient now owed A 30 and B 60.

The old republican *consortium* among co-heirs mentioned by Gaius 3. 154*a* need not be discussed in this book since in classical times it no longer existed.

526.
Bonorum
possessores;
bonorum
possessor
and heres
If there was a plurality of *bonorum possessores*, similar rules applied. They were not co-owners, but the praetor treated them as if they were. The rule *nomina ipso iure divisa sunt* applied; each possessor might demand his share from the debtor, *ficto se herede*. Sometimes a *bonorum possessor* competed with an *heres*; then the legal situation was technically somewhat complicated.

Suppose that a father had two sons, A in *potestate*, B emancipated. The father died intestate. A was universal heir *iure civili*. Both A and B might apply for *bonorum possessio unde liberi*, each to one-half; A did not apply for it, while B obtained *bonorum possessio*. Thus B was *bonorum possessor* of the whole estate, but *cum re* only to one-half. *Iure civili* there was no co-ownership, but the praetor treated A and B as if they were co-owners (leaving aside the *interdictum quorum bonorum*; below, s. 537).

SOURCES

s. 522. Read *D.* (50. 17) 59.
s. 523. Read Gai. 4. 34.
s. 525. Read XII Tab. v. 9 (*FIRA* i, p. 41).

BIBLIOGRAPHY

s. 523. Lenel, *Edict.* (1927), 183.

s. 525. On the maxim *nomina ipso iure divisa sunt* see Berger, *Zur Entwicklungsgeschichte der Teilungsklagen* (1912), 5, and *Studi Riccobono*, i (1936), 609 ff. For further literature see above, ss. 86, 87, Bibliography. On *consortium* see *FIRA* i, p. 42, with references; Frezza, *Rivista di Filologia*, lxii (1934), 27 ff.; Maschi, *Disertiones* (1935).*

4. *The heir and the debts of the de cuius*

The *heres* who had acquired the estate was liable for the debts without any regard to the assets. He succeeded *in locum defuncti* and for that reason was responsible for the debts even *ultra vires hereditatis*, and no remedy was available to him in order to limit his liability to the value of the assets. We have already mentioned this harsh Roman principle and may refer to our previous discussion (above, ss. 371 f.).

527. Liability ultra vires hereditatis

A *suus* who acquired the estate automatically (above, s. 488), might avail himself of the *beneficium abstinendi* (above, s. 490) and thereby set himself free from the debts. An *heres voluntarius* who acquired the estate by a legal act (*cretio* or *pro herede gestio*; above, s. 492) might apply for *in integrum restitutio* if he discovered after the *aditio* that the estate was insolvent. If he was *minor XXV annis*, the *in integrum restitutio* was available to him as a matter of course (above, s. 329), but if he was *maior XXV annis* it was only exceptionally granted, apparently only by imperial decree.

528. Beneficium abstinendi. In integrum restitutio

There was, however, a case in which the classical law already deemed it just to reduce the severity of this liability, namely, the case of the *heres necessarius*. We have already pointed out (above, s. 502) that a testator might set free his slave by will and institute him heir. The freedman acquired the estate automatically and had, unlike the *sui*, no *beneficium abstinendi* (above, s. 502). Under classical law, however, the freedman had the right to separate any property which he gained after the patron's death from the estate, thereby securing it against the hereditary creditors.

529. Beneficium separationis heredis necessarii

Modern students call this right the *beneficium separationis* of the *heres necessarius*, though this term is certainly not classical and is even misleading. Available sources on this *beneficium* are extremely scanty, but among them is a passage in Gaius' *Institutes* (2. 155). Gaius states that whatever the freedman acquired after the patron's death was 'reserved' to him (*ipsi reserventur*); the hereditary creditors could not sell it with the estate. But what does that mean? This *beneficium* has been keenly discussed by modern students, but they have apparently overlooked the fact that under classical law there existed such a thing as execution on the person (above, s. 43). The freedman was the debtor of the hereditary creditors, and if they could not obtain full payment by selling the assets of the inheritance and if, on the other hand, they were debarred from the property which the freedman had acquired after the patron's death, there still remained their right of execution upon the freedman's person. This is not impossible, but hardly probable, for, if that was the law, the *beneficium* would have been of little use to the freedman, since as a rule he would have willingly abandoned his own property to the creditors in order to avert execution upon his person. Hence we believe that the *beneficium* entailed more than the separation of the freedman's property from the estate, viz. that therewith he was set free from the threat of execution upon his person as far as hereditary debts were concerned. On the history of the *beneficium* we know nothing. The *lex Iulia de cessione bonorum* may have expressly stated that the freedman escaped execution upon his person by abandoning the estate to the hereditary creditors (a special kind of *cessio bonorum*). Or the praetor may have granted him a sort of *beneficium competentiae* (below, s. 793), restricting his liability to *in quantum facere potest ex hereditate*. Both ways lay open, but which of them was actually chosen we cannot tell. Be that as it may, the classicality of the *beneficium* should no longer be suspected. Within the history of Roman private law it was the first example of a liability *cum viribus hereditatis* and as such possesses a peculiar interest.

A further step was taken by the Emperor Gordianus, who confined the liability of a soldier to the estate.

530.
Gordian's
rescript.

Apart from these two cases the old harsh liability of the *heres* (*ultra vires hereditatis*) remained unaltered, and it was only Justinian who in A.D. 531 by the *beneficium inventarii* enabled the heir to transfer his unlimited liability into a liability *cum viribus* or *pro viribus hereditatis* (the words of Justinian's constitution, *C.* 6. 30. 22, are in this respect ambiguous).

Justinian's
beneficium
inventarii

Where there was a plurality of heirs, the rule *nomina ipso iure divisa sunt* (above, s. 525) again applied. If A was heir to one-third and B to two-thirds and the *de cuius* owed C 90, then A now owed 30 to C, and 60 to B. If the debt was indivisible, each heir owed the whole (*in solidum*; see below, s. 827).

531.
Plurality
of heirs

A *bonorum possessor* was liable for the debts like an *heres*; the creditors might sue him *ficto eo herede*.

532.
Bonorum
possessor

With the acquisition of the inheritance the estate is absorbed by the property of the heir; the heir has now only one property (Windscheid, *Pand.* iii, § 605 n. 6), which comprehends both the inheritance and the property which the heir possessed before the acquisition of the inherited estate. On the other hand, the creditors of the *de cuius* are now the creditors of the heir on equal terms with those creditors of the heir who already existed before the acquisition of the estate. Both groups of creditors compete and can secure execution upon the estate as well as the other property of the heir. However, the Edict contained a rubric *De separationibus* (Lenel, *Edict.* § 223). The wording of the Edict has not been preserved to us, but apparently the praetor granted the hereditary creditors a right to separate the inherited estate from the other property of the heir. The estate was thereby reserved to the hereditary creditors, and the creditors of the heir were excluded from it so long as the hereditary creditors were not yet fully paid off. On the other hand, the hereditary creditors were now definitely excluded from the non-inherited property of the heir. This so-called *beneficium separationis creditorum* was only available to the hereditary creditors, not to the other creditors of the heir.

533.
Beneficium
separationis
creditorum

Available sources on that *beneficium* are scanty and mostly spurious. In these circumstances the task of unravelling the classical law is past hope unless fresh sources turn up. The whole *beneficium separationis* is for the time being a problem. What was the underlying *ratio*? It might be said: 'The estate is encumbered with the debts of the *de cuius*; it is, so to speak, "mortgaged" to his creditors. It is but just, therefore, that the estate should be first and foremost reserved to these creditors in preference to the special creditors of the heir.' But why cannot the special creditors of the heir say likewise: 'the property which the heir possessed before acquiring the estate is quasi mortgaged to us, and the hereditary creditors must not have access to it so long as we have not obtained full payment'? It is said in spurious texts: 'the special creditors of the heir have no right to complain of the competition on equal terms of the hereditary creditors, since every debtor might otherwise render the position of his creditors worse by contracting new debts'; but this is hardly a convincing argument, though it has much impressed modern students and legislators. Thus not even the fundamental idea of the institution is clearly discernible, to say nothing of the details. In such a case the historian is allowed, nay bound, to pronounce a *non liquet*.

SOURCES

s. 528. Read *D.* (4. 4) 11. 5 with Beseler, *St. Riccobono*, i. 306; Gai. 2. 163.

s. 529. Read Gai. 2. 155 to *venient*.

s. 530. Read *C.* (6. 30) 22 pr.; cf. *Inst. Iust.* (2. 19) 6.

s. 533. Read *D.* (42. 6) 1 pr.–2 (entirely spurious); (42. 6) 1. 5 (spurious); (42. 6) 1. 17 (from *cuius rei ratio* spurious).

BIBLIOGRAPHY

s. 528. Solazzi, *Diritto ereditario romano*, ii (1933), 265 ff.

s. 529. Solazzi, l.c. 252 ff.; Guarino, 'Il beneficium separationis dell' heres necessarius', Z lx (1940), 185 ff.; Beseler, *Scritti Ferrini*, iii (1948), 272.*

s. 530. Solazzi, l.c. 275, 283 ff.; Windscheid, *Pand.* iii (1906), § 606.

s. 531. On *nomina ipso iure divisa sunt* see above, s. 525, Bibliography.

s. 533. Windscheid, *Pand.* iii, § 607; Lenel, *Edict.* (1927), § 2230; Baviera, *Il commodum separationis nel diritto romano* (1901); Ferrini,

Scritti, iv (1930), 67–192; Solazzi, *Bull.* xi (1898), 248 ff., xiii (1901), 247 ff.; Tumedei, *La separazione dei beni ereditari* (1917). See further German *BGB.* § 1981; *Code civ.* 878, 881 with Planiol–Ripert, *Traité élémentaire de droit civ.* iii (1946), s. 2635.

5. *Legal protection of the heir*

An *heres* had the usual actions to protect every right 534. attaching to the estate. If, for example, a slave of the *de* Survey *cuius* was not in the possession of the *heres,* the latter might sue the *possessor* with the ordinary *rei vindicatio*; if the successor was a *bonorum possessor,* a *rei vindicatio utilis* was available to him *ficto eo herede.* Actions of this kind need no further discussion (above, s. 523). There were, however, three remedies with which we have to deal in this place: (1) the *hereditatis petitio* of the *heres*; (2) the *interdictum quorum bonorum* available to the *bonorum possessor*; (3) the *actio familiae erciscundae* brought in order to dissolve the community existing among co-heirs.

i. *Hereditatis petitio*

This action lay first and foremost where an estate (or 535. something belonging to it) was in the possession of a per- Hereditatis son who contested the plaintiff's heirship. Suppose that P petitio was in possession of a piece of land which H demanded from him. H pleaded *in iure* (before the praetor; above, s. 17) that the land formerly belonged to A and that he (H) was A's *heres.* P contested the plaintiff's heirship, pleading that he himself (P) was the true heir of A, or he simply denied H's heirship without pretending to be A's heir. In such cases H might sue P with the *hereditatis petitio.* The formula probably ran as follows:

'Si paret hereditatem L. Titii qua de agitur Auli Agerii esse ex iure Quiritium neque ea res Aulo Agerio restituetur, quanti ea res erit, tantam pecuniam iudex Numerium Negidium Aulo Agerio condemnato, si non paret absolvito.' (Compare the *formula* of the *rei vindicatio*; above, s. 58.)

This is obviously the *formula* of an *actio in rem* (above, s. 58) which implies (above, s. 56) that the defendant was not bound to accept the *iudicium*; he was free to abandon the things which he had in his possession. If he neither accepted the *iudicium de hereditatis petitione* nor abandoned the things in his possession, the plaintiff might ask for the *interdictum quam hereditatem* (Lenel, *Edict.* § 229).

The *hereditatis petitio* lay in addition where the *possessor* did not contest the plaintiff's heirship but pleaded that he himself was a *bonorum possessor cum re.* In such cases an *exceptio doli* (above, s. 96) was inserted in the *formula* of the *hereditatis petitio* (Gai. 2. 120).

When the *possessor* had acquired the thing in question on a so-called singular title—e.g. by sale and *mancipatio*—he had no need to contest the plaintiff's heirship and to accept a *iudicium de petitione hereditatis*; in such a case the *rei vindicatio* was the proper action. Nevertheless, he was entitled to accept *iudicium de petitione hereditatis*, if suggested by the plaintiff; it is therefore erroneous to say that the *hereditatis petitio* only lay against a *pro herede possessor* or a *pro possessore possessor* (below, s. 537).

So far we have only considered the *hereditatis petitio* within the formulary procedure. Whenever the *hereditatis petitio* was to be brought before the court of the *centumviri*, the old procedure *per legis actionem* (*legis actio sacramento*) had to precede the trial of the issue (Gai. 4. 31). Here the defendant was bound to assert that he himself was the true heir.

536.
Senatus
consultum
Iuven-
tianum
Further details of the *hereditatis petitio* cannot be described here. In this respect available sources are extremely difficult on account of numerous and radical interpolations. The thorough going-transformation of the classical texts was mainly caused by the *senatusconsultum Iuventianum* of A.D. 129. Under the consuls Juventius Celsus (the famous Proculian lawyer; Schulz, *History*, 105, 119) and Julius Balbus a *senatusconsultum* was issued concerning the *vindicatio caducorum* by the *aerarium populi Romani.* We have already mentioned above (s. 509) that under the *lex Iulia et Papia Poppaea* an inheritance or parts of it sometimes fell to the *Aerarium* (later to the *fiscus*). This *vindicatio caducorum* was a special kind of *hereditatis petitio* (= *vindicatio hereditatis*), but the regulations established by the *senatuscon-*

sultum differed considerably from those governing the *hereditatis petitio* of private persons. During the classical period the rules of the *senatusconsultum* were extended to the *vindicatio* of *bona vacantia* (above, s. 424), but never to the *hereditatis petitio* of private persons. In post-classical times, however, perhaps only at the hands of Justinian's compilers the rules of the *senatusconsultum* were amalgamated with those of *hereditatis petitio* of private persons. For that purpose the classical texts were ruthlessly altered and the title in the *Digest, De hereditatis petitione* (5. 3), presents a most confused aspect, especially as the texts are further marred by other kinds of interpolations.

Ulpian dealt with the *hereditatis petitio* in the 15th book of his big commentary on the Edict. He began with an exposition of the law concerning the *hereditatis petitio* of private persons (Lenel, *Palingenesia*, ii. 497); then he turned to the interpretation of the *senatusconsultum Iuventianum* (Lenel, *Palingenesia*, ii. 500 ff.). This is an indisputable fact and one can conclude from it that under classical law the *senatusconsultum* did not apply to the private *hereditatis petitio*; otherwise Ulpian would have begun with the interpretation of that enactment. This argument is irrefutable and final. According to the texts in the *Digest* Ulpian began his discussion without mentioning the *senatusconsultum*; then he abruptly stopped and turned to the *senatusconsultum* with the following words (*D.* 5. 3. 20. 6):

'Praeter haec multa repperimus tractata et de petitione hereditatis, de distractis rebus hereditariis, de dolo praeterito et de fructibus; de quibus cum forma senatus consulto sit data, optimum est ipsius senatus consulti interpretationem facere verbis eius relatis' (the text of the *senatusconsultum* follows with commentary).

We cannot possibly credit Ulpian with such an absurdity. Suppose you are reading an English book on the sale of goods. The author begins by expounding the law without mentioning the Sale of Goods Act. All of a sudden he stops and declares: 'I have found more material on the issues which I have discussed so far; but since there is such a thing as the Sale of Goods Act, it will be best to comment on that Act'; then follows a commentary on the Sale of Goods Act. Surely your verdict would be that the author must be mad. The text *D.* (5. 3) 20. 6 was written by the compilers and shows that it was their purpose to amalgamate the *senatusconsultum* with the common law of *hereditatis petitio*. Hence the following text must likewise be attributed to them:

D. (5. 3) 20. 9: 'In privatorum quoque petitionibus senatus consultum locum habere nemo est qui ambigit, licet in publica causa factum sit.'

Also interpolated is *C.* (3. 31) 1 pr.

'Senatus consultum auctore divo Hadriano avo meo factum, quo cautum est, quid et ex quo tempore evicta hereditate restitui debet, non solum ad fisci causas, sed etiam ad privatos hereditatis petitores pertinet.'

The genuine rescript said the opposite: 'ad aerarii causas non ad privatos hereditatis petitores pertinet.' The text is the first in the Codex-title *De petitione hereditatis,* just the proper place for the compilers to pronounce their new principle.

This is not wild radicalism but on the contrary sound common sense and historical criticism. It is, of course, quite another question whether we are able to recover the classical law in all details from available sources. But any student who wishes to attempt it must hold fast to the principle that 'under classical law the *senatusconsultum Iuventianum* did *not* apply to the *hereditatis petitio* of private persons'. This principle is irrefutably proved, and no 'reaction from interpolationistic research' can ever hope to wipe it out.

ii. *Interdictum quorum bonorum*

537. Interdictum quorum bonorum   The ordinary actions of the *heres* were granted to the *bonorum possessor* by way of a fiction (*ficto eo herede*), but the *hereditatis petitio* was not available to him. The *Digest* has a short title *De possessoria hereditatis petitione* (5. 5), but the two fragments which we read there originally dealt with the *actiones ficticiae singulares* and not with *hereditatis petitio* afforded to a *bonorum possessor*. The *hereditatis petitio possessoria* is a post-classical invention.

The *bonorum possessor* did not need the *hereditatis petitio* because he had a special remedy; it was not an *actio* in the classical sense (above, s. 37) but an interdict (above, s. 106), called *interdictum quorum bonorum* after the initial words of the interdict. The interdict was available to any *bonorum possessor*, including the *bonorum possessor sine re*. It lay against any possessor of the estate or of a part of it who did not possess upon a singular title; in other words, it only lay against a *possessor* who possessed as an *heres* or *bonorum possessor* (*pro herede possessor*, i.e. *qui putat se heredem esse*), or who possessed without any title (*pro possessore possessor*, i.e. *qui sine causa aliquam rem hereditariam possidet*). The interdict was an *interdictum restitutorium*. For this and for all further details we may refer to our discussion of the interdicts in general (above, s. 106).

iii. *Actio familiae erciscundae*

The object of this action is the dissolution of the community among co-heirs; it is one of the so-called *iudicia divisoria* which we have described above (ss. 86, 87).

538. Actio familiae erciscundae

SOURCES

s. 537. Read Gai. 4. 144 [*vel etiam . . . pertinere*].

BIBLIOGRAPHY

ss. 535, 536. Windscheid, *Pand.* iii (1906), §§ 611 ff., with references; W. Francke, *Exegetisch-dogmatischer Commentar über den Pandectentitel de hereditatis petitione* (1864, antiquated but still useful); G. Beseler, *Beiträge*, iv (1920), 4 ff.; *Scritti Ferrini*, iii (1948), 289; Fliniaux, 'Le Sénatusconsulte Juventien et la litis contestatio', *RH* ii (1923), 82 ff., 187 ff.; Lenel, *Z* xlvi (1926), 4 ff.; *Edict.* (1927), § 65; Dénoyez, *Le Sénatusconsulte Juventien* (1926); Lewald, *Z* xlviii (1928), 638 ff.; F. Bozza, *Sulla competenza dei Centumviri* (1928), 67 ff.; Appleton, 'Le Vrai et le faux Sénatusconsulte Juventien', *RH* ix (1930), 1 ff., 621 ff.; G. Longo, *L'hereditatis petitio* (1933); A. Carcaterra, *La hereditatis petitio* (1940, not available); Santi di Paola 'La litis contestatio nella cognitio extra ordinem', *Ann. Catania*, 1948, Estratto pp. 27 ff. On the *interdictum quam hereditatem* see Lenel, *Edict.* § 229; Berger, *PW* ix. 1658.

s. 537. On the *hereditatis petitio possessoria* see Lenel, *Edict.* § 67; on the *interdictum quorum bonorum* see Lenel, § 227; Berger, l.c. 1666; De Martino, *Atti Napoli*, lviii. 348 (not available); Solazzi, *SD* vi (1940), 329.

s. 538. See references above, ss. 86, 87, Bibliography.

CHAPTER VII

LEGACIES

(*Legata et Fideicommissa*)

1. *Introduction*

539.
Etymology

LEGARE is derived from *lex*.

Lex means rules, regulations of any kind, comprehending the *lex publica* (regulations made by the State) as well as the *lex privata* (e.g. *lex contractus*, terms of a contract). As *donare* means '*donum facere*', *terminare* '*terminum facere*', etc., so *legare* originally meant '*legem facere*'. In this sense the term was used in the famous rule of the Twelve Tables (v. 3): 'Uti legassit super pecunia tutelave suae rei, ita ius esto.' However, *legare* was also used in the sense of *delegare* (to delegate). Thus *legare aliquem* means to send somebody under a *lex*, charged with a commission; hence *legatus* = ambassador. From this usage derived the legal term *legare aliquid alicui* = 'to confer something on somebody by and under a *lex testamenti*'. *Legare* as used in the Twelve Tables covered any provision made by a testator in his will. But *legare rem alicui* inevitably had a much narrower scope; it could not comprehend the *institutio heredis* since the *heres* is a *successor in locum defuncti*; *tutoris datio* and *manumissio testamento* (above, ss. 140, 285) were likewise excluded. Thus was reached the classical legal conception of *legare* and *legatum*.

540.
Definition

The classical *legatum* was a gift which a testator conferred on somebody in his will by charging his *heres*, his *heredes*, or one of them. We will illustrate this definition by the following remarks.

541. No legatum legitimum

1. A *legatum* is a gift. An *heres* might be appointed by law (intestate succession) but there was no such thing as *legatum legitimum* under classical law. The so-called *quarta divi Pii* implied a right to succeed as *heres*.

542.
Legatum not a donatio

2. *Legatum* is a gift *mortis causa*. *Donatio mortis causa* is likewise a gift *mortis causa*, but it is made by agreement between donor and donee (below, s. 574), whereas the *legatum* is left by will.

543.
Legatum to be left by testament or confirmed codicil

3. Any *legatum* must be left by will. It might be written in the *tabulae testamenti*; but as it is a charge imposed upon an *heres*, it must come after the institution of the heir. A *legatum* might also be left in a codicil confirmed by a will

(*codicilli testamento confirmati*), whereas an *heres* could not be instituted in a *codicil*.

Codicilli means a booklet made of small wooden tablets tied together; the tablets were covered with a layer of wax. To this extent *codicilli* did not differ from the *tabulae testamenti*. Under classical law no particular form was required for a codicil; hence it might be written on a papyrus roll, though a roll is, strictly speaking, not a 'small codex'. The classical lawyers used *codicilli* only in the plural (*D*. 50. 16. 148). Where we meet the singular *codicillus* in classical writings, the text is either corrupt or interpolated; see *Voc. Iur. Rom.* i. 766, but also *Thes. Ling. Lat.* iii. 1408; Beseler, Z liii (1933), 31.

4. Only a person instituted heir in a will could be charged with a *legatum*.

(*a*) Any other person who received something from the *de cuius*, in particular a legatee, could not be so charged.

(*b*) An *heres ab intestato* could not be charged with a *legatum*. This is obvious. A will which contained nothing but legacies was void because the *institutio heredis* was essential (above, s. 426). As long as there was a valid will, there was no intestate succession; and if the will collapsed, the *legata* collapsed also. However, the praetor sometimes maintained *legata* by charging the intestate heirs; we shall return to this point later (below, s. 566).

5. The classical *legatarius* is never a *successor in locum defuncti* like the *heres*. The important consequence is that he never succeeds to the debts of the *de cuius*.

6. The classical lawyers never attempted to give a definition of *legatum*. Gaius has none (cf. 2. 192), and if any other lawyer had given one, we would surely find it in our law-books, since post-classical lawyers, including Justinian's compilers, loved definitions. The two definitions which we find in the *Digest* are of post-classical origin; one of them was adopted by the compilers of Justinian's *Institutes* (2, 20, 1).

D. (30) 116 pr. 'Legatum est delibatio hereditatis, qua testator ex eo, quod universum heredis foret, alicui quid collatum velit.' The word *delibatio* (= *deminutio*, taking away from, diminishing) occurs in the whole of Latin literature (leaving aside ecclesiastical literature) only in this passage (*Thes. Ling. Lat.* v. 437. 46). This is final: no classical lawyer can possibly have used such a singular word.

D. (31) 36. 'Legatum est donatio testamento relicta.' This confusion

544.
Persons to be charged with a *legatum*

545.
Legatarius not a successor

546. Post-classical definitions

between *legatum* and *donatio* cannot be credited to Modestinus; it is in conformity with the post-classical tendency to assimilate *donatio mortis causa* to *legatum* (below, s. 575). Moreover, Modestinus' *Pandectae* from which the text was taken is a very untrustworthy work (see Schulz, *History*, 222).

547. Terminology 7. According to classical terminology the legatee was called *legatarius*. Later continental students also termed him *honoratus* because the classical lawyers regarded it as an honour to receive a *legatum*. The heir who was charged with a *legatum* was called *heres a quo legatum est*. Thus when Gaius 2. 271 states *A legatario legari non potest*, this must not be translated 'no legacy can be left by a legatee', but rather ' a legacy cannot be charged on a legatee'. Modern students term the *heres* charged with a *legatum* shortly *oneratus*, again an unclassical term, though the classical lawyers speak of *heres oneratur legato*.

548. Evolution of fideicommissum In republican times there already existed another kind of legacy, namely the *fideicommissum*. *Fidei alicuius committere* means to 'commit something to the good faith of a person'. A testator, for instance, entreated his future heir informally to do something in favour of a third person (e.g. to hand something over to him, to set a slave free), trusting that he would fulfil his wish, although he was not legally bound to do so. This was the original conception of a *fideicommissum*, viz. a trust, a charge which entailed no legal obligation but was binding in honour upon the party charged and constituted an appeal to his loyalty. Provisions of this kind certainly originated in cases in which *institutio heredis* or *legatum* was not available to the testator. A testator, for example, wished to leave his property to a woman, but was prohibited by the *lex Voconia* (Gai. 2. 226); or he wished to leave it to a *peregrinus*. However, the character of the *fideicommissum* was fundamentally changed under Augustus when it became legally binding. Though an *actio* in the classical sense (above, s. 37) was not granted to the beneficiary, he might by an *extraordinaria cognitio* compel the party charged to fulfil the wish of the *de cuius*. The authorities competent to initiate this procedure were from the times of Claudius the consuls, a special *praetor fidei-*

commissarius (in the provinces the governors), but not the
praetor urbanus; hence the Edict (i.e. the Edict of the *praetor
urbanus*) is silent upon the *persecutio fideicommissi*. After the
fideicommissum had thus become actionable, its name only
implied that it was excluded from the ordinary procedure
per formulas and that good faith determined the measure
of such performance as might be due; compared with the
actio ex testamento (below, s. 564) the *petitio fideicommissi*
might indeed be described as a *petitio bonae fidei*.

In contrast to *legatum*

1. A *fideicommissum* might be charged on anybody who
received something *mortis causa* from the *de cuius*; not only
on an *heres* but also on a legatee or a recipient of a *donatio
mortis causa*. Even the fisc to which *bona vacantia* were
expected to fall might be charged with a *fideicommissum*.

2. A *fideicommissum* might be left not only in a will or in
a codicil confirmed by will, but in any codicil and even
orally. Accordingly an intestate heir might be charged with
a *fideicommissum*, though, as aforesaid, not with a *legatum*.

3. The beneficiary is sometimes *heredis loco* and, for that
reason, liable for the hereditary debts. We shall return to
this point later (s. 568).

We may now give a plain definition of the classical *fideicommissum*; it was a gift *mortis causa* expressed in an informal
request which was addressed to a person who himself
acquired something *mortis causa* from the grantor.

The classical terminology concerning *fideicommissum*
needs further examination. Taking, however, into account
the profound differences between *legatum* and *fideicommissum*, it seems incredible that the classical lawyers ever used
the terms *legare* and *legatum* with regard to *fideicommissum*;
wherever we meet this usage we have interpolations
before us.

> The classical expression for 'to leave a trust' was *fidei* (dative) *alicuius
> committere; dare, relinquere per fideicommissum, relinquere fideicommissum*
> are also classical terms. The beneficiary was termed *fideicommissarius*.
> *Fideicommittere alicui* = 'in favour of somebody' is not classical. The
> trustee was designated as *is cuius fidei* (dative) *committitur* or *is a quo
> fideicommissum relictum est*; but *fideicommittere alicui,* 'to charge a trust

549.
**Fideicom-
missum in
contrast to
legatum**

**550. Ter-
minology**

on somebody', is hardly classical. *Fiduciarius* is not (as it is often erroneously assumed) a classical term to designate the trustee. Only in a few texts do we meet *heres fiduciarius*.

551.   The classical lawyers have studied the law of legacies
Character (*legata* and *fideicommissa*) with unconcealed predilection.
of the   classical The classical writings, particularly the *Digesta*, *Responsa*,
law of   and *Quaestiones*, are full of subtle and detailed inquiries
legacies concerning legacies. In Justinian's *Digest* seven books (30–6) are devoted to the law of legacies, not to mention the numerous texts outside these books. What we have said above (s. 359): 'the law of succession is the focus of the Roman will to law', is in particular true of the law of legacies, and whoever wishes to obtain a vivid and impressive picture of classical jurisprudence must needs study this domain of Roman law. However, this achievement of the classical lawyers reveals their limitations as well as their greatness. Studying these discussions in full detail, one cannot help wondering whether it was really justifiable to spend so much time and labour on these difficult and tortuous questions, the practical importance of which was so slight. It should not be forgotten that the lawyers who wrote these ample treatises on legacies had no care for the fate of illegitimate children (above, s. 278), failed to develop the law of corporations (above, s. 147), had no eyes for peregrine law—not even for the law of Roman and Latin *municipia*—and refrained from discussing any issues in which public administrative law was involved. On the whole classical jurisprudence remained within the magic circle described by the republican lawyers. These were *iuris consulti*, i.e. lawyers who gave *responsa*, legal opinions, and advice when consulted by parties. Their sphere of interest was, therefore, inevitably limited, but questions on legacies were just the matters most frequently brought before them, since their clients mainly, if not exclusively, belonged to the *beati possidentes*. In this respect the classical lawyers remained true to the republican tradition. Absorbed in the spinning of their fine network, they not only neglected other issues which were of much greater importance, but they apparently failed to realize how complicated

the law of legacies grew under their hands. The magnificent achievement of classical jurisprudence, here as elsewhere, was dearly purchased.

In the post-classical period a radical simplification of the classical law of legacies was attempted. The different kinds of *legata* which we shall presently mention were reduced to one, and the distinction between *legata* and *fideicommissa* ceased to exist with the disappearance of the formulary procedure. The first text in the first book of the *Digest* dealing with legacies (D. 30. 1) declares: *Per omnia exaequata sunt legata fideicommissis*. It was, of course, the compilers and not Ulpian (to whom the text is attributed) who pronounced this new principle, as was already recognized by the Bolognese Glossators:

> 'Glossa Accursii ad *D*. (30) 1: Dic quod aliquid est hic detractum a verbis Ulpiani a compilatoribus iuris.'

Justinian's *Institutes* (2. 20) 2 and 3 make that quite clear. These fundamental innovations led inevitably to numerous alterations of the classical texts, but to carry them through with complete thoroughness was beyond the power of the post-classical lawyers and even of Justinian's compilers. Moreover, such a radical destruction of the classical texts would not have been in harmony with the classicistic tendency of the Byzantine law-schools. Thus the compilers on the whole abstained from radical interpolations and a considerable part of the interpolations is to be attributed to pre-Justinianic hands. The compilers on the whole held it sufficient to pronounce the new principle and left it to the law schools to carry it through.

It is small wonder that critical analysis of the vast mass of available material is still in its infancy. For the time being no sufficiently critical work on the whole law of legacies exists. In this book we confine ourselves according to our plan to the broad outlines of the classical institutions. It is their general scope and object which we wish to make as clear as possible. The intricate details of classical law, the republican law, and the highly interesting post-classical development *relinquimus pertinacibus*.

552. Post-classical law

553. Modern literature

SOURCES

s. 539. Read *D.* (50. 16) 120.

s. 543. Read Gai. 2. 229, 270*a*; *Inst. Iust.* (2. 25) pr.

s. 544. Read Gai. 2. 270, 271.

s. 548. Read *Inst. Iust.* (2. 23) 1; (2. 25) pr.

s. 549. Read Gai. 2. 260, 271; *D.* (30) 114. 2; Gai. 2. 270*a*; *D.* (40. 5) 47. 4.

s. 552. Read *Inst. Iust.* (2. 20) 3.

BIBLIOGRAPHY

ss. 539 ff. Glück, *Erläuterung der Pandecten*, xlvi–xlix (1869–89); Ferrini, *Teoria generale dei legati e fedecommessi* (1889); Windscheid, *Pand.* iii (1906), 573 ff.; Biondi, *Successione testamentaria* (*Trattato di diritto romano*, ed. E. Albertario, x. 1943), 269 ff.; Kaser, *Altröm. Jus* (1949), 147 ff.

s. 539. Stolz–Schmalz, *Lat. Grammatik* (1928), 196.

s. 541. On the *quarta divi Pii* see F. E. Vassalli, *Miscellanea critica del diritto romano*, i (1913), 59; Beseler, *Subsiciva* (1929), 2.

s. 548. Brückner, *Zur Geschichte des Fideikommisses* (1893); Schulz, *History*, 11, with references; Guarino, *SD*, 1944, pp. 317 ff.; Z lxii (1942), 252 ff.

s. 550. Biondi, l.c. 303, with references.

s. 552. Riccobono, *Mélanges Cornil*, ii (1926), 348 ff.; Biondi, l.c. 302 ff.

2. *Creation and revocation of legacies (legata and fideicommissa)*

554. Four classical types of legata The classical *legatum* was created by charging a testamentary heir in a will or in a codicil confirmed by a will (above, s. 543). In the classical period there were two main types of *legatum*, the *legatum per vindicationem* and *per damnationem*. Two further types, the *legatum sinendi modo* and *per praeceptionem*, were of minor importance and in the second century A.D. already moribund; we may, therefore, ignore them in this book.

1. *Legatum per vindicationem*

555. Legatum per vindicationem On the strength of this sort of *legatum* the legatee acquired ownership of the thing left to him; there was no need for an act of transfer on the part of the heir. The legatee might claim the thing with the *rei vindicatio* (above, s. 58, and below, s. 640), from the heir as well as from any other person in possession of it.

The testator who wished to create such a *legatum* had to observe certain forms. The usual formula was *do lego* (e.g. *fundum Cornelianum Titio do lego*), and the *legatum per vindicationem* was, therefore, often described as *do lego legatum* (*do lego legare*). Other permissible formulas were *sumito, capito, rem sibi habeto*: they all implied that the legatee should acquire ownership without an act of transfer to be effected by the heir. *Fundum Cornelianum Titio relinquo* was certainly not sufficient. The post-classical author of the *Epitome Ulpiani* asserts (24. 1): 'Legatum est quod legis modo, id est imperative, testamento relinquitur.' This is obviously wrong: the cardinal formula *do lego* is not an imperative.

The testator must be the owner of the thing at the time when he created the legacy and also at his death; ownership at the latter moment alone was sufficient when fungible things were left. The testator might also create a usufruct or a *servitus* (below, ss. 673, 688) by this sort of *legatum*.

As regards the legatee, a *persona certa* was required; in this respect we may refer to earlier remarks (above, s. 450). A *substitutio vulgaris* was permitted as in instituting an heir (above, s. 455). If there was a plurality of heirs, one of them might be a legatee (*praelegatum*).

> Suppose that a testator instituted A, B, and C heirs, each to one-third; he further left his slave Stichus to C by *do lego legatum*. C acquired ownership of the slave, but on the strength of the legacy only to two-thirds, since to one-third he was already owner as *heres*. A little more complicated is the following case. A and B were instituted heirs each to one-half. *Fundus Cornelianus* was left to B, X, and Y, one-third to each of them. A and B become co-owners of the land as heirs, each to one-half. B's *praelegatum* is void so far as it lies upon his own share and falls to X and Y. Thus B obtains only one-sixth from A; X and Y together receive five-sixths of the land. *D.* (30) 116. 1.

2. *Legatum per damnationem*

By this sort of *legatum* the testator charged an obligation upon the heir. If, for example, a piece of land was left in this way, the heir was bound to transfer ownership to the legatee by *mancipatio* (below, s. 597).

The usual formula to be used by a testator contained the

556.
Legatum
per damna-
tionem

words *damnas esto* (e.g. 'Heres meus Stichum servum meum Titio dare damnas esto'), but an imperative of another kind (e.g. *dato*) was regarded as sufficient.

By such a *legatum* the heir might be bound by the testator to perform anything in favour of the legatee; important special types were

(a) The *legatum* of a thing which did not belong to the testator. If the heir also was not owner of it, he was bound to acquire it or to pay its value.

(b) *Legatum nominis.* Here the testator left a claim which he had against his debtor to a third person. The heir was bound to assign the claim to the legatee.

(c) *Legatum liberationis.* Here the testator granted his debtor liberation from his debt. The heir was bound to release him.

(d) *Legatum debiti.* Here the testator left to his creditor what he owed to him. Under classical law such a legacy always implied an advantage to the creditor, since he had now, in addition to the action which he already had and with which he might sue the heir, the *actio ex testamento* (below, s. 564) and the latter was one of those actions *in quibus lis infitiando crescit in duplum* (above, s. 74, and below, s. 564).

(e) *Legatum partitionis.* The testator left part of the inheritance (N.B. not the whole) to somebody by a *legatum per damnationem* (below, s. 561).

As regards the person of the legatee (*persona certa, substitutio vulgaris, praelegatum*), we may refer to our remarks on *legatum per vindicationem* (above, s. 555).

3. *Senatusconsultum Neronianum*

557.
Senatus-
consultum
Neronia-
num

A *senatusconsultum* under Nero dealt with the following case. A testator had left by *legatum per vindicationem* a thing which had never been in his ownership. According to our previous remarks (above, s. 555) this legacy was void. The Senate, however, 'confirmed' it by declaring that it should be regarded as *utile atque si optimo iure relictum esset.* The meaning of this decree was that the legacy should be regarded as a *legatum per damnationem* since only this kind of *legatum* was admissible in the case submitted to the Senate. The conversion was effected *iure praetorio* by order of the Senate, whereas *iure civili* the legacy remained void. The classical lawyers applied the *senatusconsultum* to other similar cases, but apparently always by converting the invalid *legatum* into a *legatum per damnationem*.

> Suppose a testator left a certain slave Stichus by *legatum per vindicationem*. The slave was in the testator's ownership at the time of his (the testator's) death but not when he created the legacy. The *legatum per vindicationem* was void (above, s. 555). It might have been converted into a *legatum sinendi modo* (Gai. 2. 211) but apparently it was actually converted into a *legatum per damnationem* as being *optimum ius* (Gai. 2. 210).

However, the classical lawyers never went so far as to abandon all formalities concerning *legata*. The testator had to use one of the recognized formulas required for a *legatum per vindicationem*, *per praeceptionem*, or *sinendi modo*, and if the formula chosen by the testator was in the individual case not the proper formula, the lawyers converted it into a *legatum per damnationem* as if the conditions of the latter were satisfied. Thus when a testator had written *Stichum servum meum Titio relinquo*, the legacy was void and inconvertible. The statement which we read in the post-classical *Epitome Ulpiani* (24. 11*a*) is inaccurate:

> 'Senatusconsulto Neroniano cautum est, ut quod minus aptis verbis legatum est, perinde sit ac si optimo iure legatum esset.'

In post-classical times this classical formalism concerning *legata* was abandoned (*C.* 6. 37. 21) and the different classical types of *legata* were amalgamated. This led to numerous alterations of the classical texts; in particular the classical distinctions in the texts inserted in Justinian's *Digest* and *Codex* were radically eliminated.

558. Post-classical law

No formalities were required to create a *fideicommissum*. The usual formulas were *fidei committo*, *rogo*, *peto*, but other formulas were also permitted provided that they sufficiently expressed the intention to create a *fideicommissum*. The post-classical *Epitome Ulpiani* (24. 1; 25. 2) asserts that a *fideicommissum* had to be left *precativo modo*, but this is obviously

559. Creation of fideicommissa

untrue: the word *volo* was permitted (Gaius 2. 249), which is certainly not a *verbum precativum*. However, though fixed formulas were not required for a *fideicommissum*, the classical lawyers demanded at least an express declaration and were reluctant to acknowledge implied *fideicommissa* unless supported by an imperial rescript or a *senatus-consultum*.

> Take the following example. A testator instituted L. Titius sole heir and added: *Peto, L. Titi, contentus sis decem aureis.* This was regarded as implying a *fideicommissum* of the whole inheritance minus 10 aurei in favour of the intestate heirs, but only on the strength of an imperial rescript. *D.* (31) 69 pr.

The details cannot be fully discerned from our mutilated and interpolated sources; much, of course, depended on the peculiarities of the individual case. But one thing should be firmly kept in mind: formulas required for the creation of a *legatum* were unfit to create a *fideicommissum*. When such formulas were used and the *legatum* turned out to be void in the individual case and could not be confirmed under the *senatusconsultum Neronianum*, a conversion into a *fideicommissum* was out of the question. A testator might expressly declare: 'in case the *legata* left in my testament should be void, I wish them to be maintained as *fideicommissa*', but without such a declaration a conversion did not take place. Even the institution of an heir might be converted into a *fideicommissum* on the strength of such a declaration.

> Suppose that a testator instituted Titius as his sole heir, adding: 'in case this testament should be void, I wish it to be regarded as a codicil' (above, s. 543). If the will turned out in fact to be void, on the strength of such a *clausula codicillaris* the intestate heirs were charged with a *fideicommissum hereditatis* in favour of Titius.

Two special kinds of *fideicommissa* must be given special notice.

1. *The fideicommissum libertatis*

560. Fidei-
commissum
libertatis

In contrast to *manumissio testamento* (above, s. 140), this is an indirect mode of bestowing liberty by will; the party charged was here bound to set the slave free. As the beneficiary was a slave and could not act as a plaintiff, the obligation of the trustee had at first merely a moral character, but in the second century A.D. the slave might apply to the magistrate when the trustee refused to fulfil the *fideicommissum*. By *senatusconsulta* and imperial constitutions a set of rules was developed for this kind of *fideicommissum* which we will not describe in detail.

2. *Fideicommissum hereditatis*

A *legatum hereditatis* was only possible in the form of a *legatum partitionis* (above, s. 556), but the whole inheritance as well as a part of it might be left by *fideicommissum*. Thus a testator might institute Titius heir and order by *fideicommissum* that the inheritance should be restored to Seius after Titius' death: 'Titius heres esto; cum Titius heres meus mortuus erit, volo hereditatem meam ad Seium pertinere.' Though Titius remained *heres* and Seius was only *fideicommissarius*, the legal position of the latter was assimilated to that of an *heres* by two *senatusconsulta*, the *Trebellianum* and the *Pegasianum*, to which we shall presently return. Substantially, therefore, *fideicommissum hereditatis* was a substitute for an *institutio heredis* forbidden by the rule *semel heres, semper heres* (above, s. 456): 'Titius heres esto; cum Titius mortuus erit, Seius heres esto'. Modern students term the *fideicommissum hereditatis* a *substitutio fideicommissaria* (in contrast to *substitutio vulgaris* and *pupillaris*; above, ss. 455, 458); the *Code civil* (art. 896) simply calls it 'substitution', forgetting that there is such a thing as *substitutio vulgaris*. A testator might go farther and charge the *fideicommissarius* with a similar *fideicommissum*: 'Titius heres esto. Cum Titius mortuus erit, volo hereditatem meam ad Seium pertinere; cum Seius mortuus erit, volo hereditatem meam ad filios eius pertinere', etc. Thus the 'nuisance of substitutions' (above, ss. 363, 456) and particularly a family *fideicommissum* might have developed. However, any *fideicommissarius* had to be alive at the testator's death; moreover, a *senatusconsultum* under Hadrian required that the *fideicommissarius* must be a *persona certa* (above, s. 450). Thus *substitutiones fideicoumissariae* were kept within very narrow limits and the history

561. Fideicommissum hereditatis

of the *fideicommissum familiae relictum* began only in post-classical times.

562.
Revocation
of legacies
Legacies, *legata* as well as *fideicommissa*, were revocable. No formality was required for the revocation of a *fideicommissum*. A *legatum*, however, could only be revoked by an express declaration (*non do, non lego, heres meus ne dato*) contained in a will or in a codicil confirmed by will.

> Suppose a testator wrote on the tablets of his will a *legatum* in favour of L. Later, but still before the performance of *mancipatio* (above, s. 434), he changed his mind and decided not to leave anything to L. The testator might simply strike out the relevant line in the will or he might cancel the whole tablet in which the *legatum* was written. He might further revoke the *legatum* by adding an express negative declaration in the *tabulae testamenti*. When the *mancipatio* had already been performed, two ways were still open to revoke the *legatum*: (1) the testator might make a new will by which the former will was annulled; (2) the testator might revoke the *legatum* in a codicil provided it was confirmed by will.

Informal revocation of a *legatum* did not render it void *iure civili*, but the heir might raise an *exceptio doli* when sued by the legatee. Suppose the testator after having performed the *mancipatio* opened the *tabulae testamenti* and struck out the line which contained the *legatum*; or he revoked the *legatum* in a codicil not confirmed by will. In such cases the *legatum* remained valid *iure civili*, but if the legatee sued the heir, the latter was protected by *exceptio doli*.

563.
Implied
revocation
A *legatum* as well as a *fideicommissum* might be revoked even by implication. Thus where the testator alienated the thing left by *legatum per damnationem* or *fideicommissum*, he was regarded as having revoked the legacy; the *fideicommissum* was void *ipso iure*, the *legatum* voidable by *exceptio*. Where the testator had created a *legatum per vindicationem* and had later alienated the thing so that he was no longer the owner at his death, the legacy was void *ipso iure* (above, s. 555). Nor could it be confirmed under the *Neronianum* (above, s. 557), for if he had made a *legatum per damnationem*, the alienation would have entailed an *exceptio doli*. It would have been absurd to grant the legatee an *actio ex testamento utilis* (above, s. 557) which could be repelled by the *exceptio doli*.

SOURCES

s. 554. Read Gai. 2. 192.

s. 555. Read Gai. 2. 193, 194, 196, 229, 281, 238; *D.* (30) 116. 1.

s. 556. Read Gai. 2. 201–4, 262; *D.* (32) 14. 2, *legatum (per damnationem*); [*vel . . . vendat*]; Gai. 4. 9 [*certa*]; Gai. 2. 282; 4. 171; Paul. *Sent.* (1. 19) 1; *Epit. Ulp.* 24, 25. *

s. 557. Read Gai. 2. 197; *Epit. Ulp.* 24. 11a.

s. 558. Cf. *Fr. Vat.* 44 with *D.* (30) 120. 2.

s. 559. Read Gai. 2. 249; Paul. *Sent.* (4. 1) 6; *D.* (31) 88. 17.

s. 560. Read *Epit. Ulp.* 2. 7–10; Gai. 2. 263.

s. 561. Read Gai. 2. 250, 271, 277, 287; *D.* (31) 32. 6 [*et qui . . . extenderit*].

s. 562. Read *Epit. Ulp.* 24. 29; *Inst. Iust.* (2. 21) pr.; *D.* (34. 4) 3. 8; *D.* (34. 4) 22.

s. 563. Read Gai. 2. 198.

BIBLIOGRAPHY

s. 554. Biondi, *Successione testamentaria* (1943), 271 ff.*

s. 555. On *praelegatum* see Windscheid, *Pand.* iii (1906), § 627; Biondi, l.c. 466 ff.

s. 556a. Schulz, *Epitome Ulpiani* (1926), 27, with references; Biondi, l.c. 421 ff.

s. 556b. Biondi, l.c. 448.

s. 556c. Biondi, l.c. 457.

s. 556d. Beseler, Z xlvii (1927), 65 ff.; Biondi, l.c. 450.

s. 556e. Biondi, l.c. 442.

s. 557. Ciapessoni, 'Sul senatusconsulto Neroniano', *St. Bonfante*, iii (1930), 651 ff.; Grosso, *AG* cvii (1932), 103 ff.; Biondi, l.c. 282 ff.; Beseler, *St. Albertoni*, i (1935), 432; Solazzi, *Scritti Ferrini* (ed. Archi, 1946), 144.

s. 559. Mitteis, *RP* i (1908), 196; Biondi, l.c. 291 ff.

s. 560. Buckland, *Roman Law of Slavery* (1908), 513 ff., 611 ff.

s. 561. Biondi, l.c. 477; on *fideicommissum familiae relictum* in particular Windscheid, *Pand.* iii, § 637; Declareuil, *Mélanges Gerardin* (1907), 135 ff.; Biondi, l.c. 498.

ss. 562, 563. Koschaker, 'L'alienazione della cosa legata', *Conferenze romanistiche tenute nella R. Università di Pavia 1939* (1940), 89 ff., with references; Biondi, l.c. 399 ff.; Solazzi, *Scritti Ferrini* (ed. Archi, 1946), 145, with references.

3. *Legal effects of legacies (legata and fideicommissa)*

As regards the acquisition of a *legatum* there were two days of particular importance which modern students usually term *dies cedens* and *dies veniens*. Though these

564. Dies cedens and dies veniens

terms are certainly not classical, they are indispensable and we shall use them in the following discussion.

1. At the *dies cedens* the legatee acquired not the *legatum* itself, but an expectancy transmissible to his heirs. If he died before the *dies cedens*, the *legatum* was not transmitted to his heirs. Before the *lex Papia Poppaea* the day of the testator's death was the *dies cedens* but under the *lex Papia* it was the day at which the will was officially opened (above, s. 501). If the legacy was made conditional and the condition not yet fulfilled, then the day of the fulfilment was *dies cedens*. When this day had arrived, the classical lawyers said *dies legati cessit*; the time before and after that day they termed *tempus ante* (or *post*) *diem legati cedentem*. This singular use of *cedere* is confined to Roman legal language and has not yet been fully explained linguistically; the legal meaning is quite clear. *Dies legati cedit* means 'the legacy begins to display its effects'. In any case, the term *dies cedens* as used by modern students is not classical.

2. At the so-called *dies veniens* the legatee acquired the *legatum*; this was the day at which the heir on whom the legacy was charged acquired the inheritance (automatically or by *aditio hereditatis*; above, ss. 501 ff.).

(*a*) As regards the *legatum per vindicationem* there was a controversy between the two Roman law schools. According to the *Proculiani* the thing was now *sine domino* but the legatee might acquire ownership by claiming it from the heir. According to the *Sabiniani* the legatee became owner automatically on the *dies veniens*, but if he refused the legacy, ownership attached to the heir as if it had never been acquired by the legatee. The details of the controversy need not be described here; apparently the Sabinian doctrine, somewhat modified by Julian, eventually prevailed. Where the legacy was left *ex die*, the legatee did not acquire ownership before that day had arrived (*dies venit*).

(*b*) Where the legacy was left *per damnationem*, the legatee became creditor on the so-called *dies veniens*. Was he entitled to refuse the legacy? It is generally said that if he did not wish the legacy, he might simply omit to claim it from the heir. But perhaps he was charged with a *fidei-*

commissum; it is hardly credible that he could not free himself from that *fideicommissum* by refusing the legacy. When a *legatum per damnationem* was left *ex die* and that day had not yet arrived, the legatee nevertheless became creditor; it was a case of a debt not yet due: *incipit deberi pecunia, sed peti non potest*. When that day arrived, the classical lawyers said *dies* (scilicet *debiti*) *venit*. On the strength of a *legatum per damnationem* an *actio ex testamento* lay against the heir (Lenel, *Edict.* § 170). The *formula* cannot be fully reconstructed, but it was framed *in personam* (above, s. 56), did not contain the clause *ex fide bona* (above, s. 60), and had a *condemnatio* (above, s. 30) which authorized the judge to condemn the defendant *in duplum* if he denied his debt; the action was one of those *in quibus lis infitiando crescit in duplum* (Lenel, *Edict.* p. 368).

A *fideicommissum* was acquired under similar rules. The so-called *dies cedens* was the day at which the *de cuius* died leaving an intestate heir who was charged with a *fideicommissum*. When the 'trust' was created in a will, *dies cedens* was probably the day at which the will was opened (above, s. 564). *Dies veniens* was the day at which the heir charged with the *fideicommissum* acquired the inheritance, or the day at which the legatee charged with the *fideicommissum* acquired *legatum*. With the acquisition of the *fideicommissum* the *fideicommissarius* became creditor, as did the legatee of a *legatum per damnationem*; but we have already mentioned that an *actio ex fideicommisso* did not lie (above, ss. 41, 548): the beneficiary had to pursue his claim *ex fideicommisso* in an *extraordinaria cognitio*. Since the judge in such a *cognitio* applied *bona fides* to a considerable extent, the obligation resulting from a *fideicommissum* differed widely from that in *legatum per damnationem* (above, s. 548).

Where the same thing was left *per vindicationem* to a plurality of persons, the legatees became co-owners *pro parte*, and if one of them refused the legacy, his share accrued to the others in so far as the *lex Papia* did not come in. We may refer in this connexion to our earlier remarks (above, s. 520 f.). If the same thing was left to two or more persons *per damnationem* or *per fideicommissum*, each of

565.
Plurality of legatees

them might claim the whole thing without reference to the co-legatees.

Suppose the testator had left by *legatum per damnationem* his slave Stichus to A and also to B. Each of the legatees might claim the slave, so that the heir was bound to give the slave to one of them and to the other the value of the slave. Only if the thing was left to them *coniunctim* (e.g. *Titio et Seio*) were the legatees merely entitled to claim a part, and if one of them refused the legacy, his share did not accrue to his co-legatees.

566.
Legacy a charge imposed upon a person
Any legacy, *legatum* as well as *fideicommissum*, was a charge imposed upon a person who acquired something *mortis causa* from the *de cuius*. Thus when the heir charged with a legacy refused to accept the inheritance, the legacy broke down. Suppose A was instituted sole heir and charged with legacies. A refused to accept the inheritance and intestate succession took place. The legacies broke down since the intestate heirs were not bound to pay them. When a legatee was charged with a *fideicommissum* and the legatee refused to accept the *legatum*, the *fideicommissum* broke down. There were, however, exceptions to this principle.

1. Suppose the testator instituted his only son heir and charged him with *legata*. The son whom the father had emancipated and who, therefore, was not a *suus* refused to accept the inheritance. Therewith the whole will including the legacies broke down and intestate succession ensued. The son being the next heir *ab intestato* applied for *bonorum possessio unde liberi* (above, s. 405). In such a case the praetor granted the legatees *actiones utiles* (*ficticiae*; above, s. 49) against the intestate heir. Although the legacies had become void *iure civili*, the praetor maintained them *causa cognita* (Lenel, *Edict.* § 168).

2. The testator instituted A sole heir and charged him with legacies; he further appointed B as *heres secundo gradu* (*substitutio vulgaris*; above, s. 455). After the testator's death A refused the inheritance, and B became universal heir. Until the time of Septimius Severus B was not charged with the legacies; they were, however, maintained by a rescript of Severus.

3. The testator instituted A and B as heirs and charged A

with a *legatum per damnationem*. A refused to accept the inheritance; let us assume that his hereditary portion thereby accrued to B even under the *lex Papia* (above, ss. 520, 565). The *legatum* broke down since B was not bound to pay it. The principle *portio transit cum suo onere* was, however, finally recognized on the strength of Severus' rescript which we have just mentioned.

In order to encourage the heir charged with *legata* to accept the inheritance, a *lex Falcidia* (a plebiscite of 40 B.C. moved by the *tribunus plebis* P. Falcidius) granted the heir a quarter of the net inheritance free from *legata* (*quarta Falcidia*). Where the *legata* exceeded three-quarters of the net inheritance, they were proportionately diminished.

567.
Quarta
Falcidia

> Suppose H was instituted sole heir and charged with two *legata per damnationem*, viz. to pay 60 to A and 40 to B. The net value of the inheritance was 120 and so the heir was entitled to keep 30. Thus 10 must be deducted from the *legata* in correct proportion. The method is the following:
>
> x = the amount to be deducted from A's legacy.
> y = the amount to be deducted from B's legacy.
> $x+y = 10.$ $x:y = 60:40.$ $x = 6; y = 4.$
>
> Thus the heir owes A 54 and B 36 and himself keeps 30.

Simple as this rule seems to be at first sight, it leads to innumerable awkward problems, and as, moreover, the relevant texts in our sources are variously interpolated, the law concerning the *quarta Falcidia* is particularly difficult and vexatious.

The *lex Falcidia* granted the *quarta* only in case of *legata*. With regard to *fideicommissa* the 'trustee' had never to pay more than he received from the *de cuius*, but was not entitled to keep the quarter. However, the *senatusconsultum Pegasianum* (below, s. 568) granted the quarter to a testamentary heir in the case of *fideicommissa* and Antoninus Pius accorded the same right to intestate heirs. To other persons charged with *fideicommissa*, particularly to legatees, the privilege was not extended.

Finally we have to consider the legal effects of a *fideicommissum hereditatis* (above, s. 561) imposed upon a testa-

568.
Senatus-
consultum

mentary heir. The classical law was based upon the *senatus-consultum Trebellianum* (under Nero) and *Pegasianum* (under Vespasian). Let us confine ourselves to the simplest case: a testator instituted H as sole heir and charged him with a *fideicommissum* to restore the inheritance to F after three years. When H accepted the inheritance he was now bound to restore it to F after three years. If he did so— which might be done by an informal declaration—he remained nevertheless *heres iure civili*, but F was now *heredis loco*. By order of the Senate the praetor granted F an *hereditatis petitio utilis* (above, s. 535), a so-called *hereditatis petitio fideicommissaria* (Lenel, *Edict.* § 68); he granted him in addition the hereditary actions as *actiones utiles* and the hereditary creditors might sue him with *actiones utiles* (Lenel, *Edict.* § 68). On the other hand, the praetor denied the hereditary actions to the *heres* and protected him against the hereditary creditors. These rules established by the *senatusconsultum Trebellianum* were modified by the *senatusconsultum Pegasianum*. As already stated (s. 567), it granted the heir the *quarta Falcidia*, but unfortunately combined this reasonable innovation with very complicated regulations.

The *Pegasianum* distinguished the following cases:

1. The *fideicommissum* amounted to three-quarters of the inheritance. If the heir accepted the inheritance and restored three-quarters of it to the beneficiary, the *senatusconsultum Trebellianum* applied. The result was that H was *iure civili heres* of the whole inheritance, F was *heredis loco* to three-quarters. Hence H had the hereditary actions *iure civili* but could only make use of them to one-quarter; F had the hereditary actions *iure praetorio* to three-quarters. The hereditary creditors might sue H to one-quarter *iure civili*, F to three-quarters *iure praetorio*.

2. If the *fideicommissum* covered more than three-quarters of the inheritance, the *Pegasianum* made the following secondary distinction.

(*a*) The heir voluntarily accepted the inheritance. He was then entitled to keep a quarter of the inheritance, but whether he availed himself of this right or not, the beneficiary was not *heredis loco* and stipulations between him and the heir were required to secure the transfer of the hereditary rights and liabilities.

(*b*) The heir refused to accept the inheritance. Then he might be compelled to accept by a magistrate. If he thus accepted under official duress, he lost the right to keep the *quarta*, but on the other hand the beneficiary was now *heredis loco* according to the *Trebellianum*.

We have expounded these artificial and complicated
regulations because they are so significant for classical
jurisprudence and legislation. A clear and simple position
might have been easily achieved by allowing the testator
to institute H as his heir for three years and F as his heir
after the lapse of this time. But this would have offended
against the maxim *semel heres, semper heres* (above, s. 456)
which, though created by lawyers and not owing its origin
to any statute or to the intervention of the praetor, had
become an article of faith to the classical lawyers. Instead
of making an exception to that sacred rule they built up
this intricate law.

Justinian abolished the *Pegasianum* and restored the
Trebellianum, retaining from the former only the right of
the heir to keep the *quarta* and the right of the magistrate
to compel the heir to accept the inheritance. But not even
Justinian dared to contravene the maxim *semel heres, semper
heres*. The compilers of Justinian's *Digest* and *Codex* carried
the new law through by interpolating the classical texts;
they radically struck out the *Pegasianum* wherever they
met it in classical texts and replaced it by the *Trebellianum*.
It is of course easy to discover these interpolations since
we possess Gaius' account. Moreover, the authors of
Justinian's *Institutes* and Justinian himself (*Const. Tanta*,
6) had no scruples about revealing their work for the
benefit of the law schools.

569.
Justinian's
Laws
exploso
senatus-
consulto
Pegasiano

SOURCES

s. 564. Read *Epit. Ulp.* 24. 31; *D.* (36. 2) 5 pr.; Gai. 2. 194, 195,
200, 201–4; *D.* (50. 16) 213 pr.; Gai. 4. 9 [*certa*]; 2. 282; 4. 171.

s. 565. Read Gai. 2. 199, 205.

s. 566. Read Gai. 2. 254 to *extinguebantur fideicommissa*; read the
Edict *si quis omissa causa etc.* in Lenel, *Edict.*, p. 364; *D.* (30) 74 pr.
[*Licet*]; [*tamen . . . dicendum est*]; (31) 29. 1 and 2; (31) 49. 4; (31) 61. 1.
Further exceptions not mentioned in the text above: *Epit. Ulp.* 17. 3;
D. (30) 96. 1.

s. 567. Read Gai. 2. 227, 254; *D.* (35. 2) 18 pr. to *propter fideicommissa*.

s. 568. Read Gai. 2. 253–9.

s. 569. Read *D.* (36. 1) 17. 1 [*Trebelliano*] ⟨*Pegasiano*⟩, 17. 2 [*sive*]
⟨*si*⟩ *suspectam*; [*sive sponte . . . actiones*]; *Inst. Iust.* (2. 23) 3–7; *Const.
Tanta*, 6.

BIBLIOGRAPHY

s. 564. Biondi, *Successione testamentaria* (1943), 338 ff., with references; on *actio ex testamento in duplum* see Beseler, Z xlvii (1927), 65 ff.

s. 565. Biondi, l.c. 322.

s. 566. Sanfilippo, *Studi sull' hereditas*, i (1937), 158 ff.; Biondi, l.c. 325 ff. On Gai. 2. 254 see Solazzi, *Scritti Ferrini* (1946), 184. Beseler, *Scritti Ferrini*, iii (1948), 274.

s. 567. Windscheid, *Pand.* iii, §§ 650 ff.; Biondi, l.c. 381 ff.; F. Schwarz, Z lxiii (1943), 314 ff.

s. 568. Biondi, l.c. 477 ff.; Bartosek, 'Il Sc. Trebelliano', *Scritti Ferrini*, iii (1948), 308 ff.

4. *Modus*

570.
Conception

Let us start with the following simple case: A testator left by *legatum* (*per vindicationem* or *per damnationem*) a piece of land to L requesting him to build a monument on that land in memory of the testator. This was not a *legatum* left under the suspensive condition that the legatee should build the monument. On the other hand, one could not take the testator's request as *fideicommissum* imposed upon the legatee since there was no beneficiary. It is a clear case of what Justinian's compilers called a *legatum sub modo* (*D.* 35. 1; *C.* 6. 45). Though this term is not classical, we shall use it in the following account for want of a better.

571. Scope

A *modus* might be imposed upon an heir as well as upon a legatee for various purposes. The testator might in this way give instructions concerning his funeral; he might order that his birthday should be celebrated by a feast to be given to the poor; he might forbid alienation of a piece of land; he might even request that a sum of money should be given to a certain person, but without using the proper formulas required for the creation of a legacy, e.g. 'Titio fundum Cornelianum do lego ita ut centum Maevio det'. We may now give a definition: *Modus mortis causa* was a charge imposed by the testator upon an heir or legatee which did not involve the creation of a legacy (*legatum* or *fideicommissum*).

572. Legal relevance

Provisions of this kind were very well known to the classical lawyers, but a special term to designate them did

not yet exist in their day. In principle a *modus* implied only
a moral or religious obligation. When the *modus* was imposed upon a legatee, the heir might retain the thing left
to the legatee till the latter promised him to perform the
modus. Where the performance of the *modus* was to
the interest of the State or of religion, the magistrates or the
religious authorities might intervene, but our sources with
regard to this point are few and unreliable. Where the
modus was imposed for the benefit of a certain person, it
might be taken as an implied *fideicommissum*. However, as
already stated (s. 559), the lawyers (at least down to the
Severi) were loath to recognize implied *fideicommissa*.

Under Justinian's law the performance of a *modus* could 573.
always be enforced; the compilers proclaimed this new rule Justinian's
by interpolating classical texts. law

SOURCES

   s. 572. Read *D*. (35. 1) 40. 5; (5. 3) 50. 1 [*quamvis . . . voluntatis*];
D. (36. 1) 76 pr.
   s. 573. In *D*. (33. 1) 7, the last sentence is certainly spurious; see *Index
Interp*.

BIBLIOGRAPHY

  ss. 570–3. Pernice, *Labeo*, iii. 1 (1892), 32 ff.; Mitteis, *RP* i (1908),
196 ff.; Biondi, *Successione testamentaria* (1943), 567 ff.

5. *Donatio mortis causa*

The classical *donatio mortis causa* was a gift, effected by 574.
an agreement between donor and donee, which took full Conception
effect when the donor died (or died in the course of some
specified operation dangerous to life) and the donee was
still alive at that time. Like any other donation, a *donatio
mortis causa* might be effected by various means. In particular the donor might transfer ownership to the recipient
under the suspensive condition that the donee survived the
donor. If in such a case the donee died before the donor,
the latter might recover the gift by the *rei vindicatio*. The
donor might also confer unconditional ownership on the
donee and only bind him or his heir to retransfer ownership
if the donor survived the donee.

575.
Donatio
mortis
causa and
legacy

The classical *donatio mortis causa* differed greatly from a legacy. The forms required for classical *legata* and *fideicommissa* in themselves constituted an important difference from a *donatio mortis causa*. Nevertheless, from the economic point of view, *donatio mortis causa* came very near to a legacy and it is, therefore, small wonder that even in classical times a *donatio mortis causa* was in certain respects put on a par with a legacy. We have mentioned above (s. 549) that a *fideicommissum* might be imposed upon the recipient of a *donatio mortis causa* as well as a legatee. Further, on the strength of a constitution of Septimius Severus the heir might deduct the *quarta Falcidia* (above, s. 567) from a *donatio mortis causa*. On the other hand, the compilers of the *Digest* declared in an interpolated text (*D.* 39. 6. 37 pr.):

> 'Illud generaliter meminisse oportebit donationes mortis causa factas legatis comparatas: quodcumque igitur in legatis iuris est, id in mortis causa donationibus erit accipiendum.'

Likewise the authors of Justinian's *Institutes* (2. 7. 1), referring to Justinian's constitution *C.* (8. 56) 4, say:

> 'Hae mortis causa donationes ad exemplum legatorum redactae sunt per omnia . . . a nobis constitutum est, ut per omnia fere legatis connumeretur.'

Thus it was the manifest aim of the compilers to assimilate *donatio mortis causa* to legacy. In these circumstances and in default of texts outside Justinian's law-books it is of course difficult to say how far the process of assimilation went in classical times and how much is to be attributed to post-classical authors. This much seems to be certain, that under classical law a *donatio mortis causa* as such could not be revoked by the donor. The classical *donatio mortis causa* was and remained an agreement and could not be revoked by the giver like a legacy (above, s. 562). Wherever this right to revoke occurs, the texts are either spurious or had a different meaning in their original context.

SOURCES

s. 574. Read *D.* (39. 6) 2.
s. 575. Read *C.* (6. 50) 5.

BIBLIOGRAPHY

ss. 574, 575. Biondi, *Successione testamentaria* (1943), 703 ff., with full references.*

Appendix: Executor

Within the rich store of the classical law of succession one thing was completely missing, the institution of the executor, i.e. of an independent person appointed by the testator to carry out his wishes. It was a fateful omission, for with the help of this one institution the law of succession might have been thoroughly simplified, and simplification was what classical law needed badly. The republican lawyers were very near to it, for the *familae emptor* in the original testament by bronze and balance (above, s. 432) might easily have developed into an executor. Unfortunately the lawyers took a different path and the *familiae emptor* became a mere witness. _{576. Conception. Attitude of the lawyers}

Available Roman wills made within the classical period show that the executor (called *curator* or *procurator*) actually existed, but it was only a *de facto* existence. A testator might appoint his friend as a *curator* by will and give him instructions to be performed after the testator's death. The friend might loyally accept this office and attempt to carry out the testator's wishes if supported by the goodwill of the heirs and legatees; but all depended on loyalty, good faith, and goodwill. The executor was not granted any legal recognition by classical orthodoxy. The legal history of the executor only begins in the Middle Ages. _{577. Executors in Roman testaments}

SOURCES

s. 576. Read *D.* (36. 1) 80. 1.

s. 577. Read the testament of Antonius Silvanus (A.D. 142), *FIRA*, iii, no. 47, with references; Macqueron, *RH* xxiv (1943), 123.

BIBLIOGRAPHY

ss. 576, 577. Windscheid, *Pand.* iii, § 567; Mitteis, *RP* i (1908), 105 n. 30; Kübler, *PW* va. 1010; Biondi, *Successione testamentaria* (1943), 607 ff., with references; Macqueron, *RH* xxiv (1945), 150.

PART IV
LAW OF PROPERTY
INTRODUCTION

578. Scope THE subject of this Part is the classical law of owner-ship and of those rights which emanate from owner-ship and modify it. Usufruct, for example, is an emanation from ownership, since it is only by the owner of a thing that it can be created. As long as the usufruct exists, ownership is modified, as it is charged with the right of the usu-fructuary. Thus, if the owner alienated the thing to a third person, the right of the usufructuary remained intact. The usufruct will therefore be described in this Part. On the other hand, in the case of a contract of lease by which the lessor conveyed a piece of land to the lessee, although the lessee was entitled no less than a usufructuary to reap the fruits of the land, his right was under classical Roman law fundamentally different from that of a usufructuary. The right of the Roman lessee, in sharp contrast to the English, does not emanate from ownership and it is immaterial whether the lessor is or is not the owner of the land. If the lessor is owner, the right of the lessee does not modify ownership; it is not, like usufruct, a charge imposed upon ownership. Suppose the owner of a piece of land contracted to lease it for three years; after the lapse of one year he alienated the land to a third person. The new owner might at once expel the lessee; all the lessee can do is to claim damages from the lessor who concluded the contract of lease. Thus a contract of lease does not entail a modification of ownership, and the proper place to discuss it is therefore the law of obligations (below, s. 935).

579. Iura in rem Modern students are wont to comprehend ownership and those rights which modify it under the conception of *iura in re*, or according to English usage *iura in rem*, but this conception is not classical. The classical lawyers never termed ownership (*dominium*; see below, s. 587) a *ius in re* or *in rem*, nor was the term *iura in re aliena* (or *in rem* *alienam*) known to them. For that reason we need not give a definition of *ius in re* (or *in rem*) in this Part.

The liberal character of the classical law of property is so manifest and so well known that a few remarks upon it will suffice. **580. Liberal character**

1. Ownership is sacrosanct. It was not the Roman way to pronounce this principle in a solemn formula, but it nevertheless existed. **581. Ownership sacrosanct**

> Cf. *Déclaration des droits de l'homme et du citoyen*, 28th August 1789, art. 17: 'La propriété, étant un droit inviolable et sacré, nul ne peut en être privé, si ce n'est lorsque la nécessité publique, légalement constatée, l'exige évidemment, et sous la condition d'une juste et préalable indemnité.' For similar pronouncements in continental constitutions see Hedemann, *Die Fortschritte des Zivilrechts im XIX. Jahrhundert*, ii. 1 (1930), 117 f.

This principle is clearly at work in the following rules:

(*a*) The legal institution of expropriation was well known to republican and classical law; but regulations apparently did not exist and the matter was left entirely to the discretion of the magistrates. They, however, were as a rule loath to practise expropriation, and Augustus himself in this respect set a good example to others.

(*b*) Loss of property by prescription was likewise kept within very narrow limits, as we shall point out later (below, ss. 622 ff.).

(*c*) When a non-owner alienated a thing without the owner's consent, even a bona fide recipient did not acquire ownership, since to protect bona fides would have meant an expropriation of the owner. The classical lawyers did not even hold it worth while to discuss the question whether it might be in the interests of commerce to protect the bona fide recipient, for what was dear to the lawyers was not security of commerce and business intercourse but security of vested rights. Thus the owner could sue the bona fide possessor by the *rei vindicatio* and the latter could not even claim from the plaintiff the price which he had paid for it.

2. Classical ownership did not imply an unlimited right over a thing. The powers of a slave-owner were restricted by imperial constitutions. Ownership of land was limited **582. Wide bounds of classical ownership**

not only with regard to the interests of neighbours but also by public law. But it is evident that under classical law the bounds of ownership were very wide, especially when compared with medieval Germanic ownership. It was again the liberal principle which demanded that ownership should be as unrestricted as possible and that the greatest possible latitude should be given to individual action and initiative. Both real and personal property could be freely alienated and divided. Statutory provisions limiting the right of disposal were very few (above, ss. 214, 300). Such limitations as are nowadays imposed by the game, fishery, and mining laws were unknown to classical law.

583. Free ownership 3. The right of an owner to impose charges on ownership in favour of other persons was limited, for the liberal principle aimed at keeping ownership as far as possible free of restrictions. The usufruct which granted considerable rights to the usufructuary was restricted in regard to time, since these rights could not be transferred by the usufructuary to another person and at the latest ended at his death. Servitudes were severely restricted as to their possible content (below, s. 685). Mortgage was framed in such a way that it was unfit to serve as a form of capital investment; the classical mortgage was not meant to be a permanent charge on ownership (below, s. 700).

584. Co-ownership 4. Community of property was not favoured by Roman individualistic liberalism. In case of co-ownership each owner could dispose of his share (of the ownership, not of the object) and demand dissolution of the *communio* by the *actio communi dividundo* (above, s. 86). To be sure there was a form of co-ownership without disposable shares (*zur gesamten Hand*), viz. the common property of so-called legal persons (above, ss. 146, 157, 173), but these were governed by special rules. Ownership of a house as distinct from ownership of the site; ownership of a story of a house; ownership of undetached fruits—all these forms of co-ownership, well known under Germanic law, were entirely excluded by classical law. It need not be said that nothing like the Germanic overlordship and sub-ownership was permitted under classical law.

Thus the liberal trend of the classical law of property is unmistakable. A state of affairs such as existed in Germany, Austria, and France when, before the agrarian legislation of the end of the eighteenth and the beginning of the nineteenth century, land-ownership was practically stifled under the accumulation of charges, could not arise under classical Roman law. To what extent this liberal law had evil effects, how far in particular it was a factor in the development of Italian *latifundia*, we cannot tell. Be that as it may, it is just the liberal character of the classical law of property which makes it a lasting monument in European legal history.

585.
Evaluation

BIBLIOGRAPHY

s. 579. On *ius in rem* see *Voc. Iur. Rom.* v. 122. 31 (*D.* 32. 20); on *ius in re, Voc. Iur. Rom.* v. 130. 26; Windscheid, *Pand.* i (1906), § 38 n. 4; § 165 n. 1; G. Grosso, *I problemi dei diritti reali nell' impostazione Romana* (1944), 2 n. 1.

s. 581*a*. F. M. de Robertis, *La espropriazione per pubblica utilità nel diritto Romano* (1936); Schulz, *Principles* (1936), 161, 163.

s. 581*c*. Schulz, l.c. 155, 251; Beseler, 'Hand wahre Hand', *St. Besta*, i. (1939), 199.

s. 582. Schulz, l.c. 151 ff.; Scialoja, *Teoria della proprietà nel diritto Romano*, i (1928), 303 ff., 413 ff.; Bonfante, *Corso*, ii. 1 (1926), 272 ff.

s. 583. Schulz, l.c. 153 f.

s. 584. Schulz, l.c. 154; Scialoja, l.c. 425 ff., Bonfante, *Corso*, ii. 2 (1928), 3 ff.

s. 585. Mommsen, *Schr.* iii. 582; Schulz, l.c. 157 f.

z

CHAPTER I

OWNERSHIP

1. *Conception of ownership. Terminology*

586.
Definition

NO Roman definition of ownership exists in the available sources, and we may safely assume that the classical lawyers never attempted to give such a definition. We think that Roman ownership should be defined as follows:

> Ownership is that right over a corporeal thing (N.B.) which on principle endows its holder with full power over the thing, although this power may be subject to various limitations.

Obviously this definition does not disclose anything about the content of ownership in an individual case. Suppose that the owner of a piece of land has charged it with a usufruct, with servitutes and mortgages, and that the ownership is further restricted by various rules of public law. His legal power over the land is certainly very limited, but nevertheless, he is to be regarded as the owner of the land according to our definition, since the law bestows upon him in general (exceptions reserved) the full power over the land. The Roman conception of ownership has been keenly discussed and at one time the legend was current that Roman ownership implied an unlimited power, in sharp contrast to Germanic law. In fact, this conception of ownership was erroneously attributed to Roman law by modern Romanistic lawyers. As aforesaid, available sources do not contain any definition and the Roman law from which we have to construct a definition clearly shows that Roman ownership was very far from bestowing an unlimited power on its holder. To be sure the classical law was a liberal law and for that reason the bounds of ownership were very wide, much wider than under Germanic law. It is, however, not the Roman conception of ownership which is individualistic but the Roman law relating to ownership.

In classical legal language several terms are used to 587. Ter-
designate what we should call ownership.

1. *Dominium* and *proprietas*. The owner was called
dominus, proprietarius, or *dominus proprietatis*.

2. *Esse alicuius* means 'a thing is in the ownership of
somebody' (*meum est* = I am the owner).

3. *In bonis* (or *ex bonis*) *esse* or *habere*.

4. In republican times, when *dominium* and *proprietas*
had not yet become technical legal terms, ownership was
designated by describing its principal content: *habere
possidere uti frui licere*. In classical times this formula was
apparently only used to denote the private ownership of
provincial land (below, s. 591).

SOURCES

s. 587. Read *Lex Antonia de Termessibus* (71 B.C.), i, lines 12–36
(Bruns, *Fontes*, no. 14; *FIRA* i, no. 11; *ILS* no. 38; Hardy, *Roman
Laws and Charters, with a translation*, 1912, 94 ff.) with Kaser, Z lxii
(1942), 63 f.

BIBLIOGRAPHY

s. 586. Windscheid, *Pand.* i, § 167; Schulz, *Principles*, 151; Karl
Diehl, *Theoret. Nationalökonomie*, ii (1924), 214; Hedemann, *Die Fortschritte des Zivilrechts im XIX. Jahrh.* ii. 1 (1930), 119; Scialoja, *Proprietà*,
i (1928), 255 ff.; Bonfante, *Corso*, ii. 1 (1926), 190 ff.*

s. 587. M. Kaser, *Eigentum und Besitz im älteren röm. Recht* (1943),
306 ff.; Z lxii (1942), 76 n. 241, 64; Monier, 'La Date de l'apparition du
dominium', *St. Solazzi* (1948), 357 ff.

2. *Classical kinds of ownership*

i. The principal form of ownership was the *dominium ex* 588.
iure Quiritium, i.e. the ownership recognized by Roman $\frac{\text{Quiritary}}{\text{ownership}}$
ius civile. It required (1) a person capable of holding it;
(2) a corporeal thing capable of being *in dominio*.

1. Any Roman citizen was capable of holding *dominium
ex iure Quiritium*; non-Romans only if they were in possession of *ius commercii*.

2. Movable corporeal things of any kind were capable of
being *in dominio ex iure Quiritium*. As regards landed property (*fundi*, the classical lawyers avoided the term *res*

immobiles) only *fundi Italici* were capable of being in quiritary ownership, i.e. as a rule only land situated in Italy, but exceptionally '*ius Italicum*' was granted to land outside Italy.

589.
Bonitary
ownership

ii. Alongside quiritary ownership stood praetorian ownership, just as in the law of succession *bonorum possessio* stood beside *hereditas* (above, s. 377). However, praetorian ownership was of considerably less importance than *bonorum possessio*; the former had only a transitory existence, since it changed into quiritary ownership by *usucapio* after the lapse of one or two years (below, s. 622). Like quiritary ownership, praetorian ownership was only open to Roman citizens and such non-Romans who were in possession of *ius commercii*. As for landed property, only *fundi Italici* or *Italici iuris* could be in praetorian ownership. The classical lawyers designated praetorian ownership in contrast to quiritary ownership by the terms *in bonis esse* or *in bonis habere* (hence the modern term 'bonitary ownership') and never by *dominium*; Gaius, the 'odd man out', alone affords an exception (Gai. 1. 54; 2. 40, below s. 655.).

590. Res
publicae

iii. All things belonging to the Roman State were called *res publicae*. They were in the ownership of the State, but this was not quiritary ownership, indeed not private ownership at all, but public ownership, subject to special rules which differed greatly from those applied in private law. Things in public use like streets, public places, theatres, and so on (*res publicae publico usui destinatae*) were also in the ownership of the Roman State but were protected by special remedies. Thus in classical times *res publicae* were

1. All things belonging to the *Aerarium populi Romani* (above, s. 148).
2. Things belonging to the *fiscus*, at least from the times of Claudius, although even under Augustus fiscal property was not entirely subject to private law (above, s. 152).

Things belonging to Roman *municipia* were also (though incorrectly) called *res publicae*. The *municipes* were the owners (*zu gesamter Hand*; above, s. 157). In general this

ownership was subject to private law (quiritary or praetorian ownership). Public places, streets, and buildings
situated within a *municipium* were likewise in the ownership
of the *municipes* but protected by special remedies like the
res publicae publico usui destinatae in Rome.

iv. When considering land situated in the provinces we
have to distinguish:

1. The land might have received *ius Italicum*; then it was
capable of being in quiritary and praetorian ownership.

2. The land might belong to the *Aerarium populi Romani*
or to the *fiscus*; then it was *res publica*.

3. Land belonging to the territory of a *civitas libera et
foederata* (above, s. 130) lay outside the Roman State and
the provincial administration. It belonged either to the
civitas or to individual persons (Romans or peregrines),
but this was not Roman ownership but ownership according to peregrine law. Land belonging to a *civitas Latini
iuris* was in ownership according to 'Latin' law (s. 134).

4. The rest of provincial land was in the ownership of
communities or individual persons (Romans or peregrines), but this ownership was neither quiritary nor praetorian; it was an ownership of a special kind subject to a
mixture of Roman and peregrine law. To designate it the
classical lawyers apparently used the old republican formula (or parts of it) *habere possidere uti frui licere* (above,
s. 587). *Dominium* of this land was ascribed to the Roman
State, in the senatorial provinces to the *Populus Romanus*,
in the imperial provinces to the *Princeps*, but this ownership
was neither quiritary nor praetorian ownership. It was a sort
of public ownership which implied nothing else but that the
land was subject to a tax and formed part of the territory
under the administration of the provincial governors.

v. Things dedicated to a god by a Roman magistrate
with due ceremony were regarded as being in the ownership of the god (*res sacrae*). In truth they were in the ownership of the Roman State, but it was a special kind of public
ownership subject to special rules (*res divini iuris*); these
things were expressly distinguished from *res publicae*.

591.
Fundus
provincialis

592. Res
sacrae

593. Res religiosae

vi. *Res religiosae* were things devoted to religion, but only tombs had a special legal status and for that reason were the only things called *res religiosae* by Gaius (2. 4). Tombs in which human beings were legally buried were regarded as being in the ownership of the *Di Manes*; in truth they were in the ownership of individual persons or groups of persons, in particular of *collegia funeraticia*. But this ownership also lay outside the sphere of private law (the things were *res divini iuris*) and subject to special rules.

594. Attitude of the lawyers

vii. We have already emphasized repeatedly the principle of republican and classical jurisprudence which was to ignore public and sacred law and to concentrate upon private law. Accordingly the classical lawyers only mentioned briefly those forms of ownership which were entirely or partly regulated by public and sacred law. Thus Gaius (2. 3–11) is content to state that *res publicae, sacrae,* and *religiosae* lie outside the domain of private law (they are not *in bonis*); and when the classical lawyers dealt with the law concerning tombs, they most probably confined themselves to a discussion of the remedies provided by the Edict and did not give a full description of the law which the pontiffs had developed with regard to tombs. In this Part we shall follow their example and focus our attention on classical private ownership, i.e. on quiritary and bonitary (praetorian) ownership.

SOURCES

s. 588. Compare Gai. 2. 42 with *Epit. Ulp.* 19. 8.

s. 589. Read Gai. 1. 54; 2. 40–1.

s. 590. Read *D.* (50. 16) 15; Gai. 2. 11.

s. 591. 4. Read Gai. 2. 7 and 2. 21.

s. 592. Read Gai. 2. 4 and 5; *D.* (1. 8) 6. 3; Macrob. *Sat.* 3. 3. 2 = Bremer, *Jur. Antehadr.* i. 404; Frontinus, *Grom. Vet.*, p. 56 on *luci sacri: solum indubitate populi Romani est.*

s. 593. Read Gai. 2. 4 and 6; Gellius, 4. 9. 8 = Bremer, l.c. ii. 1, p. 366.

BIBLIOGRAPHY

s. 588. Mommsen, *Staatsrecht*, iii. 1 (1887), 630 f.; Kaser, Z lxii (1942), 74. On *res immobiles* see *Voc. Iur. Rom.* iii. 397; Schulz, *Epit. Ulp.* (1926), p. 43; Kübler, *St. Bonfante*, ii (1930), 347; A. Schiller, *ACI*, Roma, ii (1935), 431 ff.; Di Marzo, *Bull.* xlix/1 (1948), 236 ff.*

s. 590. Scialoja, *Proprietà*, i (1928), 204 ff.; Bonfante, *Corso*, ii. 1 (1926), 66 ff.

s. 591. 3. Kaser, Z lxii (1942), 56.

s. 591. 4. Klingmüller, *Philologus*, lxix (1910), 71 ff.; Carelli, *SD* i (1935), 379; Kaser, Z lxii (1942), 77 ff., with references; Last, *JRS* xxxiv (1944), 55, with references; F. Bozza, 'Gaio II, 7 e la proprietà provinciale', *Athenaeum*, N.S. xx (1942), 66 ff.; xxi (1943), 13 ff.; Solazzi, *SD* vii (1941), 373 ff.

s. 592. Mommsen, *Staatsrecht*, ii. 1 (1887), 59 ff.; Wissowa, *Religion und Kultus der Römer* (1912), 385, 467; Scialoja, *Proprietà*, i (1928), 141; Bonfante, *Corso*, ii. 1 (1926), 13 ff.

s. 593. Wissowa, l.c. 387; Ferrini, *Opere*, i. 1 ff.; Mommsen, *Schr*. iii. 198; Taubenschlag, Z xxxviii (1917), 244, with references; Scialoja, l.c. 158 ff.; Bonfante, l.c. 20 ff.; Albertario, *Studi*, ii (1941), 1 ff.

3. *Transfer of ownership by acts inter vivos*

Transfer of ownership (*translatio dominii*, *transferre dominium*) is a metaphorical expression which implies that the ownership of the recipient is identical with that of the previous owner, or in other words that the recipient succeeds to the ownership of the alienator. We have already stated above (s. 369) that the conception of a so-called singular or particular succession was unknown to the classical lawyers; hence it is *a priori* doubtful whether they ever used the metaphors *translatio dominii*, *transferre dominium*, *dominium transit*. Accordingly it has even been asserted that wherever these terms occur in classical writings the texts are interpolated. The classical lawyers only used the term *transferre rem* and their idea, it is argued, was that the ownership of the alienator ends and a new ownership comes into existence in the hands of the recipient. Unfortunately this theory, though widely accepted, has not been proved and cannot be proved with the available material. But even if it were true that these expressions were never used by classical lawyers (but *proprietatem transferre* in *D.* 7. 5. 7 is hardly assailable), this would not imply that the idea of a transfer of ownership was foreign to them. *Rem per mancipationem transferre* (Gai. 2. 22) is likewise a metaphorical expression which can only mean *dominium transferre*

595.
Dominium
transferre

(cf. Gai. 3. 85). Thus the whole issue is merely a matter of terminology and we may, therefore, safely continue to speak of a transfer of ownership.

596.
Survey   Under classical law there were five acts *inter vivos* by which ownership might be transferred: *mancipatio*, *in iure cessio*, *traditio*, *adiudicatio*, and *adsignatio* (by a Roman magistrate); but only the first three are private acts deserving further discussion here.

i. *Mancipatio* (*mancipium*)

597.
Anomalous cases   We have already met *mancipatio* on several occasions (*noxae datio*, above, s. 73; *coemptio*, s. 195; *adoptio*, s. 249; *emancipatio*, s. 272; mancipatory will, s. 431), but in classical times these were anomalous cases. The main and standard case was always the *mancipatio* of corporeal things and here is, therefore, the proper place to describe it.

598.
History   *Mancipatio* is a very old legal act which can be traced back to the Twelve Tables, but its long history cannot be discerned from available sources. According to our declared plan we confine ourselves to classical law, leaving entirely aside the vast mass of more or less plausible conjectures which have been brought forward with regard to the republican and prehistoric phase of its evolution.

599.
Classical ritual   The classical *mancipatio rei corporalis* was a conveyance which took the form of a fictitious sale. Its main purpose was to transfer ownership; it had in addition other effects which we shall discuss later (in particular the so-called *actio auctoritatis*; see below, s. 920), but these were not essential and might be absent in individual cases, whereas a transfer of ownership was the inevitable effect of any valid *mancipatio* of a corporeal thing. The act had to be effected according to an old republican ritual which was stubbornly retained throughout the whole classical period. Its age should not be exaggerated since obviously the form observed in the classical period is not the original form. Anyhow, the rite to be observed in classical times was the following. In the presence of the transferor, of five witnesses, and a balance holder (*libripens*) the transferee had to pronounce the following formula:

'Hunc ego hominem ex iure Quiritium meum esse aio, isque mihi
emptus esto hoc aere aeneaque libra.'

'I declare that this slave is mine by quiritary right, and let him be
bought by me with this coin and balance.'

While speaking this formula he had to grasp the slave in
token of his ownership; the transferor remained completely
silent. The transferee now struck the balance with a coin
which he handed over to the transferor as a symbolic price.
This ritual needs some explanatory remarks.

1. The *libripens* with his balance goes of course back to
a time in which it was customary to check the weight of the
coins constituting the purchase price or in which the price
was paid by giving uncoined ingots. In classical times there
is no longer a real weighing; what the transferee gave to the
transferor was always a coin, namely a farthing (*nummus
unus*). Any classical *mancipatio* was therefore a *venditio
imaginaria* (Gai. 1. 113, 119), since the price paid in the
ritual was only a nominal price. Even when *mancipatio* was
effected *venditionis causa*, i.e. in order to perform a genuine
sale, the real price was neither mentioned nor paid within
the ritual of *mancipatio*; it was probably mentioned in a
preceding declaration (*nuncupatio*) and, if it had to be paid
at once, was paid immediately before or after the ritual was
performed. Thus the classical *mancipatio rei corporalis* was
always, as aforesaid, a conveyance formed as the performance of a fictitious cash-purchase. It might, therefore, serve
for very different purposes, e.g. for a transfer of property
donationis causa, *dotis causa*, *fiduciae causa*, *solutionis causa*.

600.
Mancipatio
nummo
uno

2. *Mihi emptus esto*. The reading *esto* as given by Gai. 1.119 of the
Cod. Veronensis is certainly right since it recurs in 2. 104; 3. 167.
Boethius (*Ad Cic. Top.* 5. 28; *Ciceronis Opera*, ed. Orelli–Baiter, v
(1833), 322) citing Gai. 1. 119 gives *est* instead of *esto*, an obvious
simplification of the *lectio difficilior* '*esto*'. *Emere* meant in classical times
'to buy', 'to purchase', whatever may have been its meaning in remote
republican times.

601.
Emptus
esto

3. The transferee was bound, as Gaius 1. 121 expressly
says, to grasp the thing which was mancipated to him
('adprehendere id ipsum, quod ei mancipio datur, necesse
sit'), adding that this symbolic act was not required when
a piece of land was mancipated (1. 121 *praedia absentia*

602.
Presence of
the object

solent mancipari). However, the formula used in the *mancipatio* is similar to that of the *legis actio sacramento* (Gai. 4. 16), and with reference to the latter Gaius states that a clod from the land or a tile from the building had to be brought before the praetor (Gai. 4. 17). Most probably a similar symbolic act had originally to be performed in a *mancipatio* of land. But it may be that this sort of symbolism had in classical times already disappeared from the ritual of the *mancipatio*, whereas it was preserved in that of the *legis actio*.

603.
Acquisition
by a slave
or a son in
power

We have so far discussed the ritual in a normal *mancipatio*. As regards the status of the persons co-operating in a *mancipatio*, both parties must be Roman citizens or non-Romans in possession of *ius commercii*. Witnesses and *libripens* must be Roman citizens. A slave might acquire something by *mancipatio* for his master and a *filius familias* for his father. As both slave and son in power were incapable of having property, they could not employ the usual formula: 'hanc rem meam esse aio ex iure Quiritium'; the standard formula was modified in such cases: 'Hanc rem Lucii Titii domini (patris) mei esse aio eaque ei empta esto', etc. (Gai. 3. 167).

604. Res
mancipi

As regards the objects, comparatively few corporeal things were capable of being conveyed by *mancipatio*, namely *fundi Italici* (including *fundi* endowed with *ius Italicum*, above, s. 588), slaves, and the indigenous domestic animals *quae collo dorsove domari solent*, which are commonly broken to draught or burden, such as oxen, horses, mules, and asses. These things were termed *res mancipi*.

> *Mancipi* is genitive of *mancipium* = *mancipatio* (not dative of *manceps*); on this genitive see Stolz–Schmalz, *Lat. Grammatik* (1928), p. 268; Kaser, *Eigentum und Besitz* (1943), 163. The accent should be placed on the second syllable. Unacceptable Ferrarino, *SD* iii (1937), 434 ff.

605. Res
nec
mancipi

All other things were called *res nec mancipi* (*nec* = *non* is old Latin). Some of these are: weapons, tools, jewellery, fungible things (money, corn, etc.), wild beasts (which included elephants and camels even though they were broken to draught or burden), dogs, sheep, goats, and pigs. Modern scholars have attempted again and again to find out the reason why those particular things were regarded as *res mancipi*, but hitherto in vain. Certainly the distinction is very old; Gaius himself says (2. 16) that camels and elephants were not regarded as *res mancipi* because their very names were unknown at the time when the distinction was made. The classical lawyers probably knew no more than we do about the underlying idea; nevertheless, they were content to retain the traditional distinction: 'non omnium quae a maioribus constituta sunt, ratio reddi potest' (*D*. 1. 3. 20).

Although according to the ritual the transferee alone had to speak, the *mancipatio* was nevertheless substantially an agreement. Thus, when a certain *fundus Cornelianus* was conveyed by *mancipatio* and parties did not agree as to what piece of land was being sold (*error in corpore*)—one of them having in mind allotment X and the other allotment Y—the *mancipatio* was void. 606. Agreement

To what extent agreement on the *causa mancipationis* was required remains doubtful. If one party believed that the *mancipatio* was made *donationis causa*, the other that it was effected *dotis* or *solutionis causa*, the *mancipatio* was probably void. But if the *mancipatio* was made *solutionis causa* and the debt did not exist, the *mancipatio* was nevertheless valid and the transferee became owner. Likewise a *mancipatio dotis causa* was valid even if the marriage did not take place. 607. Causa mancipationis

On the question whether in a *mancipatio venditionis causa* ownership was only transferred when the real price was paid we need not dwell, for under classical law this effect of the *mancipatio* took place without regard to whether or not the price had been paid. It is hardly credible that republican law was in this respect different. 607a. Transfer of ownership not dependent on payment of real price

Mancipatio was, in spite of its archaic apparatus, practised throughout the whole classical period and even in post-classical times. It is mentioned in the *Codex Theodosianus* of A.D. 438, though it is questionable whether the act called *mancipatio* was still conducted in its classical form. In Justinian's law *mancipatio* was replaced by *traditio*. 608. Disappearance

609. Terminology

The classical name of the act was *mancipatio* or *mancipium*. Both terms were derived from *manu capere*, referring to the solemn grasping of the thing by the transferee which was required by the rite. *Mancipare = mancipio dare* is said of the transferor; *mancipio accipere* of the transferee. Justinian's compilers cancelled these terms wherever they found them; *mancipatio* (*mancipium*) was replaced by *traditio*; *mancipare* or *mancipio dare* by *tradere* or *dare*; *mancipio accipere* by *per traditionem accipere* or *accipere*. Students should strictly observe the following rule. Whenever the classical lawyers dealt with the conveyance of *res mancipi*, they had in mind the *mancipatio* unless special circumstances indicate that they were concerned with praetorian ownership. Thus, when we find within the *Corpus iuris* a *traditio* of a *fundus Italicus* or of a slave, we have as a rule to assume that the original text had *mancipatio* instead of *traditio*.

ii. *In iure cessio*

610. Classical ritual

We have already met this act (above, ss. 249, 287, 494), but the law of property is the correct place for its description. The act was performed *in iure*, i.e. before the praetor or the provincial governor (above, s. 17). The person who wished to acquire ownership pronounced the following formula in the presence of the transferor: Hunc ego hominem ex iure Quiritium meum esse aio.'

As in *mancipatio*, he had to grasp the slave in token of his ownership. The magistrate then asked the transferor whether or not he wished to make objections (*an contra vindicet*), but the latter remained silent. Then the magistrate confirmed the declaration of the transferee (*addictio*), who thereupon acquired quiritary ownership whether the object was *res mancipi* or *nec mancipi*. This was the classical *in iure cessio* (giving up in court) as clearly described by Gaius (2. 24).

611. Fictitious law-suit?

According to the view which still prevails this act was a fictitious lawsuit with the transferor as the defendant, the transferee as the plaintiff, and the magistrate's *addictio* as a judgment. However, this opinion rests on a very fragile basis, as has been repeatedly pointed out. Above all a judgment only *ius fecit inter partes*, whereas the *in iure cessio* transferred an ownership which was effective against everybody. In truth the classical *in iure cessio* was probably a conveyance which had to be performed in court.

Those holding the popular opinion refer to Gai. 2. 96. Gaius, it is said, excludes a son in power from *in iure cessio*, whereas he can acquire for his father by *mancipatio* using a modified formula (above, s. 603). This difference (it is said) can only be explained by assuming that *in iure cessio* was a fictitious lawsuit, since in such a suit direct agency was out of the question. In truth Gaius simply says that a son in power cannot claim a thing *as his own* by *in iure cessio* since he is incapable of having property. This is quite right, but does not exclude his being able to claim a thing for his father, using a modified formula. The right interpretation eliminates Solazzi's main argument against the text.

As aforesaid, *res nec mancipi* as well as *res mancipi* could be transferred by *in iure cessio*. However, as *res nec mancipi* could be transferred in a much simpler way, namely by *traditio* (below, s. 613), *in iure cessio* was hardly ever used for that purpose. Nor was it normally practised to convey ownership of *res mancipi*; *mancipatio* was usually preferred as it did not require parties to appear in court. However, if the five Roman witnesses and the Roman *libripens* were not obtainable, *in iure cessio* was compulsory. Thus *in iure cessio* was mainly used for other purposes (transfer of incorporeal things; below, ss. 673, 688; *adoptio*, above, s. 249; *cessio tutelae*, above, s. 287; *cessio hereditatis*, above, s. 494). {612. Function}

In post-classical times *in iure cessio* disappeared. Justinian's compilers either cancelled it altogether or replaced it by *cessio*.

iii. *Traditio*

Tradere rem means to transfer the possession of a thing, but the term was also used in a narrower sense, viz. to transfer ownership by transferring *possessio*. It is in this narrower sense that we use the term *traditio* here. *Traditio* as a mode of transferring ownership may therefore be defined as a conveyance of a corporeal thing performed by transferring *possessio*. {613. Tradere}

This act is also very old, at least as old as the rule which established the list of *res mancipi*, for it is not credible that at any time people were bound to alienate *res nec mancipi* by *in iure cessio*. In classical times *traditio* was the proper act for transferring quiritary ownership of *res nec mancipi*. It required at any rate that both parties should agree on the {614. Age and legal character} transferring of ownership (not only of *possessio*) and on the object, so that *error in corpore* rendered the act void.

615. Causa traditionis It is a vexed and keenly discussed question whether and in what sense a *causa traditionis* was required under classical law. Available sources are heavily interpolated and Gai. 2. 20 is too vague to be of much help. Thus there is hardly any hope of reaching a *communis opinio doctorum* on this subject, unless fresh sources are discovered. Taking everything into account we think that the classical lawyers probably observed the following two rules:

1. A *causa traditionis* was required, but this only meant that agreement on the legal purpose of transferring ownership was required, i.e. whether *traditio* was made *venditionis causa*, *donationis causa*, *dotis causa*, *solutionis causa*, *mutui causa*. When such agreement did not exist, *traditio* was void. Thus when somebody gave a sum of money to A as a donation and A accepted it as a loan (*mutuum*), there was no *causa traditionis* since the parties did not agree on the purpose of the transfer of ownership; hence ownership was not transferred to A and neither *donatio* nor *mutuum* resulted.

2. No *causa* of any other kind was required. Thus *dotis causa* existed when the parties agreed that the thing was given *dotis causa*, but it was not required that marriage should actually ensue. The recipient became owner, but if marriage did not result, he had to restore the thing (above, s. 208). *Solutionis causa* existed if parties agreed that the thing was given *solutionis causa*, but the existence of a debt was not required. *Venditionis causa* existed if parties agreed that the thing was given *venditionis causa*, but a valid contract of sale was not required.

616. Traditio not dependent on payment of price When a *traditio* was made *venditionis causa*, the acquisition of ownership was not dependent on the payment of the price. This at least was the rule of classical law. Whether the Twelve Tables made *traditio* conditional on the payment of the price need not be discussed. Most probably the report given in Justinian's *Institutes* (2. 1. 41) is apocryphal and the law of the Twelve Tables was in harmony with classical law.

617. Bare agreement Though *traditio* did not require any formality, the trans-

fer of *possessio*, i.e. of the actual physical power over the
thing (below, s. 751), was indispensable and a transfer of
ownership by bare agreement was unknown to classical law.

Traditio of res nec mancipi conferred quiritary ownership
on the recipient provided (1) that he was capable of holding
quiritary ownership (above, s. 588) and (2) that the object
was capable of being in quiritary ownership (above, s. 588).
Thus if a Roman made a *traditio* in favour of a peregrine,
the latter acquired therewith peregrine not quiritary ownership. *Fundus provincialis*, which was nominally in the
ownership of the Roman State (above, s. 591. 4) but
actually belonged to private persons (*habere possidere uti
frui licere*; above, s. 591. 4), was *res nec mancipi* and, therefore, not transferable by *mancipatio*; it might be transferred
by *traditio*, which of course did not confer quiritary ownership on the recipient but only *habere possidere licere* (Gai.
2. 21 is misleading).

618. Object

In post-classical times *traditio* gradually became the sole
mode of transferring ownership *inter vivos* since *mancipatio*
and *in iure cessio* disappeared (above, ss. 608, 612). On the
other hand, *traditio* degenerated, since the actual transfer
of *possessio* was increasingly replaced by symbolic acts
(*traditio ficta*) and even by simple agreement; of course, this
process resulted in the interpolation of classical texts, but
these interpolations are not as numerous as might be
expected.

619. Post-classical law

iv. The following remarks concern all the three modes of
transferring ownership which we have discussed so far.

1. Quiritary ownership was only transferred when the
alienator had a right to alienate the thing. In the absence
of such a right *mancipatio*, *in iure cessio*, *traditio* were equally
void, even when the recipient was in good faith. We have
already mentioned (above, s. 581) this uncompromising
protection of vested rights (sc. of the true owner) on the
part of the Romans; modern students are wont to express
it in the maxim 'nemo plus iuris transferre potest quam ipse
habet' (English lawyers prefer the formula *nemo dat quod non
habet*), but this maxim is misleading and of post-classical

620. Nemo plus iuris transferre potest quam ipse habet

origin. Let us consider the following cases. A piece of land was given as *dos*; although the husband alone was owner of the *fundus dotalis* (above, s. 213), he could not alienate it under the *lex Iulia de fundo dotali* (above, s. 214), i.e. he could not transfer a right which he himself held. On the other hand, suppose that the alienator was not the owner of the thing but that he acted with the owner's consent or on the strength of a pledge; in such cases the alienator transferred quiritary ownership though he was not owner himself. The rule *nemo plus iuris*, etc., is therefore obviously false.

In fact the classical lawyers knew no such maxim, as Gai. 2. 62–4 clearly shows. We read the maxim in Justinian's collection of maxims (*D*. 50. 17. 54):

'Ulpianus libro XLVI ad edictum. Nemo plus iuris ad alium transferre potest quam ipse haberet' (N.B.).

We know that Ulpian dealt in this book of his commentary on the Edict with *bonorum possessio ab intestatio* (above, s. 404), and the text probably belongs to the rubric *Unde legitimi* (above, s. 414). An *heres legitimus* might perform an *in iure cessio hereditatis* without having acquired the inheritance by *aditio hereditatis* (Gai. 2. 35; above, s. 494). With reference to this case Ulpian probably stated:

'Heres non plus iuris ad alium transferre potest quam ipse haberet si hereditatem adisset.'

The compilers changed Ulpian's words into a general maxim but forgot to write *habet* instead of *haberet*. Students should not attempt to explain the incorrect subjunctive by reconstructing an oratio obliqua:

'X scribit neminem plus iuris ad alium transferre posse quam ipse haberet.'

It is not likely that Ulpian would have cited an authority for such an elementary rule.

The same rule appears in a slightly different form in *D*. (41. 1) 20 pr.

'Ulpianus libro XXIX ad Sabinum. Traditio nihil amplius transferre debet vel potest ad eum qui accipit, quam est apud eum qui tradit. Si igitur quis dominium in fundo habuit, id tradendo transfert; si non habuit, ad eum qui accipit nihil transfert.'

The whole text seems to be spurious. The author overlooked the cases in which a non-owner could transfer ownership.

621.   2. When we survey the three classical forms of convey-
Publicity ance, it becomes evident that the classical lawyers were but mildly interested in making the conveyance publicly

known. There was no registration of property, not even of
landed property, and the six Roman citizens required for
mancipatio (the five witnesses and the *libripens*) and the
publicity entailed by *in iure cessio* were but poor substitutes
for registration. This phenomenon is the more remarkable
since the attitude of Greek and Hellenistic law was in this
respect fundamentally different. But again the liberal character of the Roman law of property (above, ss. 580 ff.) is
evident. To an English reader this Roman disinclination
for publicity and registration will perhaps not seem remarkable. Although a Land Registration Office exists (Lord
Westbury's Act, 1862, 25 and 26 Vict. c. 53; Land Transfer Act, 1875; Land Registration Act, 1925), registration
of title is, according to these statutes, only optional, and in
fact little use is made of it, apparently for the same reasons
which underlay Roman law. One can do without this
apparatus. Continental critics of Roman law, biased by
fanatical advocates of Germanic law, should keep that in
mind. (Against the German system Fr. Vinding Kruse, *Das
Eigentumsrecht*, ii (1935), 1070 ff.). Classical law was not
primitive but liberal.

SOURCES

s. 598. Read XII Tab. vi. 1 (*FIRA* i, p. 43).

s. 599. Read Gai. 1. 119, 121.

s. 603. Read Gai. 3. 167.

s. 604. Read Gai. 1. 120; 2. 14*a*; *Epit. Ulp.* 19. 1.

s. 605. Read Gai. 2. 16; *Epit. Ulp.* 19. 1.

s. 606. Read *D.* (41. 1) 36, first sentence [*traditur*] ⟨*mancipatur*⟩;
[*traditio*] ⟨*mancipatio*⟩; [*tradam*] ⟨*mancipio dem*⟩.

s. 607*a*. Read *Inst. Iust.* (2. 1) 41.

s. 609. Compare *D.* (7. 2) 3. 1 with *Fr. Vat.* 80; *D.* (7. 1) 12. 3 with
Fr. Vat. 89.

s. 610. Read Gai. 2. 24.

s. 611. Read Gai. 2. 96; *Fr. Vat.* 51. The latter text (formed by a
post-classical author, see Schulz, *History*, 179) refers only to the ordinary
formula of *in iure cessio*.

s. 614. Read Gai. 2. 19–20l.

s. 615. Read *D.* (41. 1) 36, second sentence [*proprietatem . . . dissen-
serimus*] ⟨*donationem non esse*⟩; *D.* (12. 1) 18 pr. to *acceperit*; *D.* (18. 1)
41. 1: *pecunia condicetur*, consequently *traditio pecuniae* was valid; Gai.
2. 84: *traditio pecuniae* is valid though a *solutio* is not achieved; Gai. 3. 91,

first sentence: *traditio pecuniae* transferred ownership, otherwise a *condictio* would not lie.

s. 616. Read *Inst. Iust.* (2. 1) 41.

s. 618. Read Gai. 2. 21.

s. 619. Read *D.* (18. 1) 74; (41. 1) 9. 6; *Inst. Iust.* (2. 1) 45 with Theoph. Paraphrasis, Riccobono, Z xxxiv (1913), 197; Schulz, *Einführung in das Studium der Digesten* (1916), 68. Compare *C.* (8. 53) 6 [*maxime*], with *Fr. Vat.* 282.

s. 620. Read Gai. 2. 20; 2. 62–4; *D.* (41. 1) 9. 4; (41. 1) 46.

BIBLIOGRAPHY

s. 595. De Francisci, *Il trasferimento della proprietà* (1924); Kaser, *Eigentum und Besitz im älteren römischen Recht* (1943), 142 and *PW* viA. 2158 ff.; Beseler, Z lxvi (1948), 281 f., with references.

s. 597 ff. Kunkel, *PW* xiv. 998 ff.; Bonfante, *Corso*, ii. 2 (1928), 135 ff.; Kaser, *Eigentum und Besitz*, 107 ff., 224. K. F. Thormann, *Der doppelte Ursprung der mancipatio* (Münchener Beiträge zur Papyrusforschung, xxxiii, 1943).

s. 600. Kaser, *Eigentum*, 158 ff.

s. 601. On the sense of *emere* see Kaser, *Eigentum*, 108, with references. On *esto* see Wlassak, Z xxviii (1907), 74. 2; Kunkel, l.c. 999.*

s. 602. See Kaser, *Eigentum*, 224 ff.

ss. 604, 605. Leonhard, *PW* iA. 623 ff.; Kunkel, *PW* xiv. 1002; Kaser, *Eigentum* 163. On *nec = non* see Stolz–Schmalz, *Lat. Grammatik* (1928), 640; Kroll, *Glotta*, xxi (1933), 100 ff.

s. 606. Kunkel, l.c. 1003; Kreller, Z lxii (1942), 185; Beseler, Z xlv (1925), 221; Kaser, *Eigentum*, 142.

s. 607. Kaser, *Eigentum*, 135 n. 6, with references.

s. 607a. Kunkel, l.c. 1008; Kaser, *Eigentum*, 111, with full references.

s. 608. Kunkel, l.c. 1005; Schulz, *History*, 294, with references.

s. 609. Naber, *Mnemosyne*, xvii (1889), 394 ff.; Gradenwitz, Z vi (1883), 56 ff.

ss. 610–12. Kipp, *PW* iii. 2000 ff. Wlassak, Z xxv (1904), 90 ff.; Rabel, Z xxvii (1906), 309 ff.; Mitteis, *RP* i (1908), 276 ff.; Beseler, *Beiträge*, ii (1911), 149 ff.; H. Lévy–Bruhl, *Quelques problèmes du très ancien droit romain* (1934), 114 ff.; Kaser, *Eigentum*, 199 ff.; Pflüger, Z lxiii (1943), 301 ff.; Kaser, *Altröm. Jus.* (1949), 104 ff.

s. 611. On Gai. 2. 96 see Solazzi, *Glosse a Gaio*, ii. 402 ff.

ss. 613 ff. Ehrhardt. *PW* viA. 1875; Bonfante, *Corso*, ii. 1 (1928), 151 ff.; Kaser, *Eigentum*, 195 ff.*

s. 614. Kaser, *Eigentum*, 195.

s. 615. Schulz, Z lii (1932), 535 ff., 546, with references; Kaser, *Eigentum*, 198, with references; Beseler, *Bull.* xlv (1938), 186, not convincing.*

s. 616. Kaser, *Eigentum*, 111, with references; Feenstra, *Réclame en revindicatie* (Amsterdam proefschrift, 1949), 11 ff. on *Inst.* 2. 1. 41.*

s. 618. On Gai. 2. 21 see Solazzi, *Glosse a Gaio*, ii (1933), 332 ff.

s. 619. Riccobono, *Z* xxxiii (1912), 259 ff.; xxxiv (1913), 159 ff.; Taubenschlag, *The Law of Greco-Roman Egypt* (1944), 39.

s. 620. On *D*. (50. 17) 54 see Lenel, *Edict*. (1928), p. 356 n. 2.

4. *Acquisition of ownership by usucapio and longi temporis praescriptio*

The etymology of *usucapio* is perfectly clear: *usu capere* means to acquire (*capere*) by *possessio* (*usu*, for *usus*, means *possessio* in old republican usage). We may therefore define classical *usucapio* as the acquisition of quiritary ownership over a corporeal thing (*res mancipi* or *res nec mancipi*) by possessing it for a certain time.

The time was fixed at one year for movables, two years for immovables. The brevity of the time comes as a surprise to us if we remember how eagerly Roman law strove to preserve and to protect vested rights. However, *usucapio* goes back to the Twelve Tables (though under that code it did not yet amount to a true acquisition of ownership) and within the comparatively small area of the primitive Roman State the short time of one or two years could hardly endanger ownership, particularly as *usucapio* of stolen things was not allowed. But even in the classical period the time was not regarded as too short (thus expressly Gai. 2. 44) since *usucapio* was kept within very narrow limits, *res furtivae* and *res vi possessae* being incapable of *usucapio*, even if they were in the hands or a *bonae fidei possessor*. Under classical law the scope of *furtum* was very wide, as it comprehended embezzlement and *furtum usus* (below, s. 981). When a thing which had been borrowed or deposited was alienated by the borrower or depositary, this was as a rule *furtum* and rendered the thing incapable of *usucapio*. A *servus fugitivus* was regarded as a *fur sui* and for that reason could not be usucapted even by a *bonae fidei possessor*. To be sure, *furtum* was confined to movables by the dominant classical doctrine; but land taken from the owner by force could not be usucapted even if it was later acquired by another in good faith.

622.
Definition
of usucapio

623.
Tempus
usucapio-
nis. Res
furtivae et
vi possessae

624.   Thus as a rule *usucapio* took place only when the owner
Function   himself had alienated a thing, but had failed to make the
of usucapio recipient quiritary owner. The two standard cases were:

1. A quiritary owner alienated a *res mancipi* by *traditio*;
    the recipient acquired quiritary ownership by *usu-
    capio*.
2. A peregrine alienated a *res mancipi*, handing it over
    to a Roman citizen by *traditio*. It was only by *usucapio*
    that the recipient could become quiritary owner.

This was the main function of classical *usucapio* and in cases
like these the time of one or two years was indeed too long
rather than too short. *Usucapio* could only arise rarely in
other cases since the character of the object as *res furtiva* or
res vi possessa as a rule prevented it. Gaius (2. 50) gives the
following case: A depositary of a movable thing died and
his heir who knew nothing of the deposit sold the thing and
conveyed it to the buyer. The latter did not acquire ownership by *traditio* or *mancipatio* even if he was in good faith
('nemo plus iuris transferre potest quam ipse habet'; above,
s. 620), but he might acquire it by *usucapio*, since the heir
did not commit *furtum* by alienating the thing in good faith.
Gaius' statement: 'In rebus mobilibus non facile procedit,
ut bonae fidei possessori usucapio competat' is not quite
accurate, since no attention is paid to the two standard
cases; but apart from that it is true and highly characteristic
for the classical law (above, s. 581).

625.   A further requirement of *usucapio* was a *iustus titulus* or
Titulus   *iusta causa usucapionis*. Unfortunately it is not quite clear
(causa)
usucapionis what this meant under classical law. The relevant texts in
Justinian's compilations are heavily interpolated and Gaius
(2. 42 ff.) does not touch the question. Moreover, as
D. (41. 3) 27 shows, there was a controversy on this very
issue among the lawyers of the second century. In such a
case we can hardly hope to obtain full certainty from available sources. A satisfactory definition of *titulus* or *causa
usucapionis* can hardly be given; let us merely consider the
following typical cases.

1. Suppose that a testator left a horse (*res mancipi*) to L by

a *legatum per vindicationem* (above, s. 555) and that L accepted the legacy and took the horse into his possession. In normal circumstances L would have acquired ownership, but let us assume that in this case the testator was not the owner of the horse. Then the legacy was void (above, s. 555), but nevertheless it afforded a *iustus titulus* (or *iusta causa*) *usucapionis*. L might acquire ownership after the lapse of one year provided he was in good faith and the horse was not a *res furtiva* (*usucapio pro legato*, D. 41. 8).

2. The owner of a horse abandoned it (*derelictio*; below, s. 631. 2) and B took it into his possession, wishing thereby to acquire ownership (*occupatio*; below, s. 631). B did not acquire ownership since *derelictio* of a *res mancipi* left the ownership of the *derelinquens* intact, but B might acquire quiritary ownership by *usucapio*, *derelictio* being a *iustus titulus usucapionis* (*usucapio pro derelicto*, D. 41. 7). Or suppose that A abandoned a dog (*res nec mancipi*) which B took into his possession. If A was the owner of the dog, he would have lost ownership by *derelictio* and B would have acquired it by *occupatio*. But if A was not the owner, then B could not acquire ownership by *occupatio* but might acquire it by *usucapio* (*pro derelicto*).

3. Somebody acquired possession by *mancipatio* or *traditio* but without becoming the quiritary owner. Suppose A owed a slave to B on the strength of a stipulation and handed the slave over to B by *traditio*. As the slave was *res mancipi*, B did not become quiritary owner by *traditio*, but *traditio solutionis causa* was a *titulus usucapionis* which the lawyers briefly termed *titulus pro soluto*. Further, suppose that A owed a slave to B on the strength of a stipulation and mancipated the slave to B, but that A was not the owner of the slave. Again B might acquire ownership by *usucapio pro soluto*. Similarly *usucapio pro dote* (D. 41. 9) took place when a thing was given *dotis causa* by *mancipatio* or *traditio*; *usucapio pro donato* (D. 41. 6) if a thing was given *donationis causa*; *usucapio pro emptore* (D. 41. 4) if a thing was given *venditionis causa*. In these cases the lawyers did not speak of *usucapio pro mancipato* or *pro tradito* but of *usucapio pro soluto*, *pro dote*, *pro donato*, *pro emptore*, but these were

merely abbreviations of *usucapio pro mancipato* (or *tradito*) *solutionis causa* and so on. The dominant doctrine of the second and third centuries apparently did not require for the title *pro soluto* that the relevant debt should exist, or for the title *pro dote* that marriage should be concluded, or for the title *pro emptore* that the contract of sale should be valid; but the earlier lawyers may have decided differently.

4. A real title (*titulus verus*) was required and it was not sufficient that the possessor believed in good faith that the title existed. However, Julian apparently held that in special cases it was sufficient that the possessor believed in the existence of the title (what modern lawyers call a 'putative title', *titulus putativus*). It is hardly credible that Julian abandoned entirely the requirement of a *titulus verus*; but on this issue it is impossible to reach any certainty since all texts which regard a putative title as sufficient are interpolated and we cannot reconstruct their original wording.

626. Bona fides A further requirement of classical *usucapio* was that of good faith on the part of the possessor at the time when he acquired *possessio*; it was irrelevant whether or not he realized later that he was not entitled to possess the thing. Modern students express this rule in the maxim *mala fides superveniens non nocet*.

627. Successio in usucapionem. Accessio temporis When after the year's or two years' time had begun to run, for example, after six months had elapsed, the thing changed its possessor, we have to distinguish two different cases.

1. The possessor died and the thing came into the possession of the heir. In this case the heir succeeded *in usucapionem*; in other words, he continued the *usucapio* begun by his predecessor. Thus if the thing in our example was a movable, he became owner after the lapse of another half-year even if he was not in good faith (*mala fides superveniens non nocet*).

2. The possessor of a thing, having possessed it for six months, alienated it, e.g. *solutionis causa*. Then a new *usucapio* began, since the new possessor was not successor to his predecessor (the classical lawyers knew no singular or particular succession; above, s. 369). Good faith of the

recipient was required at the time when he took possession of the thing, and the six months which had already passed in favour of his predecessor did not benefit him. Justinian finally granted him *accessio possessionis* so that henceforth he needed only six months' possession in order to accomplish *usucapio* (below, s. 782).

A special kind of *usucapio* was *usucapio pro herede*. It was originally *usucapio hereditatis* (*hereditas* = *ius successionis*; above, s. 375), and for that reason only one year's possession was required, whether the objects contained in the inheritance were immovables or movables. In classical times it was only a *usucapio* of the single objects, but the traditional time of one year was retained, so that even land belonging to the inheritance could be usucapted after the lapse of one year. Neither title nor good faith was required. We will not dwell on the conjectures which have been brought forward on the origin of this sort of *usucapio*. In classical times its function was merely to force the true heir to come to an early decision as to whether or not he wished to accept the inheritance (Gai. 2. 55; above, s. 500). On the strength of an unknown *senatusconsultum* under Hadrian the effect of a *usucapio pro herede* could be cancelled by *in integrum restitutio* (above, s. 117), but apparently only if the possessor was not in good faith.

A *fundus provincialis* could not be usucapted even by a Roman citizen, since it was incapable of being in quiritary ownership (above, s. 588). However, a rescript of Septimius Severus and Caracalla (A.D. 199) protected a person who had possessed such land for ten or twenty years (ten years *inter praesentes*, i.e. if both plaintiff and defendant lived in the same *civitas*; twenty years *inter absentes*). The emperors, having in mind the *extraordinaria cognitio*, granted the possessor a *praescriptio*, a defence which in the formulary procedure would have been called *exceptio* (above, s. 95). This meant that the possessor was now regarded as the owner of the land, though, of course, not the quiritary owner, since more than legally protected possession of a *fundus provincialis* was not possible (above, ss. 587, 591. 4). Title and good faith (*iustum initium*) were required

628.
Usucapio
pro herede

629. Longi
temporis
praescriptio

as for *usucapio*, but in contrast to *usucapio* only uncontested possession was held sufficient and *accessio possessionis* (above, s. 627. 2) was generally admitted. The *praescriptio* was called *longi temporis* (or *longae possessionis*) *praescriptio*.

630. Justinian's law

The post-classical development lies outside the scope of this book. Justinian amalgamated *usucapio* and *longi temporis praescriptio* since any land situated within Justinian's empire was now capable of being in full Roman ownership. He fixed the period of possession at three years for movables and at ten or twenty years for immovables (*inter praesentes* now meant parties living in the same province). The compilers of the *Institutes*, the *Digest*, and the *Codex* attempted to carry through these innovations by innumerable interpolations. They wished to confine the term *usucapio* to movables; for *usucapio* of immovables they used *longa possessione capio*, *longi temporis praescriptio*, or similar phrases. Thus, whenever they found in pre-Justinianic sources *usucapio fundi*, they replaced *usucapio* by *longa possessione capio* or a similar term; sometimes they even altered the text in this way when it spoke generally of a *usucapio rei*. It goes without saying that whenever we find *longi temporis praescriptio* (in any form whatever) in writings earlier than A.D. 199 we face interpolations; but even later lawyers rarely mentioned *longi temporis praescriptio*. Of course the compilers had also to cancel the classical *annus* or *biennium*; they replaced them by *statutum tempus*, thereby referring to Justinian's constitution *C*. 7. 31.

SOURCES

ss. 623, 624. Read XII Tab. vi. 3 (*FIRA* i, p. 44) with Kaser, *Eigentum*, 86 ff.); Gai. 2. 42, 44, 45, 50, 51, first sentence; *D*. (47. 2) 61.

s. 626. Read Gai. 2. 49–51; *D*. (41. 1) 48. 1.

s. 627. Read *D*. (41. 4) 2. 19, first sentence; (41. 3) 40 and 43 pr.; *C*. (7. 31) 1. 3.

s. 628. Read Gai. 2. 52–8.

s. 629. Read the rescript of Severus and Caracalla in Bruns, *Fontes*, no. 87; *FIRA* i, no. 84 and no. 851; Paul. *Sent.* (5. 2) 4.

s. 630. Cf. *Inst. Iust.* (2. 6) 7 with *D*. (41. 3) 38; cf. Gai. 2. 44 with *D*. (41. 3) 1: [*Bono publico*]; [*quarundam*]; [*et fere semper*]; [*statuti temporis*] ⟨*anni aut biennii*⟩. In *D*. (41. 3) 9 *maxime* was added because the compilers wished to confine *usucapio* to movables.

BIBLIOGRAPHY

ss. 622 ff. Bonfante, *Corso*, ii. 2 (1928), 204 ff.

ss. 622, 623. Kaser, *Eigentum und Besitz im älteren röm. Recht* (1943), 86 ff., 293 ff., 313 ff. On the *servus fugitivus* see Buckland, *Roman Law of Slavery* (1908), 31, 271.

s. 625. Bonfante, *Scritti*, ii (1918), 469 ff.; Beseler, Z xlv (1925), 225 ff.; Schulz, Z lii (1932), 547 f.; van Oven, 'Iusta causa usucapiendi', T xvi (1939), 435 ff.; Collinet, 'Iusta causa et bona fides dans l'usucapion d'après les Institutes de Gaius', *Mélanges Fournier* (1929); Voci, *St. Ratti* (1934), 369 ff.; Kaser, l.c. 295.*

s. 625. 1. Beseler, l.c. 226 n. 1; Ciapessoni, *St. Bonfante*, iii (1930), 692 ff.

s. 625. 2. H. Krüger, 'Derelictio und usucapio', *Mnemosyna Pappulias* (1934), 155 ff.; Kaser, l.c. 105, with references.

s. 626. Van Oven, l.c. 434 ff.; Levet, *RH* xii (1933), 1 ff.; Kaser, l.c. 296 ff., with references.

s. 627. Zanzucchi, 'La successio e l'accessio possessionis nell' usu-capione', *AG* lxxii (1904), 177 ff.; 'Sulla storia dell' accessio possessionis nell' usucapione', *AG* lxxvi (1906), 3 ff.; Beseler, Z lxvi (1948), 349.

s. 628. Beseler, Z xlv (1925), 229; Solazzi, *Diritto ereditario Romano*, i (1932), 61 ff., 169 ff.; ii (1933), 140 ff.; Collinet, 'Les variations de l'usucapion pro herede avant Hadrien', *St. Riccobono*, iv (1936), 131 ff.; H. Krüger, Z liv (1934), 80 ff.; Kaser, l.c. 48, with references.*

s. 629. Partsch, *Die longi temporis praescriptio im klass. röm. Recht* (1906); Mitteis, *Grundzüge* (1912), 286; *Chrestomathie*, no. 374; *FIRA* I, pp. 437 ff.; Taubenschlag, *Law of Greco-Roman Egypt* (1944), 184.

s. 630. E. Levy, 'Die nachklassische Ersitzung', *Bull.* x and xi. (1948), 352 ff.

5. *Other modes of acquiring ownership*

i. *Occupatio*

Ownership could be acquired by taking possession of a thing with the intent to acquire ownership. If we leave aside the occupation of *res hostiles*, which was partly regulated by public law, we may state that only those things which had no owner could be acquired by occupation (*res nullius*). The two main groups were the following:

1. Wild animals (game, fishes, birds) were *res nullius* as long as they enjoyed their natural freedom. There was no game law or fishery law, in particular the right of hunting and fishing was not reserved to landowners; thus if somebody entered the estate of another and captured game, he

631.
Occupatio

acquired ownership. This law, as already stated (s. 582), is in harmony with Roman liberalism.

2. *Res derelictae*. Things in ownership might become *res nullius* when their owner abandoned them. However, ownership of *res mancipi* was not lost by *derelictio*, and the person who took possession of them could only acquire ownership by *usucapio*; otherwise the rule 'ownership of *res mancipi* cannot be transferred by *traditio*' might have been easily evaded by combining *derelictio* with *occupatio*. It has been asserted that *res nec mancipi* became *res nullius* by *derelictio*, but that nevertheless ownership could not be acquired by occupation; under classical law this seems hardly credible.

Things that had been lost remained the property of their owners and could not even be acquired by *usucapio*. The finder had to restore them and was not entitled to demand a reward.

ii. *Thesaurus*

632.
Thesaurus

Treasure trove was certainly not open to occupation nor did it fall to the State, but our knowledge of the classical law is poor. Only things hidden in land were taken into consideration; secret drawers were apparently not yet known. In republican and early classical law a treasure was probably regarded as *pars fundi*, but under a constitution of Hadrian it fell to both the finder and the owner of the land, the two taking equal shares. Unfortunately, we know of this constitution only through the short and not quite reliable report given in Justinian's *Institutes* (2. 1. 39). Above all, what is *thesaurus*? The definition given in the *Digest* is faulty and unworkable.

D. (41. 1) 31. 1. 'Thesaurus est vetus quaedam depositio pecuniae, cuius non extat memoria, ut iam dominum non habeat.'

The assertion that the treasure has no owner is certainly inaccurate, since as a rule there would be an owner according to the Roman law of succession, though he could not be identified: *non deficit ius sed probatio*. Further, *pecuniae* is faulty, as a treasure might consist, for example, of jewellery. *Depositio* is a clumsy expression, since treasure is not a *depositio pecuniae* (i.e. a depositing of money) but rather *pecunia deposita*. The whole definition seems to be of post-classical origin and should no longer be used as a basis for any theories regarding *thesaurus*.

iii. *Increment by rivers*

Owners of land which was situated along a public river might acquire ownership through the natural action of the river.

1. The silt deposited by the river on its banks accrued to the respective landowners (*per alluvionem*). When a definite piece of land was torn away by the river (what modern lawyers call *avulsio*) and swept to another part of the bank, the owner of that part of the bank did not become owner of it until it had grown into the bank.

2. When new land was created by the river in the form of an island (*insula in flumine nata*), it accrued to the riparian owners; but the rules laid down by the lawyers are so vague and primitive that we cannot clearly discern how it was apportioned between them.

3. If the river left its bed entirely, the original bed (*alveus derelictus*) accrued to the riparian owners in the same way as a new island. None of the three modes of acquisition applied when the land of the riparian owners had been measured by official surveyors (*agri limitati*). In such cases the increment was *res nullius* and open to occupation.

iv. *Acquisition of ownership by accession and by specification*

This part of classical law has a rather odd appearance. The lawyers discussed the relevant issues with enthusiasm, but the result of their work is very far from being a glorious achievement. Important questions remained controversial and their discussions are often curiously academic and unpractical. They were perhaps influenced to some slight extent by Hellenistic philosophy, but fresh and more critical inquiries into both philosophical and legal sources are needed to determine the point. It was, however, just the scholastic character of these doctrines which rendered them dear to the law schools of late antiquity as well as of the Middle Ages; thus they lived on, though more in textbooks than in practice, and unfortunately influenced European legislators down to our own times. To be sure the classical lawyers were the first to deal with these vexed though hardly important problems and for that reason their doctrines deserve remembering. Moreover, the scholasticism of the classical law school is a phenomenon which must not be overlooked by critical historians of classical jurisprudence. Unfortunately, however, the available texts are marred by numerous interpolations; modern scholars, by repeated investigations, have proved so much, but in reconstructing the classical doctrines with anything like certainty they have not been, and perhaps cannot be, entirely successful. In these circumstances we may confine ourselves to some individual examples in order to illustrate the problems and the way in which the classical lawyers attempted to tackle them.

635.
Implantatio
1. *Implantatio*. Suppose that A, the owner of a piece of land, planted in his ground plants or trees belonging to B without the latter's consent. The plants or trees remained in B's ownership, but if they took root, A became the owner whether or not he acted in good faith. B could not demand separation, and even if A separated the plants, the ownership did not revert to B. A just and accurate separation of the plants from the soil seemed impossible to the lawyers since the plants had already extracted an undefinable quantity of nutritious substance from the soil: an almost incredible piece of academic pedantry. Moreover, it must be emphasized that B had no *condictio* against A on account of the latter's enrichment; if A did not act in good faith he was of course liable for *furtum*.

Suppose that A was not the owner but only the possessor of a piece of land which belonged to B. A planted his own plants in this ground. B became the owner of the plants as soon as they took root. A could not demand separation and if he himself separated the plants, he did not become their owner. But if B sued A with the *rei vindicatio* for recovery of the land, A might demand reimbursement of his expenses on the strength of an *exceptio doli* (above, s. 96) if he was in good faith, although an action for repayment did not lie.

One must confess that a more unpractical regulation of these simple cases could hardly be conceived.

636.
Inaedificatio
2. *Inaedificatio*. Suppose A built a house on his own ground with materials which belonged wholly or partly

to B. Though A became the owner of the building (*super-ficies solo cedit*), B remained the owner of the materials. However, B could not demand separation since the Twelve Tables (vi. 8) expressly provided *Tignum iunctum aedibus ne solvito* and the classical lawyers regarded *tignum* as covering building materials of any kind. If the materials were stolen, B had under the Twelve Tables an *actio de tigno iuncto* even if A was in good faith; this was a penal action (above, s. 72) with which B might obtain double the value of the materials; a *condictio* on account of unjustified enrichment was not available to B. Thus B's ownership of the materials was a dormant ownership; but if the building came down by accident or was deliberately demolished by A, then B's ownership 'awoke' and he might claim the materials with the *rei vindicatio*. Hence in this case *inaedificatio* did not entail acquisition of ownership of the materials by A and for that reason it is not mentioned by Gaius (2. 73).

Now let us suppose that A was only possessor of a piece of land which belonged to B. A built a house on the land with his own materials. In contrast to the first case B became at once the owner of the materials (Gai. 2. 73), and even if the house was demolished later, they did not revert to A; but if B sued A with the *rei vindicatio*, A might obtain compensation on the strength of an *exceptio doli generalis* if he was in good faith. But a *condictio* was not available to A.

These rules concerning *inaedificatio* are rendered still more difficult by the fact that they do not apply to all movables firmly connected with immovables, and it is impossible to find a workable principle. The rule that 'all things belong to the house *quibus aedes perficiantur*' (*D.* 50. 16. 245) is certainly unworkable (what about stoves, book-shelves, machines?).

As regards the connecting of movable things with each other we refer to the text-books; the classical law remains to a large extent obscure.

637. Connecting movable things with each other

3. *Specificatio*. *Specificatio* is the fashioning of materials into new product. The term *specificatio* (as well as *specificare*) is absent from our sources but was already used by the

638. Specificatio

Bolognese Glossators. The classical lawyers spoke of *speciem facere* (only once, *D.* 41. 1. 7. 7 *novam speciem facere*).

According to Labeo, Proculus, and the Proculians the manufacturer became the owner of the product even if he was not the owner of the materials, provided that he did the work for himself (*suo nomine*) and not for another who gave him the materials for that purpose. The Sabinians always attributed the product to the owner of the materials. Justinian adopted the following solution. The owner of the materials becomes the owner of the product, if the product can be reduced to the original materials; if that is not possible, the worker becomes the owner of the product. It is conceivable that Justinian's theory or a similar theory was advocated in classical times, but the relevant texts are not reliable. According to Justinian's *media sententia* a baker became the owner of the bread which he baked using somebody else's flour, since the bread could not be reduced to flour; but an artist who made a statue of bronze did not become the owner of the statue since it could be reduced to bronze.

All the three theories are crude and primitive in that they say nothing about the indemnification of the party who suffers loss from the acquisition of the thing by the other party; this is the main issue, whereas the question of ownership is less important. Further, no regard is paid to the good or bad faith of the manufacturer. Finally, Proculus' theory as well as that adopted by Justinian leaves unsolved the question as to what constitutes a new thing. Deep philosophic or economic speculations certainly did not lie at the bottom of these theories. It is erroneous to regard the Proculian theory as an offshoot of Aristotle's natural philosophy and the Sabinian doctrine as stimulated by Stoic theories. Nor, on the other hand, were the Proculians the protectors of labour and the Sabinians the champions of capital.

SOURCES

s. 631. Read Gai. 2. 66–8; *D.* (41. 1) 5. 1; *D.* (41. 7) 2, *rem* ⟨*nec mancipi*⟩; (6. 1) 67.

s. 632. Read *D*. (41. 1) 31. 1; *Inst. Iust.* (2. 1) 39: *D*. (41. 2) 3. 3.

s. 633. Read Gai. 2. 70–2; *D*. (41. 1) 7. 2–5 to *iuris gentium*; (43. 12) 1. 6.

s. 635. Read Gai. 2. 74–6; *D*. (41. 1) 7. 13; (41. 1) 9 pr.; (41. 1) 26. 1.

s. 636. Read *D*. (41. 1) 7. 10; Gai. 2. 73; *D*. (41. 1) 7. 12 [*et si scit . . . itaque*]; [*nam si scit . . . alienum*].

s. 638. Read Gai. 2. 79; *D*. (24. 1) 29. 1; (41. 1) 7. 7 [*est tamen . . . reverti possunt*]; (41. 1) 24 and 26 pr. to *corpus fieret* (hardly genuine).

BIBLIOGRAPHY

s. 631. Kaser, *PW*, Suppl. vii. 682 ff., with full references; Z lxv (1947), 220.*

s. 632. Beseler, *Beiträge*, iv (1920), 162; Z lvi (1936), 62 f.; Bonfante, *Corso*, ii. 2 (1928), 95 ff., with references; G. Hill, 'Treasure-Trove, the law and practice of Antiquity', *Proceedings of the Brit. Academy*, xix (1933), 219 ff.; Kübler, *PW* viA. 7 ff.

s. 633. Bonfante, l.c. 89 ff.; Kaser, l.c. 686; Z lxv (1947), 229.

s. 634. P. Sokolowski, *Die Philosophie im Privatrecht*, I. *Sachbegriff und Körper* (1902); Karl Reinhardt, *Kosmos u. Sympathie. Neue Untersuchungen über Poseidonios* (1926), 5 ff., 34 ff.; Guarneri Citati, *Reviviscenza e quiescenza nel diritto Romano* (1927), 33 ff.; 'La cosidetta accessione separabile e i suoi effetti nel diritto romano', *Annali Palermo*, xiv (1930); Bonfante, *Corso*, ii. 2 (1928), 68 ff.; Kaser, Z lxv. 226 ff.

s. 635. Bonfante, l.c. 86; Kaser, Z lxv. 227.

s. 636. Riccobono, 'Dal diritto romano classico al diritto moderno', *Annali Palermo*, iii/iv (1917), 445 ff., 508 ff., 652 ff.; Bonfante, l.c. 87 ff.; Beseler, *Beiträge*, iv (1920), 298; Kaser, Z lxv. 232 ff.

s. 637. Kaser, l.c. 232 ff.*

s. 638. Bonfante, l.c. 116 ff.; Weiss, *PW* iiiA. 1551; Kaser, l.c. 242.

6. *Judicial protection of ownership*

At this point we will only describe the *actiones rem per-* _{639.} *sequentes* by which an owner might protect his property; we ^{Survey} leave aside the penal actions (in particular *actio furti* and *legis Aquiliae*), the *condictio furtiva*, and the possessory interdicts. Further, we confine ourselves to the classical ordinary, i.e. formulary procedure, since our knowledge of the classical *extraordinaria cognitio* (above, s. 20) is as yet very inadequate. We shall therefore deal with the following remedies: i. *Rei vindicatio*; ii. *Interdictum quem fundum* and *actio ad exhibendum*; iii. *Actio negatoria* (or *negativa*); iv. *Actio Publiciana* (and *exceptio rei venditae et traditae*).

i. *Rei vindicatio*

640. The classical *rei vindicatio* was an action by which the
Conception plaintiff, on the strength of his quiritary ownership, de-
of rei
vindicatio manded the restitution of a thing from the defendant who
had the thing in his possession. It had two alternative forms
of procedure, *per sponsionem* and *per formulam petitoriam*.

641. Rei   1. *Rei vindicatio per sponsionem*. This procedure was
vindicatio archaic in character. It began with a wager of law or
per
sponsionem *sponsio*, the defendant promising to pay a nominal sum of
money to the plaintiff if the latter was in truth the quiritary
owner of the vindicated thing. From this *sponsio* an action
resulted for the payment of the promised sum; this action
was a normal *actio in personam* (above, s. 56). The parties in
this action reached *litis contestatio* as usual (above, s. 17) and
the plaintiff had then to prove his quiritary ownership
before the judge. If he succeeded, the judge condemned
the defendant to pay the nominal sum. This sum, however,
was not really paid, for the *sponsio* was only made in order
to bring the issue of ownership before the judge, who by
his judgment on the wager incidentally decided on the question of the quiritary ownership of the plaintiff. The *sponsio*
was, for that reason, called *sponsio praeiudicialis* (above,
s. 88). In addition to this *sponsio* the parties made *in iure*
another *sponsio* in which the defendant promised with
sureties to restore the vindicated thing (including fruits)
should he be defeated in the trial concerning the *sponsio
praeiudicialis*. This second *sponsio* was called *sponsio pro
praede litis et vindiciarum*. Let us now suppose that the
defendant was defeated in the trial regarding the *sponsio*.
As a rule he would restore the thing to the plaintiff, since
the judgment implicitly affirmed the ownership of the
plaintiff; if he refused to do so, the plaintiff had to sue him
and the sureties with another *actio in personam* on the
strength of the *sponsio pro praede*.

This procedure originated in republican times when the
legis actio sacramento was still in full vigour and had a special
purpose which we will not discuss here. But it was preserved throughout the whole classical period and dis-

appeared only in post-classical times. It is never mentioned
in Justinian's compilations; the compilers either cancelled
or interpolated the relevant texts. Thus we know very little
more of the *vindicatio per sponsionem* than what Gaius (4. 93)
tells us; nevertheless, its function under classical law is discernible. The trial on the *sponsio praeiudicialis* could be
brought to an end in a comparatively short time, since the
judge was only concerned to decide whether or not the
plaintiff was the owner. He did not need to trouble himself
with stating what the defendant was bound to restore
(fruits and damages) or with estimating its value, as he had
to do in the *vindicatio per formulam petitoriam* (below,
s. 643). Moreover, he was not concerned with *exceptiones*
since in the *sponsio praeiudicialis* there was no room for an
exceptio. If the judge came to the conclusion that the plaintiff was the owner and accordingly condemned the defendant to pay the nominal sum, the latter as a rule restored
the vindicated thing spontaneously as the result of his
defeat, and no further trial followed. Thus the *vindicatio
per sponsionem* was even under classical law a very service-
able remedy in spite of its archaic aspect. Of course it was
only suitable if the plaintiff's ownership was the sole issue
in question; if the defendant wished to defend himself with
an *exceptio*, the *vindicatio per formulam petitoriam* was the
right remedy.

2. *Rei vindicatio per formulam petitoriam*. We have already
given the text of the *formula* and explained its structure
(above, ss. 58, 68). The parties accomplished the *formula
in iure* (perhaps inserting an *exceptio* and *replicatio*; above,
ss. 91, 105) and effected *litis contestatio* (above, s. 17). They
then appeared before the judge, pleaded their case, and
brought forth their respective evidence. The plaintiff was
in particular bound to prove his quiritary ownership which
was sometimes a hard task, since classical law knew no
acquisition of ownership on the strength of the good faith
of the transferee (*nemo plus iuris*, etc.; above, s. 620) and
usucapio was kept within narrow limits (above, s. 623).
Medieval lawyers styled this proof *probatio diabolica* (in the
medieval miracle-plays the devil attempted to prove that

642. Rei
vindicatio
per
formulam
petitoriam

a soul belonged to him and generally failed); however, as the classical judge was perfectly free in his evaluation of the evidence, he might regard the ownership as proven, if a certain degree of probability was reached. The classical lawyers as usual had no eyes for this difficulty, since they were not concerned with questions of evidence.

Where the judge came to the conclusion that the plaintiff was right and that the defendant should consequently restore the thing (*restituere*), he did not at once proceed to the *condemnatio pecuniaria* (above, s. 36) but, on the strength of the clause *nisi restituetur*, pronounced an *arbitrium* in which he ordered specific restitution (above, s. 68). Placing a liberal construction on that clause, he not only ordered the restitution of the vindicated thing, but also awarded fruits and damages; on the other hand, he bound the plaintiff to compensate a *bonae fidei possessor* for his expenses. On the whole question of this *restituere* the classical lawyers evolved a fine network of rules based on the distinction between *bonae* and *malae fidei possessor*, but we will not dwell upon these details which are still to some extent uncertain.

643.
Iusiuran-
dum in
litem
When the defendant obeyed the *arbitrium* and made restitution, the procedure was ended. But if he remained obstinate, the judge had to pronounce the *condemnatio pecuniaria* (above, s. 36). For that purpose he had to find out the value of what the defendant was bound to restore according to the *arbitrium*; but he might leave it to the plaintiff to fix the value by a declaration on oath. This *iusiurandum in litem* was an expedient designed to hasten condemnation, as it spared the judge a wearisome and lengthy task. The idea was not to compel the defendant to make specific restitution by threatening him with an assessment made by the plaintiff himself, who might considerably exceed the real value. Modern historians as usual underrate Roman *fides* and piety. To be sure the Roman principle was *deorum iniuria diis curae*, but even an average Roman did not forswear himself lightly.

644. The
plaintiff
expro-
priated?
Finally the judge pronounced judgment, condemning the defendant to pay a certain amount of money to the plaintiff. The thing which the plaintiff had vindicated as

his own remained with the defendant and the plaintiff could not sue him a second time with the *rei vindicatio*. But was the defendant now the owner of the thing? The question is generally answered in the affirmative; the defendant, it is said, acquired bonitary (praetorian) ownership, the plaintiff was expropriated. This theory goes perhaps too far. On the other hand, we must not say simply that the plaintiff remained the owner and the defendant acquired no right whatever over the thing. If that were true, the condemned defendant could not make any use of the thing. If he reaped fruits, the plaintiff might demand them with a *vindicatio fructuum*; if the thing was movable, the plaintiff might sue him with an *actio furti*. Thus the *condemnatio pecuniaria* would have been senseless. The condemned defendant must have been protected by the praetor, like an owner, at any rate against the plaintiff. However, the interpolated sources need a fresh examination.

The *rei vindicatio* (*per sponsionem* as well as *per formulam petitoriam*) lay only against a person who possessed the vindicated thing at the time of the *litis contestatio*. If he was not *possessor* at that time, he could not be sued with that action, even if he had deliberately given up possession (*si dolo desiit possidere*). So much is certain; the question, however, as to what kind of possession was required cannot be answered with absolute certainty. Most probably only a possessor invested with the possessory interdicts (below, s. 753) could be sued with the *rei vindicatio* and not also a mere *detentor* (see below, s. 754) like a lessee, a depositary, or a borrower. Suppose that A was the owner of a house, that B was *possessor*, and that C had rented the house by a contract with B. Under classical law A might sue B with the *rei* vindicatio, but probably not C. If the owner of the house had himself let the house, he might sue his lessee with the *actio locati* (*ex contractu*), but certainly not with the *rei vindicatio*.

645. Possession of the defendant

The praetor might make sure that the defendant was in possession, and if he found out that he was not, he refused the *vindicatio*, but he can hardly have required that the movable thing should be brought before him. To be sure,

646. Presence of the thing in iure

the presence of the vindicated thing was indispensable in
the old *vindicatio per legis actionem*, but in old republican
times the compass of the Roman State was small; under
classical law this requirement would have implied considerable and quite unnecessary trouble.

> Imagine that two peasants A and B lived in a village in upper Italy.
> A wished to vindicate an ox from B. Both A and B travel to Rome, appear
> before the praetor, and ask for the *formula petitoria*. The praetor answers:
> 'First bring me the ox.' The defendant travels back to his village and
> eventually appears with the ox before the praetor. Now the *formula* is
> composed and the judge appointed, a matter which in this case is a mere
> formality and is finished in a few minutes. Then the defendant has to
> take the ox back to his village. This is an absurdity with which we cannot
> credit the classical praetor. Beseler's theory that the presence of a movable
> *in iure* was invariably required for its *vindicatio* cannot possibly be right.

647. Actio
in rem

The *rei vindicatio* in both forms (*per sponsionem* and *per
formulam petitoriam*) was an *actio in rem*, as Gaius 4. 91
expressly says. We have already explained the classical
meaning of that term (above, s. 56). The peculiarity of an
actio in rem lay in the procedure *in iure*, the defendant not
being bound to defend the vindicated thing. This is particularly apparent in the *vindicatio per sponsionem*. The
actions resulting from the *sponsio praeiudicialis* as well as
from the *sponsio pro praede* were both *actiones in personam*,
but as the defendant was not bound to engage these *sponsiones*, the *vindicatio per sponsionem* was termed an *actio in
rem*. If the defendant refused to defend the vindicated
thing either by making the *sponsiones* or accepting the
formula petitoria, he had to abandon it to the plaintiff. If
the thing was movable and present *in iure* the praetor pronounced a *iussum duci vel ferri rem ab actore*; if it was not
present or was an immovable, then two other remedies
came in which we have now to consider.

ii. *Interdictum quem fundum* and *actio ad exhibendum*

648. Inter-
dictum
quem
fundum

The praetorian Edict had under the title *de interdictis* a
rubric: 'a quo fundus petetur, si rem nolit defendere'
(Lenel, *Edict.* § 248). The praetor there promised an interdict to cover a case in which a plaintiff wished to vindicate
an immovable and its possessor declined to defend it (either

by executing the *sponsiones* or by accepting the *formula petitoria*). This interdict no longer existed under Justinian's law and our knowledge of it is therefore poor; but it ran apparently as follows:

> 'Quem fundum ille [the name of the plaintiff had to be inserted; *Aulus Agerius* was deliberately avoided in the form of an interdict, above, s. 111] a te vindicare vult et rem nolis defendere, eum illi restituas.'

It was an *interdictum restitutorium* for the details of which we may refer to our general remarks on *interdicta* (above, ss. 106 ff.). It lay only against a person who might be sued with the *rei vindicatio*, for only of such a person could it be said that he declined to defend the piece of land.

> Lenel's reconstruction of the interdict, though universally accepted, is nevertheless untenable:
>
> > 'Quem fundum ille a te vindicare vult, quem possides dolove malo fecisti quo minus possideres, si rem nolis defendere etc.'
>
> The *rei vindicatio* did not lie against a non-possessor who *dolo desiit possidere*; consequently a *nolle defendere* was out of the question.

The *actio ad exhibendum* was only concerned with movable things and was in some respects a counterpart of the *interdictum quem fundum*. Like the interdict it was available to a person who wished to vindicate a thing. The action lay against any possessor, not only (like the *rei vindicatio*) against a *possessor* protected by the possessory interdicts; moreover, it lay against a non-possessor who had *dolo malo* given up the possession (*qui dolo malo desiit possidere*). It was an *actio in personam* (the defendant was therefore bound to accept the *iudicium*; above, s. 56) and a so-called *actio arbitraria* (above, s. 67); before pronouncing the *condemnatio pecuniaria* the judge ordered the defendant in an *arbitrium* to discover (*exhibere*) the thing (not to restore it). 649. Actio ad exhibendum

The functions of the *actio ad exhibendum* within the sphere of the *rei vindicatio* were threefold:

1. It served as a preparation for the *rei vindicatio*. Perhaps the plaintiff wished to identify the thing before raising the *rei vindicatio*; or the thing was connected with another movable thing and the plaintiff demanded separation in order to vindicate it.

2. It afforded a remedy if the defendant declined to defend the thing against the *rei vindicatio*. When the thing was exhibited the plaintiff might take it into his possession on the strength of the praetorian *iussum duci vel ferri rem ab actore*.

3. Lastly it was a substitute for the *rei vindicatio* against a non-possessor who *dolo desiit possidere* (above, s. 645). An *interdictum quem fundum* against a non-possessor was, as aforesaid (above, s. 648), not required, since the present possessor of a piece of land is always evident, but it is often difficult to find out the present possessor of a movable thing. Thus if the owner could prove that B had been in the possession of the thing (e.g. of a ring) and had later *dolo malo* given up the possession, he might sue B with the *actio ad exhibendum* although, and indeed because, a *rei vindicatio* against him was not available.

iii. *Actio negatoria* (or *negativa*)

650.
Conception of the actio negatoria

It was the negative wording of the *intentio* (above, s. 30) which gave the classical *actio negatoria* or *negativa* its name. Let us consider the following three examples:

1. 'Si paret Numerio Negidio ius non esse, eo fundo quo de agitur, uti frui invito Aulo Agerio neque ea res restituetur, quanti ea res erit, tantam pecuniam iudex Numerium Negidium Aulo Agerio condemnato, si non paret absolvito.'

This is the proper action for an owner of land against a person who claims to have an usufruct over the land while the owner denies the existence of the usufruct.

2. 'Si paret Numerio Negidio ius non esse per fundum quo de agitur ire agere invito Aulo Agerio neque ea res restituetur etc.'

This is the action of an owner of land against a person who unjustly claims to have a right of way over the land.

3. 'Si paret Numerio Negidio ius non esse aedes suas altius tollere invito Aulo Agerio etc.'

This is the action of a landowner against a person who claims to have a right to raise a building on his own ground beyond a certain height, whereas the plaintiff contests that right. But this *formula* covers two fundamentally different cases:

(*a*) The defendant claimed to have a *servitus altius tollendi* over the land of the plaintiff which the latter denied. In this case the *actio negatoria* is as in the preceding cases an action of the owner against a person who pretends to have a servitude over the plaintiff's land.

(*b*) The plaintiff claimed to have a *servitus altius non tollendi* over the defendant's land and the latter denied the existence of that servitude. This is obviously a *vindicatio servitutis* which we shall discuss later (below, s. 692); but this *vindicatio* is an *actio negativa* since the *intentio* of its *formula* is negative.

Here we have only to consider the *actio negatoria* so far as it serves to protect ownership. We may therefore exclude the case 3*b*.

The *actio negatoria* was an *actio in rem* although, against 651. Actio in rem the general rule, the name of the defendant was mentioned in the *intentio* (above, s. 58). Gai. 4. 3 is substantially right, though the text may be corrupt. For this reason the defendant was not bound to accept the *iudicium*; if he declined to do so, he had to abandon the servitude claimed by him. When the servitude was a *servitus praediorum*, the plaintiff had the *interdictum quem fundum* adapted to that case (above, s. 648). When the servitude was a usufruct over a movable thing, the praetor issued a *iussum duci vel ferri rem ab actore* and the plaintiff had the *actio ad exhibendum*. You may ask how the defendant who claimed to have a right of way over the plaintiff's land could abandon the non-existing servitude. In fact he did so by giving a *cautio de non amplius turbando*.

If the defendant accepted the *iudicium* and the judge found that the plaintiff was right, an *arbitrium* was issued as in the *rei vindicatio* which imposed upon the defendant a *restituere*. The defendant had to restore the thing (in the case of an alleged usufruct), to remove a building which he had unlawfully erected and to pay damages. If the defendant did not obey the *arbitrium*, the *condemnatio pecuniaria* took place.

In conclusion we wish to emphasize that the *actio negatoria* did not lie when somebody interfered with the property of another without alleging a right to do so. In such cases the owner was only entitled to the remedies of self-help and the interdicts, not to the *actio negatoria*.

iv. *Actio Publiciana* and *exceptio rei venditae et traditae*

An unknown praetor Publicius, probably of the last cen- 652. The tury B.C., introduced the *actio Publiciana* into the Edict. Edict Leaving aside the republican history of this action we confine ourselves to classical law, viz. to the Edict as it was stabilized under Hadrian (above, s. 25). In this Edict the praetor under the rubric *de Publiciana in rem actione* (Lenel, *Edict*. § 60) promised to grant an action (an *actio honoraria*; above, s. 45) and as usual appended a model *formula*. The edictal promise is only preserved to us in an interpolated text and its reconstruction remains doubtful. Perhaps it simply ran:

> 'Si quis rem sibi traditam ex iusta causa et nondum usucaptam petet, iudicium dabo.'
> 'If anybody claims a thing which was conveyed to him by *traditio* and which he has not yet usucapted, I shall grant him an *actio*.'

The edictal *formula* is reliably given by Gaius (4. 36):

> 'Si quem hominem Aulus Agerius emit et is ei traditus est, anno possedisset,
> tum si eum hominem de quo agitur eius ex iure Quiritium esse oporteret,
> nisi restituetur, quanti ea res erit, tantam pecuniam etc.'
> 'If, supposing that the plaintiff had possessed for a year a slave bought by him and conveyed to him by *traditio* he would be quiritary owner of the slave etc.' *Et is ei traditus est* instead of *quique ei traditus est* is official republican usage: *lex Iul. municip.* 1. 157.

653. Scope   Under classical law the edictal *formula* was only a model *formula* which had to be adapted to other cases, for in classical times the *actio Publiciana* was available to any possessor who could acquire quiritary ownership over the thing in question by *usucapio*. Let us consider the following cases:

1. The quiritary owner of a *res mancipi* (above, s. 604) sold it to B and conveyed it to him by *traditio*. B was now merely possessor, but he might acquire quiritary ownership by *usucapio* if he remained in possession for one or two years (above, s. 623). However, before the end of the *tempus usucapionis* B lost possession and the thing came into the hands of C. B wished to recover the thing from C. The *rei vindicatio* was of course not available to B, since he was not quiritary owner; but the *actio Publiciana* was open to him. By the *formula* the judge was instructed to consider the case under the assumption that B had possessed the thing for the full *tempus usucapionis* and, if under this assumption B

would be quiritary owner on the strength of *usucapio*, to treat C as if the action were a *rei vindicatio*. Thus the judge had only to decide whether the quiritary owner had in fact conveyed the thing to B by *traditio*, for the other conditions of *usucapio* (above, ss. 623 ff., a thing capable of being *usucapted* and *bona fides*) were obviously satisfied in this case.

2. Suppose that a non-owner of a *res mancipi* or *nec mancipi* sold it to B and conveyed it to him by *traditio*. Later B lost possession and the thing came into the possession of C. B might sue C with the *actio Publiciana*. In this case the judge had not only to determine whether the thing had been conveyed to B but also whether B was in good faith and whether the thing was capable of being usucapted (not a *res furtiva vel vi possessa*; above, s. 623). Of course in such a case the defendant C might be the quiritary owner. Since the praetor did not wish to expropriate the quiritary owner, C was entitled to insert an *exceptio dominii* in the *formula*.

The edictal *formula* covered both these cases and was adapted to other similar cases. When B had acquired possession by a *traditio donationis causa*, *dotis causa*, *solutionis causa*, or when B possessed *pro legato* (*per vindicationem*) or *pro derelicto*, an *actio Publiciana utilis* (above, s. 52) was granted to him, since in these cases also B was *possessor ad usucapionem*. We may in summing up say that the purpose of the classical *actio Publiciana* was the protection of a particular type of possession, i.e. of a possession which might lead to *usucapio*; the action was an artificially framed praetorian *rei vindicatio*. A praetorian *actio negatoria* did not exist.

The edictal section *de exceptionibus* contained the form of an *exceptio rei venditae et traditae* (Lenel, *Edict.* § 276) which covered the following two cases.   654. Exceptio rei venditae et traditae

1. The quiritary owner of a *res mancipi* sold and delivered it to B. As the seller remained quiritary owner, he might sue B with the *rei vindicatio*. The praetor, however, protected B by granting him a special *exceptio*: 'si non Aulus Agerius fundum quo de agitur Numerio Negidio vendidit et tradidit'.

2. A non-owner A sold and delivered a *res mancipi* or *nec mancipi* to B. A later acquired quiritary ownership of the thing (e.g. by becoming the heir of the quiritary owner). In this case also B might protect himself with the *exceptio rei venditae et traditae* against the *rei vindicatio* of A.

This exception might function as a *replicatio* against the *exceptio dominii* which we have mentioned above (s. 653). Suppose that A, the quiritary owner of a *res mancipi*, sold and delivered the thing to B. Later B lost possession and the thing eventually returned into A's hands. B now sued A with the *actio Publiciana*. A might object that he was quiritary owner (*exceptio dominii*; above s. 653), but B might reply that A had sold and delivered the thing to him (*replicatio rei venditae et traditae*).

The edictal *exceptio* could be adapted to similar cases. When, for example, A had delivered a thing to B *donationis causa*, B was certainly protected against A's *rei vindicatio* by an *exceptio rei donatae et traditae*.

655.
Bonitary
ownership

Thus there was under classical law a sort of *possessio* protected by the praetor even against the quiritary owner. It was this kind of possession which Gaius felt no scruples about calling a sort of *dominium* and which modern lawyers are wont to call 'bonitary' or 'praetorian ownership'; we may compare it with the *bonorum possessio cum re* (above, s. 378). The classical lawyers apparently avoided the term *dominium* (Gaius' terminology is quite singular) and were content with using the ambiguous term *in bonis esse alicuius*. In the Byzantine law-school such a possessor was already called *dominus bonitarius* (δεσπότης βονιτάριος, Theophilus, *Paraphrasis*, 1. 5. 4).

v. *Justinian's law*

The post-classical development of all these remedies lies outside the scope of this book and a few remarks on Justinian's law must suffice. The classical remedies entirely changed their character and the classical texts inserted in Justinian's compilations are for that reason heavily interpolated.

1. The *arbitrium iudicis* was now an enforceable judg- 656.
ment, but the *condemnatio pecuniaria* was not entirely Praecise
teneri and
abolished. Apparently the compilers wished to give the condem-
plaintiff the choice between specific performance and natio
pecuniaria
damages; but as they have nowhere clearly expressed this
principle, there has been an endless dispute since the times
of the Glossators on the question to what extent the defendant was liable for specific performance (*praecise teneri* was
the medieval term).

2. *Rei vindicatio, actio negatoria*, and *actio Publiciana* were 657. Actio
still called *actiones in rem* and this term still implied that the in rem
defendant was not bound to defend the thing in a trial. But
if he declined to defend it, the remedies open to the plaintiff
were simplified; the *interdictum quem fundum* entirely disappeared.

3. The *rei vindicatio* was assimilated to the *actio ad exhi-* 658. Rei
bendum. Like the latter, *rei vindicatio* now lay against any vindicatio
and actio
possessor who had *facultas restituendi* and even against a ad exhiben-
person who *dolo desiit possidere*. dum

4. With the disappearance of the categories *res mancipi* 659. Res
and *res nec mancipi* the sphere both of the *actio Publiciana* mancipi
and nec
and the *exceptio rei venditae et traditae* was considerably mancipi
narrowed.

These are the main alterations which any reader of the
sources must bear in mind.

SOURCES

s. 641. Read Gai. 4. 93, 94.
s. 645. Read *D.* (6. 1) 9 [*puto . . . posse*]. See *Index Interpol.*
s. 647. Read *D.* (2. 3) 1. 1.
s. 648. Read *Ulp. Inst. Vindobon.* fr. IV (Seckel–Kübler, i. 494).
s. 654. Read *D.* (6. 1) 72 [*pretio soluto*]; [*tradiderit*] ⟨*mancipio dederit*⟩;
(21. 3) 2 [*pretio . . . Titius*], ⟨*Titius autem*⟩; (44. 4) 4. 32 [*pretio soluto*];
[*tradiderit*] ⟨*mancipio dederit*⟩.
s. 655. Read Gai. 2. 40, 41; 1. 54.
s. 656. Read *D.* (6. 1) 68, interpolated, see *Index Interp.*
s. 658. Read *D.* (6. 1) 9, last sentence; (6. 1) 27. 3 (both interpolated).
s. 659. Read *C.* (7. 31) 1. 5.

BIBLIOGRAPHY

s. 641. Bozza, 'Actio in rem per sponsionem', *St. Bonfante* ii (1930),
591 ff.; Kaser, *Eigentum und Besitz im älteren röm. Recht* (1943), 282 ff.*

s. 642. Lenel, *Edict.* (1927), § 69. On *probatio diabolica* Windscheid, *Pand.* i (1906), § 196 n. 3. On *restituere* see Kaser, *Restituere als Prozess-Gegenstand* (1932); 'Besitz und Verschulden bei dinglichen Klagen', Z li (1931), 92 ff.

s. 643. Schulz, *Principles* (1936), 229; Wenger, *CP* (1940), 199.

s. 644. Levy, 'Die Enteignung des Klägers im Formular-Prozess', Z xlii (1921), 476 ff.; Carrelli, *L'acquisto della proprietà per litis aestimatio* (1934); Ehrhardt, *Litis aestimatio* (1934), 141; Beseler, 'Litis aestimatio und Enteignung', *SD* 1937, pp. 367 ff.

s. 645. H. Siber, *Die Passivlegitimation bei der rei vindicatio* (1907); *Röm. Recht* (1928), 97; Beseler, *Beiträge*, i (1910), 20; ii (1911), 5 f., 135; *Index Interp.* ad *D.* (6. 1) 9; Herdlitczka, Z xlix (1929), 274 ff.; Kaser, *Eigentum und Besitz*, 288, 292.

s. 646. Beseler, *Beiträge*, i (1910), 10 ff.; ii (1911), 128 ff.; Lenel, 'Rei vindicatio und actio ad exhibendum', Grünhut's *Zeitschrift für das Privat- und öffentliche Recht der Gegenwart*, xxxvii (1910), 515 ff.; Kaser, Z li (1931), 100 n. 2.

s. 647. Lenel, *Edict.* (1927), p. 136; Berger, *PW* ix. 1661.

s. 648. Lenel, *Edict.* § 248; Berger, *PW* ix. 1660 f.

s. 649. Beseler, *Beiträge*, i (1910), 1 ff.; ii (1911), 128 ff.; Lenel, 'Rei vindicatio und actio ad exhibendum', l.c.; *Edict.* § 90.

s. 650. On the terminology see *Voc. Iur. Rom.* iv. 79; on Gai. 4. 3 see Beseler, Z xlvi (1926), 268; Biondi, *Actio negativa ed actio prohibitoria* (1929), 3; see further Lenel, *Edict.* §§ 72, 73; Bohacek, *Bull.* xliv (1937), 49 ff.; xlvi (1939), 142 ff.

s. 651. Lenel, *Edict.* §§ 248, 255; Berger, *PW* ix. 1660 f.; Windscheid, *Pand.* i (1906), § 198 n. 7.

s. 652. Lenel, *Edict.* § 60; Bonfante, *Corso*, ii. 2 (1928), 326 ff.; Beseler, *Beiträge*, iv (1920), 87; Pflüger, Z xlii (1921), 469. De Sarlo, *St. Solazzi* (1948), 203 ff.

s. 653. Actio Publiciana negatoria? see Windscheid, *Pand.* i, § 199 n. 3.

s. 654. Lenel, *Edict.* § 276, with references; Bonfante, *Scritti*, ii (1918), 450 ff.

s. 655. Bonfante, *Scritti*, ii (1918), 370 ff.; *Corso*, ii. 2 (1928), 314 ff.*

s. 656. Windscheid, *Pand.* i (1906), § 193 nn. 1–3; Beseler, *SD* 1937, p. 368.

s. 657. Wlassak, Z xxv (1904), 143.

s. 658. Herdlitczka, Z xlix (1929), 275 n. 1, with references.

CHAPTER II

SERVITUDES

1. *Introduction*

UNDER Justinian's law a *servitus* was a burden im- posed upon a corporeal thing by a private legal act concerning the use of that thing. This definition needs a short explanation.

1. 'Burden imposed upon a thing' is of course a metaphorical expression: the legal meaning is 'modification of ownership'. The usufruct, for example, is a *servitus* because the right of the usufructuary modifies ownership (above, s. 578), since this right is valid and is protected against any owner of the thing charged with that servitude. A lessee may have virtually the same right to use the thing, but his right is valid and is protected only against the lessor (or his heir). If the lessor alienated the thing, the lessee had no right against the new owner. The right of the lessee therefore does not modify ownership; modern students say (above, s. 579) that he has no *ius in re* (or *in rem*) but only a *ius in personam*.

2. *Servitus* concerns the use of the servient thing. As a rule *servitus* implies a right to use a thing belonging to another person, e.g. the usufruct or the *ius itineris*. Sometimes, however, a servitude only limits the use of the thing by its owner, e.g. the *servitus altius non tollendi* which prevents the owner of the servient land from raising a building beyond a certain height.

3. The ownership of landed property was limited by Roman private law in favour of neighbours. Modern lawyers called these legal restrictions *servitutes legales*, a misleading term which implies that Roman ownership in itself is an unlimited right. We will not describe these limitations here. Further restrictions upon ownership might be imposed by public law; these we will also leave aside. The servitude which alone we wish to describe here is a burden imposed by a private legal act.

661.
Classification

Servitudes fall into two classes: *servitutes personae* or *personales* (personal servitudes) and *servitutes praediorum* or *reales* (praedial or real servitudes). The difference between them lies in the manner in which the right is vested in the holder of the servitude.

1. The personal servitude is vested in an individual person; the object charged with such a servitude may be movable or immovable.

2. The real or praedial servitude must always be attached to the ownership of a thing, so that when this thing changes its owner the new owner automatically acquires the right contained in the servitude. Servitudes of this kind can only be created in favour of an owner of land (*praedium*) and the thing burdened with the servitude must also be land. Thus two immovable things are required for the creation of such a servitude, a *praedium dominans* (the term is absent from our sources, but is nevertheless useful) and a *praedium serviens* (this term occurs in our sources).

662.
Classical terminology

The classical terminology differed widely from that adopted by the compilers. The classical *servitus* comprehended only what the compilers called 'real' or 'praedial servitudes'; the term 'personal servitude' did not exist, the lawyers being content with calling the two classical personal servitudes, *usus fructus* and *usus*, by their specific names. Thus the Edict had a rubric *si usus fructus petatur* (Lenel, *Edict*. § 72; *usus* was apparently not expressly mentioned) which was followed by the rubric *si servitus vindicetur* (Lenel, *Edict*. § 73). The compilers of the *Digest* retained this order, though it was illogical since usufruct was for them a kind of servitude. Book 7 of the *Digest* deals with usufruct and other personal servitudes; book 8 with *servitutes*. In the following discussion we shall use the Byzantine terminology because it is more convenient for our purposes. The Byzantine *servitus* is by no means an empty scholastic term. It is valuable for a systematic arrangement of the law of property and for any sociological, economic, or political study. Personal and praedial servitudes form a definite unity and require a generic term in order to mark them off from *pignus* and *hypotheca*, which have a fundamentally different function. In this respect the Byzantine terminology is superior to that of the classical lawyers.

We have already (above, s. 583) touched on the general character of the classical law of servitudes. It was an undisguisedly liberal law; the tendency to preserve ownership as unrestricted as possible and to keep servitudes within comparatively narrow limits is visible throughout.

1. Classical law recognized a stock of typical servitudes; some of them were listed in the *Edict*, but even the list given in Hadrian's *Edict* was not complete and other types were recognized by the lawyers and the praetor. This group of standard servitudes was gradually developed and even in classical times the list was not yet closed. However, when a new type came to be considered by the praetor, it depended on his discretion whether it was recognized or rejected, and he as well as the lawyers was loath to deviate from the principles which underlay the well-established forms of servitudes. For example, a usufruct in favour of an owner of land (in other words, a praedial servitude with the content of a usufruct) would have been rejected in the same way as 'real charges' (below, s. 666). Parties were not perfectly free to create servitudes, but stood under a permanent and beneficial control which prevented servitudes from draining ownership of its entire content. The pernicious development of servitudes which we find in central Europe and particularly in Germany from the Middle Ages to the beginning of the nineteenth century was made impossible under that control. ^{663.} *Meaning of the classical types*

2. The classical personal servitude was indissolubly tied to the individual person of its holder. The usufruct, for example, was a personal servitude which endowed its holder with far-reaching rights—he was entitled to keep the thing (movable or immovable) in his hands, to use it and to reap its fruits—but he could not alienate it nor could he leave it to his heirs; the right ended inevitably at his death, if not earlier, and the owner thereby regained unrestricted ownership. Parties were unable to render usufruct alienable or inheritable. A usufruct could not be created in favour of a legal person (above, ss. 162, 175). ^{664.} *Personal servitudes*

665.   3. Praedial or real servitudes might continue to exist for a
Praedial very long time, since these rights were vested in the chang-
servitudes ing owner of the *praedium dominans* and not in an individual
person. But the content of such servitudes was strictly
limited, as we shall presently point out (below, s. 685). As
aforesaid (above, s. 663), it was not allowed to constitute
a usufruct as a praedial servitude because such a right
would have rendered ownership a *nudum ius* for a very long
time.

666.   4. No servitude can bind the owner of the servient thing
Servitus in to do something. The maxim *servitus in faciendo consistere*
faciendo
consistere *nequit* was not yet formulated in classical law but was never-
nequit theless a leading principle of the greatest importance. An
obligation to pay periodically a sum of money, to furnish
periodically a certain quantity of eggs, butter, flour, wood,
and so on, or to do personal services of a certain kind at
specified intervals (e.g. once a week or a month) could not
be made the content of a servitude. Such obligations might
be created by contract, but in that case only the promisor
and his heir were subject to them and not the owner for
the time being of the servient thing. Thus the pernicious
institution of *Reallast* (real charges) could not develop in
classical private law and remained confined to the sphere of
public law. The State and the *municipia* might impose such
charges, but to allow private parties to create them at their
discretion was thought too dangerous to freedom of ownership. Continental agrarian history has fully justified the
Roman attitude and modern agrarian legislation since the
French Revolution has attempted more or less vigorously
to abolish or at least to restrict real charges.

667.   Under Justinian's law there was only one exception to
Servitus the rule *servitus in faciendo consistere nequit*, namely the *ser-*
oneris
ferendi *vitus oneris ferendi*. In such a servitude the owner of the
praedium dominans was entitled to raise a building upon a
wall built upon the servient land; the owner of the latter
was bound to keep the wall in good repair. It is, however,
very doubtful whether the classical lawyers acknowledged
this obligation. They certainly took it into consideration
and discussed it, but the dominant opinion apparently

refused to recognize it. And even if this exception were classical, it would only confirm and emphasize the rule.

5. In post-classical times the liberal principles of classical law were considerably weakened. The range of personal servitudes was extended, so-called irregular personal servitudes were acknowledged, and, above all, *superficies* and *emphyteusis* entered the sphere of private law. We shall presently return to these topics (below, ss. 693 ff.). 668. Post-classical law

As a whole the classical law of servitudes is a memorable achievement, but much more so in its leading principles than in its details. Earnest attempts have been made by a number of modern scholars to rediscover the classical law, but the available texts are heavily interpolated and many issues—unfortunately not merely matters of detail—are still obscure and disputed. 669. Evaluation and sources

SOURCES

s. 660. Read *D.* (8. 1) 15. 1 (substantially classical); *Lex Urson.* cc. 73–5 (Bruns, *Fontes*, no. 28; *FIRA* i, no. 21).

s. 661. Read *D.* (8. 1) 1 (spurious); (8. 4) 1. 1; (18. 1) 47.

s. 662. Read Gai. 2. 14 (usufruct in contrast to servitude).

s. 664. Read Gai. 2. 30, last sentence; *D.* (7. 1) 56 (above, s. 162).

s. 666. Read *D.* (8. 1) 15. 1; (18. 1) 81. 1; (33. 1) 12 [*neque ... in rem*], but the whole text is corrupt (confusion of *legatum* and *fideicommissum*, above, s. 550). For public real charges read the so-called *lex Iulia munic.* (Bruns, *Fontes*, no. 18; *FIRA* no. 13) l. 20.

s. 667. Read *D.* (8. 5) 6. 2 (the text is corrupt).

BIBLIOGRAPHY

s. 660. Windscheid, *Pand.* i (1906), § 200, with references; Bonfante, *Corso*, iii (1933), 15; Biondi, *La categoria romana delle servitutes* (1938); *Le servitù prediali nel dir. rom.* (1946); G. Grosso, *I problemi dei diritti reali nell' impostazione romana* (1944); Solazzi, *Requisiti e modi di costituzione delle servitù prediali* (1947). On public servitudes see Schulz, *Principles* (1936), 30; Biondi, *La categoria*, 557 ff.

s. 662. Longo, 'La categoria delle servitutes nel dir. rom. class.', *Bull.* xi (1898), 281 ff.; Buckland, *St. Riccobono*, i (1936), 278; Biondi, *La categoria*, 673 ff.; Grosso, *SD* v (1939), 251; *I problemi dei diritti reali*, 313.

s. 663. Arangio-Ruiz, 'La cosiddetta tipicità delle servitù e i poteri della giurisprudenza romana', *Il Foro Italiano*, lix (1934); G. Grosso, 'L'evoluzione storica delle servitù nel dir. rom. e il problema della tipicità', *SD* iii (1937), 265 ff.; Biondi, *Le servitù prediali*, 39 ff.; Solazzi, *Requisiti*, 6 f.

ss. 664, 65. Jhering, *Geist des röm. Rechts*, ii. 1 (4th ed. 1880), 226 f.; Solazzi, *Bull.* xlix/l (1948), 393 ff.

s. 666. Bonfante, 'La regola servitus in faciendo consistere nequit', *St. Ascoli* (without year), 179 ff.; *Corso*, iii. 24 ff.; Biondi, *Le servitù prediali*, 98 ff., 105 ff.; Solazzi, *Requisiti*, 19; Schulz, *Principles*, 30 n. 3.

s. 667. Pernice, *Z* xix (1898), 85 f.; Scialoja, *AG* xxvii (1881), 145 = *Studi* i. 1. 84 ff.; Beseler, *Z* xlv (1925), 231 ff.; G. Segrè, *Bull.* xli (1932), 17 ff., 52 ff.; 'Le formole delle azioni relative alla servitus oneris ferendi', *St. Ascoli* (without year).

s. 669. Windscheid, *Pand.* i, §§ 200 ff.; Bonfante, *Corso*, iii (1933); Biondi, *Istituzioni* (1946), §§ 70 ff.; Arangio-Ruiz, *Istituzioni* (9th ed. 1947), cap. viii and ix.

2. *Personal Servitudes*

670.
Conception of usufruct
The outstanding classical personal servitude was the *usus fructus*. The usufructuary had the right to use the *res serviens* and to enjoy its fruits (Gai. 2. 93: *habet ius utendi fruendi*). The details of these rights were much discussed by the classical lawyers, their tendency being to restrict them; but we will not dwell upon them. On the whole these discussions bear a casuistical character; the famous general formula, 'Usus fructus est ius alienis rebus utendi fruendi salva rei substantia', is obviously inaccurate, since the usufructuary is (within certain limits) entitled to take sand, stones, minerals, lime, etc., from the servient land, which is of course impossible without diminishing the substance of the thing.

671.
Usufruct pars dominii?
The further question (recently much discussed) whether and, if so in what sense, the classical lawyers regarded the usufruct as *pars dominii* we leave entirely aside. The few relevant texts are interpolated. Actually any servitude is *pars dominii* and the popular idea that usufruct in particular is a part of ownership had hardly any influence in classical jurisprudence.

672.
Function
The chief function of the classical usufruct was to provide maintenance for an individual person. It was particularly suitable for this purpose since it necessarily ended with the death of its holder. For that reason the lawyers liked to discuss it in connexion with legacies (*de usu fructu legato*), legacy being the chief mode of creating a usufruct.

Usufruct might be created directly by *legatum per vindi-* *cationem* (above, s. 555). If a usufruct was left by *legatum per* *damnationem* or by *fideicommissum* (above, ss. 556, 559), the heir had to constitute the usufruct by an act *inter vivos*, namely by *in iure cessio* (above, s. 610). A remarkable mode of creating a usufruct was the *mancipatio deducto usufructu*; the owner of a thing mancipated it to another while retaining a usufruct in it for himself. A *legatum per vindicationem* and an *in iure cessio deducto usufructu* was also possible. Further a usufruct might be created by *adiudicatio* in a so-called *iudicium divisorium* (above, s. 86). A usufruct could probably not be acquired by *usucapio*, although the point is still disputed.

673.
Creation of usufruct

Under classical law these were the only modes of creating a usufruct. It is indeed puzzling that a usufruct over a *res nec mancipi* could not be created by *traditio*; ownership could be transferred by *traditio* and one might argue that *in maiori inest et minus*. However, this argument is not entirely cogent; the lawyers wished to preserve free ownership and were probably loath on that account to facilitate the creation of a usufruct. Be that as it may, the creation of a usufruct by *traditio* is expressly excluded by Gaius (2. 28. 30). Praetorian modes of creating a usufruct did not exist, for the praetor too was disinclined to favour servitudes. By *traditio* not even an honorarian usufruct could be created. In singular cases the praetor treated a person as if he were a usufructuary, but one can hardly speak of a praetorian usufruct in these cases.

Suppose a testator instituted H as his heir, left the usufruct over the *fundus Cornelianus* to L *per vindicationem*, and charged L by *fideicommissum* to restore the usufruct to F. L delivered the land to F. Here L is the usufructuary and not F, as the usufruct cannot be alienated (above, s. 664), but the praetor protected F against L and H, as if he (F) were usufructuary. A quite singular decision which, if genuine, was perhaps based upon a rescript.

A usufruct could not be created over a *fundus provincialis* (above, s. 588). To be sure, Gaius in a carelessly worded passage (2. 31. 32) seems to imply that a usufruct might be constituted *pactionibus et stipulationibus*, but at most this

674.
Fundus provincialis

only means an honorarian usufruct protected by the provincial governors, and even that is hardly probable since only an *actio in personam* could be created *pactionibus et stipulationibus*. Perhaps Gaius only wished to say that the parties must be content with an obligatory contract as a substitute for a true usufruct. However, certainty cannot be attained, since reliable sources do not exist.

675. Creation under Justinian's law Under Justinian's law when *mancipatio* and *in iure cessio* no longer existed (above, ss. 608, 612) a usufruct could be constituted *pactionibus et stipulationibus*, and also by *traditio ususfructus* and by *traditio rei deducto usufructu*. Numerous classical texts inserted in the *Corpus iuris* were interpolated to serve this purpose.

676. End of usufruct Since usufruct greatly impaired the rights of the owner, its duration was deliberately kept within narrow limits.

1. Any usufruct came to an end with the death of its holder, and parties were not allowed to make it inheritable. Where a testator left a usufruct to A by legacy, he could not 'repeat' the legacy (*repetitio legati*) in favour of A's heir.

2. Further, usufruct came to an end in the event of *capitis deminutio* (above, s. 123) of its holder; but a testator might provide for this by *repetitio legati*.

3. Parties might constitute a usufruct *ad tempus* (e.g. for three years) by legacy, *in iure cessio* and *adiudicatio* (*Fr. Vat.* 48). Then usufruct ended at the conclusion of the term; but if the usufructuary died or suffered *capitis deminutio* earlier, it ended before that time.

4. Usufruct came to an end by *non-usus* for one year if the thing was movable, for two years if it was immovable. The times are of course those required for the *usucapio rei* (above, s. 623).

5. Where the usufructuary wished to resign his rights, he had to make an *in iure cessio* in favour of the owner of the thing; an informal resignation led only to an *exceptio* granted to the owner against the *vindicatio ususfructus*.

6. The usufruct ended when the usufructuary became the owner of the thing (*consolidatio*), since a usufruct could not be created in favour of the owner of the thing. However,

if this rule led to unjust results, the lawyers treated the owner as if he were still a usufructuary.

7. Finally the usufruct ended not only if the thing ceased to exist but also if it was considerably altered. Thus the usufructuary of a house lost his right if the house was burnt down; it did not survive as a right over the site. The classical tendency to favour free ownership is here particularly apparent.

The usufructuary had a special action which the classical lawyers called *actio de usu fructu* or *vindicatio usus fructus*; the compilers of the *Digest* (Title 8. 5), and apparently they alone, designated it by the strange term *actio confessoria*. The *vindicatio usus fructus* originally lay only against the owner of the thing, but later—at least from the time of Julian—it lay also against any possessor who might be sued with the *rei vindicatio* (above, s. 645). The action was an *actio in rem* in the usual classical sense (above, ss. 56, 647); instead of the *interdictum quem fundum* (above, s. 648) the usufructuary had the *interdictum quem usum fructum* (Lenel, *Edict.* § 248). The formula of the *vindicatio usus fructus* ran as follows (Lenel, *Edict.* § 72): 677. Vindicatio usus fructus

> 'Si paret Aulo Agerio ius esse eo fundo, quo de agitur, uti frui neque ea res restituetur, quanti ea res erit, tantam pecuniam', etc. (above, ss. 58, 67).

As regards the actions available to the owner against the usufructuary, the *rei vindicatio* did not as a rule lie since the usufructuary was not *possessor rei* (above, s. 645). The owner had the possessory interdicts and in particular he was protected by the *cautio usufructuaria*, i.e. by the *actio ex stipulatu* resulting from that *cautio*. The usufructuary was bound to promise to use the thing *boni viri arbitratu* and to restore it at the end of the usufruct. Under the edictal title *de legatis* (Lenel, *Edict.* § 171) the praetor imposed upon him the obligation to effect such a *cautio*, and under the rubric *usufructuarius quemadmodum caveat* (Lenel, *Edict.* § 286) he pronounced its wording: 678. Cautio usufructu-aria

> 'Cuius rei usus fructus testamento Lucii Titii tibi legatus est, ea re boni viri arbitratu usurum fruiturum te et, cum usus fructus ad te

pertinere desinet, id quod inde exstabit restitutum iri dolumque malum
abesse afuturumque esse spondesne? Spondeo.'

The owner was entitled to refuse to deliver the thing
until the *cautio* was given to him. If he inadvertently
delivered the thing without having obtained the *cautio*, he
might exceptionally sue the usufructuary with the *rei vindicatio* and reclaim the thing; a *condictio cautionis* was unknown
to classical law, nor did the praetor grant the owner a special
action in order to obtain the *cautio*.

The praetor expressly granted the *cautio* only in case of
a *ususfructus legatus*. Here praetorian protection was particularly required. For if the usufruct was left *per vindicationem*, it came into existence without any act of the heir
(above, s. 504. 2); if it was left *per damnationem*, the heir
was bound to constitute the usufruct according to the
testator's will. If the usufruct was constituted by *in iure
cessio venditionis* or *donationis causa*, the owner was free to
require a *cautio* before executing the *in iure cessio*. However,
the praetorian rules were extended to all kinds of usufruct
by the lawyers. Thus, if a usufruct was created by *in iure
cessio venditionis* or *donationis causa* and the owner had forgotten to require the *cautio*, he might retain the thing till
the *cautio* was given.

679.
Quasi-
usufruct
In close connexion with the *cautio usufructuaria* stands
the quasi-usufruct over movables which can only be
enjoyed by consuming them (e.g. money, wine, and so on).
The lawyers originally regarded such a usufruct as illogical,
but it was nevertheless admitted by a *senatusconsultum* of the
first century A.D. (known already to Sabinus) when such
usufruct was left by legacy. The wording of the *senatusconsultum* is unknown to us, but the classical law based upon it
is clear. The legatee became the owner of the things concerned but was bound to restore other things of the same
quality and quantity at the end of the quasi-usufruct. The
heir was entitled to demand a *cautio usufructuaria*, and even
without such a *cautio* he might, according to the dominant
classical doctrine, recover things of the same quality and
quantity by *condictio*.

680. Usus
By the side of the usufruct stood *usus*, which was a

limited usufruct, since the *usuarius* was not entirely excluded from enjoying the fruits. The content of this personal servitude cannot be accurately discerned from available sources; the classical lawyers confined themselves to casuistical discussions which are only preserved to us in a mutilated and interpolated form. As regards creation and extinction there was no difference between *usus* and *usus fructus*. The *usuarius* had a *vindicatio usus* (apparently not mentioned in the Edict) and was bound to give a *cautio usuaria* (perhaps mentioned in the Edict, Lenel, *Edict.* § 17).

Other types of personal servitutes were unknown to classical law. *Habitatio* and *operae servorum*—special types under Justinian's law—were regarded as forms of *usus* by the classical lawyers. The so-called irregular personal servitudes, i.e. personal servitudes with the content of praedial servitudes—a mixture which the classical lawyers disliked as they disliked other mixtures—did not exist in classical law. On *superficies* and *emphyteusis* as personal servitudes—both foreign to classical private law—we shall speak below in an appendix (below, s. 693).

681. Other types

SOURCES

s. 670. Read *D.* (7. 1) 1; *Epit. Ulp.* 24. 26; *D.* (7. 1) 9 pr.–2 [*quasi ... familias*]; (7. 1) 12 pr. (substantially classical); (7. 1) 68; Paul. *Sent.* (3. 6) 19–22; *D.* (7. 1) 12. 2.

s. 671. Read *D.* (50. 15) 25 [*totum*]; [servitutis] ⟨*iuris*⟩; [*totum*].

s. 673. Read Gai. 2. 30, 33; *Fr. Vat.* 45. 47, 47*a*; Paul. *Sent.* (3. 6) 17; *D.* (33. 2) 29.

s. 674. Read Gai. 2. 31, 32.

s. 675. Read *Inst. Iust.* (2. 4) pr.–1; *D.* (7. 1) 3 pr.–1 (interpol.).

s. 676. Read Paul. *Sent.* (3. 6) 28–33; Gai. 2. 30; *D.* (7. 1) 58; (7. 4) 5 pr. [*nisi ... legaverit*]; (7. 4) 5. 2–3 (substantially classical); (7. 4) 8; *Fr. Vat.* 83.

s. 677. Read *D.* (7. 6) 5. 1; (44. 4) 4. 12.

s. 678. Read *D.* (7. 1) 13 pr. [*ut ... fiat*]; (7. 1) 13. 2 [*actionem*] ⟨*cautionem*⟩ polliceri; (7. 9) 7 pr. [*quae ... poterit*]; cf. (7. 9) 12; Gai. 2. 93.

s. 679. Read *D.* (7. 5) 1 [*vel minuuntur*]; (7. 5) 2 [*remedio introducto*]; (7. 5) 7 [*aut ... commodius est*]; (7. 9) 7. 1; (7. 9) 12.

s. 680. Read Paul. *Sent.* (3. 6) 25; *D.* (7. 8) 4. 1; (7. 8) 14. 2; (7. 9) 5. 1 [*hoc ... caveatur*].

BIBLIOGRAPHY

ss. 670 ff. Bonfante, *Corso*, iii (1933), 52 ff.

s. 670. Ebrard, Z xxxviii (1917), 329 n. 2, with references.

s. 671. Kunkel, § 84 n. 1, with references; Kaser, *Festschrift P. Koschaker*, i (1939), 458 ff.; Grosso, *SD* ix (1943), 157 ff.

s. 673. On *usucapio ususfructus* see Beseler, *Beiträge*, iv (1920), 78 ff.; on *traditio* Beseler, l.c. 82 ff.

s. 674. Beseler, *Beiträge*, iv. 82 ff.; Solazzi, *Requisiti e modi di costituzione delle servitù prediali* (1947), 109 ff.; *Bull*. viii/ix (1948), 393.

s. 675. Solazzi, l.c. 147 ff.

s. 676. Schulz, Z l (1930), 220. On *Fr. Vat.* 83, Beseler, *St. Riccobono*, i (1936), 311, 314; Sanfilippo, *Bull*. xlix/l (1948), 58 ff.; P. E. Cavin, *L'Extinction de l'usufruit rei mutatione* (1933).

s. 677. Kunkel, § 88 n. 4, with references; Bohacek, *Bull*. xliv (1937), 49 ff.; Arangio-Ruiz, *Rariora* (1946), 1 ff.; Grosso, *I problemi dei diritti reali* (1944), 132 ff.; Sciascia, *Bull*. xlix/l (1948), 471 ff.

s. 678. Lenel, *Edict.* (1927), §§ 171, 286; Siber, *Röm. Privatrecht* (1928), 115; Grosso, 'In tema di cautio fructuaria', *Atti Torino*, lxxii (1936/7), estratto, with references.

s. 679. Grosso, 'Sul quasi usufrutto', *Bull*. xliii (1935), 237 ff.

s. 680. Riccobono, 'Sull' usus', *Studi Scialoja*, i (1905); Grosso, *SD* v (1939), 133 ff., with references.

s. 681. Biondi, *Le servitù prediali* (1946), 112 ff.; Bonfante, *Corso*, iii (1933).

3. *Praedial Servitudes*

682.
Conception

Following Byzantine terminology (above, s. 661), we give the name of 'praedial (or "real") servitudes' to those servitudes which are imposed upon land (*praedium serviens*) in favour of the owner of another piece of land (*praedium dominans*). It was to these servitudes only that the classical lawyers applied the term *servitutes* (above, s. 662).

683.
Types

As we have already stated (s. 663), classical law knew a group of well-established and recognized types of praedial servitudes but that group did not yet form a closed circle. For that reason we need not enumerate the various types which are mentioned in our sources; the examples given in the course of the following description will suffice.

684.
Rustic and urban servitudes

One general distinction must not be left unmentioned. The classical lawyers distinguished two groups of praedial servitudes: *servitutes* (or *iura*) *praediorum rusticorum* and *urbanorum*. As usual they did not define these conceptions,

but we can find definitions by the study of their discussions.
A *praedium urbanum* is of course a *praedium* situated within
a town; a *praedium rusticum* a *praedium* situated outside a
town. But you must not conclude that *servitutes praediorum
rusticorum* are servitudes when either or both *praedia*
(*dominans* and *serviens*) are situated outside a town. The
classical significance of the distinction was rather the
following. *Servitutes praediorum rusticorum* are servitudes
which as a rule serve agricultural purposes; *servitutes
praediorum urbanorum* are servitudes which as a rule serve
non-agricultural purposes. The lawyers who chose these
terms had in mind only the typical cases and for that reason
they inevitably came into conflict with common usage in
atypic cases. Thus the standard types of rustic servitudes
were *iter, actus, via, aquaeductus*; in classical times *aquae
haustus, pecoris ad aquam adpulsus, ius pascendi, calcis co-
quendae, harenae fodiendae* were also recognized. As a rule,
these servitudes occurred only when the two estates were
situated outside a town. But exceptionally, they might be
constituted over and in favour of estates situated within a
town. Thus the owner of a house in a town might be interested in having a right to cross his neighbour's garden in
order to have easy access to another street. It would have
been absurd to give such a *ius itineris* different treatment
from that given to a right of way outside a town; accordingly the lawyers qualified it as a *servitus praediorum rusticorum*, i.e. as a servitude which as a rule occurred only *in
praediis rusticis*. On the other hand, a *servitus altius non
tollendi, ne luminibus, ne prospectus officiatur* are typical urban
servitudes; but exceptionally, they might be constituted in
favour of a house situated outside a town and even then they
were called *servitutes praediorum urbanorum*. This terminology is of course in conflict with common usage, but legal
terms often seem perplexing to laymen. We shall presently
return (below, ss. 688. 3, 691) to the legal significance of
this classification.

The classical tendency to restrict servitudes is visible

1. In the principle *servitus in faciendo consistere nequit*. 685. No
We have already mentioned it above (s. 666), but must servitus in
faciendo

emphasize it again here since it is of particular importance in connexion with praedial servitudes.

686.
Praedio utilis
2. In the principle that any praedial *servitus* must accommodate the *praedium dominans* (*praedio utilis*). The servitude must be closely connected with the use of the *praedium dominans* (mostly with its economic use); it must be profitable for its use. In classical times the chief purpose of this requisite was apparently to prevent rustic servitudes being for industrial purposes. Thus a *servitus* over a quarry might be constituted for the purpose of building a house upon the *praedium dominans* but not for selling the stones. A *servitus* might be created over a clay-pit in order to make pottery for use within the *praedium dominans* but not for sale. As regards urban servitudes the requisite of *utilitas praedii* was less important, but a praedial servitude over a garden creating a right to walk or dine in it could not be created; for such purposes *usus* (a personal servitude; above, s. 680) should have been employed.

687.
Vicinitas
3. In numerous texts it is mentioned in passing that the servient land was situated in the vicinity of the *praedium dominans*, but *vicinitas* was not a special requirement distinct from *utilitas praedii*. To be sure for some kinds of praedial servitudes vicinity of the estates was indispensable, for instance, for urban servitudes (*ne luminibus*, *ne prospectui officiatur*) or for *aquae haustus* or *pecoris ad aquam adpulsus*. But for others vicinity was obviously not essential; for example, a *ius pascendi* for a flock of sheep might be profitable to the *praedium dominans* even if the pasture was far distant from it. Moreover, *vicinitas* is such a vague conception that it could hardly have been a special requirement. The *servitus* must be profitable to the use of the *praedium dominans* and this requirement sometimes implied that the two estates should be adjacent.

688.
Creation
A praedial servitude could be created in the same way as a personal servitude (above, ss. 673 ff.):

1. By *in iure cessio*, *legatum per vindicationem*, and *adiudicatio*.

2. By *mancipatio rei excepta servitute*, so that the *mancipio dans* acquired the *servitus*; in the same way by *in iure*

cessio rei excepta servitute or by *legatum per vindicationem excepta servitute.*

The classical lawyers used the expressions *mancipio dare deducto usufructu, detracto usufructu,* or *excepto usufructu (Voc. Iur. Rom.* ii. 119.
41 ff.; 202. 38 ff.; 670. 42 f.; 671. 35 ff.), but apparently only *mancipio
dare excepta servitute (Voc. Iur. Rom.* ii. 670. 30 f.). We should not seek
any profound legal ideas underlying these terminological differences. In
particular *mancipare rem deducto usufructu* does not imply that in the
eyes of the classical lawyers usufruct, in contrast to other servitudes, was
pars dominii. As already observed, any servitude may be regarded as a
part or fragment of ownership (above, s. 671).

3. *Servitutes praediorum rusticorum* (above, s. 684) were
regarded as *res mancipi* (above, s. 604), and therefore could
be created by a *mancipatio* performed by the owner of the
servient land.

The reason why only rustic servitudes were classed as
res mancipi is unknown. But we have already stated (s. 605)
that we cannot explain why only those animals *quae collo
dorsove domantur* were *res mancipi.* However, the fact that
rustic servitudes were treated as *res mancipi* should no
longer be contested.

4. *Usucapio* of a *servitus praediorum* was expressly excluded by a *lex Scribonia* of unknown date, a statute significant for a true understanding of the Roman attitude
towards servitudes and towards *usucapio* in general (above,
ss. 583, 662, 623).

A praedial servitude like a personal servitude could not 689.
be created over a *fundus provincialis.* Gaius' formula, Fundus
pactionibus et stipulationibus id efficere potest, we have already provincialis
mentioned and explained (above, s. 674).

Under Justinian's law praedial servitudes were created 690.
by *traditio rei excepta servitute* (or by legacy *excepta servitute*); Creation
further *pactionibus et stipulationibus* and by *traditio servi-* under
tutis. A praedial servitude might now also be acquired by Justinian's
longi temporis praescriptio (above, s. 629). To make them law
accord with these new rules the classical texts have been
thoroughly interpolated.

Rustic servitudes were ended by *non-usus* for two years, 691.
urban servitudes by *usucapio libertatis,* i.e. by an obstruction End of
on the part of the owner of the *praedium serviens* which servitudes

lasted for two years. All praedial servitudes were ended by resignation in the form of *in iure cessio* and by *confusio*, i.e. when the ownership of both *praedia* became vested in one person (the owner of the servient land acquiring the *praedium dominans* or vice versa).

692.
Actions
The holder of a praedial servitude had a *vindicatio servitutis* which the compilers called *actio confessoria* (above, s. 677). It was an *actio in rem* like the *vindicatio usus fructus*; instead of the *interdictum quem usufructum* (above, s. 677) the plaintiff had a similar interdict (Lenel, *Edict.* § 255). The *vindicatio servitutis* lay against the owner of the servient land; whether it also lay against the mere possessor of this land or even against anybody who disturbed the holder of the servitude in making use of it remains doubtful. A special action for the protection of the *servitus aquae ductus* was the *actio de aqua* (Lenel, *Edict.* § 176). For particular rustic servitudes the praetorian Edict granted special interdicts (Lenel, *Edict.* §§ 250 ff.).

SOURCES

s. 684. Read Gai. 2. 14, 17, 29; *Epit. Gai.* 2. 1. 3; *Epit. Ulp.* 19. 1; *D.* (8. 3) 1 pr. § 1 cf. *Inst. Iust.* (2. 3) 2; *D.* (8. 2) 2; (8. 3) 2 pr. [*rusticorum*] ⟨*urbanorum*⟩. *D.* (50. 16) 198 refers to the *oratio divi Severi* (above, s. 300). N.B. Cf. *D.* (33, 10) 12.

s. 686. Read *D.* (8. 3) 5. 1; (8. 3) 6 pr.; (8. 1) 8 pr.

s. 687. Read *D.* (8. 3) 5. 1.

s. 688. Read Gai. 2. 17, 29; *Fr. Vat.* 45; *D.* (41. 3) 4. 28, first sentence.

s. 691. Read *D.* (41. 3) 4. 28 [*statutum tempus*] ⟨*biennium*⟩; (8. 2) 6 [*statutum tempus*] ⟨*biennium*⟩; [*constitutum tempus*] ⟨*biennium*⟩.

BIBLIOGRAPHY

ss. 682 ff. Bonfante, *Corso*, iii (1933), 15 ff.; Biondi, *Le servitù prediali nel diritto romano* (1946); Solazzi, *Requisiti e modi di costituzione delle servitù prediali* (1947).*

s. 682. Buckland, *LQR* (1928).

s. 684. Arnò, *Della distinzione fra servitù rustiche ed urbane* (1895); Bonfante, *Corso*, iii (1933), 29 ff.; Grosso, 'Sulle servitù altius tollendi e stilicidium non avertendi', *St. Albertoni*, i (1933), 466 ff.; Guarneri Citati, *Bull.* xliii (1935), 71; Grosso, 'Appunto storici ... sulla distinzione fra servitù rustiche ed urbane', *Riv. di diritto agrario*, xvii (1938), estratto, pp. 7 ff.; Biondi, l.c. 172 ff.*

s. 686. Biondi, l.c. 148 ff., 164 ff.*

s. 687. Bonfante, *Corso*, iii. 15 ff.; Biondi, l.c. 153 ff.; Solazzi, l.c. 29 ff.

s. 688. Rabel, *Mélanges Girard*, ii (1912), 387 ff.; Beseler, *Beiträge*, iv (1920), 82 ff.; Biondi, l.c. 191 ff.; Solazzi, l.c. 85 ff. On rustic servitudes as *res mancipi* (*Fr. Vat.* 45), see Grosso, *St. Besta* i (1939), 45, with references.

s. 690. Solazzi, l.c. 147.

s. 691. Biondi, l.c. 263 ff.; Grosso, 'Sulla genesi storica dell'estinzione delle servitù per non usus e della usucapio libertatis', *Il Foro Italiano*, lxii (1937).*

s. 692. Buckland, *LQR* xlvi (1930), 447 ff.; Biondi, l.c. 293 ff.; Grosso, *I problemi dei diritti reali nell' impostazione romana* (1944), 124 ff.; Bonfante, *Corso*, iii (1933), 367 ff.*

4. *Appendix. Superficies and Emphyteusis*

Under Justinian's law there were two species of servitudes which are obviously irreconcilable with the fundamental classical principles. Both empty ownership almost entirely of its content and assimilate the right of the holder of the servitude to ownership. *Superficies* was the right to have a building on the land of another person, that right being granted for a long time or for ever; the *superficiarius* was bound to pay a rent to the owner. *Emphyteusis* (ἐμφύτευσις, derived from ἐμφυτεύω, to implant) was a lease of agricultural land for a long time or for ever; the *emphyteuta* (ἐμφυτεύτης) had to pay a rent to the owner. Both rights were alienable and inheritable and protected by an *actio in rem*. 693. Justinian's law

It is certain that both rights originated in public law. *Superficies* as well as *emphyteusis* (in classical times called *ager vectigalis*) were originally created by the authorities of the State or of the *municipia* and were regulated by public law and the question is only whether in classical times they were already regarded as modifying private ownership, i.e. as *iura in rem*, protected by an ordinary *actio in rem*. This question has been keenly and even fanatically discussed during recent years, but no unanimity has been reached among students of Roman law. This cannot come as a surprise. Available texts within the *Corpus iuris* are without doubt thoroughly interpolated but, in default of reliable sources, we cannot reconstruct the classical texts with 694. Origin and sources certainty. Nevertheless, we believe that neither of these irregular species of servitudes was protected by an ordinary *actio in rem*.

695. Superficies As regards *superficies* it should no longer be doubted that the *actio in rem* of the *superficiarius* mentioned in our texts is not classical. It may be that the praetor protected him by a special *interdictum de superficie*. Actually the classicality of this interdict is much disputed; but even if it were classical, it would not render the right a private *ius in rem* since interdicts sometimes protected public rights.

> D. (43. 18) 1 pr. 'Ait praetor: Uti ex lege locationis sive conductionis superficie, qua de agitur, nec vi nec clam nec precario alter ab altero fruimini, quo minus ita fruamini, vim fieri veto. Si qua alia actio de superficie postulabitur, causa cognita dabo.'
>
> Whatever you may think about the interdict (probably fabricated by the compilers) the last sentence *si qua . . . dabo* must needs be spurious, simply because according to classical usage an interdict is not an *actio* (above, s. 111). The praetor could not say *alia* (N.B.) *actio* since that would have implied that the interdict is also an *actio*. Consequently the words *quasi in rem actionem polliceri* in the following § 1 cannot be genuine.

696. Ager vectigalis More difficult is the question whether the lessee of an *ager vectigalis* was protected by an *actio in rem* as early as classical times. It is generally held that Hadrian's Edict contained a special rubric *si ager vectigalis petatur* (Lenel, *Edict.* § 70) under which the praetor granted an *actio in rem* to the lessee. However, this opinion rests on very weak grounds; Gaius 3. 145 says that the lease of an *ager vectigalis* was regarded by the dominant opinion as a regular *locatio*: he could hardly have left unmentioned the *actio in rem* if it really existed.

697. Conclusion In these circumstances we are entitled to leave aside both *superficies* and *emphyteusis*. Though they were of great importance in the agrarian history of the republican, classical, and post-classical period, they lay even in classical times outside the sphere of that which the classical lawyers regarded as private law and cannot be adequately discussed within a systematic description of the classical law of servitudes.

BIBLIOGRAPHY

s. 695. Kübler, *PW* ivA, 925 ff., with references; Beseler, Z lii (1932), 287 ff.; Kaser, *Eigentum und Besitz im älteren röm. Recht* (1943), 21, with references; Arangio-Ruiz, *Istituzioni* (9th ed. 1947), cap. ix.*

s. 696. C. v. Schilling, *Studien aus der röm. Agrargeschichte* (1926), reviewed by Eisser, Z l (1930), 633 ff.; Beseler, *SD* iii (1937), 360 ff.; *Scritti Ferrini*, iii (1948), 276; Lanfranchi, *Studi sull' ager vectigalis*, I. *La classicità del actio in rem vectigalis* (1938); II. *Il problema della usucapibilità degli agri vectigales* (1939); Kaser, l.c. 21, with references; Arangio-Ruiz, l.c.*

CHAPTER III

REAL SECURITIES

(Fiducia cum creditore and Pignus)

1. *Introduction*

698.
Conception
and types
i. A REAL security is a right over a thing (movable or immovable) granted to a creditor in order to secure his claim against a debtor. Various types are possible, since the rights bestowed upon the creditor may differ greatly. In these preliminary remarks we will only mention a few of them for the sake of illustration; the types recognized in classical law we shall describe later (below, ss. 704 ff.).

1. The right granted to the creditor may be ownership. The debtor or a third person transfers ownership of a thing to the creditor on the condition that the latter restores it when the debt is discharged. The further rights of the creditor may vary. The creditor may or may not be entitled to the possession of the thing. When the debt is due and not paid, the creditor may become the absolute owner of the thing without regard to whether its value exceeds the amount of the debt or not; or the creditor may be limited to selling the thing: then he is bound to restore the price in so far as it exceeds the amount of the debt.

2. A usufruct may be conceded to a creditor on the condition that this right expires when the debt is discharged. But if usufruct inevitably comes to an end with the death of its holder (as was the case under Roman law) it must be an unsatisfactory kind of real security.

3. Possession without ownership may be accorded to a creditor as a security. This form also admits several possible variants in detail. The creditor may have merely a *ius retinendi* effective only against the person who gave him the pledge: obviously this affords only a weak security. The creditor may be granted a right effective against any owner of the thing and even against the whole world and he may be protected accordingly by *actiones in rem*; then his right

is, as modern students say (above, s. 579), a proper *ius in rem alienam*. When the debt is due and not paid, the creditor may become the absolute owner of the thing or he may only be entitled to sell it and to repay himself out of the price. Further, he may or may not have the right to use the thing and to reap its fruits.

4. The security may not even bestow possession upon the creditor but only the right to take possession of the thing when the debt is due; in its strongest form this right is protected by an *actio in rem*. The further rights granted to the creditor may vary: he may be entitled to sell the thing, to reap its fruits, etc. Modern students are wont to call such a security *hypotheca* and, though this term was foreign to the classical lawyers, we will retain it since we need a short term to designate a 'security without possession', i.e. a security which entitles the creditor to possession only when the debt is due and left unpaid.

ii. From the economic point of view real security is a special kind of credit. Where somebody has borrowed money without giving a real security, this is pure 'personal credit', and if he has given one or more sureties to the creditor, it remains personal credit. But if he has given him real security, this would be a form of 'real credit', viz. a combination of personal credit with real credit. 'Pure real credit' is possible (the creditor can then only obtain payment by means of the real security), but we will leave aside that form for the present and return to it later (below, s. 753).

699. Personal and real credit in general

Any credit means for the debtor living and working with the help of another's money; for the creditor it means a sort of investment of capital. In modern economic life pure personal credit among private persons—it is different when the State or a public community is the debtor—is of comparatively small importance and as a rule is only granted for a short time; real credit stands in the foreground and in particular real credit granted on landed property. A mortgage of land provides a landowner with capital which he will need permanently or at least for a considerable time; on the other hand, it furnishes a secure and lasting investment to capitalists. To be sure, if real security is to function in this way, a law is required which makes it fit to serve these purposes; where such a law exists, real credit as a rule develops very fast. Such a development entails both advantages and disadvantages. An owner of agricultural land may buy a machine and improve the land with the help of capital, and the capitalist obtains thereby a good investment of his capital. On the other hand, landowners become more and more accustomed to work with other people's money, the land is increasingly charged with debts, and their ownership eventually becomes a mere matter of form, the creditors being in fact the economic owners. The economic history of the Continent and particularly of Germany in the nineteenth and twentieth centuries provides an instructive picture.

700. Personal and real credit in Roman life Turning now to the law of the Republic as well as of the classical period, we have to realize the important fact that the principal form of credit was pure personal credit (with or without sureties) and not real credit. Roman *fides*, Roman pedantic accuracy, honesty, and reliability in business matters were the strong pillars of that credit. Moreover, we must keep in mind that execution on the person of the debtor was still in force (above, s. 43) and that personal credit implied in consequence much greater security for the creditor than it provides in modern times. It is certainly significant that whenever a security (*cautio*) was required by the praetor (e.g. the *cautio usufructuaria*; above, ss. 114, 678) this did not mean that real security had to be given: a *cautio* was a promise given by *sponsio* with or without sureties and real security was not even regarded as a sufficient substitute for sureties. It is no less significant that the *lex Malacitana* (cap. lx) provided that the *cautio pecuniam publicam salvam fore* required sureties; real security only, if sureties seemed to be insufficient: 'Si de ea re is praedibus (sureties of a particular kind) minus cautum esse videbitur, praedia subsignato.' On the other hand, capitalists who wished to invest their money in land preferred to buy land rather than to give a loan to a landowner on mortgage. When a capitalist like the younger Pliny,

speaking of the investment of his property, says (*Epist.*
3. 19. 8): 'Sum quidem prope totus in praediis, aliquid
tamen faenero', the meaning is that the greatest part of the
property was vested in land of which Pliny was the owner
and which was cultivated by his *coloni*; a small part of his
property was put out at interest on personal credit. Pliny
is a typical capitalist of Trajan's period: in so far as capital
was not invested in commercial or industrial enterprises it
was invested in land or personal credit but not in mortgages. Thus real security was used only within very narrow
limits down to the end of the first century A.D. In later
times it may have gained ground, being encouraged by the
development of the law, but capitalists still preferred to buy
land rather than to invest their money in mortgages; a
guardian, for example, was bound to invest the ward's
property if possible in land by buying estates and not in
mortgages.

Hence real credit developed but slowly and imperfectly
in Roman economic life and the history of the Roman law
concerning real security shows the same features. Has
economic life hampered the development of law? Or, conversely, have the shortcomings of the law checked the
growth of real credit? Perhaps economics and law have
influenced each other reciprocally. Be that as it may, the
republican law of real security was poor and only tolerable
among men who were accustomed to work mainly with
personal credit. During the first century of the Principate
this law made little progress, if any at all, but Hadrian's
Edict worked an important improvement by its general
recognition of the *actio Serviana* (below, s. 711). This was
the farthest point reached; more could have been achieved
only by an official registration of hypothecs, but that was
never taken into consideration by the Roman lawyers,
though local registration existed in parts of the Empire.
The post-classical period considerably impaired the classical achievement by recognizing general hypothecs which
charged the whole property of the debtor and which came
into existence by law (legal hypothecs), being privileged
against other hypothecs. The fisc had a legal hypothec of

701.
Develop-
ment of the
Roman law
of real
securities

this kind for its claims, and so also had a wife to secure her
actio de dote (above, s. 220). Suppose that a landowner had
charged his estate with hypothecs and that later he married.
The dotal hypothec ranked above all other hypothecs and,
of course, considerably diminished their value. It is significant that Justinian in his *Novella* 72 (A.D. 538) advised
guardians to deposit the property of their wards rather than
to put it out at interest.

> '... ne ulla necessitas ex lege incumbat curatoribus pecuniam minorum
> fenori dandi, sed ut eam tuto deponant illisque custodiant, cum praestet
> securitatem in sorte eis conservare quam usurarum cupiditate etiam sorte
> eos privari.'

Mortgage obviously afforded no sufficient security.

701a.   In modern times Justinian's law of real securities has
Evaluation been universally and emphatically condemned as unfit to
meet the demands of modern economic life. This verdict is
just and must be extended to classical law, although the
latter was at least free from the devastating general legal
hypothecs (the fiscal hypothec intruded only in the third
century). But what if the classical lawyers did not wish to
further the development of real credit? In any case they
lived in a world in which economic life widely differed from
our own; credit was far less developed than today and personal credit could and did prevail. Moreover, is the exploi-
tation of real credit in all ways a good and desirable thing?
The severe critics of the nineteenth century did not hesitate
to answer this question in the affirmative; for them the
slogan 'economic progress by real credit' did not stand in
need of proof. Meanwhile experience has taught us that
real credit is a powerful but two-edged weapon. Classical
law produced at least the desirable effect that landed property was not overcharged with debts, and free ownership,
so dear to Roman hearts, was preserved. Its evil effect was
unfortunately that it contributed to the ruin of small free
farmers: the absence of a secure mortgage of land robbed
them of the opportunity to obtain cheap credit, and, as
capitalists preferred to invest their money by buying land,
the farmers eventually sold their land and became lessees
(*coloni*). The republican and classical law of real security

was probably an important factor in the rise of *latifundia*. For historians and lawyers interested in the connexion of law with economics the Roman law of real security will for ever remain an instructive phenomenon; details are also interesting for pure lawyers; but as a whole it belongs irretrievably to the past.

iii. As regards the sources of the classical law of real security we depend almost entirely on the *Corpus Iuris*. Gaius' *Institutes* exclude on principle purely praetorian law and the corner-stone of classical pledge and hypothec, the *actio Serviana*, was a purely praetorian creation. Nevertheless classical law is fairly well discernible. 702. Sources

iv. As usual we confine ourselves to classical Roman law leaving entirely aside post-classical and non-Roman, especially Hellenistic, law, although this last is of particular interest. 703. Scope

SOURCES

s. 700. Read *D*. (46. 5) 7, substantially classical.

BIBLIOGRAPHY

ss. 698 ff. A comprehensive modern work on the Roman law of real securities does not yet exist. H. Dernburg, *Das Pfandrecht nach den Grundsätzen des heutigen röm. Rechts* i (1860), ii (1864), though of course thoroughly antiquated, is still the indispensable standard work. For further literature down to 1906 see Windscheid, *Lehrbuch des Pandektenrechts*, i (1906), §§ 224 ff. Pappulias, *Das Pfandrecht nach dem griech. und röm. Recht*, is unfinished: vol. i (1909, written in Greek, reviewed by Mitteis, Z xxx (1909), 442 ff.; Manigk, *Pfandrechtliche Untersuchungen* (1904); *PW* vi. 2287 (*fiducia*) xvii. 343 (hypotheca), 291 (*hyperocha*); *PW* xx. 1239 (*pignus*); Rabel, 'Real securities in Roman law', *Seminar*, i (1943), 32. Monographic literature will be cited later.

s. 699. J. W. Hedemann, *Die Fortschritte des Zivilrechts im XIX. Jahrhundert*, ii. 1 (1930), 94 ff., 170 ff.; ii. 2 (1935), *passim* (very valuable and interesting).

s. 700. Pernice, 'Parerga viii: Über wirtschaftliche Voraussetzungen römischer Rechtssätze', Z xix (1898), 120 ff.; Mommsen, *Schr.* i. 368; v. 611; Salvioli, *Il capitalismo antico* (a cura di Brindisi, 1929), 35, 44.

s. 701*a*. Hedemann, l.c. ii. 2, p. 6 f., with references.*

s. 703. For Greek law see Pappulias, l.c.; Mitteis, *Grundzüge* (1912), 129 ff., with references; Taubenschlag, *The Law of Greco-Roman Egypt* (1944), § 33.

2. *Kinds and creation of classical real securities*

704.
Fiducia
cum
creditore
i. The only classical real security which afforded an *actio in rem* to the creditor *iure civili* was the *fiducia cum creditore contracta*. It was created by a *mancipatio* or *in iure cessio fiduciae causa* which transferred the ownership of a thing to the creditor as a sort of trustee. The creditor acquired full ownership and was therefore protected by *actiones in rem* (*rei vindicatio* and *actio negatoria*), but he was bound to restore the object (by *mancipatio* or *in iure cessio*) if the debt was discharged; when he failed to do so, the giver of the *fiducia* (as a rule the debtor) might sue him with a special action, the *actio fiduciae*. Further rights of the creditor will be described later (below, ss. 720 ff.).

As already said, *fiducia cum creditore* could only be created by *mancipatio* or *in iure cessio*; *mancipatio* (but not *in iure cessio*) was of course limited to *res mancipi* (above, s. 604).

> A debtor certainly might transfer the ownership of a *res nec mancipi* by *traditio fiduciae causa*, for there is no reason why *fiduciae causa* should not have been regarded as a sufficient *causa traditionis* (above, s. 615). But the *actio fiduciae* was confined to *mancipatio* and *in iure cessio* and for that reason we never meet a *traditio fiduciae causa*. The debtor might have transferred ownership by *traditio* to a creditor who promised by stipulation to restore the object when the debt was paid. The *actio ex stipulatu* might have served as a substitute for the missing *actio fiduciae*. But the latter was so much more effective than the *actio ex stipulatu*, especially since it involved *infamia*, that a *traditio dominii fiduciae causa* was apparently never practised.

The *fiducia* afforded the creditor a very strong security and was in harmony with the Roman aversion to *iura in re aliena*. But it implied a considerable risk for the debtor and had the disadvantage that it could only be effected once; the same object could not be given by the debtor *fiduciae causa* to several creditors successively. Nevertheless *fiducia* was practised throughout the whole classical period. It was already known in republican times, though we cannot say whether it existed as early as the Twelve Tables. We find this sort of real security (with variations in detail) in many other legal systems; for English students the mortgage of the older English law is the nearest approach.

In post-classical times *fiducia* disappeared together with
mancipatio and *in iure cessio* (above, ss. 608, 612) and was
not replaced by a *traditio dominii fiduciae causa*; Justinian's
compilers radically eliminated *fiducia cum creditore* from
classical texts and replaced it by *pignus* which we shall
presently describe.

705.
Disappear-
ance of
fiducia

ii. Another classical form of real security was termed
pignus. The etymology of this word is obscure and disputed,
but it cannot possibly mean anything else but 'security'.
The term was used to designate things taken by a magistrate to enforce his orders (*pignoris capio*), to things taken
under the old *legis actio per pignoris capionem*, and to the
things taken by the *publicani* (*pignoris capio*); but at this
point we have only to deal with *pignus* within the sphere of
private law. Under classical private law the term *pignus*
covered two different forms of real security, pledge and
hypothec. Pledge was already known in early republican
times and is probably older than *fiducia*; *hypotheca* developed slowly and gradually from the end of the Republic
onward.

706.
Pignus

1. *Pledge*. Pledge was a form of real security created by
an informal agreement which conferred upon the creditor
merely possession (not ownership) of a thing. Further
rights of the creditor we shall discuss later (below, ss.
720 ff.); here it will suffice to state that the creditor was
originally not protected by an *actio in rem*. As he was
possessor, he had the possessory interdicts, but an *actio in
rem* (the *actio Serviana*) was granted to him only very late,
probably by Hadrian's Edict. Thus only from the second
century A.D. might the right of the pledgee be described
(using modern terminology; above, s. 579) as a *ius in rem
alienam iure praetorio*. The agreement by which a pledge
was created implied also a contract, one of the so-called
'real contracts' from which resulted *actiones in personam*.
This contract which was also termed *pignus* we shall
describe later in the law of contracts (below, s. 898).

706a.
Pignus =
Pledge

2. *Hypotheca*. The hypothec, i.e. (according to our definition above, s. 698. 4) a form of real security which gave
neither ownership nor possession to the creditor, appeared

707.
Conception
and de-
velopment

very late in the history of Roman private law. In default of sources the details cannot be discerned with full certainty, but most probably the development was as follows.

708. The test case (*a*) The original case was the case of the tenant (*colonus*) who mortgaged to his landlord the movable property which he brought into the estate (*invecta et illata*). The tenant could not possibly deliver these things as a pledge to the landlord, since he needed them himself for his work. Consequently, when he mortgaged them to the landlord, the meaning of such an agreement could originally only be that a pledge should come into existence in the future, i.e. that later, if the rent was not duly paid, the landlord should be entitled to take possession of the things as pledges; the *invecta et illata* were, as Gaius 4. 147 rightly says, 'res quas colonus pro mercedibus fundi pignori futuras (N.B.) pepigisset'. On the strength of such an agreement the landlord had of course no *actio in rem* and was dependent on self-help if the tenant later failed to deliver the things to him. Thus the right of the creditor was still very far from being a hypothec.

709. Interdictum Salvianum (*b*) An unknown praetor Salvius granted, probably at the end of the Republic, an interdict to the landlord by which he might claim the possession of the *invecta et illata* (*interdictum Salvianum*). This interdict lay only against the tenant (Lenel, *Edict.* § 266).

710. The original actio Serviana (*c*) Later, but certainly before Hadrian's codification of the Edict, an unknown praetor Servius granted to the landlord an *actio in rem* (*actio Serviana*) and inserted it in the Edict immediately after the *interdictum Salvianum*. Hereby a true hypothec amounting to a *ius in rem alienam* was created, but it was still limited to the original case.

711. The classical actio Serviana (*d*) Later praetors perhaps granted an *actio Serviana utilis* in certain other cases, but it was only Julian who, in codifying the Edict for Hadrian, took the last step. He extended the *actio Serviana* to all cases of hypothec and even to pledge. He replaced Servius' *formula* by a new *formula* which was no longer confined to the *invecta et illata* of the tenant but was applicable to any sort of *pignus* (pledge and hypothec); nevertheless, he left it in its tradi-

tional place, viz. immediately after the *interdictum Salvianum*, which as before was confined to the *invecta et illata* of the tenant (Lenel, *Edict.* §§ 266, 267).

It has come as a surprise to modern students that Julian's Edict contained nothing but the *formula* and not also—as in other cases in which a purely praetorian remedy was granted—a clause in which the praetor declared that he would be prepared to grant the *formula*. The explanation is probably that previous edicts contained such a clause but Julian could not retain it since it referred only to the original case, viz. to the *invecta et illata* of the tenant, and his new *formula* had a much wider scope. He deemed it unnecessary to replace it by a more general clause, as his draft of the Edict was to be approved by the Emperor and the Senate. Thus he simply cancelled the old clause and was content merely to give the *formula*.

This, in broad outlines, was the development of *pignus* into a *ius in rem*. As regards the terminology, *pignus* originally meant only pledge, and even in classical times the contract called *pignus* (above, s. 706a, and below, s. 898) concerned only pledge. Thus Gaius could still say:

712. Classical terminology

   D. (50. 16) 238. 2: ' "Pignus" appellatum a "pugno", quia res quae pignori dantur, manu traduntur.'

After the hypothec had been generally recognized, the classical lawyers did not coin a special term for it but called both pledge and hypothec indifferently *pignus*. The term *hypotheca* remained entirely foreign to them and intruded into the classical texts only in post-classical times. For the numerous interpolations Justinian's compilers are but partly responsible; to a considerable extent they found these interpolations already in the texts used by them. Accordingly the meaning of the term *hypotheca* is in our sources not always the same; sometimes it is used as a synonym of *pignus*, sometimes it means hypothec in contrast to pledge. With this conclusion as to terminology the theory of the Greek origin of the Roman hypothec finally collapses, for its strongest support was the Greek term *hypotheca*. The development of the Roman hypothec as we have just described it is so typically Roman that the theory is today universally abandoned.

The *formula* granted in Hadrian's Edict was called by the classical lawyers *formula Serviana*. Accordingly, classical monographs on that *formula* must have had the title *ad formulam Servianam*, but post-classical writers before Justinian have changed the title to *ad formulam hypothecariam*. The *actio in rem* granted to the creditor was termed by the classical lawyers from the time of Hadrian's Edict *formula Serviana*, *actio Serviana*, or *vindicatio pignoris*. Other terms which occur in the sources are not classical.

> Sometimes the name *actio Serviana* is confined to the original case (above, s. 708) and the *actio in rem* granted to the creditor in other cases is called *actio quasi Serviana*. This terminology occurs only three times, *Inst. Iust.* (4. 6) 7 and 31, and *D.* (16. 1) 13. 1, and is certainly not classical (Lenel, *Edict*. p. 493 n. 1).
>
> The term *actio hypothecaria* is in classical texts always spurious. Exceptionally it is used to designate the Byzantine *actio quasi Serviana*; as a rule it is a substitute for the classical term *actio Serviana*.
>
> The term *actio pigneraticia* was used by the classical lawyers only to designate the *actio in personam* resulting from the real contract called *pignus* (below, s. 898). In our sources it is sometimes used as a substitute for the classical *actio Serviana*, but the relevant texts are interpolated.

713. Legal hypothecs in general　　3. *Legal hypothecs.* So far we have dealt only with *pignus* created by an agreement of the parties. But under classical law a hypothec might also come into existence directly by operation of law without such an agreement. The number of legal hypothecs was in classical times very small.

714. Classical legal hypothecs　　(1) Where a guardian bought something for the ward with the ward's money, the guardian became the owner of the thing since he could not act as a direct agent of his ward (above, s. 301). A constitution of Severus and Caracalla granted to the ward a legal hypothec on the purchased object.

(2) Claims of the fisc were from the times of the Severi secured by a legal general hypothec on the whole property of the fiscal debtor.

Other legal hypothecs apparently did not exist in classical times.

715. Non-classical legal hypothecs　　(1) It is said in our sources that under the Emperor Marcus a *senatusconsultum* granted to a creditor who had given a loan to a landowner for the purpose of rebuilding a collapsed house a legal hypothec on that house. However, this hypothec is hardly understandable since when the creditor

wished for real security he might demand a hypothec to be created by agreement before giving the money. Apparently, under classical law, the creditor had only a *privilegium exigendi* and not a legal hypothec.

This legal hypothec occurs only once in our sources, *D.* (20. 2) 1, a text taken from the 10th book of Papinian's *responsa*; but in this book Papinian dealt with privileges and not with *pignus*. The *privilegium exigendi* of the creditor is mentioned in several passages: *D.* (42. 3) 1; (42. 5) 24. 1; (12. 1) 25. In these texts the legal hypothec would have been mentioned if it had existed.

(2) Under Justinian's law the landlord of an agricultural estate had a legal hypothec on the fruits. This hypothec is not classical. Africanus knows nothing of it; he merely says (*D.* 47. 2. 62. 8) that as a rule the tenant mortgaged the fruits to his landlord. To be sure Pomponius, *D.* (20. 2) 7 pr., states that such a mortgage is implied in the contract of lease, but the text is obviously interpolated.

(3) Under Justinian's law the landlord of a house had a legal hypothec on the *invecta et illata* of his tenant. This hypothec, too, is not classical.

D. (2. 14) 4 pr. is clearly interpolated. Hence the passages in *D.* 20. 2 which deal with that hypothec must also be regarded as interpolated, though, for the time being, we cannot reconstruct the classical texts. The formula of the *interdictum de migrando* (Lenel, *Edict.* p. 265) knows nothing of a legal hypothec.

Summing up we may state that classical law was at least free from devastating legal hypothecs and to this extent was sound.

4. *Pignus ex causa iudicati captum and pignus praetorium.* 716.

(1) In the *extraordinaria cognitio* the execution of a judgment might be effected by *pignoris capio* ordered by the judge (above, s. 44). This sort of *pignus* was not yet fully developed in classical times; in particular the *actio Serviana* was not available to the creditor. ^{Pignus ex causa iudicati captum}

(2) Sometimes the praetorian *missio in possessionem* (above, s. 44) had as its purpose the provision of a creditor with a form of real security. The legatee, for example, might demand the *missio legatorum servandorum causa* if the legacy was not yet due and the heir refused to give the *cautio legatorum servandorum causa* (Lenel, *Edict.* §§ 172, 173). In ^{717. Pignus praetorium}

such cases the Byzantines termed the right of the *missus*
a 'pignus praetorium'. This term is certainly not classical,
since, under classical law, it would have been misleading:
the *actio Serviana* was a purely praetorian remedy, hence
any classical *pignus* was a *pignus praetorium*. The classical
lawyers in discussing the legal position of the *missus* might
have occasionally used the analogy of *pignus* and even employed the term *pignus*, but it seems that in fact they never
did so since all relevant texts are interpolated. In any case
this sort of *pignus* differed widely from the true *pignus* of
classical private law; it was only Justinian who granted the
missus an *actio Serviana* (*C.* 8. 2 1. 2).

718.   iii. The *aerarium populi Romani* and the *municipia* when
Praediatura making a contract with a private person required a special
security, the *cautio praedibus praediisque*. *Praedes* were
sureties of a special kind; *praedia* were estates given as real
security. Neither ownership nor possession was transferred
to the creditor, who was only entitled to sell the estates.
This sort of security was created by a signed declaration of
the landowner (*subsignare* is said of the party who gave the
security). The *subsignatio* was registered in the records of
the State (*tabulae publicae*) or of the *municipium* (*tabulae
communes*; concerning the terminology see above, s. 1 57).
Moreover, the *subsignatio* was sometimes published *ita uti
de plano recte legi possit* (*Lex Malacitana*, cap. lxiii). This
sort of security was virtually a hypothec, but a *hypotheca
iuris publici*. Only the *aerarium* or a *municipium* could be the
holder of such a hypothec and the creditor was not protected by the *actio Serviana* or any other *actio in rem*. The
praetorian Edict had a rubric *de praediatoribus* (Lenel,
Edict. § 1 86), but *praediator* means the person who purchased the estates from the *aerarium* or the *municipia* (Gai.
2. 6 1) and the praetor only promised to protect such pur-
chasers, as the *lex Malacitana*, cap. lxv, clearly shows. No
actio in rem was granted by the praetor to the *aerarium* or
the *municipia*. Thus this sort of hypothec lies outside the
domain of private law. As always, whenever we cross the
boundary of private law we enter a new world: we find
documents, registration, and publicity, phenomena which

were entirely foreign to classical private law. The *praediatura* certainly existed as early as the second century B.C. and was still in force throughout the classical period, but no connexion with the hypothec of private law is visible. Here as always public law and private law were kept strictly apart.

Similarly the real charges in the so-called alimentary foundations fell under public law and can only be mentioned in passing.

719.
Alimentary
foundations

SOURCES

s. 704. Read Gai. 2. 59, 60; 3. 201.

s. 705. Compare *Fr. Vat.* 94, first sentence, with *D.* (24. 3) 49. 1 [*pignoris*] ⟨*fiduciae*⟩. Read *D.* (13. 7) 8. 3 [*pignus*] ⟨*fiduciam*⟩; (13. 7)34 [*pignus*] ⟨*fiduciam*⟩. Note in both passages *eam* which the compilers forgot to change into *id*.

s. 709. Read Gai. 4. 147.

s. 712. Read *D.* (20. 6) 7. 4 [*hypothecae*] ⟨*pignori*⟩; (13. 7) 9. 2, spurious; (20. 1) 5. 1, spurious; (13. 7) 1 pr.; *Inst. Iust.* (4. 6) 7; *Tract. de actionibus* (Z xiv, 1893, p. 89), s. 5.

s. 714. Read *D.* (27. 9) 3 pr.; *C.* (7. 8) 6.

s. 715. 1. Read *D.* (20. 2) 1; (42. 3) 1; (42. 5) 24. 1; (12. 1) 25.

s. 715. 2. Read *D.* (47. 2) 62. 8, first sentence.

BIBLIOGRAPHY

s. 704. Oertmann, *Die Fiducia* (1890); Manigk, *PW* vi. 2287; Longo, *Corso di diritto romano. La fiducia* (1933); Erbe, *Die Fiducia im röm. Rechte* (1940); Franceschelli, 'La garanzia reale delle obbligazioni nel diritto romano classico e nel diritto inglese', *St. Albertoni*, iii (1935), 517 ff.; Burdese, *Lex commissoria e ius vendendi nella fiducia e nel pignus* (1949), 7 ff., with references.

s. 705. Erbe, l.c. 191 ff.; Lenel, Z iii (1882), 104 ff.

s. 706a. Manigk, *PW* xx. 1239 ff.; Steinwenter, *PW* xx. 1234 ff.

s. 707. Manigk, *PW* xvii. 343 ff.; M. Fehr, *Beiträge zur Lehre vom röm. Pfandrecht in klassischer Zeit* (1910), 4 ff., 136 ff., with references.

s. 709. Lenel, *Edict.* (1927), § 266; Berger, *PW* ix. 1667.

s. 712. Lenel, *Edict.* (1927), p. 493 nn. 1 and 13; Schulz, *History* (1946), 202 ff., with references.

s. 714. 1. Dernburg, *Pfandrecht*, i (1860), 321; Windscheid, *Pand.* i (1906), § 231 n. 10; Pringsheim, *Der Kauf mit fremdem Geld* (1916), 126.

s. 714. 2. Dernburg, l.c. 334 ff.; Windscheid, l.c. § 232 n. 1.

s. 715. 1. Dernburg, l.c. 314 ff.; Windscheid, l.c. § 231 n. 9; Pringsheim, l.c. 151.

s. 715. 2 and 3. Dernburg, l.c. 294 ff.; Windscheid, l.c. § 231; Koschaker in *Abhandlungen zur antiken Rechtsgeschichte. Festschrift für G. Hanausek* (1926), 152.

s. 716. Dernburg, l.c. 417 ff.; Windscheid, l.c. § 233; Wenger, *CP*. 313.

s. 717. Dernburg, l.c. 400 ff.; Windscheid, l.c. § 233; Maria F. Lepri, *Note sulla natura giuridica delle missiones in possessionem* (1939), 3–37, with references; Branca 'Missiones in possessionem e possessio', *St. Solazzi* (1948), 483 ff.

s. 718. Mommsen, *Schr.* 1. 357 ff.; *Staatsrecht*, ii (1887), 430 ff.; P. Viard, *Le Praes* (1907); Schulz, Z xxviii (1907), 470 ff.; Lenel, *Edict.* (1927), § 186.

s. 719. Pernice, *Labeo*, iii. 1 (1892), 164 ff., 167; G. Segrè, 'Sulle istituzioni alimentarie imperiali', *Scritti*, ii (1938), 36 ff.; 'Nuove osservazioni in tema di istituzioni aliment. imperiali', *St. Albertoni*, i (1935), 349 ff.

3. *Legal content of the classical real securities*

i. *Forfeiture*

720.
Forfeiture
without
lex com-
missoria
Fiducia cum creditore was, as already stated (s. 704), created by a conveyance (*mancipatio* or *in iure cessio*) to a creditor *fiduciae causa*. The latter acquired full ownership of the thing but was bound to restore it, if the debt was properly discharged. Failure to pay the debt at the appointed time did not automatically entail forfeiture; the creditor remained a 'trustee' and had to keep the object at the debtor's disposal so that, if the debtor paid in due course the creditor was bound to re-convey the thing and if he failed to do so was liable on the *actio fiduciae*. The formalism of the Roman *mancipatio* and *in iure cessio* led inevitably to this result.

Suppose that the *pactum fiduciae* contained nothing but the following clause (cf. *Formula Baetica*, 1. 10 ff.): 'ut usque eo is fundus eaque mancipia fiduciae essent, donec ea omnis pecunia persoluta esset'. Then forfeiture could not take place automatically, even if a certain day had been fixed for the payment; the wording of the pact makes that quite clear.

721. Lex
commis-
soria effects
It was only by a special clause of the *pactum fiduciae* that forfeiture took place. Such a clause was called *lex commissoria* (*lex* = contract, agreement, clause of a contract or agreement; *committitur fiducia* = the *fiducia* is forfeited). On the strength of this clause the creditor might become absolute owner of the mortgaged object, whereupon the debt expired. When a *res nec mancipi* was given as a pledge

(*pignus*), a *lex commissoria* might also be added. If the debt was not punctually discharged, the creditor became the owner of the thing and the debt was extinguished. In such a case the agreement by which the *pignus* was created implied a conditional *traditio dominii* (the creditor shall be the owner if the debt is not duly paid), and on the strength of this *traditio* the creditor acquired ownership when the condition was fulfilled. When a *res mancipi* was given as a pledge (*pignus*) under a *lex commissoria*, the creditor could only acquire bonitary ownership (above, s. 655) since civil ownership could not be transferred by *traditio*. Of course he might become civil owner later by *usucapio*.

When a thing (*res mancipi* or *nec mancipi*) was given as hypothec (*pignus*; see above, s. 712) under a *lex commissoria*, that clause could only be effective if the creditor later (after the debt had become due) came into possession of the object.

The *lex commissoria* remained in force throughout the classical period in spite of the harshness which it implied for the debtor; eventually it was abolished by Constantine (*C. Th.* 3. 2. 1 = *C. Iust.* 8. 34. 3). 722. Disappearance of lex commissoria

ii. *Right of the creditor to sell the mortgaged object*

As regards *fiducia* the creditor (as he was the owner of the thing) had of course the legal power to sell the object and to transfer ownership to the purchaser, but if he did so without being authorized by a special *pactum de vendenda fiducia*, he was liable on the *actio fiduciae* if the debtor later discharged the debt. Examples of such a pact are furnished by our documents. 723. Pactum de vendenda fiducia

> Pompeian document of A.D. 61 (*FIRA* iii, no. 91 with Arangio-Ruiz, *Parerga*, 1945, pp. 67 ff.): '. . . Si ea pecunia omnis mihi heredive meo kalendis Novembribus primis soluta non erit, ut mihi heredive meo liceat ea mancipia, quibus de agitur, idibus Decembribus primis pecunia presenti Pompeis in foro luce palam vendere. . . .'
>
> *Formula Baetica* of the first or second century A.D. (*FIRA* iii, no. 92): '. . . Si pecunia sua quaque die L. Titio heredive eius data soluta non esset, tum uti eum fundum eaque mancipia sive quae mancipia ex is L. Titius heresve eius vellet, ubi et quo die vellet, pecunia praesenti venderet. . . .'

Without such a *pactum de vendenda fiducia* the creditor was
not entitled as between himself and the giver of the *fiducia*
to sell the object, for it is not credible that the pact was
regarded as being implied in formal acts like *mancipatio* and
in iure cessio. A *pactum de non vendenda fiducia* was for that
reason superfluous. Nevertheless, the professional scribes
might have occasionally inserted such a negative clause in
the document according to the rule *superflua non nocent*. An
apocryphal text (Paulus, *Sent.* 2. 13. 5) states that in spite
of a *pactum de non vendenda fiducia* the creditor might sell
the *fiducia* without becoming liable on the *actio fiduciae*; this
was certainly not classical law.

724.   In the case of *pignus* (pledge as well as hypothec) the
Pactum de   creditor's right to sell the mortgaged thing depended like-
pignore
vendendo   wise on a special *pactum de pignore vendendo* which in classical times was not regarded as implied in any *pignoris datio*.
Gaius (2. 64) obviously knows nothing of an implied
pactum and it is not probable that the law was in this respect
altered during the following decades. Thus under classical
law a *pactum de non vendendo pignore* was superfluous, but
it might nevertheless appear in documents (*superflua non
nocent*). Under post-classical law the creditor had the right
to sell without a special authorization; the *pactum de vendendo* was now regarded as implied in any *datio pignoris*.
Under Justinian's law the creditor had that right even
when parties had expressly excluded it by a *pactum de non
vendendo pignore*. The legal hypothecs recognized by classical law (above, s. 714) were introduced by imperial constitutions which probably afforded the *ius vendendi* to the
creditor.

725. Mode   The sale of *fiducia* and *pignus* was regulated by the pacts
of the sale of the parties, as our documents show (above, s. 723); legal
rules apparently did not exist.

726.   The creditor who sold the *fiducia* might transfer civil
Transfer of ownership to the purchaser by *mancipatio* or *in iure cessio*;
ownership
by the   if he only delivered the thing to the purchaser by *traditio*,
selling   the latter became bonitary owner (above, s. 655). When a
creditor
res mancipi was given as *pignus* (pledge or hypothec), the
creditor making use of his *ius vendendi* could render the

purchaser only a bonitary owner; neither *mancipatio* nor *in iure cessio* was available to the creditor, since (in contrast to *fiducia*) he was not the owner of the thing. When a *res nec mancipi* was given as *pignus*, the creditor selling the thing might transfer full civil ownership to the purchaser by *traditio*, since any non-owner could transfer ownership by *traditio* with the owner's consent (above, s. 620) and this consent the mortgager had irrevocably given in the *pactum de vendendo*.

The price which the creditor received from the purchaser of the *fiducia* or *pignus* automatically diminished or completely extinguished the debt. If the price was below the amount of the debt, the creditor might sue the personal debtor for the rest with an *actio in personam*. This was sometimes expressly stated in the pacts of the parties. 727. The price

> Pompeian document cited above, s. 723: 'Si quo minoris ea mancipia, quibus de agitur, venierint, in sortis vicem debebuntur mihi heredive meo quae reliqua erunt.'

But under classical law the statement was not required; even without it the creditor was entitled to claim the remainder of the debt.

When the price exceeded the amount of the debt the creditor had to restore the surplus (*superfluum*) to the mortgagor (not necessarily identical with the debtor). 728. Hyperocha

> Modern students, with rather a snobbish predilection for Greek terms, are wont to call this surplus *hyperocha* (ἡ ὑπεροχή). The term was undoubtedly foreign to classical legal language; in our sources it occurs only once: *D.* (20. 4) 20.

When the *fiducia* was sold, the mortgagor might sue the creditor with the *actio fiduciae* for the surplus. When a pledge was sold the pledgor had the *actio pigneraticia in personam* (above, s. 712) with which he might claim the surplus. This action was probably also available when a hypothec was sold; apparently, the real contract *pignus* (below, s. 898) came into existence when the creditor took the thing given as hypothec into his possession in order to sell it.

When the creditor failed to find an adequate purchaser, he might apply to the Emperor to assign the thing to him 729. Impetratio dominii (the creditor) for a certain price (*impetratio dominii*); in the case of *fiducia*, since the creditor is already owner, the expression used may have been *impetratio possessionis*. This institution scarcely existed before the Severi.

iii. *Right of the creditor to use the mortgaged object and to reap its fruits*

730.
Pledge
The creditor was not entitled to use the pledge unless the pledgor had allowed this in a special clause of the agreement; if the creditor used it without permission, he was (if the thing was movable) liable on the *actio furti* (below, s. 982). If the pledge was a fruit-bearing thing, the creditor might be authorized to reap the fruits and to keep them as his own; whether such a pact was regarded as implied remains doubtful. The value of the fruits diminished or completely extinguished the debt; when capital and interest was due, the value of the fruits had to be set off first against the interest and then against the capital. However, parties were free to regulate the matter differently. In particular it might be provided by a pact that the fruits should be kept in lieu of interest without regard to whether the value of the fruits was, or was not, equal to the amount of the debt; modern students call such a pact a *pactum antichreticum*.

The term antichresis (ἀντίχρησις) means the enjoyment of the use or the fruits of a thing (χρῆσις) in recompense for something else (ἀντί τινος), not necessarily ἀντὶ τῶν τόκων, in lieu of interest. In our sources it occurs only once since *D.*(20.1) 11.1 and (13.7) 33 are fragments of the same text; here antichresis means χρῆσις ἀντὶ τῶν τόκων, but the text does not deal with a case in which the estate *itself* was mortgaged. Thus the term *antichresis* is absent in classical legal language. It occurs but very seldom in other sources; see Ebrard, *Die Digestenfragmente ad formulam hypothecariam* (1917), 116; Liddell and Scott, *Lex.* v. ἀντιχράω. Preisigke–Kiessling, *Wörterbuch der griech. Papyrusurkunden*, iv (1944), 181; in the papyri hitherto only once: *Pap. Groning.* (ed. A. G. Ross, 1933), no. 11 col. i. 12; ii. 5.

731.
Fiducia
As regards *fiducia* the creditor might of course use the thing without making himself liable on the *actio furti*, since he was the owner. The fruits which he gained were set off against interest and capital as we have stated with regard to *pignus*.

SOURCES

s. 721. Proof of *lex commissoria* occurring in the *pactum fiduciae*: Paul. *Sent.* (2. 13) rubric with Schulz, Z xlvii (1927), 47.

s. 723. Read Paul. *Sent.* (2. 13) 5, spurious.

s. 724. Read Gai. 2. 64; *D.* (47. 2) 74; *C.* (4. 24) 4 [*vel hypothecae*]; *C.* (8. 27) 7 [*non reluctante*]; *reluctari* occurs only in this text and *C.* (2. 58) 2 Justinian, *C.* (4. 1) 12. 1*a* Justinian, *C.* (11. 59) 6. 1 Grat. Valentin. Theodos. See further Paul. *Sent.* (2. 5) 1 spurious; *D.* (13. 7) 4 [*etsi*] ⟨*si*⟩; [*hoc tamen . . . distraheretur*]; [*nisi . . . cessaverit*].

s. 726. Read Gai. 2. 64; *D.* (41. 1) 46; (41. 1) 9. 4.

s. 727. Read *D.* (20. 5) 9. 1; *C.* (4. 10) 10.

s. 728. Read *D.* (13. 7) 6. 1; the text originally dealt with *fiducia*; Paul. *Sent.* (2. 13) 1.

s. 729. Read *D.* (13. 7) 24 pr. first sentence; the text originally dealt with *fiducia*: Lenel, Z iii (1882), 111; Erbe, *Fiducia*, 28, with references.

s. 730. Read Gai. 3. 195, 196; *Inst. Iust.* (4. 1) 6; *D.* (47. 2) 55 pr.; *C.* (4. 32) 17; *D.* (36. 4) 5. 21.

s. 731. Read Paul. *Sent.* (2. 13) 1*b* = *D.* (20. 2) 8, spurious; Paul. *Sent.* (2. 13) 2; (20. 1) 23 pr. dealing with *fiducia*.

BIBLIOGRAPHY

ss. 720–2. Dernburg, *Pfandrecht*, ii (1864), 273 ff.; Manigk, *PW* vi. 2296; ix. 296, 355; xx. 1248; Erbe, *Fiducia* (1940), with references; Burdese, *St. Solazzi* (1948), 324 ff.; *Lex Commissoria e ius vendendi nella fiducia e nel pignus* (1949), 10 ff., 95 ff., 110 ff.

s. 723. Manigk, *PW* vi. 2293 ff.; Devilla, 'L'ius distrahendi nella fiducia e nel pegno', *St. Sassaresi*, xv (1938), not available; Erbe, l.c. 36 ff.; Burdese, *Lex commissoria*, 25 ff.

s. 724. Manigk, *PW* xx. 1256; Albertario in G. Rotondi, *Scritti*, ii. 582 n. 1; Messina Vitrano, *Per la storia del ius distrahendi nel pegno* (1910); Ratti, 'Sul ius vendendi del creditore pignoraticio', *St. Urbinati*, i (1927), not available; Levy, Z xlix (1929), 251; Lauria, 'Ricerche su Pauli Sententiarum libri', *Annali Macerata*, vi (1930), p. 85 f., with references; Burdese, *Lex commissoria*, 132 ff.

s. 726. Mitteis, *RP* i (1908), 208; Beseler, *Beiträge*, iv (1920), 129; *Opora* (1930), 3; Burdese, *Lex commissoria*, 165 ff.

s. 728. Dernburg, *Pfandrecht*, i (1860), 140 ff.; Manigk, *PW* xvii. 291; Kaser, *Quanti ea res est* (1935), 79; Erbe, *Fiducia* (1940), 89; Burdese, *Lex commissoria*, 195 ff.; Kreller, Z lxii (1942) 173 f.

s. 729. Dernburg, *Pfandrecht*, ii (1864), 240 ff.; Burdese, *Lex commissoria*, 206 ff.

ss. 730, 731. Dernburg, *Pfandrecht*, ii. 67 ff.; Manigk, *Gläubigerbefriedigung durch Nutzung* (1910).*

4. *Accessory character of the real security*

732.   i. Real security being a form of credit (above, s. 699) is
Types of from the economic point of view accessory to a debt, but
accessio
this dependence of the security on the debt may be legally
expressed in various ways.

733.   1. A capitalist may give a loan to a landowner, both par-
'Grund- ties agreeing that the creditor shall merely have the right to
schuld'
recover the money out of the estate. If the money is due and
not paid, the creditor may take the estate and realize it but
he cannot levy execution either on the person of the landowner or on his property apart from the estate; the owner
is not in this case a so-called personal debtor. The *Grund-
schuld* of modern German law is an example of this type of
security, but in its pure form it is hardly ever practised. It
was entirely foreign to Roman private law: it is a sort of real
charge, and real charges, as we have seen (ss. 666, 685),
were not allowed under classical private law (or under Justinian's law except in the case of the *servitus oneris ferendi*;
above, 2. 667). Classical public law had apparently no
scruples about recognizing this form of real security (*praediatura*, alimentary foundations; above, ss. 718, 719).

734.   2. The real security of classical private law was accessory
Roman   to a personal debt (*debitum*).
private
law   The *formula Serviana* (above, ss. 711, 712) began with
the following words:

> 'Si paret inter Aulum Agerium et Lucium Titium convenisse ut ea
> res, qua de agitur, Aulo Agerio pignori esset *propter pecuniam debitam*. . . .'

The security could not come into existence unless a debt
existed which might be secured by the mortgage; on the
other hand, the security came to an end when the debt was
discharged. Thus the creditor who received a real security
had as a rule two ways of obtaining satisfaction:

(*a*) He might avail himself of his claim against the personal debtor (who might be a person different from the
giver of the security) and eventually levy execution upon
his person or property.

(*b*) He might obtain satisfaction out of the object given
as a real security.

Hypotheca and *pignus* is expressly designated as *accessio* in only one 735. Ter-
passage: *D.* (46. 3) 43; the designation is implied in *D.* (46. 1) 32. Both minology
texts are interpolated, but nevertheless we retain the term.

The term *debitor personalis* (personal debtor in contrast to the owner
of the mortgaged object) was foreign to classical usage. But this term is
also indispensable.

ii. The accessory nature of the classical real security
needs some explanation and qualification.

1. The connexion of the security with the personal debt 736.
might be more or less close.   Fiducia

(*a*) The *fiducia cum creditore* conferred ownership on the
creditor *ob debitum*. If the debt did not exist, the *mancipatio
fiduciae causa* was, nevertheless, valid and the creditor
acquired ownership; moreover, if the debt ceased to exist,
ownership did not automatically revert to the mortgagor.
In both cases the creditor was only bound to *re-mancipate*
the object.

(*b*) *Pignus*, however, was more closely connected with 737.
the debt. If the debt did not exist, the creditor acquired no Pignus
right over the thing; and if the debt ceased to exist, the
creditor's right automatically lapsed.

2. A *natura debitum* (*obligatio naturalis*; see below, s. 795) 738.
was regarded as a sufficient basis for a real security. Thus if Obligatio
a slave promised something, there resulted only a *naturalis*
(i.e. not actionable) *obligatio* on the part of the slave;
nevertheless it sufficed as a basis for *fiducia* and *pignus* as
well as for the giving of a surety.

3. If the debt was discharged, the security came to an 739.
end; the *res fiduciae data* had to be re-mancipated and *pignus* Pignoris
ended automatically. It should be kept in mind that the indivisa est
personal debtor as well as the mortgagor was entitled to
repay the debt even before the term fixed for repayment.
If only a part of the debt was discharged, the security continued to exist on the whole mortgaged object, but only for
the rest of the debt; modern students express this rule by
the maxim *pignoris causa indivisa est*. The strangely worded
maxim occurs only once in an interpolated text:
D. (21. 2) 65.

Consider the following cases:
(*a*) A gave an estate as a *pignus* for a debt of 100; later he paid back 50.

The whole estate (not merely half of it) remained mortgaged for the remaining 50.

(*b*) A gave two pieces of land, each worth 120, as a *pignus* for a debt of 100; later he paid back 50. Both estates remained mortgaged for 50; the creditor was not bound to release one of them.

(*c*) C gave a loan of 100 to D, who conveyed an estate to C as *pignus*. Later D died and H1 and H2 became his heirs each of them to one-half. The two heirs are now co-owners *pro indiviso* of the estate (above, s. 525); as for the debt, each of them now owes C 50 (*nomina ipso iure divisa sunt*; above, s. 531). The debt being due, H1 paid to C what he owed him, namely 50; H2 paid nothing. The legal result is: C's *pignus* continues to exist on the whole estate for 50; not only is the quota belonging to H2 charged with the *pignus*, but also the quota of H1 who has paid what was due from him.

(*d*) C gave a loan of 100 to D and received from him an estate as *pignus*. Later C died and H1 and H2 became his heirs. Now D owes 50 to each of the two heirs (*nomina ipso iure divisa sunt*; above, s. 525) and each of them has a *pignus* on the estate for 50. If D pays 50 to H1, the latter loses his personal claim and therewith his *pignus*. H2 still has a *pignus* on the whole estate for 50.

740.
Expiring of
the debt
with or
without
satisfaction

4. Where the debt expired otherwise than by payment, the security also came to an end if the creditor had obtained satisfaction. The *formula Serviana* made the condemnation conditional on the negative fact that the creditor had not been paid or otherwise satisfied ('. . . eamque pecuniam neque solutam neque eo nomine satisfactum esse'). Thus if the creditor accepted a *datio in solutum* (below, s. 1074) or released the personal debtor, he lost the real security. Even if the creditor became the heir of the personal debtor and the debt consequently expired by *confusio*, he was regarded as satisfied, whether or not the inheritance was solvent.

Suppose that C gave a loan to D and that A mortgaged his land to C for that debt. Later D died and C became his heir. The debt was extinguished by *confusio*, but the mortgage also came to an end. It was only in complicated cases that the debt expired without affording satisfaction to the creditor: in such cases the mortgage continued to exist without a personal debt.

Consider the following cases:

(*a*) C gave a loan to D and A gave a *pignus* to secure that debt. Later C sued D with an *actio in personam* which was consumed by *litis con-*

testatio. The *pignus* remained intact 'quia neque soluta pecunia neque eo nomine satisfactum est.'

(*b*) C gave a loan to D and received S as a surety. To secure the obligation of the surety (N.B.) A gave a *pignus* to C. Later D died and S became his heir. The obligation of the surety was extinguished by a so-called 'absorbing *confusio*', but *pignus* remained intact.

SOURCES

s. 738. Read Gai. 3. 119*a*; *D.* (12. 6) 13 pr.; (20. 1) 5 pr.

s. 739*b*. Read *D.* (20. 1) 19; (45. 1) 85. 6 [*tradere*] ⟨*mancipio dare*⟩.

s. 739*c*. Read *C.* (8. 30) 1; *D.* (13. 7) 8. 2.

s. 739*d*. Read *C.* (8. 31) 1; *D.* (13. 7) 11. 4.

s. 740. Read *D.* (20. 1) 13. 4, substantially classical; (46. 3) 38. 5.

BIBLIOGRAPHY

ss. 732–4. Dernburg, *Pfandrecht,* i (1860), 514; Windscheid, *Band* i, § 225; Ratti, *Sull' accessorietà del pegno* (1927), not available; Carrelli, *Sulla accessorietà del pegno in diritto romano* (1934), not available. On *praediatura* and alimentary foundation see references in bibliography ad ss. 718, 719.

s. 735. Levy, *Sponsio, fidepromissio, fideiussio* (1907), 18; Solazzi, *Bull.* xxxviii (1930), 18; *L'estinzione della obbligazione* (1931), 290; Flume, *Studien zur Akzessorietät der röm. Bürgschaftsstipulationen* (1932), 7. 126; *Voc. Iur. Rom.* i. 78. 39 f.

s. 739. Dernburg, *Pfandrecht,* ii (1864), 28 ff.; Windscheid, *Pand.* i (1906), § 226 n. 3; Schulz, *Einführung* (1916), 88 ff.

s. 740. Dernburg, l.c. ii. 574 ff.; Windscheid, l.c. § 249; Beseler, Z xlvii (1927), 55; Solazzi, Estinzione, 290.

5. *Plurality of hypothecs on the same object*

If a thing had been given *fiduciae causa* for a certain debt, the mortgagor obviously could not give it *fiduciae causa* to another creditor, but the owner of a thing might give it as a hypothec successively to several creditors; then the order of the several hypothecs was fixed by the rule *prior tempore, potior iure*. There were, however, privileged hypothecs which ranked before all others. [741. Prior tempore, potior iure]

The classical law concerning the second and succeeding hypothecs was rather primitive.

1. The holder of a second (or further) hypothec was not entitled to the possession of the thing, nor had he the right to sell it. It would have been possible to grant the second creditor the right to sell the object (of course charged with [742. Right to take the object into possession and to sell it]

the first hypothec), but the Roman lawyers did not avail themselves of that possibility.

743.
Extinction of hypothecs by sale

2. Only the first creditor had the right to take the thing into his possession, if the debt was due, and to sell it on the strength of a *pactum de vendendo* (above, s. 724). Where he sold it he rendered the purchaser a free owner, civil or bonitary (above, s. 726), and all hypothecs—not only the hypothec of the selling creditor but also all further hypothecs—came to an end.

744.
Second creditor cannot claim the hyperocha

3. It is said that if the price which the first creditor received from the purchaser exceeded the sum which was due to him, he had to restore the surplus (*hyperocha*; above, s. 728) to the second creditor. But as regards classical law this opinion must be wrong simply because the second creditor had no action against the first creditor with which he might claim the surplus. Under classical law the surplus had to be restored to the mortgagor (above, s. 728).

745.
Second hypothec raised to the first rank if first hypothec expired

4. When the first creditor was paid off, the second hypothec rose to the first rank. This is a primitive rule. The second creditor usually stipulated higher interest than the first because his risk was greater; if the second hypothec now obtained the first rank, the rate of interest was not automatically reduced. Again we have to realize that the classical hypothec was not designed to serve as a permanent investment of capital (above, s. 700). The classical lawyers would probably have replied to our objection with the argument that if the second creditor, who by the extinction of the first hypothec obtained the first rank, was not prepared to reduce the rate of interest, the debtor might pay him off with the help of another capitalist who was willing to lend him the money at a lower rate of interest, viz. at the rate which was usual when the creditor was secured by a hypothec of first rank. Of course this reply would not fully satisfy us.

746. Ius offerendi et succedendi

5. The second creditor had a *ius offerendi et succedendi*. Under classical law this only meant that the second creditor was entitled to pay off the first creditor and thereby to raise his own hypothec to the first rank. He acquired neither the

personal claim of the first creditor nor his hypothec but, apparently on the strength of an imperial constitution, he might sell the mortgaged object and keep from the price even the sum which he had paid to the first creditor and not merely the amount of his own claim.

Suppose A mortgaged an estate to C1 for 50 and to C2 for 100. Later C2 paid 50 to C1. Thereupon the personal claim of C1 expired as well as his hypothec; the hypothec of C2 rose to the first rank. Now C2 sold the estate for 200; he was entitled to keep $100 + 50$, the rest he had to restore to A.

This *ius succedendi* also took place when a third creditor paid off the first creditor.

Suppose C1 had a hypothec for 50, C2 for 60, C3 for 100. Later C3 paid 50 to C1. The result was that the hypothec of C1 was extinguished; the hypothec of C3 up to 50 now occupied the first rank. Thus the estate was now charged as follows: (i) hypothec of C3 for 50; (ii) hypothec of C2 for 60; (iii) hypothec of C3 for 50.

SOURCES

s. 741. Read *C.* (8. 17) 3; *D.* (20. 4) 9. 3, heavily interpolated, the original text probably dealt with *fiducia*: Beseler, Z xlv (1925), 440; Erbe, *Fiducia* (1940), 76 f.

ss. 742, 743. Read *C.* (8. 17) 8; (8. 19) 3; Paul. *Sent.* (2. 13) 8.

s. 744. Read *D.* (20. 4) 12. 5 [*et quod . . . restituat*].

s. 746. Read *D.* (20. 4) 11. 4; *D.* (20. 4) 12. 6; *D.* (20. 5) 5 pr.; *C.* (8. 13) 22; *C.* (8. 17) 5.

BIBLIOGRAPHY

s. 741. Dernburg, *Pfandrecht*, ii (1864), 411 ff.; Windscheid, *Pand.* i (1906), § 242; Koschaker, *Scritti Ferrini*, iii (1948), 233; Beseler, Z lxvi (1948), 325 sub v. 'invertere' (right).

s. 742. Dernburg, l.c. 482 ff.

s. 743. Dernburg, l.c. 224.

s. 744. Dernburg, l.c. 487; Beseler, *Beiträge*, iv (1920), 138; Kaser, *Quanti ea res est* (1935), 79.

s. 746. Schulz, Z xxvii (1906), 104 ff.; Windscheid, l.c. § 233*b* n. 11; Dernburg, l.c. 489, 518.

6. *Judicial remedies*

It seems convenient to wind up our discussion by gathering together the various judicial remedies resulting from *fiducia* and *pignus*. We have already mentioned them before, but some additional remarks are required.

747. Actio
fiduciae

From *fiducia cum creditore* resulted two actions, the *actio fiduciae directa* and *contraria* (on the terminology see above, ss. 70 ff.). The *actio directa* was the action of the mortgagor against the creditor by means of which he might claim the re-mancipation of the mortgaged object and damages in addition. It was an *actio bonae fidei*, though the *formula* perhaps did not contain the usual clause *ex fide bona* (above, ss. 61, 62). The condemnation involved *infamia* (above, s. 80). Further details of the *formula* remain doubtful. The *actio contraria* was the action of the creditor against the mortgagor by which he might claim indemnification for expenses.

748. Actio
Serviana

The *actio Serviana* as contained in Hadrian's Edict (above, s. 711) can be reconstructed with certainty (Lenel, *Edict.* § 267):

> 'Si paret inter Aulum Agerium et Lucium Titium convenisse, ut ea res, qua de agitur, Aulo Agerio pignori esset propter pecuniam debitam, eamque rem tunc, cum conveniebat, in bonis Lucii Titii fuisse eamque pecuniam neque solutam neque eo nomine satisfactum esse, neque per Aulum Agerium stare quo minus solvatur, nisi ea res restituetur, quanti ea res erit, tantam pecuniam iudex Numerium Negidium Aulo Agerio condemnato, si non paret absolvito.'

This *formula* is *in factum concepta* (above, s. 47) since the action was an *actio honoraria* (see above, ss. 46, 50). The action was an *actio in rem* (above, s. 56) like the *rei vindicatio* and lay like the latter against any *possessor* of the object. Obviously the wording of the *formula* covered both pledge and hypothec. As the edictal *formula* only mentioned *pignus conventionale*, an *actio utilis* (above, s. 52) had to be granted to the creditor in the case of a *pignus legale* (above, s. 720); an *actio utilis* was also required in other more difficult cases (see Lenel, l.c. p. 494) on which we will not dwell. If the same object was charged with two hypothecs of different rank, the second creditor might sue a third person with the *actio Serviana*; but if he himself obtained possession, the first creditor might sue him with the *actio Serviana*, since as between first and second creditor only the former was entitled to possession (above, s. 742). If the second creditor sued the first with the *actio Serviana*, the latter was protected by an *'exceptio si non* Numerio Negidio (the first creditor) ante pignori res obligata est'.

The *interdictum Salvianum* was a remedy available to the lessor of agricultural land against a lessee who had mortgaged the *invecta et illata* (above, s. 709). The interdict was, as Gaius 4. 147 rightly says, an *interdictum adipiscendae possessionis*; its *formula* is not transmitted to us, but most probably it was framed as an *interdictum prohibitorium* (above, s. 109). The compilers modified the interdict by granting it (like the *actio Serviana*) against any possessor of the mortgaged objects. 749. Inter-dictum Salvianum

The actions resulting from the real-contract *pignus*—the *actio pigneraticia directa* and *contraria* (above, s, 70)—will be described later (below, ss. 898 ff.). 750. Actio pignera-ticia

SOURCES

s. 747. Read Paul. *Sent.* 2. 13. 6–7.

s. 748. Read *D.* (20. 4) 12 pr.

s. 749. Read *D.* (20. 1) 10; (43. 33) 1. 1; *C.* (8. 9) 1 [*debitoremve*] perhaps only a gloss.

BIBLIOGRAPHY

s. 747. Lenel, *Edict.* (1927), § 107; W. Erbe, *Die Fiducia im röm. Recht* (1940), 86 ff., 106 ff. with references; Kreller, Z lxii (1942), 143 ff., 183 ff. (hardly acceptable); Burdese, *St. Solazzi* (1948), 324 ff.

s. 748. Lenel, l.c. § 267; Kreller, Z lxiv (1944), 334.

s. 749. Lenel, l.c. § 266; Berger, *PW* ix. 1668; Kreller, Z lxiv (1944), 320 ff.

CHAPTER IV

POSSESSION

1. *Introduction*

751.
Conception
of possessio

THE word *possidere* contains of course the word *sedere* (to sit), and though the first syllable (*pos*) is linguistically doubtful, the meaning of *possidere* can hardly be anything else than 'to sit upon a thing'; accordingly *possessio* means 'sitting', *possessor* 'a person settled upon a thing'. The terms originally referred only to land and even the Twelve Tables apparently did not apply them to movables. The semasiological history of these terms we will not pursue in this place; according to our plan we confine ourselves to fixing their legal meaning under classical private law. Here their meaning was highly technical: *possessio* meant physical control of a corporeal thing (a *iuris quasi possessio* did not exist under classical law) in contrast to ownership and other kinds of rights. *Possessor* was a person who had physical control of a corporeal thing, whether or not he had any right to have the thing under his control. The owner might also be, and as a rule was, the *possessor* of the thing; but if he lost the thing or if it was stolen, he was no longer *possessor*, though he was still the owner; on the other hand, the thief was *possessor*. Thus *possessio* was a matter of fact and not of right, but it was a fact which was, within certain limits, endowed with legal consequences and, in fact, the classical lawyers only described physical control as possession when it was recognized by the law. Only exceptionally was *possessio* ascribed to a person who had no physical control over the thing; here *possessio* meant that the person concerned was in the legal position of a true *possessor* (see below, s. 756).

As regards the legal effects of *possessio* we must distinguish between *ius civile* and *ius honorarium*.

752. Ius
civile

Under classical *ius civile* possession was relevant in the following cases:

1. Ownership of *res nec mancipi* was transferred by *traditio ex iusta causa* (above, ss. 613 ff.).

2. One of the requirements of *usucapio* was possession (above, s. 622).

3. The *bonae fidei possessor* of a thing acquired the fruits *iure civili*. A *bonae fidei possessor* of a slave acquired, within certain limits the acquisitions of his slave.

4. Ownership was acquired by *occupatio* when the thing was taken into possession (above, s. 631). Where a wild animal escaped, both ownership and possession continued to exist 'si in conspectu sit nostro nec difficilis eius persecutio sit' (Gai. 2. 67). Wild animals which had the *consuetudo revertendi* remained in the possession of their owner even when they strayed abroad (Gai. 2. 68).

In all these cases the *possessor* has the thing in his control *qua* owner.

As regards *ius honorarium*, the praetor protected a certain group of possessors by special remedies, the so-called possessory interdicts, *unde vi*, *uti possidetis*, and *utrubi*. We shall describe these remedies in detail later (below, ss. 776a ff.); here we are only concerned with determining the group of persons to whom they were available. **753. Ius honorarium**

1. Any person who had a corporeal thing under physical control *qua* owner was protected by those interdicts. Even the thief was protected, though not against the person robbed.

> Suppose that A stole a thing from B and sold it to a purchaser C, who was in good faith. Later B found the thing in C's hands and took it from him. C might sue B with the *interdictum utrubi* and B could not meet it by the objection that he was the owner.

2. Persons who had the physical control of a thing but not *qua* owner were only exceptionally protected by the interdicts.

(*a*) The *tutor impuberis*, *curator furiosi* and *prodigi* were possessors of the property of their wards and protected by the possessory interdicts.

(*b*) A person who possessed a thing *qua* pledge (*pignus*) had the interdicts. They were already granted to him in republican times when the *actio Serviana* did not yet exist (above, s. 706*a*); the interdicts were then the only remedies available to him. The mortgagor was not afforded the interdicts, although as regards *ius civile* (*usucapio*, acquisition of fruits) he was possessor.

(*c*) A person who possessed a thing by way of *precarium* was vested with the possessory interdicts. What is *precarium*? Our sources are poor and apparently inaccurate. It is said that *precarium* was a gratuitous grant revocable at will. However, when somebody borrowed a book for a week, that was certainly *commodatum* and the borrower was not entitled to the interdicts, as we shall presently see. If the loan of the book could be terminated at the lender's will, the legal position of the borrower cannot possibly have been better. Apparently *precarium* was confined in the classical period to those special cases in which the borrower might reasonably expect to become the owner of the object. When a *fiducia cum creditore* was made, the creditor might hand over the object to the mortgagor by way of *precarium*: the latter could expect to regain ownership by discharging the debt. Further, when the seller of a thing handed it over to the purchaser by way of *precarium* under an agreement that the latter should become owner if the price was fully paid, the purchaser might expect to become the owner. The *precario dans* was debarred from the interdicts, but he was probably possessor *iure civili*, in particular *quoad usucapionem*; this at any rate was Sabinus' opinion. Against the *precario accipiens* the *precario dans* had a special interdict, the *interdictum de precario* (Lenel, *Edict.* § 258).

(*d*) The *sequester* was equally protected by the possessory interdicts. The *sequester* was a stake-holder; two persons disputing over the ownership of a thing deposited it with a third person. The *sequester* alone was possessor. The idea apparently was that neither of the disputing parties must be regarded as possessor in order to prevent *usucapio* during the dispute.

(*e*) It is uncertain whether the holder of an *ager vectigalis* (above, s. 694) had the possessory interdicts.

(*f*) We need not discuss here the classical *missio in possessionem*, since it did not afford *possessio*. For literature see above, s. 717, bibliography.

Apart from these highly exceptional cases a person who 754. had the physical control, but not as owner, was not entitled Detentio to the possessory interdicts. Thus the lessee, the depositary, and the borrower of a thing had not the interdicts: they were available only to the lessor, the depositor, and the lender.

> The important consequence of this statement is evident. Suppose A hired a house from B for three years. After one year the lessor gave notice to A to leave the house at once. If A refused to do so, the lessor might resort to self-help without running the risk of being sued with an interdict. If A successfully resisted the lessor, the latter might sue him with an interdict; the lessee could not object that he had a right to stay in the house under the contract. Of course the lessee might claim damages by means of an *actio conducti* on the strength of the contract, but he still lost his home.

The usufructuary, like the lessee, was not granted the 755. Usu-above-mentioned possessory interdicts but he was pro-fructuary tected by special interdicts. not possessor

> The usufructuary had an interdict *si uti frui prohibitus esse dicetur* (Lenel, *Edict.* § 245, p. 468), but it was granted to him without regard to whether or not possession of the object had been acquired by him. An *interdictum uti possidetis utile* (Lenel, *Edict.* § 247, p. 473) applied only when two persons claimed the same usufruct against each other.

As already stated (s. 751), the lawyers exceptionally 756. ascribed possession to a person who had no physical con-Possessio trol at all. Thus the master of a slave acquired possession = legal through the slave even if the latter was not in his control position of (e.g. if the slave was in the hands of a *bonae fidei* or *malae* a possessor *fidei possessor*). In such cases, which we shall consider later (ss. 770 f.), *possessio* only means that the party was placed in the legal position of a true possessor.

The classical terminology was simple and clear. The 757. Ter-classical lawyers used as technical terms only *possessio, pos-*minology *sessor, possidere*. Within the domain of pure private law *possessio* meant 'actual physical control of a corporeal thing, recognized as such by the law' (*ius civile* or *ius honorarium*) or 'the legal position of such a possessor'. Other technical terms did not exist.

1. There was no term to designate physical control not recognized by the law. Modern students usually call this

sort of physical control *detentio* (*detentor*, *detinere*); they say, for example, that the lessee is merely a *detentor* and not a *possessor*. The classical lawyers occasionally used *tenere* and *detinere*, but not as technical terms, to designate physical control not recognized by the law. Nevertheless we shall retain this terminology since we need terms to describe this sort of physical control.

2. Possession protected by the possessory interdicts is called by modern students *possessio ad interdicta* (interdictal possession). This term too was unknown to the classical lawyers, but we shall nevertheless use it.

3. In our sources we find the terms *civilis possessio* and *naturalis possessio*. Their meaning has been much discussed but no consensus of opinion has been reached so far. In fact these terms were entirely unknown to classical lawyers. They occur in Justinian's *Digest* (*Fr. Vat.* 258 has only *naturaliter retinere* and the last sentence is spurious) and nowhere else; the number of relevant texts is very small and in some of them interpolation is evident. These facts (according to our well-founded method) inevitably lead to the conclusion that the whole unnecessary and ambiguous terminology is unclassical.

758.
Evaluation

The classical law of possession is an artificial creation of great interest for the historian, typical of the classical attitude and entirely unique; institutions found in other systems which at first sight seem similar turn out to be fundamentally different if examined more closely. This, however, is really all which can be said in favour of this part of classical law. The possessory interdicts are archaic and of an absurd intricacy. To debar the defendant in the interdictal procedure from any defence based on his right to possess goes too far. Moreover, the rule that ownership of *res nec mancipi* could only be transferred by transferring possession (*traditio*; above, ss. 613 ff.) was, at least in classical times, cumbersome and even senseless, particularly as the classical lawyers observed it very strictly and excluded the so-called *constitutum possessorium* (see below, s. 767). Transfer of ownership by agreement was on the way, but the classical lawyers obstinately stuck to the traditional rule. As a whole the classical law of possession was already thoroughly antiquated in classical times.

Lawyers of the post-classical period attempted to reform the law on this point. The cumbrous interdictal procedure was abolished and the interdicts were replaced by possessory actions. The classical rules concerning *traditio* were rendered less rigorous: the *constitutum possessorium* was recognized (below, s. 767) and symbolic *traditio* was held sufficient. But these and other reforms were carried through by interpolating classical texts; a drastic reform was beyond the strength of that period and even Justinian's compilers did not dare to attempt it.

759. Postclassical law

Thus the sources of the Roman law of possession are in a chaotic state; the texts are bristling with interpolations, reliable sources are scarce. To apply this law as a living law has proved a most difficult task and from the Glossators it has tormented generations of lawyers. Since Savigny's famous book *Das Recht des Besitzes* (1803) the Roman law of possession has been a favourite subject of continental Romanistic students, but owing to their uncritical and speculative methods their writings are (with few exceptions) today hardly more than collections, and often misleading collections, of materials. Through the application of modern critical and philological methods, from the time of Alibrandi, the outlines of the classical law have been ascertained, but numerous details are still doubtful. Exposition of the post-classical development, including Justinian's law (as usual much more difficult than that of the classical law), is still in its infancy. A modern work comprehending the whole Roman law of possession does not yet exist.

760. Sources and literature

SOURCES

s. 751. Read *D.* (41. 2) 3 pr.; Gai. 4. 139 [*quod tum . . . contenditur*]; *D.* (41. 2) 1 pr.; (43. 17) 1. 2; (37. 1) 3. 1 [*Hereditatis autem*] *bonorum*[*ve*], see above, s. 377.

s. 752. Read Gai. 2. 92; *D.* (41. 1) 48. 1 [*per longum tempus*] ⟨*usu*⟩; [*longum tempus*] ⟨*usucapio*⟩.

s. 753. 2*b.* Read *D.* (41. 3) 16 [*adeo . . . dedit*].

s. 753. 2*c.* Read Gai. 2. 59, 60; *D.* (43. 26) 20, shortened by the compilers; *C.* (4. 54) 3; *D.* (41. 2) 3. 5 to *accepit*; (43. 26) 15. 4.

s. 753. 2*d*. Read *D*. (16. 3) 17. 1.

s. 754. Read *D*. (43. 26) 6. 2.

s. 755. Read Gai. 2. 93; *Fr. Vat.* 90, first sentence; *D*. (41. 2) 12 pr. [*naturaliter*] ⟨*non*⟩; *D*. (43. 26) 6. 2.

s. 757. 2. Read *D*. (6. 1) 9: 'possessionem . . . quae locum habet in interdicto uti possidetis vel utrubi.'

s. 757. 3. Read *D*. (10. 4) 3. 15 [*non solum . . . possessioni*]; (41. 2) 1 pr. 1 [*naturaliter*]; [*naturali*]; (41. 2) 12 pr. [*naturaliter*] ⟨*non*⟩.

BIBLIOGRAPHY

s. 751. On the etymology of *possessio* see Bonfante, *Scritti*, iii (1926), 516 ff.; Stolz–Schmalz, *Latein. Grammatik* (1928), pp. 162, 501. On *iuris possessio* see Albertario, *Studi*, ii (1941), 307 ff.; Arangio–Ruiz, *Istituzioni* (1947), 281 f.; Biondi, *Istituzioni* (1946), 243; G. Segrè, *Scritti*, ii (1938), 653 ff.; Dénoyez, *Festschrift P. Koschaker*, ii (1939), 304 ff.; Monier, *St. Solazzi* (1948), 369, with references; Sargenti, *Scritti Ferrini*, ii (1947), 226 ff.

s. 752. 3. Beseler, *SD* iii (1937), 375; Aru, *Bull.* xlv (1938), 191 ff.*

s. 753. 2. M. Kaser, 'Zum römischen Fremdbesitz', *Z* lxiv (1944), 389 ff.; Albertario, 'La involuzione del possesso del precarista del creditore pignoratizio e del sequestratario nel diritto post-classico e giustinianeo', *Studi*, ii. 141 ff.

s. 753. 2*b*. M. Kaser, *Eigentum und Besitz* (1943), 353 f.; Z lxiv. 391.

s. 753. 2*c*. Kaser, *Eigentum und Besitz*, 349 ff., 354; Z lxiv. 391; Ciapessoni, 'Il precarista detentore', *Atti del primo congresso nazionale di Studi Romani*, ii (1929), 199 ff., with references; Scherillo, Locazione e precario, *Rend. Lomb.* lxii (1929); E. Levy, Z lxvi (1948), 1 ff.; Branca, *St. Solazzi* (1948), 500.

s. 753. 2*d*. Kaser, *Besitz und Eigentum*, 354; Z lxiv. 394; Branca, l.c.

s. 753. 2*e*. Albertario, 'Il possesso del ager vectigalis', *Studi*, ii. 387.

s. 754. Albertario, 'Possessio e detentio', *Studi*, ii. 161 ff.; Radin, *St. Bonfante*, iii (1930), 153 ff.

s. 755. Albertario, *Studi*, ii. 307, 359; Arangio–Ruiz, Segrè, ll.cc.

s. 757. Brassloff, *Possessio in den Schriften der röm. Juristen* (1928, not available).

s. 757. 1. Albertario, *Studi*, ii. 161 ff.; Radin, l.c.

s. 757. 3. Bonfante, *Scritti*, iii. 534 ff.; Riccobono, Z xxxi (1910) 321 ff.; *Scritti Chironi* (1915), 377 ff.; Albertario, *Studi*, ii, 213; Beseler, *Jurist. Miniaturen* (1929), 90 ff.; Kunkel, 'Civilis und naturalis possessio', *Symbolae Friburg. in honorem Ottonis Lenel* (1933), 40 ff.; C. A. Maschi, *La concezione naturalistica del diritto e degli istituti giuridici romani* (1937), 112 ff.; Kaser, *Eigentum u. Besitz* (1943), 369.

s. 760. Savigny, *Das Recht des Besitzes*, 1st ed. 1803 (on later editions see Landsberg, *Geschichte der deutschen Rechtswissenschaft*, iii. 2, Noten (1910), 96). Italian translation by Conticini (1839); French translation by Staedler (1870). For the literature of the 19th century, see Windscheid,

Pand. i (1906), §§ 148 ff. On the whole see Bonfante, *Corso,* iii (1933), 130 ff.; Albertario, 'Il possesso', *Bull.* xl (1932), 3 ff. = *Studi,* ii (1941), 107 ff.; M. Kaser, *Besitz und Eigentum im älteren röm. Recht.* (1943). Bozza, *Sull' origine del possesso* (1931), and Carcaterra, *Possessio, Ricerche di storia e di dogmatica* (1938), were not available. Monographic literature will be given below in due course.*

2. *Acquisition of possession*

At this point we have only to deal with the acquisition of what the classical lawyers called *possessio rei* (above, ss. 751 ff.). Possession was acquired *corpore et animo,* 'with body and mind', i.e. by deliberately obtaining physical control of a corporeal thing.

761. Corpore et animo

> The well-known phrase 'with body and soul' is not, as Beseler held (*Juristische Miniaturen,* 1929, p. 90), a translation of the legal formula but derives from the biblical ψυχὴ καὶ σῶμα, *anima et corpus,* Matth. x. 28.

i. *Physical control*

What is physical control? We must not answer this question by giving an abstract definition. Any general formula would be useless and only replace one word by others which again would need definition. We can only answer the question in a casuistic way by considering typical cases. One can merely venture the general observation that the classical lawyers required for the acquisition of possession a fuller physical control than for its continuance; the reader should compare the following examples with those given below (ss. 772 ff.).

762. Conception of 'physical control'

1. When a hunter had wounded a wild animal so that it could be captured, he had not yet acquired the possession of it.

763. Occupatio

2. As we have already said (s. 754), a lessee, depositary, or commodatary was not possessor but merely detentor. Where such a person resolved never to give back the thing, he did not thereby acquire possession of it; the maxim *nemo sibi causam possessionis mutare potest* was applied to this case. But if, for example, the depositary diverted some deposited money to his own use, he acquired possession of it.

764. Embezzlement

765.
Traditio
brevi manu

3. A handed a valuable ring to B on deposit. Later A sold this ring to B, both parties agreeing that the purchaser should at once become the owner. B acquired possession (and thereby ownership) on the strength of that agreement even if the parties were far away from the ring. This form of *traditio* is called *brevi manu traditio* by modern students. Of course it takes place when such an agreement has been made between lessor and lessee just as between borrower and lender.

766.
Traditio
longa manu

4. A sold a movable to B. At B's request A placed the thing in B's house. B acquired possession at once, even if he was not at home when A brought the thing.

5. A sold goods lying in a storehouse to B and delivered the key to him, both agreeing that B should at once become the owner. B acquired possession (and thereby ownership) immediately, provided the key was given to him near the storehouse. Ultimately Justinian disregarded the requirement of proximity. Where D owed something to C and at C's request put the thing in a certain place in view of the creditor, the latter acquired possession at once. A sold a piece of land to B, both agreeing that B should be possessor. B might acquire possession by walking round the land; but the agreement was also effective if it was made in the vicinity or at least in sight of the land, for example, on a tower from which the land was visible. In such cases even the classical lawyers spoke of a *traditio longa manu*.

767. Con-
stitutum
posses-
sorium

6. A sold an estate to B. The parties agreed that B should acquire possession at once, but that A should keep the estate for a year as B's lessee. Under Justinian's law B acquired possession. Modern students call this mode of acquiring possession *constitutum possessorium*, a term which is not found in our sources.

> The term was derived from *D*. (41. 2) 17. 1: '. . . possessio autem recedit, ut quisque constituit nolle possidere'.

The classical lawyers knew no such thing as a *constitutum possessorium*. A transfer of possession by mere agreement was unknown even if it was embodied in a document and the document was handed over to the acquirer; all texts conflicting with this rule are spurious. The extent to which

Justinian wished to recognize *constitutum possessorium* is a question which does not concern us here.

7. Acquisition of possession by inheritance or *legatum per vindicationem* was unknown under classical and post-classical law; when the heir acquired the inheritance, he became the owner of the inherited property but not also the possessor. In order to acquire possession he had to take the corporeal things belonging to the inheritance under his physical control. It has indeed been recently asserted that a *suus heres* (above, s. 384) acquired possession automatically when he acquired the inheritance, but this opinion cannot be right. Such a case of acquiring possession *sine corpore et animo* would have left conspicuous traces in our sources; in fact, however, all relevant texts state the contrary.

768. Le mort saisit le vif?

ii. *Animus possidendi*

Animus possidendi means 'the will to have a thing under physical control' and nothing else. Possession could not be acquired without *animus possidendi*, but the requirement of *animus* is actually of little importance since there are but few cases in which physical control can be acquired without *animus*.

769. Conception and importance of animus possidendi

> Children at play throw a ball into my garden without my noticing it; I do not possess the ball since I have no *animus possidendi*.
>
> In my absence somebody parks a car upon my land. I am possessor of the land but not of the car.
>
> A pickpocket pursued by the police hurries through a crowd and puts a stolen watch into my pocket without my noticing it; though I have physical control of the watch I have no *animus possidendi* and therefore do not possess it.
>
> Somebody puts a book on my bed while I am asleep. I do not acquire possession since I have no *animus possidendi*.

The requirement of *animus* becomes more important if we remember that the law as a rule requires a qualified will. A *furiosus* (above, s. 344) was held incapable of acquiring possession since his will was not recognized by the law. An *impubes infantia maior* (above, s. 302) might acquire possession even without his guardian's co-operation; this rule can never have been disputed among the lawyers since such an *impubes* was capable of effecting any acquisitive act (see in particular Gai. 2. 83. 84). Apparently an *infans* (above, s. 302) was entirely incapable of acquiring possession.

iii. *Acquisition of possession by an intermediary*

The acquisition of possession with the help of an intermediary was subject to special rules.

770.
Acquisition through persons in power

1. Whatever a person in power (*in potestate*) acquired fell automatically to the holder of the *potestas* (above, s. 262). This old and fundamental Roman rule was applied without hesitation to possession. Thus the holder of *potestas* acquired possession through his son in power or his slave whether or not he knew of the acquisitive act (Gai. 2. 89). Justinian, however, confined this mode of acquiring possession to acts executed on behalf of the *peculium*.

In these cases also possession was acquired *corpore et animo*, but the body and mind in question were those of the son or slave, not of the holder of *potestas*; neither physical control nor *animus possidendi* on the part of the latter was required. But some lawyers seem to have said that a master could only acquire possession through his slave if he was in possession of the slave.

> Suppose that a slave belonging to M was in the hands of a *bonae fidei possessor* P; a third person made a gift to the slave. M acquired both possession and ownership of the gift, though obviously he had neither physical control nor *animus possidendi* (Gai. 2. 92). Only a slave *in fuga* was incapable of acquiring possession for his master.

This possession acquired by the holder of *potestas* through his son or slave is a special kind of possession; *possessio* means here only 'the legal position of an ordinary possessor' (above, s. 751); the classical lawyers were well aware of this peculiarity and occasionally emphasized that it was admitted for practical reasons, *utilitatis causa iure singulari receptum*.

771.
Acquisition through free persons

2. Acquisition through free agents was on principle excluded by classical law: *per extraneam* (or *liberam*) *personam nobis adquiri non potest*, 'we cannot acquire anything through a person who is not in our *potestas*'. This maxim also applied to *possessio* down to the second century A.D., but already in the first half of that century some lawyers were inclined to make an exception to the old rule in the

case of the *procurator*, stating *per procuratorem possessio
nobis adquiri potest*. Unfortunately in the relevant passage
of Gaius' *Institutes* (2. 95) the decisive word is illegible,
but today it can hardly be doubted that Gaius after having
stated the old maxim continued: 'tantum de possessione
quaeritur an per procuratorem nobis adquiratur.' In any
case the lawyers of the second century made an exception
only with regard to a *procurator* and not any other free
agent. The classical *procurator* was a free person (not a slave,
but often a freedman) permanently entrusted with the
administration of his principal's property, not a simple
mandatary who had to execute a single business for his
principal; a *procurator unius rei* (except the *procurator ad
litem*) was not a *procurator* in the technical classical sense.
The question was still disputed at the time of Gaius, but
the issue became clearer in the course of the second century
and from Septimus Severus onward it was an established
rule: 'Per procuratorem ignoranti quoque adquiritur possessio'. Evidently *possessio* in this rule also (see above,
s. 770) means only 'the legal position of an ordinary possessor' and not a physical control recognized by the law. The
principal acquired through the *procurator* the legal position
of an ordinary possessor but not necessarily physical control as well; of course he might obtain that later. Here, too,
the classical lawyers emphasized that this sort of possession
was only *utilitatis causa recepta*.

The new rule *per procuratorem possessio nobis adquiri
potest* was, in classical times, not extended to any other free
agent, apparently not even to a *tutor impuberis* or a *curator
furiosi vel prodigi*. Further, it remained strictly confined to
possession; thus, if the *procurator* wished to acquire the
ownership of a *res nec mancipi* for his principal, the will
(*animus*) of the latter to obtain ownership was required:
dominium per procuratorem ignoranti non adquiritur.

Justinian's compilers extended the classical rule to any
free agent and also to the acquisition of ownership. Under
Justinian's law, therefore, the rule runs as follows: 'Per
liberam personam possessio etiam ignoranti adquiritur et
per hanc dominium.'

SOURCES

s. 761. Read Paul. *Sent.* (5. 2) 1, with Beseler, *Beiträge*, iv. 64; Gai. 4. 153, last sentence (*nec ulla*, etc.); *D.* (41. 2) 3. 1, first sentence.

s. 763. Read *D.* (41. 1) 5. 1.

s. 764. Read *D.* (41. 5) 2. 1 [*Quod . . . propterea*]; (41. 2) 3. 18, 19; (47. 2) 68 pr. [*nec enim . . . furtum est*]; [*nec refert . . . destinaverit*].

s. 765. Read *D.* (41. 1) 9. 5; (12. 1) 9. 9 [*animo . . . condici*].

s. 766. Read *D.* (41. 2) 18. 2 [*mercato*]; (18. 1) 74; (41. 1) 9. 6 ⟨*apud horreum*⟩ *tradiderit*; (46. 3) 79; (41. 2) 3. 1.

s. 767. Read *D.* (41. 2) 48; *Fr. Vat.* 263 [*citra stipulationem*]; *D.* (41. 2) 19 pr. (the text does *not* say that the owner is now possessor); (41. 2) 21. 3 [*possessio . . . revertitur*] ⟨*possessionem amisisse videtur*⟩; *C.* (8. 53) 1, spurious.

s. 768. Read Paul. *Sent.* (2. 31) 11 ex Cod. Vesontino (N.B.); *D.* (41. 2) 23 pr. [*naturaliter*]; this text taken from Javolenus' *Epistulae* considers a case which was submitted to the lawyer and in which the *possessio* of the instituted heirs was at issue; obviously the text is only an abridgement of the original; (41. 2) 30. 5.

s. 769. Read *D.* (41. 2) 1. 3, heavily interpolated.

s. 770. Read Gai. 2. 89; *D.* (41. 2) 34. 2, first sentence; (41. 2) 4 [*peculiari nomine*] (a *peculium* is here quite out of the question); (41. 2) 44. 1 to *inquirere* [*ex peculii causa*]; [*ne . . . inquirere*]; (41. 2) 1. 5 [*earum . . . tenent*]; [*quia . . . permiserimus*]; [*ex causa peculiari*]; (41. 2) 3. 12 [*peculiariter*]; (41, 1) 21.

s. 771. Compare *Inst. Iust.* (2. 9) 5 with Gai. 2. 95. Read Paul. *Sent.* (5. 2) 2; *C.* (7. 32) 8 [*et . . . etiam*]; *C.* (7. 32) 1 [*liberam personam*] ⟨*procuratorem*⟩; *C.* (4. 27) 1 pr. [*liberam . . . subdita*] ⟨*procuratorem*⟩; *D.* (3. 5) 23; (41. 1) 13 [*id est proprietas*]; [*et tutor . . . ignorantibus*]; (41. 1) 20. 2 [*quasi*]; [*liberam personam*] ⟨*procuratorem*⟩, (41. 1) 53 [*quemlibet . . . nobis*] ⟨*procuratorem*⟩.

BIBLIOGRAPHY

ss. 761 ff. K. Olivecrona, 'The Acquisition of Possession in Roman Law', *Lunds universitets årsskrift*, N.S. Afd. 1, vol. xxxiv. 6 (1938). The paper is based on A. Hägerström's ideas (*Der röm. Obligationsbegriff*, i, 1927).

s. 764. Jolowicz, *Digest XLVII*, 2 *De Furtis* (1940), 104.

s. 765. Schulz, *Einführung* (1916), 63 ff.

s. 766. Schulz, l.c. 66 ff.; Beseler, *Beiträge*, iv (1920), 317.

s. 767. Schulz, l.c. 73 ff.; Beseler, *Juristische Miniaturen* (1929), 94; Riccobono, *Z* xxxiii (1912), 278 ff., 283; Luzzatto, 'Il constitutum possessorium', *AG* cviii (1932), 244 ff.; Buckland *RH* iv (1925) 355 ff.; Pflüger, *Zur Lehre vom Erwerbe des Eigentums* (1937), 65 ff., wrong.

s. 768. Windscheid, *Pand.* iii (1906), § 605 n. 5; Solazzi, 'Sul possesso dell' heres suus', *Bull.* xxxix (1931), Fasc. iv–vi, pp. 5 ff.; *Diritto ereditario romano*, ii (1933), 145; Kaser, Z lxii (1942), 31; *Eigentum und Besitz* (1943), 242.

s. 769. Beseler, *Juristische Miniaturen* (1929), 90, 95; Riccobono, Z xxxi (1910), 365; Lewald, Z xxxiv (1913), 450; Vassalli, *Miscellanea critica*, ii (1914), 31; G. Rotondi, *Scritti*, iii. 220; G. Longo, Bull. xlii (1934), 469 ff.; Albertario, *Studi*, ii (1941), 233 ff.; Lauria, *St. Solazzi* (1948), 784 f.

s. 770. Beseler, *Beiträge*, iv (1920), 61 ff.; Z xliii (1922), 417; *SD* iii (1937), 381; *Juristische Miniaturen* (1929), 91. On *servus fugitivus* see Albertario, *I problemi possessori relativi al servus fugitivus* (1929) = *Studi*, ii. 271 ff.; Carcaterra, 'Il servus fugitivus e il possesso', *AG* cxx (1938), 158; Pringsheim, *St. Solazzi* (1948), 603 ff.

s. 771. Mitteis, *RP* i (1908), 211 ff.; Lewald, Z xxxiv (1913), 449 ff.; Schulz, *Einführung* (1916), 74 ff.; Beseler, *Beiträge*, iv (1920), 51 ff.; *Juristische Miniaturen* (1929), 91; Albertario, *Studi*, iii (1936), 495 ff.; Arangio-Ruiz, *Il mandato in diritto Romano* (1949), 8 ff., 49 ff.; Serrao, *Il procurator* (1947), not available; Solazzi, 'Il procurator ad litem', *Atti Napoli*, lxii (1948).

3. *Continuance and loss of possession*

Whereas possession was acquired *corpore et animo* (neither *solo corpore* nor *solo animo*), it was lost *aut corpore aut animo*. We have to start from this general rule, though we shall presently mention exceptions. If a crucial text (D. 41. 2. 8) states that possession was only lost *corpore et animo*, this cannot be classical: either the original text has been deliberately altered or it has been shortened and referred only to those exceptional cases.

772. Amittitur possessio aut corpore aut animo

If somebody lost a ring, he lost possession at once even if he did not immediately discover his loss. If the ring was stolen, the thief acquired possession at once and the person robbed lost possession at once. These are clear cases of loss of possession *solo corpore*. On the other hand, if a *bonae fidei possessor* hired the thing from the owner, he lost possession and became merely a *detentor* (above, s. 754), although the owner (in default of *constitutum possessorium*; above, s. 767) did not acquire possession. Further, suppose that the *procurator omnium bonorum* of A was owner and possessor of a thing. He sold that thing to A and henceforth wished to hold it for A. The *procurator* ceased to be possessor and A acquired possession, since the latter could acquire possession through a *procurator* (above, s. 771), even by *constitutum possessorium*. These are clear examples of losing possession *solo animo*.

773.
Classical
interpreta-
tion and
exceptions

Thus classical *possessio* was on principle lost *aut corpore aut animo*. However, the classical lawyers tackled the question of the loss of possession in a truly lawyer-like way, keeping always in mind the legal consequences of their decision. Possession was held to be still existent whenever it seemed just and equitable having regard to the legal effects of possession (above, ss. 752–3). Hence they required considerably less for the continuance than for the acquisition of possession (above, ss. 752 ff.). Thus they arrived at the following two important rules.

774.
Retinere
posses-
sionem
corpore
alieno

1. 'Retinere possessionem possumus per quemlibet, qui nostro nomine sit in possessione.' This was the case even though possession could not be acquired through any person *qui nostro nomine sit in possessione* but only through persons *in potestate* or through a *procurator omnium bonorum*. When a possessor delivered the object to his lessee, commodatary, or depositary (i.e. to a person who was merely a *detentor*; above, s. 754), he continued to be possessor, possession being retained through the *detentor*. When a possessor gave the object as a pledge, the pledgee became possessor; the pledgor lost possession *ad interdicta* (above, 2. 757), but retained possession *quoad usucapionem* (above, s. 753).

775.
Animo
retinere
posses-
sionem

2. *Retinere possessionem possumus solo animo* although possession could not be acquired *solo animo*. The classical meaning of this rule was the following:

(*a*) A possessor continued to possess even if he was nowhere near the object, provided that he had the *animus revertendi*. The borderline case was the *saltus aestivus* or *hibernus*, i.e. land only to be used during the summer or during the winter. According to the classical doctrine the possessor of a *saltus aestivus* continued to possess during the winter and the possessor of a *saltus hibernus* remained in possession during the summer; the possession was retained *solo animo*. Obviously possession was also retained in the much less extreme cases, viz. when the land was used throughout the whole year but the possessor was not permanently in the vicinity of the land. It would have been absurd not to preserve possession in the latter cases and to preserve it in the case of a *saltus aestivus vel hibernus*.

Suppose a farmer had land at a considerable distance from his dwelling-place; he remained in possession during the time when he was away from the land. When he left his plough on the land he continued to possess the plough during his absence. It would have been absurd to deny the continuance of possession in these cases after the possession of a *saltus aestivus* during the winter had been recognized.

(*b*) A possessed land through a slave or through a tenant; later the slave or the tenant died or became of unsound mind. The master of the slave or the lessor retained possession for a while *animo*. The sources say expressly that this continuance of possession was recognized *utilitatis causa*, i.e. for practical reasons.

(*c*) A special case was the *servus in fuga*. Such a slave was still *in dominio* but he was not *in potestate* so far as the *actio noxalis* was concerned. Further, he remained in the possession of the person from whom he had fled but it was only a *possessio ad usucapionem*. If he had taken a thing with him belonging to the person from whom he had fled, the latter also retained the possession of that thing *ad usucapionem*. Whatever a *servus in fuga* acquired by *stipulatio* or *mancipatio* fell automatically to his master, but *possessio* acquired by the slave did not fall to the master and consequently neither did ownership of a *res nec mancipi* on the strength of a *traditio* made to the slave. The compilers, however, have cancelled this prohibitive rule.

Post-classical law added two further cases of *animo retinere possessionem*.

(*a*) Somebody possessed land through a slave or a tenant; later the slave or the tenant left the land without *animus revertendi*. The possessor retained his possession, whereas under classical law he lost it.

(*b*) When a possessor possessed land *solo animo* and another thrust himself into control of it, the former lost his possession only if he came to know of the intrusion and attempted in vain to recover the land. Under classical law

776. Post-classical cases of animo retinere possessionem

possession was always lost if another person took possession of the object.

SOURCES

s. 772. Read *D.* (41. 2) 21. 3 [*possessio . . . revertitur*] ⟨*possessionem amisisse videtur*⟩; (41. 2) 18 pr., interpolated.

s. 773. Read *D.* (41. 3) 31. 3 [*peculiari . . . nomine*]; (41. 3) 4. 3; (41. 2) 27.

s. 774. Read Gai. 4. 153; *D.* (41. 3) 16 [*adeo . . . dedit*].

s. 775. 2*a.* Read Paul. *Sent.* 5. 2. 1(with Beseler, *Beiträge*, iv. 64); Gai. 4. 153; *D.* (41. 2) 3. 11; (41. 2) 27; (43. 16) 1. 25 (genuine).

s. 775. 2*b.* Read *D.* (41. 2) 25. 1; 40. 1, first sentence.

s. 775. 2*c.* Read *D.* (41. 2) 1. 14 [*licet . . . usucapi*], substantially classical; ⟨*non*⟩ *adquiri*; (47. 8) 2. 25 ⟨*non*⟩ *sunt*; ⟨*non*⟩ *possum*; *Fr. Vat.* 89, cf. *D.* (7. 1) 12. 3; Paul. *Sent.* (2. 31) 37; *D.* (47. 2) 17. 3.

s. 776*a.* Read *D.* (41. 2) 31, genuine; (41. 2) 40. 1 vv. *aliud . . . discesserit* (classical); (41. 2) 3. 8 vv. *quod si . . . possessionem*, non-classical; (41. 4) 7 pr., non-classical decision; (4. 3) 31 [*non*] *amittitur.*

s. 776*b.* Read *D.* (41. 2) 46, entirely spurious; (41. 2) 25. 2, interpolated.

BIBLIOGRAPHY

s. 772. On *D.* (41. 2) 8 see *Index Interpol.*; on *D.* (41. 2) 21. 3 see Schulz, *Einführung* (1916), 78; on *D.* (41. 2) 18 pr. see Schulz, l.c.; Beseler, *Juristische Miniaturen* (1929), 95.

s. 775. G. Rotondi, 'Possessio quae animo retinetur', *Bull.* xxx (1921), 1 ff. = *Scritti*, iii. 94 ff.; Albertario, '*D.* (41. 2) 8 e la perdita del possesso nella dottrina giustinianea', *Annali Macerata*, v (1929) = *RH* x (1931), 1 ff. = *Studi*, ii. 245; Beseler, *Beiträge*, iv (1920), 70 ff.; *Juristische Miniaturen* (1929), 91; Rabel, *St. Riccobono*, iv (1936), 203 ff. On *servus fugitivus* see above s. 770, bibliography.

s. 776. Beseler, *Beiträge*, iv (1920), 70 ff.; Albertario, ll. cc.

4. *Possessory interdicts*

776a.
Conception and kinds

Under Republican and classical law possession was protected not by actions but by interdicts. We have already dealt with interdicts in general above (ss. 106 ff.); here we are only concerned with the so-called possessory interdicts. The term *interdicta possessoria* (or similar expression) was unknown to the classical lawyers; nevertheless, we shall use it to designate those interdicts by which possession was protected against aggression. Under classical law there were four possessory interdicts: (1) the *interdictum de vi armata*;

(2) the *interdictum de vi non armata*; (3) the *interdictum uti possidetis*; (4) the *interdictum utrubi*.

We shall describe these remedies in detail later (s. 779 ff.), at present we only wish to emphasize their common character. They were available to a possessor whether or not he had a right to possess, and lay against anybody who violated another's possession, again without regard to whether he had or had not a right to possess. Suppose that a thief sold and delivered the stolen thing to a *bonae fidei emptor* P. Later the owner of the thing O found the thing in P's hands and took it away by self-help. P might sue O with the *interdictum utrubi* since O had violated P's possession and O could not defend himself by asserting and proving his ownership. To this defence the praetor would have answered: 'First make good your breach of the peace; afterwards we will talk about your right. I decline to discuss title with a peace-breaker.' Thus O had to restore the thing to P; afterwards he might sue P with the *rei vindicatio*, the *iudicium possessorium* being strictly separated from the *iudicium petitorium*.

Consider in contrast to the possessory interdicts the following interdicts which we have mentioned earlier.

1. The *interdictum Salvianum* was available to a *locator* against a *colonus* who had mortgaged the *invecta et illata* for the rent (above, s. 749). This was obviously not a possessory interdict since its purpose was not the protection of possession, the locator not being possessor of the *invecta et illata*. The tenant might of course object that he had never mortgaged the *invecta et illata* or that he had duly paid the rent, i.e. he might defend himself by referring to his right to retain the things.

2. Nor was the *interdictum quorum bonorum* a possessory interdict. It was available to a person who had obtained *bonorum possessio* (above, s. 537), but *bonorum possessio* was not a *possessio rerum* and the interdict was like the *interdictum Salvianum* an *interdictum adipiscendae possessionis*. To be sure, when the *bonorum possessio* was *sine re* (above, s. 378), and the defendant was the heir *ex iure civili*, the latter apparently could not defend himself by asserting that he was *heres*. Nevertheless, the interdict was not a possessory interdict, since its purpose was not to protect *possessio rei*.

3. For the same reason the *interdictum de precario* (above, s. 753, 2c) cannot be described as a possessory interdict. The defendant could even defend himself by asserting that he was the owner of the object.

Let us now consider the possessory interdicts in detail.

i. *Interdictum de vi armata*

This interdict was available to a possessor of land against a person who had expelled him with the help of armed men; it was an *interdictum recuperandae possessionis* and an *interdictum restitutorium* (above, s. 113*d*).

1. In Hadrian's Edict the formula of the interdict ran as follows:

> 'Unde tu illum vi hominibus coactis armatisve deiecisti aut familia tua deiecit, eo illum quaeque ille tunc ibi habuit restituas.'

> 'Bring the plaintiff back to the place from which (*unde*) you have expelled him by armed force and restore also the things which the plaintiff had in that place.'

2. After the praetor had pronounced this interdict, the defendant might demand a *formula arbitraria* (above, s. 109). We know nothing about the wording of this *formula*; perhaps it ran as follows:

> 'Quod Numerius Negidius Aulum Agerium vi hominibus coactis armatisve de fundo Corneliano, quo de agitur, deiecit, nisi restituetur, quanti ea res erit, tantam pecuniam Numerium Negidium Aulo Agerio condemnato, si non paret absolvito.'

With this or a similar *formula* the parties appeared before the judge and the usual procedure *apud iudicem* began. This needs no further description (above, ss. 32 ff.).

3. If the defendant failed to demand the *actio arbitraria* in time, the *sponsiones* (*sponsio* and *restipulatio*) were made (above, s. 110). The plaintiff asked the defendant:

> 'Si contra edictum praetoris non restituisti, tot nummos mihi dare spondes?'

The defendant answered: *Spondeo*.
Now the defendant asked the plaintiff (*restipulatio*):

> 'Si ex edicto praetoris restitui, tot nummos mihi dare spondes?'

The plaintiff answered: *Spondeo*.

The archaic words of the *restipulatio* '*si ex edicto praetoris restitui*' were regarded as covering also a case in which the defendant had indeed not restored the land but was in fact not bound to do so according to the Edict (for example, if he had not expelled the plaintiff).

4. Now the *formulae* for the two *sponsiones* were framed;

to the *formula* of the plaintiff was added a *secutorium iudicium*. The *formula* for the plaintiff probably ran as follows:

'Si paret Numerium Negidium Aulo Agerio tot nummos dare oportere, tantam pecuniam Numerium Negidium Aulo Agerio condemnato, si non paret absolvito.

'Et si Aulus Agerius Numerium Negidium sponsione vicerit neque is fundus restituetur, quanti ea res erit, tantam pecuniam', etc.

The *formula* for the defendant concerning the *restipulatio* ran as follows:

'Si paret Aulum Agerium Numerio Negidio tot nummos dare oportere, tantam pecuniam', etc.

5. Now the parties left the praetor and appeared with their *formulae* before the judge.

If the judge found that the plaintiff was right, he condemned the defendant to pay the sum stipulated in the *sponsio* and further (on the strength of the *iudicium secutorium*), if the defendant refused to restore the land, to pay *quanti ea res erit*; with respect to the *restipulatio* he absolved the plaintiff.

If the judge found that the defendant was right, he condemned the plaintiff to pay the sum stipulated in the *restipulatio* and acquitted the defendant with respect to the *sponsio* and the *iudicium secutorium*.

6. The defendant could not defend himself by asserting and proving that he was the owner or was entitled on some other ground to expel the plaintiff. Only if the plaintiff had earlier expelled the defendant by *vis armata* might he demand an *exceptio* to be inserted in the formula of the interdict (N.B.).

ii. *Interdictum de vi non armata*

780. Interdictum de vi non armata

The interdict was available to a possessor of land against a person who had expelled him by force; it was an *interdictum recuperandae possessionis* and an *interdictum restitutorium* (above, s. 113*d*).

1. In Hadrian's Edict the formula of the interdict ran as follows:

'Unde in hoc anno tu illum vi deiecisti aut familia tua deiecit, cum ille possideret, quod nec vi nec clam nec precario a te possideret, eo illum quaeque ille tunc ibi habuit restituas.'

'Bring the plaintiff back to the place from which in the course of this year you have expelled him, and restore also the things which the plaintiff had in this place, provided that the plaintiff had not obtained possession from you *vi, clam*, or *precario*.'

This formula differed from the *interdictum de vi armata* in two important respects:

(*a*) It was only available within a year to be calculated from the *deiectio*. After the lapse of this year the praetor would grant an *actio in factum*, but no longer the interdict.

(*b*) This interdict contained the *exceptio vitiosae possessionis*; if the plaintiff had obtained possession from the defendant *vi, clam*, or *precario* (above, s. 753. 2*c*), his possession was called *possessio vitiosa*.

Suppose A was possessor of a piece of land; B expelled him by force. Later B was expelled by C. Now B sued C with the *interdictum unde vi*. Although B had obtained the possession by force, it was not *possessio vitiosa* since B had not acquired the possession by force from C. (N.B.)

2. In other respects the same rules applied to the *interdictum de vi non armata* as to the *interdictum de vi armata*.

781. Inter- iii. *Interdictum uti possidetis*
dictum uti
possidetis   This was a very complicated remedy. Like the *interdicta unde vi* it was confined to immovables, but otherwise it differed greatly from them.

1. Let us start from the formula of the interdict as expounded in Hadrian's Edict:

'Uti nunc eas aedes, quibus de agitur, nec vi nec clam nec precario alter ab altero possidetis, quo minus ita possideatis, vim fieri veto.'

'I forbid force to be used to prevent him of you two who is at present in a faultless possession of the disputed building from possessing it as he at present does.'

2. According to its form the interdict was an *interdictum prohibitorium* and *retinendae possessionis*; nevertheless it served sometimes as a remedy to recover lost possession, as we shall presently point out, and had a so-called recuperative function. Students must keep that firmly in mind and must not be misled by the classical terminology.

3. The interdict was an *interdictum duplex*, because the praetor addressed both parties; accordingly each party acted, and was bound to act, both as plaintiff and defendant. Each party was bound to plead present possession even if only one of them was actually in possession.

4. After this formal pleading the praetor pronounced the above-mentioned interdict addressed to both parties.

5. Now each of the parties executed a symbolic act of violence against the disputed land (*vis ex conventu*) and then returned to the praetor.

6. Possession of the land was now provisionally attributed to one of the parties, but we will not dwell on the details of this part of the procedure.

7. Now the *sponsiones* were made. Whereas in the *interdicta unde vi* only one *sponsio* and one *restipulatio* was required (in all, therefore, two stipulations), in the *interdictum uti possidetis*, since it was an *interdictum duplex*, two *sponsiones* and two *restipulationes* (in all, therefore, four stipulations) had to be made.

A's *sponsio*: A asked B
 'Si adversus edictum praetoris possidenti mihi a te nec vi nec clam nec precario vis facta est, tot nummos mihi dare spondes?'
 B answered: *Spondeo*.

B's *restipulatio*: B asked A
 'Si adversus edictum praetoris possidenti tibi a me nec vi nec clam nec precario vis facta non est, tot nummos mihi dare spondes?'
 A answered: *Spondeo*.

B's *sponsio*: B asked A
 'Si adversus edictum praetoris possidenti mihi a te nec vi nec clam nec precario vis facta est, tot nummos mihi dare spondes?'
 A answered: *Spondeo*.

A's *restipulatio*: A asked B
 'Si adversus edictum praetoris possidenti tibi a me nec vi nec clam nec precario vis facta non est, tot nummos mihi dare spondes?'
 B answered: *Spondeo*.

8. Now the four *formulae* for those four stipulations were drafted and in addition a *formula* for a *iudicium secutorium* (above, s. 779) against the party who had obtained provisional possession of the disputed land.

9. With these *formulae* the parties now appeared before

G g

the judge who, according to the result of his examination of the case, condemned one party and acquitted the other.

10. Let us now illustrate the whole procedure by considering two cases.

(*a*) A was possessor of a piece of land and B had disturbed his possession. The parties appeared before the praetor and executed their pleadings; the interdict was issued, the symbolic act of force was performed, and the provisional possession was granted to B. Now the *sponsiones* were made and the parties appeared with their *formulae* before the judge. Let us assume that the judge came to the conclusion that A was right. Then he condemned B to pay the money which he had promised according to A's *sponsio* and *restipulatio* and acquitted A with respect to B's.*restipulatio* and *sponsio*. If B refused to restore the land (which he had provisionally obtained), he further condemned him to pay its value (*quanti ea res erit*). In this case the interdict functioned as a remedy *retinendae possessionis*. For B either restored the land to A (in which case A regained the possession which he had at the beginning of the whole procedure, and in addition the money promised on his *sponsio* and *restipulatio*) or B refused to restore the land (in which case A obtained the value of that land and in addition the money promised on his *sponsio* and *restipulatio*).

(*b*) Now consider another case. A was possessor of a piece of land and was ejected by B. Now A sued B with the *interdictum uti possidetis*. The same procedure followed which we have just described. At the end of the procedure *apud iudicem* the judge came to the conclusion that A was right. Then he condemned B and acquitted A in the same way as in the preceding case. Thus in case (*b*) the *interdictum possidetis* had a recuperative function; it worked like an *interdictum recuperandae possessionis*, though the classical lawyers described it as an *interdictum retinendae possessionis*, an obviously inaccurate designation. This statement will perhaps puzzle the reader. He might object that in case (*b*) the *interdicta unde vi* are the proper remedies. This is quite true and whenever an *interdictum unde vi* was available, the plaintiff will hardly ever have used the *interdictum uti possi-*

detis since the latter involved a greater risk since, if he did not succeed, he had to pay a double fine on the defendant's *restipulatio* and *sponsio*, whereas the *interdictum unde vi* was not an *interdictum duplex*. But suppose B had occupied the land in A's absence (*clam*). Then an *interdictum unde vi* did not lie at all and the *interdictum uti possidetis* in its recuperative function was the only possessory remedy available to A.

iv. *Interdictum utrubi*

This interdict was only concerned with movables. Its formula as laid down in Hadrian's Edict ran as follows:

> 'Utrubi hic homo, quo de agitur, maiore parte huiusce anni nec vi nec clam nec precario ab altero fuit, quo minus is eum ducat, vim fieri veto.'

> 'He of you who for the greater part of the preceding year possessed the slave faultlessly may take him and I forbid force to be used to prevent him from doing so.'

According to its wording this is an *interdictum prohibitorium*. The classical lawyers further described it as an *interdictum retinendae possessionis*, though as a rule it was actually a remedy to recover lost possession, for the victor in this procedure was always he who had possessed the thing faultlessly for the greater part of the preceding year, the period being counted backwards from the issue of the interdict. The recuperative function of this interdict is prominent, since mere disturbance of the possession of a movable is hardly thinkable.

Suppose A possessed a thing from the 1st of December to the 1st of April following. At that date the thing was stolen and later sold to a *bonae fidei emptor* B. The latter possessed the thing from the 1st of October to the 20th of November; at the latter date A came and took the thing from B by force. On the 1st of December B sued A with the *interdictum utrubi*. A succeeded, since he had been in faultless possession for four months of the preceding year (1st of December to 1st of April), whereas B had only been possessor for 1 month and 19 days. In this case the interdict functioned as a remedy *retinendae possessionis*.

Suppose, on the other hand, that A was possessor of a movable from the 1st of December to the 1st of April. At that date the thing was stolen and eventually sold to a *bonae fidei emptor* B on the 1st of October. Later A discovered the thing in B's hands and sued him with the *interdictum utrubi* at the 1st of December. A was successful. Here the interdict had a 'recuperative function'.

782. Interdictum utrubi

In calculating the period each party could make use of the faultless possession of his predecessor, for example, of the person from whom he had bought the thing. This was the classical *accessio temporis* which stimulated Justinian's compilers to admit *accessio temporis* in *usucapio* (above, s. 627).

In conclusion, the *interdictum utrubi* was an *interdictum duplex* like the *interdictum uti possidetis* and *sponsiones* and *formulae* were made similar to those in the *interdictum uti possidetis*.

783.
General
character
of the
possessory
interdicts

As we have already said above (s. 777), the *iudicium possessorium* was strictly separated from the *iudicium petitorium*, since the right to possess was not at issue in the possessory procedure. This separation is a conspicuous feature of the classical possessory interdicts and makes them summary remedies: obviously in a possessory *iudicium* judgment might be obtained in a considerably shorter time than in a *iudicium petitorium* where the right to possess was at issue. Hence the interdictal procedure was sometimes followed by a *iudicium petitorium* in which the party who was victorious in the interdictal procedure enjoyed the better legal position since as possessor he was not bound to prove his right to possess: the well-known phrase *beati possidentes* had originally a purely legal significance. Nevertheless, it is wrong to describe the possessory interdicts as preliminary remedies granted in order to prepare for the *iudicium petitorium*. The misleading remark in Gaius' *Institutes* (4. 148) is possibly interpolated. Sometimes the parties acquiesced in the result of the interdictal procedure and sometimes the interdict was the only available remedy. If a pledgee had lost possession of the pledge, he had only the interdict so long as the *actio Serviana* did not exist (above, s. 706a); also a *precario accipiens* and a *sequester* had no remedy other than the interdicts. The suspect text Gai. 4. 148 entirely ignores these cases. In classical times the main purpose of the possessory interdicts was to protect possession against aggression and thereby to preserve the peace. For this purpose they were very efficient remedies, particularly since the question of right to possess was entirely excluded. Their penal character is obvious, for the *spon-*

siones were *sponsiones poenales* and not *praeiudiciales*, as
Gaius 4. 94. 141 expressly states.

The post-classical period abolished the archaic classical
procedure and changed the interdicts into actions. Justinian's compilers amalgamated the two *interdicta unde vi*,
cancelled the *interdictum utrubi* altogether, and extended
the *interdictum uti possidetis* to movables; the 'recuperative
function' of the *interdictum uti possidetis* was apparently forgotten even in pre-Justinianic times. Thus under
Justinian's law there were only two possessory interdicts,
the *interdictum unde vi* and the *interdictum uti possidetis*, the
latter having no 'recuperative function'. The compilers
seem to have overlooked the fact that there was now no
longer a possessory remedy to recover possession of a
movable. The medieval *actio spolii* filled the gap but on an
entirely different basis. The details of the post-classical and
medieval development lie outside the scope of this book.

784. Post-
classical
law

SOURCES

s. 778. Read Gai. 4. 144, 147.

ss. 779, 780. Read Gai. 4. 154, 155 [*nam ... possessionem*]; Beseler,
Z xlvii (1937), 359. On *scuta et gladios* see Cic. *pro Caec*. 15. 43; 21. 60;
22. 62; 23. 64 (apparently overlooked by Beseler, l.c.).

s. 781. Read Gai. 4. 148 [*solet ... gratia*]; 4. 149, 150; 4. 160 [*nec
quisquam ... loquitur*] (Beseler, Z lvii (1937), 25; lxvi (1948), 342); 4.166–8.

s. 782. Read Gai. 4. 148, 151, 152; Paul. *Sent*. (5. 6) 1.

s. 783. Read Gai. 4. 148 [*solet ... gratia*].

s. 784. Read *Inst. Iust.* (4. 15) 4. 4*a*, 6. 8; *D*. (43. 31) 1; Paul. *Sent*.
(5. 6) 1; observe Paul. *Sent.*: *is potior est, qui redditi interdicti tempore ...
possidet* in contrast to Gai. 4. 150: *eum potiorem esse praetor iubet*, etc.
Gaius refers only to the wording of the interdict and does not exclude its
recuperative function.

BIBLIOGRAPHY

ss. 776*a* ff. Berger, art. 'interdictum', *PW* ix. 1609 ff., with references,
particularly col. 1706; Windscheid, *Pand*. i (1906), §§ 158 ff., with references; Bonfante, *Corso*, iii (1933), 348 ff.

s. 779. Lenel, *Edict*. (1927), p. 467; Berger, l.c. 1680, 1692 ff.; v.
Bethmann-Hollweg, *Der Civilprozess des gemeinen Rechts*, ii (1865),
365 ff.

s. 780. Lenel, l.c. pp. 461 ff.; Berger, l.c. 1677 ff.

s. 781. Lenel, l.c. § 247; Berger, l.c. 1682, 1695 ff.; v. Bethmann-
Hollweg, l.c. 372 ff.; P. Krüger, *Kritische Versuche* (1870), 78 ff., 93 ff.;

LAW OF PROPERTY

Ciapessoni, 'Appunti sul testo edittale degli interdetti "uti possidetis" e "utrubi",' *St. Albertoni*, ii (1934), 15 ff.; Beseler, Z lxvi (1948), 342. On the recuperative function of the *interdictum uti possidetis* see in particular Windscheid, l.c. § 159 n. 10; Siber, *Röm. Privatrecht* (1928), 149, 151.

s. 782. Lenel, l.c. § 264; Berger, l.c. 1684; E. Fränkel, Z liv (1934), 312 (rightly against Lenel); Ciapessoni, l.c. 103 ff.; Beseler, Z lxvi (1948), 342.

s. 783. Beseler, Z xliii (1922), 421 ff.; *Juristische Miniaturen* (1929), 96 ff. (not acceptable).

s. 784. See above, ss. 112, 113; Windscheid, l.c. §§ 162, 162*a*; Ruffini, *L'actio spolii* (1889); E. Levy, 'Possessory Remedies in Roman Vulgar Law', *Scritti Ferrini*, iii (1948), 109 ff.

PART V

LAW OF OBLIGATIONS

INTRODUCTION

THE Latin word *obligare* is comparatively old (we find it as early as Plautus' comedies) and its meaning is 'to bind', the word being used literally (*obligare tabellam*, Plautus, *Bacch.* 748) and metaphorically. In legal language it occurs in two connexions: *obligare rem* = 'to bind a thing', 'to give it as a mortgage, *pignus* or hypothec', and *obligare personam* ≐ 'to impose a duty upon a person'. *Obligare* was still used in both senses in classical and post-classical times. In contrast to *obligare* the noun *obligatio* appeared very late: it was not yet current at the end of the Republic. It is entirely absent from Plautus' plays and occurs only once in Cicero's voluminous works (*epist. ad Brutum*, 1. 18. 3); both *obligare* and *obligatio* are absent from the writings of Caesar, Vergil, Tacitus, and Apuleius. These statistics are in any case significant and one must not object that the noun *obligatio* cannot have been of late origin since the verb *obligare* existed from early times. The Latin language was reluctant to admit nouns: *contractus* is also late (below, s. 799), though *contrahere* was used by Plautus; the verb *adstringere* was used by the classical lawyers, but not the noun *adstrictio*. In classical times *obligatio* was a well-known legal term used like *obligare* in connexion with things and persons (*obligatio rei*, *obligatio personae*). We are here only concerned with *obligatio personae* and *obligare personam*; we wish to ascertain the technical meaning of these terms within the domain of classical private law.

785. Obligare and obligatio

First and foremost we have to emphasize that the classical lawyers never attempted to define *obligatio*. The two world-famous definitions which we find in our sources (*D.* 44. 7. 3 pr.; *Inst. Just.* 3. 13 pr.) are of post-classical origin, and from that fact we are entitled to conclude that a classical definition did not exist, since if it had existed, the

786. No classical definition of obligatio

compilers would have been only too glad to insert it in their compilations. This is in harmony with the general attitude of the classical lawyers: they were loath to define fundamental conceptions and just as there was no definition, for example, of *actio* and *legatum*, so a definition of *obligatio* was wanting. We must therefore try to discover the meaning of *obligatio* by examining the usage of the classical lawyers.

787. Classical conception of obligatio

The dominant classical doctrine confined the terms *obligatio* (*personae*) and *obligare* (*personam*), when used in the sphere of private law, to *ius civile*. *Obligatio* was a legal bond between two persons which implied a duty of one towards the other, recognized by *ius civile* and enforceable by an *actio in personam* (above, s. 56). Let us explain the significance of this definition.

1. *Obligatio* was a conception confined to *ius civile*, as were *dominium*, *heres*, and *hereditas*. There was no such thing as an *obligatio honoraria* any more than there was *dominium honorarium* (or *praetorium*) or *heres honorarius* (or *praetorius*). When a person was bound *iure praetorio* to perform something, the terms *obligatio* and *obligare* were avoided; the classical lawyers said in such cases *actione* (e.g. *de dolo*) *tenetur*, or they used the terms *debere* or *adstringere*, which embraced duties of any kind. The Edict, as far as we can see, avoided *obligatio* and *obligare* and the lawyers accordingly confined these terms to *ius civile*.

2. When a duty was only enforceable in the *extraordinaria cognitio* (above, s. 20), the terms *obligatio* and *obligare* were again avoided, for only a duty enforceable by an *actio in personam* was called *obligatio*. Thus when a *fideicommissum* was imposed upon an heir, the latter was bound to perform something for the benefit of the *fideicommissarius*, but this duty was not called *obligatio* since the *persecutio fideicommissi* was not an *actio* (above, s. 41). The lawyers might say *heres restituere debet hereditatem fideicommissario* (Paul. *Sent.* 4. 3. 2), but this did not imply an *obligatio* in the classical sense.

3. Duties resulting from a *ius in rem* and enforceable by an *actio in rem* (above, s. 56) were not called *obligationes*. Thus, the owner might by the *rei vindicatio* claim the restitution of a thing, including in his claim fruits and damages.

The lawyers when describing these rules said *rem, fructus restituere debet* or *restituere eum oportet*, but the terms *obligatio* and *obligare* were avoided.

This was the simple classical conception of *obligatio*.

The post-classical period attempted, here as elsewhere, to fuse together *ius civile* and *ius honorarium*. *Obligatio honoraria* was now no longer regarded as a contradiction in terms and wherever a praetorian *actio in personam* lay, the jurists did not hesitate to use the term *obligatio*. Moreover, as the classical distinction between ordinary and extraordinary procedure no longer existed, duties which in classical times could only be enforced in the *extraordinaria cognitio* were now termed *obligationes*. This new conception of *obligatio* found its way into classical texts by glosses and interpolations which obscured the classical terminology. 788. Post-classical conception

This process of amalgamation was completed in the post-classical period, but its tentative beginnings are already visible in classical times. Once more Gaius stands out in his anticipation of the post-classical development. 789. Gaius' conception

In his section on *obligationes ex delicto* (3. 182 ff.) Gaius deals with the *actiones furti, vi bonorum raptorum, legis Aquiliae,* and *iniuriarum.* Now the *actio furti manifesti, vi bonorum raptorum,* and the *actiones iniuriarum* were *actiones honorariae* as well as the *actiones legis Aquiliae utiles;* nevertheless, he terms them *obligationes.* He did not go so far as to include other praetorian penal actions like the *actio de dolo* or *metus causa,* but confined himself to those which were closely connected with *ius civile. Furtum manifestum* was already punished by the Twelve Tables, although the penalty was not a fine as under praetorian law. The *raptor* was a sort of *fur (fur improbior).* The *actiones legis Aquiliae utiles* were of course closely connected with the *lex.* As for *iniuria,* the provisions of the Twelve Tables were the historical basis of the praetorian rules governing *iniuria.* Though Gaius on principle confined his *Institutes* to *ius civile,* he paid regard to honorarian law whenever that seemed suitable to his purpose. Just as he dealt with *bonorum possessio* in his description of the law of succession, so he discussed these praetorian penal actions in his section on *obligationes ex delicto.* He could not properly deal with *furtum* without mentioning the praetorian *actio furti manifesti;* in dealing with the *lex Aquilia* he could not leave aside the *actiones utiles,* and when he wished to expound the rules of the Twelve Tables concerning *iniuria* he could not omit the rules of the Edict. This induced him to apply the term *obligatio* to all obligations resulting from *furtum, damnum iniuria datum,* and *iniuria,* without regard to whether they were enforceable by *actiones civiles* or *honorariae*. Gaius was perhaps the inventor of this new and rather vague conception of *obligatio* and was probably not followed during the classical period, just as his idea of a *duplex dominium* (*dominium civile* and *dominium honorarium*; above, s. 655) was ignored by other lawyers. *Iniuriarum obligationes* occurs only once in the *Vocabularium Iurisprudentiae Romanae* (iii. 748, 749) and in this single text (*D.* 4. 5. 7. 1) is certainly spurious; *iniuriarum obligari* never occurs. Possibly Gaius also described the duties resulting from *fideicommissum* as *obligatio* (Gai. 2. 184, *per fideicommissum obligemus*; 2. 277, *heredem suum obligatum reliquit de fideicommisso restituendo*), but the second of these two passages is certainly interpolated and in the first *obligemus* may have taken the place of an original *rogemus*. Be that as it may, according to the dominant usage of the classical lawyers the duty resulting from *fideicommissum* was not termed *obligatio*.

790.
Sources
and
method
The classical conception of *obligatio* has been keenly discussed since Perozzi's *Le obligazione romane* (1903), but the literature in general lacks method. As already stated, the available texts are interpolated and these interpolations could be made by very slight alteration of the classical texts. If, for example, a classical text dealing with the praetorian *actio institoria* said *in solidum dominus tenetur* (*D.* 14. 3. 5. 1), a post-classical author or editor had only to replace *tenetur* by *obligatur*—Paul. *Sent.* 2. 6. 1: *in solidum dominus obligatur*. Such an interpolation left no further traces and it is for that reason sometimes not possible to prove the interpolation of a text, particularly if it is examined in isolation without paying regard to other texts; the whole mass of available materials must be taken into consideration and a conclusion reached from the general impression given by them.

1. It is a fact that the classical lawyers said *furti obligare* (*Voc. Iur. Rom.* ii. 979. 26 ff.; *furti obligatio* only in *D.* 27. 3. 1. 22, itp.) but never *doli obligare* or *ob dolum* or *propter dolum obligare* (*Voc. Iur. Rom.* ii. 324 ff.; iv. 374). Likewise they never said *iniuriarum obligare* (*Voc. Iur. Rom.* iii. 749); *iniuriarum obligatio* occurs only once in an interpolated text, as already pointed out. Gaius alone says that 'obligatio ex delicto nascitur si quis iniuriam commiserit'; this must needs be a special Gaian usage.

2. It is a fact that the classical lawyers did not describe as *obligatio* the duty resulting from a *fideicommissum*. Within the domain of the *Vocabularium Iurispr. Rom. obligare* in connexion with *fideicommissum* occurs (apart from Gaius' *Institutes*) only in four passages (*D.* 36. 1. 78;

(35. 2) 32. 4; 36. 1. 18; 34. 5. 7). They are all interpolated. If Gai.
2. 184, 277 are genuine, then we have before us again a special Gaian
usage.

3. Sometimes the interpolations are obvious, as in the texts concerning
fideicommissum which we have just cited. Another good example is
D. (46. 4) 8. 4. This text deals with the *actiones adiecticiae* which were
actiones honorariae. Ulpian rightly said *filius patrem non obligat,* but the
compilers wrote *civiliter non obligat,* since they regarded the *actio
adiecticia* as an *obligatio honoraria,* as they expressly said a few lines later:
honorariae obligationes si quae sunt adversus dominum. Obviously *obligationes* has replaced the original *actiones,* for *obligatio est adversus
aliquem* is not Latin. Wherever we meet this phrase (or *obligatio contra
aliquem*) the compilers have changed *actio* into *obligatio*: *D.* (12. 1) 36;
(12. 2) 9. 3; (17. 1) 45 pr.; (21. 2) 51. 3; (24. 3) 64. 4; (46. 1) 21. 2;
(46. 1) 47 pr.

4. These facts are conclusive. The dominant classical usage confined
the conception of *obligatio* to *ius civile.*

Nevertheless, since we cannot exclude honorarian law from
the following discussion, we shall adopt the post-classical
usage which comprehended the classical *obligatio* as well as
what in the post-classical period was called *obligatio honoraria.* As already stated, *debitum* and *debere* had too wide a
scope to be used as technical terms.

The creditor might exceptionally resort to self-help in 791.
order to obtain satisfaction. Thus the lessor might take back Self-help
the hired object, since the lessee was not *possessor* (above,
s. 754); the *precario dans* might take back the object given
as *precarium,* since the *precario accipiens,* though *possessor,*
was not protected against the *precario dans* (above, ss. 780,
781, 782). Apart from such cases self-help was forbidden
and, according to an enactment of the Emperor Marcus
(*decretum divi Marci*), recourse to it involved the loss of the
creditor's claim. The creditor had to be content with his
action (*actio civilis* or *honoraria, persecutio* by *extraordinaria
cognitio*). When the debtor was condemned, execution
on his person and on his property was available (above,
s. 43).

However, this liability of the debtor was restricted in
special cases.

1. A son in power was capable of being a debtor and 792. Son
might be sued by his creditor, but execution on the person as debtor

was excluded out of regard for *patria potestas* (above, s. 267).

793. Con-
demnatio
in id quod
debitor
facere
potest2. In some cases execution on the person seemed too harsh and was in practice avoided by limiting the debtor's liability to the value of his property. A *taxatio* (*dumtaxat in id quod facere potest*) was inserted in the *formula*, which authorized the judge to condemn only in so far as the debt was covered by the property of the debtor. Where, for example, the debtor owed 100 and had a property worth 50, the judge condemned him to pay only 50. Execution on the person was legally available for the sum of 50, but the debtor might easily avoid it by paying off the creditor.

It will suffice here to mention the following cases.

(*a*) A *socius omnium bonorum* sued by means of the *actio pro socio* (below, s. 952) was only condemned *in quantum facere potest* on the strength of a special clause of the Edict.

(*b*) Where a son in power owed something *ex contractu* and was later emancipated, the praetor declared in his Edict that he would only grant an action against the son *in quantum facere potest*. The same restriction of his liability took place when the son had become *sui iuris* upon the death of the father without becoming his heir.

(*c*) On the strength of a rescript of Antoninus Pius a person who had promised a gift was only liable *in quantum facere potest*.

(*d*) A husband liable on the *actio rei uxoriae* (above, s. 217) was only condemned *in quantum facere potest*; here a *taxatio* in the *formula* was apparently not required.

794. Bene-
ficium
competen-
tiaeUnder Justinian's law the debtor in these cases of re-stricted liability was even entitled to retain a part of his property in order to guarantee his living. Because in medieval Latin *competentia* meant 'sufficiency of means for living' (from which is derived the English *competence* or *competency*) the lawyers since the sixteenth century have called this privilege *beneficium competentiae*. As far as classical law is concerned, this term is misleading and should be entirely avoided, for under classical law the debtor was not entitled to keep a competence, not even if he were a donator. All texts in which this idea occurs are certainly interpolated.

795.
Obligatio
naturalisA slave was incapable of being a debtor towards his master as well as towards a third person. However, where a slave had promised something to a third person, the praetor granted an *actio de peculio* against the master. The *formula* authorized the judge to inquire whether the slave would be bound if he were a free man and, if he decided that he would, to condemn the master up to the amount of the *peculium*:

'Si paret Stichum qui in Numerii Negidii potestate est, si liber esset ex iure Quiritium, Aulo Agerio centum dare oportere, iudex Numerium Negidium Aulo Agerio centum dumtaxat de peculio condemnato, si non paret absolvito.'

In calculating the amount of the *peculium* the master might deduct what the slave owed to him. Accordingly the classical lawyers spoke of *debita* and *debere* of slaves. They were fully aware that they were not using these terms in their proper sense, but the terms were convenient and hardly likely to cause confusion. Those debts though not actionable were none the less genuine debts, so that if they were paid, a *condictio indebiti* did not lie; moreover, they might be secured by a *fideiussio* or *pignoris datio*. The terms *obligatio* and *obligare* were apparently avoided by the classical lawyers, but in one single passage of Gaius' *Institutes* (3. 119*a*) the debts of the slave are termed *obligationes naturales*. This term comes as a surprise, since we find it in the *Institutes* only in this place and Gaius does not explain it. The decisive words *at ne . . . adiciatur* look like an addition, but Gaius himself may have written it. Gaius was possibly the first to apply the term *obligatio naturalis* which in post-classical times was in general use.

The obligation of a slave was the prominent case of an *obligatio naturalis*, but not the only one. The legal status of a *filia familias* was in this respect very similar to that of a slave, since she was equally incapable of being a debtor (above, s. 267); her debts to her father and to a third person were likewise regarded as *obligationes naturales*. A son in power was capable of binding himself by contract (above, s. 267), but not towards his father; accordingly his debts to his father were *obligationes naturales*. However, under classical law natural obligations did not exist except in the case of persons in power and it was only in post-classical times that other cases were acknowledged. Thus when a pupillus made a promise without *auctoritas tutoris*, he was not even *naturaliter obligatus* (above, s. 302); his debt was apparently a *causa solvendi*, but it could not be secured by *fideiussio*. In our sources it is sometimes termed *obligatio naturalis*, but the texts are not reliable. We will not dwell further on the artificial phenomenon of a non-actionable debt. Available texts are heavily interpolated and the position is not yet fully clear, in spite of much modern investigation.

796.
Evaluation
The Roman law of obligations has always met with particular admiration and has influenced European law more than other parts of Roman law. Even Otto Gierke, a fanatical champion of Germanic law, declared:

> 'The victory of Roman law was more complete in the domain of the law of obligations than in any other. Undoubtedly this law was the greatest and most perfect creation of the Roman legal genius, applicable to a world-wide commerce and trade and logically developed down to the finest issues, which under Germanic law had hardly been raised. Besides, it had a universal character and was not as closely connected with the special conditions of Roman social and economic life as were other parts of Roman law. Thus it ascended the throne and has maintained its sovereign power down to the present.'

This eulogy is on the whole justified with regard to modernized Roman law as practised from the sixteenth to the nineteenth century. As regards classical and Justinianic law a more sober evaluation is required.

1. It is true that the Romans were the first to study obligations thoroughly; the wealth of problems raised and discussed in the sources is admirable and other laws not inspired by Roman law seem in this respect primitive, being mainly concerned with the law of persons, family law, law of succession, and property. It will suffice to quote the words with which Maitland opened his chapter on contract:

> 'The law of contract holds anything but a conspicuous place among the institutions of English law before the Norman Conquest. In fact it is rudimentary. Many centuries must pass away before it wins that dominance which we at the present day concede to it. Even in the schemes of Hale and Blackstone, it appears as a mere supplement to the law of property.'

Seen from this point of view the Roman law of obligations is indeed a great and unique achievement in the history of human civilization.

2. Turning to details, we may observe that institutions like the consensual contracts and the actions for recovering an unjustified enrichment are very valuable and quite original. The principle *pacta sunt servanda* was unflinchingly carried through; *bona fides* played a dominant part, the classical *actio iniuriarum* was a vigorous and quite unique remedy for the protection of immaterial interests, the *actio de dolo* was an effective weapon against fraud of any kind.

3. We must, however, not overlook the grave defects of this much praised part of Roman law. In this field as elsewhere the sterile conservatism of the classical lawyers prevented modernization of the law when it was due. The central figure within the scheme of contracts, the *stipulatio*, had archaic features; nevertheless, the lawyers obstinately preserved it instead of replacing it by a written contract. The law of sale was unnecessarily intricate, particularly in respect of the warranty of the seller for defects in the object. The hiring of lodgings and of free labour was insufficiently developed. The reluctance to admit assignment led to artificial and cumbrous substitutes. The law of *furtum* was complicated and in part archaic. This list might be easily enlarged. The post-classical lawyers, in particular Justinian's compilers, had the intention to modernize the antiquated classical law, but the task was beyond their strength. Carelessly made interpolations only paved the way to futile and endless controversies; the fundamental question, for instance, whether, and if so, to what extent, a creditor might claim specific performance (*an debitor praecise teneatur*) remained in dispute for many centuries.

Within the framework of this book we confine ourselves to describing in outline the main classical institutions and refer for all further details to other books. A modern comprehensive work on the law of obligations does not yet exist.

797. Scope of this book

SOURCES

s. 786. Read *D.* (44. 7) 3 pr.; *Inst. Iust.* (3. 13) pr.

s. 791. Read *D.* (4. 2) 13; (48. 7) 7.

s. 793. Read *D.* (14. 5) 2 pr.; (14. 5) 7 [*sed . . . potest*]; (42. 1) 16 [*id est . . . alieno*]; (17. 2) 63 pr. [*etiam*]; [*attamen*] ⟨*non*⟩; *Inst. Iust.* (4. 6) 38; (50. 17) 28; (46. 2) 33 [*exceptionem*] ⟨*taxationem*⟩.

s. 794. Read *D.* (50. 17) 173 pr.; (42. 1) 19. 1, both texts interpolated.

s. 795. Read Gai. 3. 119*a*.

BIBLIOGRAPHY

ss. 785–90. See above all Albertario, 'La cosidetta obligatio honoraria', *Studi*, iii (1936), 19 ff.; 'La cosidetta obligatio ex causa fideicommissi', *Studi*, iii. 43 ff.; *Corso di diritto romano. Le obbligazioni, Parte generale* (1947), 7 ff. Further Cornil, 'Debitum et obligatio', *Mélanges Girard*, i (1912), 199 ff.; G. Segrè, 'Obligatio, obligare, obligari nei testi della giurisprudenza classica e del tempo di Diocleziano', *St. Bonfante*, iii (1930), 499 ff.; Radin, *PW* xvii. 1917 ff.; Grosso, *Obbligazioni Contenuto e requisiti della prestazione, obbligazioni alternative e generiche* (1947). On Hägerström, *Der röm. Obligationsbegriff im Lichte der allgemeinen röm. Rechtsanschauung* (1927), see rightly J. Binder, *Kritische Vierteljahresschrift*, xxiv (1931), 269 ff.

s. 786. Marchi, 'Le definizioni romane dell' obbligazione', *Bull.* xxix (1916), 5 ff.; Albertario, 'Le definizioni dell' obbligazione romana', *Studi*, iii. 1 ff.; Schulz, *Principles* (1936), 47; Arangio-Ruiz, 'Noterelle Gaiane', *Festschrift für L. Wenger*, ii (1944), 56 ff.

s. 791. Schulz, *Einführung* (1916), 46.

ss. 793, 794. Zanzucchi, 'Sul cosi detto beneficium competentiae', *Bull.* xxix (1916), 100 ff.; Levet, *Le Bénéfice de compétence* (1927); Beseler, *St. Bonfante*, ii (1930), 60; Solazzi, *L'estinzione della obbligazione* (1931), 190 ff. (the 2nd ed. of this work (1935) was not available); Guarino, 'Il beneficium competentiae del promissor dotis', *Riv. It.* xiv (1939); 'Il beneficium competentiae dei milites', *Rend. Lomb.* lxxii (1938/9); 'Sul beneficium competentiae dell' extraneus promissor dotis', *Festschrift P. Koschaker*, ii (1939), 49 ff.; 'Studi sulla taxatio in id quod facere potest I', *SD* vii (1941).*

s. 795. Siber, *Naturalis obligatio* (1925); Pringsheim, *Z* xlvi (1926), 350 ff.; Beseler, *T* viii (1928), 318 ff.; *Bull.* xlv (1938), 187 f.; Albertario, 'A proposito di obligatio naturalis', *AG* cii (1929), 230 ff. = *Studi*, iii (1936), 57 ff.; *Corso di diritto romano, de obbligazioni, Parte generale* (1947), 29 ff.; Vážný, 'Naturalis obligatio', *Studi Bonfante*, iv (1930), 129 ff.; Flume, *Studien zur Akzessorietät der röm. Bürgschaftsstipulationen* (1932), 70 ff.; Maschi, *La concezione naturalistica del diritto e degli istituti giuridici romani* (1937), 122 ff.*

s. 796. Gierke, *Deutsches Privatrecht*, iii. *Schuldrecht* (1917), 4; Stobbe–Lehmann, *Handbuch des deutschen Privatrechts*, iii (1898), 114 f.; Pollock and Maitland, *History*, ii (1911), 184.

CHAPTER I

LAW OF CONTRACTS

1. *Introduction*

THE classical lawyers did not develop a systematic theory of what we call today 'contract'. As a rule they were content to discuss the individual types of contracts, and when exceptionally they dared to advance more general remarks, these remained rudimentary; the classical lack of interest in generalization and systematization is apparent throughout. The post-classical law-schools showed in this respect a greater interest, but on the whole it is to the jurisprudence of Roman common law that we owe a general theory of contract. Let us first consider the classical terminology. 798. Absence of a systematic theory

The verb *contrahere* is old and was used both literally and metaphorically (*Thes. L.L.* iv. 757 ff., 764). If used metaphorically *contrahere* means as a rule (*Voc. Iur. Rom.* i. 1001) 'to effect', 'to perpetrate', 'to bring on oneself (*admittere, committere, constituere*): *contrahere invidiam, offensionem, amicitiam, inimicitias, culpam, crimen, stuprum, incestum, aes alienum, societatem, nuptias,* etc. Students must beware of believing that in common Latin usage *contrahere* meant primarily 'to make a contract'. Even the classical lawyers used *contrahere* in the wide sense we have indicated. Some of the relevant texts are spurious, but when Gaius (*Inst.* 2. 14) said: 'Incorporales res sunt quae tangi non possunt qualia sunt . . . obligationes quoquo modo contractae', he certainly had in mind the *obligationes ex delicto* as well as obligations arising *ex contractu*. 799. Contrahere and contractus

In contrast to the verb *contrahere* the noun *contractus* appeared very late (*Thes. L.L.* iv. 753 ff.). We cannot trace it back farther than to the age of Cicero. It is entirely absent from the writings of Caesar, Cicero, Sallustius, Livy, Tacitus, Suetonius, and Pliny (*maior* and *minor*). Cicero sometimes speaks of *res contracta* (or *contrahenda*) but never uses the word *contractus*. Our first non-legal text is Varro, *De re rustica* 1. 68. Here *contractus* means the shrivelling of grapes; even in later non-legal literature down to the fourth century the term occurs but rarely. Our first legal text occurs in the *liber de dotibus* of Servius Sulpicius, the well-known friend of Cicero. Dealing with betrothal he stated (Gellius 4. 4 = Bremer, *Jurispr. Antehadriana*, i. 226; Seckel–Kübler, *Jurisprud. Antejust*. i. 33): *Is contractus stipulationum sponsionumque dicebatur sponsalia*. One should translate: 'This making (*contractus*) or *sponsiones* was called *sponsalia*.' Obviously the legal term *contractus* was coined by the lawyers of the late Republic, perhaps by Servius himself. Originally it meant nothing but 'the making' and therefore was used in connexion with a noun in the genitive: *contractus stipulationis* (the making of a stipulation), *contractus emptionis* (the making of a sale); but as the lawyers applied the new term only to contracts, it obtained for itself the meaning of contract. Labeo attempted to give a definition of *contractum* (not of *contractus*). Unfortunately the relevant text (*D*. 50. 16. 19) is corrupt and beyond restoration; but it is evident that he confined the term to contract. Pedius apparently declared (*D*. 2. 14. 1. 3): 'nullum esse contractum qui non habet in se conventionem.' We cannot discuss all the texts in which the term *contractus* occurs; they are partly interpolated and need a careful critical examination. But a few remarks on some well-known passages in Gaius' *Institutes* are indispensable since they have confused all modern discussion of the topic. Gaius in his love for classification was bold enough to declare (3. 88):

'Nunc transeamus ad obligationes. quarum summa divisio in duas species diducitur; omnis enim obligatio vel ex contractu nascitur vel ex delicto.'

Obviously this is a classification of all possible obligations; consequently *contractus* must needs embrace any legal act from which obligations resulted, delicts alone being excluded, so that even the *condictio* for unjustified enrichment, the *actio negotiorum gestorum*, the *actio tutelae*, and the obligation resulting from a *legatum per damnationem* (above, s. 556), fall into the class of *obligationes ex contractu*. So much is clear or at any rate should be clear; the usual argument 'Gaius did not seriously mean what he said; in an elementary textbook he might be inaccurate', will not do. The dichotomy returns in *Inst.* 4. 2. and 4. 182 and in the latter passage the *actio tutelae* is expressly ranged among the *obligationes ex contractu*. On the other hand, in the description of *obligationes ex contractu* as given in 3. 89 ff. Gaius confined himself to what we call today 'contracts' and in 3. 91 he states that the *condictio indebiti* does not arise from an *obligatio ex contractu*, thus revealing that his dichotomy is insufficient, since the *condictio* is certainly not an *actio ex delicto*. To be sure, 3. 91 may be interpolated, but even if we cancel the second sentence, sed ... contrahere, the fact remains that 3. 92 ff. are only concerned with contracts in the modern sense. We can only explain these glaring contradictions by assuming that we are dealing with unfinished lecture-notes not published by Gaius himself. Two points should, however, no longer be disputed:

1. Gaius' statement 'omnis obligatio vel ex contractu nascitur vel ex delicto' cannot have been derived from a republican text-book as has been assumed again and again. Even if such a book existed (in fact it is only the shadow of a dream), it cannot have contained such a sentence, since neither *obligatio* nor *contractus* was a current legal term in republican times.

2. Gaius' broad conception of *contractus* was foreign to the classical lawyers both before and after him. The few texts which have been cited to prove the contrary are unreliable.

D. (3. 5) 15. Here *negotiorum gestio* seems to be described as *contractus*, but the original text dealt with a *procurator* under *mandatum*.

D. (42. 4) 3. 3 and (42. 4) 4: 'videtur impubes "contrahere" cum adit hereditatem. Sed et is qui miscuit se, "contrahere" videtur'. The meaning here is that the term 'contrahere' used in the edictal clause *quod cum pupillo contractum erit* (Lenel, *Edict.* § 204) embraces the *aditio hereditatis*.

D. (50. 17) 19 pr. '. . . cum (heres) non sponte cum legatariis contrahit'. This text probably dealt with the *cautio legatorum servandorum causa*.

D. (11. 7) 1 The text cannot be genuine; see *Index Interp.*

D. (5. 1) 57. The text proves nothing but can scarcely have been written by Ulpian; see *Index Interp.*

In Gaius' *Res cottidianae* the dichotomy was dropped and replaced by a trichotomy:

D. (44. 7) 1 pr. 'Obligationes aut ex contractu nascuntur aut ex maleficio aut proprio quodam iure ex variis causarum figuris.'

This may be a post-classical text, but as the whole work was probably written in early post-classical times, it corroborates the fact that Gaius' conception of *contractus* was not adopted by the classical lawyers who came after him. This conception was probably an audacious creation of Gaius like his conception of *obligatio* itself (above, s. 789) and *duplex dominium* (above, s. 655) which he himself failed to carry through and which was adopted by none of the leading lawyers.

Aristotle, *Eth. Nic.* 1131a, 1 ff. says:

τῶν γὰρ συναλλαγμάτων τὰ μὲν ἑκούσιά ἐστι τὰ δ' ἀκούσια. ἑκούσια μὲν τὰ τοιάδε οἷον πρᾶσις, ὠνή, δανεισμός, ἐγγύη, χρῆσις, παρακαταθήκη, μίσθωσις . . . τῶν δ' ἀκουσίων τὰ μὲν λαθραῖα, οἷον κλοπὴ . . . τὰ δὲ βίαια, οἷον . . . θάνατος, ἁρπαγὴ . . .

Aristotle uses here the term synallagma (in contrast to Greek legal usage) in the sense of 'act which entails an obligation'. Hence we must translate:

'Acts which entail an obligation are either voluntary or involuntary. Voluntary like sale, loan of money, surety, loan of things, deposit, hire. . . . Involuntary acts are performed either secretly like theft . . . or by force like . . . murder, robbery. . . .

Or in other words: 'omnis obligatio vel ex contractu nascitur vel ex delicto.'

Gaius probably read Aristotle's text either in Aristotle's work or in an intermediate source.

J. Partsch, *Aus nachgelassenen und kleineren verstreuten Schriften* (1931), 12; Beseler, Z lii (1932), 294; Bortolucci, *Acta CI* i (1935), 261, are not satisfactory.

Thus we come to the conclusion that although *contrahere* was still used in a wide sense, *contractus* in the usage of the dominant lawyers of the high-classical age meant 'contract', i.e. an agreement recognized by *ius civile* and made by the parties in order to create an obligation.

800.
Kinds of
contractus

Gaius (3. 89) distinguishes four kinds of contract and only four.

1. Real contracts (*re contrahitur obligatio*).

2. Verbal contracts (*verbis contrahitur obligatio*).

3. The literal contract (*litteris contrahitur obligatio*).

4. Consensual contracts (*consensu contrahitur obligatio*).

This classification is by no means well contrived and was possibly invented by Gaius.

Re contrahitur obligatio means that the obligation comes into existence by the handing over of a corporeal thing (*mutuum, depositum, commcdatum, pignus*); otherwise the contracts assembled in this group have nothing in common.

Verbis contrahitur obligatio signifies that these contracts require certain spoken (not written) words. This group comprehends in the first place the *stipulatio*, but also the *dotis dictio* (above, s. 209) and the sworn declaration of a freedman by which he promised services to his patron (Gai. 3. 95*a*). The name of this group is misleading since strictly speaking it implies that other contracts were not made by words but by signs.

Litteris contrahere obligationem does not simply mean 'to make a written contract' (see below, s. 870).

Consensu contrahitur obligatio means that the obligation comes into existence *nudo consensu* (*emptio venditio, locatio conductio, societas, mandatum*). Again the name is unsatisfactory, since *consensus* is required for any contract. Apart from their lack of form the contracts of this group have little in common and form a rather mixed company.

Substantially the classification is accurate; there were indeed no classical *contractus* other than those enumerated in this scheme. *Mancipatio, in iure cessio*, and *traditio* were not classed among the *contractus*. We may regard them as agreements, but as they were primarily conveyances they were not termed *contractus*. Even the *mancipatio fiduciae causa* was apparently not called *contractus*. Gaius does not mention it in his description of contracts (3. 90 ff.), though in a later passage (4. 182) he describes the *actio fiduciae* as an *actio ex contractu*; but the latter text is no sufficient proof as to the usage of the leading lawyers since, as said above (s. 799), it also classes the *actio tutelae* among the *actiones ex contractu*.

The term 'quasi-contract' is entirely absent from our sources, but a group of obligations (resulting from *tutela, negotiorum gestio*, legacy, *communio*, and unjustified enrichment) is described as *obligationes quae nascuntur quasi ex contractu* or *non proprie ex contractu*. Both terms are of postclassical origin; the first is apparently Byzantine. The 801. Quasi-contracts whole classification is merely scholastic and has no practical value.

802.
Pactum
conventum

We may list as ancient expressions *pacere, pagere, pacisci, pactio, pactum, convenire, conventio, pactum conventum*. They were suitable for designating agreements of any kind and indeed were sometimes used in this general sense. But originally *pacere* and *pacisci* meant 'to compromise', 'to come to an understanding'; *pactum* meant '*compromise*', 'arrangement', and not a contract like sale, hire, and loan.

> XII Tab. 1. 7: 'Ni pacunt, in comitio aut in foro ante meridiem *causam coiciunto*'. If the parties do not come to an understanding, they shall begin their pleadings.
> XII Tab. 8. 2: 'Si membrum rupsit, ni cum eo pacit, talio esto'. If somebody tore off a limb of another man and did not come to an understanding with him, he shall suffer retaliation.

In classical technical terminology *pactum* means 'compromise' and also any informal additional pact. If somebody had promised by stipulation to pay a sum of money on the 1st of July and later obtained an extension of the period from the creditor, this was called a *pactum de non petendo*. Pacts added to a *mancipatio* were likewise called *pacta*, e.g. the *pactum fiduciae*; the *pactum de pignore vendendo* we have already mentioned (above, s. 724) and we might cite other examples. The praetorian Edict had a special rubric, *De pactis conventis*. This was the true wording of the rubric. Under this rubric the praetor declared:

> 'Pacta conventa, quae neque dolo malo neque adversus leges plebis scita, senatus consulta, edicta decreta principum neque quo fraus cui eorum fiat facta erunt, servabo.'

This rather high-sounding pronouncement had in fact a quite modest aim. In fact it referred only to compromise, and additional pacts which aimed at the limiting or at the discharging of an obligation, and the praetor promised by this clause to protect such pacts by granting an *exceptio pacti*. The praetor was by no means prepared to accord an action on the strength of every informal pact that did not have an unlawful object. Where, for example, somebody received a loan of money and promised to pay interest by *pactum* (not by stipulation), the creditor had no action for the interest. Only exceptionally was a *pactum* actionable. Thus the *pactum fiduciae* was protected by the *actio fiduciae*. Further, pacts added to a contract from which resulted a *iudicium bonae fidei* (e.g. sale) were actionable, since the judge had to recognize them on the strength of the formulary clause *ex fide bona* (above, s. 60). Whether this rule was confined to *pacta in continenti adiecta* (pacts added at the making of the contract) remains a matter of doubt; available texts are heavily interpolated. A few informal agreements were mentioned in the Edict as enforceable *iure praetorio* (e.g. the *constitutum debiti*; below, s. 963); modern students usually call them *pacta praetoria* (below, s. 962), but they were not termed *pacta* either in the Edict or by the lawyers. Lastly, the praetor might protect any agreement by granting an *actio in factum* (above, s. 47) not provided in the Edict, but he did so only very rarely (below, ss. 901 ff.).

The conclusion to be drawn from these statements is that the classical law knew only a fixed series of typical contracts (*iuris civilis* and *honorarii*). Within certain limits the parties might adapt these types to their individual purposes and the *stipulatio* covered a very wide range, but the contracting parties could not make entirely new types; they could not, for example, make the written contract a substitute for *stipulatio*. Informal contracts were recognized to a great, perhaps a too great, extent, but outside their strictly defined sphere was the realm of formality in which the *stipulatio* reigned. This classical system was already seriously shaken in post-classical times by the recognition of the so-called innominate contracts (below, s. 901); eventually it was destroyed altogether by the pulling out of its corner-stone, the *stipulatio*. Under the influence of canon and natural law the *stipulatio* was from the Middle Ages replaced by the informal contract. This was a veritable piece of folly as a result of which informal contract gained a position which it had never enjoyed under the already too liberal Roman law; even for a dangerous contract like surety no form was required. Certainly the *stipulatio* was out of date, but the right substitute would have been the written contract.

803. Decline and fall of the classical system

804. Scope of this book   In this book we are only concerned with the classical law of contracts. We leave aside its republican history and will only just touch on the post-classical law. The medieval and modern development of the Roman law of contracts lies completely outside our treatment.

SOURCES

s. 799. Read Gai. 2. 14, 38; 3. 88, 89, 91; 4. 2. 182.

s. 800. Read Gai. 3. 89, 92, 95*a*, 96, 135, 136; *D*. (44. 7) 1. 1–3, 5–6.

s. 801. Read *Inst. Iust.* (3. 27) pr.–6; *D*. (44. 7) 5 pr., 1 [*sed quia . . . videntur*]; 2. 3 [*quasi . . . datione*].

s. 802. Read Paul. *Sent.* (2. 14) 1; consult. 4. 9; *C*. (4. 65) 27; *D*. (2. 14) 7. 5 (certainly a post-classical text); *D*. (19. 5) 23; (19. 5) 1. 1 [*civilem*].

BIBLIOGRAPHY

s. 799. Pernice, 'Zur Vertragslehre der röm. Juristen', *Z* ix (1888), 195 ff. (by far the best work on this subject, though not sufficiently critical); Perozzi, *Le obbligazioni Romane* (1903), 31 ff.; Mitteis, *RP* i (1908), 146; Riccobono, 'Dal diritto classico al diritto moderno', *Annali Palermo*, x (1915), 263 ff., 689 ff.; *St. Bonfante*, i (1930), 123 ff.; Bonfante, *Scritti*, iii (1926), 107 ff., 135 ff.; Segrè, 'Sulla classificazione di cause delle obligationes nelle istituzioni di Gaio', *Rend. Accad. Lincei*, v (1929), 49–57; Bortolucci, *Acta CJ* i (1935), 246 ff., with references; Albertario, 'Le fonti delle obbligazioni', *Scritti*, iii (1936), 71 ff.; 'Ancora sulle fonti delle obbligazioni', ibid. 95 ff.; Nocera, 'Le definizioni bizantine di contratto', *Riv. It.* 1936; Lauria, 'Contractus, delictum, obligatio', *SD* iv (1938); P. Voci, *Scritti Ferrini* (1946), 383 ff.; Maschi, 'Cenni intorno alla definizione di "contractus",' *Annali Triestini*, xvi (1947), 159; Solazzi, *Bull.* il/1 (1948), 360 ff. On *D*. (50. 16) 19 and (2. 14) 1. 3 see *Index Interp.* On the character of Gaius' *Institutes* see Schulz, *History* (1946), 159 ff. On Gaius' *Res cottidianae* see Albertario, *Studi*, iii. 97; Schulz, l.c. 167; Di Marzo, *Bull.* x/xi (1947), 1 ff.*

s. 800. Pernice, l.c. 220 ff.; Perozzi, 'Il contratto consensuale classico', *Studi Schupfer*, i (1898), 163 ff.; Arangio-Ruiz, *Il mandato* (1949), 80; Brasiello, 'Obligatio re contracta', *St. Bonfante*, ii (1930), 541 ff.; R. de Ruggiero, 'La classificazione dei contratti et l'obbligazione letterale nel diritto class. e nel giustinianeo', *St. Perozzi* (1925), 369 ff. On *fiducia* as *contractus* see Erbe, *Die Fiducia* (1940), 19 ff., with references.*

s. 801. Riccobono, 'Dal diritto class.', l.c. 263 ff.; Kübler, *Z* xxxix (1918), 214, with references; Albertario, 'Ancora sulle fonti', l.c. 131 ff.*

s. 802. Manenti, 'Contributo critico alla teoria generale dei patti secondo il diritto romano', *St. Senesi*, vii/viii (1891); 'Pacta conventa', ibid. xxxi (1915); Pernice, l.c. 218 f.; Lenel, *Edict.* (1927), pp. 32, 64; Riccobono, *FIRA* i (1941), 339; Mitteis, *RP* i (1908), 148. On *pacta adiecta* see Viard, *Les Pactes adjoints aux contrats en droit rom. class.* (1929);

Rotondi, *Scritti*, ii. 210 ff.; Siber, *Z* xlii (1921), 80 ff.; Grosso, *Efficacia dei patti nei bonae fidei iudicia* (1928), in particular 18 ff.; Stoll, *Z* l (1930), 551 ff.*

s. 803. L. Seuffert, *Geschichte der obligatorischen Verträge* (1881); O. Gierke, *DP* iii (1917), 344.

2. *The stipulation in general*

The classical *stipulatio* was a formal contract, but its form 805. was very simple. The future creditor (*stipulator*) asked the Classical form future debtor (*promissor*) whether he was prepared to make a certain promise; the latter thereupon immediately gave this promise. Even in the time of Cicero the promisor was not bound to repeat the content of the question in his answer; he might give his promise with a single word (Cicero, *pro Caecina*, 3. 7: 'si quis, quod spopondit, qua in re verbo se obligavit uno . . .').

> Thus the simplest type of a *stipulatio* is the following:
> *Stipulator: Centum mihi dari spondes?*
> *Promissor: Spondeo.*

Note *dari*, not *dare*. The legal style used *spondere* and *promittere* with accusative and infinitive in the passive voice. Where classical texts have *dare*, it is probably due throughout to the scribes. See for materials the *Voc. Iur. Rom.* ii. 296; further Stolz–Schmalz, *Lat. Gramm.* Syntax, § 170.

No precise *formula* was required as in the *mancipatio*; there were not even any fixed catchwords. The use of the Greek language (in the third century A.D. apparently also the use of any other language) was permitted whether the parties were Roman citizens or peregrines. Only the *sponsio* (i.e. a *stipulatio* in the form *spondesne?—spondeo*) was reserved to Roman citizens and had to be made in Latin.

Thus few rules had to be observed in the making of this contract, but those few had to be observed scrupulously.

1. The classical stipulation was an oral contract. Both parties must speak and be capable of understanding each other. Signs and writing were no substitute for the oral declarations and both mute and deaf men were excluded.

2. Both parties must be present during the whole act; the question must invariably come first and the answer

must follow immediately (*unitas actus*). If the promisee began by saying *centum tibi dari promitto* and the promisor replied *accipio*, that was a *stipulatio non existens*.

3. The answer must correspond precisely to the question. If the stipulator spoke in Latin, the promisor could not answer in Greek: if the stipulator asked *dari spondes?* the promisor must not answer *promitto*; if the stipulator asked *100 mihi dari spondes?* and the promisor answered *150* (or *50*) *tibi dari spondeo*, the *stipulatio* was entirely void.

This was the *stipulatio* as practised throughout the whole classical period. It was a very old Roman institution and mentioned in the Twelve Tables (Gai. 4. 17*a*). It is therefore idle to speculate on its origin and its original form. The etymology of *stipulari* and *stipulatio* is obscure and what the ancient authors say in this respect is merely guess-work. If in truth the *stipulatio* was originally effected by a symbolic act, e.g. by a symbolic binding of the promisor with a haulm (*stipula*), this was all long forgotten by the time of the later Republic and the ancient etymologists could have had no knowledge of it.

806. Stipulari, stipulatio, stipulatus   The verb *stipulari* is a deponent and means 'to stipulate', 'to demand a promise'. When *stipulari* is used in the sense of *promittere* or in the passive, the text is corrupt or interpolated.

D. (4. 3) 1. 4: ['ut puta, si de dolo stipulatum sit'.]

D. (38. 1) 10 pr.: ['itaque patrono dari stipulandum est'.]

D. (46. 3) 5. 2: 'si forte usurae non sint debitae et quis simpliciter solverit [quas omnino non erat stipulatus]'.

D. (13. 4) 7. 1 (corrupt); (12. 6) 26. 13 (corrupt).

Stipulatio or *stipulatus* means the whole contract, not only the act of questioning.

807. Roman character   The Roman stipulation is entirely a Roman creation and has no parallel in any other system. It is founded on Roman *fides*, which with an almost religious sanction binds a man to keep his word, and it shows the true Roman predilection for accuracy, brevity, and simplicity.

1. Psychologically the binding force of a formal oral promise given in the presence of the other party is (at least for Romans) much greater than that of a formal document which the promisor might sign without having fully read or understood it.

2. Non-committal preliminary discussions clearly form no part of the contract. The formal question and answer left no room for a doubt about the moment at which preliminary negotiations ended and the contract came into existence.

3. A contract made in the presence of both parties offers less opportunity for misunderstanding than a contract made *inter absentes*.

4. The precise correspondence between question and answer makes it quite clear that *consensus* has been reached.

5. The form of the *stipulatio* (in contrast to that of the *mancipatio*) was not designed to furnish evidence that the contract had in fact been made. This is in conformity with the Roman inclination to separate law and evidence, which is visible throughout in classical jurisprudence. The contract was valid even if it was made without witnesses and not reduced to writing; *non ius deficit sed probatio*, and Roman *fides* afforded a sufficient security. However, the drafting of a written document based on the stipulation was already practised in early Republican times and was carried out as a matter of course in the classical period; parties might also refer to the document for the details of their declarations as the testator in a mancipatory will might refer to the *tabulae testamenti* (above, s. 432). But the document was purely evidentiary and in no way a substitute for the oral declarations, which alone were the constitutive acts; counter-evidence might always be brought forth. If, for example, it was said in the document that the stipulation had been made in Rome on the 1st of July, the defendant might prove that he was not in Rome at that time.

This was the form of the classical *stipulatio*, a form reverently preserved by the lawyers as a palladium of Romanity. The presence of both parties was of course a cumbrous requirement since direct agency was excluded; but a son in power or a slave might act as a stipulator for the father or master and also as a *promissor* at least *iure praetorio*. Moreover, in numerous cases other kinds of contracts were available (in particular sale, hire, and loan) which could be made *inter absentes*. The requirement of presence of the

808. Degeneration of the stipulation

parties could not be abandoned without destroying the stipulation altogether and to such a bold step the lawyers could not reconcile themselves. But with the *constitutio Antoniniana* (A.D. 212) the stipulation was doomed. It was too closely connected with Roman customs and the peculiar Roman temperament and too alien to Eastern legal thought to be fully understood and properly applied by the vast mass of new Roman citizens. Now at last a contract in writing ought to have been substituted for the *stipulatio*, but no such step was taken. Diocletian was here as elsewhere a true champion of classical law. After him, however, the stipulation suffered an inevitable decline. The classical form was no longer observed scrupulously and the written document more and more took the place of the oral declaration. The professional scribes of documents persistently emphasized that the oral stipulation had been carried out, but we may reasonably doubt the truth of such statements, and, if they were true whether the classical form was at all carefully observed. In Justinian's law-books the stipulation was on principle preserved thanks to the classical tendency of Justinian and his compilers; but its form was considerably modified and in legal practice the written document actually formed the substitute for the oral stipulation. This highly interesting process of degeneration cannot be described here in any detail, but we must always remember it in reading the classical sources, since this evolution has inevitably led to numerous alterations of the classical texts.

809. Actio ex stipulatione   There arose from any valid stipulation an *actio civilis in personam*. The classical lawyers apparently did not yet possess a general name for this action, but as we need one we may safely call it *actio ex stipulatione*.

i. Under the rubric *si certum petetur* (Lenel, *Edict.* § 95) the praetorian Edict offered three *formulae*.

1. The *formula certae creditae pecuniae* ran as follows:

'Si paret Numerium Negidium Aulo Agerio sestertium decem milia dare oportere, iudex Numerium Negidium Aulo Agerio sestertium decem milia condemnato, si non paret absolvito.'

The *actio* was called *actio certae creditae pecuniae*, perhaps also *condictio certae pecuniae*; *condictio certi* is a Byzantine term. The *formula* was applicable to an *actio ex stipulatione* when a certain sum of money had been promised.

2. Another *formula* ran as follows:

'Si paret Numerium Negidium Aulo Agerio tritici Africi optimi modios centum dare oportere, quanti ea res est, tantam pecuniam iudex Numerium Negidium Aulo Agerio condemnato, etc.'

This was the proper *formula* for an *actio ex stipulatione* when a definite quantity of something had been promised. The Byzantine, but not the classical, lawyers called this action *condictio triticaria* or *condictio incerti*.

3. A third *formula* had the following wording:

'Si paret Numerium Negidium Aulo Agerio servum Stichum dare oportere, quanti ea res est, tantam pecuniam iudex Numerium Negidium Aulo Agerio condemnato, etc.'

This was the *formula* for an *actio ex stipulatione* when a certain individual thing had been promised. The classical name of the action is unknown (*condictio certae rei?*); the Byzantines called it like no. 2 *condictio triticaria* or *condictio incerti*.

None of the three formulae was confined to the *actio ex stipulatione*, as the edictal rubric clearly shows; thus the *formula certae creditae pecuniae* was also the *formula* for the *actio ex mutuo*. We shall return to this point later (below, s. 879).

ii. Under another rubric of the Edict, which probably ran 'si cum eo agatur qui incertum promiserit' (Lenel, *Edict.* § 55), there appeared the following *formula*:

'Quod Aulus Agerius de Numerio Negidio incertum stipulatus est, quidquid ob eam rem Numerium Negidium Aulo Agerio dare facere oportet eius, iudex Numerium Negidium Aulo Agerio condemnato etc.'

This *formula* (in contrast to the three other *formulae*) was confined to the *actio ex stipulatione*; it was the proper *formula* when an *incertum* had been promised (i.e. neither *certa pecunia* nor *certa res* or *quantitas*. In particular it applied when a *facere* had been promised (e.g. *aedificium mihi fieri spondes?*). Modern students call this particular action and only this (not also the actions mentioned above, sub. i) *actio ex stipulatu*, but this is an absurd Byzantine usage. If the classical lawyers used the term at all, they certainly did not confine it to the *actio ex stipulatione incerta*.

The term *actio ex stipulatu* is absent from *Gai Inst.*, from the *Epitome Ulpiani*, the *Fragmenta Vaticana*, the *Collatio legum Mosaicarum et Romanorum*, and from the so-called *Consultatio*. In Paul's *Sententiae* it occurs only once (2. 22) 2, where [*ex stipulatu*] is certainly an interpolation; *Sent.* (5. 5A) 1 has only *ex stipulatu petere*. *Sent.* (1. 1) 3 has *ex stipulatione peti* and not *ex stipulatu* (rightly E. Levy, *Pauli Sent.* (1945) 51). In Caracalla's rescript given in Appendix I of the Visigothic *Lex Romana* (Mommsen, Krüger, Studemund, *Collectio*, iii. 253 f.) the text is corrupt and Mommsen's conjecture certainly wrong; the final sentence (*quo si . . . dabitur*] seems to be spurious. In these circumstances we are entitled to eliminate the term *actio ex stipulatu* from the classical vocabulary.

The *formula* of the classical *actio ex stipulatione* was invariably abstract, i.e. the *causa stipulationis* (e.g. *dotis causa*) was never mentioned in it. Further, it did not contain the clause *ex fide bona* (above, s. 60) even when it was technically possible to insert it (i.e. when the *intentio* began with *quidquid*; above, s. 61). Nevertheless, we must not describe the *actio ex stipulatione* as an *actio stricti iuris* (or a *iudicium stricti iuris* or a *iudicium strictum*) or the *stipulatio* as a *contractus stricti iuris*. These terms were never used by the classical lawyers and with good reason, for the defendant might always demand an *exceptio doli* to be inserted in the *formula* and on the strength of that *exceptio* the judge had to take *bona fides* into account to a considerable extent. To be sure the freedom of the judge was much greater in a *bonae fidei iudicium*. In the *iudicium venditi*, for example, the judge might award payment of interest if the defendant was *in mora*, while in the *iudicium ex stipulatione* he could only do so if interest was expressly stipulated. Obviously the *exceptio doli* could never work to the advantage of the plaintiff. But if the creditor had granted an extension of the period of payment by an informal *pactum* and now sued the promisor *ex stipulatione* without regard to that *pactum*, the judge had to acquit the defendant on the strength of the *exceptio doli*.

810.
Domain
of the
stipulation
The scope of the *stipulatio* was immense. It might be made *donationis* or *dotis causa*; the numerous *cautiones* which we meet throughout Roman private law were stipulations

(e.g. the *cautio usufructuaria*, above, s. 678; the *cautio de conferendis bonis*, above, s. 409; the *cautio legatorum servandorum causa*, Lenel, *Edict.* § 287, etc.); the promisor might promise to give a *mutuum*, a *commodatum*, or a *pignus*; he might promise a fine for non-fulfilment of a contract, and so on. Even when an informal contract was available, parties might prefer to make a stipulation. The recipient of a loan (*mutuum*) might promise by stipulation to return it. Instead of making a consensual contract of sale parties might promise by stipulation to deliver the goods and to pay the price. In short, any obligation might be created by stipulation provided it was not prohibited by law. When a betrothal was made by means of stipulations, no obligations resulted (above, s. 184); not even a penalty could be stipulated for breach of promise. A husband might promise a penalty for taking a concubine but not for divorcing his wife (above, s. 223).

The wording of the stipulation might mention the *causa stipulationis* (e.g. *centum mihi dotis causa dari spondes?*) or be silent on the point (e.g. *centum mihi dari spondes?*); in the latter case we speak of an abstract stipulation. The *formula* of the *actio ex stipulatione* was always abstract, whether or not the stipulation was abstract. The obligation resulting from an abstract stipulation was abstract, i.e. not dependent on the existence of a *causa stipulationis*. If the *causa* was mentioned in the stipulation, the obligation was apparently likewise abstract, provided the obligation was not expressly made conditional on the *causa*.

811. Abstract stipulatio, abstract formula, abstract obligation

> Suppose the stipulation ran: *centum mihi dari spondes? spondeo.* Both parties agreed that the stipulation was made *dotis causa*. Undoubtedly the obligation came into existence even if the marriage had not yet taken place, or if the engagement was dissolved later. If the stipulation was expressly made *dotis causa*, the effect was probably the same; *D.* (23. 3) 21 originally referred to *dotis dictio*, not to the *stipulatio dotis*. See Riccobono, *Bull.* viii/ix (1948), 39.

The abstract nature of the *obligatio ex stipulatione* must not be overrated. On the strength of an *exceptio doli* or other kind of *exceptio* the judge had to take the *causa* into account. Students should never forget this essential point. Of course the defendant when referring to the *exceptio* had to prove his objections. Further, it must be borne in mind that any *exceptio* had to be inserted before *litis contestatio* (above, s. 17).

Let us consider the following cases.

1. The stipulation ran: *centum mihi dari spondes? spondeo.* The promisor gave the promise because the stipulator had informally promised to give him 100 as a loan (*mutuum*). Later the stipulator refused to give the loan and died. His heir found a document evidencing the stipulation among the papers of the *de cuius* and sued the promisor with the *actio ex stipulatione*. Undoubtedly the promisor was bound *ex stipulatione*, but on the strength of an *exceptio doli* inserted in the *formula* he might object before the judge that the stipulation was made *mutui causa* and that he had never received the money. If he could prove his statement, the judge had to acquit him (Gai. 4. 116).

2. The same stipulation was made *dotis causa*; later the engagement was dissolved. The promisor was undoubtedly bound, but if he was sued by the *stipulator*, he might avail himself of the *exceptio doli* and thereby obtain acquittal.

3. The parties instead of making a consensual contract of sale made two stipulations, the vendor promising the delivery of certain goods, and the buyer promising to pay the price. The vendor sued the buyer with the *actio ex stipulatione* without having delivered the goods. The buyer might refuse payment and on the strength of an *exceptio mercis non traditae* (so-called *exceptio non adimpleti contractus*) the judge had to acquit him. It is often said that the stipulation was a strictly one-sided contract involving the binding of only one of the parties. This is true, but it must be borne in mind that an *exceptio* might connect two reciprocal stipulations with each other.

812.
Exceptio
non
numeratae
pecuniae
Imperial constitutions of the third century introduced a special *exceptio non numeratae pecuniae*. Its existence is irrefutably proven by a rescript of Diocletian inserted in the Visigothic *Lex Romana* of A.D. 506 (*Collectio librorum*, ed. Mommsen, Krüger, Studemund, iii, p. 234), but the function of this new exception is disputed since all other relevant texts are interpolated. We cannot discuss here the various theories which have been advanced, but will merely expound our own opinion. Suppose the promisor promised by stipulation to pay a sum of money which the stipulator had informally promised to give him as a loan. Later the stipulator sued the promisor with the *actio ex stipulatione*, but the defendant objected that he had not received the

loan. In the time of Gaius (*Inst.* 4, 116) the defendant might defend himself with an *exceptio doli*, but he had to prove that the stipulation was made *mutui causa* and that he had not in fact received the money. On the strength of the new *exceptio non numeratae pecuniae* it was the plaintiff who had to prove that he had given the loan even if the promisor had admitted in writing that he had received it. This privileged *exceptio* was only available for one year; after the lapse of this period the promisor had to rely on the *exceptio doli* and the burden of proof rested on him. It can hardly have been otherwise. The emperors cannot have abolished the *exceptio doli*, which had no time-limit. The *exceptio non numeratae pecuniae* could only operate when the stipulator brought his action and he might delay doing so till the year had elapsed. Without the *exceptio doli* the promisor would have been unprotected against this trick, for he could not compel the stipulator to bring the action before the lapse of the year, nor had he an action for release (*condictio liberationis*) against him. This was the late classical *exceptio non numeratae pecuniae*. Diocletian granted it for five years, Justinian for two. But Justinian's compilers amalgamated the *exceptio non numeratae pecuniae* with the *exceptio doli* so that under Justinian's law the defendant no longer had an *exceptio doli* after the lapse of the two years. If the stipulator did not sue him within this period, the promisor might, under Justinian's law, sue the stipulator within the two years' period for release (*condictio liberationis*).

The promisor was responsible for *dolus* and *culpa* (negligence). If he failed wilfully or negligently to fulfil the obligation in due time—*si per eum steterit quominus solveretur* (if the non-fulfilment was due to him)—he was *in mora debitoris*. Suppose the promisor was bound to furnish a certain slave (*Stichus*) on the 1st of July. He forgot the day and believed that his debt was due a week later. From the 2nd of July onward he was *in mora*, for it cannot be admitted that *mora debitoris* included only wilful delay in discharging an obligation. Thus so far the promisor was responsible for *culpa in non faciendo*. The *mora* had no legal effect, if money or other fungible things (e.g. a quantity of wheat) had been

813. Responsibility

promised; the judge was not entitled to award interest on account of the *mora*. But in the case of a *stipulatio certae rei* (about the *stipulatio incerta*, e.g. *aedificium fieri*, we know nothing) the *debitor in mora* was responsible for *casus* (accident). When *Stichum dari* was stipulated and some days later Stichus died in an accident, the obligation was discharged. But if the promisor was *in mora* when Stichus died in an accident, the obligation remained intact, *perpetuatur obligatio*; the stipulator might sue the promisor with the usual *formula* (above, s. 809) 'si paret Numerium Negidium Aulo Agerio Stichum dare oportere', though Stichus no longer existed, and might obtain damages. Apart from *mora* the promisor was only responsible for *dolus* and for negligence in the execution of a positive act (*culpa in faciendo*). Thus if the debtor owed a certain slave and manumitted him, he was responsible; if he flogged the slave and inadvertently killed him, he was equally responsible—'per eum stetit quominus solveretur; obligatio perpetuatur'. But if he failed to care for a slave during an illness and the slave died, the obligation was discharged.

SOURCES

s. 805. Read Gai. 3. 92, 93; *D.* (45. 1) 1. 4 [*nisi in decem*]; [*licet . . . inesse*]; Paul. *Sent.* (2. 3) 1; (5. 7) 1; (5. 7) 2, first sentence; *C.* (4. 32) 1; *D.* (45. 1) 137 pr. [*ut tamen . . . possit*]; [*ceterum . . . spopondisset*]; *D.* (45. 1) 65, *sed* [*et*] *si*; [*non*] *obesse*; ⟨non⟩ *obligaberis*; ⟨non obligaberis⟩.

s. 807. Read *C.* (4. 2) 14; *D.* (13. 5) 24 to *successisse*.

s. 808. Read Paul. *Sent.* (5. 7) 2; *D.* (2. 14) 7. 12 [*non tantum . . . paciscentium*]; *D.* (45. 1) 1 (heavily interpolated) with Riccobono's commentary, Z xxxv (1914), 247 ff. and *Index Interp.*; *C.* (8. 37) 10 and 14; *Inst. Iust.* (3. 15) 1; (3. 19) 12; (3. 20) 8.

s. 809. For the Byzantine terminology see *D.* (13. 3) 1 pr. (spurious); (46. 2) 12 vv. [*condictione incerti . . . esset*]; *Inst. Iust.* (3. 15) pr.

s. 811. Read Gai. 4. 116; *D.* (19. 1) 25, first sentence with Schulz, *Principles*, 94 n. 3; Gai. 4. 126a.

s. 812. Read Gai. 4. 116 with *Inst. Iust.* (4. 13) 2 and note that the compilers substituted *pecuniae non numeratae* to *doli*; *C.* (4. 30) 3 [*seu doli seu*]; Diocletian's rescript in Mommsen, Krüger, Studemund, *Collectio librorum*, iii. 234.

s. 813. Read *D.* (22. 1) 32 pr. [*id est . . . solverit*]; (44. 7) 45; (12. 1) 5;

(46. 3) 33. 1, first sentence; (45. 1) 91 pr. (substantially classical); (45. 1) 91. 3 (substantially classical).

BIBLIOGRAPHY

s. 805. Weiss, *PW* iiiA. 2540 ff.; Riccobono, Z xxxv (1914), 243 ff.; Brandileone, 'La stipulatio nell' età imperiale romano e durante il medievo', *Scritti di storia del diritto privato italiano*, ii (1931), 419 ff.; Kaser, *Altröm. Jus.* (1949), 256 ff. On the etymology see A. Walde, *Lat. Etym. Wörterbuch* (1910), vv. 'stipo' and 'stips'; Ernout–Millet, *Dictionnaire étym. de la langue lat.* (1939), v. 'stipulari'; Weiss, l.c.; Beseler, *Beiträge*, iv (1920), 107; Z xlv (1925), 430; Kaser, *Altröm. Jus.* (1949), 267.*

s. 806. Beseler, Z lvi (1936), 195.

s. 807. Schulz, *History* (1946), 25.

s. 808. Riccobono, Z xxxv (1914), 214 ff.; xliii (1922), 262 ff.; 'Punti di vista critici', *Annali Palermo*, xii (1928), 522 ff.; Brandileone, l.c. and against him Riccobono, *Annali Palermo*, l.c. 540 ff.; Taubenschlag, *Law of Greco-Roman Egypt* (1944), 299.*

s. 809. Lenel, *Edict.* (1927), §§ 95, 55. Robbe, 'L'autonomia dell' actio certae creditae pecuniae e la sua distinzione della condictio', *SD* vii(1941), 35 ff. (not acceptable).*

s. 812. H. Kreller, 'Zur Geschichte der exceptio non numeratae pecuniae', *St. Riccobono*, ii (1936), 283 ff., with references; H. Krüger, 'Querella non numeratae pecuniae', Z lviii (1938), 1 ff.; Lemosse, *St. Solazzi* (1948), 470 ff.

s. 813. Siber, Z xxix (1908), 47 ff.; Gradenwitz, Z xxxiv (1913), 255 f.; Genzmer, Z xliv (1924), 86 ff., 92 ff., 118 ff., 121 ff.; Montel, *La mora del debitore* (1930, not available, but see Felgenträger's review, Z li (1931), 523 ff.); Arangio-Ruiz, *Responsabilità contrattuale in diritto romano* (2nd ed. 1933), 9 ff.; Guarneri Citati, *Annali Palermo*, xi (1923), 229 ff., 269 ff.; Beseler, Z lvi (1936), 77.

3. *Special types of stipulation*

We will now consider a series of special types of stipulation which are of general importance. The law governing these was developed in republican times and accordingly bears the unmistakable trade mark of the republican jurisprudence: it is formalistic, simple, and clear. The only exception is the law of *fideiussio* which originated at the end of the Republic or at the beginning of the Principate. 814. General character

i. *Novatio*

The classical institution termed *novatio* was a *stipulatio* which, if fully effective, substituted a new obligation for an 815. Conception and kinds existing obligation. Let us consider the various cases which fell under this conception.

1. A and B made a contract of sale. Afterwards they made a stipulation; A (the seller) asked B: 'Quod tu mihi debes ex vendito dari mihi spondes?' B answered: 'Spondeo.' What is the legal result? A modern lawyer might say: there are now two obligations, one resulting from sale, the other from the stipulation, but if one of them is fulfilled, the other expires automatically. The republican and classical rule was different: the *obligatio ex vendito* expired and the *obligatio ex stipulatione* took its place whether or not the parties had the *animus novandi*. The new obligation differed from the old one since the *actio venditi* was an *actio bonae fidei* and the *actio ex stipulatione* was not.

If B received 100 from A as a loan and afterwards promised by stipulation to repay this sum, the *obligatio ex mutuo* was discharged and only the *obligatio ex stipulatione* remained. To be sure the action resulting from *mutuum* was the same as that coming from stipulation, namely the *actio certae creditae pecuniae* (above, s. 809), but the obligation *ex stipulatione* differed from that *ex mutuo* since only an obligation *ex stipulatione* could be discharged by *acceptilatio* (Gai. 3. 169) and secured by *sponsio* or *fidepromissio* (Gai. 3. 119; below, s. 845). Thus the new obligation brought a new advantage to the creditor and the novation was for that reason effective. However, if B owed 100 to A *ex stipulatione* and afterwards promised these same 100 to A by another stipulation, the latter was apparently void, at least under classical law, since it introduced nothing which was not already contained in the earlier stipulation (Gai. 3. 177). It was of course valid if the second stipulation contained a *dies* or a *condicio* absent from the prior stipulation.

A plurality of obligations might be novated by the same stipulation and consequently all obligations by which the promisor was bound to the stipulator at the time of the stipulation might be novated *uno actu*. It was to meet this latter case that Aquilius Gallus, a friend of Cicero's, drafted a precedent, the so-called *stipulatio Aquiliana*.

2. D owed something to C *ex vendito*, *mutuo*, or *stipulatione*. Afterwards B promised C by stipulation to pay what D owed to C. Again a modern lawyer might say that both D and B are now C's debtors, but if one of them pays off the creditor, the other becomes free. Under republican and classical law, however, this was a case of *novatio* irrespective of whether the parties had the *animus novandi*; thus B alone was now C's debtor. D's consent was not required since B might as well have paid off D's creditor without D's consent. In this case the new obligation invariably contained something new, viz. a new debtor.

3. D owed something to C *ex vendito*, *mutuo*, or *stipulatione*. Afterwards D promised B by stipulation to pay him what D owed to C. This was also a case of *novatio*, provided that C had given his consent, however informally expressed; thus C lost his claim and B alone was now D's creditor. A special *animus novandi* was not required.

Obviously these are very simple but also very formalistic rules. The post-classical lawyers required *animus novandi*; Justinian went a step farther by providing (*C*. 8. 41. 8) that a *novatio* should only take place when the parties expressly declared their *animus novandi*. The numerous classical texts in which the requirement of *animus novandi* is mentioned are all interpolated; Gaius knows nothing of it. 816.
Animus
novandi

We have now to give some additional rules. 817. Prior
and new
obligation

1. Suppose the stipulation ran: 'Quod Titius mihi debet tu, Seie, mihi dari fieri spondes? Spondeo.' If Titius actually owed nothing at all, Seius too owed nothing. And if Titius owed something, but could invalidate the creditor's action by *exceptio*, Seius too might avail himself of that *exceptio*.

2. The earlier obligation came to an end and with it all accessory right of the creditor (surety and *pignus*).

3. Under republican law, at any rate according to the doctrine of Servius Sulpicius, the old obligation expired even if a new obligation did not come into existence; apparently the creditor was regarded as having abandoned bis claim. The classical lawyers mitigated this harsh rule by the following rather artificial distinction:

(*a*) If the novating stipulation was a *stipulatio non existens*, the prior *obligatio* remained intact. This of course occurred if the general form of the stipulation was not observed, and also if the promisor was a peregrine and used the word *spondeo* (which was only available to Roman citizens; above, s. 805) or if he was a slave.

(*b*) But if the promisor in the novating stipulation was a *pupillus* or a woman who acted without *auctoritas tutoris*, the earlier obligation perished. The stipulation was not a *stipulatio non existens*, although the promise given by the *pupillus* or the woman was void and did not create an obligation.

818.
Functions

The classical *novatio* operated substantially like a *datio in solutum*, the creditor of the original obligation receiving satisfaction which was not owed to him. When the stipulator in the novating stipulation was not the creditor in the original obligation, *novatio* was a substitute for the non-existent assignment. If the promisor in the novating stipulation was not the debtor in the original obligation, the *novatio* functioned as substitute for the missing transfer of debts upon another debtor.

819.
Literal
contract?
Novatio
necessaria?

Apparently a *novatio* could only be made by *stipulatio*; at any rate Gaius only mentions this mode. It is generally assumed that the so-called literal contract (below, s. 870) also operated as a *novatio*, which is possible but not certain. Further, modern students usually say that *litis contestatio* worked as a *novatio* (so-called *novatio necessaria* in contrast to the *novatio voluntaria* by stipulation) in cases in which the original *obligatio* was consumed by *litis contestatio*. In fact Gaius deals with the discharge of an obligation by *litis contestatio* immediately after his chapter on *novatio* (Gai. 3. 180, 181), but he does not describe it as a *novatio*. He mentions the republican *dictum*:

'ante litem contestatam dare debitorem oportere;
post litem contestatam condemnari oportere;
post condemnationem iudicatum facere oportere.'

However, *condemnari oportere* certainly does not imply an obligation on the part of the defendant. Moreover, a *pignus* was not lost by *litis contestatio* in the personal action. The idea of a *novatio necessaria* was apparently quite foreign to the classical lawyers and should be abandoned altogether, though we meet it already in a few post-classical pre-Justinianic texts.

ii. *Alteri stipulari*

Modern students, for long accustomed to the conception of a 'contract in favour (or 'for the benefit') of a third person', are impelled to ask whether and to what extent such a contract was valid under Roman law. However, the general conception of such contracts embracing heterogeneous cases was unknown to the classical lawyers and is not helpful for an analysis of classical law. 820. Contractus in favorem tertii

1. B promised A by stipulation to pay a sum of money to a third person (Titius). Under classical law this stipulation was absolutely invalid; neither Titius nor A had an action against B. The stipulation was valid if A was Titius' slave or his son in power: in this case Titius and he alone became the creditor and acquired the *actio ex stipulatione*. This rule is expressly stated by Gaius: 821. Alteri stipulari nemo potest

> 3. 103. 'Inutilis est stipulatio, si ei dari stipulemur, cuius iuri subiecti non sumus.'
>
> 3. 163. 'Expositis generibus obligationum, quae ex contractu nascuntur, admonendi sumus adquiri nobis non solum per nosmet ipsos, sed etiam per eas personas quae in nostra potestate manu mancipiove sunt.'

Any attempt to whittle down this statement is futile: a *stipulatio alteri* was entirely invalid unless the stipulator was in the power of the third person. One must not say that the stipulation was only invalid in so far as it did not involve a binding obligation towards the third person. Nor must we say that the stipulation could be enforced by the stipulator if he was interested in the fulfilment of the stipulation. This is escapism of the worst kind; such interpretations are irreconcilable with Gaius' text.

2. Romanists have repeatedly searched for the reason underlying the classical rule. Certainly, it was not any lack of interest on the part of the stipulator which caused the nullity of a *stipulatio alteri*, for such an interest was practically always existent. No sensible man would even stipulate 822. Reason of the classical rule

in favour of a third person without having an interest in its fulfilment; even if he only wished to make a gift to the third person, this would be a reasonable interest. The classical lawyers cannot possibly have ignored this point. On the other hand, a slave stipulating for the benefit of his master lacked interest and his stipulation was nevertheless valid. The true reason was simply this: Classical private law excluded on principle direct agency; this principle was rather inadequately expressed in the well-known maxim: 'per extraneam personam adquiri nobis non potest.' From this maxim it followed immediately that the promisor was not bound to the third person and that the latter had no action against him. But the maxim further implied that any stipulation which attempted to create a right in the third person was entirely void. Such a stipulation was in the eyes of the republican lawyers (for we can trace back the rule concerning *alteri stipulari* to Q. Mucius) *stipulatio alteri*, for according to its wording its sole aim seemed to be to bind the promisor to the third person. The republican lawyers could not as yet distinguish between *alteri stipulari* and *stipulari* in the name of the third person (direct agency); indeed this subtle distinction has puzzled lawyers of much later centuries. Thus the rule *alteri stipulari nemo potest* was one result of the general rule against direct agency. This is made abundantly clear by the exception, for as far as direct agency was admitted, a *stipulatio alteri* was valid (i.e. when the stipulator was in power of the third person).

823. Other prohibited contracts 3. If this explanation is true, it follows that not only a stipulation but also any other contract was void if it contravened the rule against direct agency.

A husband made a contract of sale expressly in the name of his wife (*nomine uxoris*); the contract was void and neither the husband nor the wife had an action. If A gave a thing to B as a deposit with the agreement that he should return the thing to Titius, the contract was invalid. A gave a sum of money to B with the agreement that B should regard it as a loan given by Titius who knew nothing of the whole business. The contract was void, but Titius had a *condictio sine causa* against B.

824. Valid contracts 4. On the other hand, contracts which did not contravene this principle were valid although they might be regarded by modern lawyers as contracts in favour of a third *in favorem* person. *tertii*

(*a*) A *mandatum aliena gratia* was valid (Gai. 3. 155). Suppose A commissioned B by a *contractus mandati* to pay a sum of money to Titius. Direct agency was here quite out of the question, for B did not promise A to pay the money to Titius but rather promised to carry through the *mandatum* which A might revoke at any time.

(*b*) 'Centum mihi dari spondes si Titio centum non dederis?' The stipulation was valid since direct agency was not involved.

(*c*) A and B made a *locatio conductio operis* in which the contractor B promised to raise a building on A's land (*fundus Cornelianus*). B then hired workers for that purpose. These contracts were of course valid. B might also make a *locatio conductio operis* with an architect in which the latter promised B to raise a building on A's *fundus Cornelianus*. B might even make a stipulation in which the architect gave that promise. All these contracts in favour of a third person were valid since B clearly did not act as a direct agent of A.

(*d*) 'Mihi et Titio dari spondes?' The promisor was bound solely to the stipulator and the question was only whether he might claim 100 or only 50 (Gai. 3. 103).

(*e*) 'Mihi aut Titio dari spondes?' The promisor was only bound to the stipulator, but he was entitled to pay to Titius (as a *solutionis causa adiectus*) and thereby to discharge his obligation towards the stipulator.

(*f*) A made a deposit with B with the agreement that the depositor A might claim the deposit and that after his death Titius might do so. The contract was valid, but A alone might claim the deposit and, after his death, his heir.

5. A made a donation to B with the informal under- 825. standing that B should pass on the donation to Titius after Donatio a specified period. This was a so-called *donatio sub modo* *sub modo* (below, s. 974); neither A nor Titius had an action to enforce the agreement. But in the high classical age (end of the second century and third century) imperial constitutions granted an action to Titius *benigna iuris interpretatione* (*Fr. Vat.* 286); in classical times this case remained an exception.

6. Justinian's law differed from the classical in two main 826. particulars. Justinian's law

(*a*) The principle *alteri stipulari nemo potest* was preserved but it was now founded on the erroneous assumption that an interest on the part of the stipulator was usually lacking. When a *stipulatio alteri* was made by the stipulator in order to set himself free from an obligation towards the third person, it was regarded as valid since the stipulator had a reasonable interest.

(*b*) In a series of cases Justinian granted an action to the third person. All classical texts in which this action appears are interpolated with the single exception of those dealing with the *donatio sub modo* which we have just mentioned (*Fr. Vat.* 286 = *C.* 1. 8. 54. 3). It was probably this exceptional classical case which inspired the compilers to provide the third person with an action; the *fideicommissum a debitore relictum* stood too far away.

iii. *Plures rei stipulandi et promittendi*

827. Form of the stipulation
In one and the same stipulation two or more persons might act as stipulators or promisors. Such stipulations had to be made in the following way.

1. Maevius and Seius asked Titius:

> Maevius: Decem mihi dari spondes?
> Seius: Eadem decem mihi dari spondes?
> Titius: Utrique vestrum dari spondeo.

The legal result of this stipulation was what modern lawyers call 'active solidarity'. Maevius as well as Seius might claim 10 from Titius, but if Titius paid 10 to Maevius, his obligation towards Seius was also discharged and if Maevius released Titius by *acceptilatio*, both obligations ceased to exist. Even if Maevius sued Titius, both obligations were destroyed by the consumptive force of *litis contestatio*.

2. Titius asked Maevius and Seius:

> Titius: Maevi, decem mihi dari spondes?
>   Sei, eadem decem mihi dari spondes?
> Maevius and Seius: Spondeo.

The legal effect of this stipulation was what modern lawyers call 'passive solidarity'. Maevius as well as Seius owed 10 to Titius, but if Maevius paid 10, both obligations were discharged, and if Titius released Maevius by *acceptilatio*, Seius too was free. Even if Titius sued Maevius, both obligations were destroyed by *litis contestatio*.

These types of solidarity were called 'correality' (active and passive correality) by the Romanists of the nineteenth century in contrast to 'simple solidarity' where the *litis contestatio* by one stipulator or with one promisor left the other obligation (or obligations) intact. This terminology is entirely absent from our sources, *correus* occurs only once (*D. 34. 3, 3. 3*) and then not in a technical sense. *828. Correality*

Whether, and if so, to what extent correality could be created by other modes under classical law—by other contracts, for example, by *commodatum* or *depositum*, or even outside the sphere of contracts, e.g. by *legatum per damnationem* or by theft (for example, a *condictio furtiva* lay against each of two thieves)—is a crucial question which we cannot even touch upon here. The relevant texts are interpolated and hitherto no unanimity has been reached about the classical law. It must, however, be borne in mind that under classical law two or more penal actions of the same kind were invariably cumulated (above, s. 73) so that there was neither correality nor simple solidarity in this domain. It was left to the compilers to tone down the classical cumulation to solidarity in some cases (below, s. 977). *829. Scope of correality*

Justinian abolished the consumptive power of *litis contestatio* in the classical cases of passive correality, thereby changing it into simple solidarity. As regards active correality the classical law was apparently preserved. *830. Justinian's reform*

iv. *Adstipulatio*

An *adstipulatio* was made in the following way: *831. Conception and form*

> Maevius: Titi, decem mihi dari spondes?
> Titius: Spondeo.
> Seius (asking with Maevius' consent): Titi, eadem decem mihi dari spondes?
> Titius: Spondeo.

The second stipulation was called *adstipulatio* and Seius was called *adstipulator*. The *adstipulatio* was accessory to a preceding complete stipulation and was added for the benefit of the prior stipulator.

1. The two stipulators were not *plures rei stipulandi* since there was no *unitas actus* (see above, s. 827); the *832. Stipulator and adstipulator*

adstipulatio followed after the principal stipulation had become completed by Titius' first *spondeo*. In classical times the *adstipulatio* followed immediately upon the preceding stipulation, but there was no legal objection to making it after an interval. The *adstipulator* might further use a form of words other than that used by the principal *stipulator*; for example, he might ask *promittis?* whereas the principal *stipulator* has asked *spondes?*

2. The adstipulation was accessory to a principal stipulation, not to a principal obligation. A principal stipulation had to precede in which the form of the stipulation was properly observed (above, s. 805), but the adstipulation was valid even if the principal stipulation did not succeed in creating an obligation.

> Consider the following case:
>
> Maevius: Titi, decem mihi post mortem meam dari spondes?
> Titius: Spondeo.
> Seius: Titi, eadem decem mihi dari spondes?
> Titius: Spondeo—
>
> The principal stipulation was ineffective since a *stipulatio post mortem stipulatoris* was *inutilis* (Gai. 3. 100), but the adstipulation was effective. Gaius even tells us that in his time this was almost the only case in which adstipulation was employed (Gai. 3. 117).

The accessory nature of the adstipulation is clearly revealed by the rule that the adstipulator might stipulate for less but never for more than the principal stipulator.

3. The *adstipulatio* had not the effect of a *novatio* (above, ss. 815 ff.). When the second stipulator asked: 'Titi, quod debes Maevio id mihi dari spondes?' this would have been *novatio* (above, s. 815), but that formula was carefully avoided in the *adstipulatio*.

4. When an obligation did arise from the principal stipulation, the *adstipulatio* added a second; the promisor was now the debtor of each of the two stipulators. This was a case of active solidarity (above, s. 827). The promisor had only to pay once; if he paid one of the two stipulators, both obligations were discharged, and if one of them released the promisor by *acceptilatio*, the effect was the same, since *acceptilatio* was regarded as an *imaginaria solutio* (Gai. 3.

169). On the other hand, the *adstipulator* as well as the principal stipulator might claim payment from the promisor. This makes it quite clear that an *adstipulatio* could only be made with the informal consent of the principal stipulator, just as a *novatio* by a new stipulator could only be made with the consent of the original creditor (above, s. 815. 3).

5. We are unable through lack of sources to say anything definite about *litis contestatio*. Apparently there was no correality and *litis contestatio* by one of the two creditors did not affect the other. Likewise the *novatio* of one of the two obligations did not affect the other (*D*. 45. 2. 2 deals with *plures rei stipulandi* and not with *adstipulatio*). _{836. Litis contestatio and novatio}

6. The *adstipulator* was a sort of trustee. For that reason his right was strictly personal and not transferable to his heir. A slave might act as a stipulator, thereby acquiring for his master, but he could not act as an *adstipulator*. A son in power might be an *adstipulator*, but his father did not acquire the action resulting from the *adstipulatio*; it was reserved for the son until the time when he became *sui iuris*. The *adstipulator* had to act in the interest of the principal stipulator. If the promisor paid the *adstipulator*, the latter was bound to restore the amount received to the principal stipulator who, under classical law, had the *actio mandati* against the *adstipulator* (Gai. 3. 111). When the *adstipulator* released the promisor by *acceptilatio in fraudem stipulatoris* (i.e. of the principal *stipulator*), the latter had a special action against the *adstipulator* introduced by the second chapter of the *lex Aquilia* (below, s. 1005). Of course at the time of that statute the *actio mandati* did not yet exist (Gai. 3. 215). Under classical law this *actio legis Aquiliae* was in truth superfluous, but it was nevertheless preserved, since it implied the advantage for the principal *stipulator* that *lis infitiando crevit in duplum* (below, s. 1009). The statement in *D*. (9. 2) 27. 4: 'Huius legis (scil. *Aquiliae* secundum quidem capitulum in desuetudinem abiit' has to be regarded as a bold interpolation and not as Ulpian's text. _{837. Adstipulator a trustee}

7. *Adstipulatio* was already moribund at the end of the second century A.D. and disappeared entirely in post-classical times. It is absent from all our post-classical sources, _{838. Disappearance}

including of course Justinian's law-books. In a few Egyptian papyri of the second century A.D. scholars have recognized adstipulations, but these stipulations are unconnected with the true Roman *adstipulatio*, which was hardly known, let alone practised in Egypt.

v. *Accessory sponsio and fidepromissio*

839.
Sponsio
(termi-
nology)
Sponsio in its wider sense meant any stipulation in which parties used the word *spondere*; in the narrower sense it meant a kind of suretyship created by a stipulation in which parties used the word *spondere*. Here we are only concerned with *sponsio* in the narrower sense which we will call 'accessory *sponsio*'. This *sponsio* was an old republican institution which in classical times was still confined to Roman citizens, peregrines being excluded from all sorts of *sponsiones* (above, s. 805).

> The word *spondere* is certainly akin with Greek σπένδειν, which means 'to pour a libation' and 'to make a contract'. The contract was originally celebrated by drinking a glass of wine (Jacob Grimm, *Deutsche Rechtsaltertümer*, i, 1899, 263 f.), which in antiquity implied a libation. But this formality was long forgotten in republican times. To connect *spondere* with *pendere* is certainly erroneous, as in the *sponsio* there was no opportunity for weighing.

840. Fide-
promissio
(termino-
logy)
Another republican form of suretyship though of a less ancient origin was the *fidepromissio*. In its broader sense *fidepromissio* meant any stipulation where the parties used the word *fidepromitto*; in its narrower sense it meant a sort of suretyship which we will call 'accessory *fidepromissio*'. This form was available to peregrines as well as to citizens.

841. The
law of spon-
io and fide-
promissio
Accessory *sponsio* and *fidepromissio* were both subject to the same legal rules (leaving aside the *lex Publilia*; below, s. 854). For the sake of brevity we may therefore confine the following description to the accessory *sponsio*; the reader must throughout keep in mind that our statements refer also to the *fidepromissio* unless the contrary is expressly stated.

842. Form
The accessory *sponsio* was made in the following way:

> Titius: Maevi (the principal debtor) decem mihi dari spondes?
> Maevius: Spondeo.
> Titius: Sei (the surety) eadem decem mihi dari spondes?
> Seius: Spondeo.

The second *sponsio* is the accessory *sponsio*; in the case of a *fidepromissio* the parties used in the accessory stipulation the verb *fidepromittere* instead of *spondere*.

The accessory *sponsio* (and *fidepromissio*) is an obvious counterpart to the *adstipulatio* (above, s. 831); in the latter there was a second stipulator, an *adstipulator*, in the former a second promisor, an *adpromissor*. _{843. Adpromissio}

> The term *adpromissor*, comprehending accessory *sponsor* and *fidepromissor*, was known to the republican jurisprudence, as Festus (v. *adpromissor* (Bruns, *Fontes*, ii, p. 2)) shows, but it remains doubtful whether it was still used by the classical lawyers. It occurs only three times in our legal sources (*Voc. Iur. Rom.* i. 256) and these three texts are unreliable.

The parallel is important and should be firmly borne in mind; the reader should compare in detail the following statement with what we have said above about *adstipulatio* (ss. 831 ff.).

1. Principal debtor and accessory *sponsor* were not *plures rei promittendi*, just as principal stipulator and *adstipulator* were not *plures rei stipulandi*. The accessory stipulation followed the stipulation with the principal debtor; they were not both combined in one act (no *unitas actus*). The accessory *sponsio* might even follow after a considerable interval and differ in form from the principal stipulation. _{844. No plures rei promittendi}

> Titius: Maevi, decem mihi dari promittis?
> Maevius: Promitto.
> Titius: Sei, eadem decem mihi dari spondes?
> Seius: Spondeo.

2. Like the *adstipulatio*, the accessory *sponsio* was accessory to a principal stipulation, not to a principal obligation. _{845. Accessory character}

(*a*) A principal stipulation was invariably required. Thus an obligation resulting from a consensual contract of sale could not be secured by accessory *sponsio* unless it was previously transformed into a verbal obligatio by *novatio*.

(*b*) If no obligation resulted from the principal stipulation the accessory *sponsio* was nevertheless effective.

> Titius: Maevi, decem mihi post mortem meam dari spondes?
> Maevius: Spondeo.
> Titius: Sei, eadem decem mihi dari spondes?
> Seius: Spondeo.

The principal stipulation was ineffective, since a stipulation *post mortem stipulatoris dari* was *inutilis* (Gai. 3. 100), but the accessory *sponsio* was fully valid (Gai. 3. 119). Or, if the promisor in the principal stipulation was a *pupillus* or a woman who acted without *auctoritas tutoris*, both *pupillus* and *mulier* were free from obligation, but the surety (*sponsor* or *fidepromissor*) was bound (Gai. 3. 119).

(*c*) The accessory *sponsio* could never exceed the principal stipulation. If the principal promisor had promised 10, the accessory *sponsor* could not promise 20; this is but logical. Of course the surety might promise only 5 (Gai. 3. 126).

846. No novatio   3. The accessory *sponsio* had not the effect of a *novatio*. If the second stipulation ran, 'quod Maevius mihi debet, id tu Sei mihi dari spondes?' this would be a *novatio* (Gai. 3. 176), but this formula was carefully avoided when an accessory *sponsio* was made (Gai. 3. 116).

847. Passive solidarity   4. When an obligation resulted from the principal stipulation (which was of course the normal case), the accessory *sponsio* added a second; this was a case of passive solidarity.

848. No beneficium excussionis   (*a*) The creditor might claim the whole from either of his two debtors; he might even first claim it from the surety, who was not entitled to refer him to the principal debtor (the *sponsor* had no *beneficium excussionis*; see below, s. 865). To be sure *fides* required that the creditor first attempted to obtain payment from the principal debtor if he was as easily accessible as the surety. If the creditor wilfully applied to the surety first in order to defame the principal debtor, the latter had an *actio iniuriarum* against the creditor.

> In a comparatively small town like ancient Rome gossip played an important part. Thus when a creditor applied first to the surety, rumour spread at once that the principal debtor was insolvent (see below, s. 1016).

849. Payment   (*b*) If the surety paid the creditor, the principal debtor was free and vice versa; and if the creditor released one of his two debtors by *acceptilatio*, both obligations were discharged, since *acceptilatio* was an *imaginaria solutio*.

850. Mora and culpa   (*c*) *Mora* and *culpa* of one of the two debtors did not affect the other.

Suppose P promised *Stichum dari* and the accessory sponsor (S) promised *eundem Stichum dari*.

While S was *in mora debitoris*, the slave died by accident. S's obligation remained intact (*perpetuatur obligatio*; above, s. 813), but P's obligation was discharged since it was now impossible for him through no fault of his own to deliver the slave. As we have repeatedly emphasized, the stipulation of the accessory *sponsor* was accessory to the principal stipulation, but his obligation was not accessory to the principal obligation. Thus when the principal obligation expired (apart from payment and *acceptilatio*), the obligation of the accessory *sponsor* continued to exist.

If P was *in mora* and the slave died by accident, P's obligation was perpetuated but S was free. The contrary opinion founded on an *argumentum e contrario* taken from *D*. (45. 1) 127 is hardly justified, since that text is not reliable.

5. As regards the effect of *litis contestatio* we must start from the fact that the principal promisor and the accessory *sponsor* were not *plures rei promittendi* (above, s. 832). Accordingly there was here no correality. If the creditor sued the principal debtor, the principal obligation was destroyed by *litis contestatio*, but the obligation of the *sponsor* remained intact since its existence was not dependent on the existence of the principal obligation. If the creditor sued the accessory *sponsor*, his obligation was discharged by *litis contestatio* but the obligation of the principal debtor remained intact. Likewise novation of one of the two obligations did not destroy the other.

851. Litis contestatio

6. The obligation of the accessory *sponsor* was of a strictly personal character (just like the right of the *adstipulator*; above, s. 837). It was invariably destroyed by the death of the *sponsor* and was not transferred to his heir (Gai. 3. 120).

852. Personal character of sponsio

7. Under a *lex Furia* of unknown date (but certainly of the second century B.C.) the accessory *sponsor* became free after the lapse of two years; however the statute applied only in Italy (Gai. 3. 121, 122).

853. Prescription

8. If the *sponsor* discharged the debt and was not reimbursed within six months, a *lex Publilia* granted him a special *actio depensi* against the principal debtor. The date of the statute is unknown, but it probably belongs to the second century B.C. This action was not available to the *fideipromissor*, but under classical law both accessory *sponsor*

854. Actio depensi, mandati and negotiorum gestorum

and *fidepromissor* had an *actio mandati* or *negotiorum gestorum* for reimbursement.

So far we have only dealt with a single accessory *sponsor* or *fidepromissor*; now we have to consider a plurality of sureties (*sponsores* or *fidepromissores*).

855. Con-
sponsores
solidarity
and
correality
1. Two or more sureties might bind themselves at the same time either *uno actu* or one after the other; they might do so at different times (e.g. one today, the other tomorrow). The *sponsio* of each of them was accessory to the principal stipulation; this needs no further explanation. In every case the *consponsores* were solidary debtors. The creditor might claim the whole from any of them, but if one of them paid off the creditor, the others were free.

> Suppose the principal debtor owed 100. Three sureties A, B, C had promised *eadem sexaginta dari*. The creditor might claim 60 from each of them, but if A paid 60, the obligations of B and C were discharged; the principal debtor now owed only forty.

When the *consponsores* had bound themselves *uno actu* (but only then) there was of course correality and *litis contestatio* with one of the sureties set the others free.

856.
Beneficium
divisionis
2. These rules were modified by the *lex Furia* which we have already mentioned (above, s. 853). Under this statute the creditor was bound to divide the amount of the debt among the sureties who were alive at the time when the debt was due.

> Suppose A, B, C, D were sureties for a debt of 60. When the debt was due, D had died (above, s. 852). The creditor could only claim 20 from A, 20 from B, 20 from C.

However, the *lex Furia*, as aforesaid, applied only in Italy. In the provinces the old solidarity survived throughout the classical period; the *beneficium divisionis ex epistula divi Hadriani* (below, s. 867) was never extended to *sponsio* and *fidepromissio* in classical times (Gai. 3. 121*a* is probably entirely spurious; Italia is called a province).

857. Lex
Apuleia
3. Under a *lex Apuleia* (earlier than the *lex Furia*) an accessory *sponsor* or *fidepromissor* who had paid more than his share might recover the excess from the other sureties.

> If A, B, C were sureties for a debt of 60 and A paid the whole, he could recover 20 from B and 20 from C.

vi. *Fideiussio*

This was a third form of suretyship created like the accessory *sponsio* and *fidepromissio* by stipulation, but otherwise fundamentally different from the two older forms. *Fideiussio* is not of ancient origin; we can only trace it back to Labeo. The terms *fideiussio* and *fideiubere* are entirely absent from the works of Caesar and Cicero and, of course, from older literature; it is further absent from all *leges* known to us. Thus we may safely assume that *fideiussio* was created by the jurisprudence in the late Republic or the early Principate, probably by Servius Sulpicius or Labeo. Be that as it may, *fideiussio* is the most modern form of suretyship and it is small wonder that it eventually drove out the two older forms; in Justinian's law only the *fideiussio* survived.

858.
Origin

The legal character of the *fideiussio* in contrast to the accessory *sponsio* and *fidepromissio* can be briefly described.

859.
Character

1. The *fideiussor* did not (like the *sponsor* and *fidepromissor*) promise what the principal debtor had promised (he was not an *adpromissor* and certainly was never designated as such by the classical lawyers; above, s. 843), but he declared himself to be liable for the fulfilment of the principal obligation by the principal debtor. Let us illustrate the difference in the following way:

Accessory sponsio	*Fideiussio*
Titius: Maevi, decem mihi dari spondes?	Titius: Maevi, decem mihi dari spondes?
Maevius: Spondeo.	Maevius: Spondeo.
Titius: Sei, eadem decem mihi dari spondes?	Titius: Sei, quod Maevius mihi debet, id fide tua esse iubes?
Seius: Spondeo.	Seius: Fideiubeo.

Fideiubeo means *iubeo debitum fide mea esse*, 'I wish that the debt should rest on (or be supported by) my *fides*' (my good faith trustworthiness, faithfulness, responsibility). *Iubere* is used synonymously with *velle* as in *sic volo, sic iubeo* or *velitis iubeatis*. It should be observed that *fidepromitto* is only a stylistic variant of *promitto*; *fide mea spondeo* (Pliny, *epist.* 1. 14. 10) only differs stylistically from *spondeo*; in both cases *fide* might have been omitted. But in *fideiubeo* '*fide*' is essential; *fideiubeo* is an abbreviation of *iubeo id fide mea esse*.

2. The *fideiussio* was not, like the two older forms of

suretyship, a stipulation accessory to a principal stipulation, but rather a stipulation involving an obligation which was accessory to a principal obligation which need not necessarily have been created by stipulation.

Let us now turn to the details.

860. Character of the principal obligation

1. A principal stipulation was not required for *fideiussio*. The principal obligation might originate from any other *causa* and even a natural obligation (above, s. 795) was sufficient (Gai. 3. 119*a*). Only *obligationes ex delicto* were excluded under classical law since they had a penal character.

861. The principal obligation did not exist

2. When from the very beginning a principal obligation did not exist, the *fideiussio* was void.

The contrast to the accessory *sponsio* and *fidepromissio* is particularly palpable, if the surety secured a principal stipulation:

Accessory sponsio	Fideiussio
The principal promisor was a *pupillus* who acted without the *auctoritas* of his guardian: the accessory *sponsio* was valid.	The principal promisor was a *pupillus* who acted without the *auctoritas* of his guardian: the *fideiussio* was void.
The principal promisor was a slave: the accessory *sponsio* was void. (Gai. 3. 119.)	The principal promisor was a slave: the *fideiussio* was valid, since the slave was *naturaliter obligatus*. (Gai. 3. 119*a*.)

862. The principal obligation ceased to exist

3. When the principal obligation was afterwards discharged, the liability of the *fideiussor* automatically expired. Thus if the creditor received payment from the principal debtor or if he released him by *acceptilatio*, the *fideiussor* was free. If the principal obligation was discharged by *novatio* or *confusio* (e.g. the creditor became the heir of the principal debtor), the liability of the *fideiussor* came to an end. If the creditor sued the principal debtor and thereby consumed the principal obligation (by *litis contestatio*), the *fideiussor* was free (Paul. *Sent.* 2. 17. 16). If the fulfilment of the principal obligation became impossible through no fault of the principal debtor (e.g. he owed Stichus and Stichus died by accident), the latter was free, but so was the *fideiussor*. Even if the slave died by *dolus* of the *fideiussor*, not only the principal obligation was discharged (as the principal debtor was

not responsible for the death) but also the obligation of the *fideiussor*, since the accessory obligation could not exist without the principal obligation; in this case the creditor had an *actio de dolo* against the *fideiussor*. If, however, the slave died by *dolus* of an accessory *sponsor*, the principal obligation was discharged, as the principal debtor was not responsible for the death, but the sponsor's obligation remained intact because his obligation could exist without the principal obligation.

4. When the principal debtor was protected by an *exceptio*, the *fideiussor* might avail himself of that *exceptio* whether or not the principal debtor was bound to reimburse the surety.

863. Exceptio

5. The obligation of the *fideiussor* could of course never exceed the principal obligation. If the principal debtor owed 100, the *fideiussor* might be liable for only 50, but never for more than 100. In this respect the *fideiussio* did not differ from the accessory *sponsio* and *fidepromissio* (Gai. 3. 126).

864. Fideiussio in minus

6. The principal debtor and the *fideiussor* were solidary debtors. The creditor might apply first to the *fideiussor*, who under classical law had no *beneficium excussionis*; it was only introduced by Justinian (*Novella* 4, cap. 1). Principal debtor and *fideiussor* were not *plures rei promittendi*, accordingly there was no correality. When the obligation of the *fideiussor* was novated, the principal obligation remained intact, and when the creditor sued the *fideiussor*, the *litis contestatio* destroyed the obligation of the *fideiussor*, but not also that of the principal debtor. A widespread doctrine asserts that *litis contestatio* with the *fideiussor* consumed also the principal obligation, but this is not supported by any reliable text and only rests on dubious speculations.

865. Solidarity not correality

7. When the *fideiussor* satisfied the creditor, he might sue the principal debtor for reimbursement with the *actio mandati* or *negotiorum gestorum*. The artificial device of the *beneficium cedendarum actionum* apparently did not yet exist under classical law.

866. Reimbursement

Suppose the creditor claimed payment from the *fideiussor* and the latter declared himself prepared to pay if the creditor assigned his action against the principal debtor to him. The creditor consented and the *fide-iussor* paid. The payment might be regarded as the price paid for the action, so that this action was not discharged. If the creditor sued the *fideiussor*, he might be compelled by the judge (on the strength of an *exceptio doli*) to assign his action against the principal debtor (which, as aforesaid, was not consumed by *litis contestatio* with the *fideiussor*) to the *fideiussor*. However, this artificial device was apparently not practised under classical law; *actio mandati* and *negotiorum gestorum* were sufficient remedies.

867.
Beneficium
divisionis

8. Two or more *fideiussores* were solidary debtors and only if they had bound themselves *uno actu* were they correal debtors. Under an *epistula Hadriani* the *confideiussores* enjoyed a *beneficium divisionis*, the creditor being bound to divide the amount of the debt among those sureties who were solvent at the time of the *litis contestatio*. The view that this benefit was confined to *fideiussores* who had bound themselves *uno actu* is unfounded.

> Suppose that A, B, C were *confideiussores* for 60. If all were solvent, the creditor could claim 20 from each of them; if C was insolvent, A and B were liable for 30 each.

868. Reim-
bursement
among
confideius-
sores

9. If one of the *confideiussores* paid the creditor, the other sureties were bound to reimburse him *pro parte*. The surety who paid had against them an *actio mandati, negotiorum gestorum*, or *pro socio*; a *beneficium cedendarum actionum* did not exist under classical law.

869.
Justinian's
law

As already stated (s. 858), *fideiussio* alone survived in Justinian's law while accessory *sponsio* and *fidepromissio* were cancelled. Whenever the compilers inserted in their compilations a text dealing with the accessory *sponsio* or *fidepromissio*, they invariably substituted *fideiussio* for the older forms of suretyship. As a rule it is easy to prove these interpolations. Justinian also abolished the consumptive power of *litis contestatio* (*C*. 8. 40. 28). On other sorts of interpolations in this connexion we need not dwell. A full and critical analysis of the Justinianic texts does not yet exist.

SOURCES

s. 815. Read Gai. 3. 176, 177; *D*. (46. 2) 1 pr. [*vel . . . naturalem*]; [*transfusio atque*]; (46. 2) 8. 5 [*si hoc . . . alter liberatur*]; (46. 2) 34. 2; *Stipulatio Aquiliana*: *D*. (46. 4) 18; *Inst. Iust.* (3. 29) 2; *D*. (2. 15) 4.

s. 816. Read *Inst. Iust.* (3. 29) 3*a*; *D.* (46. 2) 2 [*ex quacumque . . . obligationes*].

s. 817. Read Gai. 3. 176, 179; *C.* (8. 40) 4 [*legitime perfecta*]; *D.* (46. 2) 18 [*legitime facta*]; (13. 7) 11. 1

s. 819. Read Gai. 3. 180, 181; *D.* (20. 1) 13. 4; (46. 2) 29 [*voluntariae*]; [*si id . . . actum est*], but the whole text is of post-classical origin; *Fr. Vat.* 263 [*si . . . novavit*]; see Beseler, Z xliii (1922), 539.

s. 821. Read Gai. 3. 103, 163; 2. 95; *D.* (50. 17) 73. 4; *C.* (5. 12) 26; (8. 38) 3 pr. [*nisi sua intersit*].

s. 823. Read *C.* (4. 50) 6. 3; (3. 42) 8 [*commodavit aut*]; [*stricto iure*]; [*utilis . . . actio*]; *D.* (12. 1) 9. 8 [*nec dubitari . . . debitori nostro*].

s. 824*a*. Read *D.* (17. 1) 6. 4.

s. 824*b*. Read *D.* (45. 1) 38. 17.

s. 824*c*. Read *D.* (45. 1) 38. 21 (text corrupt but substantially classical).

s. 824*d*. Read Gai. 3. 103; *D.* (45. 1) 110 pr.; *D.* (18. 1) 64 [*est*] ⟨*esto*⟩; [*personam . . . ideoque*].

s. 824*e*. Read Gai. 3. 103*a*; *D.* (20. 1) 33; (46. 1) 23.

s. 824*f.* Read *D.* (16. 3) 26 pr., *salva* [*ve*]; [*filio an marito*]; cf. Stephanus schol. 3 ad Bas. (13. 2) 26, Heimbach, 2. 54.

s. 825. Read *Fr. Vat.* 286.

s. 826. Read *D.* (45. 1) 38. 17 and 22 (interpol.); *Inst. Iust.* (3. 19) 19 and 20, first sentence; *C.* (8. 38) 3 pr. [*nisi sua intersit*]; *C.* (5. 14) 7 [*licet*]; [*tamen . . . actio*]; cf. Thalelaeus schol. 2 ad Bas. (29. 1) 37, Heimbach, 3. 483; *D.* (30) 77 [*quasi . . . debitori*]; [*quod cum . . . potest*]; see Beseler, Z xlv (1925), 262.

s. 827. Read *Inst. Iust.* (3. 16) pr. and § 1; *D.* (45. 2) 16, genuine; (46. 2) 31. 1 to *utrique obligationem*; [*iudicium*]; (45. 2) 2 [*aut . . . aut*]; [*et singuli . . . ideoque*]; (45. 2) 11. 2.

s. 829. Read *D.* (45. 2) 9 pr. [*fiunt . . . decem dato*] with Beseler, *St. Bonfante*, ii. 74; (30) 8. 1, spurious (Beseler, Z xlvii. 371 f.) (31) 16, spurious (Beseler, ibid. 373); Gai. 2. 205; *D.* (9. 3) 1. 10; (9. 3) 3 [*sed*] ⟨*et*⟩; ⟨*non*⟩ *liberabuntur*; cf. Bonfante, *Scritti*, iii. 231.

ss. 831 ff. Read Gail 3. 110–14, 117, 215, 216.

s. 842. Read Gai. 3. 116, first sentence.

s. 845. Read Gai. 3. 118, 119, 126.

s. 846. Read Gai. 3. 116, 176, 179 in fine.

s. 848. Read *D.* (47. 10) 19.

s. 850. Read *D.* (38. 1) 44, *debito* [*fideiussor*] ⟨*sponsor*⟩; (45. 1) 88 [*fideiussor*] ⟨*sponsor*⟩ *hominem*; [*fideiussor*] ⟨*sponsor*⟩ *autem*; (45. 1) 127 [*pupillus*] ⟨*mulier*⟩; [*fideiussorem*] ⟨*sponsorem*⟩ *dedit*; [*pupillo*] ⟨*muliere*⟩ *nec* [*fideiussor*] ⟨*mulier*⟩ *nec sponsor*⟩; [*propter . . . moram*]; [*fideiussorem*] ⟨*sponsorem*⟩ *obligatum*.

s. 852. Read Gai. 3. 120.

s. 853. Read Gai. 3. 121, 121*a*; Ulpian, Disput. lib. iii (Fragmenta Argorat. Seckel–Kübler, *Iurisprud. Anteiust.* i. 498).

s. 854. Read Gai. 3. 127; 4. 9.

s. 856. Read Gai. 3. 121.

s. 857. Read Gai. 3. 122.

s. 859. Read Gai. 3. 116.

s. 860. Read Gai. 3. 119*a*; *D.* (46. 1) 70. 5 [*non*] *sic*; [*nam ... vim habet*].

s. 861. Read *D.* (46. 1) 23.

s. 862. Read *C.* (8. 40) 4 [*legitime perfecta*]; *D.* (46. 1) 21. 3; Paul. *Sent.* (2. 17) 16; *D.* (4. 3) 19.

s. 863. Read *D.* (39. 5) 24 *legis* ⟨*Cinciae*⟩.

s. 864. Read Gai. 3. 126.

s. 866. Read Gai. 3. 127.

s. 867. Read Gai. 3. 121.

s. 868. Read Gai. 3. 122, *verb. itaque si, etc.*

s. 869. Cp. *Inst. Just* (3. 20) pr. §§ 5, 6 with Gai. 3. 115, 117, 126, 127.

BIBLIOGRAPHY

ss. 815 ff. E. Weiss, *PW* xvii. 1156 ff., with references; Beseler, Z xlvii (1927), 357; lxvi (1948), 386; Bonifacio, *St. Solazzi* (1948), 290 ff. (not acceptable); Beretta, *St. Ferrini*, iii (1947), 77 (not acceptable). On 'aliquid novi' see Beseler, Z lxvi (1948), 330, with references, 601. On the *stipulatio Aquiliana* see Wlassak, Z xlii (1921), 394 ff.; Taubenschlag, *Law of Greco-Roman Egypt* (1944), 307, 322.*

s. 816. De Ruggiero, 'Novatio legitime facta', *Bull.* xi (1898), 49; Scialoja, *St. Perozzi* (1925), 407 ff.; Cornil, 'Cause et conséquences de l'apparation tardive de l'animus novandi', *Mélanges Fournier* (1929), 87 ff.; Meylan, 'La Réforme justinienne de la novation', *Acta CI.* 1 (1935) 277.

s. 817. W. Flume, *Studien zur Akzessorietät der röm. Bürgschafts-stipulationen* (1932), 65–9.*

s. 819. I. Goldschmidt, *Prozess als Rechtslage* (1925), 53, 56.*

ss. 820 ff. Pernice, *Labeo*, iii. 1 (1892), 189, 193, 333 f.; Eisele, *Beiträge zur röm. Rechtsgeschichte* (1896), 76 ff.; Riccobono, 'Lineamenti della dottrina della rappresentanza diretta in diritto romano', *Annali Palermo*, xiv (1930), 399 ff.; Pacchioni, *I contratti a favore di terzi* (3rd ed. 1933, not available); Cornil, *St. Riccobono*, iv (1936), 241 ff.; Vazny, ibid. 359 ff.; Albertario, 'I contratti a favore di terzi', *Festschrift P. Koschaker*, ii (1939), 16 ff., with references; *Corso, Le obbligazioni* (1948), 199, 229; Beseler, *Scritti Ferrini*, iii (1948), 276. On the *stipulatio post mortem* which we have not dealt with see F. E. Vassalli, *Di talune clausole con riferimento ad 'dies mortis' nel legato e nella stipulazione* (1910); Albertario, l.c. 36 ff. On the distinction between direct agency and contracts in favour of a third person see H. Buchka, *Die Lehre von der Stellvertretung bei Eingehung von Verträgen* (1852), 121 ff. (history of the doctrine since the Glossators); O. Gierke, *DP* iii (1917), 380, 386 ff. On medieval and Dutch law see De Wet, *Die ontwikkeling van die vooreenkoms ten behoewe van 'n derde* (1940).*

s. 826. See in particular Eisele, l.c.; Albertario, l.c. 22 ff. On the *fideicommissum a debitore relictum* see K. Hellwig, *Die Verträge auf*

Leistung an Dritte (1899), 1 ff. (completely uncritical); Beseler, Z xlv (1925), 262 ff.; Windscheid–Kipp, *Pand.* ii (1905), § 316 n. 4.

ss. 827 ff. J. Binder, *Die Korrealobligationen* (1899), with references to the older literature; E. Levy, *Die Konkurrenz der Aktionen und Personen*, i (1918), 173 ff., 375 ff.; Kerr Wylie, *Solidarity and Correality* (1923); Bonfante, *Scritti*, iii (1926), 209 ff., 368 ff.; Beseler, *Beiträge*, iv (1920), 271 ff.; *St. Bonfante*, ii (1930), 74; Z xliv (1924), 387; xlvi (1926), 89 ff.; xlvii (1927), 371 f., 373; Schulz, *St. Bonfante*, i (1930), 357 ff.; Albertario, 'Sulla applicabilità della riforma giustinianea a contenuta in *C. 8. 40. 28*', *Studi Mancaleoni*, 1938 (*Studi Sassaresi*, ser. 2, vol. 10), not available; Corso, *Le obbligazioni solidali* (1948); Archi, 'La funzione del rapporto obbligatorio solidale', *SD* viii (1942), 197 ff.; *Sul concetto di obbligazione solidale* (1940).

ss. 831. ff. Pernice, Z xix (1898), 178.

s. 838. Taubenschlag, *Law of Greco-Roman Egypt* (1944), 233.

ss. 839 ff. W. Flume, *Studien zur Akzessorietät der röm. Bürgschaftsstipulationen* (1932, fundamental); E. Levy, *Sponsio, fidepromissio, fideiussio* (1907); on this book see Mitteis, *Aus röm. und bürg. Recht* (*Festgabe für E. I. Bekker*, 1907), 126 n. 1; Z xxviii (1907), 487 n. 1; Wenger, Z xxviii (1907), 487 ff.; Flume, 11; Kerr Wylie, *Solidarity and Correality* (1923); Levy, *Seminar*, ii (1944), 6 ff.; De Martino, *Studi sulle garanzie personali*, I. *L'autonomia classica della sponsio* (1937), not acceptable; Beretta, *Scritti Ferrini*, iii (1947), 77 ff., with references (not acceptable). Antiquated but still useful: Girtaner, *Die Bürgschaft nach gemeinem Civilrecht* (1850); O. Geib, *Zur Dogmatik des röm. Bürgschaftsrechts* (1894).

s. 843. Solazzi, *Bull.* xxxviii (1939), 19 ff.; Flume, 14 and 126.

s. 844. Flume, 13. 64 ff.

s. 850. Flume, 105 ff., with references; Beseler, Z lxvi (1948), 317.

s. 852. Levy, l.c. 45 ff.

ss. 853, 854. Levy, l.c. 58 ff.; G. Rotondi, *Leges publicae* (1912), 473, 476.

s. 856. Beseler, *Beiträge*, iv (1920), 111; Solazzi, *Glosse a Gaio*, ii. 313; Albertario, *Studi*, v (1937), 487; Archi, l.c. 265, 275 f.

s. 857. Levy, l.c. 58; Rotondi, l.c. 246, 506; Archi, l.c. 265 ff.

s. 858. See for literature ss. 831 ff. Bibliography. Further Buckland, 'Les Limites de l'obligation du fideiussor', *RH* xii (1933), 116 ff.; 'Principal and fideiussor. Consumptio litis', *Juridical Review*, liii (1941), 281 ff.

s. 860. Levy, l.c. 132 n. 3; Beseler, *Beiträge*, iv (1920), 273; v (1931), 80; Siber, *Röm. Privatrecht* (1928), 295.

s. 862. Flume, 105 ff., with references.

s. 863. Beseler, *St. Bonfante*, ii (1930), 75.

s. 865. Siber, l.c. 297; Buckland, 'Principal and fideiussor', l.c.

s. 867. Levy, l.c. 137 ff.; Archi, l.c. 276 ff.

s. 868. Levy, l.c. 164 ff.; Beseler, *Beiträge*, iv (1920), 275; Archi, l.c. 279 ff.

s. 869. Levy, l.c. 87 ff.; Schulz, *St. Bonfante*, i (1930), 357 ff.

4. *So-called literal contract*

870.
Literal
contract

Among the obligations created by contract Gaius mentions the *obligatio quae litteris fit* (Gai. 3. 88 and 128). It is clear that this contract was not simply a contract by deed (Gai. 3. 134), but its exact nature cannot be discerned with anything like certainty from Gaius' much too short description (3. 128–33). It is generally held that the contract was made by entries in the ledger (*codex accepti et expensi*) which it was the custom to keep. This theory cannot be proved in default of sources, but it may quite possibly be true. Perhaps the tablets found in Herculaneum will furnish fresh material. For the time being we will not dwell on this enigmatical contract. In any case it did not survive the Principate; what Justinian's *Institutiones* (3. 21) call *litterarum obligatio* has no connexion with the classical literal contract and concerns the *exceptio non numeratae pecuniae* (above, s. 812).

SOURCES

Read Gai. 3. 128–33; *Inst Iust.* 3. 21.

BIBLIOGRAPHY

Steinwenter, *PW* xiii. 786 ff.; Arangio-Ruiz, 'Les Tablettes d'Herculanum', *RIDA* i (1948), 15–17.*

5. *Real contracts in general*

871.
Conception
and kinds

We now turn to the informal contracts of classical law and begin with the so-called real contracts. We have already mentioned this group (above, s. 800) and we may repeat our definition: Real contracts were informal contracts which were made by handing over corporeal things and which bound the recipient to restore them (*re contrahitur obligatio*). The classical civil law knew only four such contracts: *mutuum, commodatum, depositum, pignus*. We will now describe these in detail. The praetorian real contract, the *receptum cauponum*, we shall discuss later among the *pacta praetoria* (below, s. 971).

872. Constitutive
factors

Two things were essential for any real contract: (1) a *traditio rei* or *rerum*; (2) the agreement of the parties on the legal purpose of the *traditio*. Both were constitutive factors of the contract: in default of an agreement there was no contract, and in default of a *traditio* the agreement was void. If A handed over a sum of money to B as a deposit and B accepted it as a loan, neither *depositum* nor *mutuum* came into existence.

From any real contract there could only spring an obligation to restore the things given and received, either the very same individual things or (in case of *mutuum*) things of the same kind. Thus if a quantity of wine was given as a *mutuum*, the recipient could not be bound by agreement to restore corn; nor could the recipient of a loan of money be bound by the real contract to pay interest. Of course if the deposited object perished and the depositary was responsible for the loss, he was liable for damages. 873. Character of the obligation

Contracts constituting a mixture of a real contract and verbal contract—so-called 'real-verbal contracts', *re et verbis contrahitur obligatio*—did not exist under classical law. A might promise B in advance by stipulation to restore a loan to be given him by B; but if afterwards B gave the loan, there was only one contract, namely the stipulation. If the stipulation followed the *datio mutui*, this was a case of *novatio* (above, s. 815). If the recipient of a loan of money promised interest by stipulation, there were two contracts: the real contract (*mutuum*) and the verbal contract. 874. Real-verbal contract

SOURCES

s. 871. Read Gai. 3. 89, 90; *D*. (44. 7) 1. 3–5.
s. 872. Read *D*. (12. 1) 18 pr. to *acceperit*; (12. 1) 18. 1 to *accepi*.
s. 873. Read *D*. (12. 1) 2 pr.
s. 874. Read *D*. (44. 7) 52 pr. 3 (spurious); (46. 2) 6. 1 [*sine stipulatione*]; [*unus contractus est*] ⟨*duo contractus sunt*⟩; [*idem*] ⟨*aliud*⟩; (46. 2) 7 [*non*] *puto*; [*quia . . . fieri*].

BIBLIOGRAPHY

ss. 871 ff. Brasiello,'Obligatio re contracta', *St. Bonfante*, ii (1930), 539 ff.*
s. 874. Pernice, 'Der sogenannte Realverbalcontract', Z xiii (1892), 246 ff.; Segrè, 'Mutuo e Stipulatio nel diritto rom. class. e giustinianeo', *St. Simoncelli* (1917), 233 ff., not available; De Ruggiero, *St. Perozzi* (1925), 375.*

6. *Mutuum and commodatum*

875. Con- 　*Mutuum* was a loan of money or other fungible things
ceptions　(wine, corn, etc.) given by transferring ownership to the
recipient, who thereby became bound to restore an equal
quantity (not the things which he had received in specie).

> The etymology of the word *mutuum* is doubtful. Gaius' explanation
> (3. 90) ' "mutuum" appellatum, quia quod ita tibi a me datum est, ex
> "meo tuum" fit' is of course silly. *Mutuum* derived from *mutare* and
> probably meant 'change', i.e. 'to give coins in order to receive other
> coins of equal value'; Varro, *De lingua Latina*, 5. 179 (Bruns, *Fontes*,
> ii. 54): *Si datum quod reddatur, 'mutuum'*.

Commodatum (= *commodo datum*) or *utendum datum* was
a loan of movable (as a rule not fungible) or immovable
things; the loan did not vest ownership in the recipient,
who was bound to restore these very same things.

876. Forms 　Both *mutuum* and *commodatum* are forms of loan; non-
of loan　legal writers felt no scruples in saying *nummos dare utendos
mutuos* or *nummos commodare* and the legal term for interest
was *usurae*, i.e. recompense for *usus*. The lawyers, however,
rightly introduced a terminological distinction between the
two forms: what is lent by *mutuum* is the value of the coins
(or other fungible things) and not the things themselves,
which need not be restored; what is lent by *commodatum* is
the individual thing.

> Maitland (Pollock and Maitland, *History*, ii. 170) says: 'Even the
> *mutuum* is not kept apart from the *commodatum* (scil. in medieval English
> legal literature.... Very often the lender is said *commodare* or *accommodare
> pecuniam*. . . . To this day Englishmen are without words which neatly
> mark the distinction. We lend books and half-crowns to borrowers; we
> hope to see the same books again, but not the same half-crowns; still in
> either case there is a loan.' Gibbon, *Decline and Fall*, c. 44: 'The Latin
> language very happily expresses the fundamental difference between the
> *commodatum* and the *mutuum* which our poverty is reduced to confound
> under the vague and common appellation of a loan.' However, this
> 'poverty' is not peculiar to the English language. The Greek term χρῆσις
> applied to both *commodatum* and *mutuum*, though Aristotle (*Eth. Nic.*
> 1131ª. 3) attempted to contrast χρῆσις (*commodatum*) with δανεισμός
> (*mutuum*); see Taubenschlag, *Law of Greco-Roman Egypt* (1944), 267.
> The French *Code civil*, art. 1874, applies the term *prêt* to both *commo-
> datum* and *mutuum*, distinguishing *prêt à usage ou commodat* and *prêt de
> consommation ou simplement prêt*. The German *BGB*. (§§ 598, 607) calls

the *mutuum* 'Darlehen' and the *commodatum* 'Leihe', an unhappy terminology and foreign to common German usage which persists in styling the *mutuum* 'Leihe'. The Swiss *Obligationenrecht* (art. 305 and 312) calls both contracts 'Leihe', distinguishing between 'Gebrauchsleihe' (*commodatum*) and 'Darlehen' (*mutuum*). Earlier Germanic law did not differentiate between the two forms, describing both as 'Leihe' and in Latin sources *res praestita* (Gierke, *DP* iii. 575). In short the Roman terminology is unique; even this trifle reveals the particular strength of Roman legal thought and its tendency towards *proprietas verborum* (Quintilian, *Inst. or.* 5. 14. 34).

i. *Mutuum*

A *mutuum* could not come into existence unless the ownership of the money or other fungible things was vested in the recipient. For the sake of brevity we will only speak of the loan of money in the following discussion.

877. Transfer of ownership

1. The simplest case was of course that of an owner of money who transferred ownership by *traditio mutui causa*. If the lender was not the owner of the coins, he could not transfer ownership (above, s. 620) and accordingly there was no *mutuum*. But what if the recipient mixed up the coins with his own money and thus acquired ownership, or if he became the owner by *usucapio*? Apparently a contract of *mutuum* did not come into existence. The lender had now a *condictio* against the recipient, but this was a *condictio sine causa* and not a *condictio ex mutuo*.

2. A owed 100 to B. The creditor B ordered his debtor A to pay 100 to C as a loan to be made by himself, B. By this payment a contract of *mutuum* between B and C came into existence provided that B and C had reached agreement on the legal purpose of that payment. This was the prevailing classical view; older lawyers had denied a *mutuum*, requiring a transfer of ownership from the *mutuo dans* to the *mutuo accipiens* (cf. Gai. 3. 90 *ex meo tuum fit*).

3. A owed B 100 as the result of sale. When the debt was due, A requested to keep the sum as a loan and B acquiesced. Under Justinian's law a *mutuum* came thereby into existence, but not under classical law; the classical lawyers, Julian as well as Ulpian, regarded such an agreement as void.

4. A handed over a *res nec mancipi* to B, authorizing him

to sell the thing and to keep the purchase price as a loan. Under Justinian's law B held the sum as a *mutuum* and the thing stood at his risk until he sold it. Modern lawyers call this contract unnecessarily and erroneously *contractus mohatrae*. Under classical law a *mutuum* did not come into existence in this way and the thing stood at the risk of A.

> *Mohatra* is a medieval Latin word derived from the Arabic *muchatara* (= risk): Du Cange, *Glossarium*, v. 'mohatra'. This term was used to describe the following transaction. A sold B a thing for 100 under the condition that the price should be paid, for example, after a year. Immediately after this sale had been made, A bought the same thing from B for 80, received the thing, and paid the price (80). After the lapse of the year B had to pay 100, i.e. substantially the loan of 80 plus 20 as interest. The device served to elude the canonical prohibition on stipulations for interest.

878.
Interest

Mutuum was not necessarily gratuitous, but interest could not be claimed *ex contractu mutui* since a real contract could only create an obligation to restore the things received (in the case of *mutuum* things of the same kind). However, the borrower might promise interest by stipulation. The classical limit was *usura centesima*, i.e. 1/100th monthly = 12 per cent. yearly; in the case of *faenus nauticum* a limitation did not exist.

> *Faenus nauticum* or *pecunia traiecticia* was a loan which the borrower had to repay only if a ship reached its destination safely. The risk which the lender incurred in this case seemed to justify high interest. Such a loan was in substance a contract of insurance, the interest being the premium of insurance.

879.
Actions

There was no special *actio ex mutuo* under classical law. The lender might avail himself of the *actio certae creditae pecuniae* (if money was given as a loan) or of the so-called *condictio triticaria* (if other fungible things were given). We have already mentioned these actions above (s. 809) and only wish to emphasize that *mora debitoris* was of no legal consequences: interests *ex mora* could not be claimed by means of these actions (above, s. 813), and the responsibility of the borrower could not be raised by his *mora*, since from the acceptance of the loan he was responsible for *omnis casus* like any other debtor who owed money or other fungible things.

A *senatusconsultum* of the time of Vespasian which the lawyers called *senatusconsultum Macedonianum* provided that when a loan of money was given to a son in power no action should be granted to the lender. A loan given to a son in power was *iure civili* valid, although the son did not become the owner of the money, which fell instead to his father. The lender might sue the son, but no execution of the judgment was possible, since the son had no property and an execution on his person was not permitted (above, s. 267). When the son became *sui iuris* by his father's death, the usual modes of execution were of course open to the creditor. According to the wording of the *senatusconsultum* the praetor (or privincial governor) was bound to deny the *actio certae creditae pecuniae* (*denegare actionem*; above, s. 17). Sometimes the praetor acted accordingly with a direct denial, but as a rule he was content with inserting an *exceptio* in the *formula*: 'si in ea re nihil contra senatusconsultum Macedonianum factum est' (Lenel, *Edict*. § 279). When the praetor did not deny the action, he was bound *officio suo* to insert that *exceptio*, since he had to obey the *senatusconsultum*.

880.
Senatus-
consultum
Mace-
donianum

The purpose of the *senatusconsultum* was to prevent capitalists from lending money to sons in power, as such loans were thought to be *adversus bonos mores*; not because in such cases the lender stipulated for excessive interest for the *senatusconsultum* applied even when there was no stipulation for interest, but as the lender very often could expect repayment only after the father's death, the loan seemed to endanger the father's life, since the lender might attempt to murder him. Similarly the *substitutio pupillaris* was made in separate tablets (*in secundis tabulis*) so as not to endanger the life of the *pupillus* (above, s. 458). On the other hand, the loan furnished the means of extravagant living to the son who had no need to trouble about repayment as long as he was in power, since he was legally unassailable. The purpose of the enactment was not to protect the son against the consequences of his own folly. Such a protection would have been absurd, since the son was sometimes a grown-up person; even a consul might still be in power. To be sure the punishment imposed upon the lender resulted in a protection of the son, but that was merely an inevitable reflexeffect of the punishment. Thus if the creditor did not deserve punishment, viz. if he did not know that the borrower was in power, the *senatusconsultum* did not apply. Moreover, if the son paid the loan back after having become *sui iuris*, he could not recover the money even if he had paid it by inadvertence; the Senate did not prohibit *soluti retentio* but merely decreed that an action should be denied.

Though we possess the text of the *senatusconsultum* (*D*. 14. 6. 1 pr.) it is problematical. Macedo, who gave the name to the enactment, was not a consul but a son in power whose case provoked it. Macedo had committed a crime and in the trial he declared that his debts induced him to commit it. The Byzantine professors told their pupils that Macedo, under the pressure from his creditors, had murdered his father (Theophilus, *Paraphrasis Inst.* 4. 7. 7; cf. *Inst. Iust.* 4. 7. 7; *D*. 14. 6. 3. 3). Obviously this story cannot be true, since under classical law the creditor had no chance of enforcing payment from the son in power; in this respect the son's legal position became worse not better, by his father's death, as he was now *sui iuris* and therefore liable to suffer execution. Nevertheless, it may be true that Macedo murdered his father. Perhaps he wanted more money to continue his luxurious life and could not obtain more credit on account of his debts. If he expected a rich inheritance from his father, this would enable him to pay off his creditors and to obtain fresh credit. Sex. Roscius was accused of having murdered his father. Cicero (*pro Sex. Roscio Amerino*, 14. 39) raises the question: 'luxuries igitur hominem nimirum et aeris alieni magnitudo (N.B.) et indomitae animi cupiditates ad hoc scelus impulerunt?' But be that as it may, the classical lawyers do not mention the story because it was not important for the interpretation of the *senatusconsultum*. Even if Macedo had murdered his father, the purpose of the enactment was not to protect fathers against murderous sons; it would have been an entirely inadequate measure and would have exposed fathers to greater dangers, as sons in power now could not find any credit at all.

We will not discuss further details; the relevant texts are interpolated and not yet fully cleared up. The whole institution was closely connected with the Roman *patria potestas* and the proprietary incapacity of a son in power; after that *potestas* had disappeared, it had no longer any real point. Nevertheless, the *senatusconsultum* survived in Germany down to 1 January 1900.

ii. *Commodatum*

This type of loan was made by delivering a movable or **881.** immovable thing without vesting the ownership in the **Creation** borrower; consequently, the lender might be a non-owner. The borrower did not even acquire possession in the strict legal sense; he was merely detentor and the lender retained possession (above, s. 754). As a rule only non-fungible things were the subject-matter of a *commodatum*, for the loan of fruits to be used only as a show-dish was hardly more than an academic case. The *commodatum* was strictly gratuitous; when the borrower promised a reward for the use, the contract was hire (*locatio conductio rei*) and not *commodatum*.

This contract was unknown to old republican law. Of **882. Late** course people have at all times lent and borrowed things **origin** gratuitously, particularly neighbours, relatives, and friends, but the old-Roman lawyers rightly regarded such a loan as a mere matter of friendship lying outside the sphere of law; even today *commodatum* is seldom the subject of a legal dispute. It was not a very happy idea of the later republican jurisprudence to range *commodatum* among the contracts.

The praetorian Edict as codified by Hadrian offered two **883.** *formulae* to the lender, one *in factum concepta* and the other **The two** *in ius concepta*; this is expressly stated by Gaius (4. 47). The **formulae** *formula in ius concepta* clearly shows that *commodatum* was recognized by *ius civile* at the time of Hadrian, though Gaius does not mention it 3. 90, 91. Unfortunately the wording of the *formulae* is not given by Gaius.

About the *formula in factum concepta* there can be little doubt; it must have been similar to the *formula depositi in factum concepta* as given by Gaius 4. 47:

'Si paret Aulum Agerium Numerio Negidio rem qua de agitur commodasse eamque Aulo Agerio redditam non esse, quanti ea res erit, tantam pecuniam iudex', etc.

As regards the *formula in ius concepta* it remains doubtful whether or not it contained the clause *ex fide bona*. Gaius 4. 47 suggests that it contained that clause as did the *formula depositi in ius concepta*; but on the other hand, the *actio commodati* is not mentioned in Gaius' list of *bonae fidei iudicia* (4. 62). However, Gaius had no need to give a complete list in this place (he is dealing with *compensatio*); moreover, the whole list may be a later addition. The development of the *formula in ius concepta* is hardly intelligible unless it contained the clause *ex fide bona*. The *formula in factum concepta* undoubtedly originated in republican times when *commodatum* was not yet recognized by *ius civile*. The *formula in ius concepta* must also belong to that period, but was not then regarded as being *in ius concepta*: the judge was authorized to decide the case according to *bona fides*, in contrast to *ius civile*.

It was only much later that all actions having the clause *ex fide bona* were regarded as *actiones in ius* (scil. *civile*) *conceptae* (above, s. 63). Obviously the clause *ex fide bona* was indispensable at the time when *commodatum* was not yet recognized by *ius civile*: without that clause the judge would always have been compelled to find for the defendant (that the *actio commodati* is missing in the list of *bonae fidei iudicia*, given Cic. *De off.* 3. 17. 70, does not matter, since that list is spurious: Beseler, *Bull.* xxxix (1931), 338 f.). In Hadrian's Edict the *formula* was certainly regarded as being *in ius* (*civile*) *concepta*, but Julian cannot possibly have invented the *formula*.

Thus we come to the conclusion that the *formula commodati in ius concepta* contained the clause *ex fide bona* and ran as follows:

'Quod Aulus Agerius Numerio Negidio rem qua de agitur commodavit, quidquid ob eam rem Numerium Negidium Aulo Agerio dare facere oportet ex fide bona, eius iudex', etc.

The lender had the choice between the two *formulae*. Their different construction suggests substantial differences, but it is possible that they were already assimilated in classical times. At any rate it is difficult to discern these substantial differences from available sources, since the compilers amalgamated the two actions. For that reason we confine ourselves to substantial law in the following description and leave aside the question as to which *formula* the plaintiff had to use in order to obtain what he wished.

884. Not revocable at will   In contrast to *precarium* (above, s. 753. 2*c*), *commodatum* was not revocable at will. If the thing was lent for a year and the lender claimed it back before the lapse of that year and sued the borrower, the latter could defend the action successfully (in the case of the *formula in ius concepta* on the strength of the clause *ex fide bona*, in the case of the *formula in factum concepta* on the strength of an *exceptio doli*). But if the lender took the thing back without recourse to law, the borrower had apparently as a rule no action against him, neither the *actio furti* nor the *actio commodati contraria* being available.

The borrower was liable for *dolus*, *culpa* (negligence), 885.
and *custodia* (safe keeping). The liability for *custodia* was Custodia
an archaic liability for *culpa*. The responsibility of the
borrower was defined in a casuistical or typical way; he was
absolutely liable for certain typical accidents which were
regarded as avoidable by properly watching and guarding
the borrowed thing, and on the other hand he was not liable
for other typical accidents which were invariably regarded
as not avoidable by the exercise of care. Thus if the borrowed thing was stolen by a third person, the borrower was
invariably responsible to the lender and could not excuse
himself by pointing out that he had actually looked after the
thing as well as possible. On the other hand, if the thing was
taken by invading enemies or by a gang of robbers, the
borrower was not responsible. The borrower was likewise
liable for accidents by which the borrowed thing was destroyed or damaged, as, for example, when a borrowed book
was torn or soiled by a third person; but he was not liable if
the thing was destroyed or damaged by robbers or enemies.
Slaves were usually not guarded; thus if a slave was lent,
the borrower was not liable for *custodia* unless he had expressly undertaken liability for *custodia*. A conception like
the classical liability for *custodia* cannot be expressed adequately by an abstract formula, for its essence is just that it
was demarcated in a concrete and casuistical way. If, nevertheless, we wish to have a general formula by which to distinguish the two groups of accidents, we may safely say
(using the post-classical and modern terminology): the
liability for *custodia* implied a liability for lesser accidents
(*casus minor*), i.e. for accidents not to be qualified as *vis
maior*; or shortly, a liability for any loss not to be attributed
to *vis maior*. This primitive conception of *culpa* occurs in
almost all primitive law and what comes as a surprise to us
is the fact that we still find it in classical law. Justinian's
compilers toned down the classical liability for *custodia* to
a simple liability for *culpa* (or *diligentia*) *in custodiendo* by
numerous ruthless and yet superficial interpolations. The
classical texts cannot be recovered throughout, but the
character of the classical liability for *custodia*—a liability

for certain typical accidents—is (or should be) beyond any doubt.

886. Dolus and culpa   Apart from the liability for *custodia*, the liability for *dolus* and *culpa* must not be forgotten. Suppose the borrower received the thing under the express condition that he should use it only at home. Nevertheless he took it with him on a journey, was attacked by a gang of robbers, and lost the thing. The borrower was responsible, not because he was liable for *custodia* but because he wilfully committed a breach of the condition. Further, if the borrower delayed the restitution of the thing by his negligence, he was *in mora debitoris* and thereby liable for *omnis casus*, including *vis maior*.

887. Actio contraria   The *formula commodati in ius concepta* might also be used by the borrower (so-called *actio commodati contraria*; above, s. 70), who therewith might demand reimbursement of his expenses and indemnification for damages caused by the borrowed thing.

888. No actio famosa   Lastly it should be noted that the *actio commodati* did not involve *infamia*.

SOURCES

s. 875. Read Gai. 3. 90; *Ulp. Inst. Fragm. Vindobon.* fr. 2 (Seckel-Kübler, *Iurispr. Anteiust.* 1. 493); *D.* (12. 1) 2 pr.; (44. 7) 1. 2, and 3.

s. 877. 1. Read *D.* (12. 1) 13 pr. and 1.

s. 877. 2. Read *D.* (12. 1) 15 to *acceperis*.

s. 877. 3. Read *D.* (17. 1) 34 pr. to *fieri posse*; (12 .1) 15, second sentence (spurious).

s. 877. 4. Read *D.* (12. 1) 4 pr. [*qui suscepit*]; ⟨*non*⟩ *habebit*; the interpolation is palpable, since Ulpian would have written *tuo periculo est*; (12. 1) 11 pr. ⟨*non*⟩ *puto*; *quod si lancem*, etc.: the text is heavily interpolated and the original cannot be recovered.

s. 879. Read *D.* (44. 7) 1. 4 to *securus est*.

s. 880. Read *D.* (14. 6) 1 pr.; 3 pr. (substantially classical); 7. 7 [*sed et si . . . nocere*], real-verbal contract (N.B.); 7. 9.

s. 881. Read *D.* (13. 6) 1. 1; 3. 6; 4.

s. 883. Read Gai. 4. 47.

s. 884. Read *D.* (47. 2) 15. 2 and 60.

ss. 885, 886. Read Gai. 3. 206; Paul. *Sent.* (2. 4) 3; *D.* (44. 7) 1. 4 [*alias . . . poterit*]; (13. 6) 5. 9 [*diligentia*] ⟨*custodia*⟩, palpable interpolation as the last line has preserved *custodiam*; (13. 6) 5. 4 [*aut . . . accidit*]; 5. 5 [*etiam diligentem*]; 5. 6; 5. 7 to *meum erit periculum*; 5. 10; 5. 13 [*culpam*] ⟨*custodiam*⟩; [*nisi . . . culpam*]. On *D.* (13. 6) 19 and (19. 2) 41, see Beseler, Z l (1930), 54. H. J. Wolff, *Seminar* VII (1949) 69 ff.

s. 887. Read *Coll.* (10. 2) 5; (47. 2) 60; (47. 2) 15. 2; (13. 6) 21 pr.;
(13. 6) 18. 2 [*sed et . . . pertineant*]; (13. 6) 17. 1–3 (post-classical tract).

BIBLIOGRAPHY

s. 875. On the etymology of *mutuum* see Mommsen, *Röm. Geschichte*, i
(6th ed. 1874), 155, Engl. translation by Dickson, i (1894), 200.

s. 877. Pernice, *Labeo*, ii. 2. 1 (1900), 94 ff.; P. E. Viard, *La mutui
datio*, i (1939).

s. 877. 3. Beseler, *T* x (1930), 205; Z liii (1933), 25.

s. 877. 4. Beseler, *T* x (1930), 206 note; Sachers, *Festschrift Paul
Koschaker*, ii (1939), 80 ff., 86 ff.

s. 878. On *foenus nauticum* see Windscheid, *Pand.* ii (1906), § 371 n. 7;
Taubenschlag, *Law of Greco-Roman Egypt* (1944), 239.

s. 880. G. Mandry, *Das gemeine Familiengüterrecht*, i (1871), 431 ff.;
Vassalli, 'Iuris et facti ignorantia', *St. Senesi* xxx (1914), not available;
Beseler, *Beiträge*, iv (1920), 130, 176; Siber, *Naturalis obligatio* (1925),
52 ff.; Daube, Z lxv (1947), 261 ff.; *Index Interp.* ad *D.* 14. 6, with
references; Windscheid, l.c. § 373; Stobbe–Lehmann, *Handbuch des
deutschen Privatrechts*, iv (1900), 436 f.

ss. 881 ff. Ferrini, 'Storia e teoria del contratto di commodato nel
diritto romano', *Scritti*, iii (1929), 81 ff.; Cicogna, *Bull.* xix (1907),
235 ff.; De Ruggiero, 'Depositum vel Commodatum', *Bull.* xix (1907), 5 ff.

s. 883. Lenel, *Edict.* (1927) § 98, with references; Beseler, Z xlvii
(1927), 366; Kaser, *Quanti ea res est* (1935), 69, 75; *Eigentum und
Besitz* (1943), 23.*

s. 884. Kaser, *Eigentum und Besitz* (1943), 29.

s. 885. Schulz, Z xxxii (1911), 23 ff.; Z *für vergleich. Rechtswissenschaft*, xxv (1911), 459 ff.; xxvii (1912), 145 ff.; Vazny 'Custodia', *Annali
Palermo*, xii (1926), 101 ff.; Paris, *La Responsabilité de la custodia en
droit romain* (1926); Beseler, *T* viii (1928), 286; Z lxvi (1948), 346;
Arangio-Ruiz, *Responsabilità contrattuale in diritto romano* (2nd ed. 1933),
cap. iii–v; Luzzatto, *Caso fortuito e forza maggiore*, I. *La responsabilità per
custodia* (1938); Jolowicz, *Digest XLVII, 2 De Furtis* (1940), pp. xxxi ff.;
De Martino *Riv. di diritto di navigazione*, 1936, 61 ff. (not available);
Pflüger, Z lxv (1947), 121 ff.; Krückmann, Z lxiv (1944), 1 ff. F. Haymann's unmethodical and misleading paper, Z xl (1919), 167 ff., should be
ignored.*

s. 887. Lenel, *Edict.* (1927), § 98 in fine; see above, ss. 70, 71, Bibliography.

7. *Depositum and Pignus*

i. *Depositum*

This contract was made by entrusting a movable or im- 889.
movable thing to a person for safe custody. The depositary ^{Conception}
did not acquire either ownership or possession; like the

commodatary he was merely *detentor* and the depositor remained *possessor*. The contract was, like *commodatum*, strictly gratuitous.

890. The Twelve Tables *Depositum* is a time-honoured contract and is found among the earliest legal institutions in all systems; in primitive times especially people frequently needed to give valuable things into the custody of a trustworthy person. It is therefore small wonder that the Twelve Tables already protected the depositor by a special action for double the value of the deposited thing. This was a special penal action for breach of faith and not the ordinary actio *furti nec manifesti*, since at the time of the Twelve Tables *furtum* meant only 'carrying away a thing' (*furtum* derived from *ferre*). The details of this action are unknown as it had practically disappeared in republican times, the praetor not granting a *formula* for it.

891. The Edict The praetorian Edict as codified by Hadrian contained four formulae:

1. A *formula in factum concepta* for double the value in case of a so-called *depositum miserabile*, i.e. of a deposit made *tumultus, incendii, ruinae, naufragii causa*. This was of course a penal action like the action granted by the Twelve Tables.

2. A *formula in factum concepta in simplum* for ordinary cases of deposit.

3. A *formula in ius concepta* for deposits of any kind. The two latter formulae are given in full by Gaius (4. 47); the *formula in ius concepta* contained the clause *ex fide bona*.

4. Lastly the Edict contained a special *formula sequestraria* for a deposit made jointly by two or more persons who were disputing over the deposited thing. The *formula* is not transmitted to us. We have already stated above (s. 753) that in this case the depositary (sequester) was *possessor*.

892. Liability Under classical law the depositary was only liable for *dolus* and not for *culpa* or *custodia*. Of course his liability was increased by *mora debitoris*.

893. Actio contraria The *formula in ius concepta* might be used for an *actio contraria* by means of which the depositary (like the commodatary) might demand reimbursement of his expenses and indemnification for damages caused by the deposited thing.

In contrast to the *actio commodati* the *actio depositi*, the *actio directa* as well as the *actio contraria*, involved *infamia*. 894. Actio famosa

This was the classical law at the time of Gaius. Undoubtedly *depositum* was then recognized by *ius civile*, as the *formula in ius concepta* clearly shows. That both *commodatum* and *depositum* are unmentioned in Gaius' chapter on real contracts (3. 90, 91) can only be explained by the literary character of the *Institutes*: they were lecture-notes left unfinished or incomplete by the author and published posthumously. 895. Age of the actions

The development of the praetorian remedies remains obscure, but they probably already existed in republican times, the *formula in ius concepta* being of course of a more recent date than the *formula in factum concepta*. It comes as a surprise that the so-called *lex Iulia municipalis* (l. 110) does not mention the *actio depositi* among the *actiones famosae*, but it is hardly credible that at the end of the Republic that action did not yet involve *infamia*. That *lex*, as we know today, is not an absolutely reliable source; moreover, the *actio depositi* may be covered by the clause *deve dolo malo condemnatus est*.

A deposit might be made by vesting the ownership of the deposited thing in the depositary.

1. *Fiducia* could be used for that purpose (*fiducia cum amico contracta* in contrast to *fiducia cum creditore contracta*; above, s. 704), but it was confined to *res mancipi*. A *res nec mancipi* might be transferred to the depositary by *traditio*, the latter promising by stipulation to re-transfer it at the depositor's request; but we know nothing of such transactions. At any rate such a transaction was not called *depositum*. 896. Fiducia cum amico

2. Money and other fungible things might of course be given as an ordinary deposit (e.g. by handing the money over in a box or in a sealed basket); the recipient was then bound to restore the very same things which he had received. But was it possible to deposit fungible things (in particular money) by vesting the ownership of these things in the depositary and binding him to restore things of the same kind? The classical answer was a clear 'No'; such a 897. Depositum irregulare

transaction was invariably regarded as a *mutuum* whether parties qualified it as a *depositum* or as a *mutuum*. The so-called *depositum irregulare* did not exist under classical law; all texts in which we find it are interpolated. In fact that kind of *depositum* is a hybrid and entirely superfluous institution, which only leads to unnecessary difficulties. To be sure, if such a deposit were recognized, the depositor might demand interest promised by an informal pact by bringing the *actio depositi in ius concepta* while the action *ex mutuo* could not be used for that purpose. But that was no reason why the classical lawyers should acknowledge a *depositum irregulare*. If the recipient was prepared to pay interest, he might promise it by stipulation. In the eyes of the classical lawyers the stipulation was not an inconvenience but was made as a matter of course; it was only Justinian who wished to spare parties the stipulation. For the sake of clearness and simplicity the classical law rightly rejected the *depositum irregulare*. Continental European law has unfortunately retained this unhappy institution of Byzantine law while English law is in harmony with the classical law.

ii. *Pignus*

898.
Conception
This contract was made by handing over a movable or immovable thing to a creditor as a pledge. *Pignus* as a *ius in rem* has already been discussed above (ss. 706 ff.). Further, we have already stated (s. 753) that the creditor was *possessor* of the pledged thing. Here we are concerned with the obligations resulting from *pignus* as a real contract.

899. The
Edit
The praetorian Edict as codified by Hadrian contained two *formulae*, one *in factum concepta* and the other *in ius concepta*. The existence of the latter, which contained the clause *ex fide bona*, should no longer be disputed. It is attested by the unassailable rescript *C.* (4. 24) 6. Moreover, *pignus* is ranged among the *contractus iuris civilis* in the *libri rerum cottidianorum* attributed to Gaius, and though this work was probably written in early post-classical times, its author could not write that unless there was a classical *actio in ius concepta*. Lastly, there was an *actio pigneraticia contraria*

which is only conceivable in the form of an *actio in ius concepta*. The wording of the *formulae* is not transmitted to us.

The creditor was liable for *dolus*, *culpa*, and *custodia*. Liability for *custodia* implied, as aforesaid, an absolute liability for loss by *casus minor* (above, s. 885). The compilers as usual (above, s. 885) have scaled down the classical liability for *custodia* to a liability for *diligentia in custodiendo*. When the creditor availed himself of his *ius vendendi* (above, s. 724), he was bound to restore the price as far as it exceeded the amount of the debt (above, s. 728). The pledgor might demand the *superfluum* by bringing the *actio pigneraticia directa*. With the *actio pigneraticia contraria* the creditor might claim reimbursement of his expenses.

900.
Liability

SOURCES

s. 889. Read *D.* (16. 3) 1 pr.; 1. 8; 17. 1.

s. 890. Paul. *Sent.* (2. 12) 11.

s. 891. Read *D.* (16. 3) 1. 1; Gai. 4. 47.

s. 892. Read Paul. *Sent.* (2. 12) 6; *Coll.* (10. 2) 1; *D.* (44. 7) 1. 5 [*magnam . . . cadere*]. Cp. *Coll.* (10. 8) 1 with *C.* (4. 34) 1.

s. 893. Read *Coll.* (10. 2) 5.

s. 894. Read Gai. 4. 182; *Coll.* (10. 2) 4.

s. 896. Read Gai. 2. 60 to *essent*.

s. 897. Read *D.* (12. 1) 9. 9.

s. 898. Read *D.* (44. 7) 1. 6.

s. 899. Read *C.* (4. 24) 6.

s. 900. Read Gai. 3. 204 (*unde* irrefutably proves that the owner is not entitled to the *actio furti*, *quia eius non interest*; but his interest is only absent if the pledgee is liable for *custodia*); *D.* (13. 7) 13. 1 (shortened by the compilers but substantially classical); (47. 2) 15 pr. [*sed . . . preaestabit*], with Beseler, *Z* lxvi (1948), 379; *D.* (47. 2) 88 (genuine); *C.* (4. 24) 6 and 7, 1.

BIBLIOGRAPHY

s. 889. G. Rotondi, *Scritti*, ii. 56.

s. 890. Schulz, *Z für vergleich. Rechtswissenschaft*, xxv (1911), 464; xxvii (1912), 144 ff.

s. 891. Lenel, *Edict.* (1927), § 106, with references; Rotondi, *Scritti* ii. 1 ff.; Beseler, *Z* xlvii (1927), 366; Kaser, *Quanti ea res est* (1935), 69 ff.; *Eigentum und Besitz* (1943), 23.

s. 892. Rotondi, *Scritti*, ii. 91 ff.; Sachers, 'Die Verschuldungshaftung des Depositars', *Festschrift P. Koschaker*, ii (1939), 80 ff.

s. 894. Lenel, *Edict.* (1927), p. 77 n. 10.

s. 895. On the character of Gaius' *Institutes* see Schulz, *History of Roman Legal Science* (1946), 163 f.; on the so-called *lex Iulia munic.* see Schulz, ibid. 88.

s. 896. W. Erbe, *Die Fiducia in röm. Recht* (1940), 121 ff.

s. 897. Bonifacio, 'Ricerche sul deposito irregolare in diritto romano', *Bull.* viii/ix (1948), 80 ff. Schulz, *Scritti Ferrini* 4 (1949), 254.

s. 898. Dernburg, *Das Pfandrecht*, 1 (1860), 138 ff.; La Pira, *St. Senesi*, xlvii. 61 ff. (not available).

s. 899. Lenel, *Edict.* (1927), § 99, with references; Beseler, Z xliii (1922), 429, with references; Kaser, *Quanti ea res est* (1935), 78 ff.; Kreller, Z lxii (1942), 167 ff., 173 n. 127 (references), 181–3.

s. 900. Schulz, Z xxxii (1911), 43 ff., 92; Kaser, *Quanti ea res est* (1935), 148 ff., with references; Beseler, Z lxvi (1948), 379; Pflüger, Z lxv (1947), 139 ff. See further literature on *custodia* above, s. 885, bibliography.

8. *So-called innominate real contracts*

901. Conception and kinds
Under Justinian's law there was a group of contracts which modern Romanists call 'innominate real contracts'. This group embraces the following types: (1) *do ut des*; (2) *do ut facias*; (3) *facio ut des*; (4) *facio ut facias*. The peculiarity of these contracts was that they only came into existence if one of the parties fulfilled his part of the agreement. The simplest example is barter. A and B informally agreed that A should give his house in exchange for B's house. Under Justinian's law this was not a consensual contract but an innominate real contract. Thus if A conveyed his house to B, the latter was bound to convey his house to A. The mere agreement had in itself no binding force, but by A's performance B was bound; one might say: *re obligatur.* A could now demand performance by means of an action which the compilers called *actio in factum civilis* (a term which would have made the classical lawyers shudder) or *actio praescriptis verbis.* Instead of demanding performance A might claim his house back with a *condictio ob causam datorum*; in other words, A had a *ius paenitendi.* Other cases of innominate real contracts were treated similarly.

902. The term
The term innominate real contract is somewhat puzzling, since one such a contract had a technical name, namely barter (*permutatio*); but it should not be denied

that they were indeed real contracts coming into existence by a performance (a delivery of things) like *mutuum, commodatum, depositum, pignus*. They come particularly near to *mutuum*. Loan of money might conceivably be a consensual contract, but under Roman law it was a real contract which required a *datio*. Likewise barter might be a consensual contract, but under Justinian's law it was a real contract which required performance by one of the parties.

The Justinianic doctrine is definitely not classical, but the compilers did not invent it; it existed in pre-Justinianic times in a more or less developed form although the classical lawyers themselves knew nothing of it. The compilers have ruthlessly forced the post-classical doctrine upon the classical texts, but since we lack reliable texts outside the *Corpus iuris* it is difficult to prove the interpolations. We cannot discuss details, but our conclusion is that the classical principle was that where an agreement could not be regarded as a consensual contract, there was no action for its fulfilment. The party transferring something under the agreement might recover it with a *condictio ob causam datorum*; if this action did not lie, only the *actio de dolo* was available. _{903.}

903.
Classical
principle

1. The classical law of barter is particularly clear. The Sabinians rightly regarded barter as a sort of sale, i.e. as a consensual contract, but unfortunately their view did not prevail. According to the dominant classical doctrine barter was no contract. Thus if one of the parties A had fulfilled his part of the agreement and the other B refused to fulfil his part, A might sue B for restitution with a *condictio ob causam datorum*, but he had not an *actio in factum* or *praescriptis verbis* for fulfilment.

904.
Permutatio

2. A delivered a thing to B under the agreement that B should try to sell the thing and that if the price exceeded a certain sum fixed in advance by A and B the latter might keep the surplus and pay B only the assessed value (*aestimatum*); if B did not sell the thing, he had to restore it to A. The classical lawyers disputed as to the action to be granted to A. The *actio mandati*, *actio locati*, and *actio pro socio* were all considered. The details of this dispute are not fully

905.
So-called
contractus
aestima-
torius

discernible from available sources, but apparently the dominant opinion in the third century A.D. favoured the *actio pro socio*. The Edict did not contain a special action to meet this case; *D.* 19. 4 is a bold fabrication of the compilers and the *actio aestimatoria* (or *de aestimato*) *praescriptis verbis* was quite unknown to classical law.

906.
Aversion to stipulation
The development of the innominate real contracts must be understood as a stage in the post-classical fight against the stipulation. The classical lawyers would have said to parties in such cases: if you wished to make a binding contract, you ought to have made a stipulation. But the post-classical lawyers wished to spare parties the stipulation.

SOURCES

s. 901. Read *D.* (19. 5) 5 pr. and § 1.

s. 903. Read *D.* (19. 5) 9 [*incerti actione*] ⟨*condictione*⟩; [*itaque . . . sequetur*]; cf. *D.* (12. 4) 4; *D.* (19. 5) 18 [*melius . . . agere*] ⟨*depositi agere possum*⟩; (19. 5) 22 [*placet . . . verbis*] ⟨*obligatio nulla est*⟩; cf. Gai. 3. 143; *Inst. Iust.* (3. 24) 1; (19. 5) 25 to *acciperet* [*praescriptis . . . agere*] ⟨*condicere*⟩; *C.* (2. 20) 4.

s. 904. Read Gai. 3. 144; *D.* (18. 1) 1. 1; *C.* (4. 64) 3 and 7.

s. 905. Read *D.* (17. 2) 52. 7; (17. 2) 44 [*si animo . . . sit*]; [*si minus . . . verbis*]; (19. 5) 13 pr. [*placet*] ⟨*ille scripsit*⟩; [*neque . . . neque*]; [*sed . . . excepit*].*

BIBLIOGRAPHY

ss. 901 ff. Lenel, *Edict.* (1927), § 112; De Francisci, *Synallagma* i (1913), 41 ff.; Meylan, *Origine et nature de l'action praescriptis verbis* (1919); Beseler, *Beiträge*, ii (1911), 156 ff.; iv (1920), 134 f.; Buckland, *Mélanges Cornil*, i (1926), 139 ff. = *LQR* xliii (1927), 74; *LQR* xlviii (1932), 495.*

9. *Consensual contracts in general*

907.
Conception and varieties
The name 'consensual contracts' denotes those contracts which could be concluded *nudo consensu*, by formless consent. Consent was required here as in any other contract, but nothing more—no deed, no witnesses, no symbolic acts, no formulas, and no delivery of a thing as in real contracts. Consensual contracts could be made *inter absentes*, by messenger or by letter. The classical *ius civile* recognized only four such contracts: *emptio venditio* (sale),

locatio conductio (hire), *societas* (partnership), and *mandatum* (mandate, agency). The *formulae* available to the parties in consensual contracts were invariably formed in the same style: they were *formulae in ius conceptae* and contained the clause *ex fide bona*. We have already discussed this type of *formula* and may refer to our earlier remarks (above, ss. 60 ff.).

The consensual contracts are a remarkable achievement of republican jurisprudence and are the offspring of *fides Romana*. The making of the contract entailed no cumbrous formalities; the content of the obligations created were flexibly defined by reference to good faith; the judge had a wide discretion which enabled him to take into account the particularities of the individual case. All these facts reveal the bold, liberal, and creative spirit of the republican lawyers. The contracts described as 'consensual' were selected with a rare instinct, for it was just to those four contracts that the republican regulation was suitable; it should be noted that suretyship, the promise of a gift or a *dos*, the promise to give a loan were rightly excluded and banned into the domain of the stipulation. One may doubt whether it was a good idea to make mandate a contract at all; but it arose comparatively late and was closely connected with the customs of Roman social life. One may hold that for the sale of land, some formality ought to have been required, but Roman liberalism had no sense of the fundamental social difference between land and movable things. On the whole the republican lawyers were on the right path. But after these proud beginnings the late republican and classical law is somewhat disappointing. The law of sale is by no means a masterpiece; it is surprisingly stiff, complicated, and in part primitive. The law of hire is ill suited to social needs and rather poor; the reader need only compare the *Digest* title 19. 2 (which comprehends both hire of things and hire of labour) with the books on legacy (30–6). The law of partnership is impaired by its extreme individualism. Nor was the clause *ex fide bona* quite as effective as might have been expected; the classical lawyers—for it was the lawyers who were responsible and not the Roman

908.
Evaluation

judges, who were entirely dependent on the lawyers—hesitated to avail themselves of the full power entrusted to them by that clause; they were much too conservative and uncreative. We shall emphasize this when considering the single contracts.

SOURCES

s. 907. Read Gai. 3. 135–7; *D.* (44. 7) 48.

BIBLIOGRAPHY

ss. 907, 908. Perozzi, 'Il contratto consensuale classico', *St. Schupfer* (1898, not available); Arangio-Ruiz, *Il mandato* (1949), 90.*

10. *Sale (emptio venditio)*

i. *Conception and formation*

909.
Definition

1. We may state in very general terms that sale (*emptio venditio*) was a contract by which goods were exchanged for money. More precisely we must define *emptio venditio* as a formless contract the purpose of which was the exchange of goods for money and which gave rise (actually or potentially) to obligations. From an academic point of view the ordinary *emptio venditio* is a contract in which both conveyance of the thing and payment of the price are postponed to a later date. Two obligations come into existence as a result of the contract; the seller is bound to convey the thing and the buyer to pay the price. But in many thousands of cases both the thing and the price are exchanged immediately upon the conclusion of the contract. Then only potential obligations are in question (e.g. if the thing turned out to be defective); it would be artificial and unrealistic to say that the obligations to convey the thing and to pay the price came into existence and are discharged at the same moment.

910.
Sale and
conveyance

2. *Emptio venditio* is in no sense a conveyance. If somebody bought a *res nec mancipi*, he acquired ownership not by the contract of sale but by *traditio*; and at this point we must remember that *constitutum possessorium* was unknown to classical law (above, s. 767). If he bought a *res mancipi*, he acquired ownership by *mancipatio* or *in iure cessio* and not

by *emptio venditio*. Thus sale and conveyance were strictly separated from each other. The consequence was that the sale of a thing not belonging to the seller was on principle quite valid and the maxim 'nemo plus iuris transferre potest quam ipse habet' (above, s. 620) did not apply. Sale belongs solely to the law of obligations; on the other hand, the transfer of ownership was under classical law not dependent on the payment of the price (above, s. 616).

3. Instead of making a consensual contract of sale the parties might execute two stipulations, the seller promising a thing and the buyer a sum of money. Economically this was sale, but legally it was not *emptio venditio* and the law of *emptio venditio* did not apply. To be sure the two verbal obligations resulting from the stipulations were connected with each other (above, s. 811), so that if the seller sued the buyer for the price with the *actio ex stipulatione* without having delivered the thing or without offering it, the defendant might protect himself with an *exceptio mercis non traditae*. There was indeed one kind of sale which could only be made by two stipulations, viz. the sale of a quantity of fungible things, or the sale of a thing described only generically and not specifically, for example, 'a horse' or 'a slave'. *Emptio venditio* was available if a quantity from a specific existing stock of the seller was sold or if, for example, a quantity of tiles to be made by the seller was sold, but apart from such cases a pure generic *emptio venditio* was unknown to classical law. To this extent the classical law was incomplete and primitive, though it must be admitted that the rules suitable for a generic sale differ considerably from those suitable for the sale of a specific thing. In the following description we will deal solely with the sale of individual things. Moreover stipulations accessory to a consensual sale played a considerable part in classical law although formless pacts (*pacta adiecta*; above, s. 802) were actionable on the strength of the formulary clause *ex fide bona*. We shall discuss such stipulations below.

4. *Emptio venditio* was only concerned with the exchange of goods for money.

(*a*) The subject-matter might be any right which could

911.
Sale and
stipulation

912. Subject matter

be vested in the buyer by the seller: ownership, usufruct, praedial servitudes, and even a claim. The mere use of a thing or of human labour could not be *merx*. If A 'sold' the use of his land, this was *locatio conductio rei*, and if a worker 'sold' his labour, this was *locatio conductio operarum*. A future thing might be sold, but then the contract was conditional, the condition being fulfilled when the thing came into existence. The bold idea of an *emptio spei*, i.e. the sale of a pure chance, stands quite alone.

913.
Pretium
(*b*) The price must invariably be money. We have already mentioned (above, s. 904) that the Sabinians rejected this rule and regarded barter as a kind of sale but unfortunately their view did not prevail. According to the victorious Proculian doctrine barter was not sale and consequently was no contract at all (above, s. 904). However, the buyer might promise something in addition to money, a.compromise between the two conflicting opinions, which like many other compromises lead to difficult questions.

It was disputed among the lawyers whether parties might leave it to a third person to fix the price. In other respects parties were entirely free to fix the price; classical liberalism and realism knew no such thing as a *pretium iustum*. The post-classical development, including Justinian's fatal rules on *laesio enormis*, lies outside the scope of this book.

914.
Consent.
Error in
corpore and
in sub-
stantia
5. Sale, being a contract, required the consent of the parties. We cannot give a general theory of legal acts or even of contracts, because the Romans had no such theory. The classical lawyers occasionally dealt with issues pertaining to that theory in their casuistic way, but refrained from attempting a comprehensive theory. Hitherto we have left aside these questions almost entirely, but at this point a few remarks are indispensable for the understanding of our forthcoming description of the seller's liability for defects (below, ss. 925 ff.). The classical lawyers did not clearly distinguish between intention and declaration of intention; accordingly they did not distinguish a discrepancy between the two declarations of the contracting parties and a discrepancy between intention and declaration of intention.

Thus in cases of *error in corpore*, i.e. if the seller had in mind one individual thing and the buyer another, in the eyes of the lawyers there was no *consensus* and a contract did not come into existence. But such cases will occur but rarely. Much more important is the question, to what extent, if at all, *error in qualitate* excluded consent under classical law. Unfortunately the available texts are so heavily interpolated that it seems a hopeless task to eradicate post-classical additions and corruptions and to reconstruct the classical texts; only the classical law is discernible.

(*a*) *Error in qualitate* did not on principle prevent *consensus*. The seller might be liable for defects and faults of which the buyer was ignorant (we shall come to that presently; below, ss. 925 ff.), but the contract was valid.

(*b*) From the time of Julian the prevailing classical opinion was that where both parties were in error about a vital quality of the thing sold (*error in substantia*), the contract was void. Thus if a table was sold, both parties believing that it was of solid silver whilst in truth it was only plated, the contract was regarded as invalid, because the consent concerned a thing which did not exist (*D*. 18. 1, 41. 1, genuine). The crucial and in truth insoluble question which qualities are vital and which not, the lawyers only answered in a casuistic way. And yet they were compelled to distinguish between essential and non-essential qualities, for otherwise they would have overthrown the rules governing the seller's liability for latent defects (below, ss. 925 ff.). Julian's theory which inevitably led to this question was very unhappy and was rightly but unsuccessfully opposed by Marcellus, who adhered to the earlier doctrine which only paid regard to *error in corpore*.

(*c*) Julian's doctrine was extended by the post-classical lawyers, who denied the existence of consent even if only one of the parties, the seller or the buyer, was in error about the substance of the thing.

This ill-starred law of *error in substantia* has greatly influenced continental European law and has confused the seller's liability for defects; English law has fortunately kept clear of it.

ii. *The two principal obligations resulting from sale*

915.
Content
of the
obligations
1. The two principal obligations which sprang from *emptio venditio* were (1) the obligation of the seller to deliver the thing to the buyer; (2) the obligation of the buyer to pay the price. To enforce these obligations the seller had the *actio venditi* and the buyer the *actio empti*. Only the content of the seller's obligation requires further discussion. Let us confine ourselves to the simplest cases, viz. to the sale of a *res mancipi* or *nec mancipi*. If a *res mancipi* was sold, the seller was bound to execute the *mancipatio* or *in iure cessio* and to transfer possession; if a *res nec mancipi* was sold, he was bound to make a *traditio venditionis causa*. But suppose the seller was not the owner of the thing sold and was not authorized by the owner to alienate it; or that he was the owner of the piece of land which he had sold but could not alienate it because it was *fundus dotalis* (above, s. 214). In such cases *mancipatio* or *traditio* could not transfer ownership to the buyer. Could the buyer, after having discovered that he had not acquired ownership, sue the seller by bringing the *actio empti*? Was it not the duty of the seller to make the buyer owner of the thing? One would certainly expect an affirmative answer. The *actio empti* was an *actio bonae fidei* and on grounds of good faith the seller would seem bound to relieve the buyer in his distress. To be sure the buyer was *possessor*, but after having discovered that he was non-owner possession was of small value for him. If the thing was movable, he was not allowed to use it; for he would commit *furtum* by doing so. If the thing was immovable, he could not acquire the fruits, since only *bonae fidei possessor fructus suos facit* (above, s. 752. 3) and the buyer was no longer in good faith. Certainly the buyer might acquire ownership by *usucapio* since *mala fides superveniens non nocet* (above, s. 626), but a stolen movable or a *fundus vi possessus* could not be usucapted (above, s. 623), and where a valid *mancipatio* or *traditio* did not transfer ownership, the thing was as a rule a *res furtiva* or *vi possessa*. The position of the buyer was indeed awkward and seemed to call for redress. Julian boldly declared the *bona*

fide emptor before eviction to be a *bonae fidei possessor* even after having discovered that he was non-owner (*D.* 22. 1, 25. 2). But the seller was *not* bound to make the buyer owner of the thing sold. It was his duty to execute the legal act required for transferring ownership and to render the buyer *possessor*; when he had done that, he had fulfilled his obligation resulting from the contract. When the buyer discovered that he had not become owner, the *actio empti* did not lie, under republican and early classical law, even in case of 'eviction', i.e. if the true owner had successfully sued him with the *rei vindicatio* (*evincere*). Eventually (from Julian onward; below, s. 923) the classical lawyers advocated the *actio empti* in case of eviction, and in a few special cases, particularly if the seller was *in dolo* where eviction had not taken place; but they obstinately persisted in preserving the rule that the seller was not bound to make the buyer the owner; he had fulfilled his obligation by affording the buyer the *habere possidere licere*. It was Julian himself who, by granting the *actio empti* against a seller who knew that he was non-owner, emphasized the old rule:

> *D.* (19. 1) 30. 1: '. . . quamvis enim aloquin verum sit venditorem hactenus teneri, ut rem emptori habere liceat, non etiam ut eius faciat, quia tamen dolum malum abesse praestare debeat, teneri eum, qui sciens alienam non suam ignoranti vendidit.'

We find similar regulations in the primitive law of other peoples, but what comes as a surprise to us is that the classical law was still so stiff and primitive. Once again we have to realize that the creative strength of the classical lawyers was rather limited.

2. The two obligations were connected with each other, one being the exchange for the other, but this connexion was not emphasized by the classical lawyers as strongly as we might expect.

(*a*) Suppose that the thing had to be delivered and the price to be paid a month after the conclusion of the contract. After the lapse of this time the seller demanded the price without delivering the thing. The buyer was entitled to refuse payment as long as the thing was not offered to him, and if the seller sued him for the price with the *actio venditi*,

916.
Exceptio non adimpleti contractus

he was protected by the judge on the strength of the clause *ex fide bona*. Modern students often speak of an *exceptio non adimpleti contractus*, but in truth there was no such *exceptio* under classical law since the clause *ex fide bona* was sufficient (above, ss. 60 ff., 96. 3).

917.
No ius
paenitendi
(*b*) Suppose that the seller had already delivered the thing but that the buyer delayed payment. The seller might sue the buyer for payment with the *actio venditi* but he could not reclaim the thing. This was an iron rule of Roman law which the classical lawyers unflinchingly observed, never yielding to Greek ideas, which advocated an action for the restitution of the thing.

918.
Genetic
connexion
(*c*) If one of the two obligations did not come into existence, the other too did not arise. Thus where an animal was sold which had already perished at the time of the contract, the seller was not bound (*impossibilium nulla obligatio*) and neither was the buyer. But this principle was not fully carried through; we have already mentioned the *negotium claudicans* (above, s. 303). Suppose a *pupillus* bought a thing without the *auctoritas* of his *tutor*; the obligation of the seller came into existence but not that of the *pupillus*. To be sure, if the *pupillus* (or his *tutor*) sued the seller with the *actio empti*, the latter might refuse delivery and refer to the clause *ex fide bona*. But what if the seller had already delivered the thing to the *pupillus* without having received the price? He had no *actio venditi* for the price, since the *pupillus* was not bound by the contract; and he could not reclaim the thing, since by delivering it he had merely discharged his obligation. At any rate under republican and early classical law the seller had no remedy (above, s. 303).

919. Peri-
culum est
emptoris
(*d*) *Perfecta emptione periculum est emptoris*. The meaning of this rule is quite clear within the framework of the *Corpus iuris*; it is that with the formation of the contract the risk passes to the buyer. Thus if the thing perished by accident after the conclusion of the contract the seller was free since he was only liable for *dolus* and *culpa*, but the buyer was, nevertheless, bound to pay the price. This famous rule has vexed generations of lawyers for centuries down to our own time, but here we are only concerned with classical law.

The rule existed as early as classical times, but it had then a very different significance. *Perfecta emptione periculum est emptoris* meant as in Justinian's law that with the formation of the contract the risk passed to the buyer, for *emptio perfecta* cannot possibly mean anything else but the conclusion of the contract. However, under classical law the seller was liable for *custodia*, i.e. for *casus minor* (above, s. 885). Thus, if the thing perished by *casus minor*, the seller was responsible for the loss; the buyer was of course still bound to pay the price and the two obligations might be set off against each other. If the thing perished by *casus maior* and *sine dolo aut culpa venditoris*, the seller was certainly free from any obligation on his own side, but nevertheless, he deserved to obtain the price. The seller had bound himself to treat the thing like a thing belonging to the buyer; he owed the fruits of the thing to the buyer and had taken over a liability for *culpa* and *custodia*. For all this he deserved a recompense, and this he received in the form of the price. The rule in the classical context, so far from being unjustified, is an ideal solution of the problem. Under Justinian's law the seller was only liable for *culpa* and the recompense is perhaps a little too high compared with the duties which he had undertaken, but the opposite rule *periculum est venditoris* is still worse. Details cannot be discussed here; the relevant texts are heavily interpolated and reliable texts outside the *Corpus iuris* are not available.

iii. *Warranty against eviction*

We have already touched upon the seller's liability for the buyer's eviction (above, s. 915) and will now describe the remedies available to the buyer.

1. The so-called *actio auctoritatis*. When a *res mancipi* was sold and the *mancipatio* was executed, the buyer had, in case of eviction, an action against the seller for double the price. This implied warranty was called *auctoritas* (Paul. *Sent.* 5. 10 rubr. *De contrahenda auctoritate*), and accordingly we call the action *actio auctoritatis*, its classical name being unknown. The action goes back to early republican times, perhaps even to the Twelve Tables; it still existed in the

920. Actio auctoritatis

praetorian Edict as codified by Hadrian, but disappeared
in post-classical times together with the *mancipatio* and is
therefore absent from the *Corpus iuris*. Available sources
are very poor (the most important text is Paul. *Sent.* 2. 17. 1
and 3, unfortunately a bad post-classical text) and leave us
in doubt about the character of the action. It was perhaps
conditional on the payment of the price; if that was so, then
the *duplum* included the price paid by the buyer and the
action was, therefore, perhaps not regarded as a penal
action.

921.
Stipulatio
duplae

2. *Stipulatio duplae* (scil. *pecuniae*). This stipulation ran
as follows:

> 'Si quis eum hominem partemve quam ex eo evicerit, quo minus me
> eumve, ad quem ea res pertinebit, habere recte liceat, qua de re lis tibi
> recte denuntiata erit, tum quanti is homo emptus est, tantam pecuniam
> duplam partemve eius duplam dari spondes?'

Parties made such a stipulation principally when a *mancipatio* had not been executed and thereby they created a
warranty similar to the implied warranty contained in the
mancipatio. The seller was bound to pay double the price in
the event of eviction and our documents seem to indicate
that the stipulation was only made after the price had been
paid, just as the *actio auctoritatis* was probably conditional
on the payment of the price.

922.
Optional
and
compulsory
stipulation

3. The *stipulatio duplae* was optional. Instead of it the
parties might conclude a *stipulatio simplae*, or indeed a
stipulatio triplae or *quadruplae*. Parties might omit a stipulation altogether, but then, under republican and early classical law, the buyer had no remedy in the event of eviction,
for the *actio empti* did not lie in that period. The stipulation
could be made compulsory by *pactum adiectum*; the buyer
might then demand the stipulation with the *actio empti*.

923. Actio
empti in
case of
eviction

4. Eventually the *actio empti* was granted in case of eviction *in id quod interfuit emptoris rem habere*; apparently
Julian was the first to take this step, thereby endowing the
consensual contract of sale with an implied warranty for
eviction.

924. Sti-
pulatio ha-
bere licere

Besides the *stipulatio duplae* Varro, *De re rust.* 2. 3. 5; 2. 4. 5; and
2. 2. 6. mentions a *stipulatio habere licere* which ran: 'eam rem recte

mihi habere licere spondes?' But in classical times the purpose of this
stipulation was to protect the buyer against interference from the seller
or his heirs, but not against eviction by a third person.

iv. *Warranty against latent defects*

The seller of an individual thing—we are only concerned
with a sale of this kind (above, s. 911)—can never be bound
to deliver a thing free of all defects; he has to deliver the
individual thing which was the object of the contract and
nothing else. But the law may make him responsible for
faults, and it is this liability which we have now to discuss.

A. *Classical ius civile.* The leading principle was *caveat*
emptor (though this maxim is not Roman); neither *manci-*
patio nor consensual sale implied a liability of the seller for
qualitative defects of the thing. The seller was only liable

925. Ius
civile

> (1) for *dicta et promissa in vendendo* (not *in mancipando*),
>   i.e. for express descriptions or formless promises
>   (*pacta adiecta*; above, s. 802) declared in the making
>   of the *emptio venditio* (Lenel, *Edict.* p. 555 n. 10;
>   269 n. 1);
>
> (2) if the seller had concealed defects *dolo malo*;
>
> (3) if he had undertaken a warranty by stipulation.

In the first two cases the buyer had the *actio empti* for
damages; we will not discuss here the precise measure of
damages which the buyer might claim. Thus the seller's
liability for defects according to *ius civile* was rather
limited; it must, however, not be forgotten that, from
Julian onward certain latent defects (*error in substantia*;
above, s. 914) excluded consent and rendered the whole
contract void.

B. *Classical aedilician law.* By the side of the very limited
warranty for qualitative defects established by *ius civile*
stood the honorarian liability created by the *aediles curules*.
These magistrates had a jurisdiction (above, s. 18) competing with that of the praetor over sales concluded in the
market of the City of Rome. In their Edict (*edictum*
aedilium curulium, aedilician edict) they promised to grant
actions in the style of the praetorian Edict and their edict
was ultimately codified by Julian and Hadrian together

926. The
aedilician
Edict

with the praetorian Edict. The stabilized aedilician Edict
dealt with sale under two rubrics: *de mancipiis vendendis*
(sale of slaves) and *de iumentis vendendis* (sale of draught
cattle). The text of the Edict as far as it concerned the
seller's liability for defects is preserved to us by the *Digest*
(*D*. 21. 1. 1. 1 and 21. 1. 38 pr.); on the whole it is reliable
but it is not quite complete. An aedilician Edict existed
even in republican times, but we know little of its content.
An occasional glimpse of the pre-Hadrianic Edict furnished by Gellius (4. 2. 1) shows that its wording differed
from that of the stabilized Edict; whether there were substantial differences remains a matter of dispute. In these
circumstances we must confine ourselves to Hadrian's
Edict and try to describe its content in broad outline.

927.
Domain of
the Edict

1. The aedilician Edict applied only to sales in the
market of Rome, for only such contracts lay within the
jurisdiction of the *aediles*. It was, further, only applicable
to proceedings before the *aediles*; when the buyer preferred
to sue the seller before the praetor, the aedilician Edict did
not apply. In the provinces there were as a rule no *aediles*,
but in the so-called senatorial provinces (*provinciae populi
Romani*) the provincial *quaestores* functioned instead of
them and issued the aedilician Edict as their own. In the
so-called imperial provinces (*provinciae Caesaris*) there
were neither *aediles* nor *quaestores* and the aedilician Edict
did not apply. This is expressly stated by Gaius (1. 6) and
we have to accept it.

928. Kinds
of sale

2. The aedilician Edict was only concerned with sales of
slaves and draught cattle; other kinds of cattle fell under the
Edict only as far as the Edict referred to diseases of animals
('Quae de iumentorum sanitate diximus, de cetero quoque
pecore omni venditores faciunto').

929. Kinds
of defect

3. According to the Edict the seller was liable for certain
specified qualitative defects. Both Edicts (on slaves and on
cattle) established a general liability for diseases and faults
('quid morbi vitiive cuique (scil. *servo*) sit'; 'quid in quoque
eorum (scil. *iumentorum*) morbi vitiive sit'). The Edict on
the sale of slaves mentioned in addition some other special
defects, for example, the case of a slave who was a runaway

(*fugitivus*) or a vagabond (*erro*) or who had committed a delict so that his master was subject to an *actio noxalis* (*noxa caput sequitur*).

4. The seller was liable for those defects whether or not he had or could have had knowledge of them. Nor was the liability conditional on express descriptions or promises of the seller (*dicta et promissa*). The edictal liability was implied in the contract of sale.

5. The edictal liability was as follows. The buyer might claim rescission of the contract, i.e. repayment of the price for redelivery of the thing. For that purpose the *aediles* granted him a special honorarian action, the *actio redhibitoria*, available within six months to be counted from the date of the contract. 930 Actio redhibitoria

(*a*) The Edict on the sale of slaves stated: *iudicium dabimus ut id mancipium redhibeatur*, which meant that the seller had to take back the slave (*re-habere*, but the lawyers sometimes used *redhibere* in the sense of *reddere*). The edict on the sale of cattle used a different formula: *de inemptis faciendis iudicium dabimus*; but the legal meaning was the same: the buyer could reclaim the price on restoring the animal. In spite of an enigmatical text (*D*. 21. 1. 45) the buyer was not entitled to demand double the price. The *actio redhibitoria* lay also on account of *dicta* and *promissa*, which involved a liability according to *ius civile* (above, s. 925); the Edict on the sale of slaves said: 'sive adversus quod dictum promissumve fuerit (scil. *mancipium*), cum veniret, fuisset quod eius praestari oportere (scil. *iure civili*) dicetur'. The clause is absent from the *edictum de iumentis*.

(*b*) According to the prevailing opinion the *aediles* granted another action as an alternative to the *actio redhibitoria* with which the buyer might within a year demand a proportional reduction of the price. This was called *actio quanto minoris* (scil. *res fuit ob vitium cum veniret*) or *actio aestimatoria*. Undoubtedly this was Justinian's law. As regards classical law the dominant doctrine rests on a weak foundation. It is our view that this action was entirely foreign to classical law. 931. Actio quanto minoris?

The *edictum de mancipiis* as transmitted to us has no mention of the *actio quanto minoris*. It is mentioned in the *edictum de iumentis*: 'vel quo minoris cum venirent fuissent (scil. *iumenta*) in anno iudicium dabimus', but this clause is interpolated as the word *vel* instead of *sive* shows (see Eisele, Z xxi, 1900, 3 ff.). Other relevant texts in the *Digest* are likewise suspect. Gellius, 4. 2. 5 furnishes no proof for the classicality of this action.

932.
Stipulatio
duplae
6. Lastly the buyer might demand from the seller a stipulation in which the latter assumed liability for certain faults and in addition promised double the price in case of eviction. The form of this stipulation is illustrated by the Transsylvanian tablets. If the seller refused to make this stipulation, the Edict granted the buyer an *actio redhibitoria* —in this case only available within two months and for double the price (and not alternatively an absurd *actio quanto minoris* within six months)—a remedy designed to enforce the *stipulatio duplae*. The compilers have cancelled this part of the Edict (*D.* 21. 1. 28 was left, but the absurd *actio quanto minoris* was added to the text).

933. Post-
classical
develop-
ment
C. *Post-classical law*. This was the classical law regarding the seller's liability for qualitative defects. In post-classical times the jurisdiction of the *aediles* and *quaestores* disappeared and the aedilician actions might now be brought before any law-court. Of course they were now no longer confined to sales made in the market. Whether they applied to sales of things other than slaves and cattle remains doubtful; at any rate Justinian's compilers extended them to sales of any kind, including sale of land, and by a bold interpolation pronounced this entirely unclassical principle at the head of the *Digest* title 21. 1, attributing it with a queer sense of humour to Labeo. The *actio quanto minoris* was invented. The *actio empti* was amalgamated with the aedilician actions, so that rescission of the contract and reduction of the price might also be claimed with the *actio empti*.

934.
Evaluation
D. *Evaluation*. 1. The Roman rules governing the seller's liability for qualitative defects has long been praised and has impressed continental legislators for centuries. In particular the liability introduced by the *aediles*—a general warranty against qualitative defects of any kind; an implied

warranty not dependent on *dicta et promissa* or *scientia* of the seller; on the other hand, a liability not for damages but only for rescission of the contract or reduction of the price— this seemed to generations of continental legislators to be an ideal system. Gradually we have become sceptical as we have begun to realize that the Roman law leads to serious difficulties. The rules of the German *BGB*. based on Roman law are indeed, as Gierke has admitted, very intricate, in part artificial and often obscure; a modern German writer has confessed to looking with envy on the rules of Anglo-American law which are in harmony with the principles of German law before the reception of Roman law. The English law is perhaps preferable after all since it is much more simple and workable than Roman law.

2. A diverting assault upon the whole *Digest* title 21.1 was launched in the beginning of this century by a passionate champion of the so-called *Freirechtsbewegung* (Ernst Fuchs) who declared: 'Nobody can read that title without the utmost disgust.' This author, somewhat lacking in historical sense, was shocked at the republican and classical discussions on *morbus* and *vitium*. These do indeed appear rather partly odd and scholastic in character. After the Edict had put *morbus* and *vitium* on a par, it was no longer required to distinguish between them; nevertheless, the old discussions were continued. However, classical jurisprudence was not entirely free from scholastic pedantry (see, for example, their treatment of *implantatio* and *specificatio* above, ss. 635, 638); but to disparage the classical lawyers for that is as absurd as to overrate them.

SOURCES

s. 910. Read *D*. (18. 1) 28 [*nam ... venditio*].

s. 911. On *exceptio mercis non traditae* see above, s. 811, Sources. On generic sale read Gai. 3. 147; *D*. (18. 1) 65 to *conductionem* with Beseler, Z l (1930), 39.

s. 912. Read *D*. (18. 1) 8 with *Index Interp*.

s. 913. Read *D*. (19. 1) 6. 1; Gai. 3. 140–1; *D*. (19. 2) 22. 3; (4. 4) 16. 4; *Epit. Ulp*. 2. 11 [*iusto pretio*].

s. 914. Read *D*. (18. 1) 41. 1 (genuine); (18. 1) 9 pr.–2 (heavily interpolated).

s. 915. Read Gai. 4. 131a; Paul. *Sent.* (1. 13a) 4; (19. 1) 30. 1 [*id est* ... *vendiderit*] with Lenel, Z li (1931), 42;(22. 1) 25. 2.

s. 916. Read *D.* (19. 1) 13. 8, with *Index Interp.*

s. 917. Read *G.* (3. 32) 12; (4. 49) 1 and 6 [*facile*].

s. 918. Read *D.* (18. 1) 15 pr.; (50. 17) 185.

s. 919. *Inst. Iust.* (3. 23) 3; *D.* (18. 6) 3 [*talem*]; praestare ⟨*eam*⟩; [*ut ... adhiberet*]; (47. 2) 14 pr. [*mandare ... oportebit*]; [*dummodo*⟨*sed*⟩]; [*præstet*] ⟨*praestare debet*⟩; (47. 2) 81 pr. [*sine culpa mea*]; [*dominium ... teneor*] ⟨*custodiam praestare debeo*⟩. On fruits see Paul. *Sent.* (2. 17) 7; *Fr. Vat.* 15.

s. 920. Read Paul. *Sent.* (2. 17) 1 and 3.

s. 921. Read the Transsylvanian document Bruns, *Fontes*, no. 130 = Lenel, *Edict.* (1927), 567 = *FIRA* III no. 88, with Arangio-Ruiz's note and Maylan, *Rev. des études Lat.* xxi/xxii (1945), 34.

s. 922. Read *D.* (21. 2) 60 [*et ex ... interest*]; (21. 2) 56 pr. [*simpla ... vel*]; [*nisi ... convenerit*].

s. 923. Read *D.* (21. 2) 8; *Fr. Vat.* 17, first sentence.

s. 926. Read the Edict in Lenel, *Edict.* (1927), 535 and 565 or *FIRA* i, no. 66; translation: De Zulueta, *The Roman Law of Sale* (1945), 139 and 145. Read further *C.* (4. 58) 2 [*etenim ... est*].

s. 931. Read Gellius, 4. 2. 5 = Seckel–Kübler, i. 92. The text should be read as follows: '... sed cui morbus est, idem etiam vitiosus est ... quam ob rem cum de homine morboso agetur (scil. actione redhibitoria), aeque inquit, ita dicetur: quando ob id vitium minoris fuerit.' This refers to the pleading of the plaintiff who wished to justify the *actio redhibitoria.* Lenel, *Edict.* p. 561 gives a wrong and misleading text.

s. 932. Read Lenel, *Edict.* (1927), § 296.

s. 933. Read *D.* (21. 1) 1 pr. (spurious); (21. 1) 63 (spurious); Paul. *Sent.* (2. 17) 6.

s. 934. 2. Read Gellius, *Noct. Att.* 4. 2; Seckel–Kübler, *Iurispr. Anteiust.* 1. 61, nos. 28, 29; 1. 92, no. 1.

BIBLIOGRAPHY

ss. 909 ff. A modern comprehensive work on the Roman law of sale does not exist. Bechmann, *Der Kauf nach gemeinem Recht* (i, 1867; ii, 1884; iii, 1905; iv, 1908) is out of date. A valuable sketch was given by F. de Zulueta, *The Roman Law of Sale*, Introduction and select texts (1945). See further (out of date) Pernice, *Labeo*, i (1873), 454 ff.; Mommsen, *Schr.* iii (1907), 132 ff.; Ferrini, *Opere*, iii (1929), 49 ff.

s. 910. Kaser, *Eigentum und Besitz* (1943), 111, with references; De Zulueta, l.c. 1 f.

s. 911. On generic sale see Seckel–Levy, Z xlvii (1927), 122 ff.; Beseler, Z l (1930), 34 ff.; Krückmann, Z lix (1939), 7 ff.; De Zulueta, l.c. 14.

s. 913. De Senarclens, 'La maxime "pretium debet esse verum certum iustum",' *Mélanges Fournier* (1929), 685; De Zulueta, 16 ff., with references; Albertario, *Studi*, iii (1936), 401; Solazzi, *Bull.* xxxi (1921), 51 ff.; Scheuer, *Z für vergl. RW.* xlvii (1932), 77.

s. 914. Beseler, *Byzantinisch-Neugriech. Jahrbücher*, i (1920), 343 ff.; Z xlv (1925), 213 ff.; *Bull.* xii (1948), 103; Lenel, *Archiv f. d. zivil. Praxis*, cxxiii (1925), 161 ff.; Simonius, *Festschrift P. Koschaker*, i (1939), 358 ff.; De Zulueta, l.c. 25 ff.; W. Flume, *Eigenschaftsirrtum und Kauf* (1948), 64 f.

s. 915. Monier, *Mélanges Cornil*, ii (1926), 139 ff.; further literature see below, ss. 920 ff., Bibliography.

s. 917. Felgenträger, *Antikes Lösungsrecht* (1933), 27 ff.

s. 919. F. Haymann, Z xl (1919), 254 ff.; xli (1920), 44 ff.; xlviii (1928), 314 ff. (unmethodical and unacceptable inquiries); Rabel, Z xlii (1921), 543 ff.; Seckel–Levy, Z xlvii (1927), 117 ff. (rightly against Haymann); Beseler, *Bemerkungen zu Z 1927* (1927), 7 ff.; *T* viii (1928), 279 ff.; Z l (1930), 34 ff. (Beseler's doctrine is right though his reconstructions of the classical texts are often problematic); Vogt, *Festschrift P. Koschaker*, ii (1939), 162 ff.; Krückmann, Z lix (1939), 1 ff.; lx (1940), 1 ff.; De Zulueta, l.c. 30 ff. See further literature on *custodia* above, s. 885, Bibliography; Pflüger, Z lxv (1947), 205.*

ss. 920 ff. Girard, *Mélanges de droit romain*, ii (1923), 1 ff. (fundamental); Rabel, *Die Haftung des Verkäufers wegen Mangels im Rechte* (1902); De Zulueta, l.c. 42 ff.

s. 920. Girard, l.c. 5 ff., 153 ff.; Rabel, l.c. 5 ff.; Lenel, *Edict.* (1927), § 290; Beseler, *Beiträge*, iv (1920), 307; Z xlvi (1926), 96; M. Kaser, *Eigentum und Besitz* (1943), 107 ff., 115 ff., 128, 129 ff.*

s. 921. Girard, l.c. 46 ff.; Kaser, l.c. 202 ff. On *satisdatio secundum mancipium* see Lenel, *Edict.* 546 ff.; Kaser, l.c. 66; Maylan, *RH* xxvi (1948), 1.

s. 922. Kaser, l.c. 204 n. 9; 210 n. 27.

s. 923. Kaser, l.c. 221; Z liv (1934), 162 ff., 169.

s. 924. Kaser, *Eigentum und Besitz*, 210 ff.

s. 925 ff. R. Monier, *La Garantie contre les vices cachés dans la vente romaine* (1930); De Zulueta, *The Roman Law of Sale* (1945), 46 ff.; Flume, *Eigenschaftsirrtum und Kauf* (1948), 57 ff.

ss. 925. F. Haymann, *Die Haftung des Verkäufers für die Beschaffenheit der Kaufsache*, i (1912), 1 ff., 44 ff.; Beseler, *Beiträge*, iv (1920), 306, rightly against Partsch, Z xxxiii (1912), 601 ff.; Monier, l.c. 3 ff., 113 ff.; Flume, l.c. 57 ff., 60 ff.

ss. 926 ff. H. Vincent, *Le Droit des édiles* (1922); Lenel, *Edict.* (1927), §§ 293, 294; Monier, l.c. 19 ff.

s. 926. F. Haymann, *Haftung des Verkäufers*, 19 ff.; De Senarclens, 'La Date de l'édit des édiles de mancipiis vendundis', *T* iv (1923), 396 ff.*

s. 927. E. Weiss, Z xxxvii (1916), 167 ff.; Solazzi, *Istituti tutelari* (1929), 117 f.

s. 930. Lenel, *Edict.* (1927), 556 ff., with references; Monier, *La garantie contre les vices* (1930), 56 ff.; De Senarclens, 'La Duplex condemnatio de l'action redhibitoire', *Studi Bonfante*, iii (1930), 91 ff.

s. 931. Lenel, *Edict.* l.c. 561 ff.; Monier, *La Garantie contre les vices,* 170 ff. (against Monier in vain F. Haymann, Z li (1931, 479 ff.); Giffard, 'L'Action édilicienne quanti minoris', *RH* x (1931), 682 ff.

s. 932. Lenel, *Edict.* (1927), 562 f., 567; Monier, l.c. 104.

s. 933. *Index Interp.* ad *D.* (21. 1) 1 pr.; De Senarclens, 'L'Extension de l'édit des édiles aux ventes de toute espèce des choses', *RH* vi (1927), 385 ff.; Monier, *La Garantie,* 161 ff., 186 ff.; Flume, l.c. 58.

s. 934. Gierke, *Deutsch. Privatrecht,* iii (1917), 468; Grossmann–Doerth, *Rechtsfolgen vertragswidriger Andienung* (1934), 27, cited by Flume, l.c. 59; Ernst Fuchs, *Die Gemeinschädlichkeit der konstruktiven Jurisprudenz* (1909), 170 f., 265.

11. *Hire (locatio conductio)*

935.
The non-
Roman
trichotomy

Under *locatio conductio* the classical lawyers grouped three types of contract which modern Romanists describe as follows:

1. *Locatio conductio rei.* This was a consensual contract whereby one party (the *locator*) agreed to give to the other (the *conductor*) a thing for use (agricultural land, a house, a room, a slave, an animal, or any other movable) and the *conductor* promised to give a recompense.

2. *Locatio conductio operis.* This was a consensual contract whereby one party (the *conductor*) promised to produce a certain effect or result by his work, for example, to build a house or to make a dress for a recompense to be paid by the other party (the *locator*).

3. *Locatio conductio operarum.* This was a consensual contract whereby one party (the *locator*) promised services of a certain kind (e.g. domestic work) for a remuneration to be paid by the other party (the *conductor*).

The terminology seems at first sight perplexing; the worker is termed *conductor* in no. 2 but *locator* in no. 3. Moreover, in individual cases it is sometimes difficult to distinguish *locatio conductio operis* from *locatio conductio operarum*. Somebody hired a gardener for a year at a fixed sum to keep a garden in good order. Or somebody hired musicians for a dancing party. Are these contracts cases of *locatio operis* or of *operarum*?

As a matter of fact the trichotomy is not found in the Roman sources and was not even implicitly recognized by the classical lawyers. They knew but one *locatio conductio* and on principle they applied the same rules to all varieties of this contract. The terminological differences were matters of linguistic convenience and usage and nothing more. *Locare* means (like the Greek ἐκδιδόναι) 'to place out', i.e. to entrust something to a person. The etymology of *conducere* is obscure; outside legal literature it meant 'to bring together' (*conducere populum in forum, conducere copias*), but the classical lawyers apparently took it as *secum ducere*. Thus when somebody hired a slave he was described as *conductor*, i.e. as a person who took the slave with him (*rem utendam conducere*); the man who supplied the slave was called *locator*, since he 'placed' the slave at the disposal of the conductor. If somebody received a thing in order or transport it to another place, he was called *conductor* because he took the thing with him (*rem perferendam conduxit*); the sender was called *locator* because he 'placed' the thing in the hands of the carrier. The terms *locare* and *conducere* were also used metaphorically. If somebody hired an architect to build a house, the architect was called *conductor* because he took the job (*domum aedificandam conduxit*); the other party was called *locator* (*domum aedificandam locavit*) because he 'placed' or entrusted the job to the architect. But if somebody hired workers to build a house under his own direction, it seemed more convenient to describe the workers as *locatores* (*locant operas suas in aedificio faciendo*) because they placed themselves at the disposal of the other party. However, we emphasize once more that this terminological differentiation was merely a matter of language, and in some cases the worker might style himself *locator* or *conductor* just as he pleased. In the case of the gardener which we have given above the gardener might say: *hortum curandum conduxi* or *operas meas locavi in horto curando*; the lawyers did not trouble themselves deciding which expression was more appropriate. And if somebody hired a flautist for an evening party, they did not deliberate as to whether that was a case of *locatio conductio operarum* or *operis* and whether, accordingly, the flautist was *locator* or *conductor*; that was a point of no legal importance whatever.

Somebody ordered a goldsmith to make a golden ring with his (the goldsmith's) own material. The dominant classical doctrine regarded this contract as sale, but Cassius described it as a sale of the gold combined with a *locatio conductio operarum* (Gai. 3. 147). Note *operarum*, not *operis*, as modern students might expect. Gaius does not say whether Cassius called the goldsmith *locator* or *conductor*; in fact this was of no legal consequence. He might have called him *conductor* (*anulum faciendum conduxit*) or *locator* (*operas suas locavit in anulo faciendo*). Thus we should certainly abandon the trichotomy altogether. It is a product of continental legal scholasticism and leads to unnecessary difficulties and even to errors, since it suggests legal differences where there were in fact none. The questions of liability and risk were not conditional on whether the contract was *locatio conductio operarum* or *operis*.

936. Definition If we now wish to have a definition of *locatio conductio* in general, we can only define it as follows: *Locatio conductio* was a consensual contract whereby one party (*locator*) placed a thing, a job, or his services at the disposal of the other party (*conductor*) for a certain purpose and whereby either the *locator* or the *conductor* promised a remuneration.

937. Character of the classical law of hire The classical law of hire seems a poor thing compared with modern standards, but economic and social conditions in Rome differed greatly from those of modern times and in this respect the classical law of hire did not more than reflect the needs of actual life. Contracts with free workers were not as frequent as today, since slave labour was more important than free labour. Factory workers were as a rule slaves. Well-to-do persons had their own artisans (shoemakers, dressmakers, and so on) among their slaves. Thus the modern problems of the law of labour could hardly arise. As regards the renting of a house, a flat, or a room, this was mostly an affair of poor people; well-to-do persons lived in their own houses. The housing shortage in Rome at the end of the Republic and during the first two centuries of the Principate was apparently appalling, since the available space was more and more occupied by public buildings and places and by the palaces and gardens of big

capitalists; new houses for poor people could not be built too far from the centre of the city for want of means of communication. Thus those who were compelled to live in hired rooms (*inquilini = incolini*) were rather at the mercy of the capitalists, who might dictate the terms of their contracts. Sometimes a whole block of flats (*insula*) was let to one person who sublet the single flats and rooms and acted in effect as a *procurator* of the owner. The lease of agricultural land showed similar features. According to Roman economic theory it was more profitable for big landowners to lease small allotments; thus the lessees (*coloni*) were as a rule people of small means who were equipped and supervised by the owner or his *procurator*. Sometimes a large estate was leased to one person, but he would be in the position of a *procurator* who had to sublet the allotments and to supervise the small tenants. A considerable class of prosperous and economically independent *coloni* did not exist.

Classical law of hire was in harmony with these social and economical facts. The lawyers wrote and worked for the class of the *beati possidentes* to which they themselves belonged and their social sense was ill developed. They were but mildly interested in workers, and the idea of protecting them and the poor lessees of flats or agricultural land against capitalism was quite foreign to them. Thus they hardly touched upon those questions which seem vital to us. Parties were perfectly free to form the contract as they liked, which in this case meant as the capitalist liked. Special rules for the lease of houses, flats, and rooms on the one hand, and for the lease of agricultural land on the other were not developed. The institution of giving notice was unknown; rooms, land, or services were hired for a fixed time. As regards repairs of the hired house or rooms the lawyers were content with stating that the landlord was bound to keep the lodging in repair; but the contract might reverse this rule and, no doubt, Roman capitalists found out as well as Mr. Sartorius that slums are particularly profitable. The compilers have occasionally attempted to improve the law for the benefit of the lessees, but their interpolations require a comprehensive description and evaluation.

A good illustration of the classical attitude is given by the inscription *ILS* 7457 (cf. Sueton., *Vespas.* 1; Pernice, Z vii. 1, 1886, 97 f.). There existed groups of farm workers (*turmae messorum*) who under a foreman (*ductor*) migrated every summer to certain places to gather the harvest. The classical lawyers had no eyes for this phenomenon.

After this general account of the classical law of hire we may tender our attention to some important individual rules.

938.
Merces

The lessee of a thing or the party who hired a worker had to promise a remuneration (*merces*); otherwise the contract would have been *commodatum* or *mandatum*. Under classical law *merces* must be a sum of money; the only exception was the *colonia partiaria* whereby the *conductor* promised a part of the fruits as recompense. In the absence of special pacts the remuneration had to be paid at the end of the contract.

939.
Actions

From any *locatio conductio* there arose two actions, the *actio locati* for the *locator* and the *actio conducti* for the *conductor*. The *formulae*, which originated in early republican times, were based on the same model as those of the actions resulting from sale, i.e. they were *in ius conceptae* and contained the clause *ex fide bona* (Lenel, *Edict.* § 111).

'*Actio locati.* Quod Aulus Agerius Numerio Negidio fundum fruendum (domum faciendam, operas suas) locavit, quidquid ob eam rem Numerium Negidium Aulo Agerio dare facere oportet ex fide bona, eius iudex Numerium Negidium Aulo Agerio condemnato etc. *Actio conducti.* Quod Aulus Agerius de Numerio Negidio fundum fruendum (domum faciendam, operas) conduxit, quidquid ob eam rem Numerium Negidium Aulo Agerio dare facere oportet ex fide bona etc.'

940. Sale
breaks hire

The rights resulting from the contract were only *iura in personam*; the person who received a thing from the other party (*fundum fruendum, vestimenta sarcienda*) was not even *possessor* but merely *detentor* (above, s. 754) and was therefore not protected by the possessory interdicts. This is a glaring illustration of his social and economic dependency. A hired a flat from B for one year. Before the lapse of this time B might resort to self-help to expel the lessee or he might bring a possessory interdict (the *rei vindicatio* did not lie; above, s. 645). Certainly A might now bring the *actio conducti* against B, but he had lost his home. If B alienated the house before the lapse of the year, the purchaser might also expel the lessee who again had nothing but the *actio conducti* against B (not against the new owner). From the Middle Ages this law was expressed in the famous maxim *sale breaks hire*, a misleading formula, particularly as regards classical law.

> The contract of hire is in truth not broken by the alienation; on the contrary it remains intact and shall afford the lessee his only remedy, viz. the *actio conducti*. The new owner has not more rights than the lessor who might equally have expelled the lessee (under Justinian's law the lessor's *ius expellendi* was a little restricted). The only difference was that the new owner was not bound by contract and therefore could not, like the *locator*, be rendered liable on the lessee's *actio conducti*.

Both parties were responsible for *dolus* and *culpa*, but the party who received a thing from the other (whether he was termed *conductor* or *locator*) was liable in addition for *custodia* (above, s. 885). It is beyond any doubt that a fuller or tailor who received clothes in order to clean or to repair them was liable for *custodia*; this is expressly said by Gaius (3. 205, 206). When it has been realized that the trichotomy did not exist and that *locatio conductio* was a unity (above, s. 935) it follows immediately that a person who hired a slave or an animal (*rem utendam conduxit*) was also liable for *custodia*. Sometimes a *locator* was liable for *custodia*. Suppose A hired a place in a storehouse (not the whole storehouse) from B and delivered a thing to him. Then B (who was termed *locator*) was liable for *custodia* unless this liability was expressly excluded; this is stated in the *lex horreorum* preserved to us in an inscription. 941. Liability

> Bruns, *Fontes*, no. 166; *FIRA* iii, no. 145, *ILS* 5414: 'Invectorum in haec horrea custodia non praestabitur.'

We repeat once more: it was of no legal importance whether the person who received the thing was termed *locator* or *conductor*. The compilers have as usual (above, ss. 885, 900) substituted *diligentia in custodiendo* for the classical *custodia* by means of numerous interpolations.

The *locator rei utendae* was bound to furnish the hired thing to the conductor and to keep it in repair *ex fide bona*. 942. Eviction and

qualitative This simple rule was held sufficient; the complicated rules
defects as to eviction and qualitative defects which we have described in the law of sale (above, ss. 885, 900) had no
counterpart in the law of hire. A true eviction could not as
a rule take place, since the conductor was not *possessor* and
consequently the *rei vindicatio* did not lie against him
(above, s. 645). The aedilician Edict did of course not apply
since it dealt only with sales, hire not falling under the
jurisdiction of the *aediles*. If the locator failed to fulfil his
duty, the conductor might bring against him the *actio conducti*, but under classical law he had no right to give notice.
However, the compilers afforded him this right.

943.   The classical law as to risk was as follows. If A hired a
Periculum house for a year and after half a year the house was burnt
down, he had only to pay half of the rent; thus *periculum est
locatoris*. If A hired a worker for a year and the latter died
after half a year, his heir might claim half of the remuneration. If A gave gold to a goldsmith to make a ring and the
gold was stolen the goldsmith was liable for *custodia* and
could not claim a remuneration even if he had already
begun or indeed nearly finished his work (*periculum est
conductoris anuli faciendi*). If an architect had undertaken to
build a house (*domum faciendam conduxit*) and the half-
finished house was burnt down, he could not claim any
remuneration and he was even bound to build a new house
(*periculum est conductoris*), but it is doubtful whether the
classical lawyers really carried through this harsh rule without any qualification.

SOURCES

s. 938. Read Gai. 3. 142, 162; *D.* (19. 2) 19. 7.

s. 940. Read *D.* (43. 16) 1. 22 [*et si . . . est*]; *C.* (4. 65) 3 [*nisi . . . es*];
D. (19. 2) 25. 1; *C.* (4. 65) 9 [*nisi . . . emit*]; *Fr. Vat.* 44; *D.* (43. 16) 12
[*nisi . . . fecisset*].

s. 941. Read Gai. 3. 205, 206; *D.* (19. 2) 60. 9; *Coll.* 10. 9 = *C.*
(4. 65) 1; *C.* (4. 65) 28; *Inst. Iust.* (3. 24) 5 [*talis*]; [*qualem . . . adhibet*];
[*aliquo casu*] ⟨*casu maiore*⟩.

s. 942. Read *D.* (19. 2) 9 pr. [*plane . . . locatorem*]; (19. 2) 25. 2 [*certe
. . . dubitatio est*]; (19. 2) 33 (interpolated).

s. 943. Read *D.* (19. 2) 30. 1; (19. 2) 9. 1 to *est aequissimum*; (19. 2) 59
shortened but substantially genuine.

BIBLIOGRAPHY

ss. 935 ff. A modern comprehensive work on *locatio conductio* does not exist. For the older literature see Windscheid, *Pand.* ii (1906), §§ 399 ff. See further E. Costa, *La locazione di cose nel diritto romano* (1915); Pernice, *Labeo*, i (1873), 466; Z ix (1888), 239 f.; xix (1898), 89 ff.; Mommsen, *Schr.* iii (1907), 132 ff.; Brasiello, 'L'unitarietà del concetto di locazione in diritto romano', *Riv. It.* ii/iii (1927/8), estratto; F. M. de Robertis, *I rapporti di lavoro nel diritto Romano* (1946), 120 ff.

s. 935. Pernice, Z ix (1888), 239 ff.; Brasiello, l.c.; Arangio-Ruiz, *Istituzioni* (1947), 346; Olivier Martin, 'Des divisions du louage en droit romain', *RH* xv (1936), 419 ff. On *conducere* see Mommsen, l.c. 137; Pernice, Z ix (1888), 241 n. 1 in fine.

s. 937. Pernice, Z xix (1898), 89 ff.; M. Weber, *Die röm. Agrargeschichte* (1891), 232 ff.; Gummerus, 'Der röm. Gutsbetrieb', *Klio*, 5. *Beiheft* (1906); R. Pöhlmann, *Die Übervölkerung der antiken Gross-Städte* (1884); Mommsen, *Schr.* v (1908), 605 ff.

s. 938. On *colonia partiaria* see Ferrini, *Scritti*, iii (1929), 1 ff.; Longo, *Mélanges Girard*, ii (1912), 105 ff.; F. Kobler, *Der Teilbau im röm. und geltenden italienischen Recht* (1928, not available, see Eisser, Z xlix (1929), 552).

s. 940. Windscheid, l.c. § 400 n. 7; Pernice, Z xix (1898), 95 f.; Schulin, Z xli (1920), 205 ff. Germ. Abt.

s. 941. On *custodia* see literature above, s. 885, Bibliography; on the difficult texts *D.* (13. 6) 19 and (19. 2) 41 see Beseler Z l (1930), 54. See further Brasiello, l.c. 60 ff.; De Robertis l.c. 150, 164 ff.; Pflüger, Z lxv (1947), 193.*

s. 943. Arangio-Ruiz, *Responsabilità contrattuale in diritto Romano* (1933), 190; probably wrong, Beseler, *T* viii (1928), 302.

12. *Partnership (societas)*

The classical *societas* was created by a consensual con- 944. tract whereby two or more persons agreed to co-operate for Conception a common purpose. Nothing else was required for the for- and mation of this contract; in some texts a special *animus* or formation *affectio contrahendae societatis* is mentioned, but they are all interpolated. As a rule the partners, or some of them, promised to make pecuniary contributions; they might even promise to contribute their whole present and future property (*societas omnium bonorum*). Thus the parties of this contract were bound reciprocally to do or to furnish something, like the parties in the contracts of sale and hire, but the fundamental difference is that in sale and hire one obligation is the exchange or recompense for the other whilst the obligations resulting from *societas* have not this character. Nevertheless, Gaius was perfectly right in ranging *societas* under the consensual contracts and in putting it between sale and hire on the one hand and *mandatum* on the other; he was certainly not the first to do so.

945.
Contractus
civilis
The classical *contractus societatis* belonged to *ius civile*, not to *ius honorarium*; the obligations resulting from it were *obligationes civiles*, and the *actio pro socio* was accordingly *in ius concepta*. Readers of Gaius 3. 154 must not be led astray by Gaius' statement that *societas iuris gentium est*; *ius gentium* as it is here used by Gaius is not in contract to *ius civile* but to *proprium ius civile*, i.e. to those institutions of Roman law which Gaius failed to find in the laws of other peoples. Classical *societas* already existed in the last century of the Republic, and apparently already as a *ius civile* institution; whether its original form was the *societas omnium bonorum* is a question of no importance for our present purpose.

946. Con-
sortium
Gaius 3. 154*a*, 154*b* (a recently discovered text) mentions the pre-classical institution of *consortium*. This was a partnership of co-heirs (*fratrum societas*) who, wishing to delay the partition of the *hereditas*, made a *societas* by contributing their shares in the inherited estate. Other persons too might make a *consortium* after the model of *fratrum societas*. This form of partnership had some features peculiar to itself, but like classical *societas* it required an agreement (*consensus*); a *societas re contracta*, i.e. a *societas* which came into existence automatically with a *communio bonorum* never existed as far as we can see. Since the discovery of the new Gaius fragments *consortium* has become a favourite topic, but we shall not discuss this literature, since we are only concerned with classical law and under that law the old *consortium* no longer existed, as one must conclude from Gaius' remarks. It is, however, possible, though not at all certain, that the classical *societas* derived from this *consortium*.

947.
No legal
person
The classical *societas* was not a so-called legal person, or as we prefer to say, a *gesamte Hand*. It was not, like a corporation, an organization with changing members (above,

s. 146). A new member might enter, but only with the consent of each of the old members. If one partner died or left the *societas*, the whole partnership invariably came to an end, though it might be continued by a new formless contract between the remaining *socii*. The common property formed by the contributions of the partners and other acquisitions was a *communio* like any other *communio*, for example, the *hereditas* in case of a plurality of heirs (above, s. 525); each partner had a share in the ownership of which he was free to dispose *durante societate*. If A and B were *socii* and an estate belonged to the common property, both A and B had a share in the ownership and each of them might alienate his share without the consent of the other, e.g. by sale and *mancipatio*; the purchaser acquired the share, but of course did not become a *socius*. Debts of the *societas* or of *universi socii* (above, ss. 157, 173) did not exist, but only debts of the single partners.

The management of the *societas* was of course greatly hampered by the lack of direct agency. Thus the bringing of contributions of the partners into the *societas* required legal acts with each of the *socii*. Even in a *societas omnium bonorum* the property of the single partners did not become common property automatically upon the formation of the consensual contract. Texts conflicting with this are spurious. If one partner acting for the *societas* bought something, it was he who acquired ownership and was bound to pay the price to the seller; he was, however, bound to bring the thing into the common property and was, on the other hand, entitled to claim reimbursement from his partners. 948. Management

The shares in profit and loss were fixed by the contract. In this respect the parties were entirely free under classical law, except that the *societas leonina* was condemned, viz. a contract whereby one partner had a share only in loss and not also in profit. 949. Shares in profit and loss

The classical reciprocal liability of the partners is still a matter of doubt. Under Justinian's law they were responsible for 'diligentia quam quis suis rebus adhibere solet', but this was certainly not classical law. Apparently a *socius* was as a rule only liable for *dolus*, but some classical lawyers 950. Liability advocated a liability for *culpa* and *custodia* in special cases. A contract of partnership of A.D. 167 preserved to us in an inscription (Bruns, *Fontes*, no. 171; *FIRA* iii. 157) mentions only liability for *dolus*; on the other hand, the post-classical but pre-Justinianic *Sententiae Pauli* (2. 16) already recognized liability for *culpa*. We cannot dwell on this problem; available texts are heavily interpolated and resist disentanglement.

951.
Deter-
mination
Societas was inevitably determined by the death of one of the partners; the heir of the deceased did not succeed to his place in the *societas*. The contract might under Justinian's law provide for the continuation of the *societas* among the surviving partners, but never under classical law. Any partner was free to give notice at any time, contrary agreements in the contract being invalid. Such a *renuntiatio* not only entailed the retirement of the partner making it, but also the dissolution of the whole *societas*. In both cases the remaining partners were of course free to continue the *societas* by formless consent, but this was then legally a new *societas*.

952. Actio
pro socio
Each partner had against his co-*socii* the *actio pro socio*. The praetorian Edict contained a rubric *pro socio* which simply means 'for the partner'; the action was accordingly called *actio pro socio* (action for the *socius*). The *formula* is not preserved, but Lenel's reconstruction is most probably right; it was *in ius concepta* and contained the clause *ex fide bona*.

> Lenel, *Edict.* § 109: 'Quod Aulus Agerius cum Numerio Negidio societatem coiit, quidquid ob eam rem Numerium Negidium Aulo Agerio dare facere oportet ex fide bona, eius iudex Numerium Negidium Aulo Agerio condemnato', etc.

The condemnation involved *infamia* (Gai. 4. 182 and the so-called *lex Iulia municipalis* 1. 111; Bruns, *Fontes*, no. 18; *FIRA* i, no. 13). On the other hand, the *socius omnium bonorum* (and under classical law only he) enjoyed the so-called *beneficium competentiae* (above, ss. 793, 794). It is now generally thought that this action lay only if the *societas* had come to an end. This is probably true and the classical *actio pro socio* was accordingly only an action for liquidation.

Thus a partner could not be sued by means of action to enforce the making of his contributions *manente societate*. For the partition of the common property the *actio communi dividundo* (above, s. 86) and not the *actio pro socio* was available.

In this survey of the classical law of partnership its indi- vidualistic and liberalistic character is evident; the characteristically Roman aversion to associations is visible throughout. The contract entails only a minimum of obligation and the law is always anxious to preserve the freedom of the individual. Its character was not essentially altered in post-classical law. The modern forms of commercial and industrial partnership have not been developed on the basis of Roman law, which, if compared with those modern forms, appears an interesting but archaic institution.

953.
Evaluation

SOURCES

s. 944. Read Gai. 3. 148.

s. 948. Read *D*. (17. 2) 73 to *redigendam*; (17. 2) 1. 1 [*continuo*]; (17. 2), 2, entirely spurious.

s. 949. Read Gai. 3. 149; *D*. (17. 2) 29. 2 [*et nos . . . spectet*].

s. 950. Read *Inst. Iust.* (3. 25) 9. The text was taken from the *Res cottidianae* attributed to Gaius (see *D*. 17. 2. 72); the pre-Justinianic text is interpolated as follows: [*etiam*]; ⟨*non*⟩ *tenetur*; [*culpa autem . . . solet*]; Di Marzo, *Bull*. li/lii (1947), 53. Read further Paul. *Sent*. 2. 16.

s. 951. Read Gai. 3. 152; cf. *Inst. Iust.* (3. 25) 5; Gai. 3. 151.

BIBLIOGRAPHY

ss. 944 ff. Manigk, *PW* iiiA. 772 ff. with references; Pernice, *Labeo*, i (1873), 443 ff.; Z iii (1882), 48 ff.; ix (1888), 232 ff.; Ferrini, *Scritti*, iii (1829), 17 ff.; Costa, *Cicerone giureconsulto*, i (1927), 186 ff.; Del Chiaro, *Le Contrat de société en droit privé Romain sous la république et au temps des jurisconsultes classiques* (1928) with Steinwenter, Z l (1930), 592 ff.; A. Poggi, *Il contratto di società in diritto romano classico*, vol. i and ii (1930, 1934, not available); Wieacker, Z liv (1934), 35 ff.; *Societas. Hausgemeinschaft und Erwerbsgesellschaft* (1936); Daube, *Cambridge Law Journal*, vi (1938), 381 ff.*

s. 946. Solazzi, 'Societás e communio', *Atti Napoli*, lvii (1935), Estratto; Arangio-Ruiz, *St. Riccobono*, iv (1936), 357 ff.; Lévy–Bruhl, *Nouvelles Études sur le très ancien droit romain* (1947), 51 ff.; Beseler, *Scritti Ferrini*, ii (1948), 278.*

s. 948. Riccobono, Z xxxiv (1913), 188 ff.

s. 949. Beseler, *Scritti Ferrini*, iii (1948), 276 ff.

s. 950. See particularly Wieacker, Z liv, l.c.; Pflüger, Z lxv (1947), 188.
s. 952. Lenel, *Edict.* § 109; E. Levy, *Konkurrenz der Aktionen* ii. 1
(1922), 143 n. 5, with references.
s. 953. Schulz, *Principles* (1936), 149 ff.

13. *Mandate* (*mandatum*)

954.
Conception
and ter-
minology
Mandatum was a consensual contract whereby one party
(the *mandatarius*) gratuitously promised to execute a commission which the other party (the *mandator*) had given
him. This was the classical conception of the consensual
contractus mandati as described by Gaius 3. 155 ff. It required (1) a formless consent; a unilateral request, order or
authorization (*iussum*) did not suffice; (2) a binding promise
of the *mandatarius* to execute the commission. This binding of the *mandatarius* was essential for any *contractus mandati*. For that reason there was no valid *contractus mandati*
when the execution of the commission was solely in the
interest of the *mandatarius* (so-called *mandatum tua gratia*;
see below, s. 959), for in such a case the *mandatarius* had
not the intention to bind himself and this binding was
essential for the contract.

> The term *mandare* derived from *manum dare* = *in manum dare* and
> meant in common Latin usage 'to entrust something', 'to give a commis-
> sion', 'to authorize', 'to give a command'. *Mandatum* in the narrower
> sense of a consensual contract was an artificial creation of legal literature.
> It is still uncertain whether the classical lawyers sometimes used *mandare*
> and *mandatum* in the broader sense (viz. in the sense of *iussum*), but here
> we are only concerned with the *contractus mandati*.

955. Actio
mandati
Mandatum comes last in Gaius' description of the consensual contracts; perhaps it was also the youngest of the
contracts in this group. When the second chapter of the
lex Aquilia was framed (above, s. 837), the *actio mandati*
was not yet known; on the other hand, the contract was
already recognized in Cicero's age. The development during the Republic remains obscure for want of sources, but
in classical times the contract was undoubtedly a *contractus
iuris civilis*, from which resulted an action (*actio mandati*)
for each of the parties. The *formula* is not preserved, but it
was *in ius concepta* and contained the clause *ex fide bona*.

Condemnation involved *infamia*. By means of the so-called *actio mandati directa* (above, s. 70) the *mandator* might demand performance of the commission, i.e. primarily the handing over of everything which the *mandatarius* had acquired in executing the commission. By means of the so-called *actio mandati contraria* (above, s. 70) the *mandatarius* might demand reimbursement of his expenses. When a transaction was commissioned to the *mandatarius*, the rights and duties arisen from that transaction, in default of direct agency, attached to the *mandatarius*. If A requested B to buy a thing from S and B accordingly bought the thing from S, it was B who had the *actio empti* against S and S had the *actio venditi* against B for the price. But B was bound to transfer the *actio empti* to A whilst A was bound to set B free from his obligation towards S.

The genesis of this contract requires explanation. Why was it created at all by the republican lawyers? In modern times, even in continental law where the Roman *mandatum* has been adopted by the codifiers, this contract plays a very modest part; a mandate to do something for the *mandator* without reward lies as a rule outside the sphere of law, since the parties do not wish to bind themselves legally. However, in Rome, and particularly in those social circles to which the lawyers belonged, certain social customs and rules prevailed which suggested this contract. Friendship (*amicitia*) gave rise to serious and substantial duties. Roman friends made claims on each other which would cause a modern 'friend' to break off the friendship without delay. In republican Rome there was no hesitation about asking a friend for help in any situation; a friend might be asked for hospitality, to give recommendations, to execute commissions, and even to lend money. It was part of one's *officium* to support a friend as far as possible. When Cicero was in exile his family in Rome was in pecuniary embarrassment, but, as he wrote reassuringly to his wife, *Ad fam.* 14. 1. 5, 'si erunt in officio amici, pecunia non deerit'. As this view was generally accepted, a person who undertook a commission at the request of his friend did not expect or demand remuneration, but nevertheless regarded it as a

956.
Social basis
of the
contract

serious business affair. Moreover, freedmen played an important part in Roman social life. A patron liked to entrust his freedmen with business affairs and the freedman felt himself bound by his *officium* to execute his patron's commissions gratuitously. Lastly, not all sorts of services seemed suited to form the subject of a *locatio conductio*. In the case of a contract with a lawyer, an advocate, a doctor, or a teacher, *locatio conductio* did not seem the proper form since, according to the view of aristocratic Romans, such services ought to be rendered gratuitously. Cicero, for example, would have refused to be 'hired' as an advocate though he felt no scruples about accepting remuneration in a less vulgar form. In such cases *mandatum* seemed to be the proper contract.

In these circumstances there was ample room and even need for the *contractus mandati* and the republican lawyers were fully justified in admitting it. They did so with their usual discretion.

957.
Liability of
the man-
datarius
1. The *mandatarius* was only liable for *dolus* like the *depositarius*; as both rendered gratuitous services a minimum of liability seemed adequate. This was the classical, and certainly also the republican law. The ill-directed tirades of young Cicero (*pro Roscio Amerino* 38. 111 ff.) must not mislead us.

958.
Deter-
mination
2. *Mandatum* was strictly personal and was therefore determined by the death of either party.

3. Each party was entitled to give notice as long as the execution of the commission had not yet begun.

959.
Mandatum
and
consilium
As the *contractus mandati* was consensual and gratuitous, it was necessary to distinguish it from mere advice (*consilium*). It is not difficult to discriminate between them. The criterion of the *contractus mandati* is the intention of the *mandatarius* to bind himself; if this intention was absent we have to assume that there was merely the giving of advice. But the republican lawyers desiring a more definite criterion chose the following formula: a *mandatum tua gratia* (i.e. a mandate in the interest of the *mandatarius*) is merely a piece of advice, for—so they argued—in such a case the *mandatarius* has certainly not the intention to bind himself.

This formula was not entirely wrong but was nevertheless inaccurate. A advised B to invest his (B's) money in land. This is a *mandatum tua tantum gratia* (exclusively in the interest of the *mandatarius*); it is merely advice, since B had not the intention to bind himself; B is not bound to execute the commission, and if he does, A is not responsible if the advice turned out to be bad. On the other hand, if A requested B to give a loan of money on interest to C, this was also a *mandatum tua gratia* but not *tua tantum gratia*; nevertheless Servius Sulpicius, Cicero's well-known friend, took it as merely advice and it was only Sabinus who rightly regarded it as a true *contractus mandati*. At the end of the classical period we find in the *Res cottidianae* attributed to Gaius the following distinction, already quite in the style of the Bolognese Glossators: (1) *mandatum tua tantum gratia*; (2) *mandatum mea tantum gratia*; (3) *mandatum aliena tantum gratia*; (4) *mandatum mea et aliena gratia*; (5) *mandatum tua et mea gratia*; (6) *mandatum tua et aliena gratia*. This is sheer scholasticism, the distinctions being superfluous and of no legal importance. The only important conception is that of a *mandatum tua tantum gratia* and the statement that such a mandate is merely advice. Thus these distinctions are only interesting as examples of classical scholasticism.

Under Justinian's law the *mandatarius* was responsible for *culpa* and not only for *dolus* as in classical times. This was an ill-considered innovation since a *mandatarius* could hardly ever have been prepared to undertake such a heavy liability without reward. It is interesting to see how modern lawyers have tried to justify the liability for *culpa*. Windscheid, for example, said (*Pand.* ii. § 410 n. 4): 'The promise to execute a commission (*etwas für einen andern zu besorgen*) implies a promise to execute it carefully (*das Versprechen der Sorgfalt*) as the word "besorgen" suggests.' This implied promise is absolutely arbitrary and the linguistic argument is absurd, particularly as it is confined to the German language. As a matter of fact the liability for *culpa* is irrational and cannot be justified; the classical lawyers were perfectly right. Under modern Roman law

960. Post-classical development

the *contractus mandati* disappeared almost entirely from actual life, since the social conditions on which it was based (above, s. 956) had disappeared.

961.
Mandatum
credendi

A special type of *mandatum* was the mandate to give a third person credit. The simplest case is the following: A requested B to give a loan of money to C. When B executed his commission, B had an *actio ex mutuo* against C and an *actio mandati contraria* against A. This looks similar to a *fideiussio* and indeed it is in substance a kind of suretyship, but the differences between this kind of mandate and *fideiussio* are under classical law quite obvious. When the creditor sued the principal debtor, the *fideiussor* became free as the result of *litis contestatio* (above, s. 862); when B sued C, his *actio mandati contraria* against A remained intact. All *exceptiones* available to the principal debtor were also available to the *fideiussor* (above, s. 863), but A could not avail himself of the *exceptiones* available to C. In short, a *mandatum credendi* was a mandate like any other and was subject to no special rules. It was, however, the tendency of the compilers to assimilate *mandatum credendi* to *fideiussio* since they wished to push the *stipulatio* (indispensable for *fideiussio*) into the background. Thus under Justinian's law the exceptions available to C were also available to A, and in case of a plurality of *mandatores* the *beneficium divisionis* took place, whereas Hadrian's *beneficium divisionis* was confined to *confideiussores* (above, s. 867). In Justinian's law the *mandatum credendi* was no longer a mandate like any other but a *mandatum sui generis*, a form of mandate subjected to special rules. For that reason this mandate was called *mandatum qualificatum* by modern lawyers, a designation which should be avoided as far as classical law is concerned.

SOURCES

s. 954. Read Gai. 3. 135, 136; *D.* (17. 1) 1; Gai. 3. 157; *D.* (17. 1) 12. 11 with Beseler, Z liii (1933), 25.

s. 955. Read Gai. 4. 62, 182; *D.* (17. 1) 20 pr.; (17. 1) 10. 6.

s. 957. Read *Coll.* (10. 2) 3.

s. 958. Read Gai. 3. 159, 160 to *adferet*.

s. 959. Read Gai. 3. 155, 156 with Beseler, *St. Bonfante*, ii (1930), 58; *D.* (17. 1) 2; *D.* (17. 1) 16 ⟨*non esse et*⟩ *hoc*; [*deducto . . . persequi*]. Celsus was a Proculian and followed Servius' opinion; Ulpian and the compilers followed Sabinus.

s. 960. Read *D.* (50. 17) 23 interpolated; *C.* (4. 35) 11 [*tam*] *dolum* [*quam culpam*]; *C.* (4. 35) 13 [*et omnem culpam*]; [*improvisum casum*] ⟨*culpam*⟩.

s. 961. Read Paul. *Sent.* (2. 17) 16; *D.* (17. 1) 32 [*si quis . . . procul dubio est*]; *C.* (4. 30) 12 [*tam . . . quam*]; *D.* (46. 1) 32 [*ceterisque accessionibus*]; *C.* (4. 18) 3 [*mandatores et*]; [*aequitatis . . . debet*]; *D.* (27. 7) 7 [*fideiussores*] ⟨*sponsores*⟩; [*nam et . . . excludit*].

BIBLIOGRAPHY

ss. 954 ff. For the older literature see Windscheid, *Pand.* ii (1906), §§ 409 ff. The standard work is now Arangio-Ruiz, *Il mandato in diritto Romano* (1949). See further Donatuti, *Contributi alla teoria del mandato in diritto romano*, I. *L'actio mandati dell' adpromissor* (1929), II. *La volontà del mandante* (1929); 'Mandato incerto', *Bull.* xxiii (1923), 168 ff.; 'Il silenzio come manifestazione di volontà', *St. Bonfante*, iv (1930), 161 ff.; 'Mandatum praesumptum', *St. Albertoni*, i (1935), 367 ff.; Kreller, *PW* xiv. 1015 ff.; 'Zum iudicium mandati', Festgabe für Heck, Rümelin, Schmidt, *Beilageheft zu Archiv f. d. ziv. Praxis*, cxxxiii (1931), 118 ff.

s. 954. Pernice, *Labeo*, i (1873), 441 ff.; Z ix (1888), 237 ff.; Beseler, *St. Bonfante*, ii (1930), 58; Donatuti, *Contributi*, ii, l.c. On *mandatum* and *iussum* see Beseler, Z l (1930), 54 (on *D.* 17. 1. 26. 1); Consentini, 'Ratihabitio mandato comparatur', *Annali Catania*, i (1947). On the etymology of *mandare* see A. Walde, *Lat. Etymolog. Wörterbuch* (1910), 460; Ernout–Meillet, *Dictionnaire étymologique* (1939), 586; *Lexicon Plautinum*, ed. G. Lodge, ii (1926), 24; Pernice, ll.cc.

s. 955. Pernice, *Labeo*, i. 442 f.; Lenel, *Edict.* (1927), § 108; Kreller, 'Zum iudicium mandati', l.c. 120 ff. On *excessus mandati* see Pampaloni, *Bull.* xx (1908), 210 ff.; Pringsheim, *St. Besta*, i (1939), 325; Riccobono, *Festschrift P. Koschaker*, ii (1939), 382 ff.; Arangio-Ruiz, l.c. 168.

s. 956. Schulz, *Principles* (1936), 149. On operae liberales see De Robertis, *I rapporti di lavoro* (1946), 183 ff.

s. 957. Mitteis, *RP* i (1908), 325 ff.; Sachers, 'Zur Lehre von der Haftung des Mandatars im klass. röm. Recht', Z lix (1939), 432 ff.; Pflüger, Z lxv (1947), 169 ff.

s. 959. Mancaleoni, 'Mandatum tua gratia e consilium', *Riv. It.* xxvii (1899), not available; Beseler, Z xliii (1922), 542; *St. Bonfante*, ii (1930); 58; Rabel, ibid. iv (1930), 283 ff.; Kreller, 'Zum iudicium mandati', l.c. 142 ff.

s. 961. Bortolucci, 'Il mandato di credito', *Bull.* xxvii (1914), 129 ff., xxviii (1915), 191 ff., particularly 239 ff.

14. *Pacta praetoria*

After having described the contracts recognized by the Roman *ius civile* we now turn to the so-called *pacta praetoria*,

962. Conception

i.e. to informal contracts from which resulted a praetorian action. We have already said (above, s. 802) that the term *pacta praetoria* was not known to the classical lawyers, nor did they speak in these cases of *pacta* at all; but in fact these agreements were pacts, informal contracts, and for that reason we may retain the traditional and convenient term. The proper place for discussing them in this book is after the consensual contracts. We confine ourselves to classical law, or more precisely to the law of Hadrian's Edict, and for this purpose a few brief remarks will suffice. In truth, these pacts are of comparatively small importance.

i. *Constitutum debiti*

963. Edict and formula   1. Under the rubric *de pecunia constituta* the praetor (according to Hadrian's Edict) promised to grant an action with the following words:

> 'Qui pecuniam debitam constituit se soluturum esse, in eum iudicium dabo.'

Constituere in this connexion does not mean 'to confirm', 'to corroborate', but to fix a certain day on which a debt has to be paid. If D promised by stipulation to pay 100 to C on the 1st of January, this might be called *constituere*, but it was not a *constituere* in the sense of this edictal clause; it was not *constituere debitam pecuniam* since the fixing of a day was part of the contract. The edictal *constitutum* was conditional on the existence of an obligation. But if D promised by stipulation to pay 100 to C on the 1st of January and later C and D agreed that the debt should be paid on the following 1st of July, this was a *constitutum* in the sense of the Edict, i.e. the fixing by special agreement of a day for the discharge of an already existing obligation. From this act resulted the praetorian *actio de constituta pecunia*. The *formula* is not preserved, but Lenel's reconstruction must be right, since only a *formula* framed in this way renders intelligible the genesis and function of the whole institution. The *formula* was of course *in factum concepta* and framed in such a way that the plaintiff could obtain with it not only the amount of the original debt but also damages for the delay in its payment.

'Si paret Numerium Negidium Aulo Agerio sestertium decem milia constituisse se soluturum,

neque fecisse quod constituit neque per Aulum Agerium stetisse quo minus fieret quod constitutum est, eamque pecuniam cum constituebatur debitam fuisse, quanti ea res est, tantam pecuniam iudex · Numerium Negidium Aulo Agerio condemnato', etc.

The words *neque fecisse quod constituit* imply that *quanti ea res est* comprehends damages for delay as well as the amount of the debt. The plaintiff in this action was entitled to demand a wager of law. At his request the defendant had to promise by *sponsio* one-half of the amount which the plaintiff claimed by the praetorian action, to be paid if he, the defendant, was defeated in the trial; on the other hand, the plaintiff had to promise half of the same sum, to be paid if the defendant won his case (*sponsio et restipulatio dimidiae partis*). Although this *dimidia pars* was meant to be a fine and the *sponsiones* were *sponsiones poenales*, the praetorian action itself was not a penal action; it lay against the heir of the *constituens* and need not be brought within a specified period (it was not an *actio annua*; see above, s. 85).

2. A *constitutum* could only be made if an obligation already existed. The Edict only mentioned pecuniary obligations (*de constituta pecunia*); in fact its scope was originally still narrower, being confined to pecuniary obligations enforceable by an *actio certae creditae pecuniae* (above, s. 809). But the lawyers extended by their interpretation the original sphere of the *constitutum*. When a quantity of fungibles was owed by stipulation or *mutuum*, the obligation might equally be constituted; eventually any obligation on *certa pecunia* or *certa quantitas* (e.g. the obligation of the buyer to pay the price) was apparently regarded as a sufficient basis for a *constitutum*. As only a *debitum* could be constituted, the *constitutum* could not exceed the amount of the original debt; nor could the *constitutum* contain a subject-matter different from that of the original debt. 964.
Conditions

3. The *constitutum* had not the effect of a novation (above, s. 815). Thus if the original debt was created by stipulation, the creditor had now two actions against the debtor, the *actio ex stipulatione*; and the *actio de constituta pecunia*. Of 965.
Effects

course the debtor had only to pay once, and even if the *obligatio ex stipulatione* was discharged by *acceptilatio* (*imaginaria solutio*) the debtor was protected by an *exceptio* against the praetorian action. But if the original obligation was destroyed in some other way, i.e. not by fulfilment or *imaginaria solutio*, the praetorian action remained intact; *constitutum*, though conditional on the existence of an obligation at the time when the *constitutum* was made, was not dependent on the continuance of that obligation.

> Consider the following case. D owed 100 to C by stipulation; S owed these same 100 as an accessory *sponsor* (above, s. 839). Later S constituted his debt *ex sponsione*. Now remember that the obligation of a *sponsor* was discharged by the sponsor's death (s. 852). Thus if S died, his obligation *ex sponsione* came to an end, but the praetorian action resulting from the *constitutum* remained intact and lay against S's heir. Further, according to the *lex Furia*, the *sponsor* became free after the lapse of two years (s. 853). Thus after the lapse of this time S was free from his obligation *ex sponsione*, but the praetorian action against him remained intact.

966.
Function

4. What was the purpose of this complicated apparatus? What was the practical function of the *constitutum debiti*? The question has been much discussed and we can give today a clear answer. The praetorian action protected the creditor against the possibility of the determination of the principal obligation by the death of the debtor or by lapse of time, but the primary purpose of the *constitutum* was the following. Let us remember that in the *actio certae creditae pecuniae* damages could not be awarded to the creditor in case of *mora debitoris* (above, s. 813). If a debtor was bound by stipulation to pay 100 on the 1st of July and did not pay at that date, the creditor could not obtain interest *ex mora debitoris* with the *actio certae creditae pecuniae*, since the condemnatio of the *formula* (above, ss. 809, 30) was a *condemnatio certa*. In this respect the *constitutum* brought a relief, for the *formula* of the praetorian action authorized the judge to award damages for the delay in payment. This was and remained the main purpose of the *constitutum*. Moreover, the *sponsio dimidiae partis* implied a further advantage for the creditor. We have already said (above, s. 964) that *constitutum* was originally only concerned with obligations

enforceable by an *actio certae creditae pecuniae*; here the need for the edictal remedy is evident. Later the *constitutum* was extended to other kinds of obligations. But if a sum of money was left by a legacy, the situation was the same, for with the *actio ex testamento* the legatee could not claim damages in case of *mora debitoris*. Of course, when the constituted obligation was enforceable with an *actio bonae fidei* (e.g. the *actio venditi*), the creditor might claim damages for delay in the *iudicium bonae fidei* on the strength of the formulary clause *ex fide bona* (above, s. 64) and the advantage implied in the *constitutum* was only the *sponsio dimidiae partis*. But it was not for such obligations that the praetor had devised the remedy.

5. Hitherto we have only considered the case of a *constitutum* which a debtor made with his creditor (*constitutum debiti proprii*), but the Edict also regulated the *constitutum debiti alieni*. D owed 100 to C by stipulation. On this obligation A made a *constitutum* with C. The result was that C had the *actio ex stipulatione* against D and the praetorian action against A. This resembles suretyship and this was realized by the praetor. Although in this case also the praetorian action was not a penal action (above, s. 963), it could only be brought within a year (*actio annua*) and was determined by the death of the constituting person. The praetor imitated the rules on the accessory *sponsor* which we have just mentioned (above, s. 965), only he substituted one year for the *biennium* of the *lex Furia*. The *constitutum debiti alieni* was indeed a sort of suretyship for which a stipulation was not required. Nevertheless it was not an entirely satisfactory substitute for *fideiussio*, principally because the risk of the wager of law was too great.

6. In post-classical times the whole artificial institution suffered a decline since it was too closely connected with the formulary procedure. The wager of law disappeared entirely, the *constitutum debiti proprii* was no longer practised. The *constitutum debiti alieni* survived but was assimilated to *fideiussio* by Justinian's constitution of A.D. 531 (*C.* 4. 18. 2); obligations of any kind might now be the basis of a *constitutum*. Justinian's tendency to push the

967. Constitutum debiti alieni

968. Post-classical law

stipulation (necessary for *fideiussio*) into the background and to replace it by a formless pact is again evident (above, s. 961).

969. ii. *Receptum argentarii*

This *receptum* was an informal pact whereby a banker promised to pay the debt of his client. A owed C 100. A requested his banker B to promise C these same 100 (*recipere solvi*). If B did that, the praetor granted a special praetorian action (*actio recepticia*) to C against the banker. The *receptum* closely resembled the *constitutum debiti alieni* and Justinian amalgamated the two.

> *Recipere* means here and in the two following *recepta* 'to take upon one's self, undertake, accept the performance of a task consigned or intrusted to one'; Cic., *Divin. in Caecil.* 8. 26: 'ego in hoc iudicio mihi Siculorum causam receptam, populi Romani susceptam esse arbitror'.

970. iii. *Receptum arbitrii*

Parties might make an agreement to submit their dispute to arbitration and appoint an arbitrator. Of course the appointed person was not bound to undertake this task, but when he accepted by a formless pact (*recipere arbitrium*) he was bound, though not *iure privato*. The parties had no action against him, but the praetor might compel him on the strength of his *imperium*, i.e. by *multae dictio* or *pignoris capio*. But the praetor applied compulsion only when the parties had secured the execution of the sentence by two penal stipulations; plaintiff and defendant each had to promise the other to pay a fine if he did not obey the sentence of the arbitrator. The Edict ran as follows:

> 'Qui arbitrium pecunia compromissa receperit, eum sententiam dicere cogam.'

Pecunia compromissa refers to the two penal stipulations (*com-promissa*, promised together) which have given the agreement of arbitration the name of *compromissum* (not of course to be translated by English 'compromise').

971. iv. *Receptum nautarum, cauponum, stabulariorum*

These *recepta* were informal pacts whereby a carrier by water (*nauta*), an innkeeper (*caupo*), or a stablekeeper (*stabularius*) undertook to be responsible for the safety of the goods brought into the ship, the inn, or the stable (*rem salvam fore recipere*). The praetor declared in his Edict (Lenel, *Edict.* § 49):

'Nautae, caupones, stabularii quod cuiusque salvum fore receperint nisi restituent, in eos iudicium dabo.'

According to the wording of the Edict and the *formula* the liability which these *recepta* entailed was unlimited but the classical lawyers scaled it down to a liability for *custodia* (above, s. 885), and in these cases the compilers have not changed *custodia* into *diligentia in custodiendo*. The basis of this liability was an express pact, and although no form was required for it, it was not sufficient to bring the goods into the ship, the hostel, or the stable; but under Justinian's law the pact was implied in the bringing in of the goods.

One may raise the question why a special action was created by the praetor for these cases. The contract with the *nauta*, *caupo*, and *stabularius* was as a' rule a *locatio conductio* and the *locator* and *conductor* was liable for *custodia* (above, s. 941). However, the edictal liability was originally not confined to *custodia* and even under classical law the *actio locati* or *conducti* was not always an efficient remedy. When a guest brought his things into his own room in the hostel, the *locator* was certainly not responsible for *custodia* under the *actio conducti*. A text in the *Digest* declares that the praetorian action against the *caupo* was called for because *caupones* were unreliable people who might co-operate with thieves. But this is a silly post-classical attempt to justify the severe liability. To be sure *caupones* were in bad repute, but that was not the reason why the praetor introduced the action. *Nautae* and *stabularii* were not in bad repute and yet he imposed on them the same severe liability; the *nautae* are even mentioned first in the edictal clause. Hence this post-classical attempt at justification should be definitely abandoned.

The *receptum nautarum* etc. in its Justinianic form (viz. as an implied pact) is the only praetorian pact which survives; it served as a model for the liability of the carrier and innkeeper in modern continental law.

SOURCES

ss. 964, 965. Read *D.* (13. 5) 18. 1, substantially genuine; *D.* (13. 5) 30 [*duobus*] *pecuniam* ⟨*quam tibi debet*⟩ *constituerit* ⟨*se*⟩ *tibi aut Titio* ⟨*soluturum*⟩ [*etsi stricto*] ⟨*ipso*⟩ *iure* [*propria . . . constitutae*]; [*tamen*] ⟨*sed petente te*⟩ with Beseler, Z xlv (1925), 439 and Koschaker, Z lxiii (1943), 475; *D.* (13. 5) 1. 8, substantially genuine, Astuti, 2. 217.

s. 967. Read Paul. *Sent.* (2. 2) 1.

s. 971. Read *D.* (4. 9) 5; (4. 9) 1. 1, entirely spurious; *D.* (4. 9) 3. 1 with Lenel, Z xlix (1929), 1 ff. Read the significant inscription *ILS* 7478.

BIBLIOGRAPHY

ss. 963 ff. G. Bruns, 'Das constitutum debiti', *Z für Rechtsgeschichte*, i (1861), 28 ff. (fundamental, but today out of date). The principal work is now G. Astuti, *Studi intorno alla promessa di pagamento. Il costituto di debito,* i (1937); ii (1941). See further Beseler, *Das Edictum de eo quod certo loco* (1907), 104; *Beiträge,* iv (1920), 260; *T* viii (1928), 333; Koschaker, Z lxiii (1943), 469 ff.; Lenel, *Edict.* (1927), § 97 with Beseler, *Beiträge,* iv. 260, note.*

s. 969. Lenel, *Edict.* (1927), § 50; Wenger, *PW* iA. 372 ff.

s. 970. Lenel, *Edict.* § 48; Wenger, *PW* iA. 358 ff.

s. 971. Klingmüller, *PW* iA. 356 (insufficient; Schulz, *Z für das Privat- und öffentliche Recht der Gegenwart,* xxxviii (1911), 9 ff.; *Krit. Viertel- jahresschrift,* xiv (1912), 27 ff.; Z xxxii (1911), 68 ff.; Lenel, Z l (1930), 1 ff.; *Edict.* § 49. See further the literature on *custodia* above, s. 885, Bibliography, and the references in the *Index Interpolationum, Digest* title 4. 9. On modern Roman law see Gierke, *DP* iii (1917) 740.*

Appendix: Donatio and Intercessio

i. *Donatio* (*donation, gift*)

972.
Conception
and
formation

1. *Donatio* was not a contract. For that reason it could not be discussed in the law of contract, but as its traditional place is within the law of obligations, we have placed it in an appendix to the law of contract.

The classical *donatio* was a legal act which entailed the enrichment of one person at the expense of another, both parties agreeing that the act was made *donationis causa*. The term *donationis causa* can only be defined in a negative way; an act was made *donationis causa* if both parties agreed that the enrichment had no other legal purpose than to enrich the recipient.

Suppose D owed 100 to C; A paid this sum to C. A has not made a donation to C, for he paid *solvendi causa*. On the other hand, D is enriched at the expense of A, since D is set free from his debt to C. However, A's payment does not always mean a donation to D; for example, A might have acted as D's *mandatarius* or *negotiorum gestor*. But if A and D agreed that the only purpose of the payment was to enrich D then A's payment is at the same time a *solutio* in respect of C and a *donatio* in respect of D. The agreement might precede or follow the payment, but if an agreement did not take place (and there was no other *causa* to the enrichment), the enrichment was unjustified and rendered D liable to a *condictio sine causa*.

Thus any legal act which entailed an enrichment of one person at the expense of another might be a *donatio*: a *traditio*, a *mancipatio*, a *stipulatio*, an *acceptilatio*, a *pactum de non petendo*. Even a sale might be made *donationis causa*: A sold a thing to B, both parties agreeing that the price was less than the equivalent of the thing (then B is a donee) or more than the equivalent (then A is a donee). This *negotium mixtum cum donatione* is a sale to which the law of donation partly applied. If, for example, such a sale was made between husband and wife, it was void since donations between husband and wife were prohibited (above, s. 206).

An agreement on the *causa donandi* was required throughout for any donation, but there was no requirement of an *animus donandi* distinct from that agreement; wherever we find this *animus* in classical texts, we have to recognize interpolation.

This broad description of *donatio* needs some qualification. *Commodatum, depositum, mandatum* are no species of *donatio*; nor is a *fideiussio* a donatio either towards the creditor or towards the principal debtor. Neither *institutio heredis* nor the leaving of a legacy is a *donatio*. Let us suppose that a testator instituted A and substituted B (*substitutio vulgaris*; above, s. 455). A refused to accept the inheritance, which now fell to B. This is not a *donatio*, even if A and B had made an agreement to that effect.

We have already dealt with *donatio mortis causa* (above, s. 574) and confine ourselves here to *donatio inter vivos*.

2. Some varieties of donation were prohibited under classical law. We have already mentioned gifts between husband and wife (above, s. 206). A *lex Cincia* of 204 B.C. 973. **Lex Cincia**

prohibited in general terms donations exceeding a certain amount; only donations to certain persons, mostly near relatives, were excepted from the prohibition (*personae exceptae*). Although this prohibition is very often mentioned, and although we possess the title *ad legem Cinciam* in the *Fragmenta Vaticana*, the sources preserve an obstinate silence on the amount fixed by the *lex Cincia*. The lawyers regarded the statute as a *lex imperfecta* and accordingly a prohibited donation was valid *iure civili*. But the praetor enforced the enactment, though only by granting an *exceptio* (*exceptio legis Cinciae*) to the donor as long as he had not yet completely executed the donation (*donatio imperfecta*); a *donatio perfecta* could no longer be impugned. Moreover, that *exceptio* might be invalidated by a *replicatio doli* if the donor had died without having revoked the donation (*morte Cincia removetur*).

Consider the following cases: (1) The donor had delivered a *res mancipi* to the donee by *traditio*. The donor might sue the donee with the *rei vindicatio* and if the defendant availed himself of the *exceptio rei donatae et traditae* (above, s. 654) the donor might meet it with a *replicatio legis Cinciae*. (2) The donor mancipated a *res mancipi* to the donee without handing it over to him. If the donee sued the donor with the *rei vindicatio*, the latter was protected by the *exceptio legis Cinciae*. (3) The donor promised something to the donee by stipulation. If the donee sued the donor with the *actio ex stipulatione*, the latter was protected by the *exceptio legis Cinciae*. But if the donor fulfilled his promise, the *donatio* was *perfecta* and could no longer be impugned. The *condictio indebiti* mentioned in *Fr. Vat.* 266 is certainly spurious.

In post-classical times the *lex Cincia* was abolished. This must have occurred after A.D. 438, as it is mentioned in the *Codex Theodosianus*, 8. 12. 4. Justinian introduced other restrictions which the compilers have sometimes substituted for those imposed by the *lex Cincia*.

974.
Donatio
sub modo
3. The *donatio sub modo* ('gift under a restriction') was a donation by which the donor by informal agreement with the donee imposed upon the latter the duty of making some performance in favour of the donor or some third person. Somebody, for instance, might give A a house *donationis causa*, imposing on him the duty of granting a flat for life to the donor or to a third person. Under classical law the

modus was not enforceable; neither the donor nor the third person had an action for fulfilment. But the donor might in case of non-fulfilment revoke the donation and reclaim the thing with a *condictio*. When the donee was required to pass on the donation after a certain time to a third person, certain classical emperors (their names are not known) granted an action for fulfilment to the third person. Under Justinian's law the donor had a *condictio* when the donee did not fulfil the *modus* and, moreover, an *actio praescriptis verbis* for its fulfilment; the latter action was also accorded to the third person in favour of whom the donee was required to make a performance.

As regards the terminology, *modus* in a technical sense was unknown to the classical lawyers, though they were well acquainted with the legal phenomenon which it describes. As a technical term we find *modus* in Justinian's *Corpus iuris*: *D.* (35. 1) rubr. 'De condicionibus et demonstrationibus et causis et modis eorum, quae in testamento scribuntur'; *C.* (6. 45) rubr. 'De his quae sub modo legata vel fideicommissa relinquuntur; *C.* (8. 54) rubr. 'De donationibus quae sub modo vel condicione vel ex certo tempore conficiuntur.'

ii. *Intercessio*

Intercessio, like *donatio*, was not a special contract. The classical conception of *intercessio* was founded on the *senatus consultum Vellaeanum* (under Nero, not as it is traditionally said A.D. 46). This was an outspokenly reactionary enactment in conformity with the general attitude of the Senate which at that period was the centre of reaction. Once more the Senate proclaimed the old Roman principle (above, s. 312): *mulieres virilibus officiis fungi non est aequum*, and for that reason (not on account of the *imbecillitas sexus*; above, s. 311) prohibited legal acts whereby women rendered themselves liable for the debts of other persons (*pro aliis reae fieri*). This superficial and clumsily worded enactment expressly mentioned two cases: (1) suretyship (*sponsio, fidepromissio*, and *fideiussio*; above, ss. 839 ff.); (2) the making of a loan of money to a woman who immediately passed it on to another person.

975. Senatus consultum Vellaeanum

The text of the *senatusconsultum* is only preserved to us by the *Digest* (*D.* 16. 1. 2). The compilers have cancelled *sponsio* and *fidepromissio* and substituted the clumsy *oportet* for the traditional *placeret*. The words 'mutui dationes pro aliis quibus intercesserint feminae' mean: 'a loan of money given to a woman on behalf of another person for whom (*quibus = pro quibus*) the woman intervened'.

On this basis the classical lawyers developed the artificial conception of *intercessio*. It is hardly possible to define it precisely by a general and intelligible formula. We can merely state that *intercessio* was any legal act whereby a woman undertook liability for a debt which economically was not her own, but this definition can only be rendered intelligible by giving individual cases.

One example must suffice. Suppose Seia asked C for a loan of money. C gave the loan to D, who passed it on to Seia, whilst Seia bound herself as *fideiussor* to C. Legally Seia undertook the debt of D, but economically it was her own debt. Thus, although the *senatusconsultum* expressly mentioned *fideiussio*, the *fideiussio* did not in this case fall under the prohibition.

A legal act of a woman which fell under the *senatusconsultum* was not void *iure civili*, but the praetor granted an *exceptio* which was inserted in the formula *officio praetoris* (*exceptio senatus consulti Vellaeani*).

Under the rubric *ad senatus consultum Vellaeanum* the praetorian Edict did *not* deal with that *exceptio*, but with two actions which the praetor granted to the creditor who had suffered a loss by the intervention of the woman.

1. D owed C 100. Seia undertook the obligation by *novatio* (above, s. 815) without receiving an equivalent from D. Seia was now protected by the *exceptio* and C had lost his action against D. The praetor granted to C a new action against D (*actio restitutoria*) with a *formula ficticia* ('Si Seia non intercessisset, tum si Numerium Negidium (in this case D) Aulo Agerio centum dare oporteret' . . .).

2. C was prepared to make a loan of money to D; by Seia's intervention he gave the loan to Seia, who passed it on to D. The praetor granted an *actio* to C against D (*actio institutoria*) as C would have had the *actio ex mutuo* had it not been for Seia's intervention.

The ill-starred enactment survived with small modifications in Justinian's law and, with further modifications, in continental law from the Middle Ages down to modern times; even today it is still in force in South Africa. The classical law of *intercessio* is still interesting as an instructive example of the classical technique of interpreting an enactment; and also because it marks the beginning of a reaction against the emancipation of women which had been achieved at the end of the Republic (above, ss. 194, 195, 313).

SOURCES

s. 972. Read *D.* (12. 1.) 18 pr. to *acceperit*.

s. 973. Read *Fr. Vat.* 275, 310, 311, 312, first sentence; *D.* (39. 5) 21. 1, first sentence [*immodicae*]; [*donationis*] ⟨*legis Cinciae*⟩; (39. 5) 24 [*supra . . . legis*].

s. 974. Read *Fr. Vat.* 286 (cf. above, s. 825); *C.* (4. 6) 2 [*condictionis*]; (8. 53) 9 [*incerto . . . verbis*] ⟨*condictione*⟩; [*ut . . . provideat*].

s. 975. Read *D.* (16. 1) 2. 1.

BIBLIOGRAPHY

ss. 972–4. Mitteis, *RP* i (1908), 153 ff.; Biondi, *Successione testamentaria. Donazioni. Trattato di diritto Romano* ed. Albertario, x (1943), 631 ff.; Biondi, 'Il concetto di donazione', *Scritti Ferrini*, i (1947), 102 ff.

s. 972. Windscheid, *Pand.* ii (1906), § 395 n. 18; Stock, *Zum Begriff der donatio* (1932); Biondi, l.c. 631 ff.

s. 973. Rotondi, *Leges publicae* (1912), 261; Mitteis, l.c. 153 ff.; Lenel, *Edict.* (1927), § 279; Siber, Z liii (1933), 136; Archi, *St. Solazzi* (1948), 740 ff.; Radin, 'La disparition de la loi Cincia', *RH* vii (1928), 248 ff., hardly right: Arnobius ('Adversus nationes', 2. 67, *Corpus Scriptorum Eccles. Lat.* 4. 102) knew that a *donatio perfecta* was valid in spite of the *lex Cincia* and deduced from that that the statute had been partly or completely abolished.

s. 974. Pernice, *Labeo*, iii. 1 (1892), 87 ff.; Mitteis, l.c. 194 ff., 200 ff.; F. Haymann, *Die Schenkung unter einer Auflage* (1905); Schulz, 'Interpolationenkritische Studien', 3 ff. (*Festschrift für Zitelmann*, 1913), wrong as far as the *condictio* is concerned; Beseler, *Beiträge*, iv (1920), 309 ff.; Biondi, l.c. 710 ff.; Giffard, 'L'actio civilis incerti et la donation avec charges dans le droit classique', *ACI* 1933, Roma, ii (1935), 135 ff.

s. 975. Bachofen, *Ausgewählte Lehren des röm. Civilrechts*, I. *Das vellejanische Senatskonsult* (1848); Windscheid, *Pand.* ii (1906), § 485; Lenel, *Edict.* (1927), § 105; *Index interp.* ad *D.* 16. 1; Beseler, Z lxvi (1948), 601. On the date of the *senatusconsultum* see Hülsen, *Mitteilungen des archäolog. Instituts*, xix (1904), 324; Hohl, *PW* x, 1099 f.; Kübler, in Mommsen, *Schr.* iii. 29 note. Still for A.D. 46 O'Brien Moore, *Suppl.* vi, *PW*, 810. On modern Roman law see Lee, *An Introduction to Roman Dutch Law* (3rd ed. 1946), 315 f.; Stobbe–Lehmann, *Handbuch des deutschen Privatrechts*, iii (1898), 378 ff.; Brissaud, *Manuel d'Histoire du droit Français* (1898), 1140 ff.

CHAPTER II

LAW OF DELICTS

1. *Introduction*

976.
Conception of delictum and obligatio ex delicto
IN the legal language of the dominant classical lawyers *delictum* meant an offence from which resulted *iure civili* a penal obligation (*obligatio ex delicto*) and a penal action (*civilis actio poenalis*). Instead of *delictum* the lawyers used sometimes the term *maleficium*. We have already described above (ss. 72 ff.) the general character of a penal action and may ask the reader to read again our earlier remarks.

Thus *delictum* (*maleficium*) and *obligatio ex delicto* were confined to *ius civile*. There were honorarian penal actions, e.g. the *actio de dolo*, but with respect to them these terms were avoided.

Crimen was used by the classical lawyers to designate an offence which was punished by public criminal law.

This was the terminology of the leading classical lawyers and perhaps also of the imperial chancery. Gaius, however, who was not one of the dominant lawyers, went his own way. We have already pointed out above (s. 789) that he designated certain praetorian penal actions, though not all, as *obligationes ex delicto*. Apparently he did not find followers during the classical period, but the post-classical lawyers caught up his idea and developed it further; the fusion of *ius civile* with *ius honorarium* led them to apply the classical terms in principle to all honorarian penal actions. *Crimen* was now also used to designate offences from which resulted penal actions.

In this book we will ignore the classical terminology and adopt the post-classical usage, for we want terms which cover both *ius civile* and *ius honorarium* (above, s. 790). For that reason we define delict as follows: *Delictum* was an offence from which resulted a penal obligation and a penal action, either *iure civili* or *iure honorario*.

The classical penal actions afforded a powerful protection
for material and immaterial interests (above, s. 78); nevertheless, the wide scope of these actions comes as a surprise
to us. Within the civilization, and particularly legal civilization, of the classical period they seem to us very primitive
and old-fashioned, for we hold today that it is on principle
the duty of the State to punish its subjects and that private
law should be confined to actions for damages; a private
penal action seems justified only for the protection of immaterial interests (*actio iniuriarum*). However, Roman public
criminal law at the end of the Republic was still far below
the standard of civil law; two centuries of revolution and
war had paralysed the administrative activity and had prevented the development of criminal law; the statutes of
quaestiones were insufficient. Thus the penal actions served
as a supplement to the unsatisfactory criminal law.

977.
Function
and dis-
appearance
of the
classical
penal
actions

> See Pollock and Maitland, *History*, ii (1911), 522: 'Under Edward I
> a favourite device of our legislators is that of giving double or treble
> damages to "the party grieved". They have little faith in "communal
> accusation" or in any procedure that expects either royal officials or
> people in general to be active in bringing malefactors to justice. More
> was to be hoped from the man who had suffered. He would move if they
> made it worth his while. And so in a characteristically English fashion
> punishment was to be inflicted in the course of civil actions: it took the
> form of manyfold reparation.' This is also a good description of the legal
> situation in Rome at the end of the Republic.

Under the Principate, criminal justice was administered
more promptly, but the private penal actions remained
unaltered; they were codified in Hadrian's Edict and were
in force throughout the whole classical period. Most probably the competing criminal procedure in which the judge
was also entitled to award damages to the offended came in
practice to supersede gradually the private penal actions,
particularly in the provinces; but the classical lawyers in
Rome as usual took no notice of this development and continued to discuss eagerly the law of penal actions as if it were
still living law. The post-classical history of the penal
actions is still obscure; not even Justinian's law has been
fully analysed. But this much is clear: the penal actions
were not abolished by Justinian. A long title of the *Digest*

was, for instance, devoted to the *actio furti* (*D.* 47. 2), though in the last text of that title the compilers confessed that 'today the offended party preferred to apply to the criminal court', *meminisse oportebit nunc furti plerumque criminaliter agi*. It is also certain that the compilers have by numerous interpolations minimized the penal element of the penal actions, in particular by restricting the principle of cumulation (above, s. 73). In modern Roman law the penal actions gradually developed into mere actions for compensation; in England they served as a model to the legislators under Edward I.

978. Scope of this book   It is not our intention to give a full survey of the numerous and widely varying penal actions. We will select a few which are of more general importance and illustrate by these examples the character of the classical penal actions and the tendencies of Justinian's compilers.

SOURCES

s. 976. Read Gai. 3. 88; 3. 182. Compare Gai. 4. 182 with *Inst. Iust.* (4. 16) 2: the compilers have added the *actio de dolo* which Gaius had deliberately omitted since it was a purely praetorian remedy without any basis in *ius civile*. Read further *D.* (44. 7) 1 pr.

BIBLIOGRAPHY

s. 976. Albertario, *Delictum e crimen nel diritto romano classico e nella legislazione Giustinianea* (1924) = *Studi*, iii (1936), 143 ff. with references; *Maleficium, St. Perozzi* (1925) = *Studi*, iii (1936), 199; De Visscher, 'Les Origines de l'obligation ex delicto', *RH* vii (1928), 335 ff. = *Études de droit Romain* (1931), 255 ff. See further literature on the conception of *obligatio*, above, ss. 785 ff. Bibliography. On the verb *delinquere* see Volterra, 'Delinquere nelle fonti giuridiche romane', *Riv. It.* v (1930); on *flagitium* see Volterra, 'Flagitium nelle fonti giuridiche romane', *AG* cxi (1934), 39 ff.*

s. 977. On penal actions in modern Roman law see Windscheid, *Pand.* ii (1906), § 326 n. 5; Stobbe–Lehmann, *Handbuch des deutschen Privatrechts*, iii (1898), 503 ff.; Gierke, *DP* iii (1917), 881. On English law see Pollock and Maitland ii. 522, but Maitland's scepticism about the Roman influence is hardly justified.

2. *Furtum* (*theft*)

i. *Conception*

979. No definition   We are accustomed to render *furtum* by 'theft' and we may safely continue to do so provided we keep in mind that the Roman *furtum* differed very greatly from modern theft. The classical conception of *furtum* was an artificial and unhappy creation of republican and classical jurisprudence, it covers cases so widely different that an accurate and intelligible definition by means of an abstract formula can hardly be given. We must confine ourselves to a consideration of the typical cases.

1. The original case of *furtum* which always remained the principal is revealed by its etymology. *Fur*, like the Greek φώρ, derived from *fero* (φέρω) and meant a man who asportated a movable thing which was in the possession or detention (above, s. 754) of another person. *Furtum* covered both the act of stealing and the stolen object. Persons in power were also possible objects of *furtum*, so that this first case embraced any asportation of objects which were in the possession, detention, or power of another person. Hence one might even steal one's own thing (*furtum rei suae*). The pledgee, for example, was *possessor* of the pledge (above, s. 753); if the pledgor unlawfully deprived the pledgee of his possession, he was liable for *furtum* (Gai. 3. 200). 980. Asportation

2. As early as the second century B.C. the practice of the law-courts had extended the original conception of *furtum* without regard to the natural meaning of the term. If somebody entrusted a thing to another person (*depositum* or *commodatum*) and the latter used it in a manner contrary to the agreement, he was held liable for theft. Q. Mucius Scaevola (†82 B.C.) asserts: 981. Unlawful use

> 'Quod cui servandum datum est (depositum), si id usus est, sive quod utendum accepit (commodatum) ad aliam rem atque accepit usus est, furti se obligavit.'

Hence, if a depositary used the deposited thing, he committed *furtum*, since he was not entitled to use the thing. If a commodatary used the thing in a manner contrary to the contract, he was also liable for *furtum*. If the pledgee used the pledge or alienated it without being authorized to do so by a *pactum de vendendo* (above, s. 724), he committed *furtum*. In all these cases asportation is of course quite out of the question.

982.
Furtum
without
aggression
against
possession
3. It was not a happy idea on the part of the republican jurists to extend the conception of *furtum* so far beyond the natural sense of the term. The rules were very harsh and were rightly described as such by Labeo (*acria et severa iudicia*). But classical jurisprudence went still farther on that path. In the first century A.D. the boundaries of *furtum* were still fluid. Sabinus advocated a *furtum* of land; he did not succeed, but his attempt shows that the scope of *furtum* was still *sub iudice*. It was perhaps Sabinus who established the rule that the finder of a lost thing committed *furtum* if he took it up in order to appropriate it:

> 'Qui alienum iacens lucri faciendi causa sustulit, furti obstringitur sive scit cuius sit sive nescit.'

Accordingly, a bona fide purchaser who later learnt that he had not acquired ownership committed *furtum* if he alienated the thing. Evidently in these cases *furtum* did not imply an aggression against possession.

983.
Furtum by
receiving
something
4. The jurists of the Principate seem to have acknowledged a fourth case of *furtum*. A gave a movable thing to B under the agreement that B should acquire ownership. For some reason or other the *traditio* was ineffective and B knew that. Then B committed *furtum* by accepting the thing. Thus in the event of an error as to identity the *traditio* was void. A gave a loan of money to B erroneously assuming that B was C. If B knew of that error, he committed *furtum* by receiving the money. Further, *furtum fit cum quis indebitos nummos sciens acceperit*. A gave B 100, erroneously believing that he owed that sum to B. If B knew that A owed nothing to him; the *traditio* was void and he committed a *furtum* by accepting the money.

983a.
Alienation
of a
hypothec
by the
mortgagor
4a. Somebody had given a movable as hypothec; later he alienated the object to a third person without the creditor's permission. This is regarded as *furtum* in three *Digest* texts. (1) *D*. (47. 2) 6 pr. The words [*sive . . . obligaverat*] are obviously interpolated. (2) *D*. (47. 2) 19. 6. The text looks odd and cannot be genuine. Huvelin, *Études sur le furtum* (1915), 560. (3) *D*. (47. 2) 62. 8. A *colonus* mortgaged the fruits to his landlord; later he carried the fruits away from the land without the landlord's permission. Julian might have granted the *actio furti* against the tenant who had deprived the landlord of the *interdictum Salvianum* which lay only against the tenant (above, s. 749).

5. Fraud was not *furtum*; here the *actio de dolo* was the proper action and not the *actio furti*. But whenever fraud led to such a situation as is described under no. 4, the trickster was liable on the *actio furti* as an accomplice (*furtum ope consilio factum*). 984. Fraud is not furtum

Consider the following case reported by both Ulpian and Paulus, obviously from the same source (*D*. 47. 2, 52. 21, and 67. 4). A capitalist C wished to invest a certain sum of money by lending it to a person of good credit. He applied to Seius who recommended to him Titius. C made inquiries and learnt that Titius was indeed a man of substance. Now Seius brought Sempronius to C pretending that Sempronius was Titius. C gave the money to Sempronius, who knew of the fraud. Obviously this is a case falling under no. 4, since C acted under an error as to identity. Consequently Sempronius committed *furtum* by accepting the money, but Seius too was liable on the *actio furti* as an accomplice. If Sempronius knew nothing of the fraud, C had only an *actio de dolo* against Seius.

The text of Mela's famous decision (*D*. 47. 2, 52. 22) must be corrupt; the proper action was the *actio de dolo* (compare *D*. 4. 3, 18. 3).

6. To destroy a thing or to cause it to deteriorate never amounts to *furtum*; here the *actio legis Aquiliae* (*directa* or *in factum*) was the proper action. Conflicting texts should be regarded as interpolated. If somebody *dolo malo* caused the loss of a thing without destroying it, he did not commit *furtum*, but he might be liable on the *actio furti* as an accomplice.

985. Destruction not furtum

A had a wild bird in a cage; B opened the cage *dolo malo* and the bird flew away. A had against B the *actio de dolo* or an *actio legis Aquiliae utilis* but not the *actio furti*. Titius had coins in his hands; Seius knocked them out. His accomplice Sempronius then grabbed them and ran away with them. Sempronius committed *furtum* and Seius was liable for *furtum* as an accomplice (*furtum ope consilio factum*).

Surveying these cases in which the lawyers acknowledged *furtum* we recognize at once features common to all of them.

1. The object of *furtum* can only be a movable thing or a person in power. Sabinus, as aforesaid, attempted to extend *furtum* to land, but he did not succeed.

986. Objects

2. The thing must be owned by somebody, though not necessarily by the person robbed.

987. Things in dominio

If somebody caught a wild animal on my estate, he did

not commit *furtum*. Again no *furtum* could be committed of things belonging to a *hereditas iacens*, since they were not *in dominio*; we have already explained above (s. 512) why the lawyers could not abandon this rule.

988.
'Invito domino'
3. The theft must have been committed against the will of the offended party.

989.
Dolus malus and animus furandi
4. The offender must have acted *dolo malo*; there was no such thing as a *furtum culpa commissum*.

> If a finder of a lost thing took it up in order to appropriate it because he believed that it had been abandoned by the owner, he was not a *fur*. Neither did he commit *furtum* if he took it up in order to bring it to the owner.

The post-classical lawyers liked to speak of an *animus furandi* or *adfectus furandi* and these terms intruded into classical texts. Sometimes such interpolations are harmless, viz. when these terms are only used as substitutes for *dolus malus*. But sometimes *animus* (or *adfectus*) *furandi* was distinguished from *dolus malus* and *furtum* was denied for want of *animus furandi* in cases in which the classical lawyers had acknowledged *furtum*. On the other hand, destruction of a thing was termed *furtum* when the offender had acted *animo furandi* (e.g. if he destroyed a legal document).

990.
Lucrum
5. The offender must have acquired something as the direct result of his act. Destruction, as aforesaid, was not *furtum*, but a specific *animus lucri faciendi* was not required. We sometimes meet in classical texts *animus lucri faciendi* or similar expressions. Some of these are interpolated, but when Sabinus in a text given by Gellius says: 'Qui alienum iacens lucri faciendi causa sustulit furti obstringitur', there is nothing objectionable since *lucri faciendi causa* is only a substitute for *dolo malo*.

991.
Furtum not always an inroad on possession
6. *Furtum* is sometimes an offence against possession but not in the cases found in group 2. *Furtum* of a lost thing is certainly not an inroad on possession, and if a bona fide purchaser later learnt that he had not acquired ownership but nevertheless alienated the thing, he committed *furtum*, but without offending against possession. Accordingly no classical lawyer can ever have asserted that *furtum* could not be committed of a thing which was not in possession.

D. (47. 4) 1. 15 cannot be genuine:

'Ulpianus libro XXXVIII ad edictum. Scaevola ait possessionis
furtum fieri [*denique si nullus sit possessor, furtum negat fieri*].' Cervidius
Scaevola (end of the second century A.D.; Q. Mucius Scaevola is quite
out of the question as the preceding § 10 shows) cannot have written
this text; *denique . . . fieri* must be a silly gloss.

7. Apparently Sabinus was the first to use the words
adtrectare and *contrectare* as technical terms. The natural
meaning of these old Latin words was 'to touch', 'to handle',
but Sabinus gave them a particular legal significance. He
sought for a suitable term to designate all acts which were,
or ought to be, recognized as *furtum* and he chose *adtrectare*
and *contrectare*; his choice was generally approved. Of
course those terms, taken in their natural sense, were too
wide: If A rent B's garment, this was certainly 'a handling',
i.e. *contrectare* in the popular sense of the word, but it was
not *contrectare* in the legal sense since destroying or damaging a thing was not regarded as *furtum*. But such a discrepancy between legal and common usage did not disturb
the lawyers. *Contrectatio* was now a legal term of art. On the
one hand, a physical touching was apparently not required
(though we should remember that the *lex Aquilia* applied
only if the damage was done *corpore*; see below, s. 1006);
on the other hand, some sorts of handling (e.g. destroying
a thing) were not *contrectatio* in the legal sense. The question
what is *contrectatio* must be answered as any act which
was regarded as *furtum*. The classical lawyers when dealing
with an individual case never asked whether this was a
handling in the popular sense. They asked rather whether
this was an offence recognized as *furtum*, and, whenever
they answered this question in the affirmative, they called
this act 'a handling' in the legal sense (*contrectatio*).

*992. Con-
trectatio*

ii. *Supposedly classical definitions of furtum*

The classical lawyers had no definition of *furtum*. Masur-
ius Sabinus, who was particularly interested in the doctrine
of *furtum*, did not give a definition; if he had done so, the
Sabinian Gaius would have mentioned it. Gellius believed

*993.
Sabinus*

that he had found two definitions in Sabinus' *libri iuris civilis*:

> Gellius 11. 18, 19–21: 'Quam caste autem ac religiose a prudentissimis viris quid esset furtum definitum sit, praetereundum non puto, ne quis eum solum esse furem putet, qui occulte tollit aut clam subripit. Verba sunt Sabini ex libro iuris civilis secundo: Qui alienam rem adtrectavit, cum id se invito domino iudicare deberet, furti tenetur. Item alio capite: Qui alienum iacens lucri faciendi causa sustulit, furti obstringitur, sive scit cuius sit, sive nescit.'

In fact these were not definitions as the non-lawyer Gellius erroneously believed, but rather *dicta* propounded in the sententious style in which Sabinus wrote his elementary textbook. Gellius has detached them from the context, so that they now look like definitions.

> The first so-called definition refers only to cases in which a thing was unlawfully used by a person to whom it was entrusted (depositary, commodatary, lessee, pledgee; above, group 2); Gaius 2. 195, 196 makes that quite clear. In this connexion Sabinus' words are perfectly correct; if taken as a definition of *furtum* in general the word *alienam* would be wrong, since there was such a thing as *furtum rei suae* (Gai. 3. 200). The word *rem* would also be incorrect, since there was a *furtum* of free persons in power (Gai. 3. 199).
>
> The second 'definition' obviously refers only to the case of a finder of a lost thing who appropriated it.

994. Certainly *D.* (47. 2) 1. 3 was meant by the compilers to
D. (47. 2) serve as a definition, but the text was manufactured by the
1. 3 compilers and not by Paulus to whom it is attributed.

> *D.* (47. 2) 1. 3: 'Paulus libro XXXIX ad edictum. Furtum est contrectatio fraudulosa lucri faciendi gratia vel ipsius rei vel etiam usus eius possessionisve.'
>
> In the whole of Latin literature *fraudulosus* occurs only in this text, as the *Thesaurus Linguae Latinae* irrefutably proves. Since the classical lawyers strictly refrained from employing unusual words, we may be sure that Paulus did not write it. Nor can Paul have written the clumsy expression *vel ipsius . . . possessionisve*. They depend on *lucri*, but *lucrum facere rei vel usus possessionisve* is hardly Latin; *lucrum facere ex re* or *lucri facere rem* would be correct. In any case the trichotomy which is generally given in text-books—(1) *furtum rei*; (2) *furtum usus* (e.g. a depositary using the deposited thing); (3) *furtum possessionis* (e.g. the pledger stealing the pledge)—is unclassical and misleading. The classical lawyers knew only a *furtum rei*. When a depositary used the deposited thing, this was *furtum rei*; the thing became *res furtiva* and

the *actio furti* lay for double the value of the thing. Students should ignore the trichotomy altogether; it occurs only in this text.

The classical lawyers had no definition of *furtum*. Reading the long texts in the *Digest* title *de furtis* one realizes at once that they were discussing particular cases and not illustrating a definition.

iii. *Actions resulting from furtum*

Classical law knew many such actions; they were all registered in Hadrian's Edict, but not all in the title *de furtis*. We are content to give a list of these actions with reference to Lenel's *Edict* (1927) and will discuss only those which are of general importance, viz. the *actio furti nec manifesti*, the *actio furti manifesti*, and the *actio vi bonorum raptorum*.

995. Survey

List of the classical actiones ex furto

1. Actio furti nec manifesti. Lenel, pp. 322, 324.
2. Actio furti concepti. Lenel, p. 322.
3. Actio furti oblati. Lenel, p. 322.
4. Actio de tigno iuncto. Lenel, pp. 322, 330.
5. Actio furti manifesti. Lenel, pp. 322, 332.
6. Actio furti prohibiti. Lenel, p. 323.
7. Actio furti non exhibiti. Lenel, p. 323.
8. Actio furti adversus nautas caupones stabularios. Lenel, p. 333.
9. Si familia furtum fecisse dicetur. Lenel, p. 355.
10. Quod familia publicanorum furtum fecisse dicetur. Lenel, p. 335.
11. Actio vi bonorum raptorum. Lenel, pp. 391, 394.
12. De incendio ruina naufragio rate nave expugnata. Lenel, p. 396.
13. Quod publicanus vi ademerit. Lenel, p. 387.

1. *Actio furti nec* (= *non*; above, s. 605) *manifesti*. This action was available in all cases of *furtum*. It was a civil action founded on the Twelve Tables for double the value of the stolen object. The *formula*, which was of course *in ius concepta* (above, s. 47), is partly preserved by Gaius and has been reconstructed by Lenel. Condemnation involved *infamia*.

996. Actio furti nec manifesti

2. *Actio furti manifesti*. It was a praetorian action for four times the value of the object. The *formula*, which was of course *in factum concepta* (above, s. 47), is not preserved. Condemnation involved *infamia*.

997. Actio furti manifesti

Furtum manifestum meant a theft which is evident, in the legal sense a theft in which the thief was caught in the act of stealing. The exact meaning of the term was still disputed in Gaius' time, but we will not dwell on these rather dull discussions.

Manifestus means in common Latin usage 'manifest', 'evident'; the etymology is quite obscure: Rabel, Z lii (1932), 473 f.

Under the Twelve Tables the penalty was much more severe. A free *fur manifestus* was beaten and assigned for life by the magistrate to the person from whom he had stolen (*addictio*); a slave was beaten and put to death. This law was still in force in the second century B.C., for when the elder Cato said in a speech (Gellius, 11. 18. 18) 'fures privatorum furtorum in nervis atque compedibus aetatem agunt', he must have had in mind the *addictio*. But in the second or first century B.C. the praetor declined to apply this severe penalty and substituted for it the *actio furti manifesti*. This was one result of the republican humanistic movement (above, ss. 180 ff.). It has recently been asserted that the action came much later, viz. in the first decades of the Principate, but this is hardly possible; it cannot be later than the *actio vi bonorum raptorum*, as we shall presently see. In any case the action was known to Sabinus.

998. Actio vi bonorum raptorum 3. The *actio vi bonorum raptorum* was a praetorian action for four times the value of the object (after a year for the simple value) and lay in cases of robbery 'si dolo malo hominibus armatis coactisve (see above, s. 779) . . . cuius bona vi rapta esse dicentur'. The *formula* was *in factum concepta*; condemnation involved *infamia*.

The action was introduced by the praetor M. Terentius Varro Lucullus in 76 B.C. At that time the *actio furti manifesti* must already have existed; otherwise the robber (*fur improbior*) would have been in a better position than a simple *fur manifestus*. Lucullus knew the *actio furti manifesti* and applied it in cases of robbery; a special action was required since the robber, not being taken in the act of stealing, was not a *fur manifestus*.

999. Evaluation 4. The distinction between *furtum manifestum* and *nec manifestum* is a primitive one since there is no difference in

guilt between the two cases; the *fur nec manifestus* was sometimes even the more dangerous man as he perpetrated the
theft without being taken. However, the distinction, which
we also meet in other primitive systems, is far from being
enigmatical. Primitive law is scrupulous concerning evidence. In the eyes of a primitive judge theft was fully
proven only if the thief was caught in the act of stealing;
only then was the theft manifest and the infliction of the
severest penalty justified. Of course in classical times the
distinction was an anachronism; nevertheless it was preserved even in Justinian's law.

After the introduction of the *actio furti manifesti* thieves
were no longer subject to the death penalty in republican
law. Graver cases fell under public criminal law, but here
too the death penalty was not inflicted; even under the
criminal law of the Principate the death penalty applied but
rarely: a characteristic feature of Roman *humanitas*. In
modern European systems the death penalty for theft was
only abolished in the course of the eighteenth and nineteenth centuries.

5. The *actio furti* (*manifesti* and *nec manifesti*) was, according to the republican rule, available to anybody who had an
interest in the safety of the thing: 'furti actio ei competit,
cuius interest rem salvam esse licet dominus non sit' (Gai.
3. 203). But the classical lawyers considerably restricted
the application of this maxim by interpretation. Though
they did not substitute another abstract maxim for that of
republican law they did in fact observe the following rules
in their discussion of cases:

(*a*) On principle the owner was entitled to the *actio furti*.
This is self-evident.

(*b*) Whenever a person was liable for *custodia* and thereby
for the loss of the thing by theft, he and he alone was
entitled to the *actio furti*, provided he was solvent.

1000.
Who was
entitled to
the actio
furti?

The commodatary, for instance, was liable for *custodia* (above, s. 885).
If the borrowed thing was stolen by a third person, the commodatary
was entitled to the *actio furti*, provided that he was solvent (otherwise
the *commodator* had the action) and the lender had only the *actio commodati* against the commodatary. Suppose the value of the borrowed

thing was 50. The lender could obtain 50 from the commodatary since the latter was solvent and, on the strength of his liability for *custodia*, unconditionally responsible for the loss by theft. The commodatary could claim 100 from the *fur nec manifestus* and 200 from the *fur manifestus*. The surplus over 50 was the premium for the commodatary's risk.

The creditor C had received a pledge (value 100) for a claim of 20. The pledgee was liable for *custodia* (above, s. 885). When the pledge was stolen by F, the pledgee had the *actio furti* for 200 (in case of *furtum nec manifestum*) and was bound to pay 100 to the pledgor (*actio pigneraticia*; above, s. 900).

(*c*) In cases of *furtum rei suae*, the person from whom the thing was stolen had the *actio furti* against the owner. When the pledgor stole the pledge from the pledgee, the latter had the *actio furti* against the owner. It is doubtful whether these three rules cover all cases of the *actio furti*; one may dispute over the cases in which a man was liable for *custodia*. But the three rules themselves should no longer be contested. They were in any case the principles which guided the classical lawyers. The compilers, who reduced the classical liability for *custodia* to a mere liability for *diligentia in custodiendo*, had to modify those classical rules. Taking the republican maxim *actio furti ei competit cuius interest* in its literal sense they interpolated the classical texts ruthlessly and carelessly. The result was the appalling confusion evident in our sources, particularly in the *Digest* title *de furtis*. It is, therefore, small wonder that the classical rules given above are still disputed, particularly as some of the study devoted to the question has been uncritical. This is not the place to examine again the difficult texts; nor are we concerned with elaborating Justinian's law.

1001.
Who was entitled to the actio vi bonorum raptorum?
6. Who was entitled to the *actio vi bonorum raptorum*? The rules concerning the *actio furti* did not apply, since liability for *custodia* did not include liability for loss by robbery (above, s. 885). Hence only the owner (*iure civili* or *iure praetorio*; above, s. 655) appears to have been entitled to this action. However the relevant texts are few and corrupt.

1002. Penal character of the actio furti
7. The *actio furti* (*manifesti* and *nec manifesti*) was a pure penal action subject to the general rules which we have expounded above (ss. 72 ff.). In particular the action

expired with the death of the thief and the principle of cumulation applied. When two thieves had co-operated, an *actio furti* lay against each of them, so that in the case of a *furtum nec manifestum* the man from whom the thing was stolen obtained double the value twice over. We hardly need emphasize that this is not solidarity (above, s. 827) but cumulation, though the sources speak quite rightly of *in solidum teneri*. If one person perpetrated a *furtum manifestum* and another had acted as an accomplice (*ope consilio*), the *actio furti manifesti* lay against the thief and the *actio furti nec manifesti* against the accomplice, so that the person from whom the thing was stolen obtained in all the fourfold value plus double the value. Further, *the actio furti* and any *actio rem persequens* (above, s. 734) could be cumulated. Thus the offended person had the *actio furti* against the thief and in addition the *rei vindicatio* against the *possessor*, who might of course be the thief himself. These rules remained unaltered throughout the whole post-classical period and were even preserved by Justinian.

8. The classical *actio vi bonorum raptorum* was also a pure penal action and no classical lawyer can have ever contested that. Gai. 4. 8 must be interpolated.

1003. Penal character of the actio vi bonorum raptorum

Gai. 4. 8: 'Poenam tantum persequimur velut actione furti [et iniuriarum et secundum quorundam opinionem actione vi bonorum raptorum]; nam ipsius rei et vindicatio et condictio nobis competit.'

This is the only text in which we meet any doubt about the penal character of the *actio vi bonorum raptorum* and for that reason alone the text is suspect. Gaius has no doubt on the matter in *D*. (47. 8) 5. The words *et iniuriarum . . . raptorum* must be a gloss; the interpolation is revealed by the sentence which follows it and which is not applicable to the *actio iniuriarum*.

Justinian's compilers have scaled down the penal character of the *actio vi bonorum raptorum in quadruplum*. This action was now an *actio mixta*.

Inst. Iust. (4. 2) pr.: 'Quadruplum autem non totum poena est et extra poenam rei persecutio, sicut in actione furti manifesti diximus; sed in quadruplo inest et rei persecutio, ut poena tripli sit.'

Perhaps this was already the law before Justinian or, at least, was advocated by pre-Justinianic lawyers; the interpolation in Gai. 4. 8 would then be explained.

SOURCES

s. 980. Read Gai. 3. 195, 199, 200; *D*. (47. 2) 15. 1; 20. 1.

s. 981. Read Gellius 6. 15. 2 = Seckel–Kübler, i. 17 = Jolowicz, *Digest*, xlvii, 2, p. 131; Gai. 3. 195, 196.

s. 982. Read Gellius 6 (7). 15. 1 = Jolowicz, l.c.; Gellius 11. 18. 13 = Seckel–Kübler, i. 74 = Jolowicz, 132; *D*. (47. 2) 25 pr.; Gellius 11. 18. 21 = Seckel–Kübler, i. 73 = Jolowicz, 133; Gai. 2. 50.

s. 983. Read *D*. (13. 1) 18, first sentence; (47. 2) 43 pr.; 52. 21; 67. 4.

s. 984. Read *D*. (47. 2) 52. 21; 67. 4; 52. 15; 43. 3 (substantially genuine).

s. 985. Read *D*. (47. 2) 31 pr. (genuine); (47. 2) 58 (substantially genuine); (9. 2) 27. 21, cf. Gai. 3. 202; *D*. (47. 2) 22 pr. [*quod ... contrectaverit*]; *D*. (47. 2) 27. 3 [*tantum*]; [*etiam*]; *D*. (19. 5) 14. 2 [*damni dandi ... faciendi*]; (4. 3) 7. 7 [*si non ... misericordia*]; (41. 1) 55, last sentence (*summam* etc.), substantially classical.

s. 989. Read Paul. *Sent*. (2. 31) 1. Compare Gai. 3. 197 with *Inst. Iust*. (4. 1) 7. Read *D*. (47. 2) 25. 2 [*furandi animo*]; (47. 2) 39 compared with Paul. *Sent*. (2. 31) 12 and 31; *D*. (47. 2) 83. 2; (47. 2) 22 pr. [*quod ... contrectaverit*]; (9. 2) 41. 1 (interpolated); (47. 2) 46. 7 (substantially classical); (47. 2) 43. 6. Sabinus (Gellius 11. 18. 20) *iudicare deberet* instead of *sciret* is inaccurate.

s. 990. *D*. (47. 2) 55. 1 (substantially classical); (19. 5) 14. 2 [*damni dandi ... faciendi*].

s. 996. Read Gai. 3. 190; 4. 182.

s. 997. Read Gai. 3. 184, 189; Gellius 11. 18. 6–8 = Jolowicz, p. 132.

s. 998. Read Gai. 3. 209; 4. 182.

s. 1000. Read Gai. 3. 203–7; *Coll*. (10. 2) 6; *D*. (47. 2) 15 pr. [sed praestabit]; (47. 2) 88 (genuine).

s. 1002. Read *D*. (47. 4) 1. 19; *C*. (4. 8) 1; Gai. 4. 8; *D*. (47. 2) 55. 3; Paul. *Sent*. (2. 31) 13; *C*. (6. 2) 12; (3. 41) 5.

BIBLIOGRAPHY

ss. 979 ff. Hitzig, *PW* vii. 384; Ferrini, *Opere*, v (1930), 107 ff., 129 ff.; P. W. Huvelin, *Études sur le furtum dans le très ancien droit romain*, i (1915); *NRH* xlii (1918), 73 ff.; Buckland, '*D*. 47. 2 (de furtis) and the Methods of the Compilers', *T* x (1930), 117 ff.; Daube, 'Furtum proprium and furtum improprium', *The Cambridge Law Journal*, vi (1938), 217 ff.; Jolowicz, *Digest XLVII, 2 De furtis* (1940) with a valuable introduction, pp. i–xci; Kaser, *Altröm. Jus* (1949), 213 ff.; see further *Index Interpolationum* ad *D*. 47. 2, with references.*

ss. 981, 982. For texts see Windscheid, *Pand*. ii (1906), § 452 nn. 8–10.

s. 983. F. Fitting, *Sciens indebitum accipere* (Thèse Lausanne, 1926). For texts see Windscheid, l.c. § 426 n. 16; § 427 n. 4; § 452 n. 8; for literature on these texts see *Index Interp*.

s. 989. Albertario, 'Animus furandi', *Studi*, iii (1936), 209 ff. with references.

s. 990. Huvelin, 'L'animus lucri faciendi dans la théorie romaine du vol', *NRH* xlii (1918), 73 ff.

s. 992. Buckland, 'Contrectatio', *LQR* lvii (1941), 467 ff.

s. 994. Schirmer, Z v (1884), 207 ff.; Albertario, *SD* ii (1936), 160.

s. 996. Lenel, *Edict*. (1927), 324; Kaser, *Quanti ea res est* (1935), 132 ff.

s. 997. Lenel, 332; Kaser, 132 ff., 138; Wlassak Z xxv (1904), 95 ff.; De Visscher, 'Le fur manifestus', *RH* xlvi (1922), 442 ff. = *Études de droit Rom*. (1931), 137 ff.; Arangio-Ruiz, 'La répression du vol flagrant et du vol non flagrant dans l'ancien droit romain', *Rariora* (1946), 197 ff. with references. On the date of the *actio furti manifesti* see Huvelin, *Études*, 657.

s. 998. Lenel, *Edict*. § 187, p. 394; Mommsen, *Röm. Strafrecht* (1899), 654 f.; E. Levy, *Die Konkurrenz der Aktionen*, i (1918), 429; Schulz, Z xliii (1922), 219.

s. 1000. Schulz, 'Die Aktivlegitimation zur actio furti', Z xxxii (1911), 23. This paper needs revision, since its author almost forty years ago was much too conservative; Beseler, who in the main accepted it, has corrected the theory by many clever remarks (see *Index Interp*. on the relevant texts). See further Kaser, l.c. 147 ff.; Jolowicz, l.c. pp. xxviii f. (too conservative) and the literature on *custodia* above, s. 885, Bibliography.*

s. 1002. Levy, l.c. 480 ff., 416 ff.

s. 1003. Levy, 429 ff.; Beseler, Z xlvii (1927), 65; *Scritti Ferrini*, iii (1948), 283; P. Voci, *Risarcimento e pena privata* (1939), 94 ff.

3. *Damnum iniuria datum* (*Loss caused by injury to things*)

i. *Lex Aquilia*

1. The basis of the classical law was the *lex Aquilia*, a *plebiscitum* of unknown date, but most probably of the third century B.C. The text is only preserved to us in a mutilated form by Justinian's *Digest*, but we possess Gaius' description of the classical law (3. 210 ff.). Here of course we are only concerned with the classical law and not with the form and the original meaning of the old statute. *1004. Date and transmission*

2. The statute contained three chapters. The second chapter dealt with *adstipulatio* and granted an action against an *adstipulator* who fraudulently released the debtor. We have already mentioned this chapter, which was still in force in classical times (above, s. 837), and will ignore it at this point. The first and third chapters dealt with loss which *1005. Content of the statute*

the owner of a corporeal thing suffered through injuries inflicted on the thing by other persons. If somebody killed a slave or a four-footed beast in the class of *pecudes* (*quadrupes pecus*, cattle), he was liable to the owner for the highest value which the thing had had within the year previous to the injury (chapter i). If somebody caused any other loss by burning, breaking, or rending a thing (*urere*, *frangere*, *rumpere*), the owner might claim the highest value (according to the classical interpretation) which the thing had had within the previous thirty days (chapter iii). The statute provided further that in any case the action should be classed among those *in quibus lis infitiando crescit in duplum* (above, s. 74).

1006. Classical interpretation 3. These were the rather primitive provisions of the statute which both republican and classical jurisprudence interpreted rather strictly, always anxious not to deviate too far from its wording.

(*a*) If the third chapter was originally only concerned with animate things, it was later extended to inanimate things (Gai. 3. 217). Further, the lawyers took the term *rumpere* as equivalent to *corrumpere* (to spoil), so that now any loss caused by the destruction or damaging of a thing might fall under the statute (Gai. 3. 217). On the other hand, the lawyers insisted on the primitive requirement of direct causation; the offender must have established direct connexion between the thing and his body, or as Gaius (3. 219) puts it:

'Placuit ita demum ex ista lege actionem esse, si quis corpore suo damnum dederit' (the usual but unclassical and misleading formula *damnum corpore corpori datum* should be abandoned).

A decision of Labeo reported and approved by Ulpian is particularly instructive (*D*. 9. 2. 9 pr.): A midwife gave some medicine to a female slave and thereby caused the death of the slave. Labeo made the following distinction. If the midwife had administered the medicine with her own hands to the patient, the statute applied; but if the midwife gave the medicine to the patient and the latter administered it to herself, the *actio legis Aquiliae* did not lie.

(*b*) The first chapter spoke of *iniuria occidere*; and the third chapter of *urere, frangere, rumpere iniuria*. The lawyers took *iniuria* not only as meaning 'unlawful, contrary to the law' but as implying the existence of *culpa*; they required in the case of both chapters that the injury should be done either wilfully (*dolo*) or by negligence (*culpa*).

(*c*) As regards the value of the injured thing the lawyers regarded as relevant that value which the thing might have had for any possible owner, not the value which it had for its actual owner. The compilers, however, abandoned that rule and substituted the interest of the actual owner. Their principle is given in

> *D.* (9. 2) 21. 2: 'Sed utrum corpus eius solum aestimamus, quanti fuerit cum occideretur, an potius quanti interfuit nostra non esse occisum? Et hoc iure utimur, ut eius quod interest fiat aestimatio.'

ii. *Actio legis Aquiliae*

1. This action was only available to the owner of the injured thing; the statute expressly attributed it to the *erus* and the lawyers stuck to the wording. Thus the doctrine of *custodia* was not relevant here and the problems which we have met concerning the *actio furti* (above, s. 1000) did not arise. _{1007. Ero competit}

> *Erus* is the old Latin term for *dominus* and was used by the statute: *D.* (9. 2) 11. 6, cf. *Thes. Linguae Lat.* v. 848. The compilers substituted *dominus* for *erus* in *D.* (9. 2) 2. 1 and (9. 2) 27. 5.

2. The classical *actio legis Aquiliae* was a penal action (Gai. 4. 112) and not an action for indemnification. To be sure, the amount of the fine was only the simple value of the injured thing (though the highest value within a certain period, within the previous year according to chapter i, within the previous thirty days according to chapter iii), but that does not render the *actio legis Aquiliae* an action for indemnification (see above, s. 72); the *actio de dolo* was also an *actio in simplum* but was nevertheless a penal action. _{1008. Penal action}

3. The classical action was a *pure* penal action and not an *actio rem et poenam persequens* as is said in Gai. 4. 9. The whole sentence [*quod . . . sunt*] has been added by a man who had in mind Gai. 4. 171. It is true that the *actio legis* _{1009. Pure penal action}

Aquiliae was an *actio qua lis infitiando crescit in duplum*; as
the action itself was a penal action, it might be called an
actio poenam et poenam (per infitiationem) persequens but never
an *actio rem et poenam persequens*. Justinian described the
actio legis Aquiliae as an *actio mixta* (*Inst. Iust.* 4. 6. 19) not
only because *lis infitiando crescit in duplum*, but also because
the offender had to pay the highest value which the injured
thing had within a certain period and not the value at the
time when the injury was done. This idea was quite foreign
to the classical lawyers, who simply styled the action a pure
penal action (Gai. 4. 112).

1010.   4. The penal character of the classical *actio legis Aquiliae*
Conse-   is revealed by the following rules.
quences of
the penal   (*a*) If a thing only suffered deterioration and was not
character completely destroyed, the offender had to pay the full value
of the thing. This rule cannot come as a surprise to anybody
who keeps in mind the penal character of the action. Thus
the penalty was the same when a dog (which did not rank
among *pecudes*) was killed and when he was only wounded.
It is of course primitive not to distinguish between the
two cases, but the old statute shows primitive features
throughout.

(*b*) As a penal action the *actio legis Aquiliae* was not
passively transmissible, and therefore was extinguished
with the offender's death.

(*c*) In the event of a plurality of offenders the principle of
cumulation applied; each of them was liable for the full
fine, and if one of them paid it, the other did not become
free.

(*d*) The *actio legis Aquiliae* and a competing action resulting from contract were also cumulated. Thus if a commodatary injured the borrowed object, two actions lay against
him: (1) the *actio commodati* (an *actio rem persequens*); (2) the
penal *actio legis Aquiliae*. Both actions were cumulated, the
inevitable consequence of the penal nature of the *actio legis
Aquiliae*. Justinian, however, abandoned this sort of cumulation; under Justinian's law the plaintiff must be content
with one of the two actions. All texts within the *Corpus
iuris* in which we meet this 'elective concurrence' are inter-

polated. But the compilers were not the first to tone down the penal character of the *actio legis Aquiliae* in this way: we find the elective concurrence in the pre-Justinianic *Collatio legum Mosaicarum et Romanarum* (12. 7. 9), but the interpolation of this text has long been recognized.

5. The *formula* of the *actio legis Aquiliae* is not preserved; it was of course *in ius concepta*.

iii. *Actio legis Aquiliae utilis*

1. Owing to the rigid interpretation of the statute the *actio legis Aquiliae* did not lie whenever there was no *damnum corpore datum* (above, s. 1006). But in such cases the lawyers, even in republican times, advocated an *actio utilis*, and in the classical period the praetor apparently granted such an action as a matter of course in all cases of *causam mortis praestare* and *causam damni praestare* which did not fall under the statute. The *actio utilis* was of course a penal action like the *actio directa*, but had, in contrast to the *actio directa*, a *formula in factum concepta*. It remains doubtful whether the term *actio in factum* which we find frequently in the *Digest* title 9. 2 as a substitute for *actio utilis* is classical (above, s. 51).

1011.
Actio utilis

2. As a rule the *actio utilis* like the *actio directa* was only available to the owner of the injured thing, but in classical times it was granted exceptionally to a non-owner (the usufructuary, the pledgee, and the *bonae fidei possessor*), but apparently only if the owner himself did the injury. It is, however, hardly credible that an *actio utilis* was ever granted in classical times when a free person had suffered injury. These and other details remain more or less obscure. The compilers of the *Digest* title 9. 2 have so drastically shortened and interpolated the classical discussions on the *actio utilis* that it is not possible to clear up all details.

iv. *Other classical actions resulting from damnum iniuria datum*

1012.
Other
actions

Besides these *actiones legis Aquiliae* the classical law recognized other actions resulting from injuries to property. Lucullus' Edict, for instance (above, s. 998), covered not only *rapina* but also *damnum iniuria datum*: 'si cui dolo malo

hominibus armatis coactisve damni quid factum esse dicetur sive cuius bona vi rapta esse dicentur'. The action for
forcible injuries to things was an *actio in quadruplum* during
the first year like the *actio vi bonorum raptorum* (above,
s. 998), after that year *in simplum*. We will not dwell further
on these actions, but only give a survey with references to
Lenel's *Edict*.

1. Actio de deiectis vel effusis. Lenel, § 61.
2. Actio de pauperie. Lenel, § 75.
3. Actio de pastu pecoris.
4. Actio in factum adversus nautas caupones stabularios. Lenel, § 78.
5. De vi turba incendio ruina naufragio rate nave expugnata. Lenel, §§ 187–9.

SOURCES

s. 1004. Read *D.* (9. 2) 1.

s. 1005. Read *D.* (9. 2) 2; Gai. 3. 210, 214; *D.* (9. 2) 27. 5; Gai. 3. 217, 218, first sentence.

s. 1006*a*. Read Gai. 3. 219.

s. 1006*b*. Gai. 3. 211 (substantially classical, cf. Beseler, *Beiträge*, iv. 114; Z lvii (1937), 41.

s. 1006*c*. Read Gai. 3. 212 with Beseler, Z l (1930), 25.

s. 1009. Read *Inst. Iust.* (4. 6) 19.

s. 1010*b*. Read *D.* (9. 2) 23. 8 [*ceterique successores*]; [vel *ceteros*] [*nisi . . . sit*]; Gai. 4. 112.

s. 1010*d*. Read *Coll.* (12. 7) 9 [*vel lege Aquilia*]; [*ita . . . agendum*].

s. 1011. 1. Read Gai. 3. 219; *D.* (9. 2) 7. 6 and 9. 3.

s. 1011. 2. Read *D.* (9. 2) 12 [*pro . . . fructus*]; (9. 2) 17; (9. 2) 5. 3 [*sed lege . . . dubito*]; (19. 2) 13. 4 [*sed et . . . diximus*] with Schulz, *Einführung* (1916), 55 f.; (9. 2) 13 pr. [*suo nomine*] ⟨*nec*⟩, [*directam . . . habet*].

BIBLIOGRAPHY

ss. 1004 ff. Taubenschlag, *PW*. xii. 2325, with references; J. B. Thayer, *Lex Aquilia. Text, Translation, and Commentary* (1929); Jolowicz, 'The Original Scope of the lex Aquilia and the Question of Damages', *LQR* xxxviii (1922), 220 f. and against him Lenel, Z xliii (1922), 575 f.; G. Rotondi, *Teorie postclassiche nell' actio legis Aquiliae* (1914) = *Scritti*, ii. 411 ff.; Kunkel, Z xlix (1939), 158 ff.; Beseler, *Beiträge*, iv (1920), 258 ff., 299; Z xliv (1924), 364 ff.; *Juristische Miniaturen* (1929), 128 ff.; Z l (1930), 25 ff.; Kaser, *Quanti ea res est* (1935), 167 ff.; *Altröm. Jus* (1949), 219 ff.; Daube, 'On the Use of the Term Damnum', *Scritti Solazzi* (1948), 93 ff., with references to Daube's earlier papers on the *lex Aquilia*.*

s. 1004. On the date see Schulz, *History* (1946), 30, with references.

s. 1006*c*. Beseler, Z l (1930), 25; P. Voci, *Risarcimento e pena privata* (1939), 66 ff.

s. 1009. On Gai. 4. 9 see Beseler, Z xlvii (1927), 65; *Scritti Ferrini*, iii (1948), 283; Voci, l.c. 94 ff.

s. 1010*a*. Lenel, Z xliii (1922), 577.

s. 1010*c*. E. Levy, *Konkurrenz der Aktionen*, i (1918), 484.

s. 1010*d*. On *coll*. (12. 7) 9 see Beseler, Z l (1930), 74; Niedermeyer, *Atti del Congresso internazionale*, 1933, Roma, i (1934), 379. The still dominant opinion regards the elective concurrence as classical: Beseler, Z xliv (1924), 364 ff.; Levy, *Privatstrafe und Schadensersatz* (1915), 134 ff.; *Konkurrenz*, ii. 1 (1922), 1 ff., 36 ff.

s. 1011. Ferrini, 'La legittimazione attiva nell' actio legis Aquiliae', *Scritti*, v (1930), 191 ff.; De Medio, 'La legittimazione attiva nell' actio legis Aquiliae', *St. Scialoja*, i (1905); Rotondi, *Scritti*, ii. 444; Arnò, *Bull.* xlii (1934), 195; Carrelli, 'La legittimazione attiva dell' actio legis Aquiliae', *Riv. It.* ix (1934), Estratto.

4. *Iniuria (offences against the personality)*

The term *iniuria* in its broadest sense embraced any 1013. illegal act; as used in the *lex Aquilia* it embraced *culpa* Conception (above, s. 1006); in the edictal rubric *de iniuriis* (Lenel, *Edict.* p. 397) it meant a wilful offence against a man's personality. Here we are only concerned with *iniuria* in the sense employed by the edictal rubric.

The classical *actio iniuriarum* was a honorarian action, 1014. The but genetically it was based on the Twelve Tables and for Twelve Tables that reason Gaius ranged it among the *obligationes ex delicto* (3. 182) and described it in his *Institutes* (3. 220 ff.) which on principle were confined to *ius civile* (see above, s. 789). The praetor started—apparently in the second century B.C. —from the following rules of the Twelve Tables (viii. 2–4):

1. If somebody tore off a man's limb, the penalty was retaliation unless the parties came to an agreement as to compensation.

2 If he broke a man's bone, the penalty was 300 asses when the injured person was a free man, 150 asses when he was a slave.

3. *Si iniuriam faxit, XXV poenae sunto.*

The term *iniuria* was only used in the third rule and originally meant any injury which was not provided for elsewhere in the law of delicts. Thus *furtum* and *damnum iniuria datum* were not regarded as *iniuria* in this sense and the close connexion of this rule with the two preceding rules suggested that *iniuria* should be taken to mean lesser physical injuries, boxes on the ear, blows, and trivial assaults generally. Later *iniuria* came to include the offences contemplated by the first two rules, so that the term denoted any wilful injury to a man's body.

1015. These very primitive rules became obsolete. The crude
The Edict. penalty of retaliation seemed no longer compatible with *humanitas* and was no longer practised; apparently the praetor made an agreement as to compensation compulsory. The fixed fines lost their point owing to the depreciation of the *as*. Eventually the praetor intervened and granted an *actio de iniuriis aestimandis*. In the *formula* he authorized the judges (for it was a procedure with *recuperatores*; above, s. 19) to fix the penalty as it seemed 'good and equitable' to them ('quantam pecuniam recuperatoribus bonum aequum videbitur ob eam rem condemnare'). Modern students are wont to call this action *actio iniuriarum aestimatoria*, but the term is unclassical.

> Gellius, 20. 1. 13: 'Labeo . . . in libris quos ad duodecim tabulas conscripsit. . . . L. Veratius fuit egregie homo improbus atque immani vecordia. Is pro delectamento habebat os hominis liberi manus suae palma verberare. Eum servus sequebatur ferens crumenam plenam assium; ut quemque depalmaverat, numerari statim secundum duodecim tabulas quinque et viginti asses iubebat. Propterea, inquit, praetores postea hanc abolescere et relinqui censuerunt iniuriisque aestumandis recuperatores se daturos edixerunt.'

Originally the edictal clause referred only to what was called *iniuria* at that time, i.e. to physical injuries to the body of a free man (for injuries to a slave were now covered by the *lex Aquilia*; above, s. 1005); but the praetor (perhaps gradually) added other cases which went far beyond the old conception of *iniuria*. The praetor did not describe these offences as *iniuria*, but he promised an action in connexion with the *actio iniuriarum aestimatoria*. The Edict as codified by Hadrian mentioned the following cases:

> 1. 'Qui adversus bonos mores convicium cui fecisse cuiusve opera factum esse dicetur, quo adversus bonos mores convicium fieret, in eum iudicium dabo.'
> *Convicium adversus bonos mores facere* meant assembling at somebody's house and raising an insulting and abusive clamour.

2. *Adtemptare pudicitiam*. The text of this clause is not preserved, but it mentioned removing a companion or attendant from a *mater familias* or a young man or woman (*comitem abducere adversus bonos mores*) and 'following' or 'accosting' such a person (*appellare* and *adsectari adversus bonos mores*).

3. 'Ne quid infamandi causa fiat. Si quis adversus ea fecerit, prout quaeque res erit, animadvertam.'

This clause comprehended any kind of defamation, not merely what would amount to libel or slander in English law.

4. 'Qui servum alienum adversus bonos mores verberavisse deve eo iniussu domini quaestionem habuisse dicetur, in eum iudicium dabo.'

We are not informed about the *formulae* in these four cases, but they were certainly similar to the *actio iniuriarum aestimatoria*, though the praetor was perhaps sometimes content with appointing a single judge instead of the *recuperatores*. These were the clauses as contained in Hadrian's Edict, but they existed in substance as early as the first century B.C. At that period they were already regarded as forming a unity; all offences covered by the Edict were now termed *iniuria* and the action resulting from any of them was always called *actio iniuriarum*. Thus *iniuria* meant now an offence against the personality of a free man and this included physical injuries.

The classical lawyers have carefully interpreted the edictal clauses, in particular that on defamation. The Romans were highly sensitive regarding defamation of any kind and this led them very far. If a creditor claimed payment from a surety although he might have easily obtained it from the principal debtor, this was regarded as *iniuria*, since it implied that the latter was insolvent. Even mentioning the name of a decent person in a trial might be regarded as *iniuria* and the orators were therefore wont to add *quem honoris causa nomino* after the name. For the details we must refer to the sources and literature on the subject.

1016. Classical interpretation of the Edict

But the classical lawyers were not content with a liberal interpretation of the edictal rules. They discussed other cases of offence against the personality not covered by the Edict and suggested the granting of an *actio iniuriarum*. Thus if somebody *dolo malo* claimed a person as his slave,

1017. Doubtful cases

some lawyers advocated an *actio iniuriarum*. Again, if one man prevented another from fishing in the sea, from sitting in the theatre, from using public baths, and so on, the lawyers, or some of them, were disposed to grant an *actio iniuriarum*. Even if somebody was prevented from using his own property, this seemed to be *iniuria*. Our knowledge of this group of actions is scanty, since the compilers have shortened the classical discussions and sometimes seem to have granted the *actio iniuriarum* where the lawyers had either denied it or not mentioned it. Thus some cases remain doubtful, for example, the entering of another's house against his will. *Domum vi introire* fell under the *lex Cornelia* (see below, s. 1020), but was not mentioned in the Edict. Did the praetor grant an *actio iniuriarum*? Ulpian (*D*. 47. 10. 5. 2–6) discussed the delict only in connexion with the *lex Cornelia* and *D*. (47. 10) 23 may also refer to that statute. In case of *domum clam introire* Ulpian (*D*. 47. 2. 21. 7) granted an *actio iniuriarum*, but the text is interpolated and Paul, *Sent*. 2. 31. 35 seems to depend on that interpolated text. A husband apparently had no *actio iniuriarum* in the case of adultery, either against his wife or against the adulterer. Insults between man and man, no other person being present, were not regarded as *iniuria*. The Romans were too proud to make an issue of such things. But though such details remain more or less doubtful, two points are quite clear.

1. There were cases of offences against the personality not covered by the Edict in which an *actio iniuriarum* was granted. In such cases it was within the discretion of the praetor to grant an action or to deny it. Theoretically this group of cases was never closed in classical times.

2. On the other hand, there were cases of offences against the personality in which there was no *actio iniuriarum*.

For that reason the classical lawyers never attempted to give a definition of *iniuria* in the sense of the Edict; the boundaries of *iniuria* remained fluid. But we may at least say that the sphere of the *actio iniuriarum* was that of injury to the personality, so that *furtum* and *damnum iniuria datum* (even if it was done wilfully) remained outside that sphere.

Dolus malus was always required for any *actio iniuriarum* which simply means that the injury must have been done wilfully. Thus in case of physical injury the offender must have acted wilfully and not merely negligently, but no further *animus iniuriandi* was required. In the case of defamation the offender must have had the intention to defame somebody; the Edict said expressly: *ne quid infamandi causa fiat*. The Edict *de adtemptata pudicitia* applied where a man had wilfully acted *adversus bonos mores*, no further *animus iniuriandi* being required. When a man 'accosted' a decent girl in the street, he acted wilfully *adversus bonus mores*, but it is plain that he had not the intention to insult her. If he accosted a decent woman who was dressed like a prostitute, he had no intention of acting *adversus bonos mores* and consequently his action did not come within the Edict: *D.* (47. 10) 15. 15 must be interpolated (cf. *D.* 47. 10. 18. 4). The classical lawyers expressed the requirement of *dolus* in various ways (*iniuriae causa*, *infamandi causa*, *in iniuriam facere*), but the terms *animus iniuriae faciendae* and *adfectus iniuriae faciendae* are certainly unclassical. The term *animus iniuriandi* which modern lawyers like to use does not occur in our sources at all.

1018. Animus iniuriandi

The classical *actio iniuriarum* was a pure penal action (Gai. 4. 112) and condemnation involved *infamia* (Gai. 4. 182).

1019. Penal character

1. Like any other penal action it was not passively transmissible but it was also what is called an *actio vindictam spirans* (above, ss. 73, 77), i.e. not even actively transmissible (Gai. 4. 112).

2. When a number of persons had committed *iniuria*, each of them was liable for the whole amount and the actions were cumulated.

3. Sometimes an *actio iniuriarum* and an *actio legis Aquiliae* resulted from the same offence. For example, if somebody whipped another's slave the offence fell under the Edict *de iniuriis* (above, s. 1015), but, if the slave was wounded, also under the *lex Aquilia*. Or if somebody had attacked a free man and thereby rent his clothes, again the offender was liable on both an *actio iniuriarum* and an *actio*

legis Aquiliae. Under classical law the two penal actions were cumulated: 'quia altera actio ad damnum pertinet culpa datum, altera ad contumeliam; duae erunt aestimationes alia damni alia contumeliae.' This was at any rate Ulpian's doctrine. Whether there were classical lawyers who advocated an elective concurrence in one way or the other remains obscure, since the only available text (*D*. 44. 7. 34 pr.) is hopelessly corrupt and perhaps from *iniuria enim* onwards entirely spurious. Probably it was only the post-classical pre-Justinianic lawyers who advocated an elective concurrence (above, s. 1010). Be that as it may, the compilers abolished cumulation; where the plaintiff had in one action obtained the fine he could demand with the other only what was over the amount of the earlier fine. If, for example, he had obtained 60 with the *actio legis Aquiliae* and might have obtained 100 with the *actio iniuriarum*, he could now only demand 40 with the latter action.

1020. Lex Cornelia de iniuriis   By the side of the edictal rules stood a *lex Cornelia de iniuriis* of the time of Sulla. It introduced a public procedure (*quaestio de iniuriis*) for certain cases of *iniuria* (*verberare, pulsare, domum vi introire*) which led to a *condemnatio pecuniaria*. The statute must be later than the praetorian Edict which introduced an *actio iniuriarum aestimatoria*, for the story of L. Veratius as given by Labeo (above, s. 1015) would be meaningless if the *lex Cornelia* had already existed at that time. The text of the statute is not preserved and our knowledge of it is on the whole poor. But it should no longer be contested that the statute did not prevent the praetor from granting an *actio iniuriarum* in those cases which were covered by the statute; Gaius is entirely silent on the *lex Cornelia*.

1021. No Greek influence   The law of *iniuria* is genuinely Roman law. The whole development—primitive rules of the Twelve Tables, praetorian reform, liberal interpretation of the Edict by the lawyers—is typically Roman. The rules of the Edict show the true Roman feeling for decency, privacy, and good repute and are closely connected with Roman customs and manners. Greek influence, which has been alleged by some, is neither proven nor probable.

The *actio iniuriarum* afforded a strong and efficient pro- 1022.
tection against injuries to immaterial interests, particularly Evaluation
against defamation of any kind, but it was not a happy idea
to tie together offences against the body with injuries to
immaterial interests. This combination was due to the
starting-point of the development, namely the rules of
the Twelve Tables regarding physical injuries, but it was
an artificial thing and turned out to be fatal, since it prevented adequate protection of a free man's body. The *actio
iniuriarum* was as aforesaid an *actio vindictam spirans*. This
was all right in cases of injuries to immaterial interests,
but when applied to physical injuries the inevitable consequence was that if a free man was killed and not merely injured, his heirs were not entitled to bring an *actio
iniuriarum* even if they were the wife and children of the
murdered man. Further, the *actio iniuriarum* required *dolus*
(above, s. 1018). This requirement might be justified in the
case of injury to immaterial interests, but *dolus* was equally
required in the case of physical injuries so that an *actio
iniuriarum* did not lie where the body of a free man was
injured by negligence, and as the *lex Aquilia* did not apply
either, there was no action at all in such case. It was for this
reason that the post-classical lawyers extended the *actio
legis Aquiliae* to cover injury to free persons (above, s.
1011). Thus the classical conception of *iniuria* as a wilful
injury to the personality was (like the conception of *furtum*)
not a happy creation and has justly disappeared from
modern law.

SOURCES

s. 1014. Read XII Tab. 8. 1–4 (Bruns, *Fontes*, p. 29; *FIRA* i, p. 53);
Gai. 3. 223.

s. 1015. Read Gai. 3. 224; *D*. (47. 10) 15. 3–10; (47. 10) 15. 16–23;
Auct. ad Herennium, 4. 25. 35.

s. 1016. Read *D*. (47. 10) 19.

s. 1017. Read *D*. (47. 10) 11. 9, first sentence (Beseler, Z liii (1933), 9);
(47. 10) 13. 7 to *conveniri potest*; (43. 8) 2. 9 [*sed in . . . est*], substantially
classical; (19. 1) 25 with Beseler, Z xlv (1925), 439.

s. 1018. Read *D*. (25. 4) 1. 8; (47. 10) 26; (44. 7) 34 pr.; (47. 10) 3. 1;
(47. 10) 18. 4. On these texts see *Index Interp*.

s. 1019. 1. Read Gai. 4. 112; *D*. (37. 6) 2. 4.

s. 1019. 2. Read *D*. (47. 10) 34; (47. 10) 11. 3–6.
s. 1019. 3. Read *D*. (47. 10) 15. 46; (9. 2) 5. 1; (44. 7) 34 pr.

BIBLIOGRAPHY

ss. 1013 ff. Pernice, *Labeo*, ii. 1 (1895), 19 ff. (fundamental); Steinwenter, *PW* ix. 1555, with references; G. Pugliese, *Studi sull' injuria*,
i (1941); Santi di Paola, 'La genesi storica del delitto di "iniuria",' *Annali
del Seminario giuridico dell' Università di Catania*, i (1947); Kaser,
Altröm. Jus (1949), 207 ff.
s. 1014. .Pugliese, l.c. 1 ff.
s. 1015. Pugliese, 96 ff.; Lenel, *Edict.* (1937), §§ 190 ff.
s. 1017. Pernice, l.c. 28 ff., 26 f.
s. 1019. 2. E. Levy, *Konkurrenz*, i (1918), 479.
s. 1019. 3. Levy, *Konkurrenz*, ii. 1 (1922), 182 ff.
s. 1020. Pugliese, l.c. 117 ff.
s. 1021. Pugliese, 39 ff.

5. *Actio metus causa* (*extortion*) *and actio de dolo* (*fraud*)

1023. **Affinity** These two actions are closely connected with each other. The offences which gave rise to them were similar (working upon another's free will); both actions were praetorian creations without any basis in *ius civile*; both originated almost at the same time (in the first half of the first century B.C.); even the *formulae* were similar.

i. *Actio metus causa*

1024. **Formula Octaviana** In about 80 B.C. a praetor Octavius introduced an action against extortioners, probably a penal action for four times the value of the extorted property. The *formula*, which was called *formula Octaviana*, contained the words *per vim aut* (or *et*) *metum auferre* whereby the praetor wished to describe extortion, i.e. what the medieval jurisprudence styled *vis compulsiva* as distinct from *vis absoluta*.

> Cicero, *In Verrem*, 2, lib. 3, cap. 65. 152: '... postulavit ab L. Metello, ut ex edicto suo iudicium daret in Apronium quod per vim aut metum abstulisset, quam formulam Octavianam et Romae Metellus habuerat et habebat in provincia.'
> Cicero, *Ad Quintum Fratrem*, 1. 1. 7. 21: '... Cogebantur Sullani homines quae per vim et (N.B.) metum abstulerant reddere.'

Thus it remains uncertain whether the *formula Octaviana* had *per vim aut metum* (or *per vim metumve*) or *per vim et metum* (or *per vim metumque*). In any case *vis aut* (or *et*) *metus* should be taken as a sort of hendiadys: 'fear caused by threat'. Otherwise the *formula* would have embraced robbery (a case of *vis absoluta*) and the *actio vi bonorum raptorum* was only introduced later by Lucullus (above, s. 998). Apparently even in Hadrian's Edict the edictal rubric ran *quod vi metusve causa gestum erit*, where *vi metusve causa* must undoubtedly be taken as a hendiadys since it covered only *vis compulsiva*.

This is all we know of the *formula Octaviana*. We are better acquainted with the *actio metus causa* as contained in Hadrian's Edict, but we cannot say whether it agreed in all details with the *formula Octaviana*. In the following description we confine ourselves to the classical action found in Hadrian's Edict.

1. The classical name of the action is unknown. The classical lawyers probably termed it according to the rubric of the Edict *actio de eo quod vi metusve causa* (or *metus causa*) *factum est*. The Byzantines called it *actio metus causa* and for the sake of convenience we will use this term. 1025. Classical name

2. The action was a penal action; it lay within a year for four times the value of the extorted things; after the lapse of a year it merely lay for their simple value. 1026. Penalty

3. The action, being a penal action, lay only against the extortioner and not also against a third person who had the extorted thing in his hands; under classical law there was no such thing as an *actio metus causa in rem scripta*. Thus if A forced B by threats to make a donation to C, the action lay only against A and not also against C. Gerhard Beseler was the first to assert this rule. His assertion has been repeatedly checked and should no longer be contested; it was the compilers who extended the action by allowing it against third persons. 1027. Not available against a third person

4. The action was a so-called *actio arbitraria* (above, s. 67). The *formula* contained a clause by which the judge was authorized to pronounce an *arbitrium* requiring the restoration of the extorted things. If the defendant complied with it, he was acquitted and escaped any penalty; if he refused to restore them, or if he was unable to do so, he 1028. Actio arbitraria

was condemned, but the condemnation did not involve *infamia*. The mildness of this procedure when compared with the *actio furti* and *legis Aquiliae* certainly comes as a surprise. But we must bear in mind that the action came late and that before the *formula Octaviana* there was no remedy at all against extortion; moreover, Octavius had Sulla's statute on *repetundae* before him, which provided no other penalty than the restitution of the extorted money.

1029. Formula   5. The *formula* is not preserved but can be confidently reconstructed; only the initial clause remains doubtful. The *formula* probably ran as follows:

> 'Si paret vi Numerii Negidii factum esse, ut Aulus Agerius Numerio Negidio fundum, quo de agitur, mancipio daret, neque plus quam annus est, cum experiundi potestas fuit, neque ea res restituetur, quanti ea res erit, tantae pecuniae quadruplum Numerium Negidium Aulo Agerio iudex condemnato, si non paret, absolvito.'

1030. Penal action   6. The action was a pure penal action, not an *actio rem et poenam persequens* nor an *actio mixta*. Like any other penal action it was not passively transmissible, but the principle of cumulation had to be modified on account of the formulary clause *nisi restituetur*. In case of a plurality of extortioners an action lay against each of them, but if one of them restored the extorted property, the other offenders were free; if in default of restitution he was condemned to pay the fine, the actions against the other offenders remained intact. This harsh but logical distinction was the inevitable consequence of the construction of the *formula* and of the penal character of the action.

1031. Exceptio and in integrum restitutio   Besides the penal action Hadrian's Edict provided two other remedies, an *in integrum restitutio propter metum* and an *exceptio metus*.

1. A legal act performed under duress was not always void. Under classical law an informal act (like sale, *traditio*, or *pro herede gestio*; above, s. 496) was invalid, but a formal act (like *mancipatio, stipulatio*, or *cretio*; above, s. 497) was valid, though voidable by *exceptio* or *in integrum restitutio*.

If, for example, A had been forced to promise something by stipulation and was sued with the *actio ex stipulatione*, he was protected by an *exceptio metus*. If A had alienated a *res*

mancipi by *mancipatio* under duress but had not yet transferred possession to the recipient, he might be sued with the
rei vindicatio but was protected by the *exceptio metus*. If A
had also transferred possession to the recipient, he might
apply for *in integrum restitutio*: the praetor annulled the
mancipatio and granted A a *rei vindicatio rescissa mancipa-
tione*.

2. Neither remedy had a penal character and for that
reason both might be granted (in contrast to the penal
action) not only against the extortioner but also against
third persons. It is, however, understandable that the classical lawyers hesitated to do so. During the first century A.D.
the *exceptio metus* was apparently only available against the
extortioner, but in Hadrian's Edict it was framed in such
a way that it might be used also against a third person. In
Hadrian's Edict the exceptio ran as follows: 'si in ea re
nihil metus causa factum est.'

It should be noted that the name of the extortioner was not mentioned
in that exception. Suppose that A had forced B to promise something
to C by stipulation and C sued B with the *actio ex stipulatione*. B might
then protect himself with the *exceptio metus*. The whole *formula* then
ran as follows:

'Si paret Numerius Negidium Aulo Agerio centum dare oportere, si
in ea re nihil metus causa factum est, iudex Numerium Negidium Aulo
Agerio centum condemnato', etc.

As regards the *in integrum restitutio* the classical lawyers
disputed over the question whether or not it might be
granted against a third person; the dominant doctrine
seems to have answered it in the affirmative.

3. The scope of neither *exceptio* nor *in integrum restitutio*
was quite identical with that of the penal action. *Exceptio*
and *in integrum restitutio* were only available where a legal
act had been induced which was valid *iure civili* (*metus
causa gestum* scil. *negotium*), whilst the action lay in the
event of any kind of extortion (*metus causa factum*) which
included the wrongful inducing of legal acts. Thus if A had
forced B to cut down a tree, B might sue A with the penal
action, whereas *exceptio* and *in integrum restitutio* were out
of the question. On the other hand, the penal action lay only

against the extortioner, whilst *exceptio* and *in integrum resti-tutio* were (at least in high classical times) also available against third persons. We cannot deal here with detailed questions as to how the three remedies worked together.

Suppose A forced B to promise him something by stipulation. B sued A with the penal action and as A refused restitution (i.e. refused to release the debtor by *acceptilatio*), he was condemned to pay fourfold damages. Now A sued B with the *actio ex stipulatione* and the defendant availed himself of the *exceptio metus*. Labeo argued—quite logically and in harmony with the penal character of the action—in favour of the cumulation of *actio* and *exceptio*, but Julian granted to A a *replicatio*. Apparently his argument ran as follows: In the penal action the defendant had the choice of restoring the extorted thing (in this case releasing the debtor) or paying the penalty. If he chose the latter case, he must be entitled to the *actio ex stipulatione*, since otherwise the choice would be a farce and B would in fact obtain both restitution and penalty.

1032. The history of these remedies in the post-classical period
Justinian's lies outside the scope of this book; we confine ourselves to
law Justinian's law. The compilers have drastically modified the classical law by ruthlessly shortening and interpolating the classical texts; for that reason the short *Digest* title 4. 2 presents unusual difficulties. We only wish to point out the two main tendencies of the compilers.

1. The compilers amalgamated *in integrum restitutio* and the penal action and granted the latter not only against the extortioner but also against a third person who had acquired the extorted things. For that reason they described the action as an *actio in rem scripta*. The *in integrum restitutio* was only preserved in a few cases in which it seemed a more con-venient remedy than the action.

Thus if somebody had been forced to accept an inheritance and thereby had become liable for the debts, the compilers granted him an *in integrum restitutio*, since otherwise he would have had to sue each of the creditors (*D*. 4. 2. 21. 5).

2. The compilers changed the penal action *in quadruplum* into an *actio mixta, rem et poenam persequens* (like the *actio vi bonorum raptorum*; above, ss. 998, 1003); they regarded only the *triplum* as penalty and the *simplum* as indemnifica-tion. In consequence any cumulation was now excluded. If there was a plurality of offenders and one of them was con-

demned to pay the four-fold and paid that sum, the other offenders were free, contrary to classical law (above, s. 1030). If A forced B to promise him something by stipulation and B sued A with the *actio in quadruplum*, the compilers established the following entirely unclassical rule: the judge had to compel A to release the debtor and moreover he had to condemn him to pay the three-fold (*D*. 4. 2. 14. 9).

ii. *Actio de dolo malo*

1. This action was introduced by Aquilius Gallus, a contemporary and friend of Cicero. Aquilius was praetor of the *quaestio de ambitu* in 66 B.C., but as such he cannot have introduced the new action. Possibly he was about that time *praetor peregrinus*, but it may also be that he introduced the action only in his private position as a famous lawyer by suggesting it to the praetor who thereupon inserted it in his Edict. In any case the action is later than the *actio metus causa*. 1033. Aquilius Gallus

2. The classical name of the action was undoubtedly *actio de dolo malo* or shortly *actio de dolo* and not *actio doli* as modern students persistently call it. 1034. Classical name

> According to the *Vocabularium Iurisprudentiae Romanae*, ii. 327, *doli actio* occurs in classical texts only once, *D.* (46. 3) 95. 1, an obviously interpolated text. *Actio doli mali* occurs once: *D.* (44. 7) 35, spurious; *doli iudicium* only once: *D.* (4. 3) 25, perhaps genuine. Within the *Codex Iustinianus doli actio* occurs only *C.* (2. 20) 8 (Constantine). For texts with *actio de dolo* see *Voc. Iur. Rom.* ii. 331; Robert Mayr, *Vocab. Codicis*, 395. Cicero, *De off.* 3. 14. 60: *de dolo malo formulas*; *De nat. deor.* 3. 30. 74: *iudicium de dolo malo*.

3. The term *dolus* as used in the *actio de dolo* originally meant nothing else than 'false pretences'. The creator of the new action himself had given this definition. Cicero reports (*De officiis*, 3. 14. 60): 1035. Conception of dolus

> 'C. Aquilius, collega et familiaris meus, . . . cum ex eo quaereretur, quid esset dolus malus, respondebat: "cum esset aliud simulatum, aliud actum"; hoc quidem sane luculente, ut ab homine perito definiendi.'

This definition clearly confined *dolus* to false pretences and it was approved by Servius Sulpicius (also a friend of Cicero's). Labeo, however, suggested a different definition.

Ulpian's text in which he reported Labeo's doctrine is corrupt (*D*. 4. 3. 1. 2), but apparently it ran as follows:

'Labeo autem ait posse et sine simulatione id agi, ut quis circumveniatur; itaque ipse sic definit: dolum malum esse omnem calliditatem fallaciam machinationem ad circumveniendum fallendum decipiendum alterum adhibitam. Labeonis definitio vera est.'

Labeo understood *circumvenire* and *fallere* in a broader sense; according to him *dolus* (in the sense of the *actio de dolo*) embraced not only false pretences but also any wilful damaging by a cunning device, intrigue, or machination. Labeo's definition was approved by Ulpian and probably by the dominant classical doctrine. Thus *damnum iniuria .datum*, even if it was done wilfully, did not fall under *dolus* in that sense, nor did *furtum*, *iniuria*, and *vis*. In general the boundaries of the conception remained fluid in classical times. Over some cases the lawyers disputed; some of them advocated the *actio de dolo*, others preferred an *actio in factum* which did not involve *infamia*. These disputes are of course not fully discernible from our sources, since the compilers as usual have shortened them. Moreover, the compilers may sometimes have substituted the *actio de dolo* for an *actio in factum* which they found in the classical text, since they were inclined to extend the domain of the *actio de dolo*. The details must inevitably remain uncertain. Let us consider the following cases.

(*a*) A legatee persuaded the heir to pay the legacy in full since, he said, the estate covered the *quarta Falcidia* (above, s. 567). If he knew that this was untrue, the heir had against him the *actio de dolo*. This was a case of false pretences (*D*. 4. 3. 23).

(*b*) A debtor forged a letter from Titius asking the creditor to release the debtor. The creditor complied with the request and released the debtor by *acceptilatio*. The creditor had the *actio de dolo* against the debtor. Here we have a clear case of a *machinatio* (*D*. 4. 3. 38).

(*c*) A promised a slave to B by stipulation; Titius wilfully killed the slave. A was set free from his debt since he was only liable for *dolus* and *culpa* (above, s. 813). According to the prevalent opinion (*plerique putant*) B had an *actio de dolo* against Titius. The question of false pretences does not, of course, arise here, but the damage was caused indirectly (*D*. 4. 3. 18. 5).

(*d*) A owed an animal on a stipulation; F was *fideiussor*. F killed the animal wilfully. The principal debtor became free and consequently the surety too (above, s. 863). Neratius and Julian granted an *actio de dolo* to the creditor against F (*D.* 4. 3. 19).

(*e*) A lent false (too heavy) weights to B who had sold goods by the weight to C; in consequence C received too much. Trebatius advocated an *actio de dolo* against A, but the imperfect tense (*dabat*) indicates that Paul did not agree with him. The compilers have shortened the original text (*D.* 4. 3. 18. 3).

(*f*) A informally allowed B to break stones on his (A's) estate. B had already made arrangements involving expenses when A revoked his permission. Ulpian (*D.* 4. 3. 34) granted an *actio de dolo* (genuine?) whilst Aristo in a similar case (*D.* 19. 5, 16. 1) took only an *actio in factum* into consideration (the last words *sed erit de dolo* are perhaps spurious).

(*g*) A promised by stipulation *Stichum aut Pamphilum dari*; the choice was reserved to the promisor. Now A killed Pamphilus wilfully, whereby the obligation was simply to give Stichus. Later Stichus died *sine dolo et culpa debitoris* so that now A was entirely free from his debt. The compilers granted the *actio de dolo* to the creditor against A, although *dolus* on the part of A is quite out of the question (46. 3, 95. 1).

4. The classical *actio de dolo* was a penal action *in simplum*. The *formula* was modelled on the pattern of the *actio metus causa* which immediately preceded it in the Edict; it was a so-called *actio arbitraria* (above, s. 1028), i.e. it contained the clause *nisi restituetur*. The action was only available for one year. Thus the *formula* ran as follows: 1036. Penalty and formula

'Si paret dolo malo Numerii Negidii factum esse, ut Aulus Agerius Numerio Negidio fundum quo de agitur mancipio daret, neque plus quam annus est, cum experiundi potestas fuit, neque ea res restituetur, quanti ea res erit, tantam pecuniam iudex Numerium Negidium Aulo Agerio condemnato si non paret absolvito.'

5. The *actio de dolo* was a subsidiary remedy; it was only granted in default of another action. The praetor expressly said this in his Edict: 1037. Subsidiarity Infamy

'Quae dolo malo facta esse dicentur, si de his rebus alia actio non erit et iusta causa esse videbitur, intra annum cum primum experiundi potestas fuerit, iudicium dabo.'

Condemnation involved *infamia*.

6. The *actio de dolo* was a pure penal action, not an *actio rem et poenam persequens*. For that reason it was not available against the heir of the offender. As regards cumulation a concurrence of the *actio de dolo* with actions of another kind was excluded by the subsidiary nature of the *actio de dolo*. In case of a plurality of offenders cumulation took 1038. Penal action

place according to the rules which we have expounded above for the *actio metus causa* (above, s. 1030).

> If A and B had committed fraud, the *actio de dolo* lay against each of them.
> 1. If A obeyed the *arbitrium iudicis* and made restitution, B too was set free.
> 2. If A was condemned to pay the penalty, the action against B remained intact. Finally the compilers abolished cumulation in this case as well (see above, s. 1032). The interpolation in *D*. (4. 3) 17 is palpable:
> 'Si plure dolo fecerint et unus restituerit, omnes liberantur; quodsi ('if however', N.B.) unus quanti ea res est praestiterit, puto adhuc ceteros liberari.'
> Ulpian obviously wrote *puto ceteros non liberari*, as *quodsi* indicates.

1039. In integrum restitutio This will suffice for the *actio de dolo*. An *in integrum restitutio propter dolum* was not promised under the edictal rubric (in contrast to the *in integrum restitutio propter metum*; above, s. 1031), but the praetor might grant it in an individual case at his discretion (*D*. 4. 1. 7. 1, though the text is completely spurious).

1040. Exceptio doli The *exceptio doli* was placed in Hadrian's Edict in the section *de exceptionibus* (Lenel, *Edict*. § 277). It ran as follows:

> 'si in ea re nihil dolo malo Auli Agerii factum sit neque fiat.'

But it is only the first part of the *exceptio* (*dolo malo factum sit*) which concerns *dolus* in the sense of the *actio de dolo*, whereas in the second part (*neque fiat* scil. *dolo malo*) *dolus* means 'contrary to *bona fides*'.

> Suppose A had induced B by false pretences to promise him 100 by stipulation. If A sued B with the *actio ex stipulatione*, B might protect himself with the *exceptio doli*, referring to its first part:
> 'Si paret Numerium Negidium Aulo Agerio centum dare oportere, si in ea re nihil dolo malo Auli Agerii factum sit neque fiat, iudex Numerium Negidium Aulo Agerio centum condemnato,' etc.
> Somebody owed 100 to a *pupillus* by stipulation. He paid that sum to the *pupillus sine tutoris auctoritate*. The *pupillus* acquired ownership of the coins, but the debt was not discharged. But if the *pupillus* now sued the debtor with the *actio ex stipulatione*, the defendant might protect himself with the *exceptio doli* (referring to the clause neque fiat) where the *pupillus* was still enriched by the money (Gai. 2. 84).

Within an *actio bonae fidei* there was no room for an *exceptio doli*, since the defendant was sufficiently protected by the clause *ex fide bona* (or a similar clause).

The age of the *exceptio doli* is unknown, but it may have existed before the *actio de dolo*; at any rate it certainly existed in republican times.

SOURCES

s. 1031. Read *D.* (4. 2) 14. 9 [*cum in . . . consecutus*]; [*quod cum . . . compellatur*].

s. 1032. Read *D.* (4. 2) 9. 8, interpolated; the original text dealt with *in integrum restitutio*; (4. 2) 14. 3 and 4, completely spurious; (4. 2) 14. 9–10, heavily interpolated; (4. 2) 14. 15 [*sed etsi . . . actionem*].

s. 1040. Read Gai. 4. 119 to *fiat*.

BIBLIOGRAPHY

ss. 1024 ff. Beseler, *Beiträge*, i (1910), 72 ff.; iv (1920), 259; Schulz, 'Die Lehre vom erzwungenen Rechtsgeschäft im antiken römischen Recht', Z xliii (1922), 171 ff.; Beseler, Z xliv (1924), 362 ff.; Lenel, *Edict.* (1927), § 39; v. Lübtow, *Der Ediktstitel 'Quod metus causa gestum erit'* (1932); G. Maier, *Praetorische Bereicherungsklagen* (1932), 91 ff.; Beseler, *St. Albertoni*, i (1933), 425, with references; C. Sanfilippo, *Il metus nei negozi giuridici* (1934).

s. 1024. Schulz, 216 ff.; v. Lübtow, 126 ff., both in error concerning the meaning of *per vim aut* (*et*) *metum*.

s. 1025. v. Lübtow, 168.

s. 1027. Schulz, 172, 240 ff.; Lenel, l.c. 113; v. Lübtow, 183 ff.; Beseler, *St. Albertoni*, i. 425.

s. 1028. Lenel, l.c. p. 113; v. Lübtow, 169 ff.

s. 1029. Lenel, l.c. p. 112; v. Lübtow, 207 f.

s. 1030. Beseler, *Beiträge*, iv (1920), 300; v. Lübtow, 273 ff., 283 with references.

s. 1031. Schulz, 171 ff. (impaired by errors); Beseler, Z xliv (1924), 171 ff.; v. Lübtow, 9 ff.; Sanfilippo, 45 ff. On *in integrum restitutio*, Schulz, 220 ff.; v. Lübtow, 99 ff. On the *exceptio*, Schulz, 225 ff.; v. Lübtow, 81 ff. On cumulation of *actio* and *exceptio*, v. Lübtow, 231 ff.

s. 1032. Schulz, 228 ff., 238; v. Lübtow, 183 ff., 218 ff., 231 ff.

ss. 1033 ff. Pernice, *Labeo*, ii. 1 (1895), 200 ff. (fundamental); Mitteis, *Röm. Privatrecht*, i (1908), 318; Lenel, *Edict.* (1927), § 40.

s. 1035. Pernice, 208 ff.; F. Litten, 'Zum Dolus-Begriff in der actio de dolo', *Festgabe für Karl Güterbock* (1910), 257 ff.; Schulz, *Einführung* (1916), 104 ff.

s. 1036. Lenel, *Edict.* § 40.

s. 1037. v. Lübtow, l.c. 262 ff.

s. 1038. Beseler, *Beiträge*, iv (1920), 300; v. Lübtow, 285 ff.

s. 1039. Lenel, *Edict.* p. 115; Schulz, Z xliii (1922), 237 n. 5; Duquesne, 'L'in integrum restitutio ob dolum', *Mélanges P. Fournier* (1929).

s. 1040. Pernice, l.c. 231 ff.

CHAPTER III

UNJUSTIFIED ENRICHMENT AND NEGOTIORUM GESTIO

1. *Unjustified enrichment*

1041.
Classical
idea
THE classical law knew actions for the recovery of an unjustified enrichment. They were *actiones in personam* (above, s. 56) founded neither on contract nor on delict but on the fact that a person was enriched at the expense of another and that this enrichment seemed legally unjustified. The idea seems simple and almost self-evident, but actually these Roman actions are quite unique and have no parallels in other laws not dependent on Roman law. They are an original and valuable Roman creation, but they must be strictly confined to certain clearly defined cases; otherwise they threaten to confuse and to shake the whole system of actions and thereby the whole system of private law. Suppose the purchaser had received the goods sold to him but had delayed payment. One might argue that the purchaser is now enriched by the goods and the vendor may accordingly claim their restitution as an unjustified enrichment. This, however, would shake the strength of the contract; under Roman law the vendor was not entitled to claim the goods but was confined to the *actio venditi* for the price (above, s. 917). We find in our sources the maxim: 'iure naturae aequum est neminem cum alterius detrimento et iniuria fieri locupletiorem'. But to the classical lawyers this was a general idea or principle, not a legal rule. They kept these actions within very narrow limits and were prepared to tolerate cases in which no action was available though an unjustified enrichment was evident. The student should keep in mind the instances of *implantatio* and *specificatio* (above, ss. 635, 638). A bona fide purchaser bought a stolen plant and planted it in his land. He acquired ownership, which undoubtedly constituted an enrichment at the expense of the owner and, as between purchaser and owner,

an unjustified enrichment; nevertheless, the purchaser was not bound to restore the enrichment to the previous owner of the plant. Likewise the owner of material had no action against the bona fide purchaser, if the latter had acquired ownership by *specificatio*. Further, under classical law *bonae fidei possessor fructus suos facit* and is not bound to restore the fruits to the owner of the thing, though the enrichment was unjustified as between owner and possessor. In short, there was under classical law no general rule that unjustified enrichment had to be restored. The idea was confined to certain groups of cases; outside these cases there was no action, not even a subsidiary remedy for the recovery of an unjustified enrichment.

The classical law was sound and cleverly contrived in spite of some gaps which ought to have been filled in; but the compilers have completely ruined the classical law. They unwisely extended the scope of these actions and unhappily modified their content by numerous interpolations which have obscured and confused the classical law without giving a clear exposition of the Byzantine law. This law is one of the worst parts of Justinian's law; it has confused and irritated generations of lawyers and exercised an evil influence on continental codifications down to our times. The German Civil Code (*BGB*) is a warning example. 1042. Justinian's law

The exploration of this part of classical law began early (in the nineties of the last century) when modern critical research was still in its infancy and students possessed neither an adequate apparatus nor a clear insight into the character of the sources. Nevertheless, the results were admirable. Later on the pace of research slowed up and even today there is no book which gives us a comprehensive analysis both of the classical law and Justinian's. 1043. Literature

Here we will leave aside special cases and remedies and confine ourselves to the central phenomenon, viz. to the *condictio* operating as a remedy for the recovery of an unjustified enrichment. 1044 Condictio

Our starting-point must be the Edict. It is an incontestable fact that the Edict contained no general *formula* for the 1045. The edictal formulae recovery of an unjustified enrichment. However, as we have already pointed out above (s. 809), under the edictal rubric *si certum petetur* there were three *formulae* which were drawn up in a very general and abstract style and which were called *condictiones* since they were similar to the *formula* in the *legis actio per condictionem* (Gai. 4. 17*b*–19): (1) the *condictio certae pecuniae*; (2) the *condictio certae rei*; (3) the *condictio certae quantitatis* (*condictio triticaria*). These *formulae* were primarily meant to serve for the actions *ex mutuo* and *ex certa stipulatione* (Lenel, *Edict.* § 95). Under another rubric—'si cum eo agatur, qui incertum promiserit', Lenel, *Edict.* § 55—stood the *formula* for the *actio ex stipulatione incerta* which was not called *condictio* (above, s. 809). The republican and classical lawyers availed themselves of the first three formulae (*condictiones*) in order to establish remedies for the recovery of an unjustified enrichment. They granted—on the analogy of the *condictio ex mutuo*—a *condictio* where somebody had acquired corporeal things (*certa pecunia, certa res, certa quantitas*) by a *datio* which entailed an unjustified enrichment. (With regard to the irregular *condictio furtiva* see below, s. 1059.) This was the very simple classical law which the compilers so horribly mutilated. Let us provisionally illustrate the classical law by the following simple example. Both A and B erroneously believed that A owed 100 to B. A paid 100 to B. The latter acquired ownership of the coins by *traditio*, for the *traditio* was made *cum causa*. The *causa traditionis* was the agreement of the parties as to the legal purpose of the *traditio* (above, s. 615); in this case the parties agree that the payment was made *solutionis causa*. Thus B acquired ownership, but this acquisition was, as between A and B, unjustified. In consequence A might reclaim the sum paid with a *condictio certae pecuniae*. The *formula* ran as follows:

'Si paret Numerium Negidium Aulo Agerio centum dare oportere, iudex Numerium Negidium Aulo Agerio centum condemnato, si non paret absolvito.'

This was the *formula* for the *actio ex mutua pecunia* and *ex stipulatione certae pecuniae*, but it was also used for the recovery of an unjustified enrichment.

The classical *condictio* for the recovery of an unjustified enrichment was, as aforesaid, conditional on a *datio* (on the *condictio furtiva* see below, s. 1059). Where an enrichment was obtained without a *datio*, a *condictio* did not lie. Thus if a bona fide purchaser of stolen material had acquired ownership by *specificatio*, there was no *condictio*, though the enrichment was, as between the owner of the material and the specificator, unjustified. 1046. Datio required

A *datio certae pecuniae* or *certae rei* (*certae quantitatis*) was required. Where somebody owed an amount of money and the debt was discharged by *acceptilatio*, this was regarded as a *datio pecuniae*. Thus if A owed 100 to B, and B wishing to give a *dos* to A released him by an *acceptilatio dotis causa*, B might demand 100 from A with the *condictio*, if the marriage did not follow. Suppose again that A erroneously believed that he owed 100 to B. A had a debtor D who owed him 100 and authorized him to promise B 100 by a novatory stipulation. According to the rule *qui delegat solvit* A was regarded as having paid 100 to B and, therefore, had a *condictio certae pecuniae* against B. If, on the other hand, A promised 100 *dotis causa* to B by stipulation and the marriage did not follow, A might protect himself with the *exceptio doli* against the *actio ex stipulatione*, but he had no *condictio* against B in order to obtain *acceptilatio*. Next, suppose that A promised 100 to B by stipulation under the informal agreement that B should give 100 to A as a loan. B never gave the loan. If B sued A with the *actio ex stipulatione*, A might protect himself with the *exceptio doli*, but he had no *condictio* against B for liberation. Under classical law there was no *condictio liberationis* (if it had existed, Gaius, 4. 116 would have mentioned it). A *condictio liberationis* would have been a *condictio incerti*, since *accepto ferre* was a *facere* and any *facere* was regarded as an *incertum* (in contrast to *certa pecunia* and *certa res*). The *condictio liberationis* was introduced by the compilers or by the post-classical lawyers. 1047. Datio certae pecuniae or rei

Datio meant a conveyance which transferred ownership to the recipient. If a *pupillus* believing that he owed 100 to B paid that sum to him *sine tutoris auctoritate*, he had no 1048. Transfer of ownership required

condictio, since B had not acquired ownership but only possession and there was no *condictio possessionis* under classical law. The *pupillus* might demand the money with the *rei vindicatio*, but if B acquired ownership of the coins by *commixtio*, the *condictio* applied: though ownership was not transferred by *datio*, the *datio* was at least the basis of the acquisition. Where the pledgee did not restore the pledge after the discharge of the debt, the pledgor had no *condictio*, as a *condictio possessionis* did not exist under classical law.

1049. No condictio incerti   We may sum up by stating that the classical *condictio* for the recovery of an unjustified enrichment was (except in the case of the *condictio furtiva*; below, s. 1059) invariably founded on a *datio certae pecuniae* or *certae rei* (*certae quantitatis*); it was always a *condictio certi* (to use the post-classical term). A *condictio incerti* did not exist under classical law. Not only is the term *condictio incerti* unclassical but also the institution itself. The Edict contained no *formula* for a *condictio incerti* (Lenel, *Edict*. § 57, p. 158); the *formula* which was provided for an *actio ex stipulatione incerta* (Lenel, *Edict* § 55) was confined to *stipulatio* and could not be used for any other purpose. The praetor might have granted a *condictio utilis* for the recovery of an *incertum*, but in fact he did not do so. Such a practice would have left conspicuous traces in our sources; we should find discussions like those on the *actiones legis Aquiliae utiles* and Julian would have inserted a *formula* in the Edict. After the codification of the Edict a *condictio incerti* could not be granted without imperial authorization, since such an action would have been a serious break with tradition, but we hear nothing of any rescripts on the matter. Above all, a *condictio incerti* would have been a contradiction in terms to the classical lawyers; to them *condictio* was a special type of *formula*: abstract, *in personam* and for *certa pecunia* or *certa res* like the *legis actio per condictionem* (Gai. 4, 17b–20). Thus we are entitled, nay bound, to eliminate the *condictio incerti* from classical law.

1050. Content of the obligation   The *condictio* lay for the recovery of the enrichment existing at the time of the *datio* and not at the time of *litis contestatio*.

(*a*) If money was given, the recipient was simply bound to pay that sum back, whether he acted *bona* or *mala fide* and whether or not he had already spent the money at the time of *litis contestatio*.

(*b*) If a quantity of fungible things was given, the *condictio* lay for the same quantity or, if it had been consumed, for its value.

(*c*) If *certa res* was given, the recipient was bound to restore the very thing; he was liable for *dolus* and *culpa*, but not for *casus*.

Since the *condictio* was not confined to the enrichment existing at the time of the *litis contestatio*, it was denied against a *pupillus* who had obtained an unjustified enrichment by a *datio sine tutoris auctoritate*. The *pupillus* acquired ownership, but the giver was not entitled to a *condictio*. At any rate this was Julian's doctrine, which was dominant in high classical times.

1051. Not available against a pupillus

The classical lawyers did not as yet distinguish types of *condictio* by fixed designations. The classifications and names which we find in the *Digest* rubrics 12.4–7 and in the *Codex* rubrics 4. 5–9 are not classical; nevertheless, they deserve consideration in order to illustrate our general remarks.

1052. Types of condictio

1. *Condictio indebiti*

1053. Condictio indebiti

A *condictio* was available in case of a *datio solutionis causa* when a debt to be discharged did not in fact exist. The term *indebiti condictio* occasionally occurs in our sources (*Voc. Iur. Rom.* 1. 897. 1 ff.), but the texts are suspect; at any rate it was not yet a technical designation in classical times.

(*a*) What was the meaning of *indebitum*? Suppose A owed B 100 by stipulation. Later B released A by an informal *pactum de non petendo* (above, ss. 93, 802). A and B died and A's heir paid 100 to B's heir since both heirs knew nothing of the *pactum de non petendo*. Has A's heir paid an *indebitum* which he can recover with a *condictio*? The classical lawyers seem to have answered in the affirmative, since the debtor (A's heir) though owing *iure civili* was protected by an *exceptio perpetua* (above, s. 103). It has been asserted that in such a case a *condictio utilis* was required as *iure civili* a *debitum* had been paid. This is possibly true, but we hear nothing of such a *condictio utilis*. The *condictio* for an unjustified enrichment was after all a creation of the lawyers and they might feel free to state its conditions. *Fr. Vat.* 266 is certainly corrupt, but the words *sed et si ... exceptionem* are perhaps only a gloss. Thus the matter remains in doubt.

(*b*) Where the recipient knew that an *indebitum* was paid to him, he committed *furtum* and did not acquire ownership (above, s. 983). The *condictio indebiti* was not available against him but of course the *condictio furtiva* was (below, s. 1059). But was that also the law when the payer owed the amount *iure civili* but was protected by an *exceptio perpetua*? We hardly think so.

(*c*) Suppose that only the payer was aware that in truth he owed nothing. Under Justinian's law the *condictio indebiti* was barred. As regards the classical law, it is widely held that the payer's knowledge of the non-existence of the debt was irrelevant; but that seems hardly compatible with the sources. It is true that such a payment does not always imply a donation, so that, if a donation was not made and a *condictio* would not be available, the payment would remain with the recipient as an unjustified enrichment; but as aforesaid (above, s. 1041) there were other cases in which an unjustified enrichment could not be claimed back. The lawyers might have said (to use the medieval maxim): *adversus factum suum nemo potest venire*.

Gaius emphasizes three or four times (3. 91; 2. 283) that the payment was made *per errorem*. It is a mere evasion to say that Gaius had only in mind the usual cases of a *solutio indebiti* and that he did not seriously regard the giver's error as an essential requirement for the *condictio indebiti*. Gai. 2. 283 can hardly be explained by referring to the particularity of the *fideicommissum*. The palpable interpolation of *D.* (12. 6) 26. 3 (cf. *Fr. Vat.* 266) does not prove that the compilers substantially modified the classical law. It is true that it is not quite accurate to require an error on the part of the payer. It is not the error which makes the *condictio* applicable; it is rather the knowledge of the payer which bars the *condictio*. But as a rule this comes to the same thing; an exceptional case like *D.* (12. 6) 26. 13 could be safely ignored by Gaius and even by other lawyers. At any rate the new doctrine is doubtful.

(d) Exceptionally the *condictio indebiti* was absolutely barred, in particular whenever the payment was made in order to discharge a non-existent obligation which, if it had existed, would be one of those *in quibus lis infitiando crescit in duplum* (above, s. 74).

2. *Condictio causā datā causā non secutā* or *ob causam datorum* (D. 12. 4 and C. 4. 6)

1054. Condictio ob causam datorum

Suppose A gave B a sum of money as *dos* (*dotis causa*); if the planned marriage did not come into existence, A might recover the money with a *condictio*. For other examples see our remarks on the so-called innominate contracts (above, s. 903) and on the *donatio sub modo* (above, s. 974).

3. *Condictio ob turpem causam* (D. 12. 5; C. 4. 7)

1055. Condictio ob turpem causam

When the recipient of a *datio* acted *adversus bonos mores*, the giver had a *condictio* against him (e.g. A gave B money in order to prevent him from murdering a third person) provided he himself was not equally *in turpitudine* (e.g. A gave B money in order that he might murder a third person).

4. *Condictio ob iniustam causam* (D. 12. 5; C. 4. 9)

1056. Condictio ob iniustam causam

Donations between husband and wife were void (above, s. 206). The giver might claim the gift with the *rei vindicatio* or, if the recipient had consumed it, with the *condictio*.

5. *Condictio ob causam finitam*

1057. Condictio ob causam finitam

This *condictio* is not expressly mentioned in our sources. But if a debtor had given a promissory note to the creditor, he might reclaim it with a *condictio* after the discharge of the debt. It should, however, be noted that the restitution of a *dos* could never be demanded with a *condictio ob causam finitam* if the marriage was subsequently dissolved: *dotis causa perpetua est*.

The special *condictio sine causa* which appears in the *Digest* rubric 12. 7 and in the *Codex* rubric C. 4. 9 and the *condictio ex lege* (C. 4. 9) did not exist under classical law.

1058. Condictio sine causa and ex lege

1059. An irregular *condictio* was the *condictio furtiva* (*D.* 13. 1;
Condictio
furtiva, *C.* 4. 8). The action was available to the owner of stolen
formula things against the thief for the restitution of those things.
A special *formula* did not exist, but the general *formulae,*
condictio certae pecuniae, certae rei, and *certae quantitatis,* were
also used in this case, though strictly speaking their wording did not cover this case. The *intentio* of those *formulae*
ran: 'Si paret Numerium Negidium Aulo Agerio . . .
dare oportere'; *dare* meant in classical times 'to transfer
ownership' and the thief was obviously unable to transfer
ownership to the owner. The lawyers have deliberately
overlooked this defect influenced, as Gaius 4. 4 says,
'odio furum, quo magis pluribus actionibus teneantur'.

1060. The *condictio furtiva* was not a penal action but an action
Character for the recovery of an unjustified enrichment; under classical law it was the only *condictio* of this kind which was not
founded on a *datio.* 'Enrichment' meant here as always
(above, s. 1050) the enrichment at the time at which it was
acquired; moreover the thief was regarded as being always
in mora debitoris (fur semper in mora), so that he was liable
not only for *dolus* and *culpa* but also for *casus.* As the *condictio* was not a penal action, it did not lie against the accomplice. On the other hand, it was, in contrast to the *actio furti,*
passively transmissible; the thief's heir succeeded to the
obligation whether or not the stolen things were in the
estate.

1061. Solo In contrast to the *actio furti* the *condictio furtiva* was avail-
domino able solely to the owner of the stolen things; at any rate this
competit was the dominant classical doctrine.

1062. Besides the *condictio furtiva* the owner had sometimes the
Competing *actio furti* and the *rei vindicatio. Condictio* and *actio furti* as
actions well as *rei vindicatio* and *actio furti* were of course cumulated
(above, s. 1002), but *condictio* and *rei vindicatio* stood only
in elective concurrence, since both were *actiones rem persequentes.*

1063. We have already mentioned above (s. 982) that Sabinus
Condictio
quasi acknowledged a *furtum* of land and granted accordingly a
furtiva *condictio furtiva* to an owner of land who had been deprived
of his possession *vi* or *clam.* Although the later lawyers con-

fined *furtum* to movable things, they seem to have followed
Sabinus with regard to the *condictio furtiva*. A *condictio
furtiva* where there was no *furtum* seems odd. We must,
however, remember that the *condictio furtiva* had not yet a
fixed name in classical times; Gaius (2. 79; 4. 4) simply calls
it *condictio*. Thus the lawyers felt no scruples about according a *condictio* (*quasi furtiva*, they might have said) to the
owner of land, though they denied the *actio furti*. Of course
this *condictio* was, like the *condictio furtiva*, a *condictio rei*,
and not a *condictio possessionis*.

SOURCES

s. 1041. Read *D*. (50. 17) 206; (12. 6) 14.

s. 1046. Read Gai. 2. 79 *in fine*; note that only the *condictio furtiva* is
mentioned.

s. 1047. Read *D*. (12. 4) 10; (16. 1) 8. 3; (23. 3) 78. 5; (12. 7) 1 pr.
(spurious); (12. 7) 3 (spurious); (46. 2) 12 (heavily interpolated).

s. 1048. Read Gai. 2. 82; *D*. (12. 1) 19. 1; (12. 1) 4. 1 (the original
text dealt with *condictio furtiva*).

s. 1049. For the classical conception of *condictio* read Gai. 4. 18: 'condictionem dicimus actionem in personam qua intendimus "dari nobis
oportere".' In Gai. 4. 5 *fierive* must needs be a gloss.

s. 1051. Read Gai. 3. 91; *D*. (26. 8) 13; (46. 3) 66 [*sed pupillus . . .
renebitur*].

s. 1053*a*. Read *Fr. Vat.* 266 to *tutus solverit*; cf. *D*. (12. 6) 26. 3.

s. 1053*c*. Read Gai. 3. 91; 2. 283; *Fr. Vat.* 266; cf. *D*. (12. 6) 26. 3
and 26. 13.

s. 1053*d*. Read *Inst. Iust.* (3. 27) 7 to *ex legato*; Gai. 2. 283 to *non potest*.

s. 1054. Read *D*. (12. 4) 7. 1 [*traditus*] ⟨*mancipatus*⟩, see *Index Interp*.

s. 1055. Read *D*. (12. 5) 4. 2–3.

s. 1056. Read *D*. (24. 1) 5. 18 [*hactenus*]; [*hactenus quatenus . . . est*].

s. 1057. Read *C*. (4. 9) 2.

s. 1059. Read Gai. 4. 4.

s. 1060. Read *D*. (13. 1) 8. 1 [*maxime . . . liberatur*]; (13. 1) 6; (50. 16)
53. 2 [*sic enim . . . non potest*]; see *Index Interp*.; (13. 1) 9 [*non . . . autem*]
(substantially classical).

s. 1061. Read *D*. (13. 1) 1; (47. 2) 14. 16; (13. 1) 12. 2 is problematical; *incerti* is certainly interpolated.

s. 1062. Read Gai. 4. 4.

s. 1063. Read *D*. (13. 3) 2 [*ceterum . . . ait*]; (47. 2) 25 pr.–1 [*possessionem*].

BIBLIOGRAPHY

s. 1042. For comparative law see Gerota, *La théorie de l'enrichement
sans cause* (1925).

s. 1043. Pernice, *Labeo*, iii. 1 (1892), 202 ff. (fundamental); R. v. Mayr, *Die Condictio des röm. Privatrechts* (1900, completely out of date); von Koschembahr–Lyskowski, *Die Condictio als Bereicherungsklage im klass. röm. Recht*, i (1903); ii (1907), thorough work with full references; H. Siber, *Röm. Privatrecht* (1928), 213 f.; G. H. Maier, *Praetorische Bereicherungsklagen* (1932); Pflüger, *Zur Lehre vom Erwerbe des Eigentums* (1937), 110 ff.; Solazzi, 'Le condictiones e l'errore', *Atti Napoli*, lxii (1947).

s. 1045. Lenel, *Edict.* (1927), §§ 55, 57, 95.

s. 1047. On the *condictio liberationis* see v. Koschembahr, l.c. ii. 273 ff.; Benigni, *AG* lxxv (1905), 320 ff.; Beseler, Z xlv (1925), 234; Archi, *St. Solazzi* (1948), 740 ff.; wrongly Kaser, Z lviii (1938), 320.

s. 1048. On *condictio possessionis* see v. Koschembahr, l.c. ii. 181 ff.; Beseler, *Beiträge*, iv (1920), 9; De Villa, 'Contributo alla storia e alla teoria della condictio possessionis', *St. Sassaresi*, x (1932, not available).

s. 1049. v. Koschembahr, l.c. ii. 78 ff.; Benigni, 'La condictio incerti', *AG* lxxv (1905), 309 ff.; Lenel, l.c. § 57.

s. 1050. Siber, l.c. 218 f., 222 in fine.

s. 1051. Siber, l.c. 316, 321 f. On *D.* (26. 8) 13 see Beseler, *St. Bonfante*, ii (1930), 70 note. On *D.* (46. 3) 66 see Guarino, *SD* xi (1945), 327.

s. 1053. Sanfilippo, *Condictio indebiti*, i (1943).

s. 1053a. Beseler, *Juristische Miniaturen* (1929), 124.

s. 1053c. Beseler, *Jur. Miniaturen*, 125; *St. Bonfante*, ii (1930), 69 n. 7; *Scritti Ferrini*, iii (1948), 292; Z lxvi (1948), 374; Solazzi, 'L'errore nella condictio indebiti', *Atti Napoli*, lix (1939); 'Ancora dell' errore nella condictio indebiti', *SD* ix (1943), 55 ff.; 'Le condictiones e l'errore', *Atti Napoli*, lxii (1947); Sanfilippo, l.c. 97; P. Voci, *L'errore nel diritto Romano* (1937), 130 ff.; *SD* viii (1942), 22 ff.; Guarino, *SD* xi (1945), 319 ff. On *D.* (12. 6) 26. 13 see Guarino, 332.

s. 1055. Beseler, 'Condictio ob causam turpem aut rem turpem dati', *SD* iii (1937), 376 ff.·

s. 1058. Pflüger, l.c.; Beseler, Z lxvi (1948), 361.

s. 1059. Bossowski, *Annali Palermo*, xiii (1927), 343 ff.; Biondi, *Bull.* xxxviii (1930), 257; Siber, *St. Riccobono*, iii (1936), 245.

s. 1061. On *D.* (13. 1) 12. 2 see Erbe, *Die Fiducia im röm. Recht* (1940), 56.

s. 1062. Levy, *Die Konkurrenz der Aktionen*, ii. 1 (1922) 90 ff.; Beseler, Z xliv (1924), 364, 371.

s. 1063. Benigni, l.c. 336 f.

2. *Negotiorum Gestio (agency without a mandate)*

1064.
Sources
and
literature
The details of the classical law of *negotiorum gestio* are still obscure in spite of repeated attempts to clear them up. The relevant texts in the *Corpus iuris* are heavily interpolated

(this is today uncontested) and reliable material outside the *Corpus iuris* is scarce. This is not the place to expound the numerous problems which with available sources are perhaps insoluble; we confine ourselves to a few remarks on the classical law under Hadrian's Edict.

The Edict contained a rubric *de negotiis gestis* (Lenel, 1065. *Edict.* § 35) which concluded the edictal title *de cognitoribus* The Edict *et procuratoribus et defensoribus*. This arrangement reveals that *negotium* in the sense of this rubric meant primarily *lis*, 'process', 'trial', and that its primary purpose was to further the defence of a person who was *indefensus* in a trial (Lenel, *Edict.* p. 32), though the praetor may have applied the Edict to other kinds of *negotium* from the very beginning or at any rate from very early times. Under this edictal rubric were three things: (1) a praetorian promise to grant an action; (2) *formulae in factum conceptae*; (3) *formulae in ius conceptae*. This statement is today uncontested.

1. The praetorian promise is only preserved to us in an interpolated form (*D.* 3. 5. 3 pr.). The classical wording most probably ran as follows:

'Si quis negotia absentis, sive quis negotia quae cuiusque cum is moritur fuerunt, gesserit, iudicium eo nomine dabo.'

The praetor confined himself to two special cases in which a *negotiorum gestio* seemed to be urgently required. The text of the *Digest* has *alterius* instead of *absentis*, but this is a palpable and today universally acknowledged interpolation; *alterius* would already have covered the second case.

2. The praetorian promise was followed by *formulae in factum conceptae*. Their construction is not known to us, but they were certainly confined to the two cases mentioned in the promise; the praetor might of course grant *actiones utiles* in analogous cases. The principal (*dominus negotii*) as well as the agent (*negotiorum gestor*) was entitled to an action. The principal might sue the *gestor* for the restitution of anything acquired by him and also for damages, if the *gestor* had acted negligently (so-called *actio directa*; see above, s. 70); the *gestor* might demand reimbursement of his expenses (so-called *actio negotiorum gestorum contraria*; above, s. 70).

3. Lastly there followed *formulae in ius conceptae* which contained the clause *ex fide bona* (Gai. 4. 62) and which were available equally to the principal and to the agent. Like the *formulae in factum conceptae* they were confined to the two cases mentioned in the praetorian promise. Lenel, and with him the dominant doctrine, held and hold that there was indeed a *formula in ius concepta* dealing with the *negotia* of a deceased person, but that another *formula* spoke quite generally of *negotia alterius* without mentioning *absentia*. He reconstructed the latter as follows:

'Quod Numerius Negidius negotia Auli Agerii gesserit, quidquid ob eam rem Numerium Negidium Aulo Agerio dare facere oportet ex fide bona, eius iudex Numerium Negidium Aulo Agerio condemnato, si non paret absolvito.'

This, according to Lenel, was the *formula* for an *actio directa*. It might be adapted to serve as a *formula* for the *actio contraria* by altering the names in the *demonstratio*, viz. *Quod Aulus Agerius negotii Numerii gesserit*, etc.

Lenel believed that this *formula in ius concepta* was (unlike the *formula in factum concepta*; Lenel, p. 103 f.) not confined to *negotia absentis*, since Ulpian when commenting on the *formula* did not mention the requirement of absence. But Lenel forgot that the compilers, as aforesaid, have changed *absentis* into *alterius* and accordingly had to delete *absentia* in Ulpian's commentary on the *formula*; thus his silence about *absentia* tells us nothing about the construction of the *formula* (Cicero, *Top.* 17. 66 is not decisive). Lenel's general formula by the side of a *formula* concerning the *negotia* of a deceased person looks odd and is highly improbable. By the side of the *formula*:

'Quod Numerius Negidius negotia quae Titii, cum is moreretur, fuerunt, gessit', etc.

stood in truth the following *formula*:

'Quod Numerius Negidius negotia Auli Agerii cum is absens fuerit, gessit', etc.

1066. Negotiorum gestio and mandatum   Certainly the praetor could grant and actually did grant similar *formulae* in other cases, but these were *actiones utiles*. It comes as a surprise that neither the edictal promise nor the *formulae* were confined to a *gestio sine mandatu*. It was at one time asserted that the text of the classical Edict contained the words *sine mandatu* or *sponte*, but these suggestions were absolutely wrong and rightly rejected by Lenel (*Edict*. p. 102). Why should the compilers have deleted those very words which were in full harmony with their own ideas?

In particular *sponte* is quite out of the question. The praetor cannot possibly have refused his remedies when a *curator prodigi absentis* had acted for his ward (although the *curator* did not act *sponte*. D. (3. 5) 3. 10 is spurious (see *Index Interp.*) or at least unreliable. See further on *sponte*, Beseler, *SD* iii (1937), 374.

The simple and convincing explanation is that the Edict originated in republican times when *mandatum* was not yet recognized as a contract (above, s. 955) and its wording remained unaltered later when that contract was acknowledged. It was the lawyers who confined the Edict to *gestio sine mandatu* after *mandatum* had become a contract, just as they did not apply the Edict to the *gestio* of a *tutor* after the *actio tutelae* had been created (above, s. 306). The praetor denied the *actiones negotiorum gestorum* when a person had acted as *mandatarius* or *tutor* of the *dominus negotii*. On the other hand, the Edict applied to the *curator furiosi* or *prodigi* (see above, ss. 339, 349) since another action did not exist; but as a rule (viz. unless the curator acted for his absent ward) *actiones utiles* were required; this is repeatedly emphasized in our sources.

The classical mechanism of the different kinds of actions —*actiones in ius* and *in factum conceptae*; *actiones directae and utiles*—is not fully discernible from available sources owing to the activity of the compilers; the classical distinctions were indeed doomed to vanish with the disappearance of the formulary procedure. Thus the compilers eliminated the classical distinction between *actio in ius* and *in factum concepta* so thoroughly that we cannot say whether the different construction of the *formula* entailed substantial differences. As regards the distinction between *actio negotiorum gestorum directa* and *utilis* the compilers declared in an entirely unclassical text (*D*. 3. 5, 46. 1) that the distinction

1067. The compilers

had lost its importance, but they fell far short of a cancellation of the term *utilis* when it occurred in texts which they inserted in their collections. As already stated (s. 1065), they changed the edictal word *absentis* into *alterius*, which implied that the classical *actiones utiles* in case of *non-absentia* were now changed into *actiones directae*. In some texts they have occasionally cancelled *utilis*, but in numerous texts they have preserved the classical *actio utilis*. Thus they styled the actions between curator and ward *utiles curationis causa actiones* (*D.* 27. 3 rubric) or *utiles curationis actiones*, abbreviations of *utiles negotiorum gestorum actiones curationis causa*, but they sometimes preserved the classical designation *actio negotiorum gestorum utilis*. Hence the sources on this point are very confused, as might be expected. The question as to when under classical law the *actio directa* was available and when an *actio utilis* was required, cannot be answered by relying on unreliable texts but by deduction from the wording of the Edict. In all cases not covered by the wording of the Edict an *actio utilis* was required.

1068.
Evaluation

On other problems we will not dwell. Much more important than the technical details is the institution of *negotiorum gestio* as a whole. It is a quite original genuinely Roman creation without parallels in the laws of other peoples not dependent on Roman law. It emanated from Roman *humanitas*. The underlying idea was that a man should help his fellow men in case of emergency. The Romans carried through this idea with their usual common sense without confusing morality and law. Nobody is legally bound to care for the affairs of another (cf. in contrast Exodus xxiii. 4–5; Deuteronomy xxii. 1–4); but the law should favour and facilitate such altruistic action by granting to the *gestor* the right to claim reimbursement of his expenses, which of course entails a liability of the *gestor*. The institution of *negotiorum gestorum* was a happy invention, quite in the bold and original style of the republican jurisprudence, although in this present age of quick postal service, telegraph, and telephone it has lost some of its importance.

SOURCES

s. 1065. 1. Read D. (3. 5) 2, substantially classical.

s. 1066. Read C. (2. 18) 4, *actione ⟨utili⟩*. That the original text had *utili* is attested by Thalelaeus; Zachariae v. Lingenthal, *Supplementum Editionis Basilicorum* (1846), p. 157, no. 15. Read further C. (2. 18) 17, genuine.

BIBLIOGRAPHY

s. 1064. Lenel, *Edict.* (1927), § 35; Kreller, *PW*. Suppl. vii (1940), 551, with full references; 'Das Edikt de negotiis gestis in der Geschichte der Geschäftsbesorgung', *Festschrift P. Koschaker*, ii (1939), 193 ff.; 'Das Edikt de negotiis gestis in der klassischen Praxis', Z lix (1939), 390 ff. (Kreller's own theory is hardly acceptable); Arangio-Ruiz, *Il mandato in diritto Romano* (1949), 19 ff.; Sachers, 'Die Haftung des auftraglosen Geschäftsführers', *SD* iv (1938) 309 ff. On Paulus, *Sent.* 1. 4 see E. Levy, *Pauli Sententiae* (1945), 86 ff.

s. 1065. On *negotium = lis* see Schulz, *JRS* xxxi (1941), 64 f.

s. 1068. Gierke, *DP*, iii (1917), 979; Kohler, 'Die Menschenhülfe im Privatrecht', *Jherings Jahrbücher*, xxv (1887), 1 ff.; *Lehrbuch des Bürgerlichen Rechts*, ii. 1 (1906), 445 ff.

CHAPTER IV

TRANSFER AND DISCHARGE OF OBLIGATIONS

1. *Transfer of obligations*

1069.
Successio
and
Novatio
UNDER classical law obligations were actively and passively transferred by succession upon death, the *heres* succeeding to the assets as well as to the debts of the *de cuius*. In the case of succession *inter vivos* (*adrogatio*; above, ss. 242, 268 and *in manum conventio*; above, ss. 193 ff.) only the assets were transferred. Apart from these cases classical law knew no mode of transferring an obligation actively or passively to another person. There were, however, two substitutes. One of them was the *novatio* which we have already described above (s. 815). Where a creditor A wished to transfer his right to B, he could not do so by *mancipatio, in iure cessio*, or *traditio*, but he might authorize B to make a *novatio* by stipulating with the debtor that the latter should give him what he owed A. If the debtor accordingly promised B what he owed A, the latter lost his right and the debtor now owed B what he had previously owed A. Economically this meant a transfer of the obligation, but legally it meant the discharge of the original obligation and the creation of a new one. Moreover, this form of assignment was only available if the debtor was prepared to co-operate, for he was not bound to make the promise to B. In the same way an obligation might be passively transferred. When a creditor to whom A owed something stipulated with B that he should pay him what A owed him (the creditor), A was set free by *novatio* and B economically succeeded to him, although in purely legal terms A's debt was discharged by the creation of a new obligation.

1070.
Cognitor in
rem suam
Another rather artificial substitute was achieved by using the institution of representation in litigation for the purpose of transferring obligations.

Where a creditor wished to transfer his right to another, he might appoint the latter his representative for the exaction of the debt and authorize him to keep what he had exacted. Under classical law the assignee was in such a case, at least as a rule, appointed as *cognitor in rem suam* (not as *procurator in rem suam*). All reliable texts speak of a *cognitor in rem suam*: *Voc. Iur. Rom.* 5. 147. 30 ff.; *Fr. Vat.* 339 is doubtful. The Byzantines have throughout interpolated *procurator* instead of *cognitor*. At any rate we will deal here with the *cognitor in rem suam*.

1. When the *cognitor* had effected *litis contestatio* with the debtor, the assignor was debarred from pursuing his claim. The debtor was condemned to perform in favour of the *cognitor* what he had owed to the assignor. This was substantially a mode of transferring an obligation which did not require the consent of the debtor; legally the right acquired by the *cognitor* was a new right and not identical with the right of the assignor.

2. Before *litis contestatio* the right of the assignee was easily assailable. The assignor might revoke his authorization at will; he might also himself demand of the debtor the fulfilment of the obligation.

3. Antoninus Pius granted an *actio utilis* to the purchaser of a *hereditas* to whom the vendor (the *heres*) had assigned the hereditary obligations as to a *cognitor in rem suam*. Later rescripts granted an *actio utilis* in other cases. As far as an *actio utilis* was available to the *cognitor*, he was at least safe against the assignor's revocation, but the assignor was still free to demand payment from the debtor and thereby to destroy the assignee's right. Eventually the compilers debarred the assignor from claiming payment, if the assignee had made a *denuntiatio* to the debtor.

In a similar way an obligation might be passively transferred. The debtor might appoint another as *cognitor in rem suam*. When the creditor effected *litis contestatio* with the *cognitor*, the debtor was free and the *cognitor* alone was responsible for the debt. But the creditor was not bound to make *litis contestatio* with the *cognitor* unless the debtor gave him security in the form of a *cautio iudicatum solvi*.

1071.
Greek and
Teutonic
law

This Roman reluctance to admit an assignment of obligations without the consent of the debtor is not a peculiarity of Roman law; we find it also in Hellenistic and Teutonic (including English) law. It could not be otherwise. A law in which execution on the person of the debtor is a living institution cannot allow a creditor to transfer his right to another without the consent of the debtor, thereby perhaps substituting a harsh creditor for a mild one. The device of making an assignment by appointing a representative for the exaction of the debt was likewise known to Greek and Hellenistic law. But this appointment again required the consent of the debtor. The consent was frequently given in advance, the debtor promising in his bond to pay to the creditor or to any other person who might present the bond (παντὶ τῷ ἐπιφέροντι). This Hellenistic clause became known through Latin documents to the Middle Ages and was applied by medieval notaries. In English documents of the thirteenth century, for instance, the clause *vel attornato* (or *nuntio*) *has litteras deferenti* was quite common. Classical law had already passed beyond this stage, since it allowed the appointment of a *cognitor in rem suam pro creditore* without the consent of the debtor. Thus, though even Justinian's law persisted in denying a full transfer of obligations by assignment, it was, nevertheless, Roman law and not Greek or Teutonic law which paved the way for modern assignment in which the obligation can be transferred without the consent of the debtor.

SOURCES

s. 1069. Read Gai. 3. 82–4; 2. 38.

s. 1070. Read Gai. 2. 39; 4. 86, 87, 101; *D.* (2. 14) 16 pr. (substantially classical); *C.* (4. 39) 7 (substantially classical); *C.* (4. 10) 2; *C.* (8–41) 3 pr. [*vel aliquid . . . denuntiaverit*]; see Bähr, *Jherings Jahrbücher*, i (1857), 378 ff.

BIBLIOGRAPHY

ss. 1069 ff. Windscheid, *Pand.* ii (1906), §§ 328 ff.; Wenger, *CP* (1940), § 9, pp. 88 ff., references, p. 93.

s. 1070. Beseler, Z lxvi (1948), 268.

s. 1071. On Greek and Hellenistic law see Beauchet, *Histoire du droit privé de la république Athénienne*, iv (1897), 515 ff., 537 ff., 540; Taubenschlag, *Law of Greco-Roman Egypt* (1944), 316, 319, 261. On Teutonic law see H. Brunner, *Forschungen zur Geschichte des deutschen und fran-zösischen Rechts* (1894), 550, 599 ff.; Gierke, *DP* iii (1917), 181. On English law see Pollock and Maitland, *History*, ii (1911), 226 f.; but Maitland's remark (p. 227 n. 4): 'Apparently Bracton f. 41*b* knew these mercantile documents under the name *missibilia*' is a mistake. Bracton obviously had in mind the *missilia* mentioned in *D.* (41. 1) 9. 7; in fact, the best manuscripts read *missilia*.

2. *Discharge of obligations*

We have already occasionally touched upon the dis-charge of obligations. Penal actions were extinguished by the death of the debtor (above, ss. 73), *actiones vindictam spirantes* by the death of the creditor (above, ss. 77, 1019); sometimes an obligation was determined by the lapse of a certain time (above, s. 854); any obligation was determined by *novatio*, etc. In this place we only wish to make some additional remarks on certain particular modes of deter-mination.

1072.
Discharge
in general

i. *Performance (solutio in the narrower sense)*

The normal mode of determination was the performance of what was due to the creditor. Under classical law due performance extinguished any obligation *ipso iure*, no formal or informal release or acquittal being required. This rule was already recognized in republican times; the maxim 'prout quidque contractum est, ita et solvi debet' can hardly ever have been a general legal rule and certainly was not so in classical times. The performance had to be made by the debtor, but if the performance was a *datio* in the classical sense (above, s. 1048) it might be made by a third person even without knowledge or against the will of the debtor. The compilers finally allowed a performance to be made by a third person where the debtor owed a *facere*.

1073.
Solutio

ii. *Datio in solutum*

Any obligation might be discharged by a performance different from that which the debtor owed to the creditor. Of course this mode of determination always required the consent of the creditor, but with this consent even a third person might make a *datio in solutum*. As regards the

1074.
Datio in
solutum

technical side of this sort of discharge, the Sabinians advocated a *liberatio ipso iure*, whilst the Proculians merely protected the debtor with an *exceptio doli*. Justinian adopted the
Sabinian view probably following the post-classical doctrine and practice. The *datio in solutum* aimed at the discharge of an obligation and was, therefore, not a contract.
The compilers, however, assimilated *datio in solutum* to a
contract of sale and granted an *actio empti utilis* to the creditor when the given object was later 'evicted' (above, s. 923);
under classical law the old obligation remained intact in
such a case.

1075. iii. *Acceptilatio*

Accepti-
latio   *Acceptilatio* was a release in the form of a stipulation
(above, s. 805). The debtor might ask the creditor: *Quod
ego tibi promisi, habesne acceptum?* The creditor answered:
Habeo. In truth the creditor had received nothing, for if he
had received payment the obligation would have been discharged under classical law by performance; the creditor's
declaration, 'I have received what was due to me', was
merely a matter of form.

Like the stipulation the *acceptilatio* was an oral agreement
(above, s. 805) and, therefore, inevitably required (in
default of telephone) the presence of the parties. Further,
only a verbal obligation could be extinguished by *acceptilatio*, i.e. primarily (above, s. 800) an obligation resulting
from a stipulation. Where parties wished to discharge obligations of another kind by *acceptilatio*, they had first to convert them into verbal obligations by *novatio* (above, s. 815).

The legal effect of a valid *acceptilatio* was the extinction
of the obligation *ipso iure*. It operated like performance and
was therefore described by Gaius as an imaginary performance (*imaginaria solutio*). So far the words *acceptum habes?
habeo* were taken literally and not as a mere matter of form.
The important consequence was that in any case of passive
solidarity (above, s. 827) a release of one of the debtors by
acceptilatio set free the other debtors; and in any case of
active solidarity the *acceptilatio* made by one of the creditors
destroyed the rights of the other creditors. Thus if the

creditor released the *fideiussor* by *acceptilatio*, the principal debtor inevitably became free as well as the surety; where the creditor wished to confine the release to the surety, he had to make a *pactum de non petendo* with the *fideiussor* and not an *acceptilatio*.

An invalid *acceptilatio* was, under classical law, absolutely ineffective and was not converted into a valid *pactum de non petendo*; thus in particular an *acceptilatio* of a non-verbal obligation was not converted into a valid *pactum*. The classical lawyers were loath to convert legal acts: an invalid will was not maintained in the form of codicils (above, s. 543), an invalid *legatum* was not converted into a *fideicommissum* (above, s. 559), etc. The attitude of the post-classical lawyers was fundamentally different; they wished to maintain an invalid *acceptilatio* as a *pactum de non petendo*. The texts in which this conversion appears are all interpolated. Under classical law an invalid *acceptilatio* was absolutely ineffective; the debt remained intact and the debtor could not even protect himself with an *exceptio doli*.

Acceptilatio still existed in Justinian's law.

iv. *Confusio*

1076.
Confusio

We have to distinguish two kinds of *confusio*.

1. Suppose the creditor became the sole heir of the debtor or, conversely, the debtor became the sole heir of the creditor. The obligation was then extinguished, since nobody can be his own debtor. Less self-evident is the extinction in the following case. A slave belonging to Titius committed a delict against Seius; the latter had an *actio noxalis* against Titius. Later Seius acquired ownership of the slave. According to the rule *noxa caput sequitur* Titius now was free from any liability and Seius was, so to speak, his own debtor. According to the Sabinians the *confusio* extinguished absolutely the obligation, but according to the Proculians the obligation was only dormant and automatically revived when the slave passed out of Seius' *potestas*. The Sabinian doctrine was adopted by Justinian. Leaving aside the Proculian doctrine we may simply state that this sort of *confusio* (i.e. when the same person becomes

creditor and debtor) extinguished any obligation *ipso iure*. Sometimes the *confusio* is described (like *acceptilatio*) as a *solutio*, but the relevant texts are interpolated. In truth the legal effects of *confusio* differed from those of *solutio*: in cases of solidarity *confusio* left the other obligations intact whilst solution extinguished them all.

Consider the following cases.

1. A and B were *plures rei promittendi* (above, s. 827). The creditor C became the heir of A or A became C's heir. The obligation of B was unaffected by the *confusio*.

2. A was C's principal debtor, B was *fideiussor*.

(*a*) If C became A's heir or A became C's heir, the principal obligation was discharged and therewith also that of the *fideiussor*, since the latter's obligation was only accessory to the principal obligation (above, s. 862).

(*b*) If C became B's heir or B became C's heir, the obligation of the *fideiussor* was extinguished, but not also the principal obligation.

2. The so-called 'absorbing *confusio*'. Suppose that A was the principal debtor and F a *fideiussor*. Later A became F's heir or F became A's heir. According to the classical doctrine the obligation of the *fideiussor* was extinguished by *confusio* with the principal obligation, but Papinian seems to have advocated protection for the creditor whenever this *confusio* involved him in substantial loss.

Consider the following case. A was principal debtor and F *fideiussor*. F died and A became his sole heir. The obligation of the *fideiussor* was extinguished by *confusio*, but this might imply a disadvantage to the creditor: if the *obligatio fideiussoria* had still existed, the creditor might have demanded *separatio bonorum*, a right which was only accorded to a *creditor hereditarius* (above, s. 533). Papinian seems to have granted *separatio bonorum* to the creditor, although after the *confusio* had happened he was no longer *creditor hereditarius* but only *creditor heredis*.

When there were two *rei promittendi* (above, s. 827) and one of them became the heir of the other, no absorbing *confusio* took place and both obligations remained in force. Similarly there was no absorbing *confusio* if there were two *rei stipulandi* and one of them became the heir of the other.

SOURCES

s. 1073. Read Gai. 3. 168, first sentence; *D.* (46. 3) 80, interpolated, reconstruction uncertain; (46. 3) 53; (46. 3) 40; (46. 3) 31 [*et hoc . . . perficiat*]; [*non consentiente stipulatore*]; *Inst. Iust.* (3. 29) pr.

s. 1074. Read Gai. 3. 168, cf. *Inst. Iust.* (3. 29) pr.; *D.* (46. 3) 46 pr. (genuine); (46. 3) 98 pr. [*promittendo obligavit*] ⟨*dixit*⟩; [*promissione*] ⟨*dictione*⟩; *C.* (8. 44) 4 [*utilis*]; [*nam . . . obtinet*].

s. 1075. Read Gai. 3. 169–70; *D.* (46. 4) 13. 7; (5. 2) 12. 3; (13. 5) 1. 4 [*cum . . . voluerit*]; [*quoniam . . . sit*]; substantially classical; (46. 4) 8 pr. (obviously spurious); (2. 14) 27. 9 [*tacita pactione*] ⟨*non*⟩; (46. 4) 19 pr. [*quidem . . . potest*]; *Inst. Iust.* (3. 29) 1.

s. 1076. Read Gai. 4. 77–8; *D.* (46. 1) 71 pr. only 'sed cum duo rei promittendi . . . confusa obligatione'; (46. 1) 21. 5; (17. 1) 11 ⟨*non*⟩ *habeo*; (46. 1) 38. 1; (46. 3) 38. 5 (see above, s. 740). On absorbing *confusio*: *D.* (46. 1) 5, substantially classical; (46. 3) 38. 5; (46. 3) 93. 2, substantially classical; (46. 1) 50; (42. 6) 3 pr., substantially classical.

BIBLIOGRAPHY

s. 1072. Windscheid, *Pand.* ii (1906), §§ 341 ff.; Solazzi, *L'estinzione della obbligazione* (1931).

s. 1073. On *D.* (46. 3) 80 see Solazzi, 10 ff. and *Index interp.* On performance by third persons see Solazzi, 35 ff.

s. 1074. H. Steiner, *Datio in solutum* (1917); Solazzi, 148 ff.

s. 1075. Solazzi, 233 ff. On the conversion of an invalid *acceptilatio* into a valid *pactum* see Beseler, Z xlvii (1927), 357 ff.; Solazzi, 246 ff.; Astuti, *Studi intorno alla promessa di pagamento, Il costituto di debito*, ii (1941), 257, with references.

s. 1076. P. Kretschmar, *Die Theorie der Confusion* (1899), a thorough work but entirely uncritical and out of date; Solazzi, 254 ff. On absorbing *confusio* see in particular Beseler, Z xlvii (1927), 53 ff. On *D.* (17. 1) 11 see Solazzi, 277 (unacceptable, since *litis contestatio* with the *fideiussor* did not consume the action against the principal debtor; above, s. 865) and Beseler, Z xlv (1925), 252 (not convincing).

INDEX

ADDENDA

s. 16, p. 16. Kaser, 'Zum Ursprung des geteilten römischen Zivilprozessverfahrens', *Festschrift für Wenger*, i (1944), 106; Wenger, 'Vom zweigeteilten römischen Zivilprozesse', *St. Solazzi* (1948), 47 ff.; Jolowicz, 'The judge and the arbitral principle', *RIDA*, ii (1949), 477.

s. 26, p. 18. Kaser, 'Die lex Aebutia', *St. Albertario* (1950).

ss. 47–51, p. 31. Philonenco, 'Intentio dans les formules in factum conceptae', *RIDA*, iii (1949), 231.

s. 56, p. 34. L. Levi, Le caractère exécutif de l'actio et l'obligation de défendre à l'encontre les actiones in personam (1938).

s. 65, p. 37. Kaser, 'Die Rechtsgrundlage der actio rei uxoriae', *RIDA*, ii (1949), 511.

ss. 70, 71, p. 41. Grosso, Il sistema romano dei contratti (1950), 249.

s. 73. 3, p. 45. Sargenti, Contributo allo studio della responsabilità nossale in diritto romano (1949).

ss. 86, 87, p. 48. Buckland, 'Finium regundorum', *RH*, xv (1936), 741.

ss. 88–90, p. 49. Siber, 'Praeiudicia als Beweismittel', *Festschrift Wenger*, i (1944), 46.

s. 97, p. 55. Collinet, *Études*, v (1947), 487 ff.

s. 103, p. 58. Solazzi, 'Sulle classificazioni delle exceptiones', *AG*, cxxxvii (1949), 4 ff.

s. 112, p. 63. Collinet, *Études*, v (1947), 479 ff.

s. 124, p. 76. Castello, *St. Solazzi* (1948), 232.

s. 136, p. 81. Alvaro D'Ors Perez-Peix, *Emerita*, xi (1943), 297; *Anuario de Historia del Derecho*, xv (1944), 162 ff.; *Sefarad*, vi (1946), 21 ff.; Arangio-Ruiz, 'L'applicazione del diritto romano in Egitto dopo la costituzione di Caracalla', *Annali Catania*, i (1947); Schönbauer, *Anzeiger der phil.-hist. Klasse der Österreich. Akademie der Wiss.*, Jahrg. 1949, p. 369.

s. 140, p. 85. Danieli, *SD*, xv (1949), 198 (manumissio censu).

s. 145, p. 89. De Visscher, 'La notion de corpus et le régime des associations privées à Rome', *Scritti Ferrini*, iv (1949), 43 ff.

s. 146, p. 89. Bruck, *Scritti Ferrini*, iv (1949), 1 ff., 18, 29 f.

s. 152, p. 92. Jones, 'The aerarium and the fiscus', *JRS*, xl (1950), 22 ff.

s. 169, p. 102. Hanslik, *Bursians Jahrbücher über die Fortschritte der klass. Altertumswissenschaft*, Jahrg. 1943, vol. 282, p. 67.

s. 180, p. 108. On *Laudatio Turiae*: van Oven, *RIDA*, iii (1949), 273; Lemosse, *RH*, xxviii (1950), 251; Durry, Éloge funèbre d'une matrone romaine (1950); Gordon, 'A new fragment of the Laudatio Turiae', *Americ. Journal of Archaeology*, liv (1950), 223.

s. 186, p. 114. H. J. Wolff, Z, lxvii (1950), 261 ff., 288.

s. 189, p. 114. Gaudemet, 'Iustum matrimonium', *RIDA*, ii (1949),

s. 191, p. 114. Gaudemet, l.c., loc. cit., 309 ff., 328 ff.

ss. 193 ff., p. 118. Düll, *Festschrift Wenger* i (1944), 204 ff.; Kaser, *AR,* 343; Maschi, *Humanitas* (1949), 75 ff.

ss. 200, 203, p. 121. On *Laudatio Turiae,* see s. 180, p. 108, Addenda.

s. 220, 4 (a), p. 128. This retentio was only available, si culpa mulieris aut patris divortium factum sit.

ss. 207 ff., p. 130. Maschi, *Humanitas* (1949), 82 ff.; H. J. Wolff, Z, liii (1933), 297.

s. 210, p. 130. H. J. Wolff, 'Dos und erneuerte Ehe', Z, lxvi (1948), 31 ff.

s. 216, p. 130. Maschi, *Humanitas* (1949), 85 ff., 91 ff.

s. 217, p. 130. Kaser, 'Die Rechtsgrundlage der actio rei uxoriae', *RIDA,* ii (1949), 511.

s. 218, p. 130. Solazzi, 'Sul consenso della filia familias all' actio rei uxoriae esercitata dal padre', *Rend. Lomb.* lxx (1937), Fasc. III.

s. 225, p. 137. H. J. Wolff, Z, lxvii (1950), 261 ff., 279 ff.

s. 231, p. 137. Kaser, Z, lxvii (1950), 493.

s. 243, p. 149. Koschaker, 'Neue Keilschriftl. Rechtsurkunden', *Abhandl. der Sächs. Akademie d. Wiss.* xxix, 5 (1928), 88 ff.

s. 244, p. 149. Kaser, *ARI* (1949), 342.

s. 245, p. 149. Prévost, 'L'adoption d'Octave', *RIDA,* v (1950), 361.

s. 249, p. 149. Kaser, Z, lxvii (1950), 474 ff.

s. 272, p. 159. Kaser, Z, lxvii (1950), 474 ff.

s. 286, p. 172. Solazzi, 'Da "tutorem do" a "tutor esto"', *SD,* xiii/xiv (1947–8, publ. 1949), 301.

s. 302, p. 177. Solazzi, L'età dell' infans, *Bull.,* viii/ix (1947), 354.

s. 306, p. 180. Kaser, 'Die Rechtsgrundlage der actio rei uxoriae', *RIDA,* ii (1949), 511; Solazzi, 'Il contratto di tutela in Gai. 4, 182, *Bull.,* viii/ix (1947), 360.

s. 313, p. 184. The passage in the *Laudatio Turiae* according to the new fragment published by Gordon, *American Journal of Archaeology,* liv (1950), 223; the traditional text of our editions (based on Mommsen's conjecture) is wrong.

s. 339, p. 199. Guarino, 'Il "furiosus" e il "prodigus" nelle XII Tabulae', *Annali Catania,* iii (1949).

s. 347, p. 200. Renier, 'Observations de la terminologie de l'aliénation mentale', *RIDA,* v (1950), 429 ff.

ss. 349 ff., p. 202. Guarino, 'Il "furiosus" e il "prodigus" nelle XII Tabulae', *Annali Catania,* iii (1949).

ss. 358 ff., p. 209. Bonfante, *Corso,* vi, 1 (1930); Solazzi, *Diritto ereditario romano* 1 (1932), 2 (1933); Albanese, 'La successione ereditaria in diritto romano antico', *Annali Palermo,* xx (1949).

s. 361, p. 209. Cassisi, 'L'editto di C. Verre et la Lex Voconia', *Annali Catania,* iii (1949).

ss. 367 ff., p. 212. Albanese, *La successione ereditaria* (1949), 228 ff.

s. 372, p. 216. Albanese, l.c. 228 ff.

s. 383, p. 225. Solazzi, 'Glosse a Gaio', *St. Riccobono*, i (1936), 80 ff.

s. 386, p. 226. Castello, 'Sulla condizione del filio concepito legitimamente e illegitimamente nel diritto romano', *RIDA*, iv (1950), 269 ff.

s. 392, p. 226. Solazzi, *Diritto ereditario romano*, i (1932), 188 ff.; Cassisi, 'L'editto di C. Verre e la "Lex Voconia"', *Ann. Catania*, iii (1949), Estratto, p. 13.

s. 402, p. 227. Solazzi, 'Glosse a Gaio', *St. Riccobono*, i (1936), 80 ff.

ss. 426 ff., p. 240. Albanese, *La successione ereditaria* (1949), 321 ff.

s. 432, p. 244. Albanese, *La successione ereditaria* (1949), 134 ff., 294.

s. 436, p. 246. Solazzi, 'Gordiano e il testamento orale pretorio', *SD*, xiii/xiv (1947, published 1949), 312 ff.

s. 438, p. 248. De Sarlo, 'Gaio II, 151 e la natura della revoca testamentaria non formale', *AG*, cxxxvi (1949), 102 ff.

s. 444, p. 251. Albanese, *La successione ereditaria* (1949), 322 ff.

s. 447, p. 256. Albanese, l.c. 316 f.

s. 452, p. 260. Solazzi, *Athenaeum*, viii (1930), 45 ff.

s. 455, p. 265. E. Weiss, *PW*, iv A, 506.

s. 458, p. 265. E. Weiss, *PW*, iv A, 507.

s. 464, p. 270. See below, s. 491, Bibliography; Albanese, l.c. 94 ff.

s. 491, p. 287. Albanese, l.c. 94 ff.

s. 492, p. 287. For texts with 'voluntarius heres' see now *Voc. Iur. Rom.* v. 1482.

s. 497a, p. 287. Biondi, *St. Solazzi* (1948), 77 with references.

s. 506, p. 291. De Zulueta, *RH*, xi (1932), 491 ff.; Aru, *AG*, cxxiv (1940), 8 ff.; Behrens, 'Coartare' (on Gai. 2, 170), *Z*, lxvii (1950), 524.

s. 525, p. 301. On *consortium* see Albanese, l.c. 9 ff., with references.

s. 529, p. 304. Solazzi, *SD*, vi (1940), 335; Guarino, 'Gai. II, 155 e il beneficium dell' heres necessarius', *SD*, x (1944), 240.

s. 554, p. 323. Kaser, *ARI* (1949), 147 ff.; 'Das legatum sinendi modo in der Geschichte des röm. Vermächtnisrechts', *Z*, lxvii (1950), 320 ff.

ss. 574, 575, p. 333. Santi di Paola, *Donatio mortis causa* (1950).

s. 586, p. 339. Brasiello, 'Brevi Note sul concetto di proprietà', *St. F. Ferrara*, Estratto, p. 30.

s. 588, p. 342. Luzzatto, 'Appunti sul ius Italicum', *RIDA*, v (1950), 79 ff., 110.

s. 601, p. 354. On 'emere' see Walde, *Lat. Etymol. WB*, i (1938), 400.

ss. 613 ff., p. 354. Pflüger, *Zur Lehre vom Erwerbe des Eigentums nach röm. Recht* (1937).

s. 615, p. 354. Pflüger, l.c. 18 ff.; P. Voci, 'Iusta causa traditionis' e 'iusta causa usucapionis', *SD*, xv (1949), 141 ff.

s. 616, p. 354. Feenstra, 'Inst. 2, 1, 91 et les origines de la "revendication" du vendeur non payé', *RIDA*, iv (1950), 455 ff.; Pringsheim, *Greek law of sale* (1950), 179 ff.

s. 625, p. 361. P. Voci, 'iusta causa traditionis' e 'iusta causa usucapionis', *SD*, xv (1949), 141 ff., 159 ff.

s. 628, p. 361. Albanese, 'La successione ereditaria in diritto romano antico' (*Annali Palermo* xx), 276 ff.

s. 631, p. 367. Lombardi, 'Libertà di caccia e proprietà in diritto romano', *Bull.*, liii/liv (1948), 273 ff.

s. 637, p. 367. Nardi, 'Un' osservazione in tema di tabula picta', *AG*, cxxi (1939).

s. 641, p. 379. Luzzatto, 'Spunti critici in tema di actio in rem per sponsionem', *St. Albertario* (1950).

s. 655, p. 380. Ciapessoni, *Studi su Gaio* (1943), 91 ff.; Franca La Rosa, 'In tema di duplex dominium', *Annali Catania*, iii (1949).

ss. 682 ff., p. 396. Solazzi, *Specie ed estinzione delle servitù prediali* (1948); *La tutela e il possesso delle servitù prediali* (1949).

s. 684, p. 396. Solazzi, *Specie ed estinzione*, 2 ff. On D. (33, 10) 12, see D'Ors, 'Varia Romana' 4, *Anuario de Historia del derecho español*, xvi (1945), 758 ff.

s. 686, p. 396. Solazzi, *Requisiti*, 21 ff., 25.

s. 691, p. 397. Solazzi, *Specie ed estinzione*, 157 ff.

s. 692, p. 397. Solazzi, *La tutela e il possesso delle servitù prediali* (1949). On the *interdictum quam servitutem* (Lenel, Edict. § 255) see Solazzi, *RIDA*, v (1950), 465 ff.

s. 695, p. 399. The standard work on *superficies* is now Heinrich Vogt, *Das Erbbaurecht des klassischen römischen Rechts* (1950). On the interdict 86 ff.; on the *actio in rem* 95 ff. Solazzi, 'Sulla superficie come servitù', *SD*, xiii/xiv (1947–8 published 1949), 307.

s. 696, p. 399. Lanfranchi, *Studi sull' ager vectigalis III. La trasmissibilità a titolo singulare del ius in agro vectigali* (1940); not available, but see Wieacker, Z, lxi (1941), 468.

s. 701a, p. 405. Savigny, *Vom Beruf unsrer Zeit für Gesetzgebung und Rechtswissenschaft* (3rd ed. 1840), 177.

ss. 730, 731, p. 419. Pringsheim, *The Greek law of sale* (1950), 311 with references.

s. 752. 3, p. 434. Kaser, Z, lxv (1947), 248 ff.

s. 753, p. 434. Kaser, 'Wesen und Wirkungen der Detention in den antiken Rechten' (Sonderdruck aus den deutschen Landesreferaten zum *III. Internationalen Kongress für Rechtsvergleichung in London*, 1950), 13 ff.

s. 757, p. 434. Kaser, 'Wesen und Wirkungen', l.c. 2 ff.

s. 760, p. 435. Kaser, 'Wesen und Wirkungen', l.c. with references.

s. 793, p. 464. Arangio-Ruiz, *La società in diritto romano* (1950), 30 f., 122.

s. 796, p. 464. Longo, 'Concetto e limiti dell' obbligazione naturale dello schiavo nel diritto romano classico', *SD*, xvi (1950), 86 ff.

s. 799, p. 472. Grosso, *Il sistema romano dei contratti* (2nd ed. 1950), 32 ff. (cap. II 'Contractus e contrahere'); Solazzi, 'Il contratto di tutela in Gai. 4, 182', *Bull.* xlix/l (1947), 360; van Oven, 'Remarques sur Gai. 3, 91', *IURA*, i (1950), 21 ff.

s. 800, p. 472. Perozzi's paper see now in Perozzi, *Scritti giuridici*, ii (1948), 563. Grosso, *Sistema*, l.c. cap. III, La 'quadripartizione delle obligationes ex contractu', p. 273 ff.

s. 801, p. 472. On quasi-contracts see Grosso, l.c. 20 ff.

s. 802, p. 473. Grosso, l.c. 186 ff.

s. 805, p. 483. Grosso, *Sistema*, 139 ff.

s. 808, p. 483. Grosso, *Sistema*, 143 ff. with references (p. 146).

s. 809, p. 483. Giffard, *RIDA*, iv (1950), 499, 501 (hardly acceptable).

s. 815, p. 504. La novazione nel diritto romano (1950).

s. 817, p. 504. Sanfilippo, 'Dubbi e riflessioni in tema di novazione mediante stipulazione nulla', *Annali Catania*, iii (1949).

s. 819, p. 504. Bonifacio, l.c. 47 ff., 62 ff.

ss. 820 ff., p. 504. Wesenberg, *Verträge zu Gunsten Dritter* (1949). On *stipulatio post mortem* see Sanfilippo, *St. Solazzi* (1948), 554; Solazzi, 'Sull' obbligazione a termine iniziale, *IURA*, i (1950), 34 ff., 49 ff. (not convincing).

ss. 871 ff., p. 507. Grosso, *Il sistema romano dei contratti* (2nd ed. 1950), 122 ff.

s. 874, p. 507. Grosso, l.c. 106: 'L'obligatio re et verbis contracta.'

s. 885, p. 517. De Robertis, *La legittimazione attiva nell' actio furti* (1950).

ss. 901 ff., p. 524. Grosso, l.c. 177 ff. Cap. VIII: Contratti innominati. On D. (19, 5) 13 pr., see Arangio-Ruiz, *La società* (1950), 148.

ss. 907, 908, p. 526. Perozzi's paper see now in Perozzi, *Scritti giuridici*, ii (1948), 563. Greek law knew no consensual contracts, see Pringsheim, The Greek law of sale (1950), 14 ff.

s. 913, p. 540. On *laesio enormis* see Carelli, *SD*, iii (1937).

s. 919, p. 541. Meylan, *RIDA*, iii (1949), 193.

s. 920, p. 541. Pringsheim, *Z*, l (1930), 433 ff.; Kaser, *ARI* (1949), 135 ff.

s. 926, p. 541. On Greek influence, Pringsheim, *The Greek law of sale* (1950), 478 ff., 480; Schulz, *Principles* (1936), 128.

s. 932, p. 538. On *D.* (21, 1), 28, see Monier, l.c. 104.

s. 941, p. 549. On the two crucial texts D. (13, 6) 19, and D. (19, 2) 41, see H. J. Wolff, 'Concerning the transmission of Julian's Digesta', *Seminar*, vii (1949), 69 ff.

ss. 944 ff., p. 553. Arangio-Ruiz, *La società in diritto romano* (1950).

s. 946, p. 553. On consortium see Albanese, 'La successione ereditaria in diritto romano antico' (Estratto dal vol. xx, degli *Annali del Seminario Giuridico di Palermo*, 1949), 9 ff. with references.

ss. 963 ff., p. 566. Bonifacio, *La novazione nel diritto romano*, 69 ff.

s. 971, p. 566. Sargenti, 'Osservazioni sulla responsabilità dell' exercitor navis in diritto romano', *St. Albertario* (1950), 367 ff.

s. 976, p. 574. Grosso, *Il sistema romano dei contratti* (2nd ed. 1950), 1 ff.; on quasi-delicts, 20 ff.

s. 979 ff., p. 586. Niederländer, *Z*, lxvii (1950), 185 ff.

s. 1000, p. 587. De Robertis, *La legittimazione attiva nell' actio furti* (1950).

ss. 1004 ff., p. 592. F. H. Lawson, *Negligence in the civil law* (1950).

s. 1049, p. 620. Giffard, 'L'action qua incertum petimus', *SD*, iv

(1938), 152 ff.; 'Observations sur l'enrichissement injuste incertain', *RIDA*, iv (1950), 499 ff. The author suggests the following formula:

Quidquid paret Numerium Negidium Aulo Agerio dare facere oportere, eius iudex Numerium Negidium Aulo Agerio dumtaxat HS. X milia condemna, si non paret absolve.

If this *formula* had existed the classical lawyers would have granted it ex furtiva causa and thereby have avoided the difficulties mentioned by Gaius 4, 4.